UNDERSTANDING EVENTS

OXFORD SERIES IN VISUAL COGNITION

Series Editors
Gillian Rhodes
Mary A. Peterson

Perception of Faces, Objects, and Scenes: Analytic and Holistic Processes
Edited by Mary A. Peterson and Gillian Rhodes

Fitting the Mind to the World: Adaptation and After-Effects in High-Level Vision
Edited by Colin W. G. Clifford and Gillian Rhodes

Human Body Perception From the Inside Out
Edited by Günther Knoblich, Ian M. Thornton, Marc Grosjean, and Maggie Shiffrar

Understanding Events: From Perception to Action
Edited by Thomas F. Shipley and Jeffrey M. Zacks

Understanding Events

From Perception to Action

EDITED BY
Thomas F. Shipley and Jeffrey M. Zacks

UNIVERSITY PRESS

2008

OXFORD

UNIVERSITY PRESS

Oxford University Press, Inc., publishes works that further
Oxford University's objective of excellence
in research, scholarship, and education.

Oxford   New York
Auckland   Cape Town   Dar es Salaam   Hong Kong   Karachi
Kuala Lumpur   Madrid   Melbourne   Mexico City   Nairobi
New Delhi   Shanghai   Taipei   Toronto

With offices in
Argentina   Austria   Brazil   Chile   Czech Republic   France   Greece
Guatemala   Hungary   Italy   Japan Poland   Portugal   Singapore
South Korea   Switzerland   Thailand   Turkey   Ukraine   Vietnam

Published by Oxford University Press, Inc.
198 Madison Avenue, New York, New York 10016

www.oup.com

Oxford is a registered trademark of Oxford University Press

Library of Congress Cataloging-in-Publication Data
Understanding events : from perception to action / edited by Thomas F. Shipley
and Jeffrey M. Zacks.
        p. cm. — (Oxford series in visual cognition ; bk. 4)
Includes bibliographical references and index.
    ISBN 978–0–19–518837–0 (cloth : alk. paper)
    1. Perception. 2. Attention. 3. Memory. I. Shipley, Thomas F.
    II. Zacks, Jeffrey M.
    BF311.U57 2007
    153.7—dc22   2007023327

9 8 7 6 5 4 3 2 1

Printed in the United States of America
on acid-free paper

This book is dedicated to our children:
Anne, Delia, Jonah, and Noah

Acknowledgments

Thomas F. Shipley would like to acknowledge the support provided by NEI grant EY13518 and NSF grant SBE0541957 for the Spatial Intelligence and Learning Center, Temple University internal study leave grant, and for collegial support on his sabbatical from Reinoud Bootsma and Jean-Louis Vercher and from the Faculté des Sciences du Sport Université de la Mediterranée Aix-Marseille II. Finally: Merci, Henri et Monique, mes amis, pour votre générosité et votre hospitalité. Ce livre est en grande partie le produit de mon congé sabbatique passé en France.

Jeffrey M. Zacks is grateful for the support of his research on event understanding from the James S. McDonnell Foundation, NIMH grant MH70674, NSF grant BCS-0236651, and NIA grant AG05681-20 for the Washington University Alzheimer's Disease Research Center. Many thanks to Corey Maley for technical assistance, and to him and the other members of the Dynamic Cognition Laboratory at Washington University for stimulating discussion.

Contents

Contributors

Dima Amso, Sackler Institute for Developmental Psychobiology, Weill Medical College of Cornell University, 1300 York Ave., Box 140, New York, NY 10021, USA. dia2004@med.cornell.edu

Alan D. Baddeley, Department of Psychology, University of York, York, YO10 5DD, UK. ab50@york.ac.uk

Dare Baldwin, Department of Psychology, 1227 University of Oregon, Eugene, OR 97403, USA. baldwin@uoregon.edu

Patricia J. Bauer, Department of Psychology and Neuroscience, Duke University, 9 Flowers Drive, Box 90086, Durham, NC 27708, USA. patricia.bauer@duke.edu

Geoffrey P. Bingham, Department of Psychological and Brain Sciences, Indiana University, 1101 E. 10th Street, Bloomington, IN 47405, USA. gbingham@indiana.edu

Roberto Casati, Institut Jean Nicod, Centre National de la Recherche Scientifique, 1 bis, avenue de Lowendal, 75007 Paris, France. casati@ehess.fr

Rama Chellappa, Center for Automation Research, University of Maryland, College Park, 4411 A. V. Williams Building, College Park, MD 20742, USA. rama@cfar.umd.edu

Martin A. Conway, Institute of Psychological Sciences, University of Leeds, Leeds LS2 9JT, UK. m.a.conway@leeds.ac.uk

Naresh P. Cuntoor, Center for Automation Research, University of Maryland, College Park, 4411 A. V. Williams Building, College Park, MD 20742, USA. cuntoor@umd.edu

Guy O. Dove, Department of Psychological and Brain Sciences, University of Louisville, Life Sciences Building, Room 128, Louisville, KY 40292, USA. godove01@louisville.edu

Michael Frank, Department of Brain and Cognitive Sciences, Massachusetts Institute of Technology, 77 Massachusetts Avenue, Cambridge, MA 02139, USA. mcfrank@mit.edu

Bärbel Garsoffky, Institut für Wissensmedien/Knowledge Media Research Center, Konrad-Adenauer-Str. 40, D-72072 Tübingen, Germany. b.garsoffky@iwm-kmrc.de

Apostolos P. Georgopoulos, Brain Sciences Center, Veterans Affairs Medical Center, One Veterans Drive, Minneapolis, MN 55417, USA. omega@umn.edu

Roberta M. Golinkoff, School of Education, University of Delaware, Newark, DE 19716, USA. roberta@udel.edu

Jordan Grafman, Cognitive Neuroscience Section, National Institute of Neurological Disorders and Stroke, Building 10, Room 7D43, MSC 1440, Bethesda, MD 20892, USA. GrafmanJ@ninds.nih.gov

Emily D. Grossman, Department of Cognitive Sciences, University of California, Irvine, 3151 Social Sciences Plaza, Irvine, CA 92697, USA. grossman@uci.edu

Bridgette Martin Hard, Department of Psychology, 1227 University of Oregon, Eugene, OR 97403, USA. bmartinhard@gmail.com

Andrea S. Heberlein, Department of Psychology, Harvard University, William James Hall, 33 Kirkland St., Cambridge, MA 02138, USA. heberlein@wjh.harvard.edu

Kathy Hirsh-Pasek, Department of Psychology, Temple University, Weiss Hall, 13th & Cecil B. Moore, Philadelphia, PA 19122, USA. khirshpa@temple.edu

Phillip J. Holcomb, Department of Psychology, Tufts University, 490 Boston Avenue, Medford, MA 02155, USA. phil.holcomb@tufts.edu

Scott P. Johnson, Department of Psychology, New York University, 6 Washington Place, New York, NY 10003, USA. scott.johnson@nyu.edu

Seong-Wook Joo, Center for Automation Research, University of Maryland, College Park, 4411 A. V. Williams Building, College Park, MD 20742, USA. swjoo@cs.umd.edu

Elissaios Karageorgiou, Brain Sciences Center, Veterans Affairs Medical Center, One Veterans Drive, Minneapolis, MN 55417, USA. karag001@umn.edu

Frank Krueger, Cognitive Neuroscience Section, National Institute of Neurological Disorders and Stroke, Bethesda, MD 20892, USA. KrugerF@ninds.nih.gov

Gina R. Kuperberg, Department of Psychiatry, Massachusetts General Hospital, Psychiatry, CNY-2, Building 149, 13th Street, Charlestown, MA 02129, USA. kuperber@nmr.mgh.harvard.edu

Daniel T. Levin, Department of Psychology and Human Development, Vanderbilt University, 230 Appleton Place #512, Nashville, TN 37203, USA. daniel.t.levin@vanderbilt.edu

Jeffery Loucks, Department of Psychology, 1227 University of Oregon, Eugene, OR 97403, USA. jloucks@uoregon.edu

Mandy J. Maguire, School of Behavioral and Brain Sciences, University of Texas at Dallas, P.O. Box 830688, GR41 (Cecil H. Green Hall), Richardson, TX 75083, USA. mjm053000@utdallas.edu

Helena Paterson, Department of Psychology, University of Glasgow, 58 Hillhead Street, Glasgow G12 8QB, UK. helena@psy.gla.ac.uk

Frank E. Pollick, Department of Psychology, University of Glasgow, 58 Hillhead Street, Glasgow G12 8QB, UK. frank@psy.gla.ac.uk

Shannon M. Pruden, Department of Psychology, University of Chicago, 5848 S. University Ave., Chicago, IL 60637, USA. spruden@uchicago.edu

Mark Sabbagh, Psychology Department, Queen's University, 348 Humphrey Hall, Kingston, ON K7L 3N6, Canada. sabbagh@post.queensu.ca

Megan M. Saylor, Department of Psychology and Human Development, Vanderbilt University, 230 Appleton Place #512, Nashville, TN 37203, USA. m.saylor@vanderbilt.edu

Stephan Schwan, Institut für Wissensmedien/Knowledge Media Research Center, Konrad-Adenauer-Str. 40, D-72072 Tübingen, Germany. s.schwan@iwm-kmrc.de

Robert Schwartz, Department of Philosophy, University of Wisconsin-Milwaukee, P.O. Box 413, Milwaukee, WI 53201, USA. schwartz@uwm.edu

Thomas F. Shipley, Department of Psychology, Temple University, Weiss Hall, 1701 N. 13th Street, Philadelphia, PA 19122, USA. tshipley@temple.edu

Sarah Shuwairi, Department of Psychology, New York University, 6 Washington Place, New York, NY 10003, USA. sms425@nyu.edu

Tatiana Sitnikova, Department of Neurology, Massachusetts General Hospital, Building 149 (2301), 13th Street, Charlestown, MA 02129, USA. tatiana@nmr.mgh.harvard.edu

V. S. Subrahmanian, Institute for Advanced Computer Studies, University of Maryland, College Park, 3143 A. V. Williams Building, College Park, MD 20742, USA. vs@cs.umd.edu

Nikolaus F. Troje, Department of Psychology and School of Computing, Queen's University, Kingston, Ontario K7M 3N6, Canada. troje@post.queensu.ca

Pavan Turaga, Center for Automation Research, University of Maryland, College Park, 4411 A. V. Williams Building, College Park, MD 20742, USA. pturaga@glue.umd.edu

Barbara Tversky, Department of Psychology, Stanford University, Stanford, CA 94305, USA. bt@psych.stanford.edu

Achille C. Varzi, Department of Philosophy, Columbia University, 1150 Amsterdam Avenue, Mail Code 4971, New York, NY 10027, USA. achille.varzi@columbia.edu

Emily A. Wickelgren, Department of Psychology, California State University, Sacramento, 6000 J Street, Sacramento, CA 95819, USA. wickelgren@csus.edu

Helen L. Williams, Institute of Psychological Sciences, University of Leeds, Leeds LS2 9JT, UK. h.l.williams@leeds.ac.uk

Phillip Wolff, Department of Psychology, Emory University, 532 N. Kilgo Circle, Atlanta, GA 30322, USA. pwolff@emory.edu

Jeffrey M. Zacks, Department of Psychology, Washington University, Campus Box 1125, St. Louis, MO 63130, USA. jzacks@artsci.wustl.edu

UNDERSTANDING EVENTS

Part I
Foundations

1

An Invitation to an Event

THOMAS F. SHIPLEY

What is an event? An event may be miraculous, mysterious, seminal, even divine—and of course, to paraphrase Ecclesiastes, there is one event that happeneth to us all. Of what do we speak when we say *event*? The Oxford English Dictionary (OED) offers the following: "Anything that happens, or is contemplated as happening; an incident, occurrence... In mod. use chiefly restricted to occurrences of some importance... In sporting language: Something on the issue of which money is staked... That which follows upon a course of proceedings; the outcome, issue; that which proceeds from the operation of a cause; a consequence, result." The term can also be used as a verb: "To come to pass... To expose to the air... To vent itself... To take part in horse trials." There are also a few notable compound phrases that incorporate "event." A *compound event* is "one that consists in the combined occurrence of two or more simple events." An *event horizon* is "a notional surface from beyond which no matter or radiation can reach an external observer." An *event-particle* is "one of the abstract minimal elements into which, according to A. N. Whitehead, space-time can be analysed."

How does this help us? It illustrates the breadth of the field of inquiry. In this book we attempt to come to an understanding about how humans think about *anything that happens*. The hubris of such an undertaking may be breathtaking, but this is not an attempt to provide a psychology of everything. The event set is not the set of all things. However, events are such a large portion of "everything" that it might be useful to consider what things are not events. Events are things that happen; events require a reference to a location in time (but not necessarily a point in time). Things that exist outside of such a temporal reference—let's call them *objects*—are not events. Physical objects (e.g., apples, mountains, clouds) are clearly not events, and so too psychological objects (e.g., ideas, concepts, goals) are not events. An object in isolation is not an event; events occur when objects change or interact. An apple is not an event, but an apple falling is. Likewise, the idea of gravity is not an event, but having the idea was an event. This usage of "object" differs from the way many use the term; it has the advantage of avoiding some messy issues such as events being prototypically short-lived and insubstantial, whereas objects are enduring and substantial. Here the continued existence of an object *is* an event (albeit a rather dull one), as it requires reference to time. The changeless existence of an object may not be a prototypical event, but it appears to have some psychological importance, as some languages explicitly mark the mutability of an object (Clark, 2001); these languages distinguish between temporary and longer-lasting states (e.g., between being wet and being made of stone).

Events may be brief or long, spanning temporal scales from fractions of a second (e.g., playing a note on a piano) to millennia (e.g., forming the Grand Canyon) and beyond. Events at these different scales may fall into different functional classes. Those on the scale of seconds may be particularly relevant to issues of safety and general motor coordination, while longer events may be more relevant to goals and plans. Very long events, such species evolution, while conceivable, may be so removed from familiar human event scales that they are difficult to understand or think about.[1]

The variety of things that can be described as events means that events also span the domains of psychology. If one looks at the history of psychology, one finds little theoretical or empirical work that is framed in terms of events. Notable exceptions include the theories of the Gestalt

---

1. The attraction of some creationist arguments may lie in their shortening time scales to a more familiar and cognitively manageable range (Klinkenborg, 2005).

psychologists (but these led to relatively little experimental work) and Gibson's ecological optics. I think event avoidance by both experimentalists and theorists reflects the practical difficulties of working with events. Researchers have been searching for truth where they can see. The advent of computers allows us to control events with greater flexibility than ever before. It is time to seriously consider the appropriate place for events in our science. At the risk of being overly polemical, events appear to be a fundamental unit of experience, perhaps even the atoms of consciousness, and thus should be the natural unit of analysis for most psychological domains. In perception, wasn't Gibson mostly right in saying that the really useful information about the world is provided over time (by motion of objects and observer through space, and by moving our eyes and head)? In cognition, to understand thinking, mustn't we try to understand how humans and other animals store information about events, retrieve that information, and use it to make plans about future events? Let me put the argument another way: Suppose humans were unable to process events. Imagine how difficult life would be. One would have to live moment to moment, without plans or expectations. Action at each instant would require an evaluation of the current static situation. How could one move out of the way of moving vehicles, or remember to bring milk home, or even have a sense of whether one is going to work early or returning home from work late? It has been hypothesized that schizophrenics are compromised in their ability to segment events (Zalla, Verlut, Franck, Puzenat, & Sirigu, 2004). If so, is it surprising that schizophrenics find it hard to interpret the actions of others? Whether the segmentation deficit is causally related to the symptoms of schizophrenia is up in the air; nevertheless, it illustrates the point: to not be able to think about events would make functional behavior nigh impossible.

Each event, each happening, reflects some interaction among objects (remember that here "objects" includes both physical and mental objects). To understand, remember, talk about, or otherwise act with respect to the event, the interaction must be perceived. Many readers may object to the use of the word *perception* to characterize the processes involved in event processing, wishing instead that I had used *cognition*, for surely any process that spans time—with environmental input at one point in time influencing processing at a latter point in time—must require memory and therefore must be cognitive. Personally, I do not find the distinction between perception and cognition very useful or easy to make. Once one admits to perception of motion, where the location of an object at one time influences processing at a later time, one has opened the door, inviting processes that span time (and thus events) into the house of perception. Once opened, it is hard to close this door, to exclude processes that take too long and thus must be cognitive. We may each have our personal limits, when we start to get embarrassed and wish to close the door—perhaps after 200 milliseconds, 1 second, or 10 minutes; there simply is no clear break in time where perception ends and cognition begins. On the positive side, thinking of the processes as perceptual offers an interesting perspective, and potential lines of research may be developed by analogy to previous work in perception. I attempt to offer a few such examples in this chapter.

It may be useful to start by considering just what we are speaking of when we say "event." Perceptual psychologists have often found it useful to distinguish between physical properties of the world and our experience of them by giving them different names. For example, "luminance" refers to the physical intensity of light and "brightness" to the psychological experience of an amount of light. In cases where the words for the physical and psychological aspects of the world are identical (e.g., "contrast"), particular care must be taken to be clear about which meaning, physical or psychological, is intended. The usage of "event" presents us with this problem: it is not always clear when "event" refers to an occurrence in the world and when it refers to our experience of things happening in the world.[2]

---

2. The lack of terminology may reflect the youth of the field. Arguably, this field does not even have a name. When I try to describe the scope of this book to colleagues, I say, "It is about the psychology of events." This gets me everything from blank looks to very narrow conceptions of the content. Perhaps the name should be taken from the field's rightful precursor, *event perception*, which I understand can be traced to Gunnar Johansson's 1950 dissertation, and, to be fair, researchers in that area have been making significant contributions for a while. The problem with that name is that it evokes either a narrow conception or an unfair dismissal as a "flaky field" due to its association with the ecological approach to perception. Finding a name for a domain is hard. *Event representation* also seems too narrow. A wag proposed *flurb*, which has the distinct advantage of being better than the more obvious *eventology*, but I am not sure it meets the more stringent criterion of being better than nothing. More seriously, the field may profit from a few terms of art. It would be useful to distinguish between an *event* as something that occurs in the environment and an *event unit* as the corresponding psychological representation of a part of a physical event.

What does it mean to perceive an event? In 1976, Ulric Neisser attempted a marriage of Gibson's perception as information pickup and information processing where detection of invariants in the ambient optic array was guided by knowledge gained from past experience. The interplay of knowledge and information pickup was characterized as a perceptual cycle. The continuous nature of a cycle captures an important aspect of event processing (Hanson & Hanson, 1996). In this cycle, information is picked up from the environment, and this then leads to recall of similar objects or events from the past; this knowledge, in the form of a schema, directs attention and guides future information pickup (Neisser, 1976; see also Reynolds, Zacks, & Braver, 2004). If incoming information fails to agree with expectations (i.e., the schema has failed to predict the evolution of an event or the content of a scene), then attention will be allocated to picking up further details. A model of how this might be achieved, including candidate neural structures, has been proposed by Zacks, Speer, Swallow, Braver, and Reynolds (2007). As events unfold there will be points of decreased predictability during which the organism is particularly likely to search for information to allow more accurate future predictions. These points of decreased predictability will be points of segmentation (e.g., after a goal has been achieved) (Wilder, 1978a, b).

We perceive events in order to anticipate the future, and we use information available in the present to guide future action; in this way we attempt to maintain a perfect coordination of our actions with the world (from looking in the right direction when watching a tennis match to placing our feet so as to avoid injury to small children running around a playground). Breaks in events are, then, the inevitable failures of coordination, points where we are off balance, zigging when we should have zagged. A break in event processing is an opportunity to take in additional information about the world, to reevaluate our models of what is happening and is likely to happen. Persistent difficulty in anticipating the future may lead to use of temporally shorter event models, in effect causing an individual to worry more about the here and now than larger temporal events.[3]

---

3. Our normally exquisite ability to coordinate action makes persistent failures of coordination meaningful. Such failures have been hypothesized to be a source of information for impaired sensory systems and used as evidence of poisoning, thus leading to motion sickness (Riccio & Stoffregen, 1991).

Coordination is not achieved by sight alone; similarly, event perception is not the exclusive domain of vision. Events are almost always multimodal. As vision can provide information about objects at great distances, it will also be able to provide information about events that evolve over space (e.g., approaching objects). Anyone who has watched a silent movie has had the experience of understanding events using exclusively visual information. What do we see during an event? When we look at objects in motion, we do not see motions; as the movie director and the psychologist know, we see actions and interactions—we see emotions and pratfalls. Visual media can communicate quite sophisticated stories. Studies of event perception highlight the level of complexity that is available to perceivers. The seminal studies in this area by Michotte (1946), Heider and Simmel (1944), and Johansson (1973), each cited over 100 times, used displays with simple geometric forms, thereby eliminating potential top-down sources of information about the past behavior of the object.

One of the simplest events—for many philosophers perhaps a prototypical event—is collision. When two objects collide, one object causes the other to move. Philosophers have found much ground to till in their consideration of the nature of causality. In a series of simple experiments, Michotte (1946) investigated the nature of the psychology of causality in simple two- and three-body interactions. He found that subjects reported the experience of causality in highly reduced visual displays, suggesting that causality was a psychological entity: certain spatiotemporal relations result in the perceptual experience of causation, just as certain combinations of wavelengths are seen as red or blue. When observers saw a small dot approach a second dot and stop upon reaching the second dot, and then saw the second dot start to move in the same direction as the first, they reported that one object caused the other to move; when spatial or temporal contiguity was broken, observers reported different sorts of causal interactions. For instance, when the first dot stopped at a distance from the second before making contact, and then the second began moving, observers reported seeing the first dot "launch" the second. When the first object did not stop but moved along with the second, subjects reported "entraining." These latter forms of causal interaction may reflect sensitivity to basic causal interactions among animate objects. Michotte noted that often the causal experience included an experience of animacy; with entraining, subjects often reported that the objects were animate—after a period of viewing, the objects appeared to move on their own. When there is action at a distance, the moving object will be seen as animate, as the interaction appears to reveal both perceptual abilities and an internal source of energy (because there was no spatially proximal cause for movement). Launching can occur when the launched object has perceptual abilities, allowing the anticipation of danger and avoidance of an approaching object. Similarly, entraining reflects a coordination of action with a distal object.

Like other perceptual phenomena, these experiences appear cognitively impenetrable to common sense or most world knowledge (Fodor, 1983). Subjects have experienced launching with impossible actors. For example, some subjects were shown a shadow or spot of light moving toward a marble; when it reached the marble, the marble began to move. The subjects reported the interaction as causal—their perception was that the shadow caused the marble to move.

The perception, detection, and recognition of animate biological interactions extend beyond simple following and avoiding to complex social interactions. Heider and Simmel (1944) showed observers films of a circle and triangles moving around a screen. When asked what they saw, almost none of the subjects reported just the temporal sequence of movements. Instead they described events as animate interactions (e.g., "He [triangle-two] attacks triangle-one rather vigorously [maybe the big bully said a bad word]" [p. 247]). These reports seem best characterized as reflecting perception of social causation. Perceivers interpret the pattern of motions, in particular the contingent motions (e.g., following, attacking, or defending), in terms of intents with goals and plans for the action. The perceptually identified goals in turn lead to using personality terms to describe the actors (e.g., "brave" for one triangle and "aggressive" for the other). Believing an object has a goal or intent means perceiving it as animate. Intentions and goals are generally conceived of as internal, invisible, even hypothetical objects. However, they can be seen in the interaction of an animate being with other objects. Thus, to perceive an action with a goal, such a catching a ball, requires picking up on the time-varying relationship between two or more objects. Experience with multiple instances of goal-directed actions may allow categorization, which in turn may subserve the linguistic representations (e.g., verbs and prepositions) of such actions (Hirsh-Pasek & Golinkoff, in press).

Research on perception of animacy is relatively limited. Some recent work has focused on the perceptual classification of an object as animate (e.g., Tremoulet & Feldman, 2000). In an important paper, Bingham and colleagues (1995) attempted to characterize the spatio-temporal patterns associated with animate events and contrasted those patterns with the patterns present in spatially similar inanimate events. The majority of studies of the perceptual processing of events that involve animate actors have been conducted under the rubric of biological motion perception.

In 1973, Gunnar Johansson published a short article describing the perception of humans when the only visible elements of a scene were small lights attached to each of the major joints of the body (shoulder, elbow, wrist, hip, knee, and ankle). The experience of seeing a person moving around in these point-light displays frequently produces marvel. These displays are intuitively notable for even a naïve observer because there is a significant discrepancy between the experience of the static display, where the lights appear as a flat constellation of points that rarely resembles anything familiar, and the moving displays, where a three-dimensional moving human is readily recognized. The sense that the point-light displays are impoverished while the perceptual content is rich may be formally analyzed in terms of the spatial structure of the actor. Recovering the spatial structure of 12 points represents a significant achievement from the point of view of degrees of freedom. If each point has six degrees of freedom (location in 3-D [X, Y, and Z] and three degrees for rotation around each axis), then 12 points represents recovery of structure given 72 degrees of freedom. To give a sense of this accomplishment, pretend for a moment that each degree of freedom is (absurdly limited to be) binary (left–right, front–back, up–down, and rotated 0 or 180 degrees in the frontal, sagittal, and horizontal planes); in this case, seeing a person walking means the system arrived at the correct solution from among 4.7×10^{21} possibilities.

Beyond the recovery of structure from motion in biological motion displays, observers can also see the action, or what the object is doing. Actions provide basic class information about the objects performing them. For example, the local actions of one point (e.g., one dot that appears to move in a pattern typical of locomotion) allow the visual system to classify an actor as animate or not; such perceptual mechanisms may serve as a simple biological-actor detector (Troje & Westhoff, 2005).

Action also provides rich information about an object and its intentions. Actions may be globally classified, for example as walking or running, independent of whether the runner is Jesse Owens or someone else. The actions may be further classified in terms of the state or emotion of the actor (e.g., happy or sad) (Dittrich, Troscianko, Lea, & Morgan, 1996; Paterson & Pollick, 2003; Troje, 2002). The perception of action may also include subtle metric properties of an action, such as how far a ball was thrown or how much a lifted box weighed (Runeson & Frykholm, 1981, 1983). Such percepts are possible because there is an intimate relationship between the visible motions in an event and the forces present in an event. An actor may pretend to be lifting something heavy when the object being lifted is actually light. Observers can recognize the intent of the actor (to deceive) as well as the truth of the weight, because the forces needed to lift heavy versus light objects are quite different, and such forces are reflected in the acceleration and locations of the joints of the actors (Runeson & Frykholm, 1981, 1983). There are significant individual differences in actions; these reflect, in part, differences in the structure of the actors. We may recognize our friends based on the way they move (Koslowski & Cutting, 1977) or categorize unfamiliar actors as female or male based on how they walk or throw (Koslowski & Cutting, 1977; Pollick, Kay, Heim, & Stringer, 2005).

Objects and Events

In point-light walker displays, we can see that motion patterns dually specify both the event and the object. Visible motion patterns reflect the shape of an object and how it is moving. Despite the intimate relationship between agent and action, object and event, research has focused on only one of these areas. The field of object perception is mature, with many years of cumulative research and established overarching theories, whereas the field of action or event perception is in its infancy. Here, I take four traditional object-perception issues and, for each, consider potential analogies to event perception.

1. Segmentation and Grouping

The words used by the OED to define events reveal an important constraint on the way humans conceive of events: we think of events as things. We use the same language to describe events and objects. The inclusion of the words "instance" and "occurrence" indicates the propensity for segmentation of events. Whether or not there might be some physical basis for segmentation is a topic of debate. For many events, the beginning and end points of the physical event are obscure. To illustrate: When does a wedding begin? When a date is set? When announcements are sent out? With the arrival of the first guest, the last guest, the wedding party, the bride, the groom? Or perhaps at the time set on the invitation? For these reasonable candidates, can the precise instant of initiation be determined? When, exactly, does someone arrive at a wedding? When he or she gets out of his or her car? When the individual first sets foot on the steps of the church? Perhaps we should borrow from horse racing and decree that arrival occurs when the nose breaks the plane of the doorway of the church. My point is not that the concept of a wedding event is incoherent; rather, it is that humans treat events as temporally well bounded, regardless of agreement about the details of the boundaries.

One might reasonably ask, "Why would events appear bounded if they are actually continuous?" The answer, I believe, is that the appearance of boundaries reflects event regularities. Within some classes of events (e.g., physical–causal interactions) the boundaries reflect physical regularities within the event; some changes in the world always occur with certain others. For example, falling precedes collision with a ground surface, which in turn precedes bouncing or breaking. The falling, colliding, and bouncing may be seen as a unit because they co-occur. When things become less predictable, a boundary will be seen. Predictable regularities influence visual processing, and event units are perceived. This idea is expanded upon in Chapter 16. Other regularities may be imperfect, perhaps learned by observation of statistical regularities among components of an event (Avrahami & Kareev, 1994). When components consistently co-occur, we come to experience them as single event unit.

Events are experienced as units—units that are the building blocks of conscious experience. Our experience of the world reflects the way we link and keep separate the various events around us. The segmenting and grouping of events in turn reflects physical regularities reflecting the physical attributes of solid objects (e.g., solidity, opacity, and continuity over time). To begin a study of event unit formation, it is useful to look at work on object perception, as the same physical regularities directly influence object and event perception.

In object perception, the basic fact of object opacity and its prevalence in natural scenes requires visual mechanisms that can interpret scenes where near objects partially obscure more distant objects and proximal parts of an object hide its distant parts. The recovery of object boundaries in cluttered scenes is one of the major challenges in computational vision. Perception must segment (identify as separate) optically adjacent pieces of different objects, and it must group (combine) optically separate pieces of a single object. Most accounts of how grouping is achieved rely on a perceptual filling-in process whereby occluded boundaries are completed based on the visible regions (for a review see Shipley & Kellman, 2001).

Occlusion, considered from the perspective of event processing, introduces some interesting processing challenges, and the potential solutions have implications for research on object perception. The opacity of surfaces in natural scenes will cause objects to temporarily go out of sight as they (or the observer) move and the object passes, or appears to pass, behind nearer objects. Accurate perception of a distal event requires recovering the changes occurring in the world despite fluctuations in visibility of the actors. Here, the visible portions of an event must be segmented from other changes and grouped together. Similarly, visual processes are needed to stitch together events fragmented by the movement of the body and eyes of the observer.

The need for segmentation may not be phenomenally obvious, as we tend to experience only one event at a time; nevertheless, many events overlap in a scene, and our inclination to attend to just one of these leads to the impression of sequences of events. Neisser and Becklen (1975) provided a nice demonstration of our ability to segment one event from a flux of events. Subjects were asked to attend to an event (e.g., two people playing a hand-slapping game) seen by one eye while a different event (e.g., basketball players throwing a ball) was shown to the other eye. Subjects accurately reported what was happening in the attended event and had little awareness of what was happening in the unattended event. This ability was undiminished when the two events were shown superimposed to both eyes; subjects could accurately reports facts about one or the other event, but not both simultaneously. Selective attention to an ongoing event is analogous to the Gestalt notions of figure and ground in object perception. Neisser's work is a precursor to recent work on change blindness (see Chapter 19 in this volume); as conceptualized here, change blindness occurs because the visual system fails to register an event that is in the background. Is the figure-ground analogy merely descriptive, or does it offer any new predictions? The answer depends on how strong the analogy is—is it possible an event could be reversible, like the perceived image in the well-known face/vase figures? Is it possible that background events are completed with a default transformation, as background surfaces continue under figures?

Grouping event fragments may be thought of as a two-stage process: the first stage involves identifying changes that take place over time and indicate a change in visibility, and the second stage provides the linkage (to a later time or from an earlier time). The first stage distinguishes changes that indicate an object's continued existence even when it is not visible from changes that indicate an object has gone out of (or come into) existence (e.g., an explosion). The optical changes associated with transitions from visibility to invisibility and vice versa are distinctive and thus can provide information about an object's existence (Gibson, Kaplan, Reynolds, & Wheeler, 1969) and shape (Shipley & Kellman, 1993, 1994).

The second stage organizes the glimpses of different parts of an event. The perception of simple events will not be disrupted by occlusion. For example, the approach of a predator may be seen as it weaves its way through tall grasses. The linking together of the various fragments of the predator's path reflects the achievement of basic object constancy—seeing "approach" requires seeing an object viewed at different points in time as the same object. Perception of longer or more spatially scattered events may require integration of multiple spatial and temporal relations. For example, the subevents of a good double play may include the pitched ball being hit, the hit ball being caught and thrown to an infielder, and the caught ball being thrown to another infielder. Although the path of the ball may help stitch together the subevents, observers need not keep all players in sight to appreciate the larger event. An additional complication arises as one moves up the temporal scale: on longer time scales, information about ongoing events may be interwoven. So, it is possible to follow the progress of a baseball game while purchasing a hot dog from a passing vendor. This, too, requires segmenting the unrelated event pieces and linking the spatially and temporally dispersed fragments.

The perception of partially occluded objects entails a completion process (Kellman, Guttman, & Wickens, 2001). What little data there are suggest that there is an analogous completion process for dealing with the spatial and temporal fragmentation of events. Michotte, Thinès, and Crabbe (1964/1991) described a case of amodal completion over time. When a moving object disappears behind an occluder and then a moving object appears from behind the occluder, the perception is of a single object moving along a continuous path, if the first and second paths are spatially aligned and the time between disappearance and appearance falls within a certain range. Michotte et al. referred to this phenomenon as *tunneling*. Event completion is not limited to interpolation of translation. Hespos and Rochat (1997) found that infants accurately anticipate changes in a spinning object that is temporarily out of sight. Whether or not filling-in of event transformations occurs with longer, more complex events is an open and important question.

2. What Makes Two Events Similar?

Recognizing events such as Jesse Owens's run or Neil Armstrong's historic small step is a significant accomplishment, despite the collective familiarity of these events, and this accomplishment is not well understood. We may see two events as similar—indeed, some events may appear so similar that we identify them as the same and say we recognize a single event. However, as noted by Zacks and Tversky (2001), we never encounter the same event twice; every event occurs at a unique location in time. Thus, when we speak of event recognition and similarity, we are really in the domain of event concepts and must wrestle with two questions: how are tokens of an event type compared, and what is the nature of event concepts?

How are events compared? The unitary nature of events naturally leads to the consideration of potential parallels to object recognition and comparison. Historically, a central issue in object perception has been shape constancy—how does the system overcome the apparent loss of information when three-dimensional objects are projected onto a two-dimensional retina? The implicit, or at times explicit, assumption was that recognition could only be achieved based on matching an experience at one instant in time with an experience at a later instant in time. In other words, how can an observer recognize an object when, inevitably, that object will not project exactly the same image when re-encountered?

Debate on this issue continues with arguments about whether or not object recognition is viewpoint specific (e.g., Beiderman & Bar, 2000, versus Hayward & Tarr, 2000), but the debate may be waning (Hayward, 2003). An analogous debate should be raging on how we recognize repeated instances of an event category. Do we encode events from the point of view from which we saw them? Or are representations of event tokens viewpoint independent? Research on event classification by infants (described in detail in Chapter 7) suggests that the ability to appreciate similarities across events develops slowly; successively greater abstraction of event properties occurs as experience of event instances accumulates.

The apparent event-category learning that occurs as infants learn verbs and prepositions offers an exciting potential for illuminating the nature of event categories. In considering how we develop categories for events, one may again look to the central questions in the object-categorization literature. For example, are event categories best conceived of as Roschian prototype-based concepts; feature-based, just-in-time concepts (Barsalou, 1983); or a mixture of different mechanisms? Work in the area of recognition from movement, where individuals may be recognized by the way they move, hints at a prototype-based mechanism (Hill & Pollick, 2000). Subjects were shown point-light actions of several actors. Some training subjects learned to differentiate between the actors based on their motions, and discrimination improved when displays were distorted to exaggerate differences in the velocities among the actors (e.g., how fast the elbow of actor A moved relative to that of actor B). These latter displays were essentially motion caricatures; the motion distortions are analogous to the shape distortions in facial caricatures, which allow better discrimination than the stimuli used for training because they emphasize the dimensions used to encode the original face as different from a central prototype. The utility of such an approach will be determined in part by success in identifying the dimensions underlying event transformations.

James J. Gibson (1979) argued that any approach to perception based on static configurations was doomed to failure; a successful theory must be based on changes (events), which provide much richer information about the world. Much of the work on the traditionally central issues of perception and cognition reflects the assumption that perceptual experience must be based on static information about the here and now, divorced from temporal context. For example, the concern with shape constancy arose from a wrong-headed conception of a system that needed to correct for distortions introduced by projecting an image onto the retina. No correction is needed if visual input is considered over time, Gibson hypothesized, because there would always be optical information available over time for the shape of an object. The task of the vision scientist is to discover what information is present and being used (e.g., what properties of an object are preserved over changes in viewing direction to allow shape recognition). Gibson referred to a property of the environment that was constant over a temporal transformation as a *structural invariant*. Structural invariants allow object recognition without having to "account" for the transformation. For example, humans can recognize individuals despite aging; to do so, humans must use some structural invariant, some property of the face that is untouched by the ravages of time. This property would remain unchanged despite the surface changes that occur as a human ages. Similarly, some invariant relation must also allow face identification despite the more transient elastic changes associated with changes of facial expressions.

Just as we may recognize a face despite a change in age or emotional state, so too may we recognize the elastic changes associated with each transformation—when we meet someone new, we have a sense of his or her age and emotional state. Robert Shaw (1974, 1975) had the critical insight that the same logic used for object perception could be applied to event perception; there is some property, a *transformational invariant*, that is present for certain transformations and allows us to identify the transformation even when it is applied to different, novel objects (Pittenger & Shaw, 1975; Shaw, McIntyre, & Mace, 1974).

Faces age in a characteristic manner; the shape changes that occur in skulls as animals grow are relatively consistent—all skulls show similar topological changes with growth (Pittenger & Shaw, 1975). Pittenger and Shaw (1975) identified two changes—sheer and strain—in skulls and investigated observers' use of these as transformational invariants for aging. Subjects were sensitive to the level of shear and strain applied to novel faces. Furthermore, when extreme values of the transformations were applied to faces, simulating ages that humans never achieve, the "super-aged" faces were perceived to be older than those in the normal range. The power of this approach is that it accounts for the appearance of age in unusual objects, such as when cartoon animators imbue naturally inanimate objects with age (e.g., creating a cute baby hammer or an elderly toaster). As noted by Pittenger and Shaw, once the transformational invariant is identified, it is possible to apply the transformation to many other things.

A transformational invariant provides the viewer with access to the essence of change. It is the change, duration of life, or degree of smile, divorced from the objects interacting in a particular event. Such information effectively forms the basis for event concepts, making concept formation an essentially perceptual achievement—the discovery of the transformational invariant. Given the limits of attention, it is likely that perception of events is based on the transformation of a small number (fewer than four) of objects or properties of objects. However, expertise may broaden the potential transformations one can process. Just as a chess master may take into account and remember the relative locations of many pieces on the board, an experienced soccer player may pass a ball based on the locations, orientation, and movement of most of his own team and the opposition.

I suspect many readers may balk at the notion of a perceptual basis to complex social events like wars or elections. But complex event concepts may be built upon simpler concepts. These simple concepts may be the early event concepts, which have a perceptual basis and may serve as the building blocks for latter ones. Baldwin and colleagues have made just such an argument for the development of attribution of intention (Baldwin, Baird, Saylor, & Clark, 2001).

Where will a transformational-invariant approach lead? Initially, perhaps to many independent research strands, each attempting to characterize the transformational invariants for a particular class of events. Whether these strands weave a structure that offers broader generalizations and understanding of event psychology or an impenetrable snarl of unrelated findings remains to be seen.

3. Representation

Events may be seen as units, but how hard can one push the analogy to objects? May we use research in the object perception literature to guide us down new avenues of research—can we bootstrap research on events using object perception? Consider the critical features of many objects—their edges, surfaces, and shape. Do events have analogous properties? To answer, consider why we perceive those features.

Visual processes tend to focus on the edges of objects because objects are relatively homogeneous and the qualities at their edges tend to be predictive of their central regions (e.g., texture and color at the edge tend to match the texture and color of the interior of the object). Thus, edges efficiently provide information about the whole object. There is a class of illusions that occur because the visual system appears to use the value for a perceptual property found at the edge of the object (e.g., lightness) and apply it to the entire object. In the Craik-O'Brien-Cornsweet illusion, for example, a circle appears to be lighter than its surround, even though the central region of the circle matches the luminance of the surround (Cornsweet, 1970). At the edge, there is a luminance cusp: from the center, which has the same luminance as the surround, there is a gradual increase in luminance up to the edge, and then an abrupt drop in luminance at the edge to the common luminance value. The visual system registers the difference at the edge—greater luminance inside the circle—and does not account for the gradual shift to a common luminance value, so the perceptual experience is one of a circle that is allover lighter than its surround.

Newtson and Engquist (1976) reported that event processing shows an analogous emphasis on the temporal regions near points of change. Subjects recall slide shows made of event breakpoints (places where one event ends and the next begins—the event analogue to objects' edges) better than slide shows made of the "central regions" of events. Attention to the event edges may reflect something about the organization of events, such that the temporal regions near points of segmentation provide efficient information about the intervening times. Observers can use the boundary properties to interpolate the missing pieces of an event, whereas event centers do not provide useful information about how the events begin and end.

If event boundaries are particularly important in understanding a scene, then one may be able to generate event illusions by analogy to object illusions. For example, abrupt, transient changes in an object may be perceived to continue throughout an event segment. If a character's face abruptly changes from neutral to angry and then gradually returns to neutral, the event may be perceived as someone getting angry and staying angry. As in the Craik-O'Brien-Cornsweet illusion, a gradual decrease in anger may be noted, but it may not be experienced as a return to neutrality.

A second reason for attending to the boundaries of objects is that shape and function are related in most objects (Gibson, 1979). So, is there an event analogy to shape? The obvious analogy is to space-time paths. Just as the physics of material objects relates form and function, so too the physics of moving objects relates space-time form to function. For example, Niko Troje (Troje & Westhoff, 2005) argues that humans can recognize local features of animate locomotion based on the patterns associated with the motion of the limbs. Here we may recognize the dynamics of locomotion based on the space-time shape of the limb motion. Similarly, bouncing balls have a unique space-time trajectory that may allow recognition of the dynamics involved in bouncing, independent of the details (shape, size, color, etc.) of the objects involved (Muchisky & Bingham, 2002). Models of how we encode object shapes are being developed (Singh & Hoffman, 2001); these may serve as a starting point for a model of event "shape" recognition (see also Chapters 15, 16, and 17 for discussions of event segmentation).

We must be able to recognize the actions in an event in order to use language to describe them. Learning labels for actions, such as verbs and prepositions, requires abstracting the action—that is, being able to recognize instances of the action despite changes in the actor. This suggests that event recognition should be transpositionally invariant. If novel motion paths have the same space-time shape despite changes in the location, size, or identity of the moving object, it should be possible to recognize the path similarity across the events (Shipley, 2005). Whether an approach involving recognition of space-time shapes can be applied to other aspects of events, such as the manner of motion, remains to be seen.

4. Feature Binding

Finally, any model of the mechanisms underlying object perception must describe how information about different aspects of an object is combined; the various features of an object may come from different neural processing streams, likely from different senses. How does this feature binding occur? How are the features of an object, such as shape, texture, color, and so forth, bound together into the phenomenologically unitary object? Treisman and Gelade (1980) have argued that the visual system employs an object file, in an analogy to a paper filing system, where all of the features of an object are kept together in a single file folder. To the extent that separate aspects of an event are processed and combined, we must consider how event-feature binding is achieved. In an event, the space-time behavior of objects must be combined. In the simple case of hitting an object, the object properties of the "hitter" object must be combined with the motion of that object, as well as with the motion and object features of the "hittee" object. Significant failures in binding would result in an observer either not experiencing or misperceiving the event. Errors within an event might lead to reversing the roles of doer and done-to. Errors across events would result in the event analogy to an illusory conjunction, where some objects or actions of one event were combined with those of another event.

Some recent attention research has considered feature binding over time. One prominent example of temporal error is the flash-lag effect (Nijhawan, 2002), in which subjects misperceive the temporal relation between punctate and ongoing events. However, most of the research on temporal errors has focused on fairly short temporal scales. How binding occurs on longer scales, particularly those relevant for coordinated action, is an open question.

One may imagine that objects, their behavior, and their spatial relations with one another are kept in a sort of event file (Hommel, 2004). The ongoing experience of events ending and beginning would then correspond to the opening and closing of such files. This is not so much a new theory as a different perspective on event-processing models put forward by Jeff Zacks and colleagues (Reynolds, Zacks, & Braver, 2004). Perhaps the analogy to work on feature binding in object perception will suggest some new directions.

In conclusion, I think it worth stepping back from our study of perceptual processing of objects so that we may consider the temporal stream in which they swim. Perhaps object perception is just a special case of the more general perceptual processes that provide information about events.

Event Taxonomy

Events, as defined here, encompass a wide range of things. The perceptual and conceptual processes that apply to one type of event may not apply to other types in the same way. For example, cyclical events may be processed differently from discrete events. In both cases, we may wish to coordinate our behavior with the world by taking advantage of event structures to help us predict the future and enable functional behavior. However, this goal may be accomplished in different ways. The recurring structure of cyclical events may be used to anticipate their future. Recurring structure in small-scale cycles may help us coordinate walking with a friend, while at longer scales recurring structures allow coordination of sleep cycles to the coming and going of daylight, and weight gains and losses to the changing of the seasons. Coordination with discrete events, in contrast, may require categorizing an event in such a way that we may take advantage of similarities in temporal structures across events. So, adaptive behavior requires recognizing an event as a member of a particular class.

There are many ways one might divide up the domain of events beyond "cyclical" or "not cyclical." As students of event processing, we would like to have some way to divide up the domain in a way that highlights regularities in how events are processed by humans. In this last section, I offer some thoughts on event taxonomies.

Perhaps the most obvious place to start is with temporal categories, as time is a key component of our definition of an event. Is it useful to group events by their duration? At the extremes, time scale must matter: events that evolve over long time scales, such as erosion of the Grand Canyon, are surely processed differently than events that occur within a single human lifetime. Furthermore, one might expect that relatively instantaneous events, such as hitting or breaking an object, might be processed differently than minute-, hour-, or day-long events. To the extent that events on different time scales are used to guide different functional classes of behavior (e.g., danger avoidance or action coordination at short scales and more vegetative or goal-directed behaviors at longer scales), we would expect an examination of observers' reactions to events of varying durations to bear fruit. In addition, the neural structures responsible for tracking longer-time-scale events may be distinct from those used for shorter scales (Gibbon, Malapani, Dale, & Gallistel, 1997). How do humans reason about events at very long time scales? I suspect by analogy (e.g., erosion of the Grand Canyon is like the erosion caused by a wave at the beach), so understanding the processing of short events may provide some basis for conceptually understanding longer time events. But is time scale the best basis for dividing up events?

As the science of events develops, the need for a functional taxonomy will become paramount. One route to take would be to attempt to construct an exhaustive list of more or less non-overlapping types of events and then see if they form any sort of hierarchy. Gibson offered an initial taxonomy, shown in Table 1.1, based in part on function, in his musings about events in *The Ecological Approach to Visual Perception* (1979). This scheme puts many of the traditional areas of perception (e.g., perception of lightness, color, and motion) into what Gibson viewed as their appropriate context—information that specified some class of events. Color perception, for example, allows perception of changes in plant, animal, and terrestrial surfaces. Motion perception allows us to perceive complex changes in layouts. The research offered by Johansson (1973) and Michotte (1946) may be seen as specifying, to some extent, the details of what information is important in each category.

A related route to developing a taxonomy has been offered by Bingham, Schmidt, and Rosenblum (1995). Building on the work of Runeson

TABLE 1.1.   James J. Gibson's Event Taxonomy

Changes in Layout

- Rigid translation and rotations of an object (displacements [e.g., falling], turns [opening a door], combinations [rolling a ball])
- Collisions of an object (with rebound and without)
- Nonrigid deformations of an object (inanimate and animate)
- Surface deformations (waves, flow, elastic, or plastic changes)
- Surface disruptions (rupturing, disintegration, explosion)

Changes in Color and Texture

- Plant surfaces (greening, fading, ripening, flowering)
- Animal surfaces (coloration of skin, changes of plumage, changes of fur)
- Terrestrial surfaces (weathering of rock, blackening of wood, rust)

Changes in Surface Existence

- Melting, dissolving, evaporating, sublimating, precipitating
- Disintegration, biological decay, destruction, aggregation, biological growth
- Construction

Adapted from Gibson, J. J. (1979). *The ecological approach to visual perception* (p. 99). Boston: Houghton Mifflin.

and Frykholm (1983), which suggests that event dynamics (the forces involved in an event) are available for perception through kinematics (the visible motions of objects), Bingham et al. (1995) argued that if event dynamics are primarily responsible for event recognition, then an event taxonomy should map onto taxonomies in the underlying physics. Bingham et al. noted the fundamental division in the physical laws describing four types of events: rigid body dynamics, hydrodynamics (the physics of fluids), aerodynamics (the physics of gases), and biodynamics. Subjects were indeed sensitive to the patterns of motions present in each type of event when shown path-light versions of events in each category, and a cluster analysis of descriptions of the events confirmed that the dynamics were more important in determining similarity than surface features of the kinematics.

How might one evaluate Gibson's taxonomy? Taxonomies should both organize existing knowledge about a domain and guide research in the domain. Gibson's categories may make sense from the perspective of physics. The information specifying the dynamics in each of the categories is likely to differ. However, it is not clear that there are any constraints on the number of categories (although Bingham et al.'s use of cluster analysis is a nice way to approach this problem). Additionally, it is hard to assess how well this taxonomy classifies the events humans care about.

This raises a question: what events do humans care about? As a rough-and-ready measure of the importance of various events, one may look to the usage frequency of English verbs. Table 1.2 lists the top hundred verbs from the British National Corpus according to frequency (Leech, 1992). The most frequent verbs (*to be* and *to have*) have achieved their standing in part by virtue of the roles they play in marking tense. As with these two, the frequency of each subsequent verb presumably reflects its relative importance. These are the events people talk about and presumably attend to most. Several things are notable about this list. The first is that many of the events described by these verbs are not obviously classifiable within the categories offered by Gibson. To be fair to Gibson, the taxonomy in Table 1.1 was not intended to be complete. Nevertheless, the nature of the unclassifiable verbs is revealing; for want of a more precise characterization, they might generally be classified as "social" verbs. Gibson seems to need a fourth class of transformations: *changes in cognitive state* (or, if you are a behaviorist, a subclass of *changes in layout* with very long-term temporal implications).

TABLE 1.2.   The 100 Most Frequent English Verbs

1. be	26. feel	51. believe	76. fall
2. have	27. may	52. allow	77. speak
3. do	28. ask	53. lead	78. open
4. say	29. show	54. stand	79. buy
5. go	30. try	55. live	80. stop
6. get	31. call	56. happen	81. send
7. make	32. keep	57. carry	82. decide
8. see	33. provide	58. talk	83. win
9. know	34. hold	59. sit	84. understand
10. take	35. follow	60. appear	85. develop
11. think	36. turn	61. continue	86. receive
12. come	37. bring	62. let	87. return
13. give	38. begin	63. produce	88. build
14. look	39. like	64. involve	89. spend
15. use	40. write	65. require	90. describe
16. find	41. start	66. suggest	91. agree
17. want	42. run	67. consider	92. increase
18. tell	43. set	68. read	93. learn
19. put	44. help	69. change	94. reach
20. work	45. play	70. offer	95. lie
21. become	46. move	71. lose	96. walk
22. mean	47. pay	72. add	97. die
23. leave	48. hear	73. expect	98. draw
24. seem	49. meet	74. remember	99. hope
25. need	50. include	75. remain	100. create

Many of the most common verbs describe mental events. This does not mean that a perception-based approach to event understanding should be relegated to remote regions of this list where physical-action verbs appear. Perception of mental events may appear to be an oxymoron, but recall that that is essentially what Heider and Simmel's subjects reported. For example, one may perceive that an object can "see" based on its behavior. If another organism moves out of the path of an object, we take this as evidence of distal perceptual abilities—it saw and avoided an approaching object. So, I think a relatively atheoretical way to begin working on understanding events would be to try to understand how humans process the events that are represented in the high-frequency verbs.

The disconnect between frequently spoken verbs and frequently researched verbs is striking. The most extensively studied event (hitting) does not make the top 100 (it is #218),[4] and the most extensively researched biological motion (walking) barely made it into the top 100 (it is #96).

Verb frequency presumably reflects the importance of events as well as the breadth of the event category (the broadest categories will tend to appear more frequently, as they can be used to refer to more events in the world). Many of the most frequent verbs are very general; they include a broad array of events (e.g., *do* and *know*, which are the broadest physical and mental event descriptors). Other verbs in the top 10 also cover very broad classes of human action (*go, get, make, take*). A few of these verbs are more specific (*say, see, know*), referring to particular types of activity (verbal action, perception, and cognition); their frequency presumably reflects their importance in human interactions.

Beyond frequency of usage, language offers some intriguing hints about how humans represent events, and its study might be a (rocky) road to a hierarchical, inclusive taxonomy of events. Hierarchical organization may be discovered by consideration of cross-linguistic patterns of verb structure. Talmy (2000) offers some potential categories for types (or features) of motion events that appear to be represented in many languages, such as path of motion, manner of motion, and whether or not the motion was causal. Their cross-cultural prevalence suggests they may reflect some of the basic units of events (see also Chapters 7 and 8 in this volume).

Finally, rather than attempting to construct a taxonomy that would encompass all events and offer meaningful subdivisions, one might try to build the taxonomy from the bottom up. Here one might start with taxonomies that have been constructed for local domains and see if they can be combined or broadened to encompass more general categories of events. For example, one might begin with dance notation or music theory. In both cases, detailed taxonomies exist for the "molecular" events, such as musical notes and body movements, as well as the more "molar" events of a movement or a pas de deux. With both music and dance, psychologists and students of the disciplines have come to some understanding of how

---

4. I suspect the verb *hitting* is most commonly used in normal speech to refer to an animate actor hitting something, not the inanimate collisions studied by psychologists in event perception. The most frequent verb for inanimate collisions would be *bouncing*, which comes in at #1137.

humans process these large-temporal-scale events. Perhaps we may use what we know about the development of dance and music appreciation to understand how humans learn about long, complex events.

Conclusion

Events, like objects, are seen to have boundaries. These boundaries may reflect the statistical structure of events as we have experienced them, either individually or as a species. Similarities in the way we conceive of events and objects may reflect underlying similarities in the function of treating objects and events as bounded. Just as we can mentally complete the form of an object partially obscured from sight (because it is not the tail of the tiger that will kill you but the rest of the tiger hidden behind the bushes), so may we anticipate the future (because it is not the crouching of the tiger that kills you but what happens beyond it). So, if you have made it this far, dear reader, you must be game; I challenge you to use the rest of this book to develop new and fruitful research programs on events.

References

Avrahami, J., & Kareev, Y. (1994). The emergence of events. *Cognition, 53*, 239–261.

Baldwin, D. A., Baird, J. A., Saylor, M. M., & Clark, M. A. (2001). Infants parse dynamic action. *Child Development, 72*, 708–717.

Barsalou, L. W. (1983). Ad hoc categories. *Memory and Cognition, 11*(3), 211–227.

Biederman, I., & Bar, M. (2000). Views on views: Response to Hayward & Tarr (2000). *Vision Research, 40*(28), 3901–3905.

Bingham, G. P., Schmidt, R. C., & Rosenblum, L. D. (1995). Dynamics and the orientation of kinematic forms in visual event recognition. *Journal of Experimental Psychology: Human Perception and Performance, 21*(6), 1473–1493.

Clark, E. V. (2001). Emergent categories in first language acquisition. In M. Bowerman & S. C. Levinson (Eds.), *Language acquisition and conceptual development* (pp 379–405). Cambridge: Cambridge University Press.

Cornsweet, T. N. (1970). *Visual perception*. New York: Academic Press.

Dittrich, W. H., Troscianko, T., Lea, S., & Morgan, D. (1996). Perception of emotion from dynamic point-light displays represented in dance. *Perception, 25*, 727–738.

Fodor, J. (1983). *The modularity of mind: An essay on faculty psychology*. Cambridge, MA: MIT Press.

Gibbon, J., Malapanic, C., Daleb, C. L., & Gallistel, C. R. (1997). Toward a neurobiology of temporal cognition: Advances and challenges. *Current Opinion in Neurobiology, 7*(2), 170–184.

Gibson, J. J. (1979). *The ecological approach to visual perception.* Boston: Houghton Mifflin.

Gibson, J. J., Kaplan, G. A., Reynolds, H. N., & Wheeler, K. (1969). The change from visible to invisible: A study of optical transitions. *Perception & Psychophysics, 5,* 113–116.

Hanson, C., & Hanson, S. J. (1996). Development of schemata during event parsing: Neisser's perceptual cycle as a recurrent connectionist network. *Journal of Cognitive Neuroscience, 8,* 119–134.

Hayward, W. G. (2003). After the viewpoint debate: Where next in object recognition. *Trends in Cognitive Sciences, 7,* 425–427.

Hayward, W. G., & Tarr, M. J. (2000). Differing views on views: Comments on Biederman and Bar (1999). *Vision Research, 40,* 3895–3899.

Heider, F., & Simmel, M. (1944). An experimental study of apparent behavior. *American Journal of Psychology, 57,* 243–259.

Hespos, S. J., & Rochat, P. (1997). Dynamic representation in infancy. *Cognition, 64,* 153–189.

Hill, H., & Pollick, F. E. (2000). Exaggerating temporal differences enhances recognition of individuals from point light displays. *Psychological Science, 11,* 223–228.

Hirsh-Pasek, K., & Golinkoff, R. (in press). *Action meets words: How children learn verbs.* New York: Oxford University Press.

Hommel, B. (2004). Event files: feature binding in and across perception and action. *Trends in Cognitive Sciences, 8*(11), 494–500.

Johansson, G. (1973). Visual perception of biological motion and a model for its analysis. *Perception & Psychophysics, 14,* 201–211.

Kellman, P. J., Guttman, S. E., & Wickens, T. D. (2001). Geometric and neural models of object perception. In T. F. Shipley & P. J. Kellman (Eds.), *From fragments to objects: Segmentation and grouping in vision* (pp 181–246). Amsterdam: Elsevier Science.

Klinkenborg, V. (2005, Aug. 23). Grasping the depth of time as a first step in understanding evolution. New York *Times.*

Koslowski, L. T., & Cutting, J. E. (1977). Recognizing the sex of a walker from a dynamic point-light display. *Perception and Psychophysics, 21,* 575–580.

Leech, G. (1992). 100 million words of English: The British National Corpus. *Language Research, 28*(1), 1–13.

Michotte, A. (1946). *La perception de la causalité.* Louvain, France: Institut Superieur de Philosophie.

Michotte, A., Thines, G., & Crabbe, G. (1964/1991). Amodal completion of perceptual structures (E. Miles & T. R. Miles, trans.). In G. Thines, A. Costall, & G. Butterworth (Eds.), *Michotte's experimental phenomenology of perception* (pp. 140–167). Hillsdale, NJ: Erlbaum.

Muchisky, M., & Bingham, G. (2002). Trajectory forms as a source of information about events. *Perception & Psychophysics, 64*(1), 15–31.

Neisser, U. (1976). *Cognition and reality: Principles and implications of cognitive psychology.* San Francisco: W. H. Freeman.

Neisser, U., & Becklen, R. (1975). Selective looking: Attending to visually specified events. *Cognitive Psychology, 7*, 480–494.

Newtson, D., & Engquist, G. (1976). The perceptual organization of ongoing behaviour. *Journal of Experimental Social Psychology, 12*, 436–450.

Nijhawan, R. (2002). Neural delays, visual motion and the flash-lag effect. *Trends in Cognitive Sciences, 6*(9), 387–393.

Paterson, H. M., & Pollick, F. E. (2003). Perceptual consequences when combining form and biological motion. *Journal of Vision, 3*(9), 786a.

Pittenger, J. B., & Shaw, R. E. (1975). Aging faces as viscal-elastic events: Implications for a theory of nonrigid shape perception. *Journal of Experimental Psychology: Human Perception and Performance, 1*, 374–382.

Pollick, F. E., Kay, J., Heim, K., & Stringer, R. (2005). Gender recognition from point-light walkers. *Journal of Experimental Psychology: Human Perception and Performance, 31*, 1247–1265.

Reynolds, J. R., Zacks, J. M., & Braver, T. S. (2004). A computational model of the role of event structure in perception. *Annual Meeting of the Cognitive Neuroscience Society*.

Riccio, G. E., & Stoffregen, T. A. (1991). An ecological theory of motion sickness and postural instability. *Ecological Psychology, 3*, 195–240.

Runeson, S., & Frykholm, G. (1981). Visual perception of lifted weight. *Journal of Experimental Psychology: Human Perception & Performance, 7*(4), 733–740.

Runeson, S., & Frykholm, G. (1983). Kinematic specification of dynamics as an informational basis for person-and-action perception. *Journal of Experimental Psychology: General, 112*(4), 585–615.

Shaw, R. E., McIntyre, M., & Mace, W. M. (1974). The role of symmetry in event perception. In R. B. MacLeod & H. L. Pick (Eds.), *Perception: Essays in honor of James J. Gibson* (pp. 276–310). Ithaca: Cornell University Press.

Shipley, T. F. (2005). Event path perception: Recognition of transposed spatiotemporal curves. *Abstracts of the Psychonomics Society, 10*, 46.

Shipley, T. F., & Kellman, P. J. (1993). Optical tearing in spatiotemporal boundary formation: When do local element motions produce boundaries, form and global motion? *Spatial Vision, 7*(4), 323–339.

Shipley, T. F., & Kellman, P. J. (1994). Spatiotemporal boundary formation: Boundary, form, and motion perception from transformations of surface elements. *Journal of Experimental Psychology: General, 123*(1), 3–20.

Shipley, T. F., & Kellman, P. J. (Eds.) (2001). *From fragments to objects: Segmentation and grouping in vision*. Amsterdam: Elsevier Science.

Singh, M., & Hoffman, D. D. (2001). Parts-based representations of visual shape and implications for visual cognition. In T. F. Shipley & P. J. Kellman (Eds.), *From fragments to objects: Segmentation and grouping in vision* (pp. 401–459). Amsterdam: Elsevier Science.

Talmy, L. (2000). *Toward a cognitive semantics: Language, speech, and communication*. Cambridge, MA: MIT Press.

Treisman, A. M., & Gelade, G. (1980). A feature-integration theory of attention. *Cognitive Psychology, 12*(1), 97–136.

Tremoulet, P., & Feldman, J., (2000). Perception of animacy from the motion of a single object. *Perception, 29*, 943–951.

Troje, N. (2002). The little difference: Fourier-based synthesis of gender specific biological motion. In R. P. Würtz & M. Lappe (Eds.), *Dynamic perception* (pp. 115–120). Berlin: AKA Press.

Troje, N. F., & Westhoff, C. (2005). Detection of direction in scrambled motion: A simple "life detector"? *Journal of Vision, 5*(8), 1058a.

Wilder, D. A. (1978a). Effect of predictability on units of perception and attribution. *Personality and Social Psychology Bulletin, 4,* 281–284.

Wilder, D. A. (1978b). Predictability of behaviors, goals, and unit of perception. *Personality and Social Psychology Bulletin, 4,* 604–607.

Zacks, J. M., Speer, N. K., Swallow, K. M., Braver, T. S., & Reynolds, J. R. (2007). Event perception: A mind/brain perspective. *Psychological Bulletin, 133*(2), 273–293.

Zacks, J. M., & Tversky, B. (2001). Event structure in perception and conception. *Psychological Bulletin, 127*(1), 3–21.

Zalla, T., Verlut, I., Franck, N., Puzenat, D., & Sirigu, A. (2004). Perception of dynamic action in patients with schizophrenia. *Psychiatry Research, 128*(1), 39–51.

2

Event Concepts

ROBERTO CASATI & ACHILLE C. VARZI

Events are center stage in several fields of psychological research. There is a long tradition in the study of event perception, event recognition, event memory, event conceptualization, and event segmentation. There are studies devoted to the description of events in language and to their representation in the brain. There are also metapsychological studies aimed at assessing the nature of mental events or the grounding of intentional action. Outside psychology, the notion of an event plays a prominent role in various areas of philosophy, from metaphysics to the philosophy of action and mind, as well as in such diverse disciplines as linguistics, literary theory, probability theory, artificial intelligence, physics, and—of course—history. This plethora of concerns and applications is indicative of the prima facie centrality of the notion of an event in our conceptual scheme, but it also gives rise to some important methodological questions. Can we identify a core notion that is preserved across disciplines? Does this notion, or some such notion, correspond to the pretheoretical conception countenanced by common sense? Does it correspond to a genuine metaphysical category?

Conceptual Tensions

Very broad umbrella notions such as *event*, *object*, and *property* are standard use in scientific practice for an obvious reason: their latitude allows for interdisciplinary circulation and theoretical track-keeping. The linguist's use of such notions may not cohere with, say, the vision scientist's, and vision scientists may themselves have changed their use and understanding of such notions over the years.[1] Yet in some broad sense we do expect the results of research about events, objects, and properties to be at least partially commensurable across disciplines and across time, and this is why researchers tend to go along with umbrella notions rather than more technically refined concepts. On the other hand, such notions are easy hostages to disciplinary idiosyncrasies. The proper methodological way to regard certain entities—or their representations—as they are "introduced" in various disciplines is to consider them as *theoretical posits*. As such, they live a life that is in the first instance intratheoretical, and we can understand what they are and how they live only by looking at their behavior within the theory that posits them—for instance, their behavior vis-à-vis certain inferences that are sanctioned by the theory.

There is thus a tension between the latitude of the umbrella notions and the invidious construal of each notion within each discipline. Latitude unifies, theory specificity divides. This is particularly striking with regard to the notion of an object (Casati, 2005), but the notion of an event suffers from a similar tension. In addition, the common-sense understanding of both notions is generally alive and kicking inside each of the specialized disciplines. In positing events as primary ingredients of semantic representation, for example, we may be using an event concept that is deferential to common sense (an event is "something that happens"), but the properties of the posits may have little in common with those of events as described by common sense (the posits may be treated as mere values of bound variables). Can we even hope to disentangle these issues?

The first thing to do, we submit, is to distinguish different *types* of notion, not only for *event* but for any umbrella notion of the same

---

1. See Casati (1994) for a historical foray into the cognate notion of visual object.

latitude. This is a necessary step to avoid equivocation, if not achieve clarity. We take it that a first taxonomy should include at least the following four notional types:

- a pretheoretical, common-sense (CS) notion;
- a philosophically refined (PR) notion, where the refinement is dictated by endogenous a priori considerations (e.g., considerations about certain internal inconsistencies of the CS notion);
- a scientifically refined (SR) notion, where the refinement is dictated by exogenous empirical considerations (e.g., considerations about the explanatory value of event-like notions for theories of space-time); and
- a psychological notion: the internal (I) representation of the CS notion, or, more generally, the I representation that subserves the explanation of a number of cognitive performances.[2]

Broadly speaking, we take it that PR and SR notions are typically introduced for the purpose of refining the CS notion, or to replace it altogether, whereas I representations may contribute to an explanation of why the CS notion has the structure it has, among other things. We also assume that the CS notion may be inadequate in many respects, and that it is precisely this inadequacy that opens the way to psychological inquiry. CS notions are, in the norm, illusions.

To illustrate, much of today's philosophical work in the metaphysics of material objects may be viewed as instantiating a refinement policy. Consider the classical puzzle of the Ship of Theseus. Exactly one ship, A, left port, but as a result of a familiar repair/assembly process, two ships, B and C, docked (one consisting entirely of new parts, carefully crafted to replace the old ones; one consisting of the old parts, first diligently stowed, then diligently reassembled). In certain contexts, we are inclined to identify A with B, the intuition being that an object can survive complete mereological change so long as the change is gradual and the shape is preserved; in other contexts we may be inclined to identify A with C instead, the intuition being that sameness of material

---

2. "I representation" is a term of art mutuated by Chomsky (1992a, 1992b, 2000), who first stressed the need to keep apart notions that are in different theoretical standing.

constitution is also sufficient for persisting through time (as when we take apart a bookcase, ship it across the country in separate batches, and put it back together). Now, of course B and C are not identical. So our two intuitions are inconsistent (A is B, A is C, but B is not C), which is to say that the CS notion of a material object is overdeterminate. Giving up either intuition (as in Chisholm, 1973, or Wiggins, 1980, respectively) yields a corresponding PR notion that is immune to the contradiction while still partly adhering to common sense.

By contrast, consider those theories that construe objects as the material content of spatiotemporal regions. Not only do such theories favor one partial intuition about what counts as an object (i.e., material constitution) over the other, they also yield a genuine replacement of the pretheoretical CS notion of an object. According to the CS notion, material objects are three-dimensional entities that occupy space and persist through time by being wholly present at each moment of their existence. According to the revised notion, they are four-dimensional entities that extend through time just as they extend through space, and which persist through time by being partly located at each moment of their existence. They have temporal parts just as they have spatial parts—they have spatiotemporal parts. Such a conception yields a PR notion or an SR notion, depending on the underlying motivation (philosophers espouse four-dimensionalism as a radical solution to the problem of change: see Sider, 2001; physicists come to four-dimensionalism from relativity theory: see Balashov, 1999). Either way, the revision yields a radical departure from common sense and determines a genuine replacement of the CS notion. In fact, construed as a four-dimensional entity, an object acquires many of the properties that common sense attributes to events, so one may even view the replacement as taking place entirely within the conceptual resources available to common sense, at least initially: the CS notion of an object is dispensed with in favor of a notion modeled on the CS notion of an event (objects are re-categorized as events), which in turn may be revised to fit specific theoretical desiderata.

Coming then to events, which are our present focus, here too common sense endorses conflicting accounts, and revisionary policies may in fact be equally varied. For example, common sense typically construes events as concrete, dated particulars (i.e., as nonrepeatable entities with a specific location and duration: Sebastian's stroll took place in Bologna, not in Paris, and it took place last Sunday, not last Saturday).

But common sense also favors a conception of events as abstract, time-less universals (i.e., as repeatable entities that may be said to recur many times and in many places: Sebastian takes the same walk every Sunday, and the lecture he gave in Bologna was the same he gave in Paris). These intuitions (nonrepeatability versus repeatability) are inconsistent, so again we can say that the CS notion of an event is overdeterminate. And giving up either intuition (as in Chisholm, 1970, or Davidson, 1970, respectively) yields a corresponding PR notion that is immune to the contradiction while still partly adhering to common sense.

As in the case of objects, there are, in addition, revisions that involve a more radical departure from the CS notion. For example, there are philosophical theories that treat events as properties of cross-world classes of individuals (Lewis, 1986a), properties of sets of world segments (von Kutschera, 1993), or tropes (i.e., particularized properties; Bennett, 1996), and there are nonphilosophical theories that treat events as very special theoretical entities—for example, as qualified points in space-time (general relativity) or as sets of outcomes (probability theory). Whether stemming from endogenous or exogenous considerations, such PR and SR notions go far beyond common sense and determine a genuine replacement of the CS notion, at least in the contexts in which these notions play an explanatory role.

Finally, a psycholinguistic reading of formal semantics provides an example of an explanatory policy, whereby an I notion explains some traits of the CS notion. The notion of an I representation of events arises in response to the need to explain certain linguistic or logical performances, such as the ability to draw and recognize the validity of the inference from "Sebastian kissed Lisa on the cheek" to "Sebastian kissed Lisa." Such an inference is clearly valid, and its validity—it can be argued—is a matter of logic rather than lexical meaning: one need not know what "on" or "cheek" means in order to reach the conclusion. Yet the inference does not wear the explanation of its validity on its sleeve, as it were. No sentential connective is available to account for the entailment between the two statements, and standard translations into first-order predicate logic are equally unable to do the job. With such translations, the premise would involve a three-place predicate (x kissed y on z) while the conclusion would involve a distinct, two-place predicate (x kissed y), and there simply is no logical link between two predicates owing to the number of their arguments. On the other hand, if we take the premise to assert that a certain event occurred (namely, a kissing between Sebastian and Lisa) *and* that it had a certain property (namely, of being on Lisa's cheek), then the entailment is straightforward (Davidson, 1967a). In other words, the inference can be explained as a form of conjunction elimination—from "Sebastian gave Lisa a kiss, and it was on her cheek" to "Sebastian gave Lisa a kiss." Now, the notion of an event that is mentioned in this explanation is a theoretical posit. Indeed, this explanation is possible at the cost of increasing the domain of admissible entities (i.e., the domain of those entities for which an underlying representation is available) so as to include events—even though such entities are not explicitly represented or visible in the surface grammar of the relevant statements. Their representation, as posited by the theory, is an I representation. The same goes for many other patterns of logical or linguistic competence, as with statements involving naked infinitives ("Sebastian saw Lisa cry"; see Higginbotham, 1983) or inferences involving mixed implicit/explicit quantification ("In every burning, oxygen is consumed. Sebastian burned some wood. Hence oxygen was consumed"; see Parsons, 1985). In all such cases, the positing of an I representation of an event at the level of "logical form" contributes an explanation of why certain inferences are justified and why certain statements mean what they mean.

It is not important here to delve into the technical ramifications (and problems) involved in such accounts (see Bennett, 1988, and Parsons, 1990). What matters here is that the event notions involved in the revision of our pretheoretical apparatus and the event notion involved in the semantic analysis of our logical and linguistic competence (for example) are of different types. The features ascribed to their respective objects by the CS, PR, and SR notions, and by I representations, can display a large variance. This is pretty obvious for the former, as PR and SR notions are expected to improve on unsatisfactory features of CS notions. But other misalignments are to be expected. The I representation of an event may predicate things that no SR notion would endorse and which many PS notions would reject, and there is no reason to suppose that the CS notion of an event and its underlying I representations share significant features either. Finally, there is no reason to suppose that the PR and SR notions are aligned. Russell (1914), for example, claimed that we only perceive events of finite extended duration and refused, on such grounds, to accept the point-events postulated by relativity theory (though, again, his full treatment of the subject required any finite part of an event to qualify as an event in its own right—an assumption that is arguably no closer to the CS notion than the physicist's conception).

Conceptual Interactions

Distinguishing different types of event notions, all of which fall under the same umbrella *as a matter of common practice*, is a first necessary step toward answering our initial questions. As soon as we take a closer look at how these notions are actually employed within the context of specific theories, we must acknowledge that the hypothesis of a unique common core can hardly be confirmed. Is there, however, a common core shared by all event notions of the same type?

Consider the CS notion first. Sure enough, unless we go with the option of relativizing it to cultural, historical, or social contexts, we may suppose that there is just one broad common-sense picture of the world, shared by all individuals, and hence a single CS notion of "event." But we have seen that this notion is both partial and incoherent, and any attempt to extract its core features immediately turns into a revisionary process that results in a corresponding SR or PR notion. SR notions, in turn, are hopelessly idiosyncratic: scientific theories come in such a variety of forms and with such diverging purposes that it would be surprising if *any* of the umbrella concepts that they employ shared significant common traits (though the possibility remains that a radical reductionist program will succeed in expressing every SR notion in terms of a common vocabulary subject to a unified body of laws). With regards to the PR notions, however, the question is by no means trivial: surely different philosophical theories will construe events differently, but that does not preclude the possibility that such notions share a common core of characteristic features—some sort of *conceptual invariant*. For example, the conception of events as concrete particulars and their conception as abstract universals diverge significantly, yet they may well agree on the invariant that every event must involve some material object (i.e., some "participant") and must be involved in some relation (e.g., causal relation) with other events. Indeed, the existence of a common core of features may seem plausible precisely on account of the fact that, typically, a PR notion is developed in an attempt to overcome certain internal inconsistencies of the cognate CS notion. And to the extent that the latter is not entirely inconsistent, the ensuing variety of PR notions need not be entirely in conflict, either.

As it turns out, things are more complicated than that. For one thing, we have already mentioned that "revision" is an ambiguous word: in some cases it may be construed as entailing a radical departure from common sense—a genuine replacement of the relevant CS notion. Secondly, and more importantly, no philosophical revision is carried out in isolation. Typically, a philosopher's endeavors proceed by taking certain CS notions and making them *interact* with other notions. And, typically, such interactions take place within the context of thought experiments designed to test the descriptive and explanatory strengths (and limits) of the notions in question. In the case of events, several such conceptual interaction projects have been put forward; the following are the most notable:

- How does the event notion interact with our understanding of *causality*?
- How does it feature in causal *explanations*?
- How does it interact with our concepts of *time* and *space*?
- How does it interact with the notion of intentional *action*?
- How does it interact with the notion of an *object*?
- How does it interact with the concepts of *identity* and *individuation*?

It is only by looking at such interaction projects, as opposed to the common CS notion that inspires them, that we may be in a position to assess the relative similarities among the ensuing PR notions. In the following sections, we review the relevant literature in this spirit. In addition, a closer look at some of these conceptual interactions may also be seen as providing useful heuristics for other projects, such as that of contributing a better understanding of the CS notions and, possibly, an explanation of such notions in terms of underlying I notions.

Events and Causation

The first two of these projects—on the interaction between the notion of an event and the notion of cause—provide a good illustration of the difficulties involved in this task. Some authors (e.g., Kim, 1973) have argued that whereas concrete particular events seem to be necessary for an analysis of causation in terms of the temporal priority of causes with regard to effects, abstract events (event types) seem necessary when it comes to analyzing causation in terms of constant conjunction of cause and effect ("All events of type C are regularly followed by events of type E"), and also to account for the possibility of subsumption under a law. If so, then there would exist no single event notion able to satisfy the requirements of a unified theory of causality, with obvious discouraging consequences for the intuition that we may look at causality to identify a core ingredient common to all PR notions.

Significantly, the same consequences follow also on the so-called singularist conception of causation, which denies the necessity of a two-fold theory of causality. In this view (Ducasse, 1926), the causal relation that may obtain between two particular events c and e is conceptually and ontologically prior to any causal law or regularity: although c and e may instantiate a regularity, it is not in virtue of this instantiation that their relationship qualifies as causal. The supposition of recurrence would therefore be irrelevant to the notion of causation, and this means once again that causal efficiency does not by itself identify a core feature of events common to all PR notions (in particular, to the two notions under discussion—events as particulars and events as universals). Even those authors who attempt to reconcile the singularist conception with the conception of causation as regularity, or constant conjunction, would reach the same conclusion. Such authors (e.g., Davidson, 1967b) draw a sharp distinction between causal *relation* and causal *explanation*. The former relates concrete particular events and holds between a cause c and an effect e no matter how these events are described or identified. (If "Sebastian's kiss" and "Sebastian's declaration of love" pick out the same event, then Sebastian's kiss caused an uproar if and only if Sebastian's declaration of love caused an uproar.) This means that we can make true assertions about singular causal transactions of the form "c caused e" without knowing a corresponding general proposition "All events of type C are followed by events of type E." We may pick out the events c and e without knowing them under the descriptions "C" and "E." On the other hand, such descriptions are relevant when it comes to providing a causal explanation of what happened, for the relata of a causal explanation are sentences or statements, not events. (If we have a law that says that every kiss causes an uproar, we don't have an explanation of why Sebastian's declaration of love caused an uproar unless we know that Sebastian's act was a kiss—in other words, unless we know that his declaration of love was a kiss.) Thus, if this distinction between causal interactions and causal explanations is accepted, then again there is no need to posit abstract event types in addition to particular events, and even if such event types were posited, there would be no need to suppose that they share the same causal features that characterize particular events: the two PR notions would, in this respect, have nothing in common.

Incidentally, that the terms of the causal relation are events is by itself a controversial philosophical tenet. There are authors who think that the proper causal relata are not events but *facts*, either always (Mellor, 1995) or in at least some cases (Bennett, 1988; Vendler, 1967). We say, for example, that the fact that the dollar fell was caused by the gradual increase in the price of oil, and it is difficult to account for the truth of such statements without taking facts (as opposed or in addition to events) at face value. Nor are facts the only competitors on the market. There is also a long tradition in the philosophy of action, according to which the causal relation may be said to hold between *agents* and events (Bach 1980; Chisholm 1964; von Wright, 1963). We say, for example, that Sebastian caused a fight, or that it was the sun that caused this year's crop. Finally, there are authors who construe causal relata as *properties* (Crane, 2001), *features* (Dretske, 1977), *aspects* (Sanford, 1985), *states of affairs* (Armstrong, 1997), or *situations* (Menzies, 1989). Obviously, once terminological issues have been disentangled and these terms are shown to refer to different entities, such a variety of views introduces considerable complications for any project designed to assess the conceptual interaction between events and causality.

Moreover, it is significant that when it comes to arguing for (or against) such views, philosophers tend to rely on considerations about the logical form of natural language (sentences expressing causality) and, therefore, on theoretical posits concerning the I representation of events. The main arguments in favor of the view that the causal relata are events are by themselves indicative of this tendency, for what such arguments are meant to establish is that reference to or quantification over events is needed in order to account for a speaker's understanding of action and causation sentences; no other rendering of the logical form of such sentences could fit the bill. To illustrate, consider a singu-lar causal statement such as "Sebastian's kiss to Lisa caused an uproar." It might be thought that such a statement can be analyzed as having the logical form of a sentential compound in which the predicate "caused" is replaced by a connective, as in "There was an uproar because Sebas-tian kissed Lisa." As Davidson (1967b) has argued, however, such an analysis would have to do justice to the following two intuitions. First, the connective "because" would have to be extensional, i.e., admit of substitution salva veritate of co-referring singular terms: if Sebastian is Fred's cousin, then the proposed paraphrase should have the same truth-conditions as "There was an uproar because Fred's cousin kissed Lisa." Second, the connective in question would have to be non-truth-functional; in other words, it should not admit unrestricted substitu-tion of materially equivalent sentences: although "Sebastian strolled in Bologna" may have the same truth-value as "Sebastian kissed Lisa," the proposed paraphrase need not have the same truth-value as "There was an uproar because Sebastian strolled in Bologna." Since these two intuitions clash with the thesis that every extensional connective is truth-functional (a thesis that seems to go back to Frege, 1892), Da-vidson concludes that the proposed paraphrase is inadequate—that is, that the statement "Sebastian's kiss to Lisa caused an uproar" can not be analyzed as having the underlying logical form of a sentential com-pound. For Davidson it is a genuine relational statement, and therefore its semantic analysis requires that we take the terms "Sebastian's kiss to Lisa" and "an uproar" at face value (as event-referring expressions). Whether this conclusion is compelling need not concern us here.[3] It is significant, however, that it depends so crucially on the need to account for the logical semantics of ordinary language statements. As with the conjunction-elimination argument reviewed above, the I notion of an event representation is posited in order to justify a certain PR notion, for the explanatory strength of the latter is tested against the need to explain certain linguistic or logical performances of competent speakers of English.

---

3. In the literature, several authors have countered Davidson's conclusion; see, for instance, Bennett (1988), Horgan (1978, 1982), Mellor (1995), and Needham (1988).

Events and Objects

Consider now the suggestion that every admissible PR notion of an event will agree on there being a certain link between events and objects: every event must involve some "participants." Since *object* is itself an umbrella notion, it is hard to assess the strength of this suggestion in generic terms. We have seen that there are PR conceptions of material objects that are radically different from the ordinary CS notion—for instance, conceptions that construe objects as four-dimensional entities that extend across time just as they extend across space. With such radical conceptions, the project of testing the interaction patterns between the two notions loses much of its heuristic value. Indeed, some philosophers would simply deny that the conceptual distinction between events and objects reflects a genuine metaphysical difference and would treat the distinction as one of degree: as Goodman (1951) put it, objects and events would only show a discrepancy in the pattern of variance among their temporal parts—"a thing is a monotonous event; an event is an unstable thing" (p. 286). Quine (1970) expresses a similar view when he describes both sorts of entity as species of the same "material inhabitant of space-time" genus (p. 30): while events appear to develop fast in time, objects are relatively "firm and internally coherent" and cohere only slightly and irregularly with their spatiotemporal surroundings; events are short-lived, and objects are long-lived fillings of spatiotemporal regions.

But let us stick to the conception of objects as three-dimensional entities—arguably a more plausible conception from the perspective of common sense. How exactly should we characterize their role as event participants? First of all, does every event require the presence of one or more objects? Some philosophers disagree, citing as counterexamples events such as changes in light or weather conditions (Brand, 1977) or, perhaps more plausibly, flashes and bangs (Strawson, 1959). On the other hand, perhaps such counterexamples are just a sign of a parochial conception of what counts as a genuine object: if we allow for objects in a wider sense, then arguably whenever a flash occurs there are photons that move; whenever a bang occurs there is air that undulates; and so on (Bennett, 1988).

Second, to the extent that objectless events are uncommon, so are eventless objects. Every object has a life, and the life of an object is an event. So the interesting question is not whether every event involves some object, or vice versa, but whether such involvement displays interesting patterns. In a radical mood, one can think of the entities in one category as being metaphysically *dependent* on entities in the other. For instance, it has been claimed that events *supervene* on their participants: two possible worlds can not be alike with respect to the truth and falsity of propositions concerning what objects there are and what properties they have and yet fail to be alike with respect to the truth and falsity of propositions concerning what events occur and when and where they occur (Lombard, 1986). But then again, a similar thesis has been put forward with respect to the dependence of objects on the events in which they partake (Parsons, 1991). In a more moderate way, one can grant equal ontological status to objects and events but maintain that either objects or events are primary *in the order of thought*. And here, interestingly enough, philosophers and psychologists tend to agree in according priority to objects. Treisman (1986), for instance, has argued that although both objects and events feature as "the fundamental units of conscious perceptual experience" and may be taken as "the basic units from which to build a descriptive system," the primacy of objects is strongly supported by phenomenological considerations. And Strawson (1959) has claimed that a pure event-based ontology would not suffice for the success of our re-identifying practices, which requires some stable, all-encompassing frame of reference, adequately provided by objects instead. In other words, in order to make reference to events in thought and language, thinkers and speakers must be able to make reference to objects. On the face of it, this is a psychological claim, anecdotally captured in the fact that ordinary parlance has expressions such as "the birth of this person" but not "the personification of this birth." On the other hand, such asymmetries must be carefully evaluated to the extent that objects, too, may and sometimes must be identified via reference to events. For example, if we track down the father of Sebastian or the author of *Waverley*, it is by identifying certain events in the first place—of fathering and of writing, respectively (Davidson, 1969; see also Lycan, 1970; Moravcsik, 1968; Tiles, 1981).

All of this suggests that the question of the respective primacy of event and object representations in explaining certain common-sense intuitions—among which is the intuition according to which all events must involve some participants—may have to be settled at a deep level that can be unearthed only through empirical investigation. It may turn out that the I representation of an object controls the unfolding of the I representation of an event, or it may turn out that there is a single I representation, accessed differently in different contexts or by different systems. This generates the intuition that events and objects are, at the common-sense level, two distinct categories (Casati, 1994, 2005; Casati & Varzi, 1999). Some interesting and seldom-noticed symmetries between the notion of an event and the notion of an object (Mayo, 1961; Wiggins, 1980) point in that direction.

Events, Time, and Space

In many PR conceptions, an important difference between objects and events concerns the way in which they are said to relate to space and time (Hacker, 1982; Quinton, 1979).[4] We have already mentioned the fact that objects, construed as three-dimensional entities, *endure* over time, whereas events, construed as particulars, *extend* over time: they have temporal parts. In addition, there is the fact that objects, being material, appear to be invidiously located in space—they appear to *occupy* their spatial location—whereas events seem to tolerate co-location. To use a standard example, if a metal sphere is simultaneously rotating and getting warm, then its rotation and its getting warm appear to be distinct events with the same spatiotemporal location (Davidson, 1967a).

If events are construed as universals, of course, it is only in an indirect way that events can be said to extend over time: they do so whenever they are instantiated. But there are variants. Some authors, for instance, would go so far as to say that events are nothing but properties of times (Montague, 1969), or *times cum description* (van Benthem, 1983). In the latter view, this morning's rising of the sun is identified by an ordered pair $\langle i, \phi \rangle$ where i is the relevant time period (corresponding to the descriptor "this morning") and ϕ is the sentence "The sun rises." (A more general account would construe events as *spatiotemporal regions cum description*, distinguishing, for instance, between this morning's rising of the sun in London and its rising in Paris.) Of course, such PR

---

4. This paragraph and the next draw on Casati and Varzi (2002).

conceptions do not do justice to some features of the CS notion—for instance, the intuition according to which events can be perceived but times can not (Gibson, 1975). The rationale for such conceptions lies, rather, in the fact that they can rely on fully developed theories of intervals along with fully developed interval-based semantics (Cresswell, 1979; Dowty, 1979). This gives them outstanding descriptive power when it comes to the fine-grained interactions between events and time.

The link between events and time has also been explored in the opposite direction, though. If events are assumed as a primitive ontological category, then one can dispense with time instants or intervals and "construe" them as derived entities. The most classical treatment of this sort proceeds by construing time instants as maximal sets of pairwise simultaneous (or partially simultaneous) events (Russell, 1914; Walker, 1947; Whitehead, 1929), but other treatments have been put forward. For example, it has been suggested that the mathematical connection between the way events are perceived to be ordered and the underlying temporal dimension is essentially that of a free construction (in the category-theoretic sense) of linear orderings from event orderings, induced by the binary relation x *wholly precedes* y (Thomason, 1989). Treatments such as these provide a reduction of time in terms of relations among events and are therefore especially germane to a relational conception of time (and, more generally, of space-time). Modal variants (Forbes, 1993), as well as mereological variants (Pianesi & Varzi 1996), of such views are also available.

The relation events have to space is more problematic. Construed as particulars, events are in space as well as in time. Sebastian's walk took place in Bologna, not in Paris. But *where* exactly in Bologna did it take place? Suppose Sebastian strolled along Main Street. Is the location of the event provided by the whole street? By the sidewalk? By the narrow portion of the sidewalk that corresponds to the trajectory of the stroll? Some authors (e.g., Davidson, 1967a; Lombard, 1986) have suggested that the spatial location of an event is indeed given (indirectly) by the location of its participants: the location of Sebastian's walk would then coincide with the sum of the regions of space that, at each time during the walk, are occupied by Sebastian's body. Yet this can hardly be generalized. Consider Brutus's stabbing of Caesar. Did this event spread *only* through Brutus and Caesar? Did it spread through their *entire* bodies? (Was Brutus's left ear involved at all in this event?) The CS notion is indeterminate in such respects, and there are philosophers who take this indetermination to suggest that events are not truly spatial entities (Hacker, 1982). On the other hand, it is not unreasonable to say that our difficulty in answering questions about the spatial location of events concerns the structure of our event talk, not the ontological makeup of events (Lewis, 1986b; Quine, 1985). According to this account, there are plenty of events out there, lots of things happening (each with precise spatiotemporal boundaries), but which ones among them correspond to the words we use may be semantically indeterminate. When we speak of Sebastian's stroll or of Brutus's stabbing of Caesar, we use descriptive phrases that are extremely poor and imprecise, because poor and imprecise is the specification of the relevant event participants, and it is simply preposterous to suppose that such descriptions should pick out a unique event. If so, however, then again we see how questions pertaining to the CS notion, as well as to specific PR notions, interact crucially with questions pertaining to the I representation of events, and the details of this interaction are no straightforward business (Borghini & Varzi, 2005; Varzi, 2002).

This in turn raises a further question that is nicely summarized in the title of a classic paper by Fred Dretske (1967): "Can Events Move?" When we say that events are "in space"—Dretske argues—the "in" is not different from the "in" of the spatial location of objects. Nevertheless, Dretske observes that events are linked to their location in a way material objects are not. A chair can be said to be in a building (at a particular time) even though most of its life is spent elsewhere, whereas a picnic can not be said to occur in a building if it just starts there but eventually winds up in the garden (we can at most say that the picnic occurs in the place that is the spatial sum of the building and the garden). The alleged reason for this asymmetry is that an event expression refers to the entirety of an event and also to the event as temporally extended. It follows that there is an incompatibility between our ascription of spatial location to events and the concept of movement—to put it in a catchy form, events can not move. This conclusion is forced upon us from a reflection on some features of the CS concept of an event. However, as we do seem to think that event motion is all but impossible, the CS concept appears to be, once more, overdeterminate.

Events and Individuation

Another theoretical issue that appears to be unresolved is the issue of identity criteria, which has been the focus of an intense debate (Pfeifer, 1989). Was Sebastian's walk the same event as his pleasant walk? Was his arm raising the same as his greeting? Some philosophers take questions such as these to be metaphysical questions—questions whose answers call for genuine identity criteria and which must therefore be answered before we are allowed to take our event talk seriously. In this sense, different PR notions tend to suggest different answers, and the many answers found in the literature range very widely—from the radical "unifiers," who take events to be as coarse-grained as objects (Quine, 1950), to the radical "multipliers," who take events to be as fine-grained as facts (Kim, 1966; Goldman, 1970, 1971). Other philosophers, however, regard questions of identity—questions about the way we talk and about what we say—to be first and foremost semantic questions. On this view, no metaphysical theory can include a general recipe for determining the semantics of ordinary event talk, and hence there is no effective way of determining the truth or falsity of an event identity statement exclusively on the basis of one's metaphysical views: what event a statement is about depends heavily (more heavily than with ordinary objects) on local context and unprincipled intuitions (Bennett, 1988). If so, then the whole identity issue is undecidable, as it stems from the hazardous attempt to bridge the chasm between semantics and metaphysics.

Once more, intuitions pull in different directions according to the context in which the event notion is made to interact. Inserting events in a causal-explanation context favors fine-grained intuitions: it wasn't just Sebastian's arm-raising but his greeting that made Lisa smile. Inserting events in a spatiotemporal context favors coarse-grained intuitions: Sebastian's greeting happens exactly when and where his arm-raising occurs. Accordingly, multipliers and unifiers have privileged either class of contexts when formulating arguments for their respective positions. Goldman (2007) suggests a *cognitive resolution* of the debate that could be framed in the following way. The CS notion of an event—if there is one—is overdeterminate, and the overdetermination is explained by *two* underlying I representations of events. There is a *perceptual* I representation of events that is movement-based (or change-based), and hence based mostly on spatial and temporal features, yielding coarse-grained individuation, and there is a *conceptual* I representation of events that is property- or fact-based, yielding fine-grained individuation.

Conclusion

The concept of an event, and of event representation, is an umbrella notion. We should therefore speak about a plurality of concepts. We have provided an overview of different ways events have been dealt with in philosophy and in linguistics and, to a minor extent, in cognitive science. This variety of positions has been construed in part as the result of different descriptive and explanatory projects. In particular, we have urged that various types of notions—common-sense, theoretically revised, scientific, and internalist psychological notions—be kept apart. The philosophical literature has applied the standard test of making different notions interact; the interactions of the notion of an event with neighboring notions, such as those of an object, of cause, or of space and time, have been tested. Results are not conclusive so far. Contextual effects abound that can pull intuitions in very different directions, and the methodology itself is largely based on material that may be in need of close scrutiny, as it draws from linguistic evidence, nonlinguistic intuitions, and sometimes examples from scientific descriptions of the external world.

On top of these largely methodological distinctions, the philosophical project of analyzing the event notion can be regarded as a contribution to psychology in the following (admittedly limited) sense. Philosophers in general articulate the CS notion of an event by drawing on inferences that involve the *concept* of an event. This applies specifically to one particular brand of philosophy, so-called descriptive metaphysics (Goldman, 1992; Strawson, 1959), the declared aim of which is to spell out the content of our prereflective thought or perception of the world—in our terms, the structure of CS representations. Descriptive metaphysicians claim, for instance, that both objects and events are denizens of the world. By contrast, other brands of metaphysics have heralded revisions of the CS notion, in particular under the pressure of scientific reconceptualizations of the world. In some cases, this has resulted in no less than a complete obliteration of the distinction between objects and events. The contrast between the opposing claims, however, may not be factual, for the theoretical demands on the notions of an event may diverge in different theories. For instance, Russell and Whitehead looked for a general theory of entities in space-time under the pressure of the new scientific image propounded by relativity theory. Admittedly, these are hardly issues that are likely to move the scholar of CS notions, as CS notions have evolved under evolutionary pressure and were not meant to address scientific changes.

Arguably, the revisions of the CS notion have an import for psychology in the sense that they could be read as "warnings" about aspects of the CS notion that could reflect just how a particular module of the cognitive apparatus contributed to the content of that very notion. If events really are not a distinct category from objects according to a PR notion of an event, then there are good reasons to think that the CS notion of an event is a form of illusion. The illusory aspects are precisely, then, those the PR notion tries to expunge. This approach is expected to predict effects in the various interactions that the notion of an event has with other notions on our list (causality, objecthood, etc.). The study of these interactions could provide templates for empirical investigations into the underlying I notions that explain why certain illusions occur at the level of the CS notion. In particular, it would be worth investigating closely at the I level the relationships between representations of events, of objects, and of regions of space, without prejudging the possibility that some of these notions are disposed of in terms of other, deeper I representations. (It may, for instance, turn out that the CS notions of event and object are, deep down, tributary to a single I representation; see Casati, 1995).

There are some consequences for philosophers as well. Contrary to the received view, the exact balancing of the philosophical issues involving the different notions at stake could be—to a surprising extent—a matter of empirical discovery.

References

Armstrong, D. M. (1997). *A world of states of affairs*. Cambridge, UK: Cambridge University Press.

Bach, K. (1980). Actions are not events. *Mind, 89*, 114–120.

Balashov, Y. (1999). Relativistic objects. *Noûs, 33*, 645–663.

Bennett, J. (1988). *Events and their names*. Oxford: Clarendon Press.

Bennett, J. (1996). What events are. In R. Casati & A. C. Varzi (Eds.), *Events* (pp. 137–151). Aldershot, UK: Dartmouth Publishing.

Borghini, A., & Varzi, A. C. (2005). Event location and vagueness. *Philosophical Studies, 128*, 313–336.

Brand, M. (1977). Identity conditions for events. *American Philosophical Quarterly, 14*, 329–337.

Casati, R. (1994). The concept of Sehding from Hering to Katz. In S. Poggi (Ed.), *Gestalt theory. Its origins, foundations and influence* (pp. 21–57). Florence: Olschky.

Casati, R. (1995). Temporal entities in space. In P. Amsili, M. Borillo, & L. Vieu (Eds.), *Time, space and movement: Proceedings of the 5th international workshop* (pp. 66–78). Toulouse: COREP, Part D.

Casati, R. (2005). Commonsense, philosophical, and theoretical notions of an object: Some methodological problems. *The Monist, 88*, 571–599.

Casati, R., & Varzi, A. C. (1999). *Parts and places: The structures of spatial representation*. Cambridge, MA: MIT Press.

Casati, R., & Varzi, A. C. (2002). Events. In E. N. Zalta (Ed.), *Stanford encyclopedia of philosophy* (http://plato.stanford.edu/). Stanford: Stanford University Center for the Study of Language and Information.

Chisholm, R. M. (1964). The descriptive element in the concept of action. *Journal of Philosophy, 61*, 613–624.

Chisholm, R. M. (1970). Events and propositions. *Noûs, 4*, 15–24.

Chisholm, R. M. (1973). Parts as essential to their wholes. *Review of Metaphysics, 26*, 581–603.

Chomsky, N. (1992a). Explaining language use. *Philosophical Topics, 20*, 205–231. Reprinted in N. Chomsky, *New horizons in the study of language and mind* (pp. 19–45). Cambridge, UK: Cambridge University Press.

Chomsky, N. (1992b). Language and interpretation: Philosophical reflections and empirical enquiry. In J. Earman (Ed.), *Inference, explanation and other frustrations: Essays in the philosophy of science* (pp. 99–128). Berkeley: University of California Press; reprinted in N. Chomsky, *New horizons in the study of language and mind* (pp. 46–74). Cambridge, UK: Cambridge University Press.

Chomsky, N. (2000). Internalist explorations. In N. Chomsky, *New horizons in the study of language and mind* (pp. 169–194). Cambridge, UK: Cambridge University Press.

Crane, T. (2001). *Elements of mind*. Oxford: Oxford University Press.

Cresswell, M. J. (1979). Interval semantics for some event expressions. In R. Bäuerle, U. Egli, & A. von Stechow (Eds.), *Semantics from different points of view* (pp. 90–116). Berlin and Heidelberg: Springer-Verlag.

Davidson, D. (1967a). The logical form of action sentences. In N. Rescher (Ed.), *The logic of decision and action* (pp. 81–95, with replies on pp. 115–120). Pittsburgh: University of Pittsburgh Press; reprinted with slight revisions in D. Davidson (1980), *Essays on actions and events* (pp. 105–129). Oxford: Clarendon Press.

Davidson, D. (1967b). Causal relations. *Journal of Philosophy, 64*, 691–703; reprinted in D. Davidson (1980), *Essays on actions and events* (pp. 149–162). Oxford: Clarendon Press.

Davidson, D. (1969). The individuation of events. In N. Rescher (Ed.), *Essays in honor of Carl G. Hempel* (pp. 216–234). Dordrecht: Reidel; reprinted in D. Davidson (1980), *Essays on actions and events* (pp. 163–180). Oxford: Clarendon Press.

Davidson, D. (1970). Events as particulars. *Noûs, 4*, 25–32; reprinted in D. Davidson (1980), *Essays on actions and events* (pp. 181–187). Oxford: Clarendon Press.

Dowty, D. R. (1979). *Word meaning and Montague grammar*. Reidel: Dordrecht.

Dretske, F. (1967). Can events move? *Mind, 76*, 479–492.

Dretske, F. (1977). Referring to events. *Midwest Studies in Philosophy, 2*, 90–99.

Ducasse, C. J. (1926). On the nature and the observability of the causal relation. *Journal of Philosophy, 23*, 57–68.

Forbes, G. (1993). Time, events and modality. In R. Le Poidevin & M. MacBeath (Eds.), *The philosophy of time* (pp. 80–95). Oxford: Oxford University Press.

Frege, G. (1892). Über Sinn und Bedeutung. *Zeitschrift für philosophie und philosophische kritik, 100*, 25–50.

Gibson, J. J. (1975). Events are perceivable but time is not. In J. T. Fraser & N. Lawrence (Eds.), *The study of time II. Proceedings of the Second Conference of the International Society for the Study of Time* (pp. 295–301). Berlin: Springer-Verlag.

Goldman, A. I. (1970). *A theory of human action*. Englewood-Cliffs, NJ: Prentice-Hall.

Goldman, A. I. (1971). The individuation of action. *Journal of Philosophy, 68*, 761–774.

Goldman, A. I. (1992). Metaphysics, mind and mental science. In A. I. Goldman, *Liaisons: Philosophy meets the cognitive and social sciences* (pp. 35–48). Cambridge, MA: MIT Press.

Goldman, A. I. (2007). A program for "naturalizing" metaphysics, with application to the ontology of events. *The Monist, 90*, 457–479.

Goodman, N. (1951). *The structure of appearance*. Cambridge, MA: Harvard University Press.

Hacker, P. M. S. (1982). Events, ontology and grammar. *Philosophy, 57*, 477–486.

Higginbotham, J. (1983). The logic of perceptual reports: An extensional alternative to situation semantics. *Journal of Philosophy, 80*, 100–127.

Horgan, T. (1978). The case against events. *Philosophical Review, 87*, 28–47.

Horgan, T. (1982). Substitutivity and the causal connective. *Philosophical Studies, 42*, 427–452.

Kim, J. (1966). On the psycho-physical identity theory. *American Philosophical Quarterly, 3*, 277–285.

Kim, J. (1973). Causation, nomic subsumption, and the concept of an event. *Journal of Philosophy, 70*, 217–236.

Lewis, D. K. (1986a). Events. In D. K. Lewis, *Philosophical papers*, Vol. 2 (pp. 241–269). New York: Oxford University Press.

Lewis, D. K. (1986b). *On the plurality of worlds*. Oxford: Blackwell.

Lombard, L. B. (1986). *Events: A metaphysical study*. London: Routledge.

Lycan, W. G. (1970). Identifiability-dependence and ontological priority. *The Personalist, 51*, 502–513.

Mayo, B. (1961). Objects, events, and complementarity. *Mind, 70*, 340–361.

Mellor, D. H. (1995). *The facts of causation.* London: Routledge.

Menzies, P. (1989). A unified account of causal relata. *Australasian Journal of Philosophy, 67*, 59–83.

Montague, R. (1969). On the nature of certain philosophical entities. *The Monist, 53*, 159–194.

Moravcsik, J. M. E. (1968). Strawson and ontological priority. In R. J. Butler (Ed.), *Analytical philosophy*, second series (pp. 106–119). New York: Barnes and Noble.

Needham, P. (1988). Causation: Relation or connective? *Dialectica, 42*, 201–219.

Parsons, T. (1985). Underlying events in the logical analysis of English. In E. LePore & B. McLaughlin (Eds.), *Actions and events: Perspectives on the philosophy of Donald Davidson* (pp. 235–267). Oxford: Blackwell.

Parsons, T. (1990). *Events in the semantics of English. A study in subatomic semantics.* Cambridge, MA: MIT Press.

Parsons, T. (1991). Tropes and supervenience. *Philosophy and Phenomenological Research, 51*, 629–632.

Pfeifer, K. (1989). *Actions and other events: The unifier-multiplier controversy.* New York and Bern: Peter Lang.

Pianesi, F., & Varzi, A. C. (1996). Events, topology, and temporal relations. *The Monist, 78*, 89–116.

Quine, W. V. O. (1950). Identity, ostension, hyposthasis. *Journal of Philosophy, 47*, 621–633.

Quine, W. V. O. (1970). *Philosophy of logic.* Englewood Cliffs, NJ: Prentice-Hall; second edition: Cambridge, MA: Harvard University Press, 1986.

Quine, W. V. O. (1985). Events and reification. In E. LePore & B. P. McLaughlin (Eds.), *Actions and events. Perspectives in the philosophy of Donald Davidson* (pp. 162–171). Oxford: Blackwell.

Quinton, A. (1979). Objects and events. *Mind, 88*, 197–214.

Russell, B. (1914). *Our knowledge of the external world.* London: Allen and Unwin.

Sanford, D. H. (1985). Causal relata. In E. LePore & B. McLaughlin (Eds.), *Actions and events: Perspectives on the philosophy of Donald Davidson* (pp. 282–293). Oxford: Blackwell.

Sider, T. (2001). *Four-dimensionalism: An ontology of persistence and time.* New York: Oxford University Press.

Strawson, P. F. (1959). *Individuals: An essay in descriptive metaphysics.* London: Methuen.

Thomason, S. K. (1989). Free construction of time from events. *Journal of Philosophical Logic, 18*, 43–67.

Tiles, J. E. (1981). *Things that happen.* Aberdeen: Aberdeen University Press.

Treisman, A. (1986). Features and objects in visual processing. *Scientific American, 254*(11), 114–125.

van Benthem, J. (1983). *The logic of time*. Dordrecht: Kluwer.

Varzi, A. C. (2002). Events, truth, and indeterminacy. *Dialogue, 2*, 241–264.

Vendler, Z. (1967). Causal relations. *Journal of Philosophy, 64*, 704–713.

Von Kutschera, F. (1993). Sebastian's strolls. *Grazer Philosophische Studien, 45*, 75–88.

von Wright, G. H. (1963). *Norm and action*. London: Routledge and Kegan Paul.

Walker, A. G. (1947). Durées et instants. *Revue Scientifique, 85*, 131–134.

Whitehead, A. N. (1929). *Process and reality. An essay in cosmology*. New York: Macmillan.

Wiggins, D. (1980). *Sameness and substance*. Oxford: Basil Blackwell.

3

Events Are What We Make of Them

ROBERT SCHWARTZ

Although we may not be responsible for everything that happens, we do help turn what happens into "events." Events are not simply out there and ready-made, waiting to be seen, recognized, or described; they are what we make of them. Appreciation of the role we play in this process of construction has, I think, implications for the study of event perception. I will leave the exploration of these implications, however, to those working in the field.[1]

A few preliminary distinctions are needed to set us on our way. It is standard in discussions of language and cognition to distinguish *count* terms and concepts from *mass* terms and concepts. "Giraffe," "chair,"

---

1. See Chapter 2 in this volume for an admirable account of philosophical issues concerning the notion of an "event." Although there may be some differences between Casati and Varzi's views on events and mine, this chapter is not meant to challenge either their positions or their account of the field. I have attempted, instead, to sidestep these issues, for I think versions of the questions I raise will come up no matter which philosophical account of events proves correct. In this chapter, I briefly explore how some of these conceptual matters may impinge on particular claims made by contributors to this volume. I would add that I am most sympathetic to Casati and Varzi's claim that there may not be much coherence to the full range of psychological studies that fall under the rubric "event perception." See references in Chapter 16 for examples of such diversity.

and "river" are count terms; "cloth," "bread dough," and "water" are mass terms. As the distinction suggests, count concepts can serve as a basis for counting: there are five giraffes here and 10 chairs there. Not so with mass concepts. By themselves, they do not sort the world in ways suitable for assigning cardinality. On the other hand, mass terms do provide a basis for the assessment of amount (e.g., there is *a lot of* bread dough resting on a *small expanse* of yellow cloth).

All counting requires the specification of units of measure, and count terms provide them. Count concepts individuate the items to which they apply by marking the boundaries between each of the things they pick out. Although count concepts are sometimes vague in their application, the items denoted can, in principle, be named. The giraffes, for example, may be labeled Tom, Dick, and Harry, or, if no obvious proper names are available, they can be individually referred to as giraffe A, giraffe B, and giraffe C. It is also not much of a problem to turn a mass concept into a count concept by adding qualifiers. "*Cup* of water" and "*molecule* of water" are count terms and supply units for measuring cardinality. The distinction between count and mass terms is not always obvious, sharp, or fixed, and it depends on how the terms are interpreted. Quine's example of "Mary had a little lamb" marvelously makes the point.

The general term "event" typically functions as a count term, denoting individually each and every event. There are also more limited event terms, such as "war," that apply not to all events but to specific types of individually nameable happenings. Although the exact beginnings and ends of wars may be fuzzy, in context the terms "the American Civil War," "World War I," and "the Vietnam War" are employed to pick them out uniquely. Count terms and names set the spatiotemporal boundaries of what they refer to; they determine where each item begins and ends.

Ontologically speaking, to say that something is an object is merely to assume there is a way to individuate it, or, what amounts to the same, a way to treat it as nameable. In this sense, any conglomeration of space-times, whether short or long, continuous or discontinuous, causally related or unrelated, is an object with respect to *all* concepts that denote it. So if events are treated as nameable, individuated space-time spans, they are objects from the standpoint of ontology. In turn, the claim that events have spatiotemporal beginnings and ends is trivial. The act of naming or applying a count term to them assures that whatever is so denoted has individuating boundaries.

What is it, then, that distinguishes those bits of space-time deemed events from all the other ontological objects? Everyday usage of the term "event" provides few clues. Many events are actions and have human causes; others occur naturally and are not in any sense intentional. Events taking place at subatomic levels are not directly perceivable in practice or theory. Some events are temporally quite extended and occupy more than a lifetime (e.g., the Hundred Years' War). Some last for only an instant (e.g., lighting a match, an explosion, or becoming the official winner of an election). The Hundred Years' War—or, for that matter, a baseball game stopped by rain and completed some weeks after—are events that are not spatially and temporally continuous. Moreover, spatiotemporal parts of events are as much events as the larger events that encompass them. "The fourth game of the 2002 World Series" denotes an event, but the third inning, the first pitch of the third inning, a strikeout, Smith's relief pitching, and so forth also fall under the category of "event."

Although the notion of an event is hard to pin down, we do in everyday talk label some things physical events and others physical objects. In work in vision theory, though, this rough-and-ready, context-sensitive, nontechnical distinction is often turned into a theoretically serious divide. Object perception is one area of study; event perception is supposedly separate and different. Yet the substantive basis for this distinction in both ordinary talk and psychological theory is elusive. Further complicating matters is that the contrasting notion "physical object" is in ways as problematic as that of "physical event." Again, ontologically speaking, any conglomeration of space-times is an object—for example, an area comprising the leg of chair D and the tip of the nose of dog E is, in essence, a thing unto itself. Analogously, the space-time segment consisting of chair D's leg breaking plus dog C's nose as it sneezes is an ontological object, only this time it is also a composite event. All of these spurious objects and events exist, can be named, and can be counted. If the notions "physical object" and "physical event" are to have specific content (i.e., not apply to any and all regions or sums of space-time), it is necessary to distinguish arbitrarily bounded ontological objects and events from those that are in some sense psychologically real.

This is not the place to go into the details of the obstacles faced in drawing lines between real physical objects and real physical events from other definable but hodgepodge sets of space-time; I have raised and discussed qualms about the concept of a "physical object" elsewhere.[2] Instead, I wish here to call attention to the fact that various ideas associated with the object/event distinction are not on firm ground. A brief look at the claim that events (as opposed to objects) are *changes* can be instructive.

An immediate problem with this claim is that intuitions vary as to how to interpret the notion "change." A car remaining parked for more than 2 hours does not seem to involve change, yet being parked for this period may be the event that is the cause of a parking ticket. Similarly, if a change in the temperature of a gas in a vessel is an event, should not the period of time the gas remains at a constant temperature also be an event? After all, the rising and the stable temperature cases are both functions of the continuously changing motion of the molecules in the gas. Might what goes on in the container be an event at a molecular level in either case, but a nonchanging state when viewed as the gas as an object maintaining a constant temperature? This would mean that the very same space-time region both is and is not an event.

Suppose, however, these and other troublesome cases are cleanly resolved, and some acceptable and serviceable notion of "change" is available. What of importance follows? An ambiguity in applying the concept "change," I believe, can lead us astray. George Washington seems to be as clear a case of a physical object as one is likely to find. The statement "George Washington changes," however, is subject to two readings—false in one, true in the other. The name "George Washington" refers to a specific space-time area that starts at the man's birth and ends at his death. "George Washington" always encompasses his unique and entire lifetime. It does not name any particular stage or time in his life. On the other hand, the object referred to by the name "George Washington" continually changes in terms of its physical, social, and political makeup.

The situation is similar with events. "The fourth game of the 2002 World Series" picks out an event: the game as a whole. The fourth game of the 2002 World Series is a single, temporally extended bit of space-time no matter how the game goes. The event so named does not

---

2. See "The concept of an 'object' in object perception" in *From Fragments to Objects*, edited by P. Kellman and T. Shipley (Elsevier, 2002).

change; it is what it is in total. But this ball game, of course, has many spatial and temporal events as parts and in this way does change from one instant to another.

If this distinction is kept in mind, certain supposed differences between objects and events no longer seem plausible. For example, it is frequently said that, given that events are changes, they must have a temporal span. Thus, at any one instant in time it is impossible to see an event in its entirety. With some long events, for instance the Hundred Years' War, it may not be possible to see the entire event through any one person's lifetime. But this fact about events and event perception does not distinguish these concepts from physical objects and object perception. First, an event itself may take place in an instant (e.g., an explosion). What changes and spans time is not the instantaneous event but the state of something before and after the happening. Second, consider the example of redwood trees, which are long-existing objects: no one person is likely to be around long enough to see a single tree go from seedling to decay. The object, a particular redwood tree R, is not different from the Hundred Years' War on this score. In addition, it is unlikely in general that there are many objects or events that are observed throughout their entire temporal dimension. Finally, the situation with the spatial dimensions of objects and events is symmetrical. In a sense, we never see an entire physical object at any single time. Indeed, the most we directly experience in a glance is the side facing us, and this is available to us for only a segment of its life.

Physical events and physical objects may both be treated as stretches of space-time. To be treated as ontological objects, they must be presumed to have individuated boundaries. In principle, they are nameable and countable. But if there is one way to pick anything out, there will always be many. To use a tried-and-true example, "Benjamin Franklin," "the first postmaster," and "the inventor of the bifocal" refer to the same person. The situation is the same in the case of events as space-time segments. "Joyce raising her arm," "Joyce voting," "Joyce voting for Tom," and "Joyce's action that triggered the revolution" may all name the same physical happening. Accordingly, it is possible for a subject S to know or perceive an object or event under one description and not under others. For instance, S may see Joyce raise her arm but have no idea that she is voting. The existence of such alternative ways to refer to or denote an event underpins the view that there are at least two distinct notions of "seeing" employed in discussions of event perception.[3]

To reconcile this ambiguity, consider another subject, S*, who is standing next to S and observing the same "Joycian" scene. S*, however, mistakes Martha for Joyce and, misperceiving the spatial layout, reports seeing "the person in front of Martha raising his arm to catch Joyce's attention across the room." In what is called the *transparent* sense of seeing, a person is said to see the same event, as long as it is the same space-time segment of the world that plays an appropriate causal role in his perception. Hence, it is correct to claim that S* sees the same event S sees. Likewise, S is seeing the same event, whether he is aware of it only as an arm raising or can offer one of the richer, true reports of his experience.

The situation is different with what is called the *opaque* sense of seeing (often labeled "seeing as" or "seeing that"). Here it would be incorrect to claim that S* sees that Joyce is voting, since he is unaware that this is taking place. In this sense, it is incorrect to claim that S* and S, who understands that Joyce is voting, are seeing the same thing. In addition, there is a factive sense of opaque seeing. On the factive reading, S*'s report of his perceptual state may be introspectively accurate. Nonetheless, S* does not "see" that the person in front of Joyce is raising his arm, since no such event took place.

In each of the above situations the viewer is face to face with a single spatiotemporal segment of the world, but the stories he or she can tell will differ depending on visual skills, attention, background knowledge, and much more. Moreover, even keeping these factors constant, the stories a person offers of his or her experience will depend on task, interest, context, appropriateness, and much more. Once all this variability is taken into account, however, I believe that prospects are slim of there being something common and theoretically important about the nature of events and the stories told about them. I think it less likely still that there are significant generalizations to be made about

---

3. Just whether, where, and how to draw the dichotomy is a matter of some debate. For a discussion of this and related issues, see the papers by philosophers and psychologists in my anthology *Perception* (Part 4: Perception and Conception) (Blackwell, 2003).

the mechanisms and processes of perception, in light of the extensive differences among types of events—the big bang, subatomic collisions, the Hundred Years' War, the fourth game of the 2002 World Series, Benjamin Franklin flying his kite, Joyce voting. Undoubtedly, in the laboratory it is possible to give particular tasks and delimit the normal sources of variability involved in perceiving, organizing, and categorizing events. Imposing such constraints very well may allow robust data to emerge. Whether such findings should be thought of as pertaining to some distinct phenomenon—event perception—is at best a terminological issue. Either way, the issues and problems earlier canvassed concerning events—"individuation," "objecthood," "change," "spurious events," and the like—remain to be coped with. As I indicated at the start, I will leave it to those working in the field to determine if any of this analysis has bearings on their research. Yet, as the title of this chapter suggests, the universe does not come parceled into events, and the events individuated do not arrive with "natural" boundaries among their parts that simply await inspection, perception, recognition, and description. So not only the events themselves but the theoretically significant concepts of "event" and "event perception," which hope to go beyond loose, unreflective, everyday talk, also require construction.

Part II
Developing an Understanding of Events

Part II

Developing an Understanding of Events: Overview

We begin at the beginning. The chapters in this section discuss the development of event perception, memory, and symbolic representation. Each chapter provides details about how children's skill at processing events develops. These discussions go beyond "children get better as they grow up." They consider how the development of event understanding contrasts with object understanding and interacts with understanding of language and of the social world. Read as a group, these chapters will illustrate the interconnections between perception, memory, and symbolic reasoning. There are a few important themes that are also brought up in later chapters on mature-adult event processes.

1. Children's early understanding of events is fragile at best. In Chapter 4, Johnson et al. review several cases, from causality to categorization, in which children are able to process only part of an event. Perception of visual events in the first 6 months of life appears to be characterized by an emerging fragile structure. This fits with the fragile structure of memories for events described by Bauer in Chapter 6. The developing strength of the memories for events may in turn contribute to the emerging ability, described by Pruden et al. (Chapter 7) and by Maguire and Dove (Chapter 8), to categorize events and represent them with prepositions and verbs. The emerging ability to perceive human

actions and social interactions may be related to the development of the temporal lobes, and fits with Grossman's and Heberlein's discussions of the importance of the posterior superior temporal sulcus in processing of social events in Chapters 13 and 14.

2. Understanding events requires understanding relations among objects (or object parts). Chapters in this part discuss how the ability to process relations in events develops over the first 2 years of life. Event representations become more robust as infants come to represent the relations among objects in an event. Both Pruden et al. (Chapter 7) and Maguire and Dove (Chapter 8) highlight the importance of conceptualizing verbs as inherently relational terms that free the concepts of events (such as running) from the details of particular events (such as who ran). As their cognitive sophistication and neural structures develop, children require fewer instances of an event to form episodic memories (see Chapter 6).

3. Among the most important relations used to understand events are the goals of actions. Detecting goals requires noting the changing relation between two objects (e.g., as an animate actor avoids obstacles to progressively approach a goal). Many important events involve animate actors and thus can best be understood, and characterized, in terms of goals (Buresh & Woodward, 2007). Baldwin, Loucks, and Sabbagh (Chapter 5) discuss how humans may take advantage of some simple rules of pragmatics to infer the action goals of others. Although simple, pragmatically oriented heuristics may bootstrap a perceiver into learning about goals, an adult-like understanding of goals is the result of a protracted developmental sequence. Some consequences of this development can be seen in the emergence of abilities to imitate actions after a delay and to effectively consolidate event representations for long-term memory (see Chapter 6).

The pattern of development of event cognition helps us understand mature event representations and highlights the importance of situating our understanding of events in the context of action.

Reference

Buresh, J. S., & Woodward, A. L. (2007). Infants track action goals within and across agents. *Cognition, 104*, 27–314.

4

Perceptual Development in Infancy as the Foundation of Event Perception

SCOTT P. JOHNSON, DIMA AMSO, MICHAEL FRANK,
& SARAH SHUWAIRI

Our subjective experience of the world is framed in terms of *events*, demarcated and carved out from the ongoing flow of perceptual input. How does our understanding of events arise during early development? Infants inhabit the same world as adults, with the same kinds of sensory information in the surrounding environment. But do infants have the same *access* to perceptual input as adults do, and do they experience the same *interpretation* of the information that specifies a meaningful event? We will address these questions by describing the nature of events to which infants are typically exposed, by characterizing the perceptual and cognitive skills infants bring to bear on the task of understanding events, and by outlining the kinds of developmental change that have been investigated by researchers. To anticipate, very young infants' visual and auditory systems are well equipped to detect the sensory input relevant to event perception and interpretation. Yet many aspects of event perception are not available to infants, due, for example, to restrictions in their ability to integrate information across space and time, as well as other cognitive limitations. These cognitive limitations are overcome with experience and maturation.

Event perception comprises detection of the meaningful units in the flow of perceptual information and integration of these units into a coherent structure. It is not necessarily easy to define some of these terms, such as "meaningful units," because what is meaningful to one observer may be unintelligible to another (e.g., two people listening to speech in a language familiar to one and foreign to the other), and what constitutes a unit may vary across observers as well. Such caveats are especially well taken when considering event perception in infancy, where behavioral measures may be related to cognitive constructs indirectly and it may be difficult to discern which aspects of any particular stimulus are most salient. To tackle the question of infants' segmentation and integration of the units of perceptual input, then, we will consider the nature of the auditory and visual environment itself and how it might appear to infants, as well as intermodal events, in particular development of infants' sensitivity to audiovisual information. Because so little is known about developments in other sensory events relative to auditory and visual events, such as haptic (tactile) sensitivity, this area will not be discussed.

We will also focus, at the end of each section, on the broader theme of developmental mechanisms—how it is that emerging sensory skills contribute to developments in cognitive capacities to segment, synthesize, and interpret information to make sense of events. Auditory and visual information processing, we will see, are dramatically different, yet some parallels can be described, such as an analysis of distributional information.

Auditory Events

Auditory inputs consist of continuous, overlapping patterns of vibration. For infants (and adults), the most meaningful of these, arguably, is human speech. In this section we will focus primarily on two distinct problems in the parsing and organization of the speech stream. The first problem is the segmentation of the *phonetic space*. Speech sounds are naturally continuous with others of their class: the difference between /ba/ and /pa/ is the amount of time between the articulatory gesture (i.e., parting of the lips) and the voicing of the vowel, known as *voice onset time*. To access the information in human speech, a listener must break down multiple continuous spaces of possible speech sounds—such as the continuum between /ba/ and /pa/—into an inventory of discrete phonemes. The second segmentation problem is the problem of temporal segmentation of the speech stream. In a typical sample of spoken speech, there are few consistent silences between words analogous to the blank spaces in written language. In fact, there is no single reliable auditory or prosodic cue to the boundaries of words in spoken language. To identify individual units of meaning, infants must learn to integrate a variety of *phonotactic* cues (i.e., the rules of language governing possible phoneme sequences), *distributional* cues (i.e., patterns of statistical association), and *prosodic* cues (i.e., patterns of sound frequency and rhythm) to infer word boundaries (Aslin, Jusczyk, & Pisoni, 1998; Kuhl, 2004).

Segmentation by Phonetic Analysis

A variety of different phoneme groups differ along one particular dimension, such as voice onset time. How do infants discover the particular boundaries that delineate the acoustic characteristics of meaningful phonemes? Infants are able to make virtually every discrimination between phonemes that adults are able to, as well as some that adults are not (Aslin, Jusczyk, et al., 1998). By 2 months of age, for example, infants discriminate vowels from one another (perhaps due to the prominence and token frequency of vowel sounds) and ignore changes in speaker gender and intonation (Marean, Werner, & Kuhl, 1992). Traditionally, these abilities have been seen as evidence that infants' auditory perceptual capacities, as they relate to speech, are innately specified. Further evidence for this claim comes from the research of Kuhl and Miller (1975), which shows that the chinchilla, a rodent with an auditory system similar to that of humans, can learn to make many of the same auditory discriminations as human infants. However, the ability to make perceptual discriminations between stimuli does not necessarily imply an ability to distinguish which of those discriminations carries meaning. Because languages' phonetic inventories vary widely, there must be some role for linguistic experience in tuning infants' auditory systems toward those distinctions used in a particular language.

Evidence for this tuning comes from two sources. First, infants in the first 6 postnatal months, who are sensitive to many phonetic contrasts to which they are never exposed outside the laboratory, still appear to show effects of the token-frequency of particular phonemes in their native language. Eimas, Siqueland, Jusczyk, and Vigorito (1971) found that infants at 1 and 4 months of age are subject to categorical perception of native speech sounds (as are adults), with superior discrimination of equidistant exemplars across categories relative to phonetic category boundaries (e.g., /b/ versus /p/). Using similar methods, Kuhl, Williams, Lacerda, Stevens, and Lindblom (1992) tested 6-month-old English- and Swedish-native infants for discrimination of English /i/ and Swedish /y/. The English-native infants grouped a wider range of /i/ tokens relative to /y/ tokens, and this effect was reversed for the Swedish infants. These results demonstrated that by 6 months of age, infants' perceptual distinctions are influenced by their native language experience. Kuhl et al. called this effect a "perceptual magnet" because nonprototypic members of a particular phonetic category are attracted toward prototypic members, causing the differences in discrimination reported in the categorical perception literature.

A second example of tuning of the infant's auditory system for speech can be observed during the second 6 months after birth. Werker and colleagues demonstrated that infants lose the sensitivity they have in the first 6 months to phonetic contrasts that are not meaningful in their native language. Werker and Tees (1983) found that English-native 4-year-olds were sensitive to contrasts present in Hindi but not in English. Werker and Tees (1984) then extended this result to English-native infants, tested in three age groups (6 to 8 months, 8 to 10 months, and 10 to 12 months) on a phonetic contrast that occurs only in Hindi. Monolingual English and Hindi adults were tested on the same contrast. Hindi-speaking adults and 6- to 8-month-old infants were able to discriminate this contrast successfully, but only some of the 8- to 10-month-olds were able to discriminate it, and the majority of the English-speaking adults and 10- to 12-month-olds were not. This study was the first strong piece of evidence demonstrating that infants' phonetic perception undergoes some sort of perceptual reorganization (Werker & Tees, 1999).

Some researchers have suggested that early attunement to the meaningful dimensions of variation in the speech signal is due to word learning. For example, learning that "bear" and "pear" differ only by the difference between /ba/ and /pa/, yet are completely separate in their associated semantics, might allow infants to notice that this particular distinction is meaningful (Jusczyk, 1985; Lalonde & Werker, 1995). But this proposed mechanism fails to explain similar effects in the domain of vowels. Polka and Werker (1994) showed that 4-month-old infants were able to discriminate both German and English vowel contrasts, while 6-month-old English-native infants were able to discriminate only the English contrasts. There is little evidence that 6-month-olds are able to segment minimally paired words from fluent speech and make semantic associations between them (in fact, the earliest evidence for this comes at 17 months; see Stager & Werker, 1997). Evidence for word segmentation in younger infants comes from Jusczyk and Aslin (1995), who found that infants at 8 months succeeded in a task at which 6-month-olds fail: recognition of single words presented in a series of repeated sentences. Six-month-olds, however, succeed at this kind of task when the tested word was the infant's own name or the word "mommy" or "mama" (Bortfeld, Morgan, Golinkoff, & Rathbun, 2005). Evidence that perceptual reorganization occurs earlier for vowels than consonants rules out a variety of general maturational and cognitive hypotheses while giving support to a possible mechanism based on token-frequency and cumulative experience, since vowels are both more prominent and more salient in speech (especially infant-directed speech) than consonants (Fernald & Kuhl, 1987).

A recent study by Maye, Werker, and Gerken (2002) provides more direct support for such a view. Six- and 8-month-old infants were familiarized to speech sounds on a continuum from /da/ to /ta/, with exemplars distributed either unimodally (grouping midway between /da/ and /ta/) or bimodally (with one group of exemplars clustered around /ta/ and another around /da/). At test, only the infants who were familiarized to the bimodal distribution were able to discriminate exemplars from the endpoints of the continuum, suggesting that the distributional frequency of training exemplars led to distinct patterns of perceptual tunings during the task.

Segmentation by Distributional and Abstract Pattern Analysis

Sounds differ in the frequency with which they are represented in real speech, and these differences in distribution may provide an important source of information for word boundaries. In the previous section, we described evidence that infants exhibit sensitivity to the distributional frequencies of phonemes. Are infants also sensitive to the distributional frequencies of words? In a series of experiments, Saffran, Aslin, and Newport (1996) and Saffran, Newport, and Aslin (1996) reported that after 2 minutes of exposure to an unsegmented speech stream of computer-synthesized syllables, 8-month-old infants were able to distinguish groups of syllables that appeared together reliably ("words") from syllable sequences that appeared together less frequently ("part-words" or "nonwords"), even though the individual syllables had all been heard during familiarization. All aspects of the stimuli except for the probabilities with which various syllable grouping co-occurred were controlled, leading Saffran and colleagues to conclude that the infants were using some type of analysis of sequential statistics to make the distinction between words and part- or nonwords. This result generalized to other kinds of auditory input (tones), implying that statistical learning is not dedicated to the task of language acquisition (Saffran, Johnson, Aslin, & Newport, 1999). In follow-up work, Aslin, Saffran, and Newport (1998) demonstrated that 8-month-olds made use of true transitional probability statistics rather than simple frequency counts: by varying the frequency of certain word pairs, Aslin et al. tested part-words that appeared with the same frequency as words but had different transitional probabilities, demonstrating that infants' sensitivity extended beyond the base rate of occurrence. Infants find it far more difficult, however, to learn statistical dependencies across syllables that are not adjacent in the sequence (Gómez, 2002).

By 7 months, infants can extract abstract patterns from sequences of phonemes, such as the "ABB" sequence inherent in the strings "ga ti ti" and "ri la la," and discriminate them from other patterns, such as "ABA" and "AAB," instantiated in new sets of phonemes (Marcus, Vijayan, Bandi Rao, & Vishton, 1999). By 12 months, infants can learn word order in *artificial grammars* (sets of tokens that are arranged according to a limited number of allowable orders) and generalize specific rules of the learned grammar to novel word sequences (Gómez & Gerken, 1999). Arguments have been made that performance in these two experiments could not rely on a purely statistical mechanism because, unlike the experiments on statistical learning, the materials presented during training and test were dissimilar, forcing the learner to rely on higher-order (i.e., abstract) relations within and across sequences (Marcus, 2000). At present, it is unknown whether statistical learning and acquisition of abstract patterns in speech or other auditory sequences are available to infants younger than 7 months, but infants as young as 2 months have been shown to be sensitive to distributional characteristics of visual sequences (Kirkham, Slemmer, & Johnson, 2002). In contrast, learning abstract patterns in similar kinds of visual sequences appears to be far more difficult, lending support to the notion of dissociable learning mechanisms for statistics versus rules, and perhaps for speech versus other kinds of sequential input as well (Marcus, Fernandes, Johnson, & Slemmer, 2004).

Segmentation by Prosodic Analysis

Real speech is rich in prosodic information, the patterns of stress and intonation used by speakers to impart meaning (e.g., the upward lilt that signals a question). Adults sometimes exaggerate prosodic content of speech when speaking to infants; this is often called "infant-directed speech," or IDS. Relative to adult-directed speech, IDS is easier for infants to interpret in a variety of ways. For example, mothers stress or highlight new words in infant-directed speech using vocal emphasis or by placing the novel words in sentence-final position (Fernald & Mazzie, 1991). Thiessen, Hill, and Saffran (2005) have shown that 7- to 8-month-old infants segment an artificial speech stream presented in IDS more readily than one presented with normal adult prosody.

In fact, infants can discriminate different samples of speech based on prosody from birth. Mehler et al. (1988) reported that neonates can make distinctions between their native language and other languages. These discriminations persisted when high-frequency information in the stimuli was eliminated using a low-pass filter, indicating that infants were probably making their judgments using low-frequency rhythmic information that was available in the womb. Further research by Jusczyk, Mehler, and colleagues has revealed that young infants can differentiate between languages of different rhythmic class (e.g., English from French) after only a few minutes of exposure (Jusczyk, Cutler, & Redanz, 1993; Nazzi, Bertoncini, & Mehler, 1998). At 5 months, infants can distinguish the rhythmic pattern of their native language from that of other languages in their language class (e.g., American English from Dutch), but not of two languages in their rhythmic class that are both unfamiliar (e.g., Dutch from German) (Nazzi, Jusczyk, & Johnson

2000). In addition, Jusczyk et al. (1993) have shown that 9-month-old infants prefer to listen to novel, word-like sound sequences that are similar to others in their language, while 6-month-olds have no such preference, indicating that by 9 months infants may have some idea of the phonological structure of words in their native language.

Cutler and colleagues have suggested that infants initially might assume that strong or stressed syllables are cues for the beginnings of words (Cutler & Butterfield, 1992; Cutler & Norris, 1988). This notion finds support from a study by Jusczyk, Houston, and Newsome (1999), who reported that at 7.5 months, infants relied primarily on stress patterns to segment speech, but by 10.5 months they were able to use other information, such as allophonic or phonotactic cues. However, infants use distributional cues to segment the speech stream before they use stress cues. As an example of this phenomenon in real language, there is some evidence that 6-month-olds recognize the words "mommy" and "daddy" to the degree that they look longer at a video of the named parent (Tincoff & Jusczyk, 1999; cf. Bortfeld et al., 2005). This phenomenon may be due to the massive token-frequency of "mommy" and "daddy," which would aid segmentation based on transitional probabilities, although it may also be due to the tendency of "mommy" and "daddy" to be presented alone or in utterance-final contexts, since infants are most successful at recognizing utterance-final words (Fernald, Pinto, Swingley, Weinberg, & McRoberts, 1998).

Summary: Auditory Events

Infants are sensitive to many aspects of phonetic, distributional, and prosodic information in the speech to which they are exposed, and they also show some ability to acquire more abstract kinds of structure. Infants, therefore, are well equipped with many perceptual and cognitive tools with which to begin to make sense of the language environment—to segment it into its constituents, and eventually to discover its semantic properties. At present it is difficult to describe a single overarching principle that can account for this wide range of data, but in recent years evidence has pointed to infants' analysis of statistical regularities in the speech signal as at least one principal determinant of success in the segmentation tasks discussed here. The work of Maye et al. (2002) on phonetic segmentation, for example, provides compelling evidence of a mechanism by which infants could make use of linguistic input to tune their developing auditory system to the particular regularities of their native language. On this sort of account, both categorical perception (e.g., Eimas et al., 1971) and the perceptual magnet effect (Kuhl et al., 1992) could be the result of the same process of statistical learning. Such a mechanism might serve as a point of entry for acquisition of information about stress patterns, allophonic variation, and phonotactic constraints in the native language by engaging in the same basic analysis of a variety of different regularities. This sort of view would imply that in early learning, infants gather information not only about transitional probabilities but also about phonetic transitions across words, phonetic variation across words, and stress variation across words.

Visual Events

Auditory and visual environments are alike in important ways: they both consist of overlapping inputs that must be differentiated and segmented. The mechanisms that carry out these processes, however, are unique to each modality. Both auditory and visual events are perceived *over time*, but visual information is inherently *spatial* in a way that auditory information is not. The ears are fixed in the head, but the eyes, of course, are movable such that visual attention can be directed toward relevant targets in the world (as we discuss subsequently, however, visual attention does not always follow the point of gaze precisely). Moreover, the observer is generally free to move around the environment, which enables exploration and discovery of new visual features unavailable from previous vantage points (Gibson, 1979). Young infants lack the capacity for free movement in the manner of adults, but, as we will see in a later section, the oculomotor (eye movement) system is largely functional shortly after birth, and infants make good use of it to learn about the world.

In the previous section, we presented evidence that infants learn fundamental aspects of speech rapidly and effectively, and it seems sensible to do so, because speech is clearly of great utility in communicating with others. In the visual environment, infants must learn about *objects*. Accurate perception of objects—their spatial layout, physical extent, typical behavior, and so on—is required for the optimal functionality of such action systems as reaching and locomotion, which reach maturity after many aspects of object perception have emerged, early in the first year after birth. (Visual events involving social interactions are the topic of Chapter 5 and will not be discussed here.) To perceive objects accurately, the infant must (a) make effective use of his or her visual attention; (b) detect the unity, boundaries, and persistence of objects; and (c) categorize stimuli as similar or dissimilar, as appropriate. Each of these will now be discussed in turn.

Visual Attention

Orienting to a location in visual space can be done *overtly*, as when we examine an object in the visual scene, or *covertly*, as when we attend to a location other than the current point of gaze. Overt attention consists of both volitional and reflexive eye movements, the former under voluntary command and the latter produced in response to the sudden onset of a stimulus (say, in the visual periphery) or when stabilizing gaze when the observer is moving (see Johnson, 2001, for a review). The most common type of volitional eye movement is the *saccade*, a quick shift of fixation from one location to another. A second type is *smooth pursuit*, the tracking of small moving targets. Saccades are functional from birth, and smooth pursuit emerges over the first several postnatal months. (Other types of eye movement, such as optokinetic and vestibulo-ocular responses, are involved in gaze stabilization and will not be discussed here; the interested reader is referred to Johnson, 2001, for a general overview of oculomotor development in infancy.)

Adult humans and many nonhuman primates move their eyes, on average, two or three times per second during everyday tasks such as scanning visual scenes, reading, and so forth (Fischer & Weber, 1993; Rayner, 1998). Infants also scan visual displays actively (Johnson, Slemmer, & Amso, 2004), and saccade patterns become more organized and systematic across the first several months after birth (Bronson, 1990, 1994). Many theories of development of visual attention have appealed to literatures on oculomotor control in monkeys, cats, and other nonhuman species that have elucidated the cortical networks that subserve overt and covert orienting. Because many kinds of attentional systems are common across species, age-related changes in orienting tasks have led to inferences about developments in certain visual pathways in humans.

This is based on the logic that an emerging observable behavior, such as a particular kind of eye movement, is rooted in maturation of the underlying cortical system. For example, Johnson (1990) proposed that the emergence of smooth pursuit across the first 2 to 3 months after birth is due to the maturation of pathways to and from a part of the visual cortex known as area MT (also known as area V5 in humans), which is known to be involved in motion processing (Newsome & Pare, 1988). However, more complex kinds of eye movement, such as fixation sequences in infants as they view intricate patterns, are less amenable to explanations involving development of a small number of cortical pathways, as they likely involve the coordination of sizable networks (Schiller, 1998).

Cognitive theories stress the infant's ability to learn from information in the environment to modify scanning, enabling increasingly efficient information extraction. For example, Johnson, Amso, and Slemmer (2003) found that infants' scan patterns are modified with short-term experience. Four-month-olds were presented with events in which a ball moved back and forth across a monitor repeatedly. The center of the ball's trajectory was occluded by a box. Thus, the ball disappeared and reappeared at (to adults) predictable intervals. The infants' eye movements were recorded. Occasionally the infants would anticipate the ball's emergence from behind the occluder, moving the point of gaze to the place in the display where the ball was to appear. More often, however, the infants moved the point of gaze to the ball after it became visible, responding rather than anticipating. Assuming that oculomotor anticipation reflects a mental representation of the ball moving on its trajectory, the behavior of these infants suggests that they had little notion of the continuing existence of the object. Six-month-olds, in contrast, produced a higher proportion of anticipations to responses, implying important developments in object representation at this time in infancy. More interesting was the behavior of a third group of infants, a group of 4-month-olds who viewed the trajectory-occlusion display after first being shown the same ball moving on an identical trajectory, but fully visible rather than partly occluded. When these infants then viewed the occlusion display, the proportion of anticipations to responses matched closely that of the 6-month-olds described previously. This result suggests that simple experience viewing a moving object provided an important learning opportunity for the younger infants; learning was rapid—occurring after only 2 minutes of exposure to the visible trajectory—and effective at guiding subsequent behavior.

In the Johnson, Amso et al. (2003) study just described, the event and behaviors in question were relatively simple and circumscribed, but in the real world events are often complex, and appropriate behaviors may be indeterminate. Little is known about how infants go about determining how to direct their gaze under such conditions. But progress has been made recently in addressing this question, in particular by considering the dual nature of visual attention. Every act of stimulus *selection* implies complementary processes of *inhibition* of the many potential inputs that must be ignored or suppressed. Inhibitory mechanisms are known to develop gradually across the first year after birth: saccades to locations in a stimulus array that were formerly occupied by an ignored object are slowed relative to control locations in infants as young as 9 months, providing evidence of inhibition of the ignored location (via covert attention; Amso & Johnson, 2005b), but this kind of inhibition appears to be less efficient in younger infants (Amso & Johnson, 2005a). The extent to which infants ignore a competing stimulus for attention depends on a host of stimulus characteristics of the target and surrounding distracters, such as their color and motion (Dannemiller, 2000, 2002), the number of distracters (Rovee-Collier, Bhatt, & Chazin, 1996), and the size and orientation of stimulus components (Adler, Gerhardstein, & Rovee-Collier, 1998; Adler, Inslicht, Rovee-Collier, & Gerhardstein, 1998).

Recently, Amso and Johnson (2006) described a model of infants' fixation sequences based on the selective and inhibitory mechanisms that determine which targets in the visual environment are fixated, presumably for subsequent processing. Three-month-old infants were tested on a visual search task in which a single target (a small red bar) was embedded among several dozen randomly placed vertical distracter elements, all identical to the target, except the target either was tilted to the right or translated back and forth. As infants viewed these arrays, their eye movements were recorded. There were individual differences in the effectiveness and latency with which the tilted (but not the moving) targets were selected. In a second task, administered on the same day, the infants were tested for their ability to perceive the unity of the two visible parts of an object moving behind an occluder that hid the moving object's center. Those infants who tended to locate more tilted targets in the search study also tended to provide evidence of unity perception, implying that scanning efficiency was an important component of success at both tasks. Interestingly, the search times for the "effective" scanners were reliably longer than those of the infants who did not show evidence of unity perception. This suggests that effective scanners engaged in qualitatively different kinds of visual search strategy relative to less effective searchers. Amso and Johnson (2006) interpreted these results as evidence that the infants who showed superior search skills were better able to inhibit the tendency to fixate the distracter elements, which in turn made them better able to determine the important visual information specifying unity in the object task—that is, the mechanisms supporting effective selection and inhibition were the same as those that led to success at disambiguating a moving object event involving occlusion.

Object and Scene Perception

There is more to the surrounding visual environment than is projected to the eye, because the full extent of objects is occluded or otherwise unseen from any single vantage point (Gibson, 1979). Yet our subjective visual experience is not one of surface *fragments* but instead one of *objects*, each with a characteristic shape, size, and distance, extending beyond what is directly visible. A perennial question of developmental and cognitive science concerns how infants, with relatively little experience in the world, may construe the visual world as fragments, as objects, or perhaps as something in between. Piaget (1936/1952) famously described a series of errors produced by infants as they attempted to search for an object concealed among a single or multiple potential hiding places (including the "A-not-B" error) and concluded that early in the first year after birth, infants experience the world as consisting of "sensorial images" that have no substance or volume. On Piaget's theory, infants initially interpret events as a consequence of their own behavior (i.e., egocentrically), as when reaching to a particular place produces a particular effect (such as making an object graspable). Later, after extensive experience interacting with objects, infants come to interpret events and objects as independent of themselves (i.e., allocentrically). Since these seminal observations, research has provided mixed support for Piaget's findings and for his theory. In the next section of the chapter, we will discuss evidence for a new perspective on infants' event perception: the visual system is partly organized at birth, and developments in sensory, motor, and cognitive skills across the first year after birth provide the foundation for accurate perception of visual events. Mechanisms of development will also be discussed.

Perception of Partly Occluded Objects

When we see a familiar object that is partly hidden by a nearer object, such as a pencil on a desk whose ends are protruding from under a stack of paper, we tend to assume that the parts of the object are joined beneath the occluder, given certain conditions—alignment of the visible parts, similar coloring, and so forth. If the visible parts were to be misaligned, on the other hand, we would tend to assume that, for instance, two pencils were under the papers. As adults, we carry with us a great deal of knowledge about how objects in the world typically behave, including pencils. Do infants perceive unity under conditions of occlusion, when they may have little or none of this "top-down" knowledge of objects in the world?

Newborn infants have been tested for unity perception, and the evidence to date indicates that they do not perceive partly occluded objects as wholes but rather as parts only (Slater, Morison, et al., 1990; Slater, Johnson, Brown, & Badenoch, 1996). In these studies, newborns (younger than 3 days old, observed in the hospital prior to going home) were presented with center-occluded object displays similar to the protruding-pencil example discussed previously and were allowed to view them repeatedly until looking times across individual trials fell to half their original level. This method of "habituation" is standard in experiments that probe infants' perceptual and cognitive development and leads reliably to a preference for novel stimuli during the second, "test" (posthabituation) phase of the study (Bornstein, 1985; Cohen, 1976). The newborns observed by Slater and colleagues reliably showed a preference for a test display consisting of a "complete" version of the partly occluded object seen during habituation, looking less at a "broken" version composed of two pieces corresponding to the partly hidden object's visible parts. In other words, the infants showed a novelty preference for a visual event that resembled a connected object. Their looking-time behavior revealed that they discerned the partly occluded object as more similar to the disconnected object parts. Several months later, the situation is reversed: 2-month-olds perceive unity in partial occlusion displays under certain circumstances (e.g., if the occluder is relatively small and the visible parts closer together), and by 4 months unity perception is more robust (Johnson, 2004).

Taken together, these findings corroborate Piaget's claims of the young infant's perception of the visual world as fragmented and unable to fully interpret occlusion. However, other research suggests that the newborn visual system is able to perceive many aspects of the environment quite accurately, such as the fact that objects retain their size and shape despite viewing distance and angle (i.e., size and shape constancy, respectively; Slater & Morison, 1985; Slater, Mattock, & Brown, 1990).

Perception of Fully Occluded Objects

A similar developmental pattern holds for infants' perception of objects that move on a visible trajectory, become occluded by a screen, and subsequently re-emerge. Johnson and colleagues (Johnson, Bremner, et al., 2003; Bremner et al., 2005) found that 2-month-olds did not perceive a partly occluded trajectory as being continuous across occlusion, but under some circumstances, such as with a narrow occluder, 4-month-olds did perceive trajectory continuity, and older infants (6-month-olds) were able to perceive continuity even in a wide-occluder display. These experiments employed 2-D, computer-generated stimuli, adopting a similar method to examine perception of object unity: habituation to an occlusion event in which an object moves repeatedly back and forth on a center-occluded trajectory, followed at test by a continuous trajectory (no occluder) alternating with two disconnected trajectory segments that correspond to the visible parts viewed in the habituation event. The use of 3-D events, rather than 2-D, may enhance young infants' ability to perceive occlusion (Smith, Johnson, & Spelke, 2003). Nevertheless, at 4 months occlusion perception remains fragile and sensitive to various display characteristics, such as occluder size, the duration for which the object is out of sight, and the path of the trajectory itself (e.g., straight versus crooked, horizontal versus oblique; Bremner et al., 2007).

The evidence described in this section and the previous section of the chapter on infants' perception of partial and full occlusion reveals an intriguing parallel. Initially in postnatal development, when infants view occlusion displays, they appear to respond solely to the visible surfaces, failing to take account of those object parts that are not seen directly. Within several months after birth, however, infants perceive occlusion under limited circumstances, and this perception becomes increasingly more robust and flexible with development. This "parts-to-whole" pattern of development is characteristic of infants' responses to moving-object events (Johnson, 2003). Younger infants typically fail to perceive the overall coherence of events that adults seem to detect with little effort. Two examples of this trend are provided by research on infants' perception of *biological motion* and *causality*, discussed next.

Perception of Biological Motion

Biological motion refers to a visual stimulus in which an animate figure is shown, such as a person walking in place on a treadmill. The person may be filmed in a darkened environment with small luminous patches attached to a small number of locations, such as hips, knees, and feet, such that the person's outline can not be seen but the positions of key joints and flexing positions of the body are revealed by the moving lights. Infants younger than 3 months perceive the individual elements in these stimuli as disconnected and, presumably, unrelated (Bertenthal, Proffitt, & Kramer, 1987). Adults, in contrast, tend to see the relations among elements easily (Nakayama, 1985). (The interested reader is encouraged to read Chapter 12 in this volume.)

Perception of Causality

Like object occlusion, causality can not be perceived directly but rather must be inferred (see the discussion in Chapter 20). Causality perception requires sensitivity to the *directionality* of events, in the sense that the ongoing events that we see are often irreversible. Development of sensitivity to temporal directionality has been assessed by showing infants "forward" and "backward" videos of real-world events, such as liquid pouring from one glass to another (i.e., *gravity-related* events) and a cookie being broken apart (i.e., *separation* events; Friedman, 2002). Four-month-olds preferred to look at a forward version of one kind of gravity-related event (liquid pouring) but not others (e.g., tumbling blocks, a dropping ball). Eight-month-olds, in contrast, showed preferences for forward versions of a variety of gravity-related events, but no preferences when viewing separation events. These results imply an emerging sensitivity to directionality across the first year after birth, perhaps based on (a) growing experience viewing events in the real world and (b) the infant's own skills and experience manipulating objects, skills that become increasingly proficient after 4 to 6 months (e.g., Thelen et al., 1993).

Interestingly, in the studies just described there appeared to be no special sensitivity to directionality in events that involved a hand (such as pouring), raising the issue of development of reactions to *animacy* in causal events. Premack (1990) suggested that infants might discriminate between two general classes of object motion in causal events: object motions initiated by contact with another object, and events involving *self-propelled* motion. Self-propelled motion was proposed to invoke perception of animacy, whereas contact events in general do not necessarily require this assumption. There is evidence that 9-month-old infants are sensitive to spatiotemporal information specifying "causation at a distance," as when a moving object (e.g., a computer-animated red square) moves toward another moving object (e.g., a green square) and seems (to adults) to make the second object move without direct contact (Schlottman & Surian, 1999). Infants younger than 8 months do not recognize "role reversal" in this kind of event, suggesting that sensitivity to so-called *social causality* develops after this time, at least in viewing computer-generated displays (Rochat, Striano, & Morgan, 2004).

Leslie and Keeble (1987) reported that by 6 months, infants appear to detect a causal relation only when there is no delay in one object launching a second object and no obvious spatial gap at the place of contact. (Presumably, the infants did not perceive the "noncausal" events as involving animacy.) More recent research reveals a complex developmental pattern in causal perception (Cohen, Amsel, Redford, & Casasola, 1998). By testing infants outside the age range observed by Leslie and Keeble, Cohen and colleagues were able to establish a developmental trajectory from processing of lower-level perceptual features to a robust and flexible comprehension of causality. Younger infants (4-month-olds) ignored causality per se and responded most strongly to the amount of continuous motion in a display. Slightly older infants (5.5-month-olds) showed a trend toward processing of spatial and temporal components of causal events, and 6.25-month-olds appeared to categorize simple events as either truly causal or noncausal. But 6.5-month-olds failed to recognize causality when complex objects were employed in the events. Ten-month-olds handled the extra processing load presented by object complexity and perceived causality in realistic object events. However, older infants, too, fell back to processing lower-level features exclusively when events were made even more complicated by changing objects *across* trials.

Taken together, results from these experiments imply that young infants detect causal relations between objects on the basis of proximity between moving objects in space and time, but information-processing demands place constraints on whether perception of causality is observed in any particular event. Perception of animacy and agent–recipient relations in causal events develops later in infancy, perhaps on the basis of noting correlations and building associations among spatiotemporal cues in events involving people and animals (Rakison, 2005; Rakison & Poulin-Dubois, 2001).

Categorization of Events

Concept formation is a fundamental aspect of human cognition; its foundation is the ability to categorize physical and perceptual information about objects and events in a systematic fashion. Initial work on adult concept learning and categorization abilities established a prototype-based model of classification behavior (Posner & Keele, 1968), which was later expanded upon by Rosch and colleagues (Rosch, 1975; Rosch & Mervis, 1975; see also Murphy, 2002). The idea behind prototype theory is that we categorize objects and events systematically based on salient perceptual attributes, or "criterial" features, that these things have in common. These major features serve as reference points for defining and assigning category membership (Rosch, 1975).

Young infants have been shown to engage in perceptual grouping based on similarity, providing evidence of early categorization skills. A seminal study by Bomba and Siqueland (1983) demonstrated that 3- and 4-month-olds show prototype effects: the infants responded as if an unfamiliar prototype of a category of geometric dot patterns (from which exemplars had been shown) was more familiar than a previously observed exemplar. Similarly, Quinn, Burke, and Rush (1993) explored the ability of infants at this age to group perceptual elements in a visual display by habituating infants to a pattern of 16 squares arranged in a 4 × 4 grid. Two alternating rows of squares were colored black and two white in either a vertical or horizontal orientation during a habituation phase, followed by a test stimulus consisting of black and white vertical or horizontal solid bars. The infants showed a preference for the novel orientation of solid bars, indicating that they grouped the similar squares into vertical columns. Notably, in both these experiments, the test stimuli were novel and had not been presented prior to test. Infant performance, therefore, was necessarily based on the ability to recognize the correspondence of stimulus attributes across habituation and test displays.

Quinn, Eimas, and Rosenkrantz (1993) used the familiarization–novelty preference paradigm with young infants to investigate acquisition of animal categories, which are more complex and abstract than the simple geometric forms discussed previously. When 3- to 4-month-olds were familiarized with photographs of different cats presented sequentially, the infants subsequently preferred to look at a novel dog photograph rather than a novel cat, suggesting that the infants had formed a category representation of "cat" that incorporated novel cats but excluded novel dogs (hence more interest in looking at the dog photograph). In contrast, when infants were initially familiarized with dog photographs, they showed no preference at test for looking at either a novel dog or a novel cat. Separate control conditions revealed that infants familiarized with either cats or dogs looked longer at photographs of birds, implying that the dog category is not overly inclusive of other types of animal stimulus. Thus the infants may have developed a category of "dog" that included novel dogs but also included novel cats, evidence of an interesting asymmetry in the exclusivity of the two perceptual category representations (cats or dogs) formed during familiarization. This asymmetry presumably resulted from the greater similarity of cats relative to dogs. The dog category incorporates a greater variety of body shapes and facial features and therefore may be more inclusive of a wider range of appearance for other animals to the naïve observer (Mareschal, French, & Quinn, 2000). Together these studies provide evidence that young infants learn to acquire prototype-based representations and perceptual categorization skills in infancy from repeated exposure to multiple, perceptually similar examples.

Relative to categorization of static visual displays, less is known about categorization of events. Recently, Baillargeon and Wang (2002) proposed a developmental trend in event categorization: when infants encounter some event involving object occlusion, they form an impression about the spatial relations among the objects and categorize the event according to the complexity of the hiding relation. For example, infants appear to have more difficulty processing containment than interposition (one object in front of another), but event categorization may aid in the resolution of this discrepancy by directing attention to different aspects of the hiding relations. The relative sizes of container and hidden object determine whether or not containment is possible but are less important for determining interposition, because the spatial relations involved in containment "fit" are more constrained. Thus, event categorization is proposed as a mechanism to guide developments in how infants process details of events—how many objects are involved, their relative sizes, their spatial relations, and whether or not a particular arrangement of objects is possible. It remains to be determined whether development of event categorization itself proceeds on the same basis as the other kinds of visual categorization discussed previously. (For further discussion of event categorization, see Chapter 7 in this volume.)

Summary: Visual Events

Infants begin postnatal life with the ability to segment visible object surfaces by virtue of differences in color, shape, motion, and texture, but the evidence to date suggests that newborns are insensitive to occlusion. Within several months after birth, however, infants begin to detect relations among individual visual features, supporting perception of object occlusion, along with biological motion, causality, categorization, and other holistic constructs. As in the case of development of responses to auditory events, it seems likely that analysis of statistical and distributional regularities in the visual environment plays a key role in infants' burgeoning ability to make sense of the events they see. Experiments that examine infants' sensitivity to probabilistic information in visual sequences (Kirkham et al., 2002) and in visual scenes (Fiser & Aslin, 2002), and others that probe infants' ability to form associations across visual events (e.g., between unoccluded and occluded trajectories; Johnson, Amso, et al., 2003), provide evidence that the cognitive skills necessary to detect correlations among visual features in the environment are in place early (cf. Rakison & Poulin-Dubois, 2001; Younger

& Cohen, 1986). In addition to statistical learning, infants participate actively in constructing knowledge of events, from manual experience (Needham, Barrett, & Peterman, 2002; Piaget, 1936/1952) and improvements in oculomotor scanning strategies (Johnson et al., 2004), both of which have been shown to improve object perception skills. In addition, growing conceptual skills may lead infants to categorize events based on relatively complex spatial relations among objects (Baillargeon & Wang, 2002).

Intermodal Events

Experiments investigating infants' perception of auditory and visual events, described in the previous sections, have provided evidence for the time course of development and also provide insights into developmental mechanisms, but it is important to note that our experience of the real world is based largely on multisensory information. For instance, when we manipulate objects, we typically see and touch them simultaneously. Also, the sight of people and the sound of their voices are co-located in space, something that also applies to sound-emitting objects in general, and when someone speaks, speech sounds correspond to facial movements in an orderly way. The ability to detect the matches existing in information from separate senses is thus a necessary condition for an integrated, multisensory awareness of the world.

Many early accounts of the development of intermodal perception concluded that detection of intersensory equivalence was possible only after the construction of intersensory links drawn from experience in the world. Piaget (1936/1952), for example, identified the need for coordination of separate schemes for looking, hearing, and touching as preconditions for intersensory awareness. On this account, infants begin postnatal life experiencing unrelated sensations from each sensory modality. However, there is long-established evidence for some form of intersensory perception early in life. For example, young infants increase visual activity in the presence of an auditory stimulus (Horowitz, 1974), and even newborns tend to look in the direction of a sound (Butterworth & Castillo, 1976). Such findings are predictable on the basis of a theory of perceptual development presented by Gibson (1969), according to which perception is largely a matter of detecting "invariants" in perceptual information (e.g., the sight of a bouncing ball hitting the floor and the sound of its contact). This principle has important implications for intersensory perception, because invariants are higher-order structural features that have generality across modalities. For instance, the radial location of an object relative to an observer is the same whether the information specifying it is picked up through sight, hearing, or touch, and processing the world at this level implies sensitivity to intersensory equivalence. Bower (1989) suggested that newborn infants may perceive such invariants. Consistent with this view, there is evidence, which will be described subsequently in this chapter, that some kinds of intermodal equivalence are detected from birth.

Audiovisual Synchrony

An extensive literature on infants' intermodal perception has followed from the early theoretical and empirical work. One productive technique involves presenting two dynamic events side by side, accompanied by a soundtrack that matches one but not the other. Spelke (1979) presented two bouncing-ball events and successively played the soundtrack (the "bounce" sound) corresponding to one visual event, and then the other, which varied in tempo. Four-month-olds appeared to search for the event that coincided with the sound (either in terms of the common frequency of the sight and sound or the co-occurrence of sound and visual impact). In experiments that presented intermodal events that were more complex, however, young infants exhibited failures to recognize audiovisual synchrony. Using a visual paired-comparison procedure, Lewkowicz (1986) tested 3-, 6-, and 8-month-olds for the ability to detect synchronous stimulus durations. Visual stimuli consisted of a flashing checkerboard that flickered in one of three ways: silently, with a sound of brief duration, or with a sound of duration to that of the checkerboard flicker. One member of the audiovisual pair always consisted of stimulus durations that were equivalent across modalities. The 6- and 8-month-old infants looked longer at the bimodally synchronous stimuli when durations were equal, but not when the audio duration was shorter than the visual. The 3-month-olds did not show any preferential looking and therefore provided no evidence of intermodal sensitivity in this paradigm.

The audiovisual events employed by Lewkowicz (1986) were undoubtedly more complex than what typically occurs in an infant's environment, but it may be as well that young infants failed to detect intermodal synchrony because the events involved would not likely occur naturally (i.e., the events were "unecological"). In experiments that tap into infants' perception of co-location, a common occurrence in the real world, infants as young as 2 months perceive invariant relationships between sight and sound, detecting the co-location of an object and the sound it emits and the synchrony between sound and object movement (Morrongiello, Fenwick, & Nutley, 1998). Although the threshold for detecting audiovisual temporal asynchrony reduces over the age range of 2 to 8 months (Lewkowicz, 1996), current evidence suggests that temporal synchrony is initially more salient than spatial co-location (Morrongiello, Fenwick, & Nutley, 1998). This may be due to young infants' limited ability to localize sounds (Morrongiello, 1988; Morrongiello, Fenwick, & Chance, 1990).

Intermodal Associations

The ability to recognize and recall simple intermodal relations in audiovisual events is present from birth. For example, newborns have been shown to "bind" a visual stimulus with an auditory stimulus to the extent that they then seem to "expect" the sound to move with the associated object (Morrongiello, Fenwick, & Chance, 1998). Slater, Brown, and Badenoch (1997) reported that newborns are also capable of learning intermodal relations between sequential visual patterns and sounds presented in tandem. Formation of such associations is facilitated by the presence of common onset and offset of stimuli in the two modalities (Slater, Quinn, Brown, & Hayes, 1999), a finding that recalls the importance of identical stimulus duration to older infants' detection of intermodal synchrony (Lewkowicz, 1986). By 6 months, infants are able to track synchronous audiovisual events to new locations, directing attention toward an empty "window" that had previously contained a visual stimulus, when they heard an audio stimulus that had been synchronized with it during an initial learning phase. This occurred even when the window moved to a unique location (Richardson & Kirkham, 2004). Evidence has also been reported in older infants of the ability to learn relations between speech sounds and object motions (Gogate & Bahrick, 1998, 2001), a finding that bears important implications for language acquisition and other cognitive achievements.

Intermodal Information and the Growth of Cognitive Capacity

In addition to being a foundation for intermodal perception of the world, detection of invariant intermodal relations may be vital as scaffolding for learning specific unimodal properties, such as the quality of sound produced by an object, the precise sound of an individual's voice, and so forth. Bahrick (2000) has drawn a distinction between *amodal* and *arbitrary* intermodal equivalences. Amodal equivalences are characterized by redundancy across modalities, and can be contrasted with arbitrary relations, in which information from one modality provides no information about the form of information in the other modality. Thus, when a person speaks, there is an amodal relation between onset and rhythm of speech and accompanying facial movements, but nothing in the facial movements provides information about the precise sound of the voice, and so this relationship is arbitrary. Bahrick suggested that in principle, detection of amodal equivalences may be available from birth, whereas arbitrary relations must be learned. The fact that newborn infants can learn arbitrary relations appears to argue against such a position, but at present it is unclear whether learning may be better facilitated by amodal, relative to arbitrary, intermodal equivalencies, because the two have not been compared directly within a single paradigm.

Summary: Intermodal Events

Infants are sensitive to intermodal relations from birth and acquire simple arbitrary intermodal associations between visual and auditory stimuli. Older infants are able to detect more complex kinds of intermodal synchrony, including events that have likely not been experienced outside a lab setting. Lewkowicz (2000) presented a theory of development of intermodal perception that is consistent with the research on perception of auditory and visual events discussed earlier in this chapter. On this account, learning starts small: initial processing restrictions force the infant learner to attend selectively to only a limited subset of available information. Temporal synchrony of amodal aspects of audiovisual events appears to be available early, and with development other kinds of relation (duration, rate, and rhythm) can be detected. Bahrick, Lickliter, and Flom (2004) suggested that early sensitivity to intermodal properties of events provides an important advantage to processing of amodal relations but can actually inhibit processing of unimodal information when bimodal information is available. Many aspects of these theoretical positions await empirical testing.

Conclusion

Understanding event perception in infancy and its underlying developmental mechanisms is of tremendous importance to cognitive and developmental science, and much progress has been made in addressing questions over the past several decades. Infants demonstrate an early sensitivity to structure in many kinds of events. Most notably, certain aspects of speech perception, detection of temporal synchrony in audiovisual events, and learning of arbitrary intermodal relations appear to be available from birth, as are the abilities to achieve figure-ground segmentation and perceive certain aspects of the layout of objects in the visual environment. Within the first several months after birth, infants detect many kinds of complex event structures, such as abstract patterns in auditory input, object occlusion, causality, and associations between sounds and object motions. Discovery of complex structure is founded in expanding cognitive capacity, such as the ability to retain progressively greater amounts of information in short-term memory (see Chapter 6) and detection of probabilistic relations among stimulus features. The literature also reflects an increasing interest in the reciprocities between developments in perceptual skills, cognitive competence, and neural maturation. These are exciting possibilities, and recent technological advances—for example, in eye tracking and recording of cortical activity in infants—are certain to contribute important knowledge in these areas. The field will benefit most from a strong focus on developmental mechanisms and on forging links across areas and paradigms.

References

Adler, S. A., Gerhardstein, P., & Rovee-Collier, C. (1998). Levels-of-processing effects in infant memory? *Child Development, 69*, 280–294.

Adler, S. A., Inslicht, S., Rovee-Collier, C., & Gerhardstein, P. C. (1998). Perceptual asymmetry and memory retrieval in 3-month-old infants. *Infant Behavior & Development, 21*, 253–272.

Amso, D., & Johnson, S. P. (2005a, April). *Insights into inhibitory development: Evidence from spatial negative priming in infants.* Poster presented at the meeting of the Society for Research in Child Development, Atlanta, GA.

Amso, D., & Johnson, S. P. (2005b). Selection and inhibition in infancy: Evidence from the spatial negative priming paradigm. *Cognition, 95,* B27–B36.

Amso, D., & Johnson, S. P. (2006). Learning by selection: Visual search and object perception in young infants. *Developmental Psychology, 42,* 1236–1245.

Aslin, R. N., Jusczyk, P. W., & Pisoni, D. B. (1998). Speech and auditory processing during infancy: Constraints on and precursors to language. In D. Kuhn & R. Siegler (Eds.), *Handbook of child psychology, 5th edition. Volume 2: Cognition, perception and language* (pp. 147–198). New York: Wiley.

Aslin, R. N., Saffran, J. R., & Newport, E. L. (1998). Computation of conditional probability statistics by 8-month-old infants. *Psychological Science, 9,* 321–325.

Bahrick, L. E. (2000). Increasing specificity in the development of intermodal perception. In D. Muir and A. Slater (Eds.), *Infant development: The essential readings* (pp. 119–136). Oxford, UK: Blackwell.

Bahrick, L. E., Lickliter, R., & Flom, R. (2004). Intersensory redundancy guides the development of selective attention, perception, and cognition in infancy. *Current Directions in Psychological Science, 13,* 99–102.

Baillargeon, R., & Wang, S. (2002). Event categorization in infancy. *Trends in Cognitive Sciences, 6,* 85–93.

Bertenthal, B. I., Proffitt, D. R., & Kramer, S. J. (1987). Perception of biomechanical motions by infants: Implementation of various processing constraints. *Journal of Experimental Psychology: Human Perception and Performance, 13,* 577–585.

Bomba, P. C., & Siqueland, E. R. (1983). The nature and structure of infant form categories. *Journal of Experimental Child Psychology, 35,* 294–328.

Bornstein, M. H. (1985). Habituation of attention as a measure of visual information processing in human infants: Summary, systematization, and synthesis. In G. Gottlieb & N. A. Krasnegor (Eds.), *Measurement of audition and vision in the first year of postnatal life: A methodological overview* (pp. 253–300). Norwood, NJ: Ablex.

Bortfeld, H., Morgan, J. L., Golinkoff, R. M., & Rathbun, K. (2005). *Mommy* and me: Familiar names help launch babies into speech-stream segmentation. *Psychological Science, 16,* 298–304.

Bower, T. G. R. (1989). The perceptual world of the new-born child. In A. Slater & G. Bremner (Eds.), *Infant development* (pp. 85–95). East Sussex, UK: Erlbaum.

Bremner, J. G., Johnson, S. P., Slater, A. M., Mason, U., Foster, K., Cheshire, A., et al. (2005). Conditions for young infants' perception of object trajectories. *Child Development, 74,* 1029–1043.

Bremner, J. G., Johnson, S. P., Slater, A., Mason, U., Cheshire, A., & Spring, J. (2007). Conditions for young infants' failure to perceive trajectory continuity. *Developmental Science, 10,* 613–624.

Bronson, G. W. (1990). Changes in infants' visual scanning across the 2- to 14-week age period. *Journal of Experimental Child Psychology, 49,* 101–125.

Bronson, G. W. (1994). Infants' transitions toward adult-like scanning. *Child Development, 65,* 1243–1261.

Butterworth, G., & Castillo, M. (1976). Coordination of auditory and visual space in newborn human infants. *Perception, 5,* 155–160.

Cohen, L. B. (1976). Habituation of infant visual attention. In T. J. Tighe & R. N. Leaton (Eds.), *Habituation* (pp. 207–238). Hillsdale, NJ: Erlbaum.

Cohen, L. B., Amsel, G., Redford, M. A., & Casasola, M. (1998). The development of infant causal perception. In A. Slater (Ed.), *Perceptual development: Visual, auditory, and speech perception in infancy* (pp. 167–209). East Sussex, UK: Psychology Press, Ltd.

Cutler, A., & Butterfield, S. (1992). Rhythmic cues to speech segmentation: Evidence from juncture misperception. *Journal of Memory and Language, 31,* 218–236.

Cutler, A., & Norris, D. G. (1988). The role of strong syllables in segmentation for lexical access. *Journal of Experimental Psychology: Human Perception and Performance, 14,* 113–121.

Dannemiller, J. L. (2000). Competition in early exogenous orienting between 7 and 21 weeks. *Journal of Experimental Child Psychology, 76,* 253–274.

Dannemiller, J. L. (2002). Relative color contrast drives competition in early exogenous orienting. *Infancy, 3,* 275–301.

Eimas, P. D., Siqueland, E. R., Jusczyk, P. W., & Vigorito, J. (1971). Speech perception in infants. *Science, 171,* 303–306.

Fernald, A., & Kuhl, P. K. (1987). Acoustic determinants of infant preference for motherese speech. *Infant Behavior and Development, 10,* 279–293.

Fernald, A., & Mazzie, C. (1991). Prosody and focus in speech to infants and adults. *Developmental Psychology, 27,* 209–221.

Fernald, A., Pinto, J. P., Swingley, D., Weinberg, A., & McRoberts, G. W. (1998). Rapid gains in speed of verbal processing by infants in the 2nd year. *Psychological Science, 9,* 228–231.

Fischer, B., & Weber, H. (1993). Express saccades and visual attention. *Behavioral and Brain Sciences, 16,* 553–610.

Fiser, J., & Aslin, R. N. (2002). Statistical learning of new visual feature combinations by infants. *Proceedings of the National Academy of Sciences, 99,* 15822–15826.

Friedman, W. J. (2002). Arrows of time in infancy: The representation of temporal-causal invariances. *Cognitive Psychology, 44,* 252–296.

Gibson, E. J. (1969). *Principles of perceptual learning and development.* New York: Appleton Century Crofts.

Gibson, J. G. (1979). *The ecological approach to visual perception.* Boston: Houghton Mifflin.

Gogate, L. J., & Bahrick, L. E. (1998). Intersensory redundancy facilitates learning of arbitrary relations between vowel sounds and objects in 7-month-old infants. *Journal of Experimental Child Psychology, 69,* 133–149.

Gogate, L. J., & Bahrick, L. E. (2001). Intersensory redundancy and 7-month-old infants' memory for arbitrary syllable-object relations. *Infancy, 2,* 219–231.

Gómez, R. L. (2002). Variability and detection of invariant structure. *Psychological Science, 13,* 431–436.

Gómez, R. L., & Gerken, L. (1999). Artificial grammar learning by 1-year-olds leads to specific and abstract knowledge. *Cognition, 70,* 109–135.

Horowitz, F. D. (1974). Visual attention, auditory stimulation, and language discrimination in young infants. *Monographs of the Society for Research in Child Development, 39,* 5–6.

Johnson, M. H. (1990). Cortical maturation and the development of visual attention in early infancy. *Journal of Cognitive Neuroscience, 2,* 81–95.

Johnson, S. P. (2001). Neurophysiological and psychophysical approaches to visual development. In A. F. Kalverboer, A. Gramsbergen (Series Eds.), & J. B. Hopkins (Section Ed.), *Handbook of brain and behaviour in human development: IV. Development of perception and cognition* (pp. 653–675). Amsterdam: Elsevier.

Johnson, S. P. (2003). The nature of cognitive development. *Trends in Cognitive Sciences, 7,* 102–104.

Johnson, S. P. (2004). Development of perceptual completion in infancy. *Psychological Science, 15,* 769–775.

Johnson, S. P., Amso, D., & Slemmer, J. A. (2003). Development of object concepts in infancy: Evidence for early learning in an eye tracking paradigm. *Proceedings of the National Academy of Sciences (USA), 100,* 10568–10573.

Johnson, S. P., Bremner, J. G., Slater, A., Mason, U., Foster, K., et al. (2003). Infants' perception of object trajectories. *Child Development, 74,* 94–108.

Johnson, S. P., Slemmer, J. A., & Amso, D. (2004). Where infants look determines how they see: Eye movements and object perception performance in 3-month-olds. *Infancy, 6,* 185–201.

Jusczyk, P. W. (1985). On characterizing the development of speech perception. In J. Mehler & R. Fox (Eds.), *Neonate cognition: Beyond the blooming, buzzing confusion* (pp. 199–229). Hillsdale, NJ: Erlbaum.

Jusczyk, P. W., & Aslin, R. N. (1995). Infants' detection of sound patterns of words in fluent speech. *Cognitive Psychology, 29,* 1–23.

Jusczyk, P. W., Cutler, A., & Redanz, N. J. (1993). Infants' preference for the predominant stress patterns of English words. *Child Development, 64,* 675–687.

Jusczyk, P. W., Houston, D. M., & Newsome, M. (1999). The beginnings of word segmentation in English-learning infants. *Cognitive Psychology, 39,* 159–207.

Kirkham, N. Z., Slemmer, J. A., & Johnson, S. P. (2002). Visual statistical learning in infancy: Evidence for a domain general learning mechanism. *Cognition, 83,* B35–B42.

Kuhl, P. K. (2004). Early language acquisition: Cracking the speech code. *Nature Reviews Neuroscience, 5,* 831–843.

Kuhl, P. K., & Miller, J. D. (1975). Speech perception by the chinchilla: Voiced-voiceless distinction in alveolar plosive consonants. *Science, 190,* 69–72.

Kuhl, P. K., Williams, K. A., Lacerda, F., Stevens, K. N., & Lindblom, B. (1992). Linguistic experience alters phonetic perception in infants by 6 months of age. *Science, 255,* 606–608.

Lalonde, C. E., & Werker, J. F. (1995). Cognitive influences on cross-language speech perception in infancy. *Infant Behavior and Development, 18,* 459–475.

Leslie, A. M., & Keeble, S. (1987). Do six-month-olds perceive causality? *Cognition, 25,* 265–288.

Lewkowicz, D. J. (1986). Developmental changes in infants' bisensory response to synchronous durations. *Infant Behavior & Development*, 9, 335–353.

Lewkowicz, D. J. (1996). Perception of auditory-visual temporal synchrony in human infants. *Journal of Experimental Psychology: Human Perception & Performance*, 22, 1094–1106.

Lewkowicz, D. J. (2000). The development of intersensory temporal perception: An epigenetic systems/limitations view. *Psychological Bulletin*, 126, 281–308.

Marcus, G. F. (2000). Pa bi ku and ga ti ga: Two mechanisms children could use to learn about language and the world. *Current Directions in Psychological Science*, 9, 145–147.

Marcus, G. F., Fernandes, K., Johnson, S. P., & Slemmer, J. A. (2004). *What's special about speech? Evidence from a contrast between rules and statistics*. Paper presented at the Boston University Conference on Language, Boston, MA.

Marcus, G., Vijayan, S., Bandi Rao, S., & Vishton, P. M. (1999). Rule-learning in seven-month-old infants. *Science*, 283, 77–80.

Marean, G. C., Werner, L. A., & Kuhl, P. K. (1992). Vowel categorization by very young infants. *Developmental Psychology*, 28, 396–405.

Mareschal, D., French, R. M., & Quinn, P. (2000) A connectionist account of asymmetric category learning in infancy. *Developmental Psychology*, 36, 635–645.

Maye, J., Werker, J. F., & Gerken, L. (2002). Infant sensitivity to distributional information can affect phonetic discrimination. *Cognition*, 82, B101–B111.

Mehler, J., Jusczyk, P. W., Lambertz, G., Halsted, N., Bertoncini, J., & Amiel-Tison, C. (1988). A precursor of language acquisition in young infants. *Cognition*, 29, 144–178.

Morrongiello, B. A. (1988). Infants' localization of sounds along the horizontal axis: Estimates of minimum audible angle. *Developmental Psychology*, 24, 8–13.

Morrongiello, B. A., Fenwick, K. D., & Chance, G. (1990). Sound localization acuity in very young infants: An observer-based testing procedure. *Developmental Psychology*, 26, 75–84.

Morrongiello, B. A., Fenwick, K. D., & Chance, G. (1998). Crossmodal learning in newborn infants: Inferences about properties of auditory-visual events. *Infant Behavior & Development*, 21, 543–554.

Morrongiello, B. A., Fenwick, K. D., & Nutley, T. (1998). Developmental changes in associations between auditory-visual events. *Infant Behavior & Development*, 21, 613–626.

Murphy, G. L. (2002). *The big book of concepts*. Cambridge, MA: MIT Press.

Nakayama, K. (1985). Biological image motion processing: A review. *Vision Research*, 25, 625–660.

Nazzi, T., Bertoncini, J., & Mehler, J. (1998). Language discrimination by newborns: Toward an understanding of the role of rhythm. *Journal of Experimental Psychology: Human Perception and Performance*, 24, 756–766.

Nazzi, T., Jusczyk, P. W., & Johnson, E. K. (2000). Language discrimination by English-learning 5-month-olds: Effects of rhythm and familiarity. *Journal of Memory and Language*, 43, 1–19.

Needham, A., Barrett, T., & Peterman, K. (2002). A pick-me-up for infants' exploratory skills: Early simulated experiences reaching for objects using "sticky mittens" enhances young infants' object exploration skills. *Infant Behavior and Development, 25,* 279–295.

Newsome, W. T., & Pare, E. B. (1988). A selective impairment of motion perception following lesions of the middle temporal visual area (MT). *Journal of Neuroscience, 8,* 2201–2211.

Piaget, J. (M. Cook, Trans.) (1952). *The origins of intelligence in children.* New York: International Universities Press. (Original work published 1936.)

Polka, L., & Werker, J. F. (1994). Developmental changes in perception of nonnative vowel contrasts. *Journal of Experimental Psychology: Human Perception and Performance, 20,* 421–435.

Posner, M. I., & Keele, S. W. (1968). On the genesis of abstract ideas. *Journal of Experimental Psychology, 77,* 353–363.

Premack, D. (1990). The infant's theory of self-propelled objects. *Cognition, 36,* 1–16.

Quinn, P. C., Burke, S., & Rush, A. (1993). Part-whole perception in early infancy: Evidence for perceptual grouping produced by lightness similarity. *Infant Behavior and Development, 16,* 19–42.

Quinn, P. C., Eimas, P. D., & Rosenkrantz, S. L. (1993). Evidence for representations of perceptually similar natural categories by 3-month-old and 4-month-old infants. *Perception, 22,* 463–475.

Rakison, D. H. (2005). A secret agent? How infants learn about the identity of objects in a causal scene. *Journal of Experimental Child Psychology, 91,* 271–296.

Rakison, D. H., & Poulin-Dubois, D. (2001). The developmental origin of the animate-inanimate distinction. *Psychological Bulletin, 2,* 209–228.

Rayner, K. (1998). Eye movements in reading and information processing: 20 years of research. *Psychological Bulletin, 124,* 372–422.

Richardson, D. C., & Kirkham, N. Z. (2004). Multimodal events and moving locations: Eye movements of adults and 6-month-olds reveal dynamic spatial indexing. *Journal of Experimental Psychology: General, 133,* 46–62.

Rochat, P., Striano, T., & Morgan, R. (2004). Who is doing what to whom? Young infants' developing sense of social causality in animated displays. *Perception, 33,* 355–369.

Rosch, E. (1975). Cognitive reference points. *Cognitive Psychology, 7,* 532–547.

Rosch, E., & Mervis, C. B. (1975). Family resemblances: Studies in the internal structure of categories. *Cognitive Psychology, 7,* 573–605.

Rovee-Collier, C., Bhatt, R. S., & Chazin, C. (1996). Set size, novelty, and visual pop-out in infancy. *Journal of Experimental Psychology: Human Perception and Performance, 22,* 1178–1187.

Saffran, J. R., Aslin, R. N., & Newport, E. L. (1996). Statistical learning by 8-month-old infants. *Science, 274,* 1926–1928.

Saffran, J. R., Johnson, E. K., Aslin, R. N., & Newport, E. L. (1999). Statistical learning of tone sequences by human infants and adults. *Cognition, 70,* 27–52.

Saffran, J. R., Newport, E. L., & Aslin, R. N. (1996). Word segmentation: The role of distributional cues. *Journal of Memory and Language, 35,* 606–621.

Schiller, P. H. (1998). The neural control of visually guided eye movements. In J. E. Richards (Ed.), *Cognitive neuroscience of attention: A developmental perspective* (pp. 3–50). Mahwah, NJ: Erlbaum.

Schlottman, A., & Surian, L. (1999). Do 9-month-olds perceive causation-at-a-distance? *Perception, 28,* 1105–1113.

Slater, A., Brown, E., & Badenoch, M. (1997). Intermodal perception at birth: Newborn infants' memory for arbitrary auditory-visual pairings. *Early Development & Parenting, 6,* 99–104.

Slater, A., Johnson, S. P., Brown, E., & Badenoch, M. (1996). Newborn infants' perception of partly occluded objects. *Infant Behavior and Development, 19,* 145–148.

Slater, A., Mattock, A., & Brown, E. (1990). Size constancy at birth: Newborn infants' responses to retinal and real size. *Journal of Experimental Child Psychology, 49,* 314–322.

Slater, A., & Morison, V. (1985). Shape constancy and slant perception at birth. *Perception, 14,* 331–344.

Slater, A., Morison, V., Somers, M., Mattock, A., Brown, E., & Taylor, D. (1990). Newborn and older infants' perception of partly occluded objects. *Infant Behavior and Development, 13,* 33–49.

Slater, A., Quinn, P., Brown, E. & Hayes, R. (1999). Intermodal perception at birth: Intersensory redundancy guides newborn infants' learning of arbitrary auditory-visual pairings. *Developmental Science, 2,* 333–338.

Smith, W. C., Johnson, S. P., & Spelke, E. S. (2003). Motion and edge sensitivity in perception of object unity. *Cognitive Psychology, 46,* 31–64.

Spelke, E. S. (1979). Perceiving bimodally specified events in infancy. *Developmental Psychology, 15,* 626–636.

Stager, C. L., & Werker, J. F. (1997). Infants listen for more phonetic detail in speech perception than in word-learning tasks. *Nature, 388,* 381–382.

Thelen, E., Corbetta, D., Kamm, K., Spencer, J. P., Schneider, K., & Zernicke, R. F. (1993). The transition to reaching: Mapping intention and intrinsic dynamics. *Child Development, 64,* 1058–1098.

Thiessen, E. D., Hill, E. A., & Saffran, J. R. (2005). Infant-directed speech facilitates word segmentation. *Infancy, 7,* 53–71.

Tincoff, R., & Jusczyk, P. W. (1999). Some beginnings of word comprehension in 6-month-olds. *Psychological Science, 10,* 172–175.

Werker, J. F., & Tees, R. C. (1983). Developmental changes across childhood in the perception of non-native speech sounds. *Canadian Journal of Psychology, 37,* 278–286.

Werker, J. F., & Tees, R. C. (1984). Cross-language speech perception: Evidence for perceptual reorganization during the first year of life. *Infant Behavior and Development, 7,* 49–63.

Werker, J. F., & Tees, R. C. (1999). Influences on infant speech processing: Toward a new synthesis. *Annual Review of Psychology, 50,* 509–535.

Younger, B. A., & Cohen, L. B. (1986). Developmental change in infants' perception of correlations among attributes. *Child Development, 57,* 803–815.

5

Pragmatics of Human Action

DARE BALDWIN, JEFFERY LOUCKS,
& MARK SABBAGH

Human action is a core contributor to many events (see Chapter 3), and thus skill at making sense of action is central to event representation. Interpreting others' actions seems at first to be a generally straightforward process, but on further reflection it seems nearly intractable. Searle (1984) provides an example that nicely captures this paradox. Let's say one observes a friend in Hyde Park, London, ambling at a relaxed pace with a contented expression. Obviously he is enjoying a pleasant Hyde Park stroll—but wait! Perhaps instead he is just passing through on his way to Patagonia, or intent merely on moving a few air molecules, or simply working hard to wear out the soles of his shoes. Any of these radically different intentional descriptions is consistent with the motions the friend exhibits through space. In fact, this conundrum is no exception: there is an infinite set of possible intentional descriptions consistent with any given behavior stream.

Despite such massive underdetermination, however, infants as well as adults seem to be skilled at homing in on appropriate descriptions. For example, adults display a high degree of agreement in the descriptions they provide for everyday intentional actions, even to the level of agreeing on specific points within the behavior stream where intentional acts begin and end (e.g., Baird & Baldwin, 2001; Hard, Tversky, & Lang, in press; Newtson, 1973; Zacks & Tversky, 2001; Zacks, Tversky, & Iyer, 2001). Infants appear to identify roughly the same kinds of distinct small-scale acts within the continuous behavior stream that adults pick out (e.g., Baldwin, Baird, Saylor, & Clark, 2001; Saylor, Baldwin, Baird, & LaBounty, 2007), and in the period between 6 and 12 months of age infants begin to display an appreciation for the intentions and goals motivating such everyday actions as grasping, pointing, and directed gaze (e.g., Tomasello, 1999; Woodward, Sommerville, & Guajardo, 2001). Taking such evidence of agreement in inferring intentions from action at face value, the interesting question then becomes, how is this achieved in the face of such a large set of possibilities?

In this chapter we offer a set of theoretical speculations grounded in the supposition that a powerful cognitive system is at play in discerning others' intentions and goals (see Baldwin, 2005, and Baldwin & Baird, 2001, for further discussion). For the most part, this system seems to operate outside conscious awareness. The basic idea we are operating with is that the functioning of this cognitive system produces multiple sources of constraint that converge on a likely candidate interpretation of a given action. However, at present much remains to be learned about these sources of constraint. Our overarching goal in this chapter is to present some novel ideas about one set of possible constraining forces that guide inferences about others' intentions and goals. In particular, we propose that action processing is guided in part by rationality assumptions akin to Grice's pragmatic principles. We begin by laying the conceptual groundwork for the proposal, which involves considering, in general terms, why such a proposal is warranted, and reminding readers of the core elements of Grice's account of the pragmatics of communication. Along the way we go to some trouble to clarify what "communicative action" means and why communicative actions of many kinds, not just language, are amenable to a traditional Gricean analysis. We then suggest ways in which a novel twist on the Gricean account makes it possible to extend the analysis in meaningful ways to what we call "simple action"—that is, action that is directed toward achieving concrete causal effects in the world. Communicative action and simple action differ along a variety of dimensions; nevertheless, we argue that analogous pragmatic phenomena can be identified in each. We pursue the proposal by outlining specific ways in which our Grice-inspired proposal can account for inferences about others' simple actions, and we review a smattering of evidence in support of the proposal's plausibility.

Pragmatics of Action Proposal: Conceptual Groundwork

Need for Principled Account of Top-Down Constraints

Recent research has focused heavily on bottom-up factors that contribute to the apprehension of others' goals and intentions. It is obvious that human action engenders a stimulus stream in need of processing, and clearly the details of that motion stream have considerable impact on the inferences an observer takes away about what intentions and goals are being enacted. In illustration, we are unlikely to infer that a man leaning contentedly back in an easy chair is at that very moment pursuing an intention to improve his aerobic fitness. Long-standing interest in human extraction of structure inherent in motion (e.g., Johansson, 1973; Chapters 10 through 13, this volume) has recently given rise to research yielding evidence of several specific mechanisms that subserve intentional action processing. In particular, for example, new evidence suggests that bottom-up mechanisms such as statistical learning (Baldwin, Andersson, Saffran, & Meyer, in press; Swallow & Zacks, submitted), detection of Gestalt-like motion patterns (Baldwin et al., in preparation; Loucks & Baldwin, 2006), and possibly detection of bursts of motion change (e.g., Martin, 2006; Newtson, Engquist, & Bois, 1977) all play a role in adults' and infants' segmentation of intentional action, which is one fundamental component of action processing (e.g., Baldwin & Baird, 1999; Newtson, 1973; Zacks, Tversky, & Iyer, 2001; also see Chapters 15 through 17, this volume).

Considerably less research has focused on top-down factors that may serve to constrain inferences about the intentions motivating others' actions. The object of our chapter is to offer some ideas on this front. Although it has long been known that observers' expectations influence the specific inferences drawn about the intentions an actor is pursuing (e.g., Zadny & Gerard, 1974), little attempt has been made to characterize, in any principled way, precisely how top-down mechanisms operate to constrain inferences about others' intentions. Our analysis is directly inspired by ongoing work in what is often thought of as a rather different domain of processing: language. In particular, we will look to analyses regarding pragmatic principles that constrain listeners' inferences about speakers' communicative intentions to generate ideas about top-down constraints that may guide observers' inferences about the intentions motivating others' actions.

Looking to Language

Language, of course, is a form of action (e.g., Austin, 1962; Wittgenstein, 1958); more specifically, it is a form of communicative action. One central object of all action processing—be it language or some other form of action—is to grasp others' intentions, whether these are communicative intentions or what we might call "simple intentions." In the language domain, substantial progress has been made regarding top-down forces that guide the interpretation of others' intentions. In particular, pragmatic principles (e.g., felicity conditions, the reality principle, and the cooperative principle) are one class of top-down constraint on processing. Perhaps such principles play a similar functional role in guiding inferences about goals and intentions motivating actions other than the linguistic type. In some respects, this is a ridiculously easy case to make. Certain other classes of action either *are* language (e.g., signed languages such as American Sign Language [ASL]) or are in key respects so much like language (e.g., conventionalized gestures) that it would be very surprising if the same pragmatic principles *failed* to operate. These are instances in which the action phenomena, like language, fundamentally concern communicative exchange.

Pragmatics of Communicative Action

Signed languages and highly conventionalized gestures are interpretable only if the addressee is sensitive to the signer's or gesturer's *communicative intentions*, just as language is fully interpretable only under these same conditions (e.g., Grice, 1975; Levinson, 1983). Understanding of others' communicative intentions requires (a) appreciating that the signer's/gesturer's intention is to communicate and (b) joining collaboratively with the signer/gesturer in ascertaining his or her specific communicative goal(s). Among other things, theoretical analyses of the pragmatics of language are specifically directed toward identifying what principles govern the collaborative process between speaker and addressee in the addressee's discovery of the speaker's communicative intent. Pragmatic theorists have explicitly pointed out that pragmatic principles extend beyond the language domain to include gesture and other social/communicative phenomena, such as, for instance, traffic lights. Levinson (1983, p. 26) illustrates in one example how Grice's ideas regarding pragmatic principles in language might also operate with respect to highly conventionalized gestures such as doffing one's cap:

> [T]here is a widespread phenomenon that Grice has called exploitation: in general, if there is some communicative convention C that one does A in context Y, then suppose instead one does B in Y, or does A but in context Z, one will not normally be taken to have simply violated the convention C and produced nonsense. Rather, one will generally be taken to have exploited the conventions in order to communicate some further pertinent message. For example, if I normally doff my cap only to my superiors, but on an occasion doff my cap to an equal, then I can effectively communicate an ironic regard, with either a joking or a hostile intent.

Here it is obvious that pragmatic inferences, guided by the cooperative principle, operate within the observer of the gesture to yield an inference regarding the gesturer's communicative intent—in this case, ironic regard. Examples of this kind—in which the interpretation of conventionalized gesture capitalizes on the same pragmatic principles driving spoken language—are probably the rule rather than the exception.

Other, nongestural forms of communicative action can also be identified. One such other form is "action pedagogy." Action pedagogy is the attempt to assist another in learning a new intentional action sequence. Teaching someone how to saddle a horse, for example, typically involves demonstrating a range of horse- and saddle-relevant actions. In action pedagogy, intentional actions are performed on objects with certain goals in mind, but this is done, in large part, for the benefit of an observer. Although gesture and signed languages have received considerable study over the years (for a recent review see Goldin-Meadow, 2006), other forms of communicative action such as action pedagogy have received little attention from cognitive psychologists until very recently (e.g., Brand, Baldwin, & Ashburn, 2002; Brand, Shallcross, Sabatos, & Massie, 2007; Csibra & Gergely, 2006; Gergely & Csibra, 2004; Rogoff, Paradise, Arauz, Correa-Chavez, & Angelillo, 2003; Zacks & Tversky, 2003), with a few striking exceptions, such as the comparative literature seeking to discover whether primates and other species are capable of genuine pedagogy (e.g., Byrne & Tomasello, 1995). Thus there is much to be learned, and investigation of the pragmatics of communicative actions other than language may ultimately enrich our general understanding of top-down forces guiding human communication, specifically, and action processing more generally.

Gricean Account of Language, and Communicative Action More Generally

Within the study of language, Grice put forward a description of reality and cooperative principles in part to explain how people understand one another despite the fact that much is technically ambiguous or left unsaid. In other words, linguistic communication seems to "work"—a message the speaker intends to communicate is indeed grasped by the observer—because both speaker and addressee cooperate and operate with common assumptions about both the nature of reality and what is entailed in cooperation.

Consider the reality principle, to start. Grice articulated the reality principle with respect to language as a charge to talk about real, everyday things in the ordinary world. For communicative action, such as action pedagogy, ASL, or conventionalized gesture, the reality principle involves assuming that people's actions are designed to communicate about real, everyday kinds of intentions. Without such an assumption, there would be nothing to ground one's inferences about the meaning or communicative significance of others' communicative actions.

With respect to the cooperative principle, Grice offered a set of sub-maxims—quality, quantity, relevance, and manner—thought to constrain inferences regarding the communicative intentions underlying others' linguistic contributions. For language, Grice stated the maxims of the cooperative principle in the following way (from Levinson, 1983, pp. 100–102):

Quality: try to make your contribution one that is true, specifically:
  (i) do not say what you believe to be false
  (ii) do not say that for which you lack adequate evidence
Quantity:
  (i) make your contribution as informative as is required for the current purposes of the exchange
  (ii) do not make your contribution more informative than is required

Relevance: make your contributions relevant
Manner: be perspicuous, specifically:
  (i) avoid obscurity,
  (ii) avoid ambiguity,
  (iii) be brief,
  (iv) be orderly

When maxims of the cooperative principle are violated, systematic inferences can be drawn regarding the speaker or actors' communicative intentions. For instance, Levinson provides a classic example of a manner violation: a parent says "Let's go to the S-T-O-R-E." By spelling out the last word, instead of just saying it in the canonical manner of speech, the speaker communicates to the addressee that there is some underlying necessity for being less perspicuous about speech than one would ordinarily be—such as the need to keep an acutely listening child in ignorance of a proposed plan. A parallel example of such a manner violation in communicative action that is nonlinguistic is when one parent waits until a child's back is turned, then raises her brows, pretends to grasp food and bring it to the mouth while staring intently at the other parent. The highly marked choice to engage in action pretense while a child's back is turned, rather than simply asking "Want to eat?," again prompts the inference that there is some necessity for keeping the child in the dark on the question at issue. A somewhat different example of a manner violation within communicative action will also be familiar to many parents: a parent asks a teenager to do something, such as head for bed, and the teenager responds with an exaggeratedly robotic version of turning on heel and jerkily heading in the direction of the bedroom. The robotic manner violates canonical motion parameters; each component of an otherwise fluid flow of motion is executed stiffly and separately. The snide message the teen communicates here is something like, "I am a puppet under your complete control, oh masterful one," which most parents need little tutoring to recognize as sarcastic.

Summing up thus far, we have simply elaborated on the noncontroversial proposal that a Gricean pragmatic analysis is applicable to communicative action in general, not just linguistic communication. Our goal in the chapter, however, is to push the Gricean envelope yet further, to encompass how humans interpret others' simple intentional acts. Making this stretch is much less intuitive but seems to account for a variety of systematic phenomena that govern how simple acts are processed by observers.

Pragmatics of Simple Action

In contrast to communicative action, such as language or action pedagogy, simple action is action aimed at achieving concrete goals in the world; everyday examples are doing the laundry or grabbing one's belongings on the way to work. Despite the name, simple actions are frequently not so simple in that they can involve long, complex, knowledge-laden, future-oriented series of activities to achieve grandiose goals, such as what it takes to sculpt a replica of Michelangelo's Pietà or to pack for a camping trip for a family of five. What we mean by "simple" is that these actions are directed toward achieving a physical change in the world rather than communicating a message to another. To understand simple action as an observer, one needs to discern which physical change (or set of changes) in the world the actor is intending to bring about.

For the moment, we will gloss over several complicating issues. One such complication is that there are many levels of analysis one can focus on in conceptualizing the intentions guiding an actor's simple act (e.g., in pressing the power button on a television remote control, the intention is to press the button, *and* to press the button in order to turn on the TV, *and* to press the button in order to turn on the TV in order to watch a program, and so on). Another is the issue that many, if not most, human intentional acts are a blend of simple action and communicative action (e.g., getting a family of five packed for camping seems to involve several million conversations about who put what where).

At first glance it seems not at all obvious why Gricean pragmatic principles would need to be invoked to account for how we discern such seemingly simple, everyday intentions as to wash a dish or plop something in the garbage bin. In simple actions, actors are not generating any kind of message that they are designing for the addressee based on the communicative affordances of the situation, so why should pragmatic principles of any kind be regarded as even remotely relevant? We argue that despite this apparently glaring disanalogy between communicative action and simple action, principles closely allied to the reality and cooperative principles we know from Grice's analysis of communicative action seem to play a core role in interpreting others' simple acts. In particular, these principles seem to help shape our judgments of whether action is or is not intentional, as well as what the actor's specific intent might be on any given occasion. What follows is an extended justification for the proposal.

Reality Principle for Simple Action

Regarding the reality principle, it behooves us to assume that actors' intentions and motions are directed toward real objects and effects in the everyday world. Without this constraint on our inferences about others' intentions, the chance of being able to make any sense at all out of others' actions would be seriously undercut. The reality principle is clearly at work when we encounter novel action streams; for example, imagine channel surfing one evening and happening upon someone gyrating wildly in midair thousands of feet above ground, hair whipping about beneath a helmet, feet locked to a board. A first reaction might be puzzlement and intense examination of the unfolding drama. Was that a smile or a grimace? Is this some terrible accident to be featured in tomorrow's headlines ("Snowboarder Falls to His Death while the World Watches"), or is this some kind of entirely new sport? Here it is fairly easy to observe pragmatic assumptions kicking in: one attempts to account for the novel scenario in terms of familiar, everyday intentional constructs, with the obvious alternatives in such a case being a bizarre accident or a strange new sport. One doesn't consider, for instance, that this might be a visitor from Pluto displaying an intention to make a grand entrance to impress earthlings, or that the actor might be in the grip of an intention to model a new mode of flying for birds, or any other unrealistic set of possible intentions.

A Twist on the Cooperative Principle: Rationality in Simple Action

Something recognizably like Grice's cooperative principle also operates in our reading of others' simple intentional acts. Again, however, simple action is not communicative; thus Grice's statement of the cooperative principle and its underlying maxims—all formulated to capture how we grasp one another's communicative intentions—must be reformulated to suit the case of simple action. We will begin there, and then take up each of the maxims in turn to show how they might operate to guide action processing, considering empirical evidence attesting to their operation. In fact, little or no empirical evidence is available to speak to adults' tendency to adhere to such principles in action processing. However, isolated studies investigating the emergence of action-processing skills in infancy yield relevant evidence that we will briefly review.

A first issue concerns the term "cooperative principle." For simple action, this would obviously be a misnomer, as simple action is directed at the world, rather than toward communicating a message to another. Probably the best substitute for the term "cooperative principle" in the case of simple action is the term "rationality principle." Our only hesitation in using this term is that it has sometimes been used by others, such as Gergely and colleagues (e.g., Gergely & Csibra, 2003), to describe what seems to be a narrower principle emphasizing minimal energy expenditure that corresponds nicely to the quantity maxim we describe below. Thus we use the term "rationality principle" with apologies to Gergely and colleagues, and we appeal to all to keep these different potential usages in mind.

Below we articulate submaxims of the rationality principle. We have taken pains to maintain as close a parallelism as possible to the traditional statement of Grice's maxims of the cooperative principle. For this reason, the submaxims are stated in terms of strictures on first-person action— the heuristics guiding people's attempts to act rationally in the world. Importantly, however, we argue that people also assume that *others* will be guided by these same strictures when taking action in the world; hence people can exploit these maxims as a basis for inferences about the likely intentions others are executing.

Quality for action: try to make your action achieve something in the world that you want done, specifically:
    (i) do not do what you believe to work against what you want to achieve
    (ii) do not do what you believe would be ineffectual *vis à vis* what you want done
Quantity for action:
    (i) make your action as effortful as is required to satisfy the intention currently at issue
    (ii) do not exert more effort than is required to satisfy the intention currently at issue

Relevance for action: make your actions relevant (e.g., to achieving the intention at issue, to prior actions, to the objects acted upon)
Manner for action: be effective, specifically:
  (i) avoid unusual, bizarre, or novel ways of acting to achieve goals,
  (ii) avoid action that might yield multiple outcomes,
  (iii) be efficient,
  (iv) be orderly

QUALITY

Taking the quality maxim up first, the idea is that it behooves people, as beings with needs and desires, to design actions in such a way as to satisfy the intentions arising from those needs and desires. People therefore assume that others likewise act to fulfill their intentions; hence people expect others to avoid acting in ways that would either interfere with or fail to culminate in the satisfaction of their intentions. Acting according to the quality maxim helps people to survive and prosper in the world; thus it is rational to assume that others will also act in accord with it. One implication of the quality maxim is that people assume others typically undertake action as an outgrowth of intentions that will result in satisfaction of their needs and desires; that is, people assume action is intentional, unless otherwise indicated. This is consistent with Dennett's (1987) suggestion that humans are deeply committed to an "intentional stance": when we watch others taking action, what we see are patterns of motion across space and time, but what we take away are a host of inferences about what intentions those motions fulfill.

In daily life, the quality maxim permeates our processing of human action. We take pains to point it out to people when we believe they are working at cross-purposes (the quality maxim leads us to assume they would not wish to); for much the same reason, we become upset with others who observe us doing something that will interfere with a stated intention and fail to inform us. Of course, we can also exploit others' tendency to adhere to quality in order to deceive them. Suppose Edgar and Gertrude both want to find buried treasure. Edgar watches Gertrude's actions closely because he assumes that Gertrude will move in the direction of the treasure (quality assumption in operation). When Gertrude moves, Edgar follows her through twists and turns and soon is lost. While Edgar is distracted, Gertrude trickily takes the chance to double back and safely reaches the now uncontested treasure. Edgar is left high and dry while Gertrude absconds with the goods. Such quality-based acts of deception, of course, can work only if people generally adhere to the quality maxim. As soon as one becomes skeptical as to whether another is acting in ways that would successfully achieve the inferred goals, one no longer falls prey to such acts of deception. This is comparable to Grice's point about how deception with language is successful only if people generally adhere to telling the truth (quality).

Finally, violations of the quality maxim in the case of simple action engender systematic inferences on the observer's part. Suppose Karen asks her daughter to sweep the patio and the daughter agrees. Later, Karen peeks out the window and notices that her daughter is giving the patio the merest, pathetic little taps with the broom, and no leaves are moving. Obviously these actions are totally ineffective for satisfying the sweeping intention that the daughter agreed to take on. Karen knows her daughter is neurologically intact and old enough to recognize that patio sweeping isn't happening; thus, this is a clear violation of the quality maxim. As an observer, one does not discard the quality maxim in the face of such violation; instead, one carries out some inferential work to retain quality at a deeper level. For example, Karen could infer that her daughter merely pretended to agree but never actually adopted the intention to sweep the patio (deception), or Karen could infer that her daughter cleverly construed the original request in such a narrow sense that all she committed to in terms of an intention on her part was to execute sweeping-like motions that need not result in any actual movement of leaves (deviousness), or, if feeling especially charitable, Karen could revise her assumption about her daughter's knowledgeability and infer that, after all, she is young and actually may not know how to use a broom to move leaves (ignorance).

Although most models of adult folk psychology seem to assume operation of the quality maxim (e.g., Perner, 1991; Wellman, 1990), to our knowledge there is no direct evidence for this. On the other hand, there are clear indicators of the quality maxim at work in developmental research exploring the emergence of folk psychology. For example, Wellman and Woolley (1990) investigated whether preschoolers appreciate that people typically act in ways that will succeed in fulfilling their desires. When asked, for example, what someone who wants a puppy will do given that a puppy is under the piano, preschoolers expect that he or she will go look under the piano—that is, children expect people to do things that will achieve their desires. Interestingly, preschoolers' well-known failures at false belief tasks (e.g., Perner, 1991; Wellman, 1990) can be construed as another source of evidence that they adhere to the quality maxim. In the classic change-of-contents task, children are faced with a character who was absent at the time a desired object was moved to a new location (thus this character is ignorant of the change in location). When asked where the ignorant character will look, 3-year-olds routinely respond that he will look where the desired object actually is, rather than where he ought to expect it to be (given his ignorance). Children's failure at attributing a false belief to the ignorant character in these studies showcases their difficulty in conceptualizing people as acting in a way that would appear to be at cross-purposes with their goals and desires, which would violate the quality maxim.

In sum, to our knowledge no one as yet has attempted a direct test of the quality maxim's operation in action processing. Nevertheless, there are hints of a quality maxim operating in action processing even in the preschool years.

QUANTITY

Recall that quantity, stated with respect to language, calls for making one's contribution precisely as informative as needed—it adjures one to say no more or less than is necessary to get the message across. It is because of the quantity maxim that one would feel seriously misled to learn that a cat, described as white by one's friend, is actually a calico with just a few white splotches. The cat is indeed white, but also black, brown, ginger, and gray. The quantity maxim enables one to assume that the speaker would provide adequate information; stopping at the mention of white in the context of a multicolored cat is not adequately informative.

With respect to simple action, the quantity maxim isn't concerned with informativeness; instead, the quantity at issue is the quantity of effort or energy expended in order to carry out an intention. As actors, we typically design our actions to avoid much outlay of energy or effort beyond what is necessary to fulfill our intentions. As observers of action, we interpret others' intentions in light of this quantity assumption. If one were to see someone dashing madly down the street, one would assume that fulfilling this individual's intentions requires that she or he get somewhere very quickly. If one later learns that in fact there was all the time in the world and thus no occasion for the rush, one would be puzzled about the rusher and wonder whether she or he is quite sane or if perhaps there is something to the story the observer was simply not privy to (the runner is training for the 50-yard dash but doesn't like track surfaces, etc.). Conversely, if one were to see someone sauntering placidly, one would assume this individual has all the time in the world to reach a destination, or has no real destination in mind at all. Suppose one later learns that, actually, this individual was on the way to the FedEx office to post a grant proposal in time to meet a deadline only 5 minutes hence (and missed the deadline). This would seem incongruous; if only she or he had rushed, the deadline might have been met. If someone didn't rush under these circumstances, an observer might assume that this individual must have been under a misapprehension about the time of day or of the deadline, or seriously ambivalent about the grant proposal. In other words, some additional inferential work will be provoked by the apparent violation of the quantity maxim. This is a point worthy of note: something like the quantity assumption must be at work, because violations of quantity predictably trigger additional inferences. In the face of such violations, the observer attempts to adhere to the maxim on a deeper level, and invokes an inference to achieve this. This phenomenon is a direct analogue to the reasoning driving Grice's theory of implicature. In Levinson's words, "it is only by making the assumption contrary to superficial indications that the inferences arise in the first place" (p. 102).

Anecdotes that implicate the quantity maxim are easy to find. Actual empirical evidence to this effect involving adults is not so easy to find. However, Gergely and colleagues have convincingly demonstrated that human infants as young as 12 months are sensitive to the quantity maxim (in their nomenclature the "rationality principle") in action processing (e.g., Gergely & Csibra, 2003). In one such study, for example, 12-month-olds watched a ball approach and then leap a barrier to reach a second ball on the far side. After becoming habituated to this display, infants viewed two different kinds of test displays with no barrier present: in one, the first ball approached the second ball along a direct trajectory (consistent with the quantity maxim), while in the other display the first ball took a leap mid-trajectory on the way toward approaching the second ball (violating the quantity maxim). It is worth noting that the leap in the quantity-violating display was perceptually identical to the leap taken by the first ball in the habituation phase; hence, in purely perceptual terms, the quantity-violating display was actually more similar to the habituation event than the quantity-consistent display. As it turned out, infants looked significantly longer at the quantity-violating leaping-ball test scenario, even though this was, in surface terms, much like the display they'd become habituated to just moments before. They apparently were struck by the quantity violation inherent in the "inexplicable" mid-trajectory leap.

Given that Gergely and colleagues presented displays involving abstract "actors"—throbbing balls capable of autonomous motion—one wonders whether these findings actually reflect how infants process everyday human action. Phillips and Wellman (2005) have extended the findings to human action, thus providing some reassurance on this point. They found that infants looked longer at a hand that took a lengthy, arcing path toward an apparently desired object when there was no obvious reason to do so, despite the fact that they had just been habituated to a hand taking that same arcing path when a barrier impeded direct motion toward the goal object. All in all, this small body of evidence makes a clear case for the quantity maxim operating, from a very early age, in human action processing.

RELEVANCE

In language processing, the relevance maxim is essential to achieving a coherent, cohesive set of inferences with respect to the topic and the whole set of utterances that speakers offer. A classic example is, "A woman dressed for a party. The pearls gleamed brightly in the mirror" (Levinson, 1983). One infers that the pearls referred to are precisely the set of pearls that the woman in question donned while dressing for the party, which she has happened to catch sight of in the mirror. Logically, of course, there is no necessity that the pearls referred to in the second sentence were ever worn by the woman referred to in the first sentence, much less that she wore them on the occasion of dressing for that particular party. However, were we to operate in this inferentially cautious way—inhibiting, or failing to generate, relevance-induced inferences linking referents across utterances and relating utterances to the general topic at hand—then conversation would be an arduous and largely intractable undertaking.

An assumption of relevance is likewise fundamental to the processing of simple action. Intentions possess a fundamental "aboutness": they relate people's actions to the world (e.g., Brentano, 1874/1970; Dennett, 1996). Not surprisingly, then, people assume others' simple actions are relevant to achieving their intended goal, to their own and others' prior goals and actions, to their own and others' subsequent and/or planned goals and actions, and to the object(s) acted upon. Like the other maxims already discussed, this all seems very commonsensical, and, given that we are arguing that relevance is a default assumption guiding people's own intentional acts as well as their processing of others' intentional acts, it should. The power of the maxims lies in how they guide expectations and inferences that enrich our understanding of others' actions well beyond the motion patterns we actually witness.

An example parallel to the language-related "pearls" illustration showcases how the relevance maxim supports us in building an integrated, coherent understanding of others' larger goal-oriented activities. Suppose you watch on a schoolday morning as I open a SpongeBob lunch box and place it on the kitchen counter. A few minutes later you notice me burrowing in the refrigerator. Chances are you will assume, via the relevance maxim, that I am locating food appropriate for the general goal of packing a child's lunch. The relevance maxim triggers so-called "bridging inferences" that relate distinct acts *vis à vis* the higher-order goal, even though distinct acts that occur in succession could, in principle, be unrelated (and sometimes are).

When we note clear-cut violations of the relevance maxim, we generate additional inferences. Typically, the inferences we draw enable us to maintain the relevance maxim at a deeper level. For instance, on viewing someone heading out the door on her way to work, we expect that she will grab belongings relevant to the day's undertakings, such as a laptop, papers, car keys, her wallet, and her cell phone. Here we are assuming that an actor's actions will be relevant to the expected goal, which is in this case a successful day at work. If she instead walks out the door holding a giant inflatable sea otter, we would take note and begin generating inferences to accommodate the apparently irrelevant item. Perhaps she is donating the swim toy to the local toddler pool and dropping it off on the way to work; perhaps she has abandoned her normal workaday goals to play serious hooky. Either of these possibilities reassesses her goals in a way that would retain relevance—either by imputing a new, secondary goal (a drop-off on the way to work) or substituting one goal (hooky) for another (work).

Other kinds of relevance violations can emerge due to ignorance or neurological damage. For instance, imagine a husband and wife visiting a new city agree that she will take care of some financial transactions at the bank while he stocks up on some necessities at the pharmacy. She then heads down the street, despite the fact that the bank is right behind her. On the surface, this woman's action was inappropriate to the object targeted and seemingly irrelevant to her acknowledged goal, but the husband viewing this puzzling scenario doesn't simply throw over the relevance maxim: he immediately infers that the wife is under a misapprehension about where the bank is located or which bank is at issue.

Oliver Sacks (1970) described a patient who exhibited seemingly inexplicable relevance violations: the man who mistook his wife for a hat. Due to neurological damage, this man was unable to categorize objects appropriately despite displaying normal visual function. As a result, he sometimes acted on objects in wildly inappropriate ways, such as trying to lift his wife's head off to put it on his own head (thinking his wife's head was a hat). In this case, the action observed violates our assumption that an actor will design action to be relevant to the object acted upon. This man's startling and debilitating disorder helps to illustrate how relevance, and more generally all the maxims of the rationality principle, supply a necessary foundation on which to build inferences about others' motions. Ordinarily, as discussed above, we respond to violations of maxims with inferences that retain the maxim at a deeper level. We charitably assume that the actor is rational and of at least normal intelligence, which licenses us to draw rationality-retaining inferences at a deeper level (see Davidson, 1980, for a related suggestion regarding charitability in language and action processing). When violations of the maxims (and hence rationality) are as striking and unresolvable as those of the man who mistook his wife for a hat, we suddenly are at a loss for how to interpret much of what this individual subsequently does, at least until we come up with some new principle to account for, and predict, his excursions from rationality (which is what Oliver Sacks offers in his essay). Even actions that seem quite normal on the surface are brought into question when faced with an individual who has shown evidence of seriously disordered action propensities. From the observer's standpoint, everything is up for grabs, inferentially speaking, and a system of inferences that normally fires off with little conscious effort suddenly becomes a quagmire of puzzlement and confusion.

As with the other maxims we've considered, some available evidence suggests that even infants operate with at least a basic assumption of relevance in their action processing. Research by Woodward and colleagues (e.g., Woodward, 1998; Woodward, Sommerville, & Guajardo, 2001), for example, indicates that infants as young as 5 months of age construe at least some basic intentional acts, such as hand grasps, as being directed toward a specific object. In other words, they assume that the grasping action is relevant to the object contacted. Interestingly, they apparently do not make this assumption when the action involved is either unfamiliar or less easily construed as intentional, such as when the actor lays the back of her hand on the object (e.g., Woodward, 1999). Also, it is not until 12 months of age that infants appreciate the fundamental relevance of pointing and directed gaze toward the object targeted by the point or gaze (e.g., Woodward, 2003, 2005). The developmental progression here highlights the role that knowledge and experience play in how assumptions such as the relevance maxim are deployed in action processing.

Research by Phillips and colleagues (e.g., Phillips, Wellman, & Spelke, 2002) clarifies that infants as young as 12 months expect that a person who chooses to look at one of two objects will subsequently act on that object. In this research, infants were especially struck by an apparent relevance violation in which the actor looked at one of the objects but then contacted the other object. These findings hint that infants regard one intentional act (looking at a specific object) as relevant to a second intentional act (grasping that object).

Finally, research by Meltzoff and others on early-emerging imitation skills delineates another way in which a basic relevance maxim guides infants' intentional action processing. Infants as young as 9 to 12 months of age are already skilled at imitation: they will imitate an action that an adult displayed just once with respect to a novel object, even across long delays, such as 1 to 4 weeks (e.g., Heimann & Meltzoff, 1996; Klein & Meltzoff, 1999). These findings clarify that infants take actions to be relevant to, and informative about, objects acted upon: presenting objects to infants triggers them to enact the relevant actions. Moreover, infants as young as 15 to 18 months are able to infer an appropriate action sequence (such as putting a loop onto a prong) when all they have actually witnessed are failed attempts to achieve this (such as bringing the loop into the vicinity of the prong and dropping it) (e.g., Meltzoff, 1995; Meltzoff & Brooks, 2001). These findings hint that infants take actions to be relevant to the goals at hand: they "read through" failed action to the intentions apparently motivating the action (but see Huang, Heyes, & Charman, 2006, for a different interpretation).

All in all, a variety of evidence speaks to infants operating with some kind of default assumption of relevance in their processing of simple action. Much remains to be learned, however; for example, we know little about how infants might resolve apparent relevance violations, or how relevance-guided inferences change as action knowledge develops.

MANNER

Communication, via language, gesture, or action, is grounded in the assumption that speakers will design their messages to avoid ambiguity and obscurity and to be brief and orderly. Obvious violations of the manner maxim trigger the listener to draw inferences consonant with the manner maxim at a deeper level. For example, a statement that is excessively convoluted and lengthy may be taken to communicate that the content under discussion is dull and incomprehensible, or that the individual under discussion is unbearably pedantic or windbaggy.

Simple action can also be characterized in terms of ambiguity, obscurity, brevity, and orderliness. It is fairly clear that, as actors, we generally strive to avoid ambiguity, in the sense that we rarely wish the outcome of our actions to be unpredictable (there are a few notable exceptions to this, such as games of chance). We avoid obscurity in action, in that we tend to produce actions in a canonical manner, and avoid odd or bizarre ways of going about things (a possible exception to this is play). We also typically strive to accomplish our intentions in as brief and orderly a manner as possible. Here, however, there is sometimes tension with the quantity maxim, in that an extensive outlay of energy up front may be necessary to achieve brevity and orderliness in action; thus brevity and orderliness may not be maximized on all occasions. An example would be the messy-garage syndrome: frequent forays to find needed items in one's disastrously chaotic garage may be lengthy and involve much random poking about. Yet this may be tolerated for months or years, given the enormous energy expenditure required to organize the mess.

Despite such exceptions, it seems plausible that we exploit our sensitivity to these dimensions of manner in our interpretation of others' simple intentional acts. Regarding ambiguity, for example, consider the act of adjusting the volume of a television using a remote control. Imagine how odd it would seem if the actor used his or her toes or threw spare change at the remote instead of using the much more ordinary and reliable method of pressing buttons with a finger. Use of toes or spare change *might* yield the outcome of changing the volume, but, since they are less precise, they might also lead to changing the channel or turning the television off. Witnessing such action might leave one quite puzzled as to what was going on, and if a query such as "What are you doing?" produced the simple answer "Trying to change the volume," one would be inclined to draw some additional inferences about the meaning or significance of the action; in this case, one might infer that the actor is a real slacker who is feeling extraordinarily lazy or deeply unconcerned about the volume level, or even entertain the possibility that he or she lacks functional hands.

One implication of our point about sensitivity to a manner maxim is that people go beyond a simple analysis of outcomes in inferring others' intentions. If people were attentive only to goal achievement, then the manner in which it was achieved would be immaterial. However, the particular manner used by an actor in achieving a given outcome can be central to inferences about the actor's intent and the overall significance of the action. Imagine, for example, how a partner might respond if one chucked a precious family heirloom his or her way rather than passing it with care: it would be all too clear that manner matters.

We recently undertook research (Sabbagh & Loucks, 2003) with the aim of gaining direct empirical evidence that even infants are sensitive to manner in their analysis of others' actions. The basic logic of our method was to devise a situation in which an alteration in the actor's manner would trigger distinct intentional inferences in the observer. To do this, we exploited an intuition that ambiguity in manner (i.e., manner associted with multiple possible outcomes) may be likely to trigger an inference that action was accidental rather than intentional, and hence that a different outcome was intended relative to what actually occurred. The action of dropping provides a particularly good example here. In comparison to placing, dropping is an ambiguous act. Whereas placing an object ensures that the object will end up in a very specific location, in a very specific orientation, dropping is considerably less precise—the object's final resting position is determined by a number of different variables (height of drop, bounciness parameters of object dropped and surface dropped upon, etc.). Given the inherent ambiguity associated with dropping, coupled with one's first-hand experience that dropping often occurs accidentally, observers witnessing someone dropping an object may seek other sources of information to resolve whether the outcome of action was intended. A variety of top-down sources could help in this respect, such as linguistic information (e.g., "Oops!"), facial expression, and environmental affordances. For example, when dropping is intentional, often there is a particular spatial location where the dropped object is to end up (a pot of water, a trash container, a basketball hoop, etc.). Based on this collection of ideas and intuitions, we hypothesized that action ambiguous in manner, such as dropping, would be susceptible to interpretation as accidental depending on the outcome context (e.g., whether the object dropped ended up inside or outside a container), whereas an action unambiguous in manner, such as placing, would be relatively impervious to such contextual influence.

To test these ideas with infants, we developed a reenactment paradigm in which infants were shown videos of a person either placing (an unambiguous manner) or dropping (an ambiguous manner) an object either inside or outside of a box (Fig. 5.1; also see color insert). We hypothesized that infants would reveal sensitivity to manner in their reenactment of the observed actions. In particular, we predicted that infants would veridically reenact the outcome of unambiguous placing actions regardless of context, whereas context would influence what form their reenactment took after viewing ambiguous dropping actions. In other words, we predicted that in the case of dropping (an ambiguous manner), infants would interpret an "outside the box" outcome as accidental and would reenact what they inferred was the likely intended outcome by placing the toy *inside* the box, rather than replicate the outcome they actually witnessed (the toy ending up outside the box). In all other scenarios, we predicted that infants would veridically reenact the outcome they actually witnessed.

The set of findings from this small-scale initial study was promising: reenactment patterns revealed that infants as young as 18 to 19 months of age were sensitive to both manner and outcome in their interpretation of these actions. In particular, infants' reenactment of the actors' actions was nicely consistent with what we would expect if they were sensitive to violations of a manner maxim. It will be important to expand this promising methodology to a broader set of action scenarios

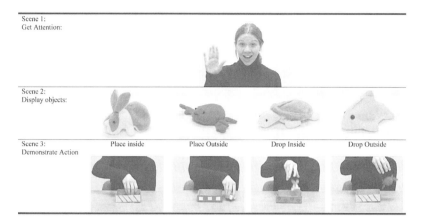

| | Place inside | Place Outside | Drop Inside | Drop Outside |

FIGURE 5.1. Scene structure and sample frames of stimulus videos from study investigating infants' sensitivity to manner and outcome in action processing.

involving other manner alterations, other activities, and other objects. As well, it will be of interest to probe the developmental emergence of the sensitivity to manner that infants displayed in this research.

Finally, before leaving the matter of a possible manner maxim guiding infants' and adults' interpretation of others' intentional acts, this seems an ideal opportunity to delineate commonalities and differences between the manner-related research we have been undertaking and the seminal research on semantic elements in verb systems such as *manner* and *path* reported by Maguire and colleagues (e.g., Maguire, 2003; Maguire, Hirsh-Pasek, & Golinkoff, 2006; Chapter 8, this volume; see also related research by Forbes & Poulin-Dubois, 1997). Despite the common focus on manner in our own research and that by Maguire et al., the investigative questions at the heart of these two research programs are fundamentally different. Our primary aim has been to understand whether infants' interpretation of intentions motivating others' actions is guided by assumptions about the standard, canonical manner in which such intentional actions would typically be performed. The central question guiding Maguire and colleagues' research, in contrast, is whether infants and young children incorporate manner information into the meaning or reference of a novel verb. One important point of commonality is that both research programs demonstrate that infants are sensitive to manner differences in how intentional actions are performed. However, Maguire and colleagues' research goes considerably further in an attempt to clarify relations between such manner sensitivity and verb learning. In particular, they have found that English-learning toddlers initially extend a novel verb on the basis of path rather than manner (consistent with a universal cross-linguistic tendency to incorporate path into verb meaning) and begin basing verb extension on manner, as is appropriate in English, at around 3 years of age at the earliest. Our own research makes a contribution along a very different dimension, demonstrating that infants alter their fundamental interpretation of an action as intended versus accidental depending on the manner (ambiguous or unambiguous) in which that action is performed.

Broader Implications, Unresolved Issues

In this chapter we have offered a twist on Gricean pragmatic analysis of language; in particular, we have suggested that principles akin to the reality and cooperative principles (and their associated maxims) operate as top-down constraints guiding reasoning about others' simple actions. We hope we have shown, via a range of illustrative examples, that crediting observers with such principles helps to account for a range of systematic inferences in human action processing. Quite probably, the pragmatic phenomena guiding action processing that we have noted do not exhaust the range of possibilities. Yet, to our knowledge, no other proposal has ever been offered that collectively accounts for this range of inferential phenomena in the action-processing arena.

It remains to be seen whether our proposal is the most elegant, or even an adequate, account of the pragmatics of simple action. As well, the traditional Gricean account comes along with a certain amount of theoretical "baggage" (e.g., a distinction between "literal" versus "figurative" meaning) that we are not yet certain we would wish to schlep around in the simple action arena. Compelling alternatives to the Gricean account of the pragmatics of communicative action are on offer (e.g., Wilson & Sperber, 2002), suggesting that accounts of simple action pragmatics diverging from ours should be entertained. We hope that others will take up the challenge to produce alternative frameworks against which the value of ours may be measured.

In this chapter we have described empirical evidence from research with human infants suggesting that core versions of our action-adapted

Gricean principles guide action processing from an early age. In many cases only a small amount of relevant evidence is available to make this case. We hope that the recent upsurge of interest in understanding human action processing will lead to a rapid expansion of knowledge on the topic. Perhaps the ideas presented here will serve as a fruitful organizing framework for guiding future investigative work.

Acknowledgments to Csibra, Gergely, and Colleagues

Some of the ideas we have offered were directly anticipated by Csibra, Gergely, and colleagues' ground-breaking research concerning what they have termed the "rationality principle" guiding event processing (e.g., Csibra, Bíró, Koós, & Gergely, 2003; Gergely & Csibra, 2003). However, our proposal seems to depart from theirs in at least two ways. As mentioned earlier, their conceptualization of the rationality principle seems to map onto what we would regard as the operation of the quantity maxim—the mandate to act with as little energy expenditure as possible while still achieving one's goals. Hence their conceptualization seems narrower than what we propose. In contrast, we believe that people's expectations for rationality in action go well beyond expectations about energy efficiency, comprising expectations of quality, relevance, and manner as well as quantity. That said, in one recent article, Gergely (2003) states that the principle of rational action directs infants to assume that "a) the basic function of actions is to bring about future goal states, and that b) agents will always perform the most efficient means action available to them within the constraints of the given situation" (p. 191). The first clause maps nicely onto the quality maxim of our proposal; thus Gergely seems to be moving toward a broader conceptualization of the rationality principle that may ultimately coincide nicely with what we propose.

Csibra, Gergely, and colleagues have also invoked nativist ideas regarding the origins of the rationality principle in some of their writing; they have specifically argued that infants arrive with an abstract notion of an agent who is expected to behave in accordance with the rationality principle (e.g., Kiraly & Gergely, 2003). We are agnostic on the nativism issue but regard it as a fascinating empirical question. We do believe, however, that a constructivist account of the rationality principle should be attempted and is far from hopelessly implausible.

Conceptual Dividing Lines?

One unresolved issue inherent in our action pragmatics proposal is a lurking question of conceptual dividing lines. Recall that we have suggested that simple action is processed via a set of principles and maxims that are related, but not identical, to the principles and maxims guiding processing of communicative action. For example, the quality maxim for communicative action emphasizes truth in the message, whereas the quality maxim for simple action emphasizes intent in the action. The obvious reason for this tweak is that simple intentional acts do not have propositional content, and therefore there is no truth—no alignment of declarative content and a state of affairs in the world—to wonder about. The quality that is at issue for action is whether motion was intended or not; fine so far. The fact that the principles take different forms for communicative action and simple action means, however, that observers must be able to identify an act as one or the other—simple versus communicative—in order to deploy the right variants of the principles and draw the right inferences about the meaning of the action. Is there any reason to believe that people can, and readily do, make such a conceptual distinction? This is an empirical question, and one not yet addressed.

To complicate matters, much human activity seems to take the form of a blend of the two kinds of action. Consider, for example, such activities as chatting over coffee or helping a friend with an engine repair. Action that is communicative (e.g., gossiping, discussing what would be the appropriate tool) occurs contemporaneously with simple action (e.g., sipping coffee, turning screws). Although the ubiquity of such blended activity seems to add a daunting layer of complexity to human action processing, our sense is that this complexity is real and not just a gratuitous theoretical tangle. People seem prone to misunderstandings that appear to have their source in misconstruing simple action as communicative, and vice versa. Two examples:

1. Helen turns her back when John enters the room, and John is enraged at what he views as Helen's obvious attempt to spite him. However, Helen was actually just turning around to locate her drink on the table behind her and thus acted without any reference to John.

2. Ben gratefully sips the water he believes Ella kindly left on the counter for him, but Ella actually just parked it there so she would have both hands free to search for a screwdriver.

In both of these examples, simple action is mistakenly taken to be communicative. The reverse mistake also seems an ordinary kind of occurrence: Ella might deliberately leave the water glass for Ben, but Ben could instead think Ella is just placing it there for herself, for example.

Given the complexities, it is perhaps surprising that such misunderstandings are relatively rare. Probably we are skilled at consulting a variety of clues to help clarify whether action is communicative or not, such as eye contact, vocal intonation and volume, body posture, and the like. If this is correct, it should be possible to systematically shape people's inferences about others' action by directly manipulating the availability of such clues. This is one possible approach to take in investigating the framework we have proposed here.

Identifying Accidents

Another unresolved issue regarding the rationality principle and its maxims is how to account for the sizable class of behaviors that appear to violate them: accidents. But perhaps it is incorrect to think of accidents as violating rationality; rather, accidents may simply not be subject to rationality concerns. When we believe another's behavior is accidental, we don't attempt to draw inferences to maintain assumptions such as quality, quantity, relevance, and manner at a deeper level; instead, we simply "write off" the behavior as unintended—the result of forces outside the agent's control. Under these circumstances, inferences about the nature of those forces come to the fore.

How do observers discriminate intended action from accident in order to know whether to invoke the rationality principle? This might seem to be challenging: accidents often take place in the midst of action that was intentionally initiated (e.g., the classic banana-peel slip that occurs in the context of an intended walk from point A to point B), and in principle the motion pattern associated with an accident can be identical in form to an intentional act (e.g., one can slip on a banana peel purposely or do it by accident). Perhaps, then, one concludes that an accident has occurred only after unsuccessful attempts to resolve rationality at a deeper level in the face of apparent rationality violations. We suspect, though, that this latter suggestion is only rarely the route to identifying accidents. Probably, discriminating action from accident depends on several sources of information. For one, certain structural properties within the motion stream are probably predictive of accidents. When action is intended, for instance, a gaze that encompasses a goal or instrument object usually precedes contact with the object; with accidents such as slipping or tripping, gaze toward the offending object usually follows contact. Second, contextual factors may promote intentional versus accidental construal (e.g., the presence versus absence of banana peels; a driver is known to be inebriated; a dropping manner is associated with an object that ends up beside a box, not in the box). Third, emotional responses accompanying accidents versus intended action often diverge (dismay/frustration for accidents versus neutrality/satisfaction for intended outcomes). If these three sources of information do not suggest an accident, an accident construal may still be considered if the observed behavior violates the rationality principle in a way one finds difficult to resolve as rational action at a deeper level. This is all to say that people may readily distinguish accidents from intentional action based on surface cues a fair amount of the time, often without needing to rely on an extended inferential check to determine that the rationality principle can not be applied. Once again, there is little in the way of empirical evidence to back these suggestions. However, what evidence there is supports the notion that observers exploit surface clues such as emotional responses to discriminate intentional versus accidental behavior. Carpenter and colleagues, for example, found that infants as young as 14 to 15 months of age are sensitive to surface emotional cues indicative of intention versus accident (e.g., "There!" versus "Whoops!"), and preferentially imitate motions taken to be intended (Carpenter, Akhtar, & Tomasello, 1998).

Possible Disanalogies Between Communicative Versus Simple Action

At the outset, we noted that a pragmatic analysis of simple action requires projecting Grice's cooperative principle from a communicative setting, trading on messages, into a rationality principle concerned with achieving causal effects in the world. The inherent disanalogy here between communicative versus simple action is, of course, what makes this analysis interesting rather than self-evident. Strikingly, simply shifting the focus from messages, as in Grice's cooperative principle, to effective causal action engenders a set of analogous maxims for simple action that appear to account systematically for a range of common-sense inferences regarding others' intentional acts.

Might the pragmatics of communicative and simple action differ in other significant ways, however, causing problems for the analysis? Quite likely they do differ, yet we are also inclined to be hopeful that these differences will not render the proposal either intractable or valueless. Consider one such possible difference: communicative action often seems to contain redundancies violating the quantity principle. Redundancies of this kind probably emerge, in many cases, as the outgrowth of a desire to avoid misunderstandings. Such redundancies (and hence quantity violations) might be less common in the context of simple action, for the reason that the potential for, or consequence of, error is not so great as with communicative action. On the other hand, however, it seems clear that quantity-violating redundancies do occur in simple action, and they seem typically to arise specifically in cases when error is recognized as possible and potentially egregious, as in the multiple backup procedures followed by airline pilots and nuclear-power-plant operators. A more ordinary example is that last, extra whack with the hammer to ensure that a nail, placed to hold up a heavy picture frame, doesn't fail. As an observer, we readily understand the pragmatic import of the redundant whack (e.g., the actor's intention is to reassure himself or herself that the nail is well and truly set in place).

In sum, while there may be differences in the typical pragmatics of the two phenomena—communicative action and simple action—these differences, at least in this case, seem explicable by means of a single underlying concern: the degree to which error is likely and/or problematic.

At the same time that interesting differences between the pragmatics of communicative versus simple action may come to the fore as our proposal is pursued, similarities between these phenomena may also be unearthed along the way. Individual variation seems a possible candidate for one such similarity. If the pragmatics of communicative action and simple action are tightly coupled conceptually, then they might also be tightly coupled in the pragmatics of an individual's behavior. We might expect, for example, correlations such that the pedant (a description of a certain pragmatic style in communication) would likely be meticulous (a description of a certain pragmatic style in simple action), whereas the flibbertigibbet would be sloppy. In fact, self-report personality measures often seem to have items probing behavior on both the communicative and the simple action level, hinting that a pragmatic coupling of communicative and simple action within the individual is not all that farfetched. In any case, we are hopeful that pursuing possible similarities and differences between the pragmatics of communicative and simple action will yield discoveries that are informative in their own right.

Linking Action Processing to Event Representation

With the focus of this chapter squarely on the pragmatics of action processing, one might wonder how it relates to the overarching theme of this volume, event representation. As mentioned at the outset, an understanding of mechanisms subserving action processing will be central to any ultimate account of event representation, as human action is a primary contributor to so many of the events humans represent. As well, there are myriad potentially interesting links between action pragmatics and the more general topic of event representation to be explored. For example, one major theme recurring throughout this volume is memory for events (see Chapter 21). We have proposed that a set of shared pragmatic principles provide top-down constraints on inferences about the intentions motivating others' actions; if this is correct, these principles are one force that structures memory for events and planning of one's subsequent action in response to events. Moreover, we would expect that a rationality principle, with its considerations of quality, quantity, relevance, and manner, would produce bridging inferences across actions from distinct event scenarios, as well as across actions and other aspects of events (see Chapter 20). Bridging inferences likely give rise to regularizations in encoding and/or retrieval that generate predictable areas of fragility and outright distortion in event memory. Finally, it seems possible that inferences about others' intentions constitute a primary crux for organization in event memory, at least for events involving human action. In other words, humans may have a strong propensity to drape memory for events around their inferences about human intentions. To the extent that this is true, pragmatic forces shaping intentional inferences about action are not merely relevant to event representation but key.

Conclusion

One upshot of this chapter is the realization of how very little is actually known about some of the fundamental processes subserving everyday human action processing. Potentially, there is great value in learning more, with possible payoffs such as a better understanding of the nature of human relations, applications for artificial intelligence, and a better ability to identify disturbances in action processing that affect social functioning, as appears to occur with disorders such as schizophrenia (e.g., Zalla, Verlut, Franck, Puzenat, & Sirigu, 2004) and autism (e.g., Blake, Turner, Smoski, Pozdol, & Stone, 2003). The specific action-pragmatics proposal we have offered generates a range of empirically testable hypotheses that we hope will help in advancing knowledge on this important topic.

Acknowledgments

Research and writing contributions to this chapter were supported in part by National Science Foundation Grant No. BCS-0214884 and a James McKeen Cattell Sabbatical Award to the first author, and funds from the Social Sciences and Humanities Research Council of Canada to the third author. Our thanks to Jeffrey Zacks, Thomas Shipley, and an anonymous reviewer for insightful comments on an earlier draft.

References

Austin, J. L. (1962). *How to do things with words*. Oxford: Clarendon Press.
Baird, J. A., & Baldwin, D. A. (2001). Making sense of human behavior: Action parsing and intentional inference. In B. F. Malle, L. J. Moses, & D. A. Baldwin (Eds.), *Intentions and intentionality: Foundations of social cognition* (pp. 193–206). Cambridge, MA: MIT Press.
Baldwin, D. A. (2005). Discerning intentions: Characterizing the cognitive system at play. In B. Homer & C. Tamis-LeMonda (Eds.), *The development of social cognition and communication* (pp. 117–144). Mahwah, NJ: Lawrence Erlbaum.
Baldwin, D., Andersson, A., Saffran, J., & Meyer, M. (in press). Adults segment dynamic human action via statistical regularities. *Cognition*.

Baldwin, D. A., & Baird, J. A. (1999). Action analysis: A gateway to intentional inference. In P. Rochat (Ed.), *Early social cognition* (pp. 215–240). Hillsdale, NJ: Lawrence Erlbaum.

Baldwin, D. A., & Baird, J. A. (2001). Discerning intentions in dynamic human action. *Trends in Cognitive Sciences, 5*, 171–178.

Baldwin, D. A., Baird, J. A., Saylor, M., & Clark, M. A. (2001). Infants parse dynamic human action. *Child Development, 72*, 708–717.

Baldwin, D. A., Baird, J. A., Malle, B., Neuhaus, E., Craven, A., Guha, G., et al. (in preparation). *Segmenting dynamic human action via sensitivity to structure in motion.*

Blake, R., Turner, L. M., Smoski, M. J., Pozdol, S. L., & Stone, W. L. (2003). Visual recognition of biological motion is impaired in children with autism. *Psychological Science, 14*, 151–157.

Brand, R., Baldwin, D. A., & Ashburn, L. (2002). Evidence for 'motionese': Modifications in mothers' infant-directed action. *Developmental Science, 5*, 72–83.

Brand, R. J., Shallcross, W. L., Sabatos, M. G., & Massie, K. P. (2007). Fine-grained analysis of motionese: Eye gaze, object exchanges, and action units in infant- versus adult-directed action. *Infancy, 11*, 203–214.

Brentano, F. (1970). *Psychology from an empirical standpoint.* London: Routledge & Kegan Paul. Translated from the original 1874 edition by L. L. McAllister.

Byrne, R. W., & Tomasello, M. (1995). Do rats ape? *Animal Behaviour, 50*, 1417–1420.

Carpenter, M., Akhtar, N., & Tomasello, M. (1998). Fourteen- through 18-month-old infants differentially imitate intentional and accidental actions. *Infant Behavior & Development, 21*, 315–330.

Csibra, G., Bíró, S., Koós, O., & Gergely, G. (2003). One-year-old infants use teleological representations of actions productively. *Cognitive Science, 27*, 111–133.

Csibra, G., & Gergely, G. (2006). Social learning and social cognition: The case for pedagogy. *Attention and Performance, XXI*, 249–274.

Davidson, D. (1980). *Essays on action and events.* Oxford: Clarendon Press.

Dennett, D. C. (1987). *The intentional stance.* Cambridge, MA: MIT Press.

Dennett, D. C. (1996). *Kinds of minds: Toward an understanding of consciousness.* New York: Basic Books.

Forbes, J., & Poulin-Dubois, D. (1997). Representational change in young children's understanding of familiar verb meaning. *Journal of Child Language, 24*, 389–406.

Gergely, G. (2003). What should a robot learn from an infant? Mechanisms of action interpretation and observational learning in infancy. *Cognitive Science, 15*, 191–209.

Gergely, G., & Csibra, G. (2003). Teleological reasoning in infancy: The naïve theory of rational action. *Trends in Cognitive Sciences, 7*, 287–292.

Gergely, G., & Csibra, G. (2004). The social construction of the cultural mind: Imitative learning as a mechanism of human pedagogy. *Interaction Studies: Social Behaviour and Communication in Biological and Artificial Systems, 6*, 463–481.

Goldin-Meadow, S. (2006). Talking and thinking with our hands. *Current Directions in Psychological Science, 15*, 34–39.

Grice, H. (1975). Logic and conversation. In P. Cole & J. L. Morgan (Eds.), *Syntax and semantics 3: Speech acts* (pp. 41–58). New York: Academic Press.

Hard, B. A., Tversky, B., & Lang, D. (in press). Making sense of abstract events: Building event schemas. *Memory & Cognition*.

Heimann, M., & Meltzoff, A. N. (1996). Deferred imitation in 9- and 14-month-old infants: A longitudinal study of a Swedish sample. *British Journal of Developmental Psychology, 14*, 55–64.

Huang, C. T., Heyes, C., & Charman, T. (2006). Preschoolers' behavioural reenactment of "failed attempts": The roles of intention-reading, emulation, and mimicry. *Cognitive Development, 21*, 36–45.

Johansson, G. (1973). Visual perception of biological motion and a model for its analysis. *Perception & Psychophysics, 14*(2), 201–211.

Kiraly, I., & Gergely, G. (2003). Shifting "goals": Clarifying some misconceptions about the teleological stance in young infants. *Consciousness & Cognition, 12*, 773–776.

Klein, P. J., & Meltzoff, A. N. (1999). Long-term memory, forgetting, and deferred imitation in 12-month-old infants. *Developmental Science, 2*, 102–113.

Levinson, S. (1983). *Pragmatics*. Cambridge, MA: Cambridge University Press.

Loucks, J., & Baldwin, D. A. (2006). When is a grasp a grasp? Characterizing some basic components of human action processing. In K. Hirsh-Pasek & R. Golinkoff (Eds.), *Action meets words: How children learn verbs* (pp. 228–261). New York: Oxford University Press.

Maguire, M. J. (2003). *Children's use of universal and language specific cues in verb learning*. Unpublished dissertation. Philadelphia: Temple University.

Maguire, M. J., Hirsh-Pasek, K., & Golinkoff, R. M. (2006). A unified theory of word learning: Putting verb acquisition in context. In K. Hirsh-Pasek & R. M. Golinkoff (Eds.), *Action meets word: How children learn verbs.* (pp. 364–391). New York: Oxford University Press.

Martin, B. A. (2006). *Reading the language of action: A model of real-time action understanding*. Unpublished doctoral dissertation. Stanford, CA: Stanford University.

Meltzoff, A. N. (1995). Understanding the intentions of others: Re-enactment of intended acts by 18-month-old children. *Developmental Psychology, 31*, 838–850.

Meltzoff, A. N., & Brooks, R. (2001). "Like me" as a building block for understanding other minds: Bodily acts, attention, and intention. In B. F. Malle, L. J. Moses, & D. A. Baldwin (Eds.), *Intentions and intentionality: Foundations of social cognition* (pp. 171–191). Cambridge, MA: MIT Press.

Newtson, D. (1973). Attribution and the unit of perception of ongoing behavior. *Journal of Personality & Social Psychology, 28*(1), 28–38.

Newtson, D., Engquist, G., & Bois, J. (1977). The objective basis of behaviour units. *Journal of Personality and Social Psychology, 35*, 847–862.

Perner, J. (1991) *Understanding the representational mind*. Cambridge, MA: MIT Press.

Phillips, A. T., & Wellman, H. M. (2005). Infants' understanding of object-directed action. *Cognition, 98*, 137–155.

Phillips, A. T., Wellman, H. M., & Spelke, E. S. (2002). Infants' ability to connect gaze and emotional expression to intentional action. *Cognition, 85*, 53–78.

Rogoff, B., Paradise, R., Arauz, R. M., Correa-Chavez, M., & Angelillo, C. (2003). Firsthand learning through intent participation. *Annual Review of Psychology, 54*, 175–203.

Sabbagh, M. A., & Loucks, J. T. (2003, April). *Infants' sensitivity to the manner and outcomes of intentional action.* Poster presented at the biennial meeting of the Society for Research in Child Development, Tampa, FL.

Sacks, O. (1970). *The man who mistook his wife for a hat and other clinical tales.* New York: Simon & Schuster.

Saylor, M. M., Baldwin, D., Baird, J. A., & LaBounty, J. (2007). Infants' on-line segmentation of dynamic human action. *Journal of Cognition and Development, 8*, 113–128.

Swallow, K., & Zacks, J. (submitted). *Sequences learned without awareness can orient attention during the perception of human activity.*

Tomasello, M. (1999). *The cultural origins of human cognition.* Cambridge, MA: Harvard University Press.

Wellman, H. (1990). *Children's theories of mind.* Cambridge, MA: MIT Press.

Wellman, H. M., & Woolley, J. D. (1990). From simple desires to ordinary beliefs: The early development of everyday psychology. *Cognition, 35*, 245–275.

Wilson, D., & Sperber, D. (2002). Truthfulness and relevance. *Mind, 111*, 583–632.

Wittgenstein, L. (1958). *Philosophical investigations.* Oxford: Blackwell Press.

Woodward, A. L. (1998). Infants selectively encode the goal object of an actor's reach. *Cognition, 69*, 1–34.

Woodward, A. L. (1999). Infants' ability to distinguish between purposeful and non-purposeful behaviors. *Infant Behavior & Development, 22*, 145–160.

Woodward, A. L. (2003). Infants' developing understanding of the link between looker and object. *Developmental Science, 6*, 297–311.

Woodward, A. L. (2005). Infants' understanding of the actions involved in joint attention. In N. Eilan, C. Hoerl, T. McCormack, & J. Roessler (Eds.), *Joint attention: Communication and other minds: Issues in philosophy and psychology* (pp. 110–128). New York: Clarendon Press/Oxford University Press.

Woodward, A. L., Sommerville, J. A., & Guajardo, J. J. (2001). How infants make sense of intentional action. In B. Malle, L. Moses, & D. Baldwin (Eds.), *Intentions and intentionality: Foundations of social cognition* (pp. 149–169). Cambridge, MA: MIT Press.

Zacks, J. M., & Tversky, B. (2001). Event structure in perception and cognition. *Psychological Bulletin, 127*, 3–21.

Zacks, J. M., & Tversky, B. (2003). Structuring information interfaces for procedural learning. *Journal of Experimental Psychology: Applied, 9*, 88–100.

Zacks, J. M., Tversky, B., & Iyer, G. (2001). Perceiving, remembering, and communicating structure in events. *Journal of Experimental Psychology: General, 130*, 29–58.

Zadny, J., & Gerard, H. B. (1974). Attributed intentions and informational selectivity. *Journal of Experimental Social Psychology*, *1*, 34–52.

Zalla, T., Verlut, I., Franck, N., Puzenat, D., & Sirigu, A. (2004). Perception of dynamic action in patients with schizophrenia. *Psychiatry Research*, *128*(1), 39–51.

6

Event Memory in Infancy
and Early Childhood

PATRICIA J. BAUER

The phrase "May you live in exciting times" is considered a curse by some. For researchers who study the development of event memory, though, it is the opposite. When I began graduate school in 1981, we knew precious little about event memory in childhood as a field; the state of knowledge about event memory in infancy was even more impoverished. Exciting times were on the horizon, however. Conceptual and methodological developments in the late 1970s and early 1980s ushered in a new era of research on event memory in preschool-age and younger children. The result has been two-plus decades of marked change in our understanding of children's and even infants' recall of events and thus, seemingly, their representations of them. In the course of this chapter, I describe the "less exciting" times during which it seemed that the study of event memory in children was an unhealthy goal for a research career, followed by some of the developments that made the soil more fertile. I then describe some of the most salient developmental changes in event memory over the first years of life and relate them to developmental changes in the neural substrate that permit the storage and later retrieval of memories of events long past. The chapter ends with suggestions of directions for future research.

130

How Are We Measuring the Development?

As discussed elsewhere in this volume, an "event" can be something as simple as a leaf fluttering in the breeze or something as complex, multilayered, and temporally extended as a world war. For purposes of this chapter, I use a definition of "event" borrowed from Katherine Nelson (1986): events "involve people in purposeful activities, and acting on objects and interacting with each other to achieve some result" (p. 11). Because purposeful activity unfolds over time, it has a beginning, a middle, and an end. Because the actions in events are oriented toward a goal or result, there are often constraints on the order in which they unfold: actions preparatory to an outcome must occur before it in time. This definition excludes simple physical transformations such as fluttering because they do not involve actors engaged in purposeful activity. In contrast, the definition includes chains of activities as complex as world wars. Importantly for present purposes, it also includes the activities in which individuals engage as they move through a typical day (such as getting ready for work in the morning and ending the day with dinner at a restaurant) as well as the unique experiences that ultimately define us as individuals. Memory for these episodes is the focus of this chapter.

K. Nelson's (1986) definition of "event" also specifies what there is to be remembered about them—namely actors, actions, objects, and the orders in which the elements combine to achieve specific goals. These elements are the subject of this chapter, which includes reviews of the literature on children's developing ability to remember the experiences of their lives, including the actors, actions, and objects of events; the order in which the activities unfold; and the goals of activities. Also discussed are age-related changes in the basic processes of memory (encoding, consolidation, storage, and retrieval) that permit children to remember more, more accurately, and for longer periods of time, as well as possible neurobiological mechanisms responsible for developmental trends. Not included in the chapter are discussions of myriad other influences on the development of memory for events, such as (a) children's understanding of concepts that allow them to place events in space and time and to appreciate their significance for the self who experienced and is remembering the event, (b) the language skills that allow children to express their event memories and that likely facilitate encoding of events, and (c) the familial and cultural environments in which children learn to remember. A single chapter can not do justice to the intricacies of the multilevel interactions of these and other influences (see Bauer, 2007, for a book-length attempt). Instead, the present chapter adopts a basic process approach aimed at addressing some of the rate-limiting factors of event memory early in development.

What We Knew Then

Suggestions of Mnemonic Incompetence

As in so many areas of cognitive developmental science, the study of memory development (and thus memory for events) got its start with Piaget (1952). Among the tenets of Piaget's theory of genetic epistemology was the suggestion that for the first 18 to 24 months of life, infants lacked symbolic capacity and, thus, the ability to mentally *re-present* objects and events. Instead, they were thought to live in a world of physically present entities that had no past and no future. Even after they had constructed the capacity for mental representation (by 1.5 to 2 years of age), children were thought to be without the cognitive structures that would permit them to organize events along coherent dimensions that would make the events memorable. Consistent with this suggestion, in retelling fairy tales, children as old as 7 years made errors in temporal sequencing (Piaget, 1926, 1969). Piaget attributed their poor performance to the lack of reversible thought. Without it, children could not organize information temporally and thus could not tell a story from beginning to middle to end.

In the 1960s and 1970s, the nature of the explanations for children's poor performance on memory tasks began to change. Rather than attributing their lackluster performance to the absence of reversible cognitive structures, children's difficulties were linked with limitations on the information-processing steps of memory encoding and retrieval. Prototypical experiments compared the performance of children 5, 7, and 10 years of age (for example) as they studied and then recalled picture lists. In such studies, the youngest children did little to help themselves remember. They did not employ strategies to facilitate encoding or to aid retrieval. Presumably as a consequence, they remembered few pictures. In contrast, the oldest children verbally rehearsed the materials and generated clusters of related items at the time of retrieval, thereby increasing the amount recalled (e.g., Flavell, Beach, & Chinsky, 1966). This pattern was replicated many times over, seemingly confirming the "fact" of young children's mnemonic incompetence.

The Dawning of "Exciting Times"

In the 1970s and early 1980s, three things happened that ushered in the "exciting times" of research on early developments in event memory. First, the field discovered the importance to memory of the organization or structure within to-be-remembered materials. A second, and related, discovery was of the importance of familiarity with the event or domain of the to-be-remembered material. Third, a means of assessing event memory in pre- and early-verbal children was developed.

STRUCTURE IS IMPORTANT

As just noted, in the 1960s and 1970s, studies of memory frequently used as stimuli lists of pictures or words. In some cases, the lists were of related items (e.g., several pictures of vehicles interspersed with several pictures of food items). However, following the tradition established in the adult literature (as early as Ebbinghaus, 1885), in many studies the materials were virtually devoid of meaning or structure. This allowed for examination of the properties of memory (e.g., speed of acquisition, decay rate) without the potentially confounding factor of familiarity (and, in the developmental literature, potentially *differential* familiarity, as a function of age and experience). Yet many of the things that individuals experience and remember are highly structured. For example, the stories that we hear and read are not made up of randomly ordered bits but of antecedent actions followed by consequences. In an influential series of studies, Jean Mandler and her colleagues (e.g., Mandler & DeForest, 1979; Mandler & Johnson, 1977) demonstrated that children are sensitive to the structure inherent in story materials: children have higher levels of recall of well-formed stories relative to stories that are less well structured (see Mandler, 1984, for a review). Findings such as these made two things abundantly clear: (1) event memory is affected by the organization or structure of to-be-remembered events, and (2) when to-be-remembered events are well organized, even young children can be expected to recall them.

FAMILIARITY IS IMPORTANT

A second formative experience for the study of developments in event memory was recognition of the importance of familiarity with a domain or event for memory performance. By asking children for reports in domains that they knew well, Katherine Nelson and her colleagues discovered mnemonic competence in children as young as 3 years of age. Instead of asking children to recall lists of words or pictures, or even stories of a protagonist's experiences, they asked, "What happens when you make cookies?" and "What happens when you go to McDonald's?" (K. Nelson, 1978; K. Nelson & Gruendel, 1986). Like those of adults, children's reports of these events seemed to follow a "script" for what happens in the course of everyday events and routines (Schank & Abelson, 1977). Impressively, children's reports were temporally organized and revealed evidence of sensitivity to the causal structure of experience as well as to the central goals of events.

THE IMPORTANCE OF A MEANS OF ASSESSMENT

The third major "event" that changed the direction of research on young children's memory was development of an experimental means of testing assumptions about limitations on the ability of infants younger than 18 to 24 months to re-present past experiences. Piaget (1952) himself suggested the means when he described his daughter's deferred imitation of a cousin's temper tantrum as an indication of the development of symbolic thought. In the first of a series of papers, Andrew Meltzoff (1985) brought deferred imitation under experimental control. He used a novel prop (a dumbbell-shaped toy) to produce a unique action (pulling the dumbbell apart), which infants were then permitted to imitate. Consistent with Piaget's suggestion that symbolic thought is available by 24 months of age, Meltzoff reported that 24-month-olds could defer imitation of the novel action for 24 hours. In contrast to Piaget's expectations, however, Meltzoff also reported 24-hour deferred imitation by infants only 14 months of age. Shortly thereafter, findings of imitation deferred for 24 hours were extended to infants only 9 months of age (Meltzoff, 1988b). At roughly the same time, Cecilia Shore and I published findings of infants as young as 17 months of age remembering, over a 6-week delay, not only individual actions but temporally ordered sequences of action (i.e., putting a ball into a cup, covering it with another cup, and shaking the cups to make a rattle) (Bauer & Shore, 1987). These findings initiated concerted efforts to map the development of event memory in the first years of life.

It is important to note that evidence of imitation after a delay was not the first indication of memory in children younger than 18 to 24 months of age. The techniques of visual paired comparison and conjugate reinforcement, for example, had been used to assess memory in infancy since the 1950s (Fantz, 1956) and 1960s (Rovee & Rovee, 1969), respectively. In visual paired comparison, two identical stimuli are placed side by side for a period of time, after which one of the stimuli is replaced by a novel stimulus. A lengthier look toward the novel stimulus is taken as evidence of memory for the familiarization stimulus. In the mobile conjugate reinforcement paradigm, infants learn the contingency between kicking their legs and the movement of a mobile suspended above them and tethered to their legs. More vigorous kicking after the contingency is introduced relative to a precontingency baseline (when the leg is not tethered to the mobile) is indicative of memory (see Rovee-Collier, 1997, for a review). What was different about the imitation procedures relative to these other paradigms was that Piaget (1952) himself had identified deferred imitation as indicative of representational ability. In contrast, visual paired comparison (and other attentional preference techniques) provided experimental demonstrations of the sorts of recognition behaviors for which Piaget saw no need to invoke representational ability. The patterns of generalization, extinction, and reinstatement exhibited by infants in the conjugate reinforcement paradigm were typical of those in operant conditioning paradigms used with a range of animal species (e.g., Campbell, 1984). As a consequence, although these other techniques had been used for many years, they did not serve as an impetus for research on event memory in the first years of life to the same extent as the findings from imitation-based tasks.

What We Know Now

Research on children's recall of stories and preschoolers' "scripts," and development of a nonverbal means of assessing event memory in infancy, proved that even young children have substantial mnemonic competence.

The findings also gave birth to research on the development of memory for events that children experience in the normal course of their everyday lives as well as for novel, one-time experiences that they encounter either in the laboratory or in the world outside it. The developments also motivated research on event memory in infancy and very early childhood: if by 3 years of age children already have well-organized event representations, then the capacity to form them must have developed earlier. Imitation-based tasks provided the means to test this critical assumption.

In this section, I outline what we have learned about early developments in event memory over the course of roughly two decades of research. The review is confined to studies that have employed imitation-based tasks. A major reason for this selective treatment is that imitation-based tasks permit tests of infants using materials that are similar to the events commonly tested with older children. In other words, infants are presented with actions or sequences of actions performed by actors on objects in order to reach a clear goal (though it is not discussed, there is evidence that infants perceive the actions and event sequences as goal-based: e.g., Carpenter, Akhtar, & Tomasello, 1998; Meltzoff, 1995; Travis, 1997). This feature of the paradigm affords a point of contact with the literature from older children. In addition, imitation-based tasks have been used with infants as young as 6 months and as old as 36 months of age. The age range thus spans the transition from infancy to early childhood, thereby permitting assessment of continuity in recall processes across two major life periods.

Contrary to the traditional conceptualization of the first 2 years of life as a period devoid of the capacity to recall the past, studies testing imitation of single actions and multistep sequences have revealed evidence of event memory at a young age, as well as pronounced developmental change along a number of dimensions. Six-month-olds, the youngest infants tested with imitation-based paradigms,[1] have fragile memories of short events that they retain for a limited period. By 24 months of age, children have robust memories for long, temporally complex se-

---

1. Neonates have been found to imitate facial and hand gestures (e.g., Meltzoff & Moore, 1977). However, because of questions concerning the robustness of the effect (e.g., Kaitz, Meschulach-Sarfaty, Auerbach, & Eidelman, 1988) and debates as to whether the mechanisms that support imitation by neonates and older infants are one and the same (e.g., Jacobson, 1979), the results of this line of research are not included in this review.

quences that they retain over extended periods of time. After outlining these normative developmental trends, I discuss what is known about the basic process and neurobiological mechanisms of development. As noted earlier, there are multiple other levels and influences on developments in event memory, discussion of which is beyond the scope of this chapter (see Bauer, 2007, and K. Nelson & Fivush, 2004, for reviews).

Event Memory Becomes More Temporally Extended

One of the most salient changes in event memory over the first 2 years of life is in the length of time over which it is apparent. Importantly—because, as with any complex behavior, the length of time an event is remembered is multiply determined—there is no "growth chart" function that specifies that children of age X should remember for Y long. Nonetheless, as summarized in Table 6.1, evidence has emerged across a number of studies to support the idea that with increasing age, infants tolerate lengthier retention intervals. In the first published study of deferred imitation by 6-month-olds, Barr, Dowden, and Hayne (1996) found that the infants remembered an average of one action of a three-step sequence (taking a mitten off a puppet's hand; shaking the mitten, which, at the time of demonstration, held a bell that rang; and replacing the mitten) for 24 hours. Collie and Hayne (1999) found that 6-month-olds remembered an average of one out of five possible actions over a 24-hour delay. These findings regarding 6-month-olds' memories for a specific event after 24 hours are remarkable in the context of traditional conceptualizations of developments

TABLE 6.1.   Lengths of Time over which Infants Exhibit Event Memory

Age Group	Length of Delay	References
6-month-olds	24 hours	Barr, Dowden, & Hayne (1996)
9-month-olds	1 month	Carver & Bauer (2001)
10- to 11-month-olds	3 months	Carver & Bauer (2001) Mandler & McDonoug (1995)
13- to 14-month-olds	4 to 6 months	Bauer, Wenner, Dropik, & Wewerka (2000) Meltzoff (1995)
20-month-olds	12 months	Bauer, Wenner, Dropik, & Wewerka (2000)

in re-presentational ability. On the other hand, such low levels of performance after 24 hours have not "inspired" researchers to examine retention over longer intervals.

By 9 to 11 months of age, the length of time over which memory for laboratory events is apparent has increased substantially. Nine-month-olds remember individual actions over delays from 24 hours (Meltzoff, 1988b) to 1 month (Carver & Bauer, 1999, 2001). By 10 to 11 months of age, infants remember over delays as long as 3 months (Carver & Bauer, 2001; Mandler & McDonough, 1995). Thirteen- to 14-month-olds remember actions over delays of 4 to 6 months (Bauer, Wenner, Dropik, & Wewerka, 2000; Meltzoff, 1995). By 20 months of age, children remember the actions of event sequences over as many as 12 months (Bauer et al., 2000).

Event Memory Becomes More Robust

Over the first 2 years there are also changes in the robustness of memory. One index of the increasing robustness of memory is reduction in the number of experiences that seem to be required in order for infants to remember. In Barr et al. (1996), infants 6 months of age required six exposures to events in order to remember them 24 hours later. If instead they saw the actions demonstrated only three times, they showed no memory after 24 hours (i.e., performance of infants who had experienced the puppet sequence did not differ from that of naïve control infants). As summarized in Table 6.2, by 9 months of age, the number of

TABLE 6.2.   The Number of Experiences Required for Infants to Form a Memory

| Age Group | Number of Experiences Required for Infants to Remember over Intervals of: | | | |
	24 hours	1 week	1 month	6 months
6-month-olds	6[a]			
9-month-olds	3[b]	2[c]	3[c]	
14-month-olds			1[d]	
20-month-olds				1[e]

[a]Data from Barr, Dowden, & Hayne (1996); [b]Data from Meltzoff (1988b); [c]Data from Bauer, Wiebe, Waters, & Bangston (2001); [d]Data from Bauer, Hertsgaard, & Wewerka (1995); [e]Data from Bauer (unpublished data).

times actions need to be demonstrated to support recall after 24 hours has decreased to three (e.g., Meltzoff, 1988b). Indeed, 9-month-olds who see sequences modeled as few as two times within a single session recall individual actions of them 1 week later; three exposure sessions supports recall over the longer delay of 1 month (Bauer, Wiebe, Waters, & Bangston, 2001). By the time infants are 14 months of age, a single exposure session is all that is necessary to support recall of multistep sequences over 1 month (Bauer, Hertsgaard, & Wewerka, 1995). Ordered recall of multistep sequences is apparent after as many as 6 months for infants who received a single exposure to the events at the age of 20 months (Bauer, unpublished data).

Another index of the robustness of memory is the extent to which it is disrupted by interference. One source of interference is change in context between the time of encoding and of retrieval. There are mixed reports of the extent to which infants and very young children are sensitive to such contextual changes. There are some suggestions that recall is disrupted if, between exposure and test, the appearance of the test materials is changed. For example, in research by Hayne, MacDonald, and Barr (1997), when 18-month-olds experienced the puppet sequence demonstrated with a cow puppet and then were tested with the same puppet, they showed robust retention over 24 hours. However, when they experienced the sequence modeled with a cow puppet and then were tested with a duck puppet, they did not show evidence of memory. Twenty-one-month-olds remembered the sequence whether tested with the same or a different puppet (see also Hayne, Boniface, & Barr, 2000, and Herbert & Hayne, 2000).

There are also reports of robust generalization from encoding to test by infants across a wide age range. In other words, infants have been shown to generalize imitative responses across changes in (a) the size, shape, color, and/or material composition of the objects used at demonstration versus test (e.g., Bauer & Dow, 1994; Bauer & Fivush, 1992; Lechuga, Marcos-Ruiz, & Bauer, 2001); (b) the appearance of the room at the time of demonstration of modeled actions and at the time of memory test (e.g., Barnat, Klein, & Meltzoff, 1996; Klein & Meltzoff, 1999); (c) the setting for demonstration of the modeled actions and the test of memory for them (e.g., Hanna & Meltzoff, 1993; Klein & Meltzoff, 1999); and (d) the individual who demonstrated the actions and the individual who tested for memory for the actions (e.g., Hanna & Meltzoff,

1993). Infants are even able to use three-dimensional objects to produce events that they have only seen modeled on a television screen (Meltzoff, 1988a; but see Barr & Hayne, 1999). Evidence of flexible extension of event knowledge extends to infants as young as 9 to 11 months of age (e.g., Baldwin, Markman, & Melartin, 1993). Thus, while there is evidence that infants' memories as tested in imitation-based paradigms become more generalizable with age (e.g., Herbert & Hayne, 2000), there is substantial evidence that from an early age, infants' memories survive changes in context and stimuli.

Event Memory Becomes More Reliable

There are two senses in which infants' event memories become more reliable over the first years of life; both concern changes in the ability to remember information about the temporal order of events (which even in adults is a more challenging task relative to item memory: e.g., Shimamura, Janowsky, & Squire, 1990). First, as summarized in Table 6.3, with age, a larger percentage of infants in a given sample show evidence of temporally ordered recall of events. Although 67% of Barr et al.'s (1996) 6-month-olds remembered some of the actions associated with the puppet sequence over 24 hours, only 25% of them remembered

TABLE 6.3. Changes in the Reliability of Temporally Ordered Event Memory

Age Group	Percentage of Infants who Remember for:		
	24 hours	1 month	6 months
6-month-olds[a]	25%		
9-month-olds[b]		≈50%	
13-month-olds[c]		78%	39%
20-month-olds[c]		100%	83%

[a]The percentage of infants who produced two or more actions in the correct temporal orader; data from Barr, Dowden, & Hayne (1996). [b]The percentage of infants who produced two or more actions in the correct temporal order; data from Bauer, Wiebe, Carver, Waters, & Nelson (2003); Bauer, Wiebe, Waters, & Bangston (2001); and Carver & Bauer (1999). [c]The percentage of infants whose ordered reproduction of actions on previously experienced events was greater than ordered reproduction of actions on new, control events; data from Bauer, Wenner, Dropik, & Wewerka (2000).

actions in the correct temporal order. Collie and Hayne (1999, Experiment 1) reported no ordered recall after 24 hours by 6-month-olds (the infants were exposed to three target events, two of which required two steps to complete). Among 9-month-olds, approximately 50% of infants exhibit ordered reproduction of sequences after a 1-month delay (Bauer et al., 2001; Bauer, Wiebe, Carver, Waters, & Nelson, 2003; Carver & Bauer, 1999). By 13 months of age, the substantial individual variability in ordered recall has resolved: three-fourths of 13-month-olds exhibit ordered recall after 1 month, whereas 100% of 20-month-olds show ordered recall over the same interval. Over longer delays, however, the memories of younger infants are less reliable relative to those of older infants. After 6 months, for example, while more than 80% of 20-month-olds show evidence of ordered recall, only roughly 40% of 13-month-olds do (Bauer et al., 2000).

The second sense in which event memory becomes more reliable over the first 2 years of life concerns infants' abilities to reproduce multistep sequences characterized by different types of temporal relations. A robust finding is that ordered recall is facilitated by enabling relations in events. Enabling relations are said to exist when, for a given end-state or goal, one action is temporally prior to and necessary for a subsequent action. For example, to enjoy a meal of pasta with sauce, one must first cook the pasta. Because alternative temporal orders of the steps of events constrained by enabling relations are physically impossible, logically unlikely, or both, they occur in an invariant temporal order. In contrast, actions in an event are arbitrarily ordered when there are no inherent constraints on their temporal position in the sequence. To continue the example, whether one consumes a salad before or after the pasta course is a matter of personal preference or cultural convention only: there is no logical or necessary reason why one course must come before the other.

From a young age, infants evidence sensitivity to enabling relations in events. They have better ordered recall of multistep sequences with enabling relations relative to sequences that are arbitrarily ordered. The advantage is apparent when children are tested immediately (e.g., Bauer, 1992) and when they are tested after a delay (e.g., Barr & Hayne, 1996; Bauer & Dow, 1994; Bauer et al., 1995; Mandler & McDonough, 1995). The advantage remains apparent even after several experiences of arbitrarily ordered events in an invariant temporal order (Bauer & Travis, 1993). (See Bauer, 1992, 1995, and Bauer & Travis, 1993, for discussions of the means by which enabling relations in events may influence ordered recall.) Moreover, the advantage is obvious quite early in development: by 11 months of age, children show superior ordered recall of events with enabling relations relative to events that are arbitrarily ordered (Mandler & McDonough, 1995). The advantage in ordered recall is observed even though the number of individual actions of sequences with and without enabling relations that infants recall does not differ. (See Chapter 19 for other examples of the psychological import of the structure inherent in events.)

Whereas infants evidence sensitivity to enabling relations in events from a very young age, development of the ability to reliably reproduce arbitrarily ordered sequences is protracted (Bauer, Hertsgaard, Dropik, & Daly, 1998; Wenner & Bauer, 1999). It is not until children are 20 months or older that they accurately reproduce arbitrarily ordered events. At that age, performance clearly is affected by the length of the sequence: children are reliable on shorter event sequences (i.e., three steps in length) but not on longer ones (i.e., five steps in length). In addition, children accurately reproduce arbitrarily ordered sequences immediately but not after a 2-week delay. In contrast, by 28 months, children recall arbitrarily ordered events even after a delay (Bauer et al., 1998). Nevertheless, seemingly across the life span, people are better able to remember events with enabling relations in them compared to events that are arbitrarily ordered (e.g., van den Broek, 1997).

Summary

Over the course of roughly two decades of research, we have learned a great deal about early developments in event memory. Contrary to the traditional conceptualization of an individual in the first 2 years of life as devoid of the capacity to recall the past, it now is apparent that developments in event memory are well underway relatively early in infancy. Within the first 2 years of life, there are substantial and significant developmental changes in the length of time over which infants and young children remember, in the robustness of infants' and children's memories, and in the reliability with which memory is observed. Indeed, by the end of the second year, children reliably show robust memories for long, temporally complex sequences, which they retain over extended periods of time. I now turn to discussion of what is known about the basic process and neurobiological mechanisms associated with these developmental changes.

Explaining Age-Related Changes in Event Memory

There is no doubt that ultimately, several factors will be found to come into play to explain developments in memory for events. They will range from changes in the neural processes and systems and basic mnemonic processes that permit memories to be formed, retained, and later retrieved to the social forces that shape what children ultimately come to view as important to remember about events, and even how they express their memories. For present purposes, I focus on "lower-level" mechanisms of change—those at the level of neural systems and basic mnemonic processes. I begin with a brief review of the neural network thought to permit recollection of specific past events in the adult, as well as what is known about its development. I then examine the basic mnemonic processes of encoding, consolidation, storage, and retrieval and evaluate their contributions to age-related changes in event memory (see Bauer, 2004, 2007, for expanded versions of this discussion).

The Temporal-Cortical Network that Supports Recollection of Events

In adult humans, formation, maintenance, and retrieval of event memories depend on a multicomponent neural network involving temporal and cortical structures (e.g., Eichenbaum & Cohen, 2001; Markowitsch, 2000; Zola & Squire, 2000).

THE SUBSTRATE IN ADULTS

As illustrated in Figure 6.1, with experience of an event, sensory and motor inputs are registered in widely distributed cortical regions (i.e., primary somatosensory, visual, and auditory cortices). Inputs from these primary sensory areas are projected to sensory association areas, each of which is dedicated to a single modality (somatic sensation, vision, or audition), where they are integrated into whole percepts of what the object or event feels like, looks like, and sounds like, respectively. The unimodal sensory association areas in turn project to

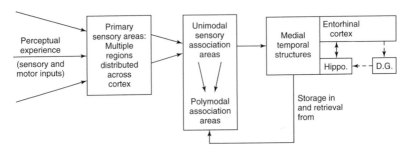

FIGURE 6.1. Schematic representation of the input and output pathways of the hippocampal formation. Information from primary sensory areas is projected to unimodal sensory and polymodal association areas in turn. It is then projected to medial temporal structures (including perirhinal and parahippocampal cortices) and to the entorhinal cortex. From the entorhinal cortex, information makes its way into the cell fields of the hippocampus in one of two ways: via the "long route" (indicated by dotted lines) through the dentate gyrus or via the "short route" (indicated by solid lines), which bypasses the dentate gyrus. (Adapted from Kandel, Schwartz, & Jessell, 2000, Fig. 62.5, p. 1232; Zola & Squire, 2000, Fig. 30.1, p. 487.)

polymodal (or multimodal) posterior-parietal, anterior-prefrontal, and limbic-temporal association areas, where inputs from the different sense modalities converge.

Ultimately, the association areas are the long-term storage sites for memory traces. Yet between the time of initial registration and commitment to long-term storage there is substantial additional processing. That processing is thought to be performed by medial temporal lobe structures—in particular, the hippocampus—in concert with the association cortices, and it results in integration and stabilization of the various inputs from different cortical regions. Whereas integration and stabilization processes begin upon registration of a stimulus, they do not end there. By some estimates, the process of stabilizing a memory trace, termed *consolidation*, continues for hours, days, months, and even years. Importantly, while they are being consolidated, memories are vulnerable to disruption and interference. Eventually, cortical structures alone are responsible for storage of memories over the long term. Prefrontal structures are implicated in the retrieval of memories after a delay. Thus, event memory depends upon multiple cortical regions, including prefrontal cortex, temporal structures, and intact connections between them.

At a general level, the time course of changes in behavior reviewed earlier is consistent with what is known about developments in the temporal-cortical network that supports explicit memory (Bauer, 2002, 2004, 2007; Nelson, 2000). In the human, many of the medial temporal lobe components of the network develop early. For instance, as reviewed by Seress (2001), the cells that make up most of the hippocampus are formed in the first half of gestation, and by the end of the prenatal period virtually all have migrated to their adult locations. In some areas of the hippocampus, synapses are present as early as 15 weeks gestational age. By approximately 6 postnatal months, the number and density of synapses have reached adult levels, as has glucose utilization in the temporal cortex (see Chugani, 1994).

In contrast to early maturation of most of the hippocampus, development of the dentate gyrus of the hippocampus is protracted (Seress, 2001). At birth, the dentate gyrus includes only about 70% of the adult number of cells. It is not until 12 to 15 postnatal months that the morphology of the structure appears adult-like. Maximum density of synaptic connections in the dentate gyrus also is reached relatively late. The number of synapses increases dramatically (to well above adult levels) beginning at 8 to 12 postnatal months and reaches its peak at 16 to 20 months. After a period of relative stability, excess synapses are pruned until adult levels are reached at about 4 to 5 years of age (Eckenhoff & Rakic, 1991).

Although the functional significance of the protracted course of development of the dentate gyrus is not clear, there is reason to believe that it is consequential. As already noted, information about events and experiences is initially distributed across regions of cortex but eventually converges on medial temporal structures (see Fig. 6.1). One of those structures—the entorhinal cortex—provides two "routes" by which information is projected into the hippocampus. By the "long route" (indicated by dotted lines in Fig. 6.1), information is projected from entorhinal cortex into the cell fields of the hippocampus, by way of the dentate gyrus; the "short route" (indicated by the solid line in Fig. 6.1) bypasses the dentate gyrus. There are suggestions that short-route processing may support some forms of memory (Nelson, 1995, 1997). However, based on data from rodents, it appears that adult-like memory behavior depends on processing of information through the dentate gyrus (Czurkó, Czéh, Seress, Nadel, & Bures, 1997; Nadel & Willner, 1989). This implies that maturation of the dentate gyrus of the hippocampus is a rate-limiting variable in the early development of event memory (Bauer, 2002, 2004, 2007; Bauer et al., 2003; Nelson, 1995, 1997, 2000). It may be especially important for ordered recall, which demands relational processing of the sort associated with intact hippocampal function (e.g., Eichenbaum & Cohen, 2001).

The association areas also develop slowly (Bachevalier, 2001). For instance, it is not until the seventh prenatal month that all six cortical layers are apparent. The density of synapses in prefrontal cortex increases dramatically beginning at 8 postnatal months and peaks between 15 and 24 months. Pruning to adult levels is delayed until puberty (Huttenlocher, 1979; Huttenlocher & Dabholkar, 1997; see Bourgeois, 2001, for discussion). It is not until 24 months that synapses develop adult morphology (Huttenlocher, 1979). Other maturational changes in prefrontal cortex, such as myelination, continue into adolescence, and adult levels of some neurotransmitters are not seen until the second and third decades of life (Benes, 2001).

The full network that supports recollection of past events can be expected to function as an integrated whole only once each of its components, as well as the connections between them, has reached a level of functional maturity. "Functional maturity" is associated with the rise to peak number of synapses; "full maturity" is associated with achievement of adult numbers of synapses (Goldman-Rakic, 1987). By this metric, we should expect to see the evidence of event memory by late in the first year of life, with significant development over the course of the second year, and continued (albeit less dramatic) development for years thereafter. The time frame is based on increases in the formation of new synapses beginning at approximately 8 months in both the dentate gyrus and prefrontal cortex, with continued synaptogenesis through 20 and 24 months, respectively. The expectation of developmental changes for months and years thereafter stems from the schedule of protracted selective reduction in synapses both in the dentate gyrus (until 4 to 5 years; e.g., Eckenhoff & Rakic, 1991) and in the prefrontal cortex (throughout adolescence; e.g., Huttenlocher & Dabholkar, 1997).

What are the consequences for behavior of the slow course of development of the network that supports recollection of past events? At a general level, we may expect that as the neural substrate develops, the behavior develops as well (and vice versa, of course). More specifically, we may ask how changes in the medial temporal and cortical structures, and their interconnections, produce changes in memory representations. To address this question, we must consider how the brain "builds a memory" and thus how the "recipe" for a memory might be affected by changes in the underlying neural substrate. In other words, we must consider how developmental changes in the substrate for memory relate to changes in the efficacy and efficiency with which information is encoded and stabilized for long-term storage, in the reliability with which it is stored, and in the ease with which it is retrieved.

Changes in Basic Mnemonic Processes

ENCODING

Association cortices are involved in the initial registration and temporary maintenance of experience. Because prefrontal cortex in particular undergoes considerable postnatal development, it is reasonable to assume that there may be changes in encoding processes over the first years of life. Consistent with this suggestion are findings of age-related differences in encoding (as measured by event-related potentials, or ERPs) that relate to age-related differences in long-term recall (as measured by deferred imitation). ERPs are scalp-recorded electrical oscillations associated with excitatory and inhibitory postsynaptic potentials. Because they are noninvasive and make no performance demands on the participant, they are ideal for use with human infants. Moreover, because they are time-locked to a stimulus (i.e., activity is recorded for a 100 ms pre-stimulus baseline, during a 500 ms visual stimulus, and for 1,200 ms after stimulus offset), differences in the latency and amplitude of the response to different classes of stimuli—familiar and novel, for example—can be interpreted as evidence of differential neural processing.

In a longitudinal study, infants were exposed to different multistep sequences at 9 months and at 10 months. To test encoding, immediately after presentation of the sequences, we recorded infants' ERPs as they looked at still photographs of the props used in the sequences, interspersed with photographs of props from novel sequences. Relative to when they were 9 months of age, infants at 10 months of age showed more robust encoding of the events (i.e., larger responses to familiar stimuli and smaller responses to novel stimuli). Importantly, the differences at encoding were related to differences at recall. That is, 1 month after each ERP, we used imitation to test recall of the events. The infants had higher rates of recall of the events to which they had been exposed at 10 months relative to the events they had been exposed to at 9 months (Bauer et al., 2006).

Age-related differences in encoding also are apparent in the second year of life. Relative to 15-month-olds, 12-month-olds require more trials to learn multistep events to a criterion (learning to a criterion indicates that the material was fully encoded). In turn, 15-month-olds reach criterion more slowly relative to 18-month-olds (Howe & Courage, 1997). Indeed, throughout development older children learn more rapidly than younger children (Howe & Brainerd, 1989).

Although age-related differences in encoding are apparent throughout the first 2 years of life, they alone do not account for the age trends in recall of events: even with encoding controlled, older children remember more than younger children. In Bauer et al. (2000), for instance, with the variance in encoding controlled statistically, across delays ranging from 1 to 12 months, older children remembered more than younger children. In samples matched for levels of encoding, younger children lose more information from memory relative to older children (Bauer, 2005). Similarly, Howe and Courage (1997) found that with level of encoding controlled via a criterion learning design, after 3 months 15-month-olds remembered more than 12-month-olds, and 18-month-olds remembered more than 15-month-olds. Findings such as these strongly suggest that changes in postencoding processes also contribute to developmental changes in event memory.

CONSOLIDATION AND STORAGE

Although they are separable phases in the life of a memory trace, at the level of analysis available in the existing developmental data, consolidation and storage can not be effectively separated, and thus I discuss them in tandem. As reviewed earlier, medial temporal structures are implicated in the consolidation process by which new memories become "fixed" for long-term storage; cortical association areas are the presumed storage sites for long-term memories. Even in a fully mature, intact adult, the process of consolidation seemingly continues for hours, weeks, and even months after an event. Throughout this time, memory traces are vulnerable: if lesions to medial temporal structures are inflicted during the consolidation period, deficits result, whereas lesions inflicted after a trace has consolidated produce no deficit (see Eichenbaum & Cohen, 2001, for a review). Consolidation may be an even more vulnerable process for the developing organism. Not only are some of the neural structures involved in the process relatively undeveloped (i.e., the dentate gyrus and prefrontal cortex) but the connections between them are still being created and thus are less than fully effective and efficient. As a consequence, younger children may experience greater vulnerability of memory traces relative to older children (Bauer, 2004, 2005a, 2005b, 2007).

To examine the role of consolidation and storage processes in event memory in 9-month-old infants, Bauer et al. (2003) combined ERP measures of encoding (i.e., immediate ERP tests), ERP measures of consolidation and storage (i.e., 1-week delayed ERP), and deferred imitation measures of recall after 1 month. As a group, the infants successfully encoded the events, as evidenced by the immediate ERP test (i.e., they showed differential responses to familiar and novel stimuli). Nevertheless, approximately half of the infants apparently experienced consolidation failure: at the 1-week delayed ERP they failed to recognize the stimuli, and they failed to recall the events 1 month later. In contrast, roughly half of the infants successfully consolidated their event memories, as evidenced by recognition after 1 week and recall after 1 month. These data strongly imply that at 9 months of age, consolidation and/or storage processes are a source of individual differences in mnemonic performance.

In the second year of life, there are behavioral suggestions of between-age group differences in consolidation and/or storage processes, as well as a replication of the finding among 9-month-olds that intermediate-term consolidation and/or storage failure relates to recall over the long term. In a study by Bauer, Cheatham, Cary, and Van Abbema (2002), 16- and 20-month-old children were exposed to multistep sequences and tested for recall immediately (as a measure of encoding) and after 24 hours. The younger children forgot a substantial amount of what they had encoded only 24 hours earlier: they produced only 65% of the target actions and 57% of the ordered pairs of actions that they recalled immediately. Among the older children, the amount of forgetting over the delay was not statistically reliable. It is not until 48 hours that children 20 months of age exhibit significant forgetting (Bauer, Van

Abbema, & de Haan, 1999). These observations suggest age-related differences in the vulnerability of memory traces during the initial period of consolidation.

Another of the experiments in the study by Bauer et al. (2002) provides additional evidence that the vulnerability of memory traces during the initial period of consolidation is related to the robustness of long-term recall. Twenty-month-old children were exposed to multistep events and then tested on some of the events immediately, some after 48 hours (a delay after which, based on Bauer et al., 1999, some forgetting was expected), and some after 1 month. The children exhibited high levels of initial encoding (as measured by immediate recall). Nevertheless, they showed evidence of significant forgetting after both 48 hours and 1 month. The robustness of memory after 48 hours predicted 25% of the variance in recall 1 month later; variability of encoding did not predict significant variance. This finding is a conceptual replication of that observed with 9-month-olds in the study by Bauer et al. (2003). In both cases, the amount of information lost to memory during the period of consolidation predicted the robustness of recall 1 month later.

RETRIEVAL

Retrieval of memories from long-term storage sites is thought to depend on prefrontal cortex. Because prefrontal cortex undergoes a long period of postnatal development, retrieval processes are a likely candidate source of age-related differences in long-term recall. Unfortunately, there are few data with which to evaluate their contribution, because in most studies there are alternative candidate sources of age-related change. In studies in which imitation is deferred until after some delay (e.g., Hayne et al., 2000; Liston & Kagan, 2002), for example, no measures of learning are obtained (i.e., no immediate imitation). As such, it is impossible to know whether developmental differences in long-term recall are due to retrieval processes or possibly to encoding processes. Even when indices of encoding are available, with standard testing procedures, it is difficult to know whether a memory representation is intact but has become inaccessible with the cues provided (retrieval failure) or whether it has lost its integrity and become unavailable (consolidation or storage failure). Implication of retrieval processes as a source of developmental change requires that encoding be controlled and that memory be tested under conditions of high support for retrieval. One study in which these conditions were met was Bauer et al. (2003; i.e., ERPs indicated that the events had been encoded; the suggestion of consolidation and/or storage failure was apparent on a recognition memory task). The results, described in the preceding section, clearly implicated consolidation and/or storage as opposed to retrieval.

Another study that permits assessment of the contributions of consolidation and/or storage relative to retrieval processes is that by Bauer et al. (2000) in which children of multiple ages (13, 16, and 20 months) were tested over a range of delays (1 to 12 months). Because immediate recall of half of the events was tested, measures of encoding are available. There was also high support for retrieval, in two ways. First, children were reminded of the to-be-remembered events both by props and by verbal labels. Second, after the test of delayed recall, the ultimate in retrieval support was provided: *the sequences were demonstrated again*, and savings in relearning was assessed. When it accrues, savings (classically, a reduction in the number of trials required to relearn a stimulus relative to the number required to learn it initially) is thought to result because the products of relearning are integrated with an existing (though not necessarily accessible) memory trace (Ebbinghaus, 1885). Conversely, the absence of savings is attributed to storage failure: there is no residual trace upon which to build. In developmental studies, age-related differences in relearning would suggest that the residual memory traces available to children of different ages are differentially intact.

To eliminate encoding processes as a potential source of developmental differences in long-term recall, in a reanalysis of the data from the study by Bauer et al. (2000), subsets of 13- and 16-month-olds and of 16- and 20-month-olds were matched for levels of encoding (as measured by immediate recall; Bauer, 2005). Performance after the delays was then examined. In both comparisons, the younger children remembered less than the older children. Moreover, in both comparisons levels of relearning by the older children were higher than those by the younger children (Bauer, 2005). Together, the findings of age-related differential memory over time and of age effects in relearning strongly implicate storage as opposed to retrieval processes as the major source of age-related differences in delayed recall early in life.

SUMMARY

Ultimately, a number of factors will be found to explain age-related variance in event memory in the first years of life. At present, developments in the basic mnemonic processes of encoding, consolidation and storage, and retrieval are one of the few sources of change to have been evaluated. Examination of their relative contributions implicates consolidation and storage as a major source of developmental change in infancy. This conclusion is consistent with the loci of developments in the neural substrate of event memory. Late in the first year and throughout the second year of life there are pronounced changes in the temporal lobe structures implicated in integration and consolidation of memory traces. A likely consequence is changes in the efficiency and efficacy with which information is stabilized for storage, with resulting significant behavioral changes in resistance to forgetting, and perhaps a shift in its locus. In other words, as temporal lobe structures develop, we might expect the functional locus of forgetting to shift from the earlier-stage processes in which they are implicated to the later-stage process of retrieval (Bauer, 2006a; though see Howe & O'Sullivan, 1997, for evidence that storage processes remain a significant source of variance throughout childhood, on a wide variety of mnemonic tasks). Testing of this hypothesis awaits future research.

Where We Might Go Next

The last two decades of the 20th century were "exciting times" for researchers of event memory in infancy and very early childhood. Research in the 1970s and early 1980s revealed previously unexpected mnemonic competence in older children's recall of stories about others, in preschoolers' understanding of the events of their daily lives, and in the ability of pre- and early-verbal infants to recall multistep events demonstrated for them by an adult. Early competence in event memory should not, however, be taken to suggest absence of developmental change. Across the first years of life there are pronounced changes in the length of time over which infants remember events, in the robustness of their event memories, and in the reliability with which they recall. It likely is more than coincidence that the changes in behavior occur at the same time the brain is undergoing postnatal development of structures implicated in event memory in adults. A more fine-grained analysis of developmental changes in the basic mnemonic processes of encoding, consolidation and storage, and retrieval suggests relations between changes in these mnemonic functions and developments in the neural structures thought to subserve them.

The search for insights into the nature and sources of developmental changes in early event memory continues. As discussed by Bauer (2006b), one task for future research is to determine how the early memory abilities tapped by paradigms such as deferred imitation relate to event memory later in development and to the deliberate memory skills tested in educational settings. Preliminary findings from ongoing studies in my own laboratory suggest substantial continuity in this regard (DeBoer, Cheatham, Stark, & Bauer, 2005; Larkina & Bauer, 2005). Especially in light of these findings, more work needs to be done to examine individual differences in event memory in school-age and older children. Whereas variability in the school years may not be as dramatic as that in infancy and the preschool years, the period is a significant part of the puzzle of how a fundamental cognitive capacity changes over the course of development. Attention to individual differences not only is important to a full description of developmental change but can be expected to shed light on the mechanisms thereof.

Through future research we may hope not only for additional description of developmental change but for advances in our knowledge of explanatory mechanisms. In particular, it is desirable to expand the focus on links between brain and behavior. Relative to the adult literature—in which there has been significant progress establishing relations between structure and function—the developmental literature is far behind. Some neuroimaging techniques, such as positron emission tomography, will never develop into "work horse" paradigms for developmental research because they require ionizing radiation, use of which in healthy children is contraindicated. Others, including ERPs and functional magnetic resonance imaging (fMRI), are already yielding insight into the neural generators of cognitive events. Specifically, high-density arrays of electrodes permit identification of the origins of electrical signals recorded on the scalp (Nelson & Monk, 2001), and fMRI scans of the brain engaged in cognitive processing can be obtained from children as young as 4 years of age (Cantlon, Brannon, Carter, & Pelphrey, 2006). Further expanding the arsenal with neural network models (Munakata & Stedron, 2001) and comparisons with performance by developing nonhuman animals (Overman & Bachevalier, 2001) will permit substantial progress in identification of the neural sources of specific behavioral change. Developments in these directions will ensure that the "exciting times" in which researchers of early event memory have been living will continue for some time to come.

References

Bachevalier, J. (2001). Neural bases of memory development: Insights from neuropsychological studies in primates. In C. A. Nelson & M. Luciana (Eds.), *Handbook of developmental cognitive neuroscience* (pp. 365–379). Cambridge, MA: MIT Press.

Baldwin, D. A., Markman, E. M., & Melartin, R. L. (1993). Infants' ability to draw inferences about nonobvious properties: Evidence from exploratory play. *Child Development, 64,* 711–728.

Barnat, S. B., Klein, P. J., & Meltzoff, A. N. (1996). Deferred imitation across changes in context and object: Memory and generalization in 14-month-old children. *Infant Behavior and Development, 19,* 241–251.

Barr, R., Dowden, A., & Hayne, H. (1996). Developmental change in deferred imitation by 6- to 24-month-old infants. *Infant Behavior and Development, 19,* 159–170.

Barr, R., & Hayne, H. (1996). The effect of event structure on imitation in infancy: Practice makes perfect? *Infant Behavior and Development, 19,* 253–257.

Barr, R., & Hayne, H. (1999). Developmental changes in imitation from television during infancy. *Child Development, 70,* 1067–1081.

Bauer, P. J. (1992). Holding it all together: How enabling relations facilitate young children's event recall. *Cognitive Development, 7,* 1–28.

Bauer, P. J. (1995). Recalling the past: From infancy to early childhood. *Annals of Child Development, 11,* 25–71.

Bauer, P. J. (2002). Long-term recall memory: Behavioral and neuro-developmental changes in the first 2 years of life. *Current Directions in Psychological Science, 11,* 137–141.

Bauer, P. J. (2004). Getting explicit memory off the ground: Steps toward construction of a neuro-developmental account of changes in the first two years of life. *Developmental Review, 24,* 347–373.

Bauer, P. J. (2005). Developments in declarative memory: Decreasing susceptibility to storage failure over the second year of life. *Psychological Science, 16,* 41–47.

Bauer, P. J. (2006a). Constructing a past in infancy: A neuro-developmental account. *Trends in Cognitive Sciences, 10,* 175–181.

Bauer, P. J. (2006b). Event memory. In D. Kuhn, R. Siegler (Volume Editors: Volume 2—*Cognition, perception, and language*), W. Damon, & R. M. Lerner (Editors-in-Chief), *Handbook of child psychology,* 6th edition (pp. 373–425). Hoboken, NJ: John Wiley & Sons, Inc.

Bauer, P. J. (2007). *Remembering the times of our lives: Memory in infancy and beyond.* Mahwah, NJ: Erlbaum.

Bauer, P. J., Cheatham, C. L., Cary, M. S., & Van Abbema, D. L. (2002). Short-term forgetting: Charting its course and its implications for long-term remembering. In S. P. Shohov (Ed.), *Advances in psychology research*, Vol. 9 (pp. 53–74). Huntington, NY: Nova Science Publishers.

Bauer, P. J., & Dow, G. A. A. (1994). Episodic memory in 16- and 20-month-old children: Specifics are generalized, but not forgotten. *Developmental Psychology, 30*, 403–417.

Bauer, P. J., & Fivush, R. (1992). Constructing event representations: Building on a foundation of variation and enabling relations. *Cognitive Development, 7*, 381–401.

Bauer, P. J., Hertsgaard, L. A., Dropik, P., & Daly, B. P. (1998). When even arbitrary order becomes important: Developments in reliable temporal sequencing of arbitrarily ordered events. *Memory, 6*, 165–198.

Bauer, P. J., Hertsgaard, L. A., & Wewerka, S. S. (1995). Effects of experience and reminding on long-term recall in infancy: Remembering not to forget. *Journal of Experimental Child Psychology, 59*, 260–298.

Bauer, P. J., & Shore, C. M. (1987). Making a memorable event: Effects of familiarity and organization on young children's recall of action sequences. *Cognitive Development, 2*, 327–338.

Bauer, P. J., & Travis, L. L. (1993). The fabric of an event: Different sources of temporal invariance differentially affect 24-month-olds' recall. *Cognitive Development, 8*, 319–341.

Bauer, P. J., Van Abbema, D. L., & de Haan, M. (1999). In for the short haul: Immediate and short-term remembering and forgetting by 20-month-old children. *Infant Behavior and Development, 22*, 321–343.

Bauer, P. J., Wenner, J. A., Dropik, P. L., & Wewerka, S. S. (2000). Parameters of remembering and forgetting in the transition from infancy to early childhood. *Monographs of the Society for Research in Child Development, 65*(4), i–vi, 1–204.

Bauer, P. J., Wiebe, S. A., Carver, L. J., Lukowski, A. F., Haight, J. C., Waters, J. M., et al. (2006). Electrophysiological indices of encoding and behavioral indices of recall: Examining relations and developmental change late in the first year of life. *Developmental Neuropsychology, 29*, 293–320.

Bauer, P. J., Wiebe, S. A., Carver, L. J., Waters, J. M., & Nelson, C. A. (2003). Developments in long-term explicit memory late in the first year of life: Behavioral and electrophysiological indices. *Psychological Science, 14*, 629–635.

Bauer, P. J., Wiebe, S. A., Waters, J. M., & Bangston, S. K. (2001). Reexposure breeds recall: Effects of experience on 9-month-olds' ordered recall. *Journal of Experimental Child Psychology, 80*, 174–200.

Benes, F. M. (2001). The development of prefrontal cortex: The maturation of neurotransmitter systems and their interaction. In C. A. Nelson & M. Luciana (Eds.), *Handbook of developmental cognitive neuroscience* (pp. 79–92). Cambridge, MA: MIT Press.

Bourgeois, J.-P. (2001). Synaptogenesis in the neocortex of the newborn: The ultimate frontier for individuation? In C. A. Nelson & M. Luciana (Eds.), *Handbook of developmental cognitive neuroscience* (pp. 23–34). Cambridge, MA: MIT Press.

Campbell, B. A. (1984). Reflections on the ontogeny of learning and memory. In R. Kail & N. E. Spear (Eds.), *Comparative perspectives on the development of memory* (pp. 117–133). Hillsdale, NJ: Erlbaum.

Cantlon, J. S., Brannon, E. M., Carter, E. J., & Pelphrey, K. A. (2006). Functional imaging of numerical processing in adults and 4-y-old children. *PLoS Biology, 4,* e125.

Carpenter, M., Akhtar, N., & Tomasello, M. (1998). Fourteen- through 18-month-old infants differentially imitate intentional and accidental actions. *Infant Behavior and Development, 21,* 315–330.

Carver, L. J., & Bauer, P. J. (1999). When the event is more than the sum of its parts: Nine-month-olds' long-term ordered recall. *Memory, 7,* 147–174.

Carver, L. J., & Bauer, P. J. (2001). The dawning of a past: The emergence of long-term explicit memory in infancy. *Journal of Experimental Psychology: General, 130,* 726–745.

Chugani, H. T. (1994). Development of regional blood glucose metabolism in relation to behavior and plasticity. In G. Dawson & K. Fischer (Eds.), *Human behavior and the developing brain* (pp. 153–175). New York: Guilford.

Collie, R., & Hayne, H. (1999). Deferred imitation by 6- and 9-month-old infants: More evidence of declarative memory. *Developmental Psychobiology, 35,* 83–90.

Czurkó, A., Czéh, B., Seress, L., Nadel, L., & Bures, J. (1997). Severe spatial navigation deficit in the Morris water maze after single high dose of neonatal X-ray irradiation in the rat. *Proceedings of the National Academy of Science, 94,* 2766–2771.

DeBoer, T., Cheatham, C. L., Stark, E., & Bauer, P. J. (2005). *Beyond the gong: Relations between elicited imitation performance at 20–40 months of age and memory at 6 years.* Poster presented at the Biennial Meeting of the Society for Research in Child Development, Atlanta, Georgia.

Ebbinghaus, H. (1885). *On memory* (Translated by H. A. Ruger & C. E. Bussenius). New York: Teachers' College, 1913. Paperback edition: New York: Dover, 1964.

Eckenhoff, M., & Rakic, P. (1991). A quantitative analysis of synaptogenesis in the molecular layer of the dentate gyrus in the rhesus monkey. *Developmental Brain Research, 64,* 129–135.

Eichenbaum, H., & Cohen, N. J. (2001). *From conditioning to conscious recollection: Memory systems of the brain.* New York: Oxford University Press.

Fantz, R. L. (1956). A method for studying early visual development. *Perceptual and Motor Skills, 6,* 13–15.

Flavell, J. H., Beach, D. R., & Chinsky, J. H. (1966). Spontaneous verbal rehearsal in a memory task as a function of age. *Child Development, 37,* 283–299.

Goldman-Rakic, P. S. (1987). Circuitry of primate prefrontal cortex and regulation of behavior by representational memory. In F. Plum (Ed.), *Handbook of physiology, the nervous system, higher functions of the brain,* Vol. 5 (pp. 373–417). Bethesda, MD: American Physiological Society.

Hanna, E., & Meltzoff, A. N. (1993). Peer imitation by toddlers in laboratory, home, and day-care contexts: Implications for social learning and memory. *Developmental Psychology, 29,* 702–710.

Hayne, H., Boniface, J., & Barr, R. (2000). The development of declarative memory in human infants: Age-related changes in deferred imitation. *Behavioral Neuroscience, 114*, 77–83.

Hayne, H., MacDonald, S., & Barr, R. (1997). Developmental changes in the specificity of memory over the second year of life. *Infant Behavior and Development, 20*, 233–245.

Herbert, J., & Hayne, H. (2000). Memory retrieval by 18–30-month-olds: Age-related changes in representational flexibility. *Developmental Psychology, 36*, 473–484.

Howe, M. L., & Brainerd, C. J. (1989). Development of children's long-term retention. *Developmental Review, 9*, 301–340.

Howe, M. L., & Courage, M. L. (1997). Independent paths in the development of infant learning and forgetting. *Journal of Experimental Child Psychology, 67*, 131–163.

Howe, M. L., & O'Sullivan, J. T. (1997). What children's memories tell us about recalling our childhoods: A review of storage and retrieval processes in the development of long-term retention. *Developmental Review, 17*, 148–204.

Huttenlocher, P. R. (1979). Synaptic density in human frontal cortex: Developmental changes and effects of aging. *Brain Research, 163*, 195–205.

Huttenlocher, P. R., & Dabholkar, A. S. (1997). Regional differences in synaptogenesis in human cerebral cortex. *Journal of Comparative Neurology, 387*, 167–178.

Jacobson, S. W. (1979). Matching behavior in the young infant. *Child Development, 50*, 425–430.

Kaitz, M., Meschulach-Sarfaty, O., Auerbach, J., & Eidelman, A. (1988). A re-examination of newborns' ability to imitate facial expressions. *Developmental Psychology, 24*, 3–7.

Kandel, E. R., Schwartz, J. H., & Jessell, T. M. (2000). *Principles of neural science*, 4th ed. New York: McGraw-Hill.

Klein, P. J., & Meltzoff, A. N. (1999). Long-term memory, forgetting, and deferred imitation in 12-month-old infants. *Developmental Science, 2*, 102–113.

Larkina, M., & Bauer, P. J. (2005). *Continuity in recall memory: Links between infancy and middle childhood.* Poster presented at the Biennial Meeting of the Society for Research in Child Development, Atlanta, Georgia.

Lechuga, M. T., Marcos-Ruiz, R., & Bauer, P. J. (2001). Episodic recall of specifics and generalisation coexist in 25-month-old children. *Memory, 9*, 117–132.

Liston, C., & Kagan, J. (2002). Memory enhancement in early childhood. *Nature, 419*, 896.

Mandler, J. M. (1984). *Stories, scripts and scenes: Aspects of schema theory.* Hillsdale, NJ: Erlbaum.

Mandler, J. M., & DeForest, M. (1979). Is there more than one way to recall a story? *Child Development, 50*, 886–889.

Mandler, J. M., & Johnson, N. S. (1977). Remembrance of things parsed: Story structure and recall. *Cognitive Psychology, 9*, 111–151.

Mandler, J. M., & McDonough, L. (1995). Long-term recall of event sequences in infancy. *Journal of Experimental Child Psychology, 59*, 457–474.

Markowitsch, H. J. (2000). Neuroanatomy of memory. In E. Tulving & F. I. M. Craik (Eds.), *The Oxford handbook of memory* (pp. 465–484). New York: Oxford University Press.

Meltzoff, A. N. (1985). Immediate and deferred imitation in fourteen- and twenty-four-month-old infants. *Child Development, 56,* 62–72.

Meltzoff, A. N. (1988a). Imitation of televised models by infants. *Child Development, 59,* 1221–1229.

Meltzoff, A. N. (1988b). Infant imitation and memory: Nine-month-olds in immediate and deferred tests. *Child Development, 59,* 217–225.

Meltzoff, A. N. (1995). What infant memory tells us about infantile amnesia: Long-term recall and deferred imitation. *Journal of Experimental Child Psychology, 59,* 497–515.

Meltzoff, A. N., & Moore, M. K. (1977). Imitation of facial and manual gestures by human neonates. *Science, 198,* 75–78.

Munakata, Y., & Stedron, J. M. (2001). Neural network models of cognitive development. In C. A. Nelson & M. Luciana (Eds.), *Handbook of developmental cognitive neuroscience* (pp. 159–171). Cambridge, MA: MIT Press.

Nadel, L., & Willner, J. (1989). Some implications of postnatal maturation of the hippocampus. In V. Chan-Palay & C. Köhler (Eds.), *The hippocampus—new vistas* (pp. 17–31). New York: Alan R. Liss.

Nelson, C. A. (1995). The ontogeny of human memory: A cognitive neuroscience perspective. *Developmental Psychology, 31,* 723–738.

Nelson, C. A. (1997). The neurobiological basis of early memory development. In N. Cowan (Ed.), *The development of memory in childhood* (pp. 41–82). Hove, East Sussex: Psychology Press.

Nelson, C.A. (2000). Neural plasticity and human development: The role of early experience in sculpting memory systems. *Developmental Science, 3,* 115–136.

Nelson, C. A., & Monk, C. S. (2001). The use of event-related potentials in the study of cognitive development. In C. A. Nelson & M. Luciana (Eds.), *Handbook of developmental cognitive neuroscience* (pp. 125–136). Cambridge, MA: MIT Press.

Nelson, K. (1978). How young children represent knowledge of their world in and out of language. In R. S. Siegler (Ed.), *Children's thinking: What develops?* (pp. 255–273). Hillsdale, NJ: Erlbaum.

Nelson, K. (1986). *Event knowledge: Structure and function in development.* Hillsdale, NJ: Erlbaum.

Nelson, K., & Fivush, R. (2004). The emergence of autobiographical memory: A social cultural developmental theory. *Psychological Review, 111,* 486–511.

Nelson, K., & Gruendel, J. (1981). Generalized event representations: Basic building blocks of cognitive development. In M. E. Lamb & A. L. Brown (Eds.), *Advances in developmental psychology,* Vol. 1 (pp. 131–158). Hillsdale, NJ: Erlbaum.

Nelson, K., & Gruendel, J. (1986). Children's scripts. In K. Nelson (Ed.), *Event knowledge: Structure and function in development* (pp. 21–46). Hillsdale, NJ: Erlbaum.

Overman, W. H., & Bachevalier, J. (2001). Inferences about the functional development of neural systems in children via the application of animal tests of cognition. In C. A. Nelson & M. Luciana (Eds.), *Handbook of developmental cognitive neuroscience* (pp. 109–124). Cambridge, MA: MIT Press.

Piaget, J. (1926). *The language and thought of the child.* New York: Harcourt, Brace.

Piaget, J. (1952). *The origins of intelligence in children.* New York: International Universities Press.

Piaget, J. (1969). *The child's conception of time.* London: Routledge & Kegan Paul.

Rovee, C. K., & Rovee, D. T. (1969). Conjugate reinforcement of infant exploratory behavior. *Journal of Experimental Child Psychology, 8,* 33–39.

Rovee-Collier, C. (1997). Dissociations in infant memory: Rethinking the development of implicit and explicit memory. *Psychological Review, 104,* 467–498.

Schank, R. C., & Abelson, R. P. (1977). *Scripts, plans, goals and understanding.* Hillsdale, NJ: Erlbaum.

Seress, L. (2001). Morphological changes of the human hippocampal formation from midgestation to early childhood. In C. A. Nelson & M. Luciana (Eds.), *Handbook of developmental cognitive neuroscience* (pp. 45–58). Cambridge, MA: MIT Press.

Shimamura, A. P., Janowsky, J. S., & Squire, L. R. (1990). Memory for the temporal order of events in patients with frontal lobe lesions and amnesic patients. *Neuropsychologia, 28,* 803–813.

Travis, L. L. (1997). Goal-based organization of event memory in toddlers. In P. van den Broek, P. J. Bauer, & T. Bourg (Eds.), *Developmental spans in event comprehension and representation: Bridging fictional and actual events* (pp. 111–138). Hillsdale, NJ: Erlbaum.

van den Broek, P. (1997). Discovering the cement of the universe: The development of event comprehension from childhood to adulthood. In P. van den Broek, P. J. Bauer, & T. Bourg (Eds.), *Developmental spans in event representation and comprehension: Bridging fictional and actual events* (pp. 321–342). Mahwah, NJ: Erlbaum.

Wenner, J. A., & Bauer, P. J. (1999). Bringing order to the arbitrary: One- to two-year-olds' recall of event sequences. *Infant Behavior and Development, 22,* 585–590.

Zola, S. M., & Squire, L. R. (2000). The medial temporal lobe and the hippocampus. In E. Tulving & F. I. M. Craik (Eds.), *The Oxford handbook of memory* (pp. 485–500). New York: Oxford University Press.

7

Current Events: How Infants Parse the World and Events for Language

SHANNON M. PRUDEN, KATHY HIRSH-PASEK, AND
ROBERTA M. GOLINKOFF

At the critical juncture between words and grammar lies the next frontier—verb learning. Serving as the architectural centerpiece of the sentence, verbs control the argument structure of grammar and describe relations between objects and events. Verbs are the means by which language conveys descriptions of events. Though verbs appear in the vocabulary of very young children (Choi, 1998; Choi & Bowerman, 1991; Choi & Gopnik, 1995; Fenson, Dale, Reznick, & Bates, 1994; Nelson, 1989; Tardif, 1996), noun acquisition has dominated the focus in the field of language development. Fundamental to developing a comprehensive theory of word learning is the study of early verb learning; fundamental to the study of verbs is the study of how young children perceive, process, and represent events. This chapter focuses on what children need to know about events before they learn their first verbs and, more broadly, their first relational terms. What are the conceptual foundations of verb learning? How do children process actions and events?

Research within the past two decades has begun to illuminate the process through which children acquire a lexicon of relational terms (see Hirsh-Pasek & Golinkoff, 2006, for a review of this research). This research shows that verbs are more difficult to learn than nouns (Gentner, 1982; also see Bornstein et al., 2004; but see Tardif, 1996, for counter-arguments). For example, Meyer et al. (2003) and Imai, Haryu, and Hiroyuki (2003) find that well into the fifth year, children have trouble determining the referent of a novel verb in both English and Japanese. Even in languages like Korean, where verbs are in perceptually favored, sentence-final positions and can appear alone in a sentence, children tend to learn verbs later than nouns (e.g., Choi & Bowerman, 1991; Choi & Gopnik, 1995; but see Tardif, 1996 for an alternative view). Further, research with adult populations, like Gillette and colleagues' (1999) "Human Simulation Project," suggests that conceptually mature adults find it hard to clearly demarcate the meaning for a verb. Asked to view silent videos of interactions between English-speaking mothers and their children, adults are fairly good at guessing which nouns the mother is likely saying (e.g., 45% correct). In contrast, when asked to guess the verbs the mother is likely saying, adults do quite poorly (e.g., 15% correct). What makes verbs and other relational terms so difficult to learn?

It has been suggested that learning verbs requires some key abilities. For example, Gentner and Boroditsky (2001) outline two critical prerequisites for acquiring verbs. According to these researchers, verb learning requires (1) the conceptualization of actions and relations and (2) the mapping of words to these actions and relations. Golinkoff and colleagues (2002) echoed Gentner and Boroditsky, suggesting that infants must pay attention to and isolate actions and relations within a larger event before they can then form categories of and map words onto these actions/relations. Thus, the conceptualization of actions and events might be part of the verb-learning problem. Further, verbs do not label whole actions but only a subset of actions, or what has been termed "semantic components." These semantic components include meaning elements like *path* (i.e., the trajectory of the object or agent; e.g., come, approach, enter), *manner* (i.e., the way in which an agent moves; e.g., walk, dance, swagger, sway, stroll), *motion* (i.e., the general fact that motion is taking place), *figure* (i.e., the primary agent or object in the event), *ground* (i.e., the reference point for the event's path), and *cause* (i.e., the cause of the figure's motion) (Talmy, 1985).

In what has been dubbed the "packaging problem" (Tomasello, 1995), these semantic components are combined or configured in different ways to generate the verb system in a particular language (Talmy, 1985; also see Langacker, 1987). For example, languages like English, German, and Chinese package the *manner* of motion in verbs, while other languages, including Spanish, Turkish, and Greek, encode manner information in other word classes. Languages like English tend to reserve information about the *path* for other word classes (e.g., prepositions such as "over"), while Spanish, Turkish, and Greek encode path information in their verbs. Infants must learn which semantic components are being encoded in a particular relational term or verb. As a result, infants may require much experience with their native language before they can recognize which semantic components are conflated in which relational terms and before they can map these semantic components themselves onto relational terms.

Most research investigating relational terms has explored either the early production of relational terms such as prepositions (Choi & Bowerman, 1991; Choi & Gopnik, 1995; Tardif, 1996) or the mapping of relational terms onto actions (Choi, McDonough, Bowerman, & Mandler, 1999; Maguire, Hirsh-Pasek, Golinkoff, & Pruden, 2003; Naigles, 1996). Little research, however, investigates whether children have the prerequisites to build an arsenal of relational terms. Can infants, for example, perceive events that will map to relational terms? Here we have mostly speculation. An example comes from Gentner (1982; also see Gentner & Boroditsky, 2001), who hypothesizes that the prerequisites for the learning of verbs and other relational terms might be in place at an early age. She writes,

> [R]elations that act as predicates over objects are, I suspect, perceived quite early. Movement, change, directionality, and so on, seem quite interesting to infants . . . [I]t is not perceiving relations but packaging and lexicalizing them that is difficult. (Gentner, 1982, p. 326)

Snedeker and Gleitman agree (2004): "vocabulary acquisition in the real case may reduce mainly to a mapping problem" (p. 280). Further, they assert, "the young child's conceptual repertoire may be rich and varied enough from the start" (p. 261).

Psychologists are not the only ones to propose that children start with a rich conceptual base for learning relational terms. Some cognitive linguists suggest that the semantic components that relational terms label (i.e., path, manner, etc.) may be prelinguistic primitives from which all other relational terms are constructed (e.g., Jackendoff, 1983; Mandler, 1991, 1992, 2004), equipping infants with a language-ready organizational system. Mandler (2004) proposes that infants construct what are called "image schemas" or "spatial representation[s] that express primitive or fundamental meanings . . . . Common image schemas are notions such as PATH, CONTAINMENT, UP-DOWN, and LINK" (p. 78). Furthermore, image schemas form the basis for conceptual categories such as animacy, causality, and agency. Children conceptualize the environment around them using these image schemas. Only after experience with their native language do infants begin to carve up these concepts into spatial categories that are particular to their native language (Hespos & Spelke, 2004).

The challenge for researchers interested in solving the verb-learning problem is to better understand the nature of events and to determine when infants understand enough about events to support the learning of relational terms. Research is just starting to focus on these issues, and our laboratories have been taking this charge seriously. In the coming sections we explore infants' ability to attend to and parse actions from ongoing events. Further, we discuss infants' ability to discriminate and categorize those semantic components and relations that are codified in relational terms. Finally, we review those factors that may hinder or aid the abstraction of the semantic components encoded in relational terms.

When Do Infants Begin to Perceive, Process, and Represent Actions and Spatial Relations?

One of the hurdles for those who want to investigate the acquisition of relational terms is that little is known about how young children process events, actions, and even spatial relations. There has been minimal research on this topic, as there is still disagreement among researchers regarding the definition of an *event* (see Chapter 1). Some define events broadly as "what happens to things" (Kable, Lease-Spellmeyer, & Chatterjee, 2002,

p. 795) or as a "basic unit in the organization of experience, memory, and meaning" (Avrahami & Kareev, 1994, p. 239). Others are more specific in their criteria for an event. Miller and Johnson-Laird (1976), for example, hold that an event must have at least two actors and include a causal relationship. In this chapter, we adopt Zacks and Tversky's (2001) definition: an event is "a segment of time at a given location that is conceived by an observer to have a beginning and an end" (p. 3). Note that these beginnings and ends are not always easy to detect. As Hanson and Hirst (1989) write,

> These boundaries may be fuzzy; the exact moment of transition between one event and the next may not be clear. As one reaches for a piece of toast and picks it up, the transition between *reaching* and *picking up* may be smooth, but the lack of a precise boundary does not imply that *reaching* and *picking up* are not discrete events. Events, like object categories, can have fuzzy boundaries and yet still be distinguished from one another. (p. 136)

As indicated above, events (such as picking up the toast) can be nested in other events (such as eating breakfast) and can be divided into smaller events or into actions units (Hanson & Hirst, 1989). As another example, consider the event of *putting gas in a car*. It can be divided into smaller units such as *purchasing the gas, opening the gas tank, lifting the gas pump hose*, and *pressing the gas pump lever*. Indeed, even the event *purchasing the gas* can be divided into *getting out a wallet, giving money to a cashier*, and so forth. Before infants map words onto these events, they must have a basic understanding of how to process events and actions in their environment (Nelson, 1997). In other words, they must understand that the events *giving money to a cashier* and *taking money from the cashier* are different before they can attach the corresponding labels *give* and *take*. Furthermore, infants need to grasp the relation between the giver and recipient of the objects they exchange.

Research investigating infants' perception of motion in events has generally looked at how infants use motion to track objects and learn about the properties of objects (see Chapter 4 for a discussion of object perception; also see Johnson & Aslin, 1995; Johnson, Cohen, Marks, & Johnson, 2003; Kellman & Spelke, 1983; Rakison, 2003; Rakison & Poulin-Dubois, 2001; Rochat & Hespos, 1996; Slater, Morison, & Town, 1985; Smith, Johnson, & Spelke, 2003; Spelke, Phillips, & Woodward,

1995; and Wang, Kaufman, & Baillargeon, 2003). The work concentrating on infants' understanding of motion itself has focused on how infants construe the physical properties of actions within an event or the "physics" of causal events.

Some have charted infants' ability to discriminate actions and spatial relations within larger events. Five-month-olds, for example, detect the invariant property of rigid motion and can differentiate between rigid movement and deformations (Gibson, Owsley, & Johnston, 1978). In this study, infants were habituated to three types of rigid motion (e.g., rotation in the frontal plane, rotation around the vertical axis, rotation around the horizontal axis). They were then shown a new example of rigid motion (e.g., looming) and an example of deformation of the object during the test phase. Infants increased their attention to the deformation but not to the new example of rigid motion, suggesting that they perceive rigidity as an invariant property of an object.

In more recent research, 5.5-month-old infants were familiarized with a repetitive activity performed by a female actor (e.g., blowing bubbles, brushing hair, or brushing teeth) (Bahrick, Gogate, & Ruiz, 2002). During test, infants were simultaneously presented with a familiar action and a novel action. They showed a significant preference for the novel action, suggesting that they could discriminate among these actions.

Casasola and Cohen (2000) demonstrated that 14-month-olds discriminate between the actions of *pushing* and *pulling*. Infants habituated to a pushing event (e.g., a toy car pushes a can across the screen) were shown two events at test: the same pushing event and an event depicting pulling (e.g., the toy car pulls a can across the screen). Infants reliably increased their looking times to the unfamiliar test event relative to the familiar test event. Thus, 14-month-old infants can discriminate between pushing and pulling actions, providing further support for infants' ability to discriminate actions within larger events. Similarly, research by Sharon and Wynn (1998; Wynn, 1996) examined infants' ability to discriminate between two actions. Six-month-old infants familiarized with a puppet performing the action of *jumping* were shown two test trials: the puppet *jumping* and the puppet *falling*. Infants increased attention to the new action (falling), indicating that they could distinguish between actions like falling and jumping. The ability to discriminate among different actions is important for verb learning (Kersten & Billman, 1997). Though this research suggests that infants are equipped with the ability to notice motion and discriminate actions, it tells us little about the sorts of cues infants are using to carve up these events.

What Cues Are Used to Carve Up Events?

Adults appear to use a number of cues, including perceptual or sensory information (i.e., "bottom-up information") and information about the goal or intention of the actor (i.e., "top-down information"), to segment events into meaningful units (Zacks, 2004). For example, adults use movement features to determine where one action ends and another begins (Newtson, 1973; Newtson, Engquist, & Bois, 1977). Adults are also sensitive to information about the goals and intentions of an actor (Hanson & Hirst, 1989; Graziano, Moore, & Collins, 1988; Markus, Smith, & Moreland, 1985; Newtson, 1973). Zacks (2004) found that adults used movement features or perceptual information to identify event segments. However, he noted that information about an actor's intention or goal modulated the processing of these movement features. Taken together, these studies suggest that both types of information—perceptual processing and intentional structure—are used to represent and segment events. What kinds of information do infants use to carve up an ongoing stream of events?

Research by Baldwin, Baird, Saylor, and Clark (2001) begins to address this issue. Baldwin and colleagues investigated infants' ability to parse continuous, everyday events. Ten- and 11-month-old infants were familiarized to continuously flowing action sequences (e.g., a woman notices a towel on the floor, reaches for and grasps it, and then moves toward a towel rack and places it on the rack). The test phase involved showing infants two different versions of the original action sequence, each containing a still-frame pause inserted at particular points in the course of the action sequence. One still frame occurred just as the actor in the action sequence completed the intended act. The other still frame occurred in the midst of the ongoing intentional action sequence. Infants looked longer at the test trial that interrupted the intended act than at the test trial that did not. These results suggest that infants as young as 10 months are able to parse continuously flowing behavior.

Baldwin and colleagues (2001) propose that infants' success in segmenting events could be attributed to both a high-level mechanism and a low-level mechanism, just as Zacks (2004) found with adults. Infants could be using high-level information about an agent's intention to parse events (as in "She wants to hang up the towel"). Alternatively, children might use low-level perceptual features of the events, such as the rapid changes in the direction of motion, to parse these events. Maguire, Shipley, Brumberg, and Ennis (2005) refer to these rapid changes in event direction as "curvature extrema" and note that adults are sensitive to them. Preliminary work from our lab suggests that between 7 and 9 months, babies are sensitive to "curvature extrema" as well (Song et al., 2007). Research using point-light displays adds credence to this latter explanation. Five-month-olds are sensitive to breaks in biological motion, indicating that they may be using low-level markers to segment events (Bertenthal, Proffitt, & Cutting, 1984). While the debate over the kind of information infants use to succeed in parsing streams of biological motion persists, these findings provide the first evidence of infants' ability to parse individual actions from the dynamic flow of events.

One more piece of evidence on early event processing shows that infants can discriminate among causal and noncausal launching events (Cohen & Amsel, 1998; Cohen & Oakes, 1993; Leslie, 1984; Leslie & Keeble, 1987; Oakes, 1994; Oakes & Cohen, 1990). By 6 months of age, infants respond to the physical changes occurring in causal events but can not yet organize these events based on causality (Leslie, 1984). In other words, infants at this age show evidence of the ability to encode the temporal order of events but do not yet show the ability to assign causal roles to objects (i.e., one object is assigned an active, causal role and the other a passive role). By 10 months of age, infants begin to process causal launching events in terms of the relationship between the objects in the event, and they organize these events based on causality (Cohen & Oakes, 1993). At this age, infants show the ability to assign causal roles to individual objects—one specific object caused the other to move.

Taken together, research on infants' processing of events demonstrates clear evidence that in the first year of life children perceive actions and events and carve up larger events into individual actions and relations (Baldwin et al., 2001; Bertenthal et al., 1984; Casasola & Cohen, 2000; Sharon & Wynn, 1998; Wynn, 1996). Yet these skills only take them so far. As Clark (2003) writes, infants also need "to know how to decompose scenes into the constituent parts relevant to linguistic expressions in the language" (p. 168)—that is, infants must also pay attention to and discriminate those components that are eventually encoded in language.

Further, in order to process events for language, infants need the ability to see objects in relation to one another. What kinds of relations are codified in the world's languages? To answer this question, researchers turned to linguists who have specified a set of semantic components present across languages (Talmy, 1985). A thorough examination of these semantic components will not only give us a sense of what might be universal across languages but may also allow us to see how these components are "packaged" in different ways across the languages of the world. Four celebrated semantic components in the literature are *containment, support, path*, and *manner*.

Discrimination of Actions and Spatial Relations

Can infants discriminate semantic components that are codified in relational terms? To better address this question, we break the research into two sections. In the first section, we discuss the research on infants' ability to discriminate the semantic components *containment, support*, and *degree of fit*. Research on semantic components that are lexicalized in relational terms has primarily focused on these relations. The second section explores the research on infants' discrimination of *path* and *manner*. Until recently, less was known about infants' discrimination of these two semantic components in events.

Discrimination of Containment, Support, and Degree of Fit

The semantic component *containment*, lexicalized by the English word "in," "is conceived of as something in any fully or partially enclosed space—that is, bounded space with an inside and an outside" (Mandler, 2004, p. 78). The semantic component *support*, lexicalized in English by the word "on," occurs "when the Figure is in contact with—typically supported by, attached to, or encircling—an external surface of the Ground" (Choi et al., 1999, p. 247). Finally, the semantic construct *degree of fit* makes a systematic distinction between interlocking surfaces (i.e., tight-fit containment and support) and those with noninterlocking surfaces (i.e., loose-fitting containment and support) (Bowerman & Choi, 2001).

In the context of the infant studies presented here, these spatial relations are actually presented as dynamic relational constructs that unfold across time where the relation is marked by the endpoint of the event—in this case, when a hand places an object in another object. Here, the endpoint denotes the relation: containment. However, as Pulverman and colleagues (2007) point out, "the crucial distinctions between the containment/support/tight-fit relations can also be derived by examining the static endpoints of the events. That is, whether something fits tightly or loosely into a container requires only perceptual examination of the boundaries around the object. Thus, it is unclear whether infants' processing of these events is based on the *dynamic* properties of motion per se" (p. 6). In other words, children may be solving these tasks using static properties rather than dynamic features of the event. Regardless of how children solve the tasks in these studies, these semantic components are important for further investigation, as they appear to be packaged in different ways across language. For example, Korean-speakers make a distinction between the degree of fit (i.e., tight fit versus loose fit) regardless of containment (e.g., fitting a peg tightly into a hole) or support (e.g., fitting one Lego tightly onto another). English-speakers, on the other hand, make a distinction between containment and support relations regardless of the degree of fit.

Findings on the spatial relations *containment* and *support* shows that young infants have an early understanding of these relations (Baillargeon, 2001, 2002; Baillargeon & Wang, 2002; Hespos & Baillargeon, 2001a, 2001b) and can discriminate instances of these types of spatial relations (Hespos & Spelke, 2004).

Baillargeon and colleagues investigated young infants' rudimentary knowledge of containment and support relations (e.g., Baillargeon, 2001, 2002; Baillargeon & Wang, 2002; Hespos & Baillargeon, 2001a, 2001b) lexicalized in English as "in" and "on." In one study, 2.5-month-old English-learning infants were shown two types of events: a possible event and an impossible event (Hespos & Baillargeon, 2001a). In the possible event, infants viewed a scene in which an object was lowered into an open container. This event depicted a possible containment relation. In the impossible event, infants saw the same object lowered into a closed container. This event depicted an impossible containment relation. Infants looked longer at the impossible event, indicating that they have some understanding of what happens in both a containment relation (i.e., when something is lowered into an open container it is a containment relation) and a support relation (i.e., when something is lowered onto a closed container it is a support relation). Infants not only discriminate between these two types of spatial relations but also have an understanding of what happens in each type of spatial relation.

Hespos and Spelke (2004) asked whether 5-month-old English-learning infants could discriminate spatial relations found in Korean but not lexicalized in English (i.e., degree of fit—tight fit versus loose fit). Infants were habituated to an event in which an object fit either tightly or loosely in a container. During the test phase, infants viewed both the familiar relation and a novel relation. For example, infants habituated to the spatial relation *tight-fit* were shown this familiar relation (i.e., tight-fit) and a novel relation (i.e., loose-fit) at test. Infants exhibited an increase in looking to the novel relation during test. Thus, they demonstrated an ability to discriminate between spatial concepts (i.e., degree of fit) that are not typically codified in their native language. These studies suggest that, at an early age, infants are predisposed to pay attention to the kinds of semantic components that may be relevant to later language learning.

Discrimination of Path and Manner

Path and *manner* are codified in many languages of the world (Jackendoff, 1983; Langacker, 1987; Talmy, 1985), although they are packaged in different ways. The semantic component of *path* may be one of the most central concepts for learning relational terms. Mandler (2004) suggests that path is a primitive used to acquire concepts like animacy and causality. A path primacy is seen in the production of relational terms in both hearing and deaf populations (Naigles, Eisenberg, & Kako, 1992; Zheng & Goldin-Meadow, 2002). Naigles and colleagues discovered that 2-year-olds produce more path expressions than manner expressions, while Zheng and Goldin-Meadow showed that path verbs were produced more often than manner verbs in both Chinese and American deaf children. Manner is equally important to study. In order for a path to be traversed, a manner is required to propel the moving figure.

A few studies have investigated infants' ability to process and discriminate components such as path and manner in nonlinguistic motion events (Casasola, Hohenstein, & Naigles, 2003; Pulverman, 2005; Pulverman et al., 2003; Pulverman & Golinkoff, 2004). For example,

Pulverman and Golinkoff (2004) studied English-learning infants' ability to pay attention to changes in path and manner in nonlinguistic motion events. Seven-month-old infants were habituated to an animated starfish performing both a path and a manner (e.g., a starfish spinning [manner] over a ball [path]). Once infants were habituated to this clip, they were shown four test trials: a control trial (e.g., starfish spinning [manner] over a ball [path]), a manner-change trial (e.g., starfish bending [manner] over a ball [path]), a path-change trial (e.g., starfish spinning [manner] under a ball [path]), and a path- and manner-change trial (e.g., starfish flapping [manner] past a ball [path]). Infants dishabituated to these test trials, suggesting that they noticed something had changed in these events.

Casasola, Hohenstein, and Naigles (2003) demonstrated that English-learning 10-month-olds could pay attention to and discriminate both path and manner in events involving naturalistic scenes and human agents (e.g., a young child crawling [manner] in front of a bush [path] versus a young child hopping [manner] in front of a bush [path]). Ten-month-olds were habituated to a young child demonstrating both a path (e.g., in front of a bush) and a manner (e.g., skipping). At test, infants were shown three clips demonstrating a change in path, a change in manner, a change in both path and manner, and the clip they saw during habituation (control). Infants increased their attention to changes in both path and manner. These results provide evidence that infants pay attention to nonlinguistic components of action events (such as path and manner) that relational terms typically encode.

Using the same stimuli and methods as those used in Pulverman and Golinkoff (2004), Pulverman and colleagues (2003) found that 14- to 17-month-olds reared in English-speaking environments, like the 7- to 9-month-olds, noticed that something in these events had changed. Unlike the younger infants, who did not show evidence of noting specific changes in path and manner, these older infants viewed path and manner as independent elements of events. For example, those infants with a higher vocabulary (as assessed by the MacArthur Communicative Development Inventory) were more attentive to the change in manner than their lower-vocabulary counterparts. These results suggest that infants at this age notice components of actions typically encoded in their language and that language may play some role in the ability to notice and attend to these components. More recently, Pulverman et al. (2007)

explored Spanish-reared infants' discrimination of path and manner. Spanish-learning infants, like English-reared infants, show evidence of the ability to notice changes in both path and manner. However, unlike their English-reared counterparts, Spanish-learning infants with a low vocabulary attended to manner as a specific element of interest, while the high-vocabulary infants did not. Taken together, these studies show that infants bring to the task of learning relational terms the ability to discriminate those components that are lexicalized in language. Additionally, they also suggest that differential focus on these semantic components can have an impact on children's lexical acquisition across language.

These studies provide us with information about infants' ability to parse dynamic events and to attend to components that are codified in motion verbs. This is only the beginning of what infants need to know to solve the verb-learning problem, however. As Oakes and Rakison (2003) state, "words refer to categories of objects and events" (p. 4)—that is, verbs label not single actions but categories of actions and events. Running, for example, is considered the same action whether performed by an Olympic runner or a child. After children have the ability to parse events into distinct actions, they must look for similarities across these actions and categorize them. Words would lose their utility if each instance of an action required a different name.

Categorization of Actions and Spatial Relations

The literature presented thus far paints a portrait of an infant capable of attending to motion, parsing events, and discriminating those semantic components that are encoded in our lexicon of relational terms. However, once children learn how to parse events into distinct actions, they also must learn how to categorize these actions into meaningful units. For objects, infants must learn that both perceptually similar and dissimilar objects can be in the same category (e.g., "vehicles" includes perceptually dissimilar airplanes and cars). Likewise, in the categorization of actions and spatial relations, infants have to learn that both perceptually similar and dissimilar actions and relations can be categorized together. For example, *Dad giving a ring to Mom* and *Brother giving a soda to Sister* are categorized as the same action—*giving*, despite their perceptual dissimilarity. Thus, the next step in processing events for language is acquiring the ability to form categories of the semantic components codified in language.

Categorization allows for "organized storage, efficient retrieval, and the capability of responding equivalently to an indefinitely large number of exemplars from multiple categories" (Quinn, 1994, p. 58). Forming categories reduces the demand on our limited memory storage and allows us to make inductive inferences about the world. Infants who form categories of spatial relations are capable of experiencing objects in a coherent spatial layout, rather than experiencing objects as spatially unrelated. Categorization of spatial relations appears to be a prerequisite to a host of skills, including spatial memory, locomotion, understanding geographic or travel maps, object recognition, reasoning about *dynamic* spatial events (like collision), and acquiring a lexicon of spatial terms (Quinn, 2003). In the next sections, we explore infants' ability to categorize spatial relations that are lexicalized in relational terms.

Categorization of Containment, Support, and Degree of Fit

Baillargeon (e.g., Baillargeon, 2001, 2002; Baillargeon & Wang, 2002; Hespos & Baillargeon, 2001a, 2001b) and Hespos and Spelke (2004) showed that infants could discriminate among the spatial relations *support, containment*, and *degree of fit*. Can infants form nonlinguistic categories for all three of these spatial relations? By answering these questions, researchers begin to address whether infants have the conceptual foundations needed for learning spatial expressions in their native languages.

McDonough and colleagues (2003) familiarized 9-month-old infants from English-speaking homes with six different scenes depicting tight-fitting containment. Infants were shown one scene depicting the same relation seen during familiarization (i.e., containment) paired with another scene showing a novel relation (i.e., support). For example, infants who were familiarized with tight-fitting containment were shown a novel scene of tight-fitting containment paired with a scene depicting loose-fitting support during the test trials. Infants looked significantly longer at the familiar relation during the test trials. These findings suggest that 9-month-old infants can abstract a common relational element and categorize the spatial relation *tight-fitting containment*.

Casasola and Cohen (2002) also examined the types of spatial relations infants categorize prior to the acquisition of spatial language. In this study, objects presented to infants during the familiarization trials varied. Nine-month-olds from English-speaking homes were habituated to four events, each depicting different pairs of objects in the same spatial relation (e.g., containment [putting a cup in a dog bowl], support [putting a cup on an inverted dog bowl], or tight-fit [fitting a green peg in a yellow block]). After habituation, infants were shown four test trials: (1) a control trial, during which they saw familiar objects in the familiar relation; (2) an object-change trial, during which they saw novel objects in the familiar relation; (3) a relation-change trial, during which they saw the familiar objects in a novel relation; and (4) an object- and relation-change trial, during which they saw novel objects in a novel relation. Those infants familiarized with containment events looked significantly longer at the novel versus familiar relationship regardless of the object change, indicating that they had formed a category of containment despite the change in objects. Infants who saw either support or degree-of-fit events during habituation did not show an increase in attention to the novel relations during test. The results suggest that 9-month-olds are unable to form a category of either support or degree of fit when the objects used to depict the relation vary.

Perhaps the most stunning of the recent demonstrations comes from Casasola, Cohen, and Chiarello (2003), who investigated whether 6-month-old infants could categorize the spatial relation *containment*. In a habituation task, infants were presented with different objects depicting a containment relation. After they habituated to the events, the experimenters presented a new example of the familiar spatial relation (i.e., containment) and an example of a novel spatial relation (i.e., support). Infants looked significantly longer at the novel spatial relation (i.e., support), indicating that they had formed a category of the spatial relation containment. This experiment replicates and extends the results reported by Casasola and Cohen (2002) of a study in which 9-month-olds demonstrated that they could categorize containment relations.

Results from these studies highlight three important points. First, preverbal infants can form nonlinguistic spatial categories of relations that are codified in relational terms. These findings provide further support for the hypothesis that infants have some of the prerequisite foundations of event processing that are needed to build a lexicon of relational terms. Second, and important to our later discussion of *abstract* spatial categorization, infants are initially unable to form categories of support and degree of fit. If older infants show evidence of this ability, it would reveal a developmental trend in the categorization of spatial relations—one in which infants initially rely on the specifics of the event to abstract the common relation. Eventually this reliance on specific objects gives way to an abstraction of the relation across varying objects, resulting in abstract spatial categories. If this hypothesis is confirmed, it would parallel the findings of Quinn and colleagues (Quinn, Adams, Kennedy, Shettler, & Wasnik, 2003; Quinn, Norris, Pasko, Schmader, & Mash, 1999), who found that the static category of *between* could be understood only in terms of the specific objects with which it was instantiated until 10 months of age.

Finally, Casasola and Cohen's (2002) data show that some spatial concepts are more accessible than others. English-learning preverbal infants were able to form a spatial category for containment but not for support, even though both are lexicalized in English. Perhaps, then, each spatial relation has its own developmental trajectory, and infants discriminate and categorize these spatial relations at different ages. These results and those from McDonough and colleagues (2003) provide empirical evidence that infants both attend to and categorize some semantic primitives in the ways proposed by both Gentner (1982; Gentner & Boroditsky, 2001) and Mandler (1991, 1992, 2004). Thus, infants bring to the task of learning relational words the ability to discriminate and categorize those components that are lexicalized in their native language.

Categorization of Path and Manner

Though less is known about the semantic components *path* and *manner*, we do have evidence that infants are capable of noticing and discriminating changes in both path and manner (Pulverman et al., 2003; Pulverman & Golinkoff, 2004) and that infants can form categories of these semantic components.

Using tightly controlled animated stimuli, we conducted two studies using dynamic events to address the following questions: (a) Can infants abstract an invariant path across multiple exemplars of manner? and (b) Can infants abstract an invariant manner across multiple exemplars of path (Pruden, Hirsh-Pasek, Maguire, & Meyer, 2004)? Using the Preferential Looking Paradigm (Hirsh-Pasek & Golinkoff, 1996), infants were familiarized to four events. Each event depicted an animated starfish performing a single manner and single path (see Fig. 7.1 for examples of the paths and manners). Three age groups—7- to 9-month-olds, 10- to 12-month-olds, and 13- to 15-month-olds—were tested. We started our investigation with infants as young as 7 months because this is the age at which infants show the ability to notice these two semantic components (Pulverman, Brandone, & Salkind, 2004).

To examine whether infants could abstract an invariant path across multiple manners, infants viewed an animated starfish performing the same exact path across four distinct manners during familiarization. During the test phase, infants were shown two events simultaneously: an event depicting the same path and a novel manner, and an event depicting a novel path and novel manner. Only 10- to 12-month-old infants showed a significant preference for the familiar test event during the test phase, while infants younger than this did not show a preference at test. These findings suggest that infants as young as 10 months can abstract the invariant path across multiple exemplars of manner (Pruden et al., 2004).

We also explored infants' ability to abstract an invariant manner across multiple exemplars of path. During familiarization infants viewed four events, each depicting the same exact manner across varying paths.

FIGURE 7.1. Examples of manners and paths to be used in stimuli. Though illustrated as a series of static postures, the manners are performed as continuous motions. *Source*: Pulverman et al., 2003.

At test, infants were simultaneously shown both an event depicting the same manner with a novel path and one depicting a novel manner with a novel path. Only the oldest age group examined, the 13- to 15-month-olds, preferred to watch the novel test event. These results suggest that infants as young as 13 months can abstract an invariant manner across multiple exemplars of path. Both of these studies indicate that infants have a fundamental ability to abstract the invariant among a series of motion events.

By asking whether infants can find an invariant path or manner, we begin to explore infants' ability to form categories of these semantic components. However, research will need to be expanded to look at when infants can move beyond simply abstracting invariant components of action events. In each of our clips, children saw the exact same path across varying manners or the exact same manner across varying paths—the invariant in each study was the semantic component that remained constant. In the real world, children rarely see such contrived scenes. Rather, children often see several different actors perform the same action at different points in time. These studies provide a first step in understanding the categorization of the semantic components *path* and *manner* by investigating children's ability to abstract an invariant action. Had children failed at these tasks, there would be little reason to move to more complex, naturalistic stimuli. Their success gives us reason to now explore the range of variability that infants can process and detect regarding categorization of path and manner.

In sum, research suggests that infants have the ability to perceive, process, and abstract four semantic components that are lexicalized in the English language: containment, support, path, and manner. Perhaps, then, as some suggest (Gentner & Boroditsky, 2001; Mandler, 2004), infants do start learning language with a set of privileged concepts used to make sense of events and spatial relations in the world.

Factors that Hinder or Support Infants' Abstraction and Categorization of Spatial Relations

Infants can form categories of spatial relations, albeit with some categories coming in earlier than others. But there is a catch: the knowledge they have is more fragile than it might first appear. For example, Baillargeon and colleagues (Aguiar & Baillargeon, 1999; Baillargeon,

2004; Hespos & Baillargeon, 2001a, 2001b; Wang, Baillargeon, & Paterson, 2005) report that young infants have great difficulty in generalizing what they know about occlusion, containment, and covering relations to new instances. Further, as Casasola and Cohen (2002) have shown, infants are unable to form categories of either support or degree of fit when the objects used to portray the relation are not those that initially depicted the relationship—they are not able to form abstract spatial categories. This research suggests that extending (or generalizing) a relation to a new set of objects is a different task from forming an initial relational category. There is also evidence in the research on verb learning that children have difficulty extending their verbs as widely as adults do (Ma et al., 2007; Seston, Golinkoff, Ma, Tomlinson, & Hirsh-Pasek, 2007). Other studies show that children have difficulty extending a newly learned verb to new referent actions (Forbes & Farrar, 1993, 1995; Maguire et al., 2002; Poulin-Dubois & Forbes, 2002). For instance, Maguire and colleagues found that 18-month-olds could not extend a novel verb to new agents.

These studies suggest that there is a developmental progression in children's ability to categorize and extend nonlinguistic spatial relations (Aguiar & Baillargeon, 1999; Baillargeon, 2004; Casasola & Cohen, 2002; Hespos & Baillargeon, 2001a, 2001b; Wang et al., 2005) as well as relations portrayed in action events and labeled by verbs (e.g., Forbes & Farrar, 1995). As Casasola (2005a) writes, "infants' initial reliance on familiar objects for recognizing a spatial relation eventually gives way to recognizing the relation with novel objects as well" (p. 279). At first, infants' spatial categories are limited to the original objects and events that depict them. Only later are infants able to break away from these original objects and events and form abstract spatial categories. For example, the English spatial term "on" applies to the spatial relation of support, regardless of the objects that are used to depict that relation.

Casasola (2005a) investigated 14-month-olds' ability to form an abstract spatial category for support. She was interested in looking at the impact of the number of category exemplars shown on children's ability to form relational categories. Infants who had habituated to only two exemplars were now able to categorize support, while those who were presented with six exemplars did not show evidence of the ability to categorize support. Casasola argued that infants failed to form a category of support in the six-exemplar condition because they were attending to the objects and not the relations, and because they did not have enough time to compare the relations. A parallel finding with verb learning is that of Maguire, Hirsh-Pasek, Golinkoff, and Brandone (2007). They found that 2.5- and 3-year-olds were able to learn and extend a novel verb to a new agent after they had seen a single actor but not after they had seen four actors.

Research has just begun to address the abstract spatial categorization of the semantic components *path* and *manner*. Pruden et al.'s (2004) research on infants' ability to abstract an invariant path and manner takes a first step in addressing the question of whether infants can form categories of actions in motion events. Song et al. (2006) built on Pruden et al.'s results and showed 10- to 12-month-old infants dynamic events of four different human actors, either jumping or marching, for familiarization. No language accompanied these events. Each actor marched or jumped in two different ways (e.g., across the scene versus up and down stairs visible in the scene). Results suggest that even 10-month-olds can form a category of a dynamic action event (marching versus jumping) performed by different actors. Babies preferred to watch the familiar action at test when performed by a novel actor. Pruden (2007) also reported that babies were able to extend an invariant category to include a new agent, at 10 months of age for path and 13 months of age for manner. Thus, the research beginning to emerge suggests that the categorization of dynamic action events may be present prior to the time that language comes on the scene. Only further work will tell whether the ambient language itself is playing a role in this categorization. The research to be reviewed below suggests that it might.

Can Language Help Infants Form Dynamic Action Categories?

A large body of research on the role of language in object category formation already exists. This research generally shows that infants' object categorization is facilitated by use of a common label and that language heightens attention to objects (Balaban & Waxman, 1997; Baldwin & Markman, 1989; Booth & Waxman, 2002; Gentner & Namy, 1999; Gopnik & Nazzi, 2003; Namy & Gentner, 2002; Waxman & Markow, 1995). By contrast, very little is known about the role of language in spatial category formation. Would the addition of language aid infants' discrimination and categorization of spatial relations?

Two possibilities exist. First, the addition of language to previous categorization tasks could heighten attention to spatial relations and facilitate categorization, as it does in object categorization studies. Support for this hypothesis comes from the literature, which shows that labels help infants form categories of objects (Waxman & Markow, 1995; Balaban & Waxman, 1997). Second, the addition of language could disrupt performance in spatial discrimination and categorization tasks, as the introduction of language may increase the processing demands. This possibility is supported by Stager and Werker's (1997) research. In a nonlinguistic discrimination task, 14-month-olds could discriminate between two minimal pair phonemes (/b/ versus /d/). However, they were able to do so only when the phonemes were presented in the absence of an object. The addition of an object increased the processing demands of the task and caused infants to fail to discriminate. Several studies have already been conducted to test this empirical question.

Casasola (2005b) tested whether language would facilitate the formation of an abstract spatial category of support. Using the same design and stimuli as those used in Casasola and Cohen (2002), she found that infants were able to form a category of support when the familiar word "on" accompanied the habituation events. Thus, the addition of a familiar word can aid in the formation of abstract spatial categories.

Pulverman, Brandone, and Salkind (2004) also examined the role of language in the processing of motion events. Using the same events from Pulverman et al. (2003), language was added to see if 14- and 17-month-old infants' processing of path and manner would be influenced. English-learning infants who heard a novel verb label during habituation noticed the manner of motion more than those infants who participated in the original, nonlinguistic version of this study. However, infants who heard the novel verb label during habituation did not increase their attention to the path of the agent. It appears that when English-learning infants hear a novel verb label while watching an event, they increase their attention to the manner of the motion. These results suggest that the addition of language to this task makes a difference by guiding infants' event processing. Furthermore, not just any label will do: this result vanishes when a noun label is used, suggesting that children are sensitive to form class of the novel word that accompanies the visual displays (Pulverman, Golinkoff, Hirsh-Pasek, Brandone, & Seston, 2006). These studies show that the introduction of a label differentially heightens attention to semantic components, while Casasola and Cohen's (2002) research suggests that labels facilitate the formation of the spatial category *support*. Does a common label also facilitate the abstraction of path or manner in those infants who were previously unable to accomplish it (Pruden & Hirsh-Pasek, 2006; also see Pruden, 2007)?

Pruden et al. (2004) found that infants younger than 10 months of age could not abstract an invariant path in a series of motion events, and that infants younger than 13 months of age could not find an invariant manner. Furthermore, in both studies, 7- to 9-month-old infants were unable to abstract an invariant path and invariant manner. This failure provides us with the opportunity to test whether the addition of language can assist in categorization of these action components. Using the same procedure and stimuli, Pruden and Hirsh-Pasek (2006; Pruden, 2007) added a label during familiarization to see if it would help infants abstract an invariant semantic component.

In the path study, we familiarized infants to four motion events, each depicting the same path (e.g., "over") but varying manner (e.g., "flapping," "spinning," "twisting," "bending"), accompanied by the novel verb label "javing." At test, infants were simultaneously shown a familiar event (i.e., familiar path, novel manner; e.g., "toe-touching over") and a novel event (i.e., novel path, novel manner; e.g., "toe-touching under") in silence. We predicted that if infants could abstract an invariant path, they would have a significant preference for one of the test events. The results were striking. Seven- to 9-month-olds benefited from the addition of a common label, showing a significant preference for the novel test event (e.g., "toe-touching under") at test. The inclusion of language appears to facilitate the abstraction of path.

In the second study, 7- to 9-month-olds viewed four familiarization events, each depicting the same exact manner across varying paths (e.g. "spinning over," "spinning around," "spinning behind," and "spinning past") (Pruden & Hirsh-Pasek, 2006; Pruden, 2007) and accompanied again by the novel verb label "javing" (repeated a total of 16 times). At test, infants were presented simultaneously with the familiar manner/ novel path and a novel manner/novel path (e.g., "spinning under" versus "twisting under"). Unlike the path study, infants did not show a significant preference for either test event. Infants were not able to use the common label to abstract the invariant manner. However, perhaps further research will reveal that 10- to 12-month-olds profit from the addition of language. Recall that manner abstraction did not occur until 13 months in the original research without language (Pruden et al., 2004).

Taken together, the results from both Pulverman et al. (2004) and Pruden and Hirsh-Pasek (2006; Pruden, 2007) suggest that, as in the object categorization tasks, labels heighten attention to features of actions within events. However, labels may not always help. For Pruden and Hirsh-Pasek's (2006) 7- to 9-month-olds, the presence of a label helped them abstract a path but not a manner. Language appears to differentially affect infants' abstraction of semantic components. On the one hand, it appears that language plays a special role in helping infants abstract semantic components. On the other hand, this facilitative effect appears to be limited at present to only one semantic component, path. There is reason to believe that path may be more fundamental than manner in learning about the world (Mandler, 2004; Pruden et al., 2004) and expressed earlier in language (Naigles et al., 1992; Zheng & Goldin-Meadow, 2002). Perhaps, then, abstracting path is easier and requires less attention than abstracting manner.

Bringing It All Together: Events, Actions, and Spatial Relations in Infancy

What have we learned about how infants and young children perceive and categorize the events that will be encoded by their language? This review has focused specifically on the underpinnings for the learning of verbs and spatial expressions, as it is these parts of language that routinely label events or their outcomes.

First, we have found that there is a developmental trend in the ability to process and categorize events. Research shows that different semantic components are processed and abstracted at different points in development. For example, Casasola and colleagues (Casasola & Cohen, 2002; Casasola, Cohen, et al., 2003) demonstrated that the ability to form categories of spatial relations develops at different times for different spatial relations. Infants could form categories of the spatial relation *containment* before they could form categories for the spatial relation *support*. Finally, in related research, Baillargeon (2004) showed that infants pay attention to different perceptual features within different types of spatial relations. In these studies, 4.5-month-olds could reason about occlusion relations when they were given height information, but they were unable to use this same information to reason about containment relations until 7.5 months of age.

Pruden et al.'s (2004) findings suggest that the categorization of semantic components like path and manner does not come online at the same time. Infants abstract invariant paths across varying manners before they can abstract invariant manners across varying paths. These results, along with Pulverman et al.'s (2003, 2004), suggest that the semantic component *path* might be more fundamental than *manner* in building a conceptual foundation for verb learning. On the other hand, the research of Song et al. (2006, 2007) found that infants could abstract a category of *manner* at 10 to 12 months of age, several months earlier than Pruden et al. (2004) found. The reason for these differences is unclear, indicating that we are just at the beginning of understanding the factors that facilitate or impede the categorization of actions. Song et al. (2006) also chose not to test for path categories. Prior work by Pruden et al. suggests that had Song and colleagues tested for path categorization, perhaps they too would have found path emerging prior to manner.

Why does path seem to be consistently favored over manner in the studies that test for both? One possibility is that path is more perceptually salient than manner. This account is supported by numerous findings. For example, Maguire (2003; Maguire et al., 2003) found that English-speaking children under 3 years of age willingly attach a novel verb label to the path rather than to the manner of action. Even when provided with additional syntactical information (e.g., "Starry is blicking over the ball"), only those children with a large arsenal of relational terms (e.g., above, on, kick, tickle) behaved like native English-speaking adults and attached the label to the manner of action. Further, research by Pulverman and colleagues (2003) demonstrated that 14- to 17-month-olds with a rich vocabulary were more attentive to manner changes than their low-vocabulary counterparts. These studies demonstrate that children are initially biased to attend to and label path, an argument consistent with that of Mandler (2004), who views path as one of the primitives needed for the conceptual development of motion. As Mandler writes, "PATH is the simplest conceptualization of any object following any trajectory through space" (p. 28). Perhaps it is more important to know where you are going (your path) than how you got there (your manner). Thus, it should come as little surprise that path seems to be processed and abstracted before manner.

The second thing that we have uncovered is that there are factors that can facilitate the categorization of dynamic events. In particular, linguistic labeling seems to heighten attention to some components of events over others (Pulverman et al., 2004) and to facilitate event categorization (Pruden, 2007; Pruden & Hirsh-Pasek, 2006). There is little understanding at present of the mechanism that is involved in this facilitation. It may be purely attentional, in that a consistent sound may cause children to watch an object or event more closely (Baldwin & Markman, 1989; Kaplan, Fox, Scheuneman, & Jenkins, 1991; Mendelson & Haith, 1976). In this case, musical notes might facilitate dynamic category formation in the same way. Or language itself may be, as Roger Brown (1958) argued long ago, "an invitation to form categories." By its sameness, it may be indicating that the diverse exemplars over which it is used share important similarities as well, a position espoused in somewhat different ways by Waxman and colleagues (Balaban & Waxman, 1997; Waxman & Markow, 1995). Clearly there is much more to be done before we can understand how infants form the nonlinguistic event categories that will ultimately by encoded by their native language.

Conclusion

To understand how relational terms are learned in young children, investigations of the conceptual foundation of verb learning are essential. As this chapter demonstrates, we are only at the beginning in our ability to comprehend how infants process and detect actions within events. How do infants' perception and conception of events map onto the world's languages? How do children learn to attend to the particular semantic components their language favors?

Much of the work done on infants' event processing has examined only a very small slice of events—motion events. Despite the limited amount of research on event processing in infancy, we are already starting to see clear evidence that infants can process key aspects of motion events. For example, we now have evidence that infants can, at the very basic level, process, abstract, and categorize those spatial relations that make up motion events. Impressively, infants in the first year of life show the burgeoning ability to discriminate and categorize the kinds of relations, including *containment*, *support*, *path*, and *manner*, that are codified in the languages of the world (Casasola, 2005a; Casasola & Cohen, 2000, 2002; Casasola, Cohen, et al., 2003; Casasola, Hohenstein, et al., 2003; Choi et al., 1999; Hespos & Baillargeon, 2001a, 2001b; Pruden et al., 2004; Pruden & Hirsh-Pasek, 2006; Pulverman et al., 2003; Pulverman & Golinkoff, 2004).

This brings us back to the question of why verbs are so much harder to learn than nouns. Researchers argue that it is not the conceptualization of actions and events that makes learning relational terms so difficult (see Chapter 8, this volume; also see Gentner, 1982; Gentner & Boroditsky, 2001; Hirsh-Pasek & Golinkoff, 2006; and Snedeker & Gleitman, 2004). Indeed, our research suggests that children have many of the prerequisite abilities needed to map relational terms onto actions. Gentner (1982) hypothesized that the problem in verb learning is with packaging relations and mapping words onto relations (see Chapter 8 for a more thorough discussion; also see Maguire, Golinkoff, & Hirsh-Pasek, 2006). The research we present here supports this hypothesis. Infants are capable of making sense of the world of both objects and events. At the very least, infants are sensitive to the spatial relations and actions embedded in events and encoded in relational terms. Despite the fact that the study of how infants view dynamic stimuli is so young, the good news is that infants are interpreting the current events in their world.

Acknowledgments

This work was supported by NSF Grants BCS0642529 and BCS9910842 and NIH Grants 3U10HD25455–0552 and 5R01HD050199. An earlier draft of this research was submitted to Temple University in partial fulfillment of the preliminary examination requirement by the first author. Portions of this research were presented at the BUCLD keynote address delivered in November of 2007 and have appeared in the *Proceedings of the 31st Annual Boston University Conference on Language Development*, the *Proceedings of the 30th Annual Boston University Conference on Language Development*, and the *Proceedings of the 28th Annual Boston University Conference on Language Development*. We would like to thank the parents and infants who generously participated in studies at Temple University and the University of Delaware. We would also like to thank the many laboratory coordinators, graduate students, and undergraduate students who worked on this research, including Natalie Sheridan, Meredith Jones, Wendy Shallcross, Amanda Brandone, Rebecca Seston, Meredith Meyer, Mandy Maguire, Rachel Pulverman, Gwen Albertson, Tilbe Göksun, and Sarah Roseberry.

References

Aguiar, A., & Baillargeon, R. (1999). 2.5-month-old infants' reasoning about when objects should and should not be occluded. *Cognitive Psychology, 39,* 116–157.

Avrahami, J., & Kareev, Y. (1994). The emergence of events. *Cognition, 53,* 239–261.

Bahrick, L. E., Gogate, L. J., & Ruiz, I. (2002). Attention and memory for faces and actions in infancy: The salience of actions over faces in dynamic events. *Child Development, 73,* 1629–1643.

Baillargeon, R. (2001). Infants' physical knowledge: Of acquired expectations and core principles. In E. Dupoux (Ed.), *Language, brain, and cognitive development: Essays in honor of Jacques Mehler* (pp. 341–361). Cambridge, MA: MIT Press.

Baillargeon, R. (2002). The acquisition of physical knowledge in infancy: A summary in eight lessons. In. U. Goswami (Ed.), *Blackwell handbook of childhood cognitive development* (pp. 47–83). Malden, MA: Blackwell Publishers.

Baillargeon, R. (2004). Infants' physical world. *Current Directions in Psychological Science, 13,* 89–94.

Baillargeon, R., & Wang, S. (2002). Event categorization in infancy. *Trends in Cognitive Science, 6,* 85–93.

Balaban, M. T., & Waxman, S. R. (1997). Do words facilitate object categorization in 9-month-old infants? *Journal of Experimental Child Psychology, 64,* 3–26.

Baldwin, D. A., Baird, J. A., Saylor, M. M., & Clark, A. M. (2001). Infants parse dynamic actions. *Child Development, 72,* 708–717.

Baldwin, D. A., & Markman, E. M. (1989). Establishing word-object relations: A first step. *Child Development, 60,* 381–398.

Bertenthal, B. I., Proffitt, D. R., & Cutting, J. E. (1984). Infant sensitivity to figural coherence in biomechanical motions. *Journal of Experimental Child Psychology, 37,* 213–230.

Booth, A. E., & Waxman, S. (2002). Object names and object functions serve as cues to categories for infants. *Developmental Psychology, 38,* 948–957.

Bornstein, M., Cote, L., Maital, S., Painter, K., Park, S.-Y., Pascual, L., et al. (2004). Cross-linguistic analysis of vocabulary in young children: Spanish, Dutch, French, Hebrew, Italian, Korean and American English. *Child Development, 75,* 1115–1140.

Bowerman, M., & Choi, S. (2001). Shaping meanings for language: Universal and language specific in the acquisition of spatial semantic categories. In M. Bowerman & S. C. Levinson (Eds.), *Language acquisition and conceptual development* (pp. 475–512). New York: Cambridge University Press.

Brown, R. (1958). *Words and things.* New York: Free Press.

Casasola, M. (2005a). When less is more: How infants learn to form an abstract categorical representation of support. *Child Development, 76,* 279–290.

Casasola, M. (2005b). Can language do the driving? The effect of linguistic input on infants' categorization of support spatial relations. *Developmental Psychology, 41,* 183–192.

Casasola, M., & Cohen, L. B. (2000). Infants' association of linguistic labels with causal actions. *Developmental Psychology, 36*, 155–168.

Casasola, M., & Cohen, L. B. (2002). Infant categorization of containment, support, and tight-fit spatial relationships. *Developmental Science, 5*, 247–264.

Casasola, M., Cohen, L. B., & Chiarello, E. (2003). Six-month-old infants' categorization of containment spatial relations. *Child Development, 74*, 679–693.

Casasola, M, Hohenstein, J., & Naigles, L. (2003, April). Ten-month-old infants' discrimination of manner and path in motion events. In M. Casasola (Chair), *From infancy to adulthood: Exploring the effect of linguistic input of the discrimination of manner and path in motion event.* Symposium presented at biennial meeting of the Society for Research in Child Development, Tampa, FL.

Choi, S. (1998). Verbs in early lexical and syntactic development in Korean. *Linguistics, 36*, 755–780.

Choi, S., & Bowerman, M. (1991). Learning to express motion events in English and Korean: The influence of language-specific lexicalization patterns. *Cognition, 41*, 83–121.

Choi, S., & Gopnik, A. (1995). Early acquisition of verbs in Korean: A crosslinguistic study. *Journal of Child Language, 22*, 497–529.

Choi, S., McDonough, L., Bowerman, M., & Mandler, J. M. (1999). Early sensitivity to language-specific spatial categories in English and Korean. *Cognitive Development, 14*, 241–268.

Clark, E. V. (2003). *First language acquisition.* New York: Cambridge University Press.

Cohen, L. B., & Amsel, G. (1998). Precursors to infants' perception of the causality of a simple event. *Infant Behavior and Development, 21*, 713–731.

Cohen, L. B., & Oakes, L. M. (1993). How infants perceive a simple causal event. *Developmental Psychology, 29*, 421–433.

Fenson, L., Dale, P. S., Reznick, J. S., & Bates, E. (1994). Variability in early communicative development. *Monographs of the Society for Research in Child Development, 59*(5, Serial No. 242), 1–185.

Forbes, J. N., & Farrar, J. M. (1993). Children's initial assumptions about the meaning of novel motion verbs: Biased and conservative? *Cognitive Development, 8*, 273–290.

Forbes, J. N., & Farrar, J. M. (1995). Learning to represent word meaning: What initial training events reveal about children's developing action verb concepts. *Cognitive Development, 10*, 1–20.

Gentner, D. (1982). Why nouns are learned before verbs: Linguistic relativity versus natural partitioning. In S. Kuczaj (Ed.), *Language development: Language, thought, and culture*, Vol. 2 (pp. 301–334). Hillsdale, NJ: Lawrence Erlbaum Associates.

Gentner, D., & Boroditsky, L. (2001). Individuation, relativity, and early word learning. In M. Bowerman & S. C. Levinson (Eds.), *Language acquisition and conceptual development* (pp. 215–256). New York: Cambridge University Press.

Gentner, D., & Namy, L. L. (1999). Comparison in the development of categories. *Cognitive Development, 14*, 487–513.

Gibson, E. J., Owsley, C. J., & Johnston, J. (1978). Perception of invariants by five-month-old infants: Differentiation of two types of motion. *Developmental Psychology, 14,* 407–415.

Gillette, J., Gleitman, H., Gleitman, L., & Lederer, A. (1999). Human simulations of vocabulary learning. *Cognition, 73,* 135–176.

Golinkoff, R. M., Chung, H. L., Hirsh-Pasek, K., Liu, J., Bertenthal, B. I., Brand, R., et al. (2002). Young children can extend motion verbs to point-light displays. *Developmental Psychology, 38,* 604–614.

Gopnik, A., & Nazzi, T. (2003). Words, kinds, and causal powers: A theory perspective on early naming and categorization. In D. H. Rakison & L. M. Oakes (Eds.), *Early category and concept development: Making sense of the blooming, buzzing confusion* (pp. 303–329). New York: Oxford University Press.

Graziano, W. G., Moore, J. S., & Collins, J. E. (1988). Social cognition as segmentation of the stream of behavior. *Developmental Psychology, 24,* 568–573.

Hanson, C., & Hirst, W. (1989). On the representation of events: A study of orientation, recall, and recognition. *Journal of Experimental Psychology: General, 118,* 136–147.

Hespos, S. J., & Baillargeon, R. (2001a). Knowledge about containment events in very young infants. *Cognition, 78,* 207–245.

Hespos, S. J., & Baillargeon, R. (2001b). Infants' knowledge about occlusion and containment events: A surprising discrepancy. *Psychological Science, 12,* 140–147.

Hespos, S. J., & Spelke, E. S. (2004). Conceptual precursors to language. *Nature, 430,* 453–456.

Hirsh-Pasek, K., & Golinkoff, R. M. (1996). *The origins of grammar: Evidence from early language comprehension.* Cambridge, MA: MIT Press.

Hirsh-Pasek, K., & Golinkoff, R. M. (2006). *Action meets word: How children learn verbs.* New York: Oxford University Press.

Imai, M., Haryu, E., & Hiroyuki, O. (2003). Is verb learning easier than noun learning for Japanese children? Three-year-old Japanese children's knowledge about object names and action names. In B. Skarabela, S. Fish, & A. H.-J. Do (Eds.), *Proceedings of the 26th Annual Boston University Conference on Language Development.* Somerville, MA: Cascadilla Press.

Jackendoff, R. (1983). *Semantics and cognition: Current studies in linguistics series, No. 8.* Cambridge, MA: MIT Press.

Johnson, S. P., & Aslin, R. N. (1995). Perception of object unity in 2-month-old infants. *Developmental Psychology, 31,* 739–745.

Johnson, S. P., Cohen, L. B., Marks, K. H., & Johnson, K. L. (2003). Young infants' perception of object unity in rotation displays. *Infancy, 4,* 285–295.

Kable, J. W., Lease-Spellmeyer, J., & Chatterjee, A. (2002). Neural substrates of action event knowledge. *Journal of Cognitive Neuroscience, 14,* 795–805.

Kaplan, P., Fox, K., Scheuneman, D., & Jenkins, L. (1991). Cross-modal facilitation of infant visual fixation: Temporal and intensity effects. *Infant Behavior and Development, 14,* 83–109.

Kellman, P. J., & Spelke, E. S. (1983). Perception of partly occluded objects in infancy. *Cognitive Psychology, 15,* 483–524.

Kersten, A. W., & Billman, D. (1997). Event category learning. *Journal of Experimental Psychology: Learning, Memory, and Cognition, 23,* 638–658.

Langacker, R. W. (1987). *Foundations of cognitive grammar*. Stanford, CA: Stanford University Press.

Leslie, A. M. (1984). Spatiotemporal continuity and the perception of causality in infants. *Perception, 13*, 287–305.

Leslie, A. M., & Keeble, S. (1987). Do six-month-old infants perceive causality? *Cognition, 25*, 265–288.

Ma, W., Golinkoff, R. M., Shun, W., Brandone, A., Hirsh-Pasek, K., & Song, L. (2007). *Carrying the load? Chinese children's knowledge of familiar verbs*. Abstract submitted for review.

Maguire, M. J. (2003). *Children's use of universal and language-specific cues in verb learning*. Unpublished doctoral dissertation. Philadelphia, PA: Temple University.

Maguire, M. J., Golinkoff, R. M., & Hirsh-Pasek, K. (2006). It's not about nouns and verbs. In K. Hirsh-Pasek & R. M. Golinkoff (Eds.), *Action meets word: How children learn verbs*. New York: Oxford University Press.

Maguire, M. J., Hennon, E., Hirsh-Pasek, K., Golinkoff, R., Slutzky, C., & Sootsman, C. (2002). Mapping words to actions and events: How do 18-month-olds learn a verb? In B. Skarabela, S. Fish, & A. H.-J. Do (Eds.), *Proceedings for the 26th Annual Boston University Conference on Language Development* (pp. 371–382). Somerville, MA: Cascadilla Press.

Maguire, M., Hirsh-Pasek, K., Golinkoff, R. M., & Brandone, A. (2007). *Less is more: Fewer exemplars facilitate children's verb extension*. Manuscript submitted for publication.

Maguire, M. J., Hirsh-Pasek, K., Golinkoff, R. M., & Pruden, S. M. (2003, April). The way you do that thing you do: Attention to path and manner in action words. In L. Wagner (Chair), *How event cognition turns into event language*. Symposium presented at biennial meeting of the Society for Research in Child Development, Tampa, FL.

Maguire, M. J., Shipley, T. F., Brumberg, J., & Ennis, M. (2005). *A geometric analysis of event path*. Unpublished manuscript, Temple University.

Mandler, J. M. (1991). Prelinguistic primitives. In L. A. Sutton & C. Johnson (Eds.), *Proceedings of the seventeenth annual meeting of the Berkeley Linguistics Society* (pp. 414–425). Berkeley, CA: Berkeley Linguistics Society.

Mandler, J. M. (1992). How to build a baby II: Conceptual primitives. *Psychological Review, 99*, 587–604.

Mandler, J. M. (2004). *The foundations of mind: Origins of conceptual thought*. New York: Oxford University Press.

Markus, H., Smith, J., & Moreland, R. L. (1985). Role of the self-concept in the perception of others. *Journal of Personality and Social Psychology, 49*, 1494–1512.

McDonough, L., Choi, S., & Mandler, J. M. (2003). Understanding spatial relations: Flexible infants, lexical adults. *Cognitive Psychology, 46*, 229–259.

Mendelson, M. J., & Haith, M. M. (1976). The relation between audition and vision in the human newborn. *Monographs of the Society for Research in Child Development, 41*(No. 4, Serial No. 167), 1–72.

Meyer, M., Leonard, S., Hirsh-Pasek, K., Imai, M., Haryu, R., Pulverman, R., et al. (2003). *Making a convincing argument: A cross-linguistic comparison of noun and verb learning in Japanese and English*. Poster presented at the Boston University Conference on Language Development, Boston, MA.

Miller, G. A., & Johnson-Laird, P. N. (1976). *Language and perception*. Cambridge, MA: Belknap Press.

Naigles, L. (1996). The use of multiple frames in verb learning via syntactic bootstrapping.*Cognition, 58,* 221–251.

Naigles, L. R., Eisenberg, A., & Kako, E. (1992). *Acquiring a language-specific lexicon: Motion verbs in English and Spanish*. Paper presented at the International Conference on Pragmatics, Antwerp, Belgium.

Namy, L. L., & Gentner, D. (2002). Making a silk purse out of two sow's ears: Young children's use of comparison in category learning. *Journal of Experimental Psychology: General, 131,* 5–15.

Nelson, K. (1989). *Narratives from the crib*. Cambridge, MA: Harvard University Press.

Nelson, K. (1997). Event representations then, now, and next. In P. W. van den Broek, P. J. Bauer, & T. Bourg (Eds.), *Developmental spans in event comprehension and representation: Bridging fictional and actual events* (pp. 1–28). Mahwah, NJ: Lawrence Erlbaum Associates.

Newtson, D. (1973). Attribution and the unit of perception of ongoing behavior. *Journal of Personality and Social Psychology, 28,* 28–38.

Newtson, D., Enquist, G., & Bois, J. (1977). The objective basis of behavior units. *Journal of Personality and Social Psychology, 35,* 847–862.

Oakes, L. M. (1994). Development of infants' use of continuity cues in their perception of causality. *Developmental Psychology, 30,* 869–879.

Oakes, L. M., & Cohen, L. B. (1990). Infant perception of a causal event. *Cognitive Development, 5,* 193–207.

Oakes, L. M., & Rakison, D. H. (2003). Issues in the early development of concepts and categories: An introduction. In D. H. Rakison & L. M. Oakes (Eds.), *Early category and concept development: Making sense of the blooming, buzzing confusion* (pp. 3–23). New York: Oxford University Press.

Poulin-Dubois, D., & Forbes, J. N. (2002). Toddlers' attention to intentions-in-action in learning novel action words. *Developmental Psychology, 38,* 104–114.

Pruden, S. M. (2007). *Finding the action: Factors that aid infants' abstraction of path and manner*. Unpublished doctoral dissertation. Philadelphia, PA: Temple University.

Pruden, S. M., & Hirsh-Pasek, K. (2006). *Foundations of verb learning: Labels promote action category formation*. In D. Bamman, T. Magnitskaia, & C. Zaller (Eds.), *Proceedings of the 30th Annual Boston University Conference on Language Development* (pp. 467–477). Somerville, MA: Cascadilla Press.

Pruden, S. M., Hirsh-Pasek, K., Maguire, M. J., & Meyer, M. A. (2004). Foundations of verb learning: Infants form categories of path and manner in motion events. In A. Brugos, L. Micciulla, & C. E. Smith (Eds.), *Proceedings of the 28th Annual Boston University Conference on Language Development* (pp. 461–472). Somerville, MA: Cascadilla Press.

Pulverman, R. (2005). *The relationship between language development and event processing: Lexical acquisition and attention to manner and path*. Unpublished doctoral dissertation. Newark, DE: University of Delaware.

Pulverman, R., Brandone, A., & Salkind, S. J. (2004, November). *One-year-old English speakers increase their attention to manner of motion in a potential verb learning situation.* Paper presented at the 29th Annual Boston University Conference on Language Development, Boston, MA.

Pulverman, R., & Golinkoff, R. M. (2004). Seven-month-olds' attention to potential verb referents in nonlinguistic events. In A. Brugos, L. Micciulla, & C. E. Smith (Eds.), *Proceedings of the 28th Annual Boston University Conference on Language Development* (pp. 473–480). Somerville, MA: Cascadilla Press.

Pulverman, R., Golinkoff, R. M., Hirsh-Pasek, K., Brandone, A., & Seston, N. R. (2006, July). *Linguistic input directs infants' attention to facilitate word learning.* Paper presented at the 15th Biennial International Conference on Infant Studies, Kyoto, Japan.

Pulverman, R., Golinkoff, R. M., Hirsh-Pasek, K., & Sootsman-Buresh, J. L. (2007). *Infants' attention to manner and path in non-linguistic dynamic events.* Under review.

Pulverman, R., Sootsman, J. L., Golinkoff, R. M., & Hirsh-Pasek, K. (2003). The role of lexical knowledge in nonlinguistic event processing: English-speaking infants' attention to manner and path. In *Proceedings of the 27th Annual Boston University Conference on Language Development* (pp. 662–673). Somerville, MA: Cascadilla Press.

Quinn, P. C. (1994). The categorization of above and below spatial relations by young infants. *Child Development, 65*, 58–69.

Quinn, P. C. (2003). Concepts are not just for objects: Categorization of spatial relation information by infants. In D. H. Rakison & L. M. Oakes (Eds.), *Early category and concept development: Making sense of the blooming, buzzing confusion* (pp. 50–76). New York: Oxford University Press.

Quinn, P. C., Adams, A., Kennedy, E., Shettler, L., & Wasnik, A. (2003). Development of an abstract category representation for the spatial relation between in 6- to 10-month-old infants. *Developmental Psychology, 39*, 151–163.

Quinn, P. C., Norris, C. M., Pasko, R. N., Schmader, T. M., & Mash, C. (1999). Formation of a categorical representation for the spatial relation between by 6- to 7-month-old infants. *Visual Cognition, 6*, 569–585.

Rakison, D. H. (2003). Parts, motion, and the development of the animate-inanimate distinction in infancy. In D. H. Rakison & L. M. Oakes (Eds.), *Early category and concept development: Making sense of the blooming, buzzing confusion* (pp. 159–192). New York: Oxford University Press.

Rakison, D. H., & Poulin-Dubois, D. (2001). Developmental origin of the animate-inanimate distinction. *Psychological Bulletin, 127*, 209–228.

Rochat, P., & Hespos, S. J. (1996). Tracking and anticipation of invisible spatial transformation by 4- to 8-month-old infants. *Cognitive Development, 11*, 3–17.

Seston, R., Golinkoff, R. M., Ma, W., Tomlinson, N., & Hirsh-Pasek, K. (2007). *Vacuuming with my mouth? Children's ability to comprehend novel extensions of familiar verbs.* Manuscript submitted for publication.

Sharon, T., & Wynn, K. (1998). Individuation of actions from continuous motion. *Psychological Science, 9*, 357–362.

Slater, A., Morison, V., & Town, C. (1985). Movement perception and identity constancy in the new-born baby. *British Journal of Developmental Psychology, 3*, 211–220.

Smith, W. C., Johnson, S. P., & Spelke, E. S. (2003). Motion and edge sensitivity in perception of object unity. *Cognitive Psychology, 46*, 31–64.

Snedeker, J., & Gleitman, L. R. (2004). Why is it hard to label our concepts? In D. G. Hall & S. R. Waxman (Eds.), *Weaving a lexicon* (pp. 257–293). Cambridge, MA: MIT Press.

Song, L., Golinkoff, R. M., Seston, R., Ma, W., Shallcross, W., & Hirsh-Pasek, K. (2006, November). *Action stations: Verb learning rests on constructing categories of action.* Poster presented at the 31st Annual Boston University Conference on Language Development, Boston, MA.

Song, L., Seston, R., Ma, W., Golinkoff, R. M., Shipley, T., & Hirsh-Pasek, K. (2007). *The path to verb learning: Seven- to nine-month-old infants are sensitive to geometric features of path.* Abstract submitted for review.

Spelke, E. S., Phillips, A., & Woodward, A. L. (1995). Infants' knowledge of object motion and human action. In. D. Sperber & D. Premack (Eds.), *Causal cognition: A multidisciplinary debate* (pp. 44–78). New York: Oxford University Press.

Stager, C. L., & Werker, J. F. (1997). Infants listen for more phonetic detail in speech perception than in word-learning tasks. *Nature, 388*(6640), 381–382.

Talmy, L. (1985). Lexicalization patterns: Semantic structure in lexical forms. In T. Shopen (Ed.), *Language typology and syntactic description* (pp. 57–149). New York: Cambridge University Press.

Tardif, T. (1996). Nouns are not always learned before verbs: Evidence from Mandarin speakers' early vocabularies. *Developmental Psychology, 32*, 492–504.

Tomasello, M. (1995). Pragmatic contexts for early verb learning. In M. Tomasello & W. E. Merriman (Eds.), *Beyond the names for things: Young children's acquisition of verbs* (pp. 115–146). Hillsdale, NJ: Lawrence Erlbaum Associates.

Wang, S., Baillargeon, R., & Paterson, S. (2005). Detecting continuity violations in infancy: A new account and new evidence from covering and tube events. *Cognition, 95*, 129–173.

Wang, S., Kaufman, L., & Baillargeon, R. (2003). Should all stationary objects move when hit? Developments in infants' causal and statistical expectations about collision events. *Infant Behavior and Development, 26*, 529–567.

Waxman, S. R., & Markow, D. B. (1995). Words as invitations to form categories: Evidence from 12- to 13-month-old infants. *Cognitive Psychology, 29*, 257–302.

Wynn, K. (1996). Infants' individuation and enumeration of actions. *Psychological Science, 7*, 164–169.

Zacks, J. M. (2004). Using movement and intentions to understand simple events. *Cognitive Science, 28*, 979–1008.

Zacks, J. M., & Tversky, B. (2001). Event structure in perception and conception. *Psychological Bulletin, 127*, 3–21.

Zheng, M., & Goldin-Meadow, S. (2002). Thought before language: How deaf and hearing children express motion events across cultures. *Cognition, 85*, 145–175.

8

Speaking of Events: Event Word Learning and Event Representation

MANDY J. MAGUIRE & GUY O. DOVE

Word learning is a conceptually difficult task that, somewhat paradoxically, very young children are readily able to accomplish. In Quine's (1960) famous example, even seemingly straightforward instances of ostension, such as a speaker of a previously unknown language pointing to a rabbit and using the word *gavagai*, are rife with potential ambiguity. There are a number of possible meanings of *gavagai*— everything from "furry thing" to "undetached rabbit parts." Remarkably, children and adults over the age of 12 months generally assume the label refers to the whole rabbit in this situation (Golinkoff, Mervis, & Hirsh-Pasek, 1994). When it comes to labeling events, though, the task appears to become much more ambiguous (Gentner, 1982; Gentner & Boroditsky, 2001). Imagine our hypothetical rabbit is not standing still but rather moving away from the child. There are an infinite number of event features that the speaker could be attempting to point out: is the rabbit going, leaving, fleeing, hopping, jumping, running, rushing, scampering, scurrying, searching, or leading the observer to Wonderland? Unlike with object labels, there is very little consensus even among adults concerning the novel event label's meaning (Gilette, Gleitman, Gleitman, & Lederer, 1999). Given the array of possible meanings, it is not surprising that children struggle to learn novel verbs as event labels up until at least 5 years of age (Imai, Haryu, Okada, Lianjing, & Shigematsu, in press). How children solve the problem of event word learning to achieve adult-like understanding of event labels provides deep insights into children's prelinguistic event concepts and how they develop and change during language acquisition.

In this chapter we outline and assess the difficulty facing children attempting to learn novel event labels. Children must overcome what has become known as the "packaging problem" (Gentner, 1982; Tomasello, 1995): they must figure out which event components among the many that co-occur are bundled, or "packaged," together within the meaning of an event word. Despite the manifest complexity of labeling events, children have some event terms in their earliest vocabularies (Fenson et al., 1994). Understanding which features of events are commonly labeled and how children acquire these labels can help us to further understand event representation in adults and children. We propose that children initially use two main sources of information to help them learn event words. The first is prelinguistic universal concepts, which give them a toehold into abstracting and labeling important event features. The second is the use of perceptual similarity across same-labeled exemplars, which initially makes verb meanings quite conservative and situation-specific. Children acquire more abstract, adult-like meanings for these words only through additional linguistic information, such as syntactic cues. In reviewing evidence for each of these strategies to action word learning, we will elucidate what each strategy teaches us about the development of event concepts in children.

The Packaging Problem

Aspects of events are labeled in various word classes, including verbs (*running*), adverbs (*quickly*), and prepositions (*up*). Although most of the event information we receive is encoded in the verbs of a language, it is important to note that what is labeled in the verbs of one language may be in another word class in another language. As a result, the research on event language acquisition focusing on verb learning should also be applicable to other word classes that encode event information.

Gentner (1982) was one of the first researchers to map out the many reasons why words that label events, particularly verbs, pose a problem for young children. Even simple event types comprise multiple components, such as manner (*walk* versus *swagger*), instrument (*hammer, shovel*), path (*ascend, descend*), and result (*open, break*). Any of these can be conflated (*sliding* generally includes a smooth manner and a downward path), and any of these can be the dominant focus for the label (*falling* highlights path; *breaking* highlights result).

To solve this packaging problem, children must discover which event features are contained within the semantic content of an event word. Adding to this difficulty, languages vary in terms of which components are prominent (Gentner, 2003; Langacker, 1987; Talmy, 1985). For example, manner is often included in English verbs (e.g., *fly away*), while path is often an integral part of French verbs (e.g., *partir en volent*, meaning "to leave flyingly"). Though both English and French contain path and manner verbs, proportionally they are quite different. As children learn to talk about events in their language, they must decide which verb to use in each instance, thus determining which event components are most important to relay to another person.

Prelinguistic Concepts

One way in which children may overcome the packaging problem is by coming to the word-learning task with some prior understanding of events. Extensive research shows that infants' knowledge of event features, such as causality and intentionality, is in fact quite robust (Baillargeon, 1995; Bertenthal, Proffitt, & Cutting, 1984; Choi, in press; Cohen & Oaks, 1993; Leslie, 1984; Leslie & Keebler, 1987; Sharon & Wynn, 1998). For a more extensive discussion of these studies, see Chapter 7 in this volume. Infants even have some prior knowledge of which event components are most important to attend to (Maguire, 2003; Pruden, Hirsh-Pasek, Maguire, & Meyer, 2003; Pulverman, Golinkoff, Sootsman, & Hirsh-Pasek, 2002). For example, children may be more likely to pay more attention to the path of the agent carrying out an action than the color of the agent's hair. Having some preconception of what event components are significant would ease the learnability problem posed by event words by constraining the range of possible hypotheses that investigators need to consider.

There are multiple lines of evidence supporting the claim that children come to the word-learning task with some universal event knowledge from which to learn event labels. One line of evidence is found by assessing the wide variety of the world's languages to find universal similarities, indicating that humans all find similar event features important to communicate. A second area of evidence is in the similar patterns of development across languages. A third line of evidence for children coming to the word-learning task with some universal event knowledge is found in errors in children's event language use unsupported by the language they are learning, indicating that they differentiate event features based on their own conceptual basis.

Similarities across the World's Languages

Many linguists, such as Jackendoff (1983), Langacker (1991), and Talmy (1985), note striking similarities in the event components that languages around the world encode in their relational terms. As Langacker (1991) points out, "certain recurrent and sharply differentiated aspects of our experience emerge as archetypes, which we normally use to structure our conceptions insofar as possible. Since language is a means by which we describe our experience, it is natural that such archetypes should be seized upon as the prototypical values of basic linguistic constructs" (pp. 294–295). In other words, because some event features are particularly salient to all humans, humans seek out ways to encode these features in their languages. Using cross-linguistic comparisons to uncover these event features allows us to (a) determine which aspects of an event *can* be encoded in the relational terms of a language and (b) determine which are most commonly encoded in the relational terms of the world's languages. As Langacker notes, these features are those that are important to human adults' conceptual structure of events.

An event contains many features, ranging in importance from the agent's eye color to whether the event was intentional or not. Any of these *could* potentially be labeled, but instead there are striking similarities across languages with respect to which features *are* encoded in relational terms (Braine, 1990; Braine, Reiser, & Rumain, 1984; Clark, 2001; Frawley, 1992; Langacker, 1987; Slobin, 2001, 2003; Talmy, 1985, 2000). There seem to be some relations that are encoded in all languages, some that are extraordinarily common across languages, and some that are rarely or never used. For example, verbs commonly encode domains such as tense (temporal relation to speech event), causality, and person (first, second, and third). In English, *walking* and *walked* vary in tense. *I walked the dog* and *I walked* vary in causality due to the latter being a transitive, as opposed to intransitive, verb. (You) *walk* and (she) *walks* vary in person. On the other hand, there are aspects of events that no language encodes in verbs, such as spatial setting (inside or outside) and the speaker's state of mind toward the event (e.g., interested or bored) (Langacker, 1987; Slobin, 2001; Talmy, 1985), meaning that although we can speak of whether something took place inside or outside, this information is never intrinsic to the verb the way person and tense are.

This seems to indicate that when talking about events, all humans feel that particular aspects are more important to convey than others. If all languages were identical, this would be a clear indication of which aspects of events are most important to human event representations; yet the commonalities are rarely absolute. While French encodes the rank of a person in the second-person verbs and pronouns, modern English does not. While Turkish demands that speakers encode whether they witnessed an event themselves or heard about it from another source (Aksu-Koc & Slobin, 1986), French and English do not. Given the manifest cross-linguistic variability, the set of true linguistic universals is bound to be quite small, and many important and indeed typical aspects of event representation may not be represented. A better approach to using cross-linguistic commonalities as a window to event representations is to expand our focus to include commonly encoded event components. These commonalities can be seen as evidence for conceptual universals. For example, aspects such as path appear to be encoded in verbs or other relational words (i.e., prepositions in English) in nearly all languages, while manner is often an optional, but rarely essential, feature to encode.

It may well be that universal concepts are not all or nothing but a hierarchy of the archetypes. For example, features such as tense, path, and intentionality appear to be salient event features necessary to the understanding of many events. On the other hand, features such as manner, listener rank, and witnessing are features that can be encoded, and are thus important to event representations but need not be conveyed to others in discussing an event. The hierarchy merely determines which features tend to be the most important to attend to and are likely to be encoded in the semantic content of an event word. Given the differences between languages, any of which a child must be able to learn, studying the relative ease and difficulty children have with particular archetypes may provide more of an insight into the development of event representations. Those that are easiest to learn may be most salient and prominent to children, while those that require more linguistic support may be more difficult for children to note and thus are not in their earliest event representations.

Similar Developmental Patterns

If children come to the event-label-learning task with prelinguistic event concepts that emerge through their early experiences, we should expect two patterns in event language acquisition: (1) all children should acquire labels for the same event concepts in the same order regardless of target language, those appearing first possibly being more prominent or salient in the hierarchy, and (2), because no language encodes all possible prelinguistic concepts, children should make errors in which they use labels to differentiate event features that are not differentiated in their target language, thereby revealing the powerful effects of some prelinguistic concepts. In this section and the next, we report support for these hypotheses, further indicating that children come to the word-learning task with some understanding of event features.

In reviewing this literature we will include work on spatial relationship terms as well, such as "on" and "in." Although in English adults tend to use these terms to refer to a steady state of being, they are often used to refer to entering that state by children—for example, a child saying "in" to tell a parent to put a block in a box. Further, the understanding of objects in relation to one another is essential to understanding events. Thus the acquisition of these terms is vital to our understanding of a developing child's event knowledge.

If event word learning is shaped by the child's prelinguistic understanding of event structure, we should find the same developmental patterns regardless of the language the child is learning. This in fact appears to be the case (Bowerman & Choi, 2001; Choi & Bowerman, 1991; Slobin, 1979). Children worldwide tend to produce terms for the same spatial event concepts in the same order. They begin with event words revolving around relationships of containment (*in, out*), accessibility (*open, close, under*), contiguity and support (*on, off*), verticality (*up, down*), and posture (*sit, stand*). Later, they learn words for proximity (*next to, between, beside*) and, lastly, words for projective relationships (*in front of, behind*). Not only is this sequence found cross-linguistically, it is also the sequence established through nonlinguistic testing by Piaget and Inhelder (1956). Although languages differ in how and where these event concepts are encoded (verbs, prepositions, adverbs, etc.), this similarity is widely evident. Thus, many developmentalists believe that once children develop these concepts independently of language, they seek out ways to express them.

Further, there is developmental support for the claim that there is a hierarchy within the range of prelinguistic universals. Some event components may emerge earlier in development and be more salient to young children, and thus be more readily encoded in language. The event component *path* is found in many more of the world's languages than *manner*. Research suggests that path is abstracted (Pulverman et al., 2002) and categorized (Pruden et al., 2003) before manner. In line with this, very young children sometimes improperly posit a path component to a verb even when this is counter to the patterns of their language. Maguire (2003) found that in an ambiguous labeling situation, English-speaking toddlers initially assume a novel verb label refers to the path of an action as opposed to the manner of an action. The pattern of labeling is quite uncommon in English, which has only a handful of path verbs (*ascend, circle*, etc.) but an abundance of manner verbs (*swagger, run, jog, skip, gallop*, etc.). The pattern of labeling does make sense, though, given the dominance of path cross-linguistically. For English-speaking children, Maguire (2003) found that around 3 years of age children begin to adhere to the more common English typography and assume the novel verb refers to the manner of the action. Given the difficulty with which children label the manner of action compared to the path, it appears that while path and manner may both be event features that children attend to, path is more prominent or salient to children than manner.

Children's Errors

The above findings indicate that children do have similar patterns and preferences in event labeling regardless of which language they are learning. This pattern holds true even when the target language does not support that preference, as in English-speaking children learning manner verbs. Strong evidence of children's initial event representations comes in the form of children's errors, especially those in which they make distinctions not encoded in their target language. Clark (2001) argues that children's errors can "offer us further insight into those categories that appear to be most salient to young children for perceptual, conceptual, and processing reasons, and hence are commonly attested in the early stages of language acquisition" (p. 381). Children's errors reveal their attempts to express universal concepts. Because these errors in linguistic expression do not have support from the language environment, they provide a unique glimpse at the child's representation of events in the world.

Clark (2001) makes the distinction between the concepts that are universal and are labeled in the native language (*robust concepts*) and those that are universal and are not labeled in the native language (*emergent concepts*). By finding the rare child error in which children express an emergent concept, we find those universal categories that children are drawn to label.

Sometimes these emergent categories make narrower distinctions than the adult language, leading to underextensions, and sometime the distinctions are much broader, leading to overextensions. For example, Budwig (1989) found that some English-speaking children use the different first-person pronoun forms (*I* and *me*) to express degree of agency. For example, children 20 to 32 months of age may use one personal pronoun (*me* or *my*) when there is full control over the action, such as *Me jump, My taked it off, My blew the candles out*. They may then use the other (often *I*) to express minimal control, such as *I like peas*, or *I no want those*. While agency is marked in many of the world's languages, it is not marked in English. As a result, English-speaking children who differentiate these concepts appear to be doing so without any linguistic input supporting the distinctions.

Another universal proposed by Clark (2001, 2003b) is the distinction between inherent and temporary states. Some properties are inherent to an object or agent (height, eye color) while others are temporary (emotions, states of being [wet, dry, cold]). This difference between inherent and temporary features is noted in the verbs of many languages. For example, Spanish has two distinct verbs for *to be* to mark this distinction. The verb *ser* in Spanish refers to inherent properties: *Jeremy is short, the dog's eyes are blue, cheetahs are fast*. The verb *estar*, on the other hand, is used when speaking about temporary features of an object or agent: *I'm hungry, the boy is sleepy, it is rainy this morning*. This distinction appears to be mastered fairly early by Spanish-speaking children (Sera, 1992). There is no such distinction encoded in English, but Clark (2003a) found that English-speaking children try to express this difference. She found that one child consistently used the suffix *-y* for inherent properties and *-ed* in contexts where he had observed some action that resulted in the acquisition of a property, making it temporary. Examples of inherent properties included *It isn't crumby* (meaning made of a crumbly material) and *There's a rocky house* (meaning a house made of rocks). On the other hand, temporary properties were consistently marked with the *-ed*: *That fork is all buttered* (meaning covered in butter) and *I want it a little bit fastened up* (meaning "Turn the faucet in a way that will release water more quickly"). Clark concluded that the distinction between inherent and temporary properties may be a fundamental one. As a result, English-speaking children find a way to express it without the support of the input of the native language. These errors are thus underextensions in which children mark distinctions more conservatively than the adult native speakers they hear.

Other errors found in children's production have been overextensions, in which children use one word across too many types. Dutch divides *on* into two kinds, distinguishing between an object being at rest when it is supported (*op*) versus requiring some kind of force or attachment for the support to be maintained (*aan*). Bowerman (1993) found that Dutch children have difficulty with the relatively unusual distinction that *aan* makes and are more apt to overextend *op* to cases in which adults use *aan* than the other way around. Mandler (1998) claims that this observation supports the view that *op* expresses a more basic or earlier analyzed aspect of support than *aan*. This would seem to indicate that a feature more akin to support is more available to children prelinguistically but that attachment must be learned through experience with the native language (though see Choi, in press, for discussion on prelinguistic understanding of support). In each of these cases children show which event features they differentiate, such as inherent and temporary properties, and which they cluster together, e.g., support and attachment, without receiving any linguistic cues for doing so.

The Role of Prelinguistic Concepts

All of this information seems to support the claim that children have and use event knowledge that is independent of their native language during language acquisition. Across the world's languages there are similar patterns regarding which event features should be encoded and which can be ignored. All children, regardless of the language they are learning, acquire some event words in the same order. Lastly, there are event features young children find so salient that on occasion they will extend words, grammatical morphemes, and constructions for their expression in ways that are not licensed in any of the speech directed to them. In terms of the development of event representations, this means that from a young age children have some knowledge of independent event components that they can use when acquiring event labels.

Claims that infants have robust event knowledge are not new (Baillargeon, 1995; Bertenthal, Proffitt, & Cutting, 1984; Choi, in press; Cohen & Oaks, 1993; Leslie, 1984; Leslie & Keebler, 1987; Sharon & Wynn, 1998). Yet here we have taken a different route by looking at children's event understandings in terms of the makeup of language, its universals, and how they are acquired. In so doing we arrive at a broader understanding of the point at which language and prelinguistic knowledge interact. Children have their own conceptualizations, and initially their event word meanings are filtered through these concepts, yet this is fleeting. There is a slight window during which robust and emergent concepts are unclear to children (Clark, 2001). By investigating children's understanding and acquisition of event labels, we learn more about event representations and development. For example, we find that universal distinctions may fall in a hierarchy that can be tracked by monitoring children's comprehension errors (as with path and manner) or their emergent category labels (as with support and attachment). Thus, children's event language proves a useful tool for learning about prelinguistic universal event knowledge.

Perception and Acquisition

Prelinguistic universals help explain how children are able to overcome the packaging problem. These provide the scaffolding for event representations and limit the space of possible solutions. As we have seen, these universals often serve as heuristics, highlighting which feature to attend to, meaning you should take note of the path of an agent instead of the degree of speaker interest. But as heuristics they represent what is likely, not guaranteed, to be encoded in a particular language. Yet prelinguistic universals are only part of the story. They do not explain how children acquire event representations that match those encoded by the particular event word. In this section, we turn to the question of how a child comes to correctly map a particular event representation to a particular event word. We survey the substantial body of evidence that supports the proposition that perceptual representations are an important component of the early representations of event words. Based on this support we extend our argument to propose that simulations of perceptual experiences may be important to children's, and eventually adults', event representations.

Let's return to our rabbit, which is moving away from the speaker of an exotic language and an uninitiated listener. However, now imagine that the native speaker is a parent and the listener is a child. Even if we are correct that universals limit the possible range of attended event features, when the parent labels the action, how does the child know what components of the event are being labeled? Is it the path (*leaving*), the manner (*hopping*), the path + manner (*fleeing*), the path + location (*exiting*), or any number of other combinations of features? Further, within any of those domains there are additional options. Even if the child knows that the word refers to the manner, there is still the question of whether the rabbit is *hopping, scurrying, jumping, scampering, running*, or *rushing*. In this section, we argue that because of their reliance on perceptually similar features across exemplars, children's initial word meanings are conservative and context-specific. It is only through experience that children can abstract the meaning from the particular agents, objects, and environments.

Many researchers argue that that the reason verbs are so hard for children to learn is that word learning is dependent on mapping labels to underlying representations and that the more abstract the representation, the harder it is to correctly map (Gentner & Boroditsky, 2001; Gillette et al., 1998; Golinkoff, Hirsh-Pasek, Mervis, Frawley, & Parillo, 1995; Maguire, Hirsh-Pasek, & Golinkoff, 2006). In general, verbs are more abstract than nouns because they refer to relations between objects. One consequence of this relatively new argument is that it moves us away from the belief in a strong dichotomy between nouns and verbs in acquisition and processing. Instead there is thought to be a conceptual continuum of concepts to be labeled (Bird, Howard, & Franklin, 2003; Black & Chiat, 2003; Gentner & Boroditsky, 2001; Gillette et al., 1999; Maguire, Hirsh-Pasek, & Golinkoff, 2006). On this continuum it is often proposed that words encoding very concrete, manipulatable items fall on one end, while words encoding linguistically bound features like prepositions and articles fall at the other end. Further, within each word class there is thought to be a range—for example, a word like *justice* would be harder to learn than a word like *juice*, and, consequently, *thinking* would be harder than *running*.

To date, the exact nature of the underlying continuum is under debate. Maguire, Hirsh-Pasek, and Golinkoff (2006) combined the most studied of these into one continuum referred to as SICI, an acronym for the various continua previously proposed: shape (Golinkoff et al., 1995), individuation (Gentner & Boroditsky, 2001), concreteness, and imageability (Bird, Howard, & Franklin, 2001; Gillette et al., 1998). As can be seen in Figure 8.1, representing SICI (from Maguire, Hirsh-Pasek, Golinkoff, & Imai, 2005), although nouns make up the more concrete end and verbs the more abstract of the continuum, there is substantial overlap between the two word classes.

In practice, the most researched of the SICI components, and thus the strongest support for SICI's claims, is imageability (Bird, Howard, & Franklin, 2000a, 2000b, 2003; Black & Chiat, 2003; Gillette et al., 1999). Imageability is defined as the ease with which a word gives rise to a sensory mental image (Paivio, Yuille, & Madigan, 1968). This is distinct from "concreteness" (Paivio et al., 1968), which refers to the ability to see, hear, and touch something. Imageability thus includes "emotion" words, like *joy* or *hate*, that one can imagine but not touch. Unlike the other components, imageability is less contingent on visual perception than are the concepts of shape, individuation, or concreteness. The argument is that children first attach labels to highly imageable event components, often conflating many more aspects than necessary and, as a result, using verbs more conservatively than adults. Through experience, children learn to abstract only those features of the event that correspond to each particular word.

It is important to note that none of the researchers claiming there is a continuum between word classes believe that any one

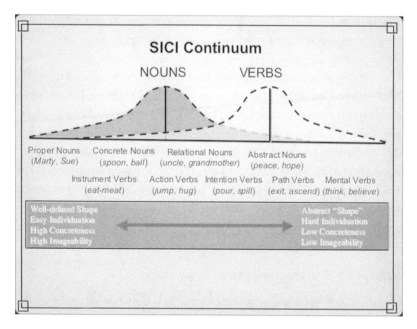

FIGURE 8.1. SICI continuum. (*Source:* Maguire, Hirsh, Pasek, Golinkoff, and Imai, 2005.)

feature—imageability, individuation, or shape—fully explains all differences between nouns and verbs in acquisition and processing. It is more the case that, all else being equal, words that are highly imageable will be easier to acquire than words that are less imageable. Two lines of evidence support these claims. First, children's initial vocabularies are filled with highly imageable nouns and verbs. Second, children's understanding of many abstract nouns and verbs is more concrete than that of adults.

Many of the verbs that appear early in children's vocabularies follow the characteristics of highly imageable words. Children's early verbs are more likely to be available to perception (such as *eat* or *run*), as opposed to later verbs that can not be as readily observed (such as *think, wish,* or *dream*) (Mandler, in press; Smiley & Huttenlocher, 1995; Snedeker & Gleitman, 2004). Other researchers have found similar evidence by correlating age of acquisition to imageability ratings. For example, Morrison, Chappell, and Ellis (1997) found that adult ratings of the age of acquisition of concrete nouns were significantly correlated with imageability ratings. Further, across word class, Bird, Howard, and Franklin

(2001) found that adult ratings of age of acquisition and imageability were correlated. To ensure that adult ratings of age of acquisition accurately portrayed actual learning, Maguire, Hirsh-Pasek, Golinkoff, and Imai (2005) used children's productive vocabulary as measured by the MacArthur Communicative Inventory (CDI; Fenson et al., 1994) as a measure of age of acquisition. The CDI is a parental checklist standardized by 1,200 parents of English-speaking children between birth and 30 months of age. These scores were compared to imageability ratings collected by Masterson and Druks (1998) for both nouns and verbs. Findings indicated that both across and within word classes (nouns and verbs), imageability ratings and age of acquisition were significantly negatively correlated.

Perceptual Representations and Imageability

Clearly, there are intriguing correlations between our intuitive understanding of the degree to which concepts are concrete or imageable and a number of developmental behavioral measures. A general weakness of the literature on imageability or SICI, though, is an absence of a theoretical explanation of what it is about our conceptual representations that gives rise to these effects. Although it is generally recognized that imageability or SICI relates to our ability to capture the event in terms of perceptual, motor, or introspective representations, there is too little consideration of how the structure of our concept representations gives rise to these effects. Part of this may be due to a reasonable effort to be empirically conservative and not precipitously exclude potential hypotheses. Another factor may be the view that the reliability of imageability ratings across subjects and across experiments is sufficient empirical justification for their use as an experimental measure of concept representation. An unfortunate side effect of this theoretical tentativeness has been a lack of interaction with the imageability literature and the cognitive science literature on concepts. In an effort to remedy this situation, we provide a brief sketch of the possible role played by perceptual representations in event concepts. In effect, we hope to give a better conceptual definition of what imageability or SICI means in terms of processing, representation, and conceptualization for adults and how children might reach adult-like levels of these. Although many of the details remain to be filled in, we feel that this account is promising and supported by evidence from a number of resources.

Within cognitive science, researchers have traditionally presumed that conceptual representations are couched in inherently nonperceptual representations. Information about objects and events is thought to be transduced through the activity of perceptual mechanisms into abstract representations that support higher cognitive functions. Recently, though, this orthodoxy has been challenged by those who hold that our conceptual representations involve perceptual symbol systems (Barsalou, 1999). On this view, the representations employed in cognitive tasks consist of modality-specific perceptual symbols (motor and introspective representations are included within this designation). Perceptual information is thus not transduced into an amodal format but is instead extracted and placed into long-term memory in such a way that preserves aspects of its structure. The critical assumption underlying this theory is that concepts rely on simulations of experience. Part of one's representation of walking, for example, consists of a simulation of the experience of seeing someone walk. This simulation will almost always be schematic in the sense that it contains only some of the perceptual states involved in this experience. Categorizing an action as an instance of walking involves the comparison of a partial simulation to the actual perception. Such simulations are the result of a kind of neurophysiological reenactment. Information concerning the neural activation patterns associated with the perception of an event is stored in long-term memory and is used to generate appropriate perceptual states (Barsalou, 1999; Damasio, 1989; Simmons & Barsalou, 2003). These simulations are generally multimodal in the sense that they involve the reactivation of perceptual states in several modalities (Barsalou, 1999; Cree & McRae, 2003).

This view fits well with the increasing body of evidence that certain cognitive tasks are handled by perceptual representations and mechanisms. For instance, sensory and motor representations have been implicated in mental imagery (Kosslyn, 1994). Behavioral and neural studies indicate that mental imagery depends in part on the activation of sensory representations (Farah, 2000; Kosslyn, 1994). Motor representations have been similarly implicated in motor imagery (Grezes & Decety, 2001; Jeannerod, 1997). Perceptual representations are also implicated in several aspects of memory (Glenberg, 1997; Martin, 2001). Thus, the claim that our event representations have a perceptual basis follows similar evidence in other areas (see similar arguments in Chapter 1).

A number of recent experiments lend more direct support to the notion that perceptually based simulation is central to some cognitive tasks (Pecher, Zeelenberg, & Barsalou, 2003, 2004). These "modality-switching" experiments build on the well-established finding that processing a stimulus in one modality is less effective when the previous stimulus was processed in another modality than when the stimuli involve the same modality (Spence, Nicholas, & Driver, 2000). For example, Pecher et al. (2003) found a modality-switching cost with a property verification task. They found that participants verified facts involving one modality, such as the fact that leaves rustle, more rapidly after verifying a fact involving the same modality, such as the fact that blenders make noise, than after verifying a fact involving a different modality, such as the fact that cranberries are tart. This result is predicted by the perceptual symbol system approach because it holds that the cognitive task of verification will be carried out by means of a simulation involving modality-specific representations.

In a related vein, Stanfield and Zwaan (2001) asked participants to affirm whether or not presented pictures depicted the action described in sentences. The sentences described actions such as driving a nail into the floor or the wall with a particular orientation. Stanfield and Zwaan found that participants responded more quickly to the pictures that had the same orientation (e.g., vertical or horizontal) as the action described. Thus, in answering questions about these events given in a linguistic frame, subjects appear to have relied on perceptual representations.

These findings are supported by lesion and brain imaging studies. There is, for instance, evidence that damage to sensory or motor areas can contribute to the loss of category-specific knowledge (Damasio & Damasio, 1994; Humphreys & Forde, 2001; Warrington & McCarthy, 1987). Further, it appears that lesions can lead to the loss of multiple categories that share sensory-motor properties (Simmons & Barsalou, 2003). Adolphs, Damasio, Tranel, Cooper, and Damasio (2000) found that damage to the somatosensory cortex was correlated with deficits in the visual recognition of facial expressions. They propose that simulation of producing facial expressions is involved in the recognition of facial expressions in others. Using functional neuroimaging and a visual naming task, Chao and Martin (2000) found increased activity in motor areas with highly manipulable objects when compared to less manipulable objects. In an fMRI study carried out by Hauk, Jonstrude, and Pulvermuller (2004), participants read individual words that referred to actions involving leg, arm, and head movements. Hauk et al. not only found that all of these word types elicited increased activation in the motor cortex but also that each type of action word produced increased activation in the particular areas within the motor cortex that became active when the participants actually carried out the relevant action. Each of these indicates that some type of perceptual processing is taking place during these comprehension and decision tasks, supporting the perceptual symbol system theory.

The most controversial aspect of perceptual symbol system theory is the claim that there are no amodal representations. A standard objection to this approach is that perceptual symbols are ill suited to represent abstract concepts such as justice, democracy, and truth. Defenders of perceptual symbol systems have offered a few responses to this objection (Barsalou, 1999; Prinz, in press), but the issue remains unresolved. For this reason, we propose to adopt an agnostic stance similar to Goldstone and Barsalou (1998)—that is, we accept that perceptual representations are central to some cognitive tasks without committing ourselves to the universal claim.

We propose that the imageability of a concept, or its SICI ranking, is the ease with which it is possible to use perceptual symbols to represent that concept. Highly imageable concepts are those that can be readily captured by means of perceptual simulation. Low imageability can arise for several possible reasons. They may be the result of a need for a disjunction of multiple perceptual representations. This could explain in part why superordinate categories such as "animal" are less imageable than basic-level categories such as "dog." Whereas most dogs share certain visual properties, few visual properties are shared by animals as a whole. To capture this category by means of perceptual symbols thus requires a disjunctive set of simulations. Low imageability may also arise from the presence of amodal representations (if there are amodal representations). This may be the case for abstract concepts such as justice. In the end, our formulation remains neutral with regard to the question of whether low imageability arises from complex processes involving modal representations or a dependence on amodal representations. The central point is that imageability can be understood as a measure of relative degree of difficulty for perceptual representation.

Imageability, Perception, and Development

We are now in a position to provide an interpretation of the developmental data correlating age of acquisition with imageability or SICI. Imageability, according to the account outlined above, is linked to perceptual simulation. A great deal of evidence indicates that children's earliest words tend to be those that are highly imageable, regardless of syntactic class. This developmental pattern suggests that young children rely more directly on perceptual simulation than do adults. By connecting imageability to perceptual symbols, we provide a novel theoretical framework for understanding this pattern of word learning.

The argument that children only learn high-imageability words, though, can be quickly countered by the fact that children do have words in their initial vocabularies that appear to be quite low in imageability or SICI, such as *love, hate, make,* and *go* (Fenson et al., 1994). While children's use of event words may at first glance appear adult-like, close examination of the use and comprehension of these words reveals clear differences. In particular, children's early verbs are more likely to be used in limited, non-metaphorical extensions as opposed to broader extensions (Behrend, 1995; Forbes & Farrar, 1993). Further, they are likely to be used in specific contexts and linked to routines as opposed to broader use in a wider range of contexts (Naigles & Hoff, in press; Tardif, in press). The process of developing mature event representations seems to be a move from straightforward perceptual simulations to more abstract, perhaps disjointed, complexes of perceptual symbols, or even to representations including amodal symbols.

Early in language acquisition children are quite conservative in their extension of novel verb labels, indicating that their event representations are more highly dependent on those aspects that are more imageable. Forbes and Farrar (1993) taught 3-year-olds, 7-year-olds, and adults novel verbs for actions and asked them to judge whether the verb applied to new situations. For 3-year-olds there could be very few perceptual changes between the exemplar and the extension in order for them to use the same word—for example, the result or the instrument of the action had to be identical for the novel verb to be extended to a new exemplar. Adults and 7-year-olds allowed for less perceptual similarity, yet there was a developmental progression between these ages. Thus, the conceptualization of the novel verb was more concrete for 3-year-olds than 7-year-olds or adults, who could abstract the meaning from the perceptual scene.

Even familiar event labels appear to be extended in a more perceptually based, context-specific way by children than by adults. Forbes and Poulin-Dubois (1997) tested 20- and 26-month-olds' extension of familiar verbs, such as *kick* and *pick up*, to novel exemplars of those events. They found that 20-month-olds were the more conservative, extending labels when the agent had changed but not the manner or the outcome. Comparatively, 26-month-olds were more liberal, extending the familiar labels when the agent or the manner had changed but not the outcome. Thus, the developmental progression of known words follows a similar pattern as the acquisition of novel words, from context-specific to more general. Further, adults can extend known labels to additional, less salient event features that children may not be using yet. Gallivan (1988) interviewed children (ages 3 to 5 years) and adults about the meaning of 10 verbs common in early vocabularies. While children gave definitions concerning perceptual similarities between exemplars (agent, object, and instrument), adults gave more conceptual responses, such as the intentions of the agents.

Theakston, Lieven, Pine, and Rowland (2002) showed that even for apparently simple verbs like *go*, which is in children's productive vocabulary by about 19 months of age (Fenson et al., 1994), children between the ages of 2 and 3 years do not have a single, unified concept of *go*, despite its frequent use. Instead, at younger ages there were very specific situations for each grammatical instantiation of the word *go*, such as *gonna*, *go away*, and *all gone*. Thus, while children appear to use a familiar verb competently, they really use it with many different, unrelated meanings. Each of these meanings is associated with its own highly imageable representation compared to the adult counterpart.

These results point to the importance of perceptual simulation in children's earliest event concepts. While adults may have event representations that allow for multiple variations, children have concrete interpretations of the same events. For children there is a strong, clear reliance on perceptual features in learning event words. Smiley and Huttenlocher (1995), for instance, found that children learned labels for actions they performed themselves up to a month before they produced that same word for actions performed by others. Self-actions are thought to be substantially more concrete than those performed by others because of the strong perceptual and motor representations involved.

While children may come to the language-learning task with some idea of which aspects of an action are most likely to be labeled, they still need to determine each word's specific meaning. In so doing, they appear to be highly reliant on perceptual features. Thus, their interpretation of an event word is more likely to include *path + manner + result*, meaning the word can only be extended to situations in which none of those features has changed. An adult's interpretation, on the other hand, may include only manner. Further, the reason that children use abstract verb labels, such as *love* and *hate*, at such young ages is that their underlying conceptualization of these words is much more concrete than that of their adult counterparts. Data from cognitive tasks and neuroimaging indicate that adults are dependent on perceptual symbols for their comprehension of event words. Children's developing event vocabularies reveal that they are even more highly dependent on these perceptual symbols. Thus, part of the process of forming an adult-like understanding of event labels may be either creating amodal representations or combining multiple, disjointed perceptual representations through exposure.

Conclusion

In learning to label events, children are faced with an enormously difficult task, given the number of event features that could potentially be labeled. Yet children appear to accomplish this task with relative ease. In this chapter we have argued that unraveling this apparent paradox can shed new light on our understanding of event representations and their development. We proposed two strategies that children use to overcome this difficulty. The first is a hierarchy of prelinguistic universal event concepts, allowing children to focus on those features of an event that are most likely to be labeled, such as path or causality. The second is a reliance on highly imageable similarities between exemplars, causing children's representations of event labels to be more conservative and context-specific than adults. In making this argument we also tried to home in on what could be meant by imageability in terms of processing and development, using a version of the perceptual symbols theory as a guide. By studying the interaction of children's prelinguistic event concepts with children's comprehension and production of language, we have added another block to our overall understanding of the development and processing of event representations.

References

Adolphs, R., Damasio, H., Tranel, D., Cooper, G., & Damasio, A. R. (2000). A role for somatasensory cortices in the visual recognition of emotion as revealed by three dimensional lesion mapping. *Journal of Neuroscience, 20,* 2683–2690.

Aksu-Koc, A., & Slobin, D. (1986). A psychological account of the development and use of evidentials in Turkish. In W. Chafe & J. Nichols (Eds.), *Evidentiality: The linguistic coding of epistemology* (pp. 185–201). Norwood, NJ: Ablex.

Baillargeon, R. (1995). A model of physical reasoning in infancy. In C. Rovee-Collier & L. P. Lipsitt (Eds.), *Advances in infancy research* (Vol. 9, pp. 305–371). Norwood, NJ: Ablex.

Barsalou, L. W. (1999). Perceptual symbol systems. *Behavioral and Brain Sciences, 22,* 577–660.

Behrend, D. A. (1995). Processes involved in the initial mapping of verb meanings. In M. Tomasello & W. E. Merriman (Eds.), *Beyond the names for things: Young children's acquisition of verbs* (pp. 251–275). Hillsdale, NJ: Lawrence Erlbaum Associates.

Bertenthal, B. I., Proffitt, D. R., & Cutting, J. E. (1984). Infant sensitivity to figural coherence in biomechanical motions. *Journal of Experimental Child Psychology, 37,* 213–230.

Bird, H., Howard, D., & Franklin, S. (2000a). Little words—not really: Function and content words in normal and aphasic speech. *Journal of Neurolinguistics, 15,* 209–237.

Bird, H., Howard, D., & Franklin, S. (2000b). Why is a verb like an inanimate object? Grammatical category and semantic category deficits. *Brain and Language, 72,* 246–309.

Bird, H., Howard, D., & Franklin, S. (2001). Age of acquisition and imageability ratings for a large set of words, including verbs and function words. *Behavior Research Methods, Instruments, and Computers, 33,* 73–79.

Bird, H., Howard, D., & Franklin, S. (2003). Verbs and nouns: The importance of being imageable. *Journal of Neurolinguistics, 16,* 113–149.

Black, M., & Chiat, S. (2003). Noun-verb dissociations: A multi-faceted phenomenon. *Journal of Neurolinguistics, 16,* 231–250.

Bowerman, M. (1993). Typological perspectives on language acquisition: Do crosslinguistic patterns predict development? In E. B. Clark (Ed.), *Proceedings of the 25th Annual Child Language Research Forum* (pp. 7–15). Stanford, CA: Center for the Study of Language and Information.

Bowerman, M., & Choi, S. (2001). Shaping meanings for language: Universal and language-specific in the acquisition of spatial semantic categories. In

M. Bowerman & S. C. Levinson (Eds.), *Language acquisition and conceptual development* (pp. 475–511). Cambridge: Cambridge University Press.

Braine, M. D. S. (1990). The "natural logic" approach to reasoning. In W. F. Overton (Ed.), *Reasoning, necessity, and logic: Developmental perspectives* (pp. 133–157). Hillsdale, NJ: Lawrence Erlbaum.

Braine, M. D. S., Reiser, B. J., & Rumain, B. (1984). Some empirical justification for a theory of natural propositional logic. In G. H. Bower (Ed.), *The psychology of learning and motivation: Vol. 18. Advances in research and theory* (pp. 313–371). New York: Academic Press.

Budwig, N. (1989). The linguistic marking of agency and control in child language. *Journal of Child Language*, *16*, 263–284.

Chao, L. L., & Martin, A. (2000). Representation of manipulable man-made objects in the dorsal stream. *Neuroimage*, *12*, 478–484.

Choi, S. (in press). Preverbal spatial cognition and language-specific input: Categories of containment and support. In K. Hirsh-Pasek & R. M. Golinkoff (Eds.), *Action meets word: How children learn verbs*. New York: Oxford University Press.

Choi, S., & Bowerman, M. (1991). Learning to express motion events in English and Korean: The influence of language-specific lexicalization patterns. *Cognition*, *41*, 83–121.

Clark, E. V. (2001). Emergent categories in first language acquisition. In M. Bowerman & S. C. Levinson (Eds.), *Language acquisition and conceptual development* (pp. 379–405). Cambridge: Cambridge University Press.

Clark, E. V. (2003a). Language and representations. In D. Gentner & S. Goldin-Meadow (Eds.), *Language in mind* (pp. 17–24). Cambridge, MA: MIT Press.

Clark, E. V. (2003b). *First language acquisition*. New York: Cambridge University Press.

Cohen, L. B., & Oaks, L. M. (1993). How infants perceive a simple causal event. *Developmental Psychology*, *29*, 421–433.

Cree, G. S., & McRae, K. (2003). Analyzing the factors underlying the underlying the structure and computation of the meaning of chipmunk, cherry, chisel, cheese and cello (and many other concrete nouns). *Journal of Experimental Psychology: General*, *132*, 163–201.

Damasio, A. R. (1989). Time-locked multi-regional retroactivation: A systems-level proposal for the neural substrates of recall and recognition. *Cognition*, *33*, 25–62.

Damasio, A. R., & Damasio, H. (1994). Cortical systems for retrieval of concrete knowledge: The convergence zone framework. In C. Koch & J. L. Davis (Eds.), *Large-scale neuronal theories of the brain. Computational neuroscience* (pp. 61–74). Cambridge, MA: MIT Press.

Farah, M. J. (2000). The neural basis of mental imagery. In M. S. Gazzaniga (Ed.), *The cognitive neurosciences* (pp. 965–974). Cambridge, MA: MIT Press.

Fenson, L., Dale, P. S., Reznick, J. S., Bates, E., Thal, D., & Pethick, S. J. (1994). Variability in early communicative development. *Monographs of the Society for Research in Child Development*, *59*(5, Serial No. 242), 1–185.

Forbes, J. N., & Farrar, J. M. (1993). Children's initial assumptions about the meaning of novel motion verbs: Biased and conservative? *Cognitive Development, 8*, 273–290.

Forbes, J., & Poulin-Dubois, D. (1997). Representational change in young children's understanding of familiar verb meaning. *Journal of Child Language, 24*, 389–406.

Frawley, W. (1992). *Linguistic semantics.* Hillsdale, NJ: Erlbaum Associates.

Gallivan, J. (1988). Motion verb acquisition: Development of definitions. *Perceptual and Motor Skills, 66*, 979–986.

Gentner, D. (1982). Why nouns are learned before verbs: Linguistical relativity versus natural partitioning. In S. A. Kuczaj II (Ed.), *Language development: Vol. 2. Language, thought, and culture* (pp. 301–334). Hillsdale, NJ: Lawrence Erlbaum.

Gentner, D. (2003). Why are we so smart? In D. Gentner & S. Goldin-Meadow (Eds.), *Language in mind: Advances in the study of language and thought* (pp. 195–236). Cambridge, MA: MIT Press.

Gentner, D., & Boroditsky, L. (2001). Individuation, relativity, and early word learning. In M. Bowerman & S. C. Levinson (Eds.), *Language acquisition and conceptual development* (pp. 215–256). Cambridge: Cambridge University Press.

Gillette, J., Gleitman, H., Gleitman, L., & Lederer, A. (1998). Human simulations of vocabulary learning. *Cognition, 73*, 135–176.

Glenberg, A. M. (1997). What memory is for. *Behavioral and Brain Sciences, 20*, 1–18.

Goldstone, R. L., & Barsalou, L. W. (1998). Reuniting perception and conception. *Cognition, 65*, 231–262.

Golinkoff, R. M., Hirsh-Pasek, K., Mervis, C. B., Frawley, W. B., & Parillo, M. (1995). Lexical principles can be extended to the acquisition of verbs. In M. Tomasello & W. E. Merriman (Eds.), *Beyond the name for things: Young children's acquisition of verbs* (pp. 185–222). Hillsdale, NJ: Lawrence Erlbaum Associates.

Golinkoff, R. M., Mervis, C. B., & Hirsh-Pasek, K. (1994). Early object labels: The case for lexical principles. *Journal of Child Language, 21*, 125–155.

Grezes, J., & Decety, J. (2001). Functional anatomy of execution, mental simulation, observation, and verb generation of actions: A meta-analysis. *Human Brain Mapping, 12*, 1–19.

Hauk, O., Johnsrude, I., & Pulvermuller, F. (2004). Somatotopic representation of action words in human motor and premotor cortex. *Neuron, 41*, 301–307.

Humphreys, G. W., & Forde, E. M. E. (2001). Hierarchies, similarity, and interactivity in object recognition: "Category-specific" neuropsychological deficits. *Behavioral and Brain Sciences, 24*, 453–509.

Imai, M., Haryu, E., Okada, H., Lianjing, L., & Shigematsu, J. (in press). Revisiting the noun-verb debate: A crosslinguistic comparison of novel noun and verb learning in English-, Japanese-, and Chinese-speaking children. In K. Hirsh-Pasek & R.M. Golinkoff (Eds.), *Action meets word: How children learn verbs.* New York: Oxford University Press.

Jackendoff, R. S. (1983). *Semantics and cognition*. Cambridge, MA: MIT Press.

Jeannerod, M. (1997). *The cognitive neuroscience of action*. Malden, MA: Blackwell Publishing.

Kosslyn, S. M. (1994). *Image and mind*. Cambridge, MA: MIT Press.

Langacker, R. W. (1987). *Foundations of cognitive grammar. Vol. 1: Theoretical perspectives*. Stanford, CA: Stanford University Press.

Langacker, R. W. (1991). *Foundations of cognitive grammar. Vol. 2: Descriptive application*. Stanford, CA: Stanford University Press.

Leslie, A. M. (1984). Spatiotemporal continuity and perception of causality in infants. *Perception, 13*, 287–305.

Leslie, A. M., & Keebler, S. (1987). Do six-month-old infants perceive causality? *Cognition, 25*, 265–288.

Maguire, M. J. (2003). Children's use of universal and language specific cues in verb learning. Unpublished dissertation. Philadelphia, PA: Temple University.

Maguire, M. J., Hirsh-Pasek, K., & Golinkoff, R. M. (2006). A unified theory of word learning: Putting verb acquisition in context. In K. Hirsh-Pasek & R. M. Golinkoff (Eds.), *Action meets word: How children learn verbs*. New York: Oxford University Press.

Maguire, M. J., Hirsh-Pasek, K., Golinkoff, R. M., & Imai, M. (2005, April). *What makes verb learning so difficult? Another perspective*. Paper presented at the biannual Society for Research in Child Development conference.

Mandler, J. M. (1998). Representation. In W. Damon (Eds.), *Handbook of child psychology: Vol. 2: Cognition, perception, and language* (pp. 255–308). New York: Wiley.

Mandler, J. M. (in press). Actions organize the infant's world. In K. Hirsh-Pasek & R. M. Golinkoff (Eds.), *Action meets word: How children learn verbs*. New York: Oxford University Press.

Martin, A. (2001) Functional neuroimaging of semantic memory. In R. Cabeza & A. Kingstone (Eds.), *Handbook of functional neuroimaging of cognition* (pp. 153–186). Cambridge, MA: MIT Press.

Masterson, J., & Druks, J. (1998). Description of a set of 164 nouns and 102 verbs matched for printed word and frequency, familiarity and age-of-acquisition. *Journal of Neurolinguistics, 11*, 331–354.

Morrison, C. M., Chappell, T. D., & Ellis, A. W. (1997). Age of acquisition norms for a large set of object names and their relation to adult estimates and other variables. *Quarterly Journal of Experimental Psychology, 50A*, 528–559.

Naigles, L. R., & Hoff, E. (in press). Verbs at the beginning: Parallels between comprehension and input. In K. Hirsh-Pasek & R. M. Golinkoff (Eds.), *Action meets word: How children learn verbs*. New York: Oxford University Press.

Paivio, A., Yuille, J. C., & Madigan, S. A. (1968). Concreteness, imagery and meaningfulness values for 925 nouns. *Journal of Experimental Psychology, 76*, 1–25.

Pecher, D., Zeelenberg, R., & Barsalou, L. W. (2003). Verying properties from different modalities for concepts produces switching costs. *Psychological Science, 14*, 119–124.

Pecher, D., Zeelenberg, R., & Barsalou, L. W. (2004). Sensorimotor simulations underlie conceptual representations: Modality-specific effects of prior activation. *Psychonomic Bulletin & Review, 11*, 164–167.

Piaget, J., & Inhelder, B. (1956). *The child's conception of space*. London: Routledge and Kegan Paul.

Prinz, J. J. (in press). The return of concept empiricism. In H. Cohen & C. Leferbvre (Eds.), *Categorization and cognitive science*. Amsterdam: Elsevier.

Pruden, S. M., Hirsh-Pasek, K., Maguire, M. J., & Meyer, M. (2003, November). *Foundations of verb learning: Infants form categories of path and manner in motion events*. Paper presented at the Boston University Annual Conference on Language Development, Boston, MA.

Pulverman, R., Golinkoff, R., Sootsman, J. L., & Hirsh-Pasek, K. (2002, April). *Infants' non-linguistic processing of motion events: One-year-old English-speakers are interested in manner*. Paper presented at the annual Stanford Language Conference, Palo Alto, CA.

Quine, W. (1960). *Word and object*. Cambridge, MA: MIT Press.

Sera, M. D. (1992). To be or to be: Use and acquisition of the Spanish copulas. *Journal of Memory and Language, 31*, 408–427.

Sharon, T., & Wynn, K. (1998). Individuation of actions from continuous motion. *Psychological Science, 9*(5), 357–362.

Simmons, W. K., & Barsalou, L. W. (2003). The similarity-in-topography principle: Reconciling theories of conceptual deficits. *Cognitive Neuropsychology, 20*, 451–486.

Slobin, D. I. (April, 1979). *The role of language in language acquisition*. Invited address at the Fiftieth Annual Meeting of the Eastern Psychological Association, Philadelphia, PA.

Slobin, D. I. (2001). Form-function relations: How do children find out what they are? In M. Bowerman & S. C. Levinson (Eds.), *Language acquisition and conceptual development* (pp. 406–449). Cambridge: Cambridge University Press.

Slobin, D. I. (2003). Language and thought online: Cognitive consequences of linguistic relativity. In D. Gentner & S. Goldin-Meadow (Eds.), *Language in mind* (pp. 157–192). Cambridge, MA: MIT Press.

Smiley, P., & Huttenlocher, J. (1995). Conceptual development and the child's early words for events, objects, and persons. In M. Tomasello & W. E. Merriman (Eds.), *Beyond the names for things: Young children's acquisition of verbs* (pp. 21–62). Hillsdale, NJ: Lawrence Erlbaum Associates.

Snedeker, J., & Gleitman, L. (2004). Why is it hard to label our concepts. In G. H. Waxman (Ed.), *Weaving a lexicon*. Cambridge, MA: MIT Press.

Spence, C., Nichols, M. E. R., & Driver, J. (2000). The cost of expecting events in the wrong sensory modality. *Perception and Psychophysics, 63*, 330–336.

Stanfield, R. A., & Zwaan, R. A. (2001). The effect of implied orientation derived from verbal context on picture recognition. *Psychological Science, 12*, 153–156.

Talmy, L. (1985). Lexicalization patterns: Semantic structure in lexical forms. In T. Shopen (Ed.), *Language typology and syntactic description: Grammatical categories and the lexicon*. Cambridge: Cambridge University Press.

Talmy, L. (2000) *Towards a cognitive semantics, Vol. 1: Concept structuring systems*. Cambridge, MA: MIT Press.

Tardif, T. (in press). But are they really verbs? In K. Hirsh-Pasek & R. M. Golinkoff (Eds.), *Action meets word: How children learn verbs*. New York: Oxford University Press.

Theakston, A. L., Lieven, E. V. M., Pine, J. M., & Rowland, C. F. (2002). Going, going, gone: The acquisition of the verb 'go.' *Journal of Child Language, 29*, 783–811.

Tomasello, M. (1995). Pragmatic contexts for early verb learning. In M. Tomasello & W. E. Merriman (Eds.), *Beyond the names for things: Young children's acquisition of verbs* (pp. 115–146). Hillsdale, NJ: Lawrence Erlbaum Associates.

Warrington, E. K., & McCarthy, R. A. (1987). Categories of knowledge: Further fractionations and an attempted integration. *Brain, 110*, 1273–1296.

Part III
Perceiving and Segmenting Events

Part III

Perceiving and Segmenting Events: Overview

The preceding section focused on how event concepts develop over childhood. We now turn to how particular events emerge online from sensation and perception. This section consists of two parts: "Perceiving Action Events" and "Segmenting Events." The first of these addresses one class of events that is particularly important for everyday activity: physical actions by other humans. In Chapter 9, Georgopoulos and Karageorgiou review research on the brain's representation of actions from the point of view of the actor—how the spatial target of an action is encoded, transformed, and re-represented in terms of a sequence of joint angles and torques that will produce the desired body movement. The following chapters by Bingham and Wickelgren, Pollick and Paterson, and Troje present accounts of how the information that is encoded when an actor prepares an action can be decoded from the visual cues that action provides to observers. Bingham and Wickelgren specifically address the possibility that action production and perception depend on a common code—that the same representations identified in Georgopoulos and Karageorgiou's studies of movement production may be used by observers to decode characteristics of human movement. However, they argue forcefully against this view, instead advocating for a Gibsonian account in which the dynamic visual information itself is sufficient to support action perception. The following chapter by Pollick and Paterson identifies specific aspects of visual information that may contribute to action understanding. Pollick and Paterson distinguish between spatial features that reflect the structural properties of the actor and environment and temporal features that reflect the dynamics of how particular actions are performed, and they show that these feature types play different roles in action understanding. Temporal features contribute uniquely to determining the manner in which a particular action is performed. For example, a bouquet of flowers might be thrown happily (at a wedding), angrily (after having been rejected by its intended recipient), or even with disgust (when discovered after having been forgotten for weeks in a vase)—and the temporal properties of the throwing motion will discriminate these cases. Chapter 12, by Troje, focuses further on how a single action, walking, may be performed differently by different people in different circumstances. He presents an elegant model that pulls out regularities in the structural and dynamic properties of movement that are correlated with meaningful features that distinguish individual walkers and different ways a particular individual may walk at any one time. As with the studies presented by Pollick and Paterson, dynamic features provide robust cues to people's mood states. The final two chapters return to the neurophysiological basis of action representations. In Chapter 13, Grossman reviews evidence for a distributed system combining information about form and motion in human action, arguing that the products of this system form the basis for perceptions of actors' intentions. Heberlein (Chapter 14) takes up the attribution of intentionality directly, again arguing for a distributed system leading to the perception of animacy from movement. One striking point of overlap between the two proposed networks is in the posterior superior temporal sulcus, a brain region that appears to be specialized for the processing of biological motion and which also appears to be critical for observers' attributions of actors' intentions.

There is an intriguing point of convergence between these chapters' characterization of adult competence and the accounts of perceptual and linguistic development given in Part II. All agree in proposing that action is analyzed into components, such as path, that are likely to be critical for representing and reproducing an actor's goal, as well as components that characterize the manner in which that goal is achieved. Chapters 11 and 12 suggest that this may result because they enable different sorts of inferences and learning.

The chapters in the first section reflect a diversity of views regarding the nature of representations involved in action understanding. However, it would not be doing too much violence to their positions to characterize the chapters by Georgopoulos, Grossman, and Heberlein as being congruent with a "common coding" (Hommel, Muesseler, Aschersleben, & Prinz, 2001; Prinz, 1997) view of action representation, in which the representations used to plan actions overlap with the representations used to understand those actions. And it would not be too great a stretch to characterize the chapter by Pollick and Paterson and that by Troje as being congruent with the argument presented by Bingham and Wickelgren against common coding views. It is worth noting that this difference in theoretical orientations covaries with differences in methodology: advocacy of common coding is associated with the use of neurophysiological and neuropsychological methods, whereas more Gibsonian approaches are associated with fine-grained formal models of behavior. In this regard, the present chapters reflect the broader state of the field. We think they highlight a potentially productive path forward, bringing together neurophysiological methods and powerful formal modeling with the hope of resolving differences between Gibsonian and common coding approaches to action understanding.

These chapters also illustrate how formal analyses might be applied in understanding some of the fundamental issues in language learning and event cognition laid out in Part II. In linguistics, a fundamental distinction is seen between describing the path of an event and describing the manner of an event. The path of an event is generally a description of the spatiotemporal trajectory of an object on its way to a goal. Bingham and Wickelgren discuss some alternative approaches to recognizing paths. In contrast, the manner is the details of the way the object moves on the path (e.g., walking). Troje, as well as Pollick and Paterson, discusses how manner might be analyzed. The chapters by Grossman and Heberlein discuss how these two aspects of an event might come together. The linking of these two aspects of an event might be critical to the uniquely human ability to reason and represent events. Consider the difference between single and linked event features: processing the path in an event would only allow the observer to emulate the action, whereas processing both path and manner allows imitation.

One of the basic problems perceptual and conceptual systems must solve is segmentation: given continuous input, perceptual systems make constant decisions about how some components of the input belong to THIS and others to THAT. Doing so reduces complexity; without segmenting continuous sensory inputs into discrete units, perception would be an intractably high-dimensional problem. (Of course, such decisions need not be conscious, and rarely are.) The chapters in the second section, "Segmenting Events," address how this happens for events. All three chapters deal with everyday events involving human actors. In Chapter 15, Schwan and Garsoffky provide a thoughtful review of research on event segmentation and outline a theoretical orientation. According to their account, event segmentation emerges from the interaction of perceptual bottom-up processes and inferential top-down processing. By grouping ongoing activity into meaningful events, perceptual systems lay down the representations that form the basis of conceptual judgments and later memory. Shipley and Maguire (Chapter 16) provide a focused look at perceptual processing, with a detailed look at the case of motion paths as a basis for segmentation. The final chapter in this section, by Tversky, Zacks, and Hard (Chapter 17), situates the dynamics of motion paths within a larger pattern that includes goals, causes, and objects. They argue that events have some analogies to objects, scenes, and language, but also some important disanalogies—a point that reinforces the empirical findings of Shipley and Maguire.

The chapters in the second section converge on a clear conclusion: the segmentation of ongoing activity into events is a central component of ongoing perception and cognition, which exerts a strong influence on judgment and memory. Together, the two sections reinforce the notion that goal-directed action is central to human perception. This makes sense: given that perceptual systems are shaped by evolution to produce adaptive action, one would expect perceptual systems to be tuned to processing such actions. The adaptive fit of representations of human action can be seen in the action production system itself, as Georgopoulos and Karageorgiou's chapter reveals. The consequences of goal-directed action for an observer are perceived events, and the rest of the chapters in this part demonstrate the power and elegance with which perceptual systems build event representations.

References

Hommel, B., Muesseler, J., Aschersleben, G., & Prinz, W. (2001). The theory of event coding (TEC): A framework for perception and action planning. *Behavioral & Brain Sciences, 24*(5), 849–937.

Prinz, W. (1997). Perception and action planning. *European Journal of Cognitive Psychology, 9*(2), 129–154.

Section I
Perceiving Action Events

9

Representations of Voluntary Arm Movements in the Motor Cortex and Their Transformations

APOSTOLOS P. GEORGOPOULOS & ELISSAIOS
KARAGEORGIOU

This chapter deals with the neural mechanisms of arm movements in space. Such movements can be made within various behavioral contexts. What, then, makes such a movement "voluntary"? Clearly, reaching to an object of interest is a voluntary motor act, but is arm-swinging during walking, or running for one's life from a predator, voluntary as well? In a way it is not, because, for example, the arms swing while we walk without us intentionally willing them to, and we run away from a predator because our life is in imminent danger and, therefore, we have no choice. However, in both of these cases, we can do otherwise if we choose to do so: we can walk without swinging our arms, and we can stay immobile when the predator approaches. However, there are other movements we can not stop. These are usually the result of brain damage, especially in a group of nuclei within the so-called basal ganglia. For example, people with lesions of the subthalamic nucleus, a small nucleus in the basal ganglia, frequently move their arm without willing it to move in wild, throwing motions—a condition called hemiballismus—and the various dyskinesias consist of movements of body parts that happen without the patient willing them to and also with the patient being unable to stop them. Therefore, these movements are called involuntary.

Strangely, the best definition of voluntary movement seems to be "the opposite of involuntary movement"—that is, a movement that can be suppressed (or not initiated at all) at will. This comes from the fact that involuntary movements are well defined and possess the cardinal feature of coming and going by themselves, and they can not be suppressed or initiated. This, then, serves as a good background against which to define voluntary movements.

The idea that a movement is "voluntary" if it can be suppressed at will is associated with the observation that neural activity in the motor cortex can change without leading obligatorily to a manifest motor output. In fact, changes in activity during imposed movement delays have been observed in practically all motor structures, including premotor cortical areas, the cerebellum, and the basal ganglia. One could suppose, therefore, that the gating of this central neural activity, so that it remains a "motor speculation," so to speak, without being translated to an overt movement, is the essence of what makes a movement "voluntary." From this it follows that an investigation of the neural mechanisms underlying this gating may lead us to the heart of the problem of the "voluntary" movement.

The study of neural mechanisms underlying intended movements was made possible by the development of a technique that allowed the monitoring of the activity of single cells in the brain of behaving animals: it is obvious that *voluntary* movements can be studied only in an awake, behaving animal. This technique has a fine grain for studying neural activity and has been used successfully during the past 30 years to study the neural mechanisms underlying voluntary movement, perception, and memory. Here we discuss the neural mechanisms of voluntary movements in the motor cortex, a major node in the brain network of initiation and control of such movements. Specifically, we discuss the neural mechanisms of reaching movements in space with respect to the encoding of movement parameters in the activity of single cells and the decoding of information from neuronal populations. This decoding scheme can be used to monitor the processing of movement-related information in various contexts and, ultimately, to drive motor prostheses.

Reaching Movements

Unlike movements about a single joint (e.g., flexion/extension at the elbow), reaching movements typically involve well-coordinated and tightly coupled motions at the shoulder and elbow joints (Soechting & Lacquaniti, 1981) and are usually directed to visual targets. The main function of a reaching movement is to bring the hand from a starting point to a desired position in space. Therefore, the hand movement can be regarded as a vector possessing direction and distance. This definition of the reaching movement, as a relative vector in a polar coordinate space centered on its starting point, is justified by the results of experiments that have shown (a) that pointing errors differ in the direction and amplitude (i.e., distance) domains (Soechting & Flanders,1989), (b) that precueing the direction or distance differentially affects the reaction time (Rosenbaum, 1980), and (c) that the processes of specifying direction and amplitude are dissociable (Favilla, Hening, & Ghez, 1989). Indeed, in accordance with these behavioral observations, it has been found that the neural specification of reaching movements deals separately with direction and amplitude. Changes in neural activity related to the direction of the upcoming movement occur in the motor and parietal cortex during the reaction time (Fu, Flament, Coltz, & Ebner, 1995; Georgopoulos, Kalaska, Caminiti, & Massey, 1982; Kalaska, 1988; Kalaska, Caminiti, & Georgopoulos, 1983; Schwartz, Kettner, & Georgopoulos, 1988), unlike those related to the amplitude of movement, which occur during the movement time (Fu, Suarez, & Ebner, 1993; Fu et al., 1995). Similar early directional effects have been found in the cerebellum (Fortier, Kalaska, & Smith, 1989) and the premotor cortex (Caminiti et al., 1991). How is the direction of an upcoming reaching movement coded in the motor cortex? It turns out that direction is encoded ambiguously in the discharge of single cells but can be decoded unambiguously from the activity of the neuronal population. We illustrate these principles below using data from the motor cortex.

Neural Coding of Direction of Reaching

Encoding in Single-Cell Activity

The activity of single cells varies in an orderly fashion with the direction of reaching (Figs. 9.1, 9.2), such that it is highest for a movement

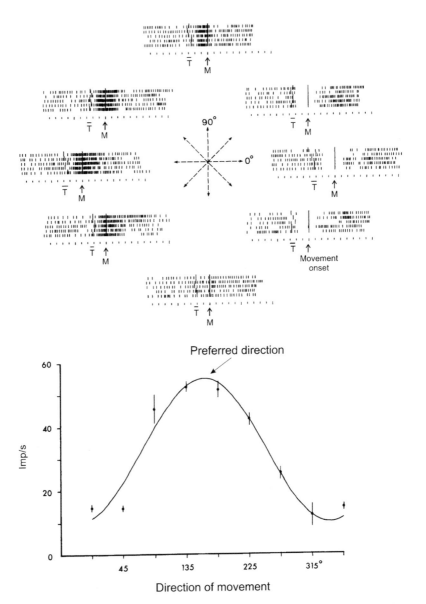

FIGURE 9.1. Directional tuning of a motor cortical cell. Upper panel: Impulse activity during five trials in which equal-amplitude movements were made in eight directions from the center of the working surface toward peripheral targets, as indicated by the diagram in the center. The rasters are aligned to the onset of movement (M). Longer vertical bars preceding movement onset denote the time of stimulus (target) onset; the range of these times is indicated by a horizontal line (T). Lower panel: Directional tuning curve. The average frequency of discharge during the time interval from the onset of the target to the end of the movement is plotted against the direction of the movement. Points are means of five trials ± SEM; the curve is a fitted sinusoidal function. (Adapted from Georgopoulos et al., 1982.)

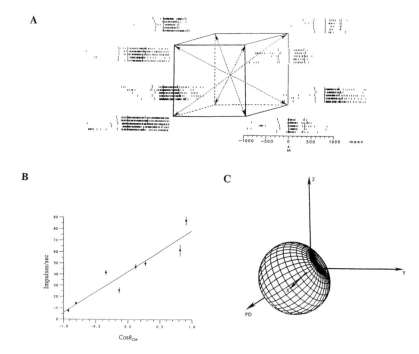

FIGURE 9.2. Directional tuning of a motor cortical cell in 3-D space. (*A*) Five trials of raster activity aligned to the onset of movement (M) (other conventions as in Fig. 9.1). (*B*) Average cell activity from the onset of the target to the end of the movement is plotted against the cosine of the angle 2 between the preferred direction C of the cell and the direction M of the movement. (*C*) Directional tuning volume and preferred direction (PD). (Adapted from Schwartz et al., 1988.)

in a specific direction and decreases progressively with movements in directions farther and farther away from the preferred one. The plot of the cell's average frequency of discharge against the direction of the movement is the *directional tuning* curve. This function has three basic characteristics: (1) it is broad, which means that cell activity varies throughout a range of directions, in both 2-D (Amirikian & Georgopoulos, 2000; Georgopoulos, Caminiti, Kalaska, & Massey, 1982; Kalaska, Cohen, Hyde, & Prud'homme, 1989) and 3-D (Caminiti, Johnson, & Urbano, 1990; Caminiti et al., 1991; Schwartz et al., 1988) space; (2) it is orderly and can be described well by a symmetric tuning function (Amirikian & Georgopoulos, 2000; Georgopoulos et al., 1982; Schwartz et al., 1988); and (3) it is unimodal, which means that there is a direction for which cell activity will be highest (the cell's "preferred direction"); the preferred directions differ for different cells and range throughout the whole directional continuum (Schwartz et al., 1988). It follows from these characteristics of the directional tuning curve that, except at the peak, the directional information provided by cell activity is ambiguous, for the same discharge rate can correspond to two different directions, on either side of the peak.

Cell activity is also modulated by the amplitude of the movement (Fu et al., 1993). The directional tuning is observed during both the reaction time and the movement time, whereas the modulation with movement amplitude is observed mostly during the movement time (Fu et al., 1995). The preferred direction of a cell is usually stable (i.e., it is invariant for different movement amplitudes) (Fu et al., 1993), but it can be influenced by the posture of the arm, as, for example, when the initial position changes (Caminiti et al., 1990) or when the posture is explicitly altered by a special mechanical arrangement (Scott & Kalaska, 1997). These findings indicate an orderly relation between cell activity and spatial movement parameters. This idea was further supported by an analysis of the time course of cell activity to assess the relations of single cell activity to evolving movement parameters, including position, velocity, and acceleration, and to the direction of the target (Ashe & Georgopoulos, 1994). It was found that cell activity was related to all of these parameters, but that target direction and movement velocity were the most important determinants of cell activity.

Decoding from Neuronal Populations

It is obvious that the directional tuning by itself does not provide for a unique coding of the direction of movement at the single-cell level, since the tuning is broad (but not as broad as previously thought; see Amirikian & Georgopoulos, 2000) and the preferred direction can be affected by posture. Any unique information, then, should rely on the neuronal ensemble of directionally tuned cells. The relatively broad directional tuning indicates that a given cell participates in movements of various directions. From this it follows that, conversely, a movement in a particular direction will involve the activation of a whole population of cells. How, then, is the direction of reaching represented in a unique fashion in a population of neurons, each of which is directionally broadly tuned? An unambiguous population code was proposed (Georgopoulos et al., 1983; Georgopoulos, Kettner, & Schwartz, 1988; Georgopoulos, Schwartz, & Kettner, 1986) that regarded the motor cortical command for the direction of reaching as an ensemble of vectors (Fig. 9.3). Each vector represents the contribution of a directionally tuned cell. A particular vector points in the cell's preferred direction and has length proportional to the change in cell activity associated with a particular movement direction; then the vector sum of these weighted cell vectors (the "neuronal population vector," or NPV) points at or near the direction of the movement (Georgopoulos et al., 1983, 1986, 1988). Therefore, information concerning the direction of movement can be unambiguously obtained from the neuronal ensemble.

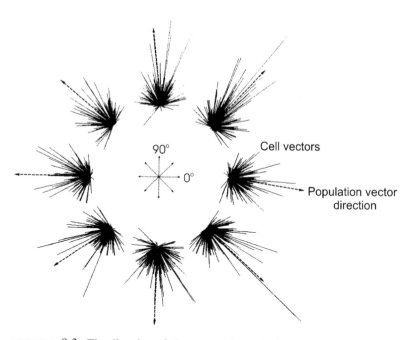

FIGURE 9.3. The direction of the neuronal population vector (NPV, dashed arrows) is shown for eight movement directions in 2-D space. Each cluster represents the directional contributions of 241 directionally tuned cells. The movement directions are shown in the diagram in the center. The population vector points approximately in the direction of the movement. (Adapted from Georgopoulos et al., 1983.)

The NPV possesses several useful characteristics. First, its direction is close to the direction of movement in space (see Fig. 9.3). Second, the calculation of the NPV is a rather simple procedure, for it (a) rests on the directional selectivity of single cells, which is apparent, (b) involves weighting of vectorial contributions by single cells on the basis of the change in cell activity, which is reasonable, and (c) relies on the vectorial summation of these contributions, which is practically the simplest procedure to obtain a unique outcome. In fact, an important aspect of the population vector analysis is that it relies on the directional tuning as defined operationally by the procedures above; no special assumptions are made or required as to how this tuning comes about. Finally, the NPV is robust. It is a distributed code, and as such does not depend exclusively on any particular cell. Its robustness is evidenced by the fact that it can convey a good directional signal with only a small number of cells (Georgopoulos et al., 1988; Salinas & Abbott, 1994). However, a much more important property of the NPV is that it is an unbiased predictor of the direction of movement when the posture of the arm changes (Caminiti et al., 1991; Kettner, Schwartz, & Georgopolous, 1988; see also Fig. 1 in Georgopoulos, 1995), even when the preferred directions of individual cells may change with different movement origins (Caminiti et al., 1990). The NPV then provides posture-free information about the direction of movement in space.

The spatial robustness of the NPV shines when it is used to construct "neural trajectories" of pointing (Georgopoulos et al., 1988) or tracing movements (Schwartz, 1994). In these experiments, monkeys were trained to track a moving light along a predetermined trajectory, such as a spiral, circle, ellipse, or figure eight. The NPV was calculated at short time intervals (e.g., 10 to 20 ms) and strung tip-to-tail to form a neural trajectory (Fig. 9.4; also see color insert). It has been found consistently that this neural trajectory is an excellent predictor of the actual trajectory. The reason for this is twofold: not only does the direction of the instantaneous NPV predict the direction of the movement, but its intensity predicts the instantaneous amplitude of the movement (i.e., speed for a fixed time bin), such that the spatially arranged NPV time series yields the upcoming movement trajectory in space. All of these findings show that accurate and robust information about movement direction can be extracted from an ensemble of directionally tuned neurons in the form of the NPV, which is invariant with respect to the posture of the arm and which, in drawing movements, carries information about the whole trajectory. In fact, this general NPV approach is being used currently to extract information about intended movements, information that has proved very effective in controlling and driving motor prostheses (Hochberg et al., 2006; Schwartz, 2004; Taylor, Tillery, & Schwartz, 2002). In addition, the NPV has been modeled as the time-varying output of a massively interconnected artificial neural network of directionally tuned neurons (Lukashin & Georgopoulos, 1993, 1994a, 1994b). This network has been successfully trained to draw accurate geometric shapes (Fig. 9.5) (Lukashin & Georgopoulos, 1994a).

Processing of Directional Information During Delayed Movement Tasks

Up to now, we have discussed issues and applications related to arm movements in space in the absence of any conditions imposed on their initiation or direction. In this section we deal with neural events under conditions that impose constraints on the upcoming movement. In fact, there are several aspects to *intending* a movement.

The most common case is when a movement is produced as soon as a stimulus appears; then some time intervenes between the occurrence of the stimulus and the beginning of the movement—the traditional reaction time. This time varies depending on the sensory modality of the stimulus and any imposed constraints on the movement, but it usually takes 200 to 300 ms. The reaction time, then, can be regarded as a time during which the movement is *intended.*

In other cases a delay can be imposed so that the movement will be initiated after a period of waiting, while the stimulus is still present. These *instructed delay paradigms* probe a step further into the representation of intended movements. Here there is no immediate motor output while the representation is being kept active.

A specific type of delayed tasks involves movements that have to be produced on the basis of information kept in *memory*. The difference from the instructed delay task is that now the stimulus defining the direction of the movement is turned off after a short period of presentation, and the movement is triggered after a delay by a separate "go"

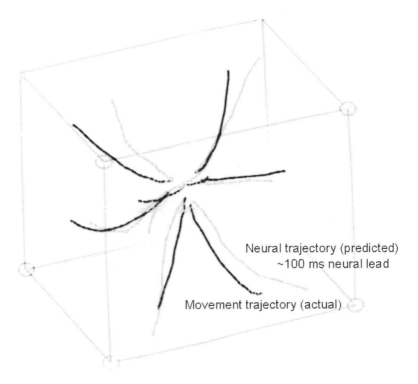

FIGURE 9.4. Neural population vector trajectories (predicted) and actual movement trajectories for eight reaching movements in 3-D space. (Adapted from Georgopoulos et al., 1988.)

signal. Thus, information concerning the intended movement has to be retained during the memorized delay.

These three tasks are illustrated in Figure 9.6. In all three cases, the representation of information about the intended movement can be studied under different conditions that impose different constraints on the system. We sought to identify and visualize the representations during the reaction time, the instructed delay, and the memorized delay periods. Since the information assumed to be represented regards direction, the neuronal population vector could be a useful tool. We computed the population vector every 20 ms (a) during the reaction time (Fig. 9.7) (Georgopoulos, Kalaska, Crutcher, Caminiti, & Massey, 1984; Georgopoulos et al., 1988), (b) during an instructed delay period (Fig. 9.8) (Georgopoulos, Crutcher, & Schwartz, 1989), and (c) during

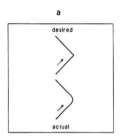
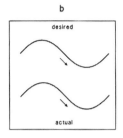
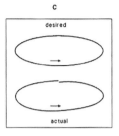

FIGURE 9.5. Plots of desired trajectories and those generated by the artificial neural network. Arrows show directions of tracing. (Adapted from Lukashin & Georgopoulos, 1994a.)

a memorized delay period (Fig. 9.9) (Smyrnis, Taira, Ashe, & Georgopoulos, 1992).

The results were clear: in all these cases the population vector pointed in the direction of the intended movement during the above time periods. In the instructed delay experiments, monkeys were trained to withhold the movement for a period of time after the onset of a visual cue signal and to move later in response to a "go" signal. During this instructed delay period the population vector in the motor cortex, computed every 20 ms, gave a reliable signal concerning the direction of the movement that was triggered later for execution (see Fig. 9.8) (Georgopoulos, Crutcher, et al., 1989). In the memorized delay experiments (Smyrnis et al., 1992), monkeys were trained to move a handle on a 2-D working surface in directions specified by a light on the plane. They first moved the handle to a light in the center of the plane and then moved the handle in the direction indicated by a peripheral light (cue signal). The signal to move (go signal) was given by turning off the center light. In the nondelay task, the peripheral light was turned on at the same time as the center light went off. In the memorized delay task, the peripheral light stayed on for 300 ms (cue period) and the center light was turned off 450 to 750 ms later (delay period). Finally, in the nonmemorized delay task, the peripheral light stayed on continuously, whereas the center light went off 750 to 1,050 ms after the peripheral light came on. Recordings in the arm area of the motor cortex (N = 171 cells) showed changes in single-cell activity in all tasks. The population vector was calculated every 20 ms, following the onset of the peripheral light.

Task without delay

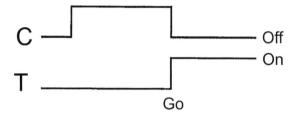

Task with memorized delay

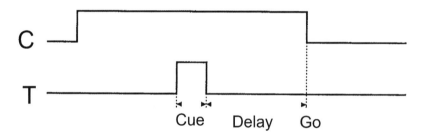

Task with instructed delay

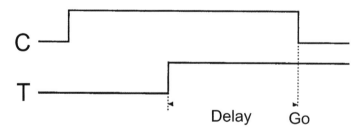

FIGURE 9.6. Schematic diagram of three reaching tasks with and without delays. C, center stimulus; T, target stimulus; Go, signal to move. (Adapted from Smyrnis et al., 1992.)

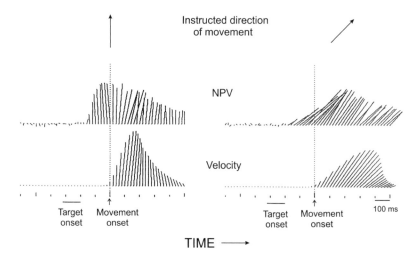

FIGURE 9.7. The neuronal population vector (NPV) points in the direction of movement well before the movement begins. The results for two movement directions in 2-D space are illustrated (top); the population vector was calculated every 20 ms (middle); the average instantaneous (20 ms bin) velocity of the movement is also shown (bottom). Before the target onset, the population vector is very small in length and its direction varies from moment to moment. Well before the onset of movement, it increases in length, and its direction points to the direction of the upcoming movement. This finding suggests that even the earliest inputs to the motor cortex are relevant to the direction of the upcoming movement. (Adapted from Georgopoulos et al., 1984.)

We were interested in two aspects of the information carried by the population vector. One concerns its direction, which can be interpreted as the directional information carried by the directional signal. The other aspect concerns the length of the population vector, which can be regarded as the strength of the directional signal. The direction of the population vector during the memorized delay period was close to the direction of the target (see Fig. 9.9). It is interesting that the population vector length was similar in the cue period but was longer during the memorized than during the nonmemorized part of the delay. This is shown in Figure 9.10, which illustrates the time course of the length of the population vector in the two delay tasks.

Three phases can be distinguished in this time course. First, there is an initial increase of the vector length during the 300 ms of the delay period, which started approximately 100 ms following the cue onset

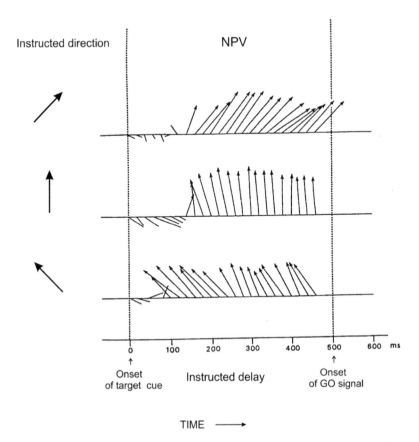

FIGURE 9.8. Time evolution of the neuronal population vector (NPV) during an instructed delay period. Results from three directions are illustrated. (Adapted from Georgopoulos, Crutcher, et al., 1989.)

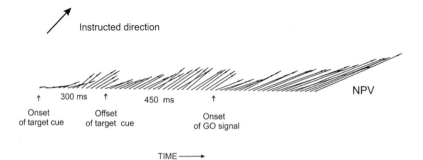

FIGURE 9.9. Neuronal population vectors (NPVs) in the memorized delay task for the direction indicated are plotted every 20 ms. (Adapted from Smyrnis et al., 1992.)

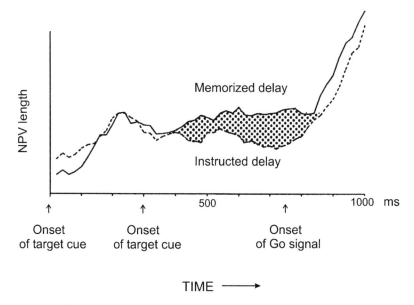

FIGURE 9.10. Length of mean resultant of the neuronal population vector (NPV) is plotted against time for two delay tasks. (Adapted from Smyrnis et al., 1992.)

and peaked at 250 ms; this increase is similar for both tasks. We interpret this initial peak as reflecting an encoding process. Second, this increase subsides during the rest of the nonmemorized delay period but continues at a somewhat higher level during the memorized delay period; the latter difference is indicated in Figure 9.10 by stippling. We interpret this as reflecting a holding-in-memory process. Finally, there is a steep increase in the population vector length following the go signal, at the end of the delay period. Thus the memorized task is distinguished from the nonmemorized one by the higher population signal during that part of the delay period in which the instructed direction had to be kept in memory. The directional information carried by the population vector in the memorized delay task identifies the memorized information in a direct fashion. Moreover, this analysis provided an insight concerning the time course of encoding and holding directional information.

These findings are interesting because the increase in the signal during the memorized delay period was observed in the absence of the target; however, one would have expected that the signal would be stronger in the presence rather than in the absence of the visual stimulus. This finding strengthens our interpretation of this increase as a memory signal, in contrast to a sensory one, and raises the more general possibility that the motor cortex may be particularly involved when only part of the visual information about an upcoming movement is provided.

In summary, these findings underscore the usefulness of the population vector analysis as a tool for visualizing representations of the intended movement and show that in the presence or absence of an immediate motor output, as well as when the directional information has to be kept in memory, the direction of the intended movement is represented in a dynamic form at the ensemble level. These results also document the involvement of the motor cortex in the representation of intended movements under various behavioral conditions.

Neural Processing of Directional Transformations

Motor Mental Rotation

In the delayed tasks described above, the movement to be made is unequivocally defined in the sense that its direction is determined by the location of a stimulus relative to the starting point. In that situation, the visual information concerning direction is used to generate the appropriate motor command to implement a movement in that direction; this movement direction has to be generated and kept available during the delay period, but it is defined from the beginning. Therefore, the direction of the intended movement is the same throughout the various times considered above. A very different situation was created in an experiment (Georgopoulos & Massey, 1987) in which the direction of the movement to be made had to be determined freshly on every trial according to a specific rule, namely that the movement direction be at an angle (counterclockwise [CCW] or clockwise [CW]) from the stimulus direction. This experiment takes us away from the case of a *fixed* motor intention; instead, this intention now has to be derived as the solution to the problem. In fact, there are many ways in which this problem can be solved (discussed in Georgopoulos & Massey, 1987). An obvious way would be to form a look-up table that contains the movement directions that correspond to the stimulus directions. Using this strategy, one would simply memorize the corresponding directions in the table and, given a stimulus direction, one would search the table to select the movement direction corresponding to the particular stimulus direction. Of course, one would not have to use numbers but simply imagine directed radii in a unit circle.

A different strategy would be to mentally rotate the stimulus direction in the instructed departure (CCW or CW) by an amount equal to the required angular shift. The look-up table and mental rotation hypotheses lead to different predictions concerning how the reaction time would change, and on this basis they can be distinguished. If the look-up table strategy is followed, the reaction time would reflect the time taken for the search, but it should not be greater for larger angles, because there is no reason to suppose that searching the table in the case of a large angle should take more time than when searching the table in the case of a small angle. In contrast, the mental rotation hypothesis predicts an increase of the reaction time with the angle because the time to be taken to rotate a radius through an angle should be proportional to the angle itself. Indeed, the results of the experiments in human subjects (Georgopoulos & Massey, 1987) showed an increase of the reaction time with the angle (Fig. 9.11), and therefore supported the mental rotation hypothesis. The average rate of the hypothesized rotation was approximately 400 deg/s. Remarkably, this is very close to the value obtained by Shepard and Cooper (1982) in experiments of mental rotation of visual images.

Another similarity in the motor rotation (Georgopoulos & Massey, 1987) and visual rotation (Shepard & Cooper, 1982) studies is that there is appreciable diversity in the rotation rates obtained among different subjects. In fact, we used this feature to test the idea that motor and visual mental rotation processes may be associated: indeed, a significant correlation was found between the two rotation rates in a group of subjects who performed both tasks (Pellizzer & Georgopoulos, 1993). This suggests that the two processes might share a common stage, or that both processes involve similar constraints.

The neural mechanisms underlying the process of mental rotation in the movement domain were investigated by training monkeys to move a handle 90 degrees CCW from a reference direction ("transformation" task); these trials were intermixed with others in which the animals

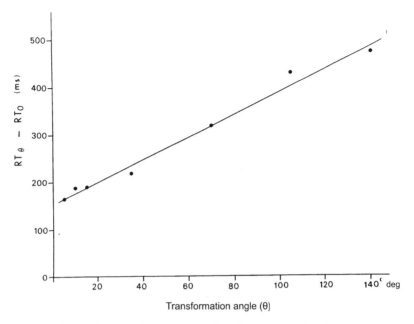

FIGURE 9.11. Average changes in reaction time between the visuomotor spatial transformation task (RT_θ) and the control task (RT_0) are plotted against the instruction angle (clockwise departure). (Adapted from Georgopoulos & Massey, 1987.)

moved in the direction of the target ("direct" task). The neural activity in the arm area of the motor cortex was analyzed at the single-cell and neuronal population levels. We found the following. The changes in the activity of single cells in the direct task were related to the direction of movement, as described previously (Georgopoulos et al., 1982). The cell activity also changed in the transformation task, but there were no cells that changed activity exclusively in this task. Therefore, at the level of the motor cortex, the required transformation did not seem to involve a separate neuronal ensemble. The patterns of single-cell activity in the transformation task frequently differed from those observed in the direct task when the stimulus or the movement was the same. More specifically, cells could not be consistently classified as "movement" or "stimulus" related, for frequently the activity of a particular cell would seem "movement-related" for a particular stimulus–movement combination, "stimulus-related" for another combination, or unrelated to either movement or stimulus for still another combination. Thus, no obvious insight could be gained from such an analysis of single-cell activity. However, an analysis of the activity of the neuronal population using the time evolution of the NPV revealed an orderly rotation of the NPV from the direction of the stimulus toward the direction of the movement through the 90-degree CCW angle (Fig. 9.12) (Georgopoulos, Lurito, Petrides, Schwartz, & Massey, 1989; Lurito, Georgakopoulos, & Georgopoulos, 1991).

Several points of interest in this analysis were surprising. First, there was no a priori reason to expect that the population vector would point to any direction other than the direction of the movement, on the simple hypothesis that the motor cortex is involved only in the production of movement. Our interpretation of the population vector, as the directional motor intention, suggests that in the transformation task the motor intention is not restricted to the movement direction but occupies intermediate directions during the reaction time. Second, there was no a priori reason to expect that the population vector would shift in an orderly fashion in the CCW direction, for no explicit instruction was given to the animals to that effect. The results obtained suggest that the directional motor intention spanned the smallest angle. This could, presumably, minimize the time and computational load involved in the required transformation. It is interesting to note that the rotation rates (direction of population vector versus time) observed (Lurito et al., 1991) were very similar to the rates (increase in reaction time versus angle) observed in the human studies (Georgopoulos & Massey, 1987). Thus, the dynamic processing of a directional transformation was successfully visualized using the NPV analysis.

Finally, the hypothesis was tested that this apparent rotation of the population vector could be the result of activation of two subsets of cells, one with preferred directions at or near the stimulus direction and another with preferred directions around the direction of movement: if cells of the former type were recruited at the beginning of the reaction time, followed by those of the second type, then the vector sum of the two could provide the rotating population vector. However, such a preferential activation of "stimulus-direction" centered and "movement-direction" centered cells was not observed. On the other hand, a true rotation of the population vector could be reflected in the engagement

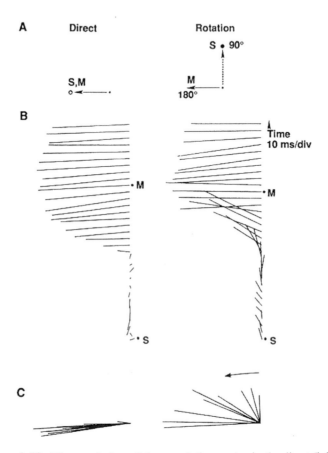

FIGURE 9.12. Time evolution of the population vector in the direct (left) and mental rotation (right) tasks. (A) Task. Unfilled and filled circles indicate dim and bright light, respectively. Interrupted and continuous arrows indicate stimulus (S) and movement (M) direction, respectively. (B) Neuronal population vectors calculated every 10 ms from the onset of the stimulus (S) at positions shown in (A) until after the onset of the movement (M). When the population vector lengthens, for the direct case (left) it points in the direction of the movement, whereas for the rotation case it points initially in the direction of the stimulus and then rotates counterclockwise (from 12 o'clock to 9 o'clock) and points in the direction of the movement. (C) Ten successive population vectors from (B) are shown in a spatial plot, starting from the first population vector that increased significantly in length. Notice the counterclockwise rotation of the population vector (right panel of [C]). (Adapted from Georgopoulos, Lurito, et al., 1989.)

of cells with intermediate preferred directions during the middle of the reaction time. Indeed, such a transient increase in the recruitment of cells with intermediate (i.e., between the stimulus and movement) preferred directions during the middle of the reaction time was observed (Fig. 9.13). This supports the idea of a true rotation of the population signal. Finally, a rotation of the population vector through several angles, including 180 degrees, has been described in a different context (Wise, di Pellegrino, & Boussaoud, 1996).

Motor Memory Scanning

When a sequence of events is predictable, it would be possible to plan a motor movement to an anticipated stimulus appearance, and thus the

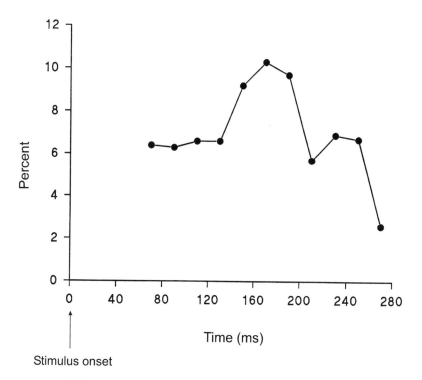

FIGURE 9.13. Transient increase during the middle of the response time of the recruitment of cells with preferred directions at or near the intermediate direction between the direction of the stimulus and the direction of the movement. Data points are centered on the middle of 20 ms bins. (Adapted from Lurito et al., 1991.)

movement would be made in a direction away from a stimulus direction based on a temporal, serial order rule (Pellizzer et al., 1995). This is a very different rule from the spatial one applied to the task described in the preceding section. Thus, in these two tasks, movements were made away from a reference stimulus direction (and at the same angular difference), but following two different rules: one that was tied to the direction of the reference stimulus and another that was tied to the serial order of the reference stimuli. It was found that the neural coding mechanisms of these two transformations of movement direction were very different.

Two monkeys were trained to perform the following motor memory scanning task: A list of two to five stimuli was presented on a circle every 0.65 s at pseudorandom locations; when one of them (except the last) changed color (test stimulus), the monkeys made a motor response toward the next light in the sequence. It is obvious that, unlike in the mental rotation task, in this task the direction of the motor response bears no consistent relation to the direction of the test (reference) stimulus. Instead, this task seems to involve a memory-scanning process in which list directions are searched until the test one is identified and the next one in the sequence selected. This kind of process was suggested by the results of early experiments in the visual domain (Sternberg, 1969) and of later experiments in the motor field (Georgopoulos & Lurito, 1991)—namely, that the response time increases as a linear function of the number of list stimuli. Indeed, this relation was also present in the monkey performance (Carpenter, Pellizzer, & Georgopoulos, 1996). The question, then, is, what are the neural mechanisms of this memory scanning process? The results of neurophysiological studies in the motor cortex (Pellizzer, Sargent, & Georgopoulos, 1995) showed that the basic element of these mechanisms involves an abrupt (approximately 40 ms) switching between the directions being searched. This was evident both at the single-cell and population levels. Specifically, single cells showed an abrupt change in activity from the pattern associated with the direction of test stimulus to that associated with the direction of the motor response (see, for an example, Figs. 2 through 4 in Pellizzer et al., 1995). At the ensemble level, the neuronal population vector switched abruptly from test to the motor direction. The difference between the neural mechanisms of this task and that of mental rotation above was further exemplified by

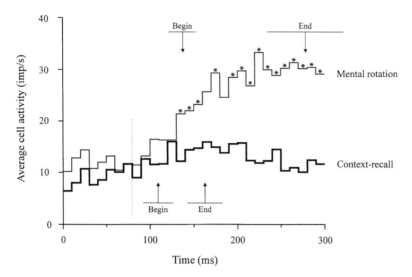

FIGURE 9.14. Peristimulus time histograms (10 ms binwidth) of the activity of cells with preferred direction at the intermediate direction (10 degrees) between the stimulus and movement directions in the mental rotation task (Lurito et al., 1991), and between the test stimulus (second stimulus in a sequence of three stimuli) and motor response (third stimulus) in the context/recall task (Pellizzer et al., 1995). In the mental rotation task, the activity of such cells (thin line) increased by more than threefold, whereas in the context/recall task cell activity remained almost constant (bold line). (*Source*: Pellizzer et al., 1995.)

analyzing the activity of cells with preferred directions intermediate between the stimulus and the movement. As discussed above, these cells were recruited selectively during the response time in the mental rotation task. In contrast, they were not engaged in the memory scanning task. This is shown in Figure 9.14. Therefore, the mental rotation and memory scanning tasks involve fundamentally different kinds of mechanisms (slow rotation versus abrupt switching), both of which were identified, remarkably, within the same (proximal arm) area of the motor cortex.

Acknowledgments

This work was supported by U.S. Public Health Service grant NS17413, the Department of Veterans Affairs, and the American Legion Chair in Brain Sciences.

References

Amirikian, B., & Georgopoulos, A. P. (2000). Directional tuning profiles of motor cortical cells. *Neuroscience Research, 36*, 73–79.

Ashe, J., & Georgopoulos, A. P. (1994). Movement parameters and neuronal activity in motor cortex and area 5. *Cerebral Cortex, 6*, 590–600.

Caminiti, R., Johnson, P. B., Galli, C., Ferraina, S., Burnod, Y., & Urbano, A. (1991). Making arm movements within different parts of space: The premotor and motor cortical representation of a coordinate system for reaching at visual targets. *Journal of Neuroscience, 11*, 1182–1197.

Caminiti, R., Johnson, P. B., & Urbano, A. (1990). Making arm movements within different parts of space: Dynamic aspects in the primate motor cortex. *Journal of Neuroscience, 10*, 2039–2058.

Carpenter, A. F., Pellizzer, G., & Georgopoulos, A. P. (1996). Context-recall memory scanning in two primate species. *Society of Neuroscience Abstracts, 22*, 1382.

Favilla, M., Hening, W., & Ghez, C. (1989). Trajectory control in targeted force impulses. VI. Independent specification of response amplitude and direction. *Experimental Brain Research, 75*, 280–294.

Fortier, P. A., Kalaska, J. F., & Smith, A. M. (1989). Cerebellar neuronal activity related to whole-arm reaching movements in the monkey. *Journal of Neurophysiology, 62*, 198–211.

Fu, Q.-G., Suarez, J. I., & Ebner, T. J. (1993). Neuronal specification of direction and distance during reaching movements in the superior precentral premotor area and primary motor cortex of monkeys. *Journal of Neurophysiology, 70*, 2097–2116.

Fu, Q.-G., Flament, D., Coltz, J. D., & Ebner, T. J. (1995). Temporal coding of movement kinematics in the discharge of primary motor and premotor neurons. *Journal of Neurophysiology, 73*, 836–854.

Georgopoulos, A. P. (1995) Current issues in directional motor control. *Trends in Neuroscience, 18*, 506–510.

Georgopoulos, A. P., Caminiti, R., Kalaska, J. F., & Massey, J. T. (1983). Spatial coding of movement: A hypothesis concerning the coding of movement direction by motor cortical populations. *Experimental Brain Research Supplement, 7*, 327–336.

Georgopoulos, A. P., Crutcher, M. D., & Schwartz, A. B. (1989). Cognitive spatial motor processes. 3. Motor cortical prediction of movement direction during an instructed delay period. *Experimental Brain Research, 75*, 183–194.

Georgopoulos, A. P., Kalaska, J. F., Caminiti, R., & Massey, J. T. (1982). On the relations between the direction of two-dimensional arm movements and cell discharge in primate motor cortex. *Journal of Neuroscience, 2*, 1527–1537.

Georgopoulos, A. P., Kalaska, J. F., Crutcher, M. D., Caminiti, R., & Massey, J. T. (1984). The representation of movement direction in the motor cortex: Single cell and population studies. In G. M. Edelman, W. M. Cowan, & W. E. Gall (Eds.), *Dynamic aspects of neocortical function* (pp. 501–524). New York: Wiley.

Georgopoulos, A. P., Kettner, R. E., & Schwartz, A. B. (1988). Primate motor cortex and free arm movements to visual targets in three-dimensional space.

II. Coding of the direction of movement by a neuronal population. *Journal of Neuroscience, 8,* 2928–2937.

Georgopoulos, A. P., & Lurito, J. T. (1991). Cognitive spatial-motor processes. 6. Visuomotor memory scanning. *Experimental Brain Research, 83,* 453–458.

Georgopoulos, A. P., Lurito, J., Petrides, M., Schwartz, A. B., & Massey, J. T. (1989). Mental rotation of the neuronal population vector. *Science, 243,* 234–236.

Georgopoulos, A. P., & Massey, J. T. (1987). Cognitive spatial-motor processes. 1. The making of movements at various angles from a stimulus direction. *Experimental Brain Research, 65,* 361–370.

Georgopoulos, A. P., Schwartz, A. B., & Kettner, R. E. (1986). Neuronal population coding of movement direction. *Science, 233,* 1416–1419.

Hochberg, L. R., Serruya, M. D., Friehs, G. M., Mukand, J. A., Saleh, M., Caplan, A. H., et al. (2006). Neuronal ensemble control of prosthetic devices by a human with tetraplegia. *Nature, 442,* 164–171.

Kalaska, J. F. (1988). The representation of arm movements in postcentral and parietal cortex. *Canadian Journal of Physiology and Pharmacology, 66,* 455–463.

Kalaska, J. F., Caminiti, R., & Georgopoulos, A. P. (1983). Cortical mechanisms related to the direction of two-dimensional arm movements: Relations in parietal area 5 and comparison with motor cortex. *Experimental Brain Research, 51,* 247–260.

Kalaska, J. F., Cohen, D. A. D., Hyde, M. L., & Prud'homme, M. (1989). A comparison of movement direction-related versus load direction-related activity in primate motor cortex, using a two-dimensional reaching task. *Journal of Neuroscience, 9,* 2080–2102.

Kettner, R. E., Schwartz, A. B., & Georgopoulos, A. P. (1988). Primate motor cortex and free arm movements to visual targets in three-dimensional space. III. Positional gradients and population coding of movement direction from various movement origins. *Journal of Neuroscience, 8,* 2938–2947.

Lukashin, A. V., & Georgopoulos, A. P. (1993). A dynamical neural network model for motor cortical activity during movement: Population coding of movement trajectories. *Biological Cybernetics, 69,* 517–524.

Lukashin, A. V., & Georgopoulos, A. P. (1994a). A neural network for coding of trajectories by time series of neuronal population vectors. *Neural Computation, 6,* 19–28.

Lukashin, A. V., & Georgopoulos, A. P. (1994b). Directional operations in the motor cortex modeled by a network of spiking neurons. *Biological Cybernetics, 71,* 79–85.

Lurito, J. L., Georgakopoulos, T., & Georgopoulos, A. P. (1991). Cognitive spatial-motor processes. 7. The making of movements at an angle from a stimulus direction: Studies of motor cortical activity at the single cell and population levels. *Experimental Brain Research, 87,* 562–580.

Pellizzer, G., & Georgopoulos, A. P. (1993). Common processing constraints for visuomotor and visual mental rotations. *Experimental Brain Research, 93,* 165–172.

Pellizzer, G., Sargent, P., & Georgopoulos, A. P. (1995). Motor cortical activity in a context-recall task. *Science, 269,* 702–705.

Rosenbaum, D. A. (1980). Human movement initiation: Specification of arm, direction, and extent. *Journal of Experimental Psychology: General, 109,* 444–474.

Salinas, E., & Abbott, L. F. (1994). Vector reconstruction from firing rates. *Journal of Computers in Neuroscience, 1,* 89–107.

Schwartz, A. B. (1994). Direct cortical representation of drawing. *Science, 265,* 540–542.

Schwartz, A. B. (2004). Cortical neural prosthetics. *Annual Review of Neuroscience, 27,* 487–507.

Schwartz, A. B., Kettner, R. E., & Georgopoulos, A. P. (1988). Primate motor cortex and free arm movements to visual targets in three-dimensional space. I. Relations between single cell discharge and direction of movement. *Journal of Neuroscience, 8,* 2913–2927.

Scott, S. H., & Kalaska, J. F. (1997). Reaching movements with similar hand paths but different arm orientations. I. Activity of individual cells in motor cortex. *Journal of Neurophysiology, 77,* 826–852.

Shepard, R. N., & Cooper, L. (1982). *Mental images and their transformations.* Cambridge, MA: MIT Press.

Smyrnis, N., Taira, M., Ashe J., & Georgopoulos, A. P. (1992) Motor cortical activity in a memorized delay task. *Experimental Brain Research, 92,* 139–151.

Soechting, J. F., & Flanders, M. (1989). Sensorimotor representations for pointing to targets in three-dimensional space. *Journal of Neurophysiology, 62,* 582–594.

Soechting, J. F., & Lacquaniti, F. (1981). Invariant characteristics of a pointing movement in man. *Journal of Neuroscience, 1,* 710–720.

Sternberg, S. (1969). Memory-scanning: Mental processes revealed by reaction-time experiments. *American Scientist, 54,* 421–457.

Taylor, D. M., Tillery, S. I., & Schwartz, A. B. (2002). Direct cortical control of 3D neuroprosthetic devices. *Science, 296,* 1829–1832.

Wise, S. P., di Pellegrino, G., & Boussaoud, D. (1996). The premotor cortex and nonstandard sensorimotor mapping. *Canadian Journal of Physiology and Pharmacology, 74,* 469–482.

10

Events and Actions as Dynamically Molded Spatiotemporal Objects: A Critique of the Motor Theory of Biological Motion Perception

GEOFFREY P. BINGHAM & EMILY A. WICKELGREN

In this chapter we describe an approach to event recognition that treats events as spatiotemporal objects whose specific form is generated by underlying dynamics. This approach is inspired, in part, by advances in the theory of the control and coordination of human and robotic actions. These theories of embodied action show that motor commands are not responsible for the essential forms of motion that are characteristic of identifiable modes of action such as bipedal walking and running. We review these developments and a series of research studies that demonstrate that trajectory forms can be detected by human observers and used as information for event recognition. We then turn to recent papers advocating a motor theory of biological motion perception, and we review and critique the arguments made for such an approach. We conclude that a motor code can not really provide very much information about recognizable biological events, because motor commands do not determine the identifiable forms of such events. Instead, we advocate a direct realist approach to event recognition. We note that this discussion is reminiscent of the debates between direct realists and motor theorists of speech perception that took place 20 years ago.

Walking is Pendulums and Running is a Bouncing Ball

In visual event recognition studies, perceptionists investigate optic flow information generated by motion in events and detected by the visual system, which uses motion to recognize different kinds of events and specific properties of those events. Human observers are known to be able to recognize a wide variety of events ranging from bouncing balls, splashing water, and trees blowing in the wind to various animate events, including human actions like walking, dancing, running, or doing gymnastics. All these events are recognized easily and rapidly. Human action events are particularly complex and may be highly variable (for instance, dancing), so the ready ability to recognize such events has justifiably attracted considerable attention.

Among studies on biological motion, those by Todd (1983) are particularly instructive. Todd attempted to discover the information that enables observers to recognize and distinguish bipedal walking and running. Todd took a strictly kinematic approach. He recorded actual human walking and running movements and used the kinematics (i.e., physical motions) to generate computer displays. He captured each type of movement in terms of motion functions for each of the joints from the hips down. He attempted to discover the most salient function for each event by mixing the functions for different joints to see if judgments would be determined primarily by one or two of the functions— that is, is running recognized primarily in terms of the way the knee joint moves over time? He found, however, that the judgment frequencies tended to reflect the mixing of the functions. The more mixed a display was, the more variable the judgments. The implication was that the whole pattern of movement of all the joints was important in each case, but it was still unclear what distinguished each pattern with respect to other possible patterns. In the end, Todd despaired of ever being able to discover the salient information for each event, because the space of kinematic possibility was simply too large.

Since then, analyses of the organization of walking and of running have revealed that they are distinguished by very well-defined dynamics. Walking is organized as a combination of upright and inverted pendulums (Alexander, 1992; Mcmahon, 1984; Mochon & Mcmahon, 1979). The stance leg performs as an inverted pendulum, while the swing leg is a compound upright pendulum. Running exhibits a bouncing-ball dynamic (Alexander, 1992). The stance leg operates as a pogo stick with an elastic spring dynamic during contact with the ground and a projectile-motion dynamic during the flight phase. The swing leg is again an upright pendulum with a shorter period produced by folding the leg to shorten the pendulum. Understanding of the dynamical structure in each case enabled the development of successful walking and running robots. McGeer (1990) designed a ballistic walker that entailed only the passive pendular dynamics with no controller. Pratt and Pratt (1998) added a controller, which simply perturbs the passive dynamics to achieve greater flexibility of movement while retaining the stability and energy-optimal character of the strictly passive organization.

Human movement scientists in the early 1980s were learning that action systems are organized to take advantage of passive dynamical organizations (e.g., joints controlled as mass springs and pendulums) to produce movements that are both stable and energetically optimal (e.g., Latash, 1993; Winters & Woo, 1990). Raibert (1986) adopted a new design strategy that imitated the organization of human running in its essential dynamical structure. The strategy yielded the first truly effective legged robots. He engineered his machines as hoppers to move with the bouncing-ball dynamic of running. He then organized a controller (that is, a finite-state automaton) around the hopper dynamic. The hopper generated a stable bouncing-ball trajectory. Raibert added sensors to detect the phases of the trajectory—that is, the flight, landing, stance, and liftoff phases. Controllers of the robot's posture and forward speed used the sensor information to perform control during appropriate phases of the trajectory. Posture was adjusted during stance, and leg angle for forward speed control was adjusted during flight.

For the event perceptionist, the most striking aspect of Raibert's running robots is that they look alive. (This can be seen via the URL for the legged robot lab at MIT: http://www.ai.mit.edu/projects/leglab/robots/.) They look like running animals, even though the structure of their legs is unlike that of any animal. Rather than having rotational joints, the legs are composed of cylinders that slid inside of one another to create a pneumatic spring. Nevertheless, when they move, the robots look animate. The essence of recognizable running is clearly the bouncing-ball dynamic and the form of the trajectories generated by this dynamic (Warren, Young, & Lee, 1986). Similarly, the essence of recognizable walking is the pendular dynamic and the form of the trajectories generated by it. The moral of this story is that event perception requires a dynamical approach. The essence of events is their dynamical structure, which, to the extent that events can be recognized, must generate the unique form and structure of their trajectories that allow them to be recognized.

This realization was the foundation of a hypothesis about the information for event recognition that is reviewed in this chapter. The central question is one consistently addressed within the ecological approach to perception: what is the information contained in optic flow that allows events to be visually perceived and recognized? Because events are inherently time extended, the information must likewise be time extended (Bingham, 1995). The significantly temporal as well as spatial character of events has made this an area of investigation that is especially challenging to representationalist (cognitivist or information-processing) approaches (see, e.g., Pylyshyn, 1987) but well suited to information-based approaches. The approach in this chapter is characteristically Gibsonian or ecological. The hypothesis is that events, as objects of perception, are indeed akin to objects (Bingham, 1987, 1995; Bingham, Rosenblum, & Schmidt, 1995; Runeson, 1974). However, whereas objects exhibit spatial forms, events exhibit spatiotemporal forms. The forms of events are those of trajectories. A trajectory consists of variations in position and velocity of a moving point. Trajectories exhibit path shapes and speed profiles along those paths. Such trajectory forms are different in different events. The oscillatory trajectory of a bouncing ball is quite different from that, for instance, of a manually oscillated hammer being used to hammer in a nail (Bingham et al., 1995). If trajectory forms are event specific, then trajectory forms might be used to recognize events, just as the shapes of objects can be used to recognize them. Again, the hypothesis is that trajectory forms provide information that allows events to be recognized. A trajectory form consists of both the path shape and the shape of the velocity profile of moving points in an event.

Events and Dynamics

Runeson (1977) argued that the physical dynamics responsible for generating the motions in an event produce unique kinematic (or motion) properties that enable observers who detect those motions to perceive corresponding dynamic properties of the events. Runeson developed this idea, which he called kinematic specification of dynamics (KSD), in the context of his work on perception of the mass of objects in collision events and on perception of the amounts of weight in a human lifting event (Runeson, 1977; Runeson & Frykholm, 1981, 1983). These are examples of the scaling problem in visual perception: how can a spatiotemporal optical pattern, which is angular (and therefore only time-dimensioned), provide information about scale properties in events other than time (e.g., distance, size, mass)? Subsequent studies showed that the timing of readily identified gravitationally governed events (pendular events, balls rolling downhill, bouncing balls, falling water, walking dogs, etc.) provides information allowing the size and distance of objects in the events to be judged (Jokisch & Troje, 2003; McConnell, Muchisky, & Bingham, 1998; Pittenger, 1985, 1990; Stappers & Waller, 1993; Twardy & Bingham, 2002; Watson, Banks, von Hofsten, & Royden, 1992). The solution revealed by these studies is that the underlying event dynamics uniquely couples spatial and temporal properties in events so that one can provide information about the other—that is, timing can provide information about spatial scale. This solution is also characteristically Gibsonian or ecological because information in this approach is law-governed. The idea is that natural laws yield the invariance that is required if information is to be reliable and informative. Dynamics is lawful.

Bingham (1995) extended Runeson's treatment of scaling problems in perception to address the problem of event recognition. Bingham et al. (1995) showed that simple events consisting of a single moving point could be distinguished and recognized using trajectory forms. Observers discriminated a freely bouncing object from one moved by hand. A freely swinging object was discriminated from one moved by hand. Furthermore, each event was recognized and, in particular, correctly identified as animate or inanimate. Other, more complex events were similarly recognized (for instance, wind-blown objects, objects moving in liquid that was stirred or splashed, a kicked ball, a ball rolling downhill). Furthermore, the trajectory forms of many of these events were asymmetric and orientation specific with respect to gravity. Bingham et al. (1995) found that when such trajectory forms were inverted, the events were no longer recognized. Similarly, observers have failed to recognize human walking when the event kinematics were inverted (Pavlova & Sokolov, 2000; Sumi, 1984). Bingham et al. (1995) also tested the effect of changes in the relative orientation of observers and events by having inverted observers judge upright event kinematics. In this case, the events were correctly identified. Finally, Shipley (2003) tested whether the effect of inversion on point-light walkers was due to the change in the characteristic posture and thus the structure of the biological object in the displays or instead due to the motion forms. Shipley tested point-light displays of people walking on their hands. Upright displays were well recognized, but inverted displays were not. Shipley concluded that inversion of the motion forms, not the object structure, caused the disruption. These results show that the events are perceived using the forms of motion as information defined relative to the generative dynamical context—that is, the downward gravitational force.

The trajectory forms of events are specific to the dynamics that deterministically generate them. If the dynamics are specific to the type of event, then trajectory forms can provide information about event types that would allow them to be recognized. Bingham et al. (1995) provided evidence that events are perceptually taxonomized in terms of the types of underlying generative dynamics.

Trajectory Forms in 3-D Perspective: Path Shape and Speed Profile

These studies provide some evidence that human observers are sensitive to trajectory forms and are able to use them to recognize events. A number of questions remain. First, trajectory forms can vary in two ways. One way is for the form of the speed profile along a given path of motion to vary. The other is for the form of the path of motion to vary for a given speed profile. Are observers sensitive to both dimensions of variation of trajectory forms? Second, trajectory forms are properties of events that must be projected into optic flow to be detected by the visual system. What are the optic flow variables, and how are the two aspects of trajectory forms—path and speed—mapped into those variables? Third, the trajectory forms of events map into spatiotemporal optical patterns via perspective projections, and thus the forms are subject to perspective distortions just as the shapes of objects are when projected into optical images. Does event recognition exhibit constancy—that is, does a given trajectory form allow an event to be recognized correctly when it is viewed from different 3-D perspectives? These questions have been addressed in a series of studies.

Muchisky and Bingham (2002) showed that adults can use the information in the speed profile of a nonlinear oscillator to recognize the event. In the experiment, an object oscillated along a straight path in a frontoparallel plane. Thresholds for both asymmetric (skewed like a parallelogram) and symmetric (more rectangular or diamond-shaped) variations in the round form of a phase space trajectory were measured, as well as the ability to use the corresponding forms to reliably recognize the corresponding events. Thresholds were found to be comparable to those established for velocity discrimination, and observers were able to use the forms to recognize events.

Wickelgren and Bingham (2001) showed that 8-month-old infants discriminated differences in trajectory forms. Infants were shown patch-light displays of events that were asymmetric in time. A patch-light ball sitting on one side of a display was hit (by an invisible pool stick) and rolled across the display to a stop at the opposite side. Visible patches on the surface of invisible water were suddenly perturbed by an invisible object splashing into the water, that then gradually settled in a damped oscillatory motion. Each of these two events looked distinctly different to adults when shown in reverse as negentropic events (that is, energy was magically gained rather than dissipated). Infants habituated to the forward events and then dishabituated to the reverse events. The only thing changed was the temporal orientation of the temporally asymmetric trajectory forms. (The spatial content and timing was the same because all the frames of the displays were the same; only the order was reversed.) Likewise, infants who were habituated to the reverse events dishabituated when shown the forward events. The infants failed to dishabituate to control events that were symmetric in time, so when they dishabituated to the experimental displays, it was really the change in trajectory form that did it.

Wickelgren and Bingham (2001) found no evidence that the infants were sensitive to the impossibility of the negentropic events. There were no differences in the looking times or time course of habituation, even though the negentropic events looked bizarre and thus were curious and interesting to adult observers. At that age, the infants seemed to be sensitive to the source of information (that is, trajectory forms), but they were not yet sensitive to the entropic invariance of events. Presumably, greater experience of events is required for children to develop sensitivity to the aspects of events reflecting lawful energy flows.

These first two studies involved only a single perspective on events with motion in a frontoparallel plane. Wickelgren and Bingham (2004) showed that adults can use the information present in the speed profile of an event to recognize the same event when viewed from different perspectives. Participants viewed an object oscillating along a straight path in a frontoparallel plane with one of five different speed profiles and identified which event they were viewing. Then, the same events were viewed from a perspective looking along the straight path extending away in depth, so that the object moved toward and away from the observer. The perspective change incurred large perspective distortions in the trajectory forms. At the same time, the optical variables changed from rigid image translation to nonrigid image expansion and contraction (Johansson, 1950, referred to these as common and relative motion components, respectively). Participants continued to be able to recognize the events despite these changes. When the path of motion was viewed from an oblique angle, the perspective distortions were carried simultaneously by both optical variables—that is, image translation and expansion/contraction—and the events were still recognized. Thus, human observers are able to detect speed profiles and use them to recognize events despite projective distortions that can occur with changes in 3-D perspective.

Trajectory forms also vary in respect to path shape. Wickelgren and Bingham (in press) investigated the use of path shape as information about event identity as well as the combination of path shape and speed profile. First, different events were created by varying the shape of the path along which an object traveled at constant speed. Observers became familiar with the events by viewing them from a perspective that placed the paths in a frontoparallel plane. Five shapes were tested, as shown in Figure 10.1. Observers learned to identify these forms as events A to E, respectively, at a reliable rate of over 95% accuracy for all the events. Subsequently, recognition was tested when the events were viewed with the motion in a horizontal plane at eye level (thus extending in depth) to determine the potential effects of perspective distortions. The closed paths were 12.5 cm across and viewed at a distance of 50 cm so significant perspective distortions would occur. Also, again the optical

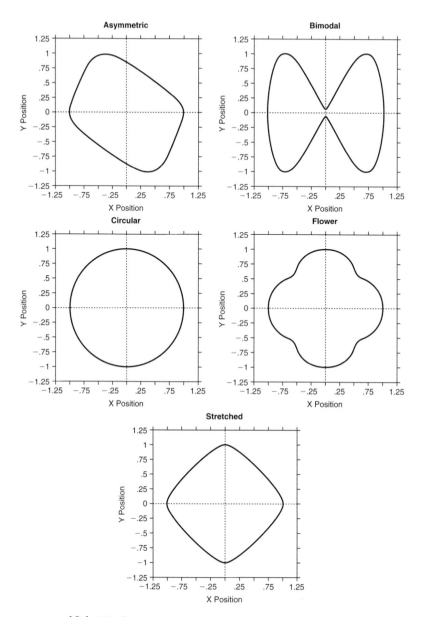

FIGURE 10.1. The five path shapes.

components carrying the trajectory form changed with the change in perspective. In frontoparallel perspective, the path shape is carried by two optical translation components, but not so in 3-D perspective. If To is the optical translation and Eo is the optical expansion/contraction component (Fig. 10.2), then the speed profile is specified by

$$V(t) = D(t) * sqrt[T_0^2(t) + E_0^2(t)] = \gamma * sqrt[T_0^2(t) + E_0^2(t)],$$

where $D(t)$ is the viewing distance. If viewing distance is large (that is, $D \gg \Delta D$, where $\Delta D = D_{max} - D_{min}$ over the course of the event), then $D(t) \approx D_c$ (that is, D constant). At closer distances, $D(t) = D_c = \gamma$ (with γ unknown—that is, assuming distance is unknown) yields perspective distortions, as also discussed and investigated by Wickelgren and Bingham (2004). The path shape requires the direction of motion, $\emptyset(t)$, in addition to the (integrated) speed. The direction is specified by

$$\emptyset(t) = arctan[E_0(t)/T_0(t)].$$

See Wickelgren and Bingham (in press) for derivations. Alternatively, path shape might be specified by the succession of image sizes coupled with the optical positions of those images.

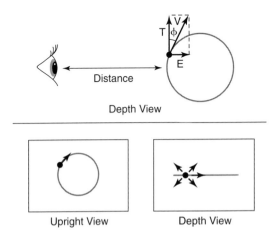

FIGURE 10.2. Viewing geometry indicating the optic flow information for the path and speed profile of an event.

Wickelgren and Bingham found that the events were recognized with an accuracy of 85%. Thus, path shapes can be used to recognize events, and such recognition exhibits constancy. Next, observers were tested with an object moving along a circular path with different speed profiles. The same five speed profiles tested by Wickelgren and Bingham (2004) were used. Previously, they had only been tested along straight paths. Once again, observers were able to recognize the events in 3-D perspective with an accuracy of over 85%.

Finally, both path shapes and speed profiles were varied. Five different path shapes were combined with five different speed profiles to create 25 different events. Observers might perceive each event as a unique integral form, and if so they would have to become familiar with each of the 25 members of the set to be able to recognize the events. In other words, it is possible that path shape and speed profile are detected as integral properties of trajectory forms, but the ability to detect these aspects separately would be more powerful and efficient. Given the availability of both speed and path in the optics, Wickelgren and Bingham expected that observers might be able to perceive these events in terms of these two separable aspects of the form rather than as a single integral form. To test this possibility, they trained observers only with the five path shapes and five speed profiles. Observers were not familiarized with the 25 events composed of these respective subsets. This was as a strong test of the hypothesis that trajectory forms provide information for event recognition because, strictly speaking, observers were not allowed to become familiar with the trajectory form for each event to be recognized. Furthermore, they were familiarized with path shapes and speed profiles viewed from a different 3-D perspective than the one in which recognition was tested. So, again, the question was whether observers would exhibit constancy.

During the training phase, observers were first trained to identify the five speed profiles observed on a circular path viewed in a frontoparallel plane. Next, they were trained to identify the five path shapes observed with a constant speed profile in a frontoparallel plane. Finally, they were tested with all 25 events viewed in depth and asked first to identify each event in terms of path shape and then speed profile. Observers were able to recognize the events, but the recognition accuracy was lower than found in the previous studies. Path shapes were recognized with 62% accuracy and the accuracy of speed profile recognition was 51%. Chance responding was 20%, so these levels were well above chance even if they were lower than recognition accuracies for each aspect in isolation. The decrement in the performance levels could have been due to the need to remember and discriminate among twice as many forms as before, as well as to the fact that both aspects had to be discriminated in each form, and this might have created attentional problems—that is, attention had to be split between the two aspects. Nevertheless, these results indicate that observers were able to identify both the path shape and speed profile of each event when viewed in 3-D perspective.

There is some evidence that observers might perceive trajectories as integral forms in which the two aspects—path shape and speed profile— are lawfully coordinated. In the 1980s, Viviani performed a number of studies in which he investigated the kinematics of human limb movements, including writing and drawing movements, reaching, and 3-D scribbling movements of the hand performed freely in the air (e.g., Lacquaniti, Terzuolo, & Viviani, 1983; Viviani & McCollum, 1983). The results revealed an invariant scaling relation between the curvature of the path of movement and the speed along that path such that the curvature and speed were inversely related by a two-thirds power law. Subsequently, Viviani and Stucchi (1992) investigated the visual perception of such movements. They systematically varied the relation between path curvature and speed and asked observers to judge which speed profiles appeared constant. They found that trajectories exhibiting the two-thirds scaling law were judged as constant speed trajectories. On the basis of this result, Viviani and Stucchi argued that human perception is especially attuned to such trajectories because they are characteristic of human limb movements.

Runeson (1974) obtained a similar result for a different type of trajectory. He also used phenomenological report measures. Observers were asked to draw the speed profiles for different trajectories including constant speed, acceleration to constant speed (which Runeson called "natural start"), constant acceleration, and constant deceleration. Motion was always along a straight path in a frontoparallel plane. Runeson found that observers judged the "natural start" displays as constant speed. Because a different trajectory type was judged as "constant speed" than that defined in Viviani and Stucchi (1992), perhaps the phenomenology should not be so strongly interpreted. Bingham (1995) noted that the important results of Runeson (1974) were that (a) observers drew different graphs for each motion, which meant that they could discriminate among the motions, and (b) observers consistently drew the same graph for each motion each time they judged it, meaning that they could recognize each of the motions (see also Bingham and Runeson, 1983). The results showed that the trajectory forms could be detected and used to recognize events.

Motor Theory and the Perception of Biological Motion

Viviani and Stucchi (1992) argued, based on their results, for a motor theory of the perception of biological motion. More recently, a number of researchers have been arguing for a "common coding theory" of biological motion perception, which is to say a motor theory (e.g. Bertenthal, 1996; Bertenthal & Pinto, 1993; Jacobs, Pinto, & Shiffrar, 2004; Jacobs & Shiffrar, 2005; Jokisch, Daum, & Troje, in press; Knoblich & Prinz, 2001; Loula, Prasad, Harber, & Shiffrar, 2005). The argument has been presented recently, and most systematically, in Jacobs, Pinto, and Shiffrar (2004) and in Loula, Prasad, Harber, and Shiffrar (2005). It is as follows: *First*, they argue that human movement is special. Human observers are especially sensitive to biological motion, and, in particular, they are especially able to recognize their own actions when they observe them in a display. Special sensitivity to human motion in general would be expected because people have more experience perceiving biological motion than other inanimate motions like bouncing balls or trees blowing in the wind. However, and *second*, the special ability to perceive self-motion would be unexpected from the perspective of empiricist theory—that is, based on the extent of past experience. People have little experience watching themselves because the only place they would get to do this is in a mirror, and such occasions are relatively rare compared to the instances when human observers get to see other people doing things. So (and *third*) the question is raised: how can observers experience superior sensitivity to a stimulus with which they have relatively little experience? The answer comes with the observation that "human motion is the only category of motion that humans both produce and perceive" (Jacobs, Pinto, & Shiffrar, 2004, pp. 823). Biological motion perception is special because a common representation is used to both produce and perceive human movements.

Because of such common coding, Loula et al. (2005) predicted that human observers should be better able to recognize their own motion than the motion of friends or strangers. Loula et al., in fact, found this to be the case, but only for certain kinds of movements. Generally, observers were able to recognize themselves and their friends equally well (and better than strangers), but when the movements were less biomechanically constrained and/or stereotypical, then they could identify themselves more readily. They could do it better with free-form dancing movements than with walking or running movements. Similarly, Knoblich and Prinz (2001) found that when observers viewed the movements of drawing either familiar or unfamiliar characters, they were able to recognize the ones that they had drawn themselves. The familiarity of the characters had no effect, from which the authors concluded that the extent of past experience in drawing the particular characters did not play a role in the ability to recognize one's own action. Because participants were not allowed to see themselves drawing the characters when they first produced them, Knoblich and Prinz concluded that the subsequent ability of the participants to visually recognize their own drawing movements supported a motor or common-coding theory of biological motion perception.

It seems that history is bound to repeat itself. Twenty years ago, speech perceptionists initiated a debate on motor theory that is to be revisited here, at least in part. Researchers at Haskins Laboratories were well known as the advocates of a motor theory of speech perception (e.g., Liberman, 1996). Their argument for motor theory also started with the supposition that "speech is special." Carol Fowler took issue with the motor theory of speech perception. Instead, she argued for a direct-realist event theory of speech perception (and production) (e.g., Fowler, 1986, 1989). We will here follow in Carol's footsteps by critiquing the motor theory of biological motion perception and advocating a direct realist approach.

Critique of the Motor Theory of Biological Motion Perception

The argument for a motor theory of biological motion perception contains a number of flaws, all of which are rooted in a common mistake. The power and extent of human perceptual abilities is simply underrepresented and underappreciated in the argument. First, the evidence that biological motion perception is special is either weak or absent. It's true that Johansson's point-light people displays were always very striking in their effectiveness. Anyone present at the First International Conference on Event Perception at the University of Connecticut in 1981 (see Warren & Shaw, 1985) would have witnessed a room of over a hundred perceptionists collectively and simultaneously giving a sharp intake of breath as Johansson demonstrated the surprising power and effectiveness of these displays. But the fact of the matter is that such point-light displays are equally effective for inanimate events like bouncing balls and splashing water (Bingham et al., 1995; Twardy & Bingham, 2002) or the perception of the movements of other species like birds, dogs, and cats (Blake, 1993; Jokisch & Troje, 2003; Pavolova & Sokolov, 2000). (For a point-light pigeon display, see http://www.biomotionlab.ca/vpigeon. php.) Furthermore, the recognition of such events, animate and inanimate alike, is disrupted by inversion every bit as much as is the recognition of point-light walkers (Bingham et al., 1995). While it is true that observers seem to be able to perceive expressions of human emotion in biological motion displays (Dittrich, Troscianko, Lea, & Morgan, 1996), we might well expect this ability to generalize to perception of emotion in other species given Darwin's seminal observations of similarity in the expression of emotion in man and animals (Darwin, 1872).

Continuity is really the issue. Continuity is at issue behind the claim that "human motion is the only category of motion that humans both produce and perceive." The claim simply is not true. A major biological motion event in Indiana occurs when a basketball is dribbled the length of the court for a successful lay-up. The dribbling is an inalienable part of this human-produced event and the dribbling is composed, in part, of a bouncing ball. More than this, and key to our argument, the running player who dribbles the ball exhibits the same bouncing-ball dynamic! The bouncing-ball dynamic is the dynamic of running, and this dynamic is the basis of the recognizable form of running. Dynamics is what relates us to our surroundings and provides a crucial common thread connecting animate and inanimate events. The projectile motion of the ball thrown for the lay-up is the very same as the projectile motion exhibited by the player executing the lay-up. Motor theory only sets up a dualism profoundly separating such events (that is, the dribbled ball versus the dribbling person) so as to render their perception as a single coherent event (ball dribbling) forever a mystery.

Warren, Kim, and Husney (1987) investigated whether observers are able to perceive the elasticity of a ball by observing someone else bounce it. They found that observers were able to use the information to gauge the impulse they applied to a ball to bounce it to a targeted height. So here, clearly, ball bouncing was an event that human observers were able to both perceive and produce, and the perception incorporated both the animate human limb motions impelling the ball as well as the inanimate ball bouncing as parts of a single coherent event. Motor theory can not provide much insight about this perceptual ability.

The problem of continuity is there in self-perception as well in the relation between perception of self and of others. The problem with the analysis in the argument for motor theory is that perception has been sold short in two ways: (1) with respect to perspective and (2) with respect to modality. First, the argument for motor theory holds that visual perception of self-motion is rare. This is simply not so. The mistake is a failure to distinguish third-person and first-person perspectives, so that the ubiquitous role of first-person perspective on self-motion is ignored. People visually perceive their own actions all the time, from a first-person perspective. The equivalent effectiveness of first- and third-person displays of biological motion has been demonstrated as follows. First, observers recognized human walking in a video display in which a walking person appeared in standard third-person perspective. Next, observers also recognized human walking in a video display when it appeared in first-person perspective. In the latter case, the camera person held the video camera on his shoulder and filmed himself getting up from a chair and walking around the room. He used the view through the lens to guide his action and filmed that view. The event was easily recognized for what it was, although no light was reflected from the walking person's surfaces into the camera. The event was easily distinguished from motion of the camera on a tripod. The first author of this chapter has performed this demonstration dozens of times in the classroom.

Bingham (1993) investigated perception of the size of people viewed in patch-light displays. In unpublished studies done in a lab class at that time, patch-light displays were filmed from first-person perspective by having actors hold the camera on their shoulder as they walked down a runway lined with a string of lights at waist height. (Image size variables were controlled in these studies.) Observers of the first-person perspective point-light displays judged actor size. Although the judgments were highly variable, they correlated significantly with the actual sizes of actors in the displays.

The point is that human actions are events that can be visually perceived from different perspectives, just as any event can. A major difference between the visual perception of self-motion and the motion of others is a difference in perspective. The important and relevant question is what difference might this difference in perspective make. Indeed, Jokisch and Troje (2003) have found that the recognition of the walking motions of oneself versus others differs in respect to the effect of perspective differences. Self-motion exhibits perspective dependence, whereas the perception of others' motions does not. (See also Troje, Westhoff, & Lavrov, 2005; Watson, Johnston, Hill, & Troje, 2005; Westhoff & Troje, in press; Zhang & Troje, 2005). In general, the interesting question that remains to be addressed in research is how first- and third-person perspectives might succeed in carrying common information about a given event. Given the characteristic forms of motion in a human walking event, how are such forms projected into different optic flows to yield common recognition?

In any case, the suggestion that visual perception of self-motion is rare is simply incorrect. So, the question "How can observers experience superior sensitivity to a stimulus with which they have relatively little experience?" is barking up the wrong tree. Observers experience good sensitivity because they have a tremendous amount of experience visually perceiving their own motions.

Self-motion is perceived not only visually from a first-person perspective but also kinesthetically. It is well recognized that kinesthetic perception is an intrinsic component of the coordination and control of actions (Latash, 1993; Winters & Woo, 1990). Another weakness in the motor theory argument is the rather striking failure to acknowledge the intrinsic importance of perception for action—that is, the lessons learned from mass-spring models of joint control and, for instance, the account in *Pride and the Daily Marathon* (Cole, 1995). Both muscle properties and reflexes (thus, sensory elements) are combined to yield joints that are controllable in terms of the stiffness and rest position of a mass spring. When the afferent (that is, sensory or perceptual) elements are removed, the system is no longer controllable, as shown by the account in Cole (1995) of someone (named Ian) to whom this happened. Ian eventually recovered the ability to move by substituting visual perception for his missing kinesthesis. Knoblich and Prinz (2001) found that observers were able to recognize their own drawing movements even though they had not been allowed to see the movements when they were originally performed. Knoblich and Prinz concluded that this finding required a motor theory account. They suggested that the motor coding for the original production was used to enable recognition of the self-generated characters. However, given the well-established role of kinesthetic perception in the control of actions, their result only requires a consideration of the relation between kinesthetic and visual perception of a given action. The drawing movements were kinesthetically perceived during the original production and visually perceived during the subsequent recognition. So the question is, how are kinesthetic and visual perceptions related? Only perceptual theory, not motor theory, need be entailed.

Visual and Kinesthetic Perception of Relative Phase and Bimanual Coordination

The earliest studies of information in visual event perception focused on phase relations among the visible moving points in an event (Johansson, 1950, 1973, 1976). The role of relative phase has been studied extensively both in visual event perception studies (Bertenthal, 1996; Bertenthal & Pinto, 1993, 1994; Bertenthal, Proffitt, & Cutting, 1984; Bertenthal, Proffitt, & Kramer, 1987; Bingham, 1995; Booth, Pinto, & Bertenthal, 2002; Todd, 1983) and in studies on perception in bimanual coordination (e.g., Bingham, 2004a, 2005b; Bingham, Schmidt, & Zaal,1999; Bingham, Zaal, Shull, & Collins, 2001; Wilson & Bingham, 2005a, 2005b; Wilson, Craig, & Bingham, 2003; Zaal, Bingham, & Schmidt, 2000). Relative phase is a measure of coordination in human movement. The event perception studies have shown that relative phase is a perceptual variable used for the perception of human movement. Bimanual coordination studies have revealed that relative phase is a perceptual variable used for the production of human movement (Wilson & Bingham, 2005a, 2005b). The coupling of movements in different limbs is mediated perceptually by perceived relative phase.

This research began with studies showing parallel results in movement studies and perceptual judgment studies (Bingham, Schmidt, & Zaal, 1999; Bingham, Zaal, Shull, & Collins, 2001; Zaal, Bingham, & Schmidt,

2000). The movement studies revealed two stable phase relations in bimanual coordination, namely 0-degree and 180-degree relative phase (Kelso, 1995). Both are stable at preferred frequencies near 1 Hz, but as frequency is increased to 3 to 4 Hz, 180 degrees becomes unstable and coordination spontaneously transitions to a 0-degree relative phase. Visual judgment studies yielded parallel results. Observers judged relative phase and phase variability of two oscillating objects in a display. Phases other than 0 and 180 degrees were judged to be intrinsically unstable (that is, highly variable). At 1 Hz, both 0 and 180 degrees were judged to be stable, but as frequency was increased to 3 to 4 Hz, 180 degrees was judged to be increasingly variable, although 0 degrees was not. The results of these visual judgment studies were all replicated in a study in which observers perceived the movements and phase relations kinesthetically (Wilson, Craig, & Bingham, 2003). The whole complex pattern of results was nearly identical in the two studies—that is, visual and kinesthetic judgments. Visual and kinesthetic perceptions of relative limb movements are symmetric, and thus the relation between them is direct and immediate. They are the same. If this symmetry extends to the detection of trajectory forms, then the results of Knoblich and Prinz (2001) are simply explained. In fact, their results could simply be interpreted as a demonstration of such symmetry.

How is a Motor Code Used to Recognize Events?

Visual recognition of events requires the detection by the visual system of optic flow information that specifies the event. What role would a motor code play in such recognition? How important would it be for the ability to recognize events? First, a motor code would only be relevant for the recognition of events involving human actions. So, general visual event recognition involving nonhuman movement, whether animate or inanimate, would entail information and processes that would not involve a motor code. The relevance of a motor code to event recognition in general is very limited. Then, within events involving human actions, it is events involving self-motions to which a motor code would be most relevant. Recognition of self-motion entails information for a unique identity—that is, a particular. Loula et al. (2005) found that self-motion was best recognized in displays of movements that were the least constrained by the dynamics of human movement. Walking movements are stereotypical, as governed by the relevant pendular dynamics, and so self-recognition is difficult. Free-form dancing is variable and allows for unique movements, and so recognition of the self is much easier. Recognizing one's own walking would also be easier if one were allowed to insert a little hop or a limp into one of the cycles of walking to make it unique and uniquely identifiable. So, the motor code helps in these cases presumably by providing a memory of the unique voluntary movement one has performed so that one can subsequently identify one's own movements.

A motor code might also be relevant to the recognition of human action events not involving self-motion. How would this work? As we have already hinted, theories of robotics and human motor control have gone through some major changes in the past 25 years. Up until the mid-1980s, a pattern-imposition approach was dominant. In motor theories and robotics, the motor plan determined a movement pattern. To impose the planned movement form on the movement apparatus (a process sometimes called "trajectory formation"), the appropriate set of executive motor commands to the muscles or motors had to be derived. These commands (or a record of them called "efference copy") actually composed the motor code. The movement of the endpoint (that is, the hand or foot) was planned, and then an inverse kinematics computation had to be performed to derive the required movements at the joints (Brady, Hollerbach, Johnson, Lozano-Perez & Mason, 1982; Hollerbach, 1982). This was followed by inverse dynamics computations to determine the torques to be applied at the joints (by muscles or torque motors) to produce the required movements. The process was computationally intensive and generally did not work. Stable movement in real time was an unachievable holy grail of the approach.

As we have reviewed above, the successes in robotics since then derived from an approach that minimized the role of explicit motor controllers (e.g., Raibert, 1986). Motor controllers merely tweak or parameterize the natural passive dynamical organizations responsible for the forms of movement exhibited by robot or human actions. The result has been effective real-time actions that are both stable and flexible. Raibert's running robots were remarkable because they could do gymnastics. Up until then, it was unusual to see truly stable reaching behavior exhibited by a robotic arm, so the ability to produce stable gymnastic movements was really a sea change. However, what makes the running or walking of such robots (and of such human actions by extension) identifiable is the dynamically generated forms of movement, not the motor code. The result of the revolution in motor theory was that the motor commands were no longer responsible for generating the forms of movement; they merely corralled them.

This was true of the mass-spring models of joint control as well. Motor programming approaches in the old style had used measurements of muscle activity (EMG) to try to infer the motor code. The effect of the mass-spring models was that the muscle activations were produced by the peripheral mass-spring organization, not by executive commands that only parameterized the mass spring (Latash, 1993). However, the mass-spring models have been elaborated in dynamical models of coordinated multi-joint movements (e.g., Winters & Woo, 1990), including the bimanual coordinated movements previously discussed (e.g., Haken, Kelso, & Bunz, 1985). These models incorporate the mass-spring organizations together with perceptual components in a coherent (typically nonlinear) dynamical organization that yields characteristic patterns of coordinated human movements as emergent phenomena that arise from the interactions of components of the perception and action systems (Bingham, 2004a, 2004b). (See, for instance, Bingham [1988], Beek and Bingham [1991], Goldfield [1995], Kelso [1995], or Turvey [1990] for extended discussion.) The important point is that the observed forms of movement are generated by dynamical organizations, not by motor commands. The conclusion is that the relevance of a motor code to visual event recognition may be limited primarily to cases where voluntary manipulation of movements generates unusual or particular movements that allow the resulting unique events to be recognized as such.

A Direct Realist Theory of Event Perception: Recognition Requires Information

A direct realist approach to event perception hypothesizes information composed of "higher-order variables" that relate uniquely to the event about which they provide information (Gibson, 1966, 1979). A lawful basis for information is hypothesized to yield the required uniqueness. The unique relation, in turn, allows the information to specify the event so that it can be visually recognized. Direct perception merely requires that the visual system detect the information. The onus on such an approach is to describe the information for event recognition and the means by which it might be detected.

A heavy hint about the information for visual event recognition comes to us from Hollywood. (See Bingham, 1995, for discussion of the dynamics of scale and scale engineering.) In the original *Godzilla* films, the monster always looks like the mechanical toy or costumed figure he is, despite attempts to set him in a context and employ a camera perspective using standard temporal scaling techniques to make him look real. The standard technique for making small-scale models of large events (collapsing bridges and buildings, giant waves of water, or sinking battleships) look real at that time was to film the events at high speed, to be replayed at slower speed. But this never really worked because the method did not alter the movement forms that revealed the actual scale. Since then, Hollywood has learned that good dynamical models of events must be used to generate the appropriate forms of movement. The dinosaurs in *Jurassic Park* look convincing thanks to the application of good computer-generated dynamical simulations for the special effects (Alexander, 1989; Magid, 1998). Similarly, the giant waves in *The Perfect Storm* were generated using the Navier-Stokes equations for fluid flows, and the result is again convincing (Magid, 2000).

The studies reviewed in the first part of this paper showed that forms of movement provide information that enables events to be recognized. Why should the visual system use trajectory forms as information? Because those forms are generated deterministically by the underlying event dynamics. To the extent that the event type, the event dynamics, and the characteristic forms of motion in an event are all unique, the motion can provide information about the event that allows observers to recognize it. In the context of dynamics, these relations are lawful, and this lawfulness provides the basis for information. So the research questions are, what are the characteristic dynamics underlying given recognizable events, and what are the characteristic forms of motion generated by those dynamics and used as information to recognize events?

The dynamics of the wide variety of different events can be taxonomized in terms of many different types of dynamics. Bingham et al. (1995) performed cluster analysis on phenomenological descriptors provided by observers of a variety of animate and inanimate point-light events and discovered that hierarchical relations emerged among the events reflecting the underlying types of dynamics, including rigid body dynamics, hydrodynamics, aerodynamics, and biodynamics. Events generated by the latter three general types of dynamics exhibited different types of nonrigid surface structure. With this, phase relations among moving elements in events became an essential part of the information analysis. Rigid body events involved only 0-degree relative phasing among the motion of various points on surfaces in the events. For instance, all the points on a point-light rolling ball move in phase with one another, and this symmetry, as suggested in Bingham (1995), might allow the visual system to achieve a significant reduction of the high degrees of freedom in the display. In contrast, nonrigid events exhibit a variety of relative phases among moving points other than 0 degrees. An example studied in both Bingham et al. (1995) and Wickelgren and Bingham (2001) is the oscillatory waves on the surface of water that has been splashed by a projectile. A point-light display of this event was created by filming white patches (like leaves) distributed on the surface of the water. The nature of the event was trivially obvious to observers: each point exhibited a damped oscillatory trajectory form. But the motions of neighboring points were phased with one another in a lawful way governed by the underlying hydrodynamics. Biological motion events also exhibit nonrigid structure in which motions of the different limbs exhibit lawfully governed phase relations (as reflected by the dynamical models thereof as described above). Thus, the motions that provide information about events are composed of trajectory forms and systematic patterns of phase relations among the distributed local forms. To the extent that the trajectory forms are the same, once again there exists a symmetry that the visual system might use to reduce the complexity of the event (again, see Bingham, 1995, for discussion).

In visual event recognition, the next question is, how are the motions in events projected into optical flows, or, alternatively, how do optical flows provide information about the motions in events? As described in the first part of this chapter, trajectory forms are carried by translatory and expansion/contraction components of the optical flows. This analysis, however, requires simplification of the full optic flow structure (Bingham, 1995). The optic flows contain information about the surface structure of objects in events—that is, the flows contain information about both object structure and motion as described in structure-from-motion (SFM) studies. SFM is the study of optical flow information about object structure—that is, the perception of objects in the context of events (Braunstein, 1994; Lind, 1996; Todd, 1995). So, advances in object perception from studies of SFM are relevant to an understanding of visual event perception. In this context, the visual system has been analyzed as composed of detectors that function like differential operators decomposing optic flow structure in ways directly relevant to information contained therein about surface structure and motion (Harris, 1994; Koenderink & van Doorn, 1977; Simpson, 1993). The problem is that these analyses are very local in time and thus they do not address time-extended information about events—that is, they do not address the detection of trajectory forms (Bingham, 1995).

A more recent model of neural mechanisms for the detection and recognition of biological motion includes separate channels for the perception of form (i.e., object structure) and motion (Giese & Poggio, 2005), although the motion channel also is hypothesized to contain optic flow information about object structure. The later stages of processing in the neural model were designed to exhibit "sequential selectivity." This sensitivity amounts to sequential expectations for samples in a position-time series. This model is the most extensively developed model specifically of biological motion measurement. However, it seems a bit awkward in that it goes from the first-order (velocity) information in optic flow back down to zero-order (position) information that is essentially the same as the frames form a video display. Nevertheless, the model is an attempt to deal with the necessarily time-extended nature of the information required for visual event identification. An alternative approach to the problem of detecting continuous temporal information in perception can be seen in models of the auditory perception of event tempo (Large & Jones, 1999; McAuley, 1995; McAuley & Kidd, 1998). In these models, internal oscillators entrain to external oscillatory events. Such models embody application of Fourier methods to the detection of trajectories. Beyond this, models that incorporate wavelet transforms are also being developed as a means by which perceptual systems might detect trajectories (e.g., Leduc, Mujica, Murenzi, & Smith, 1997).

Conclusion

The motor theory of biological motion perception hypothesizes that motor commands (or records thereof) are used to recognize human movements when they are visually perceived. However, current theories of human action render this motor theory redundant. We have reviewed advances over the past couple of decades in the understanding of the control and coordination of human movement. We have learned that motor commands are not responsible for the specific forms of different kinds of movements like running or walking. Rather, passive dynamical organizations are used to generate forms of movement that are then controlled by parametrically adjusting the dynamics. However, it is the dynamically generated movement forms that, in fact, can provide the information that allows biological motions to be perceived and recognized for what they are. This possibility has been systematically investigated in a number of studies inspired by an ecological approach to visual event perception. The approach hypothesizes that lawfully generated information must be available to allow perception and support recognition. Trajectory forms generated by event dynamics would provide such information. The studies have shown that trajectory forms can be used by human observers to recognize events.

One's own actions—that is, self-generated human actions—can be perceived in a number of ways. They can be perceived from a first-person perspective either kinesthetically or visually. This raises the question of how such visual and kinesthetic perceptions can be related to one another. We provided one possible answer, which is that if they both use the same information they can be related directly. We presented evidence that supports this possibility. One's own actions can also be perceived from a third-person perspective via a mirror or a video camera. This raises the question of how first- and third-person perspectives might be related. But this is just part of the general problem of perception: how can perception be constant despite changes in perspective? The problem of constancy is an old chestnut to perceptionists, and it's a problem to be addressed by perceptual theory. Gibson (1979) advocated that the constancy problem might be solved or replaced by a theory of perceptual information in terms of invariants and corresponding transformations. Whatever the solution, the problem is not specific to the perception of biological motion but is general to all perception of objects and events. Motor theory is not likely to provide the solution because it is simply too limited. What is required instead is an uncompromising general theory of information.

References

Alexander, R. M. (1989). *Dynamics of dinosaurs and other extinct giants.* New York: Columbia University Press.

Alexander, R. M. (1992). *The human machine.* New York: Columbia University Press.

Beek, P. J., & Bingham, G. P. (1991). Task-specific dynamics and the study of perception and action: A reaction to von Hofsten (1989). *Ecological Psychology, 3*(1), 35–54.

Bertenthal, B. I. (1996). Origins and early development of perception, action and representation. *Annual Review of Psychology, 47,* 431–459.

Bertenthal, B. I., & Pinto, J. (1993). Complementary processes in the perception and production of human movements. In E. Thelen & L. Smith (Eds.), *A dynamic systems approach to development: Applications* (pp. 209–239). Cambridge, MA: Bradford Books.

Bertenthal, B. I., & Pinto, J. (1994). Global processing of biological motions. *Psychological Science, 5,* 221–225.

Bertenthal, B. I., Proffitt, D. R., & Cutting, J. E. (1984). Infant sensitivity to figural coherence in biomechanical motions. *Journal of Experimental Child Psychology, 37*(2), 213–230.

Bertenthal, B. I., Proffitt, D. R., & Kramer, S. J. (1987). Perception of biomechanical motions by infants: Implementation of various processing constraints. *Journal of Experimental Psychology: Human Perception and Performance, 13*(4), 577–585.

Bingham, G. P. (1987). Kinematic form and scaling: Further investigations on the visual perception of lifted weight. *Journal of Experimental Psychology: Human Perception and Performance, 13*(2), 155–177.

Bingham, G. P. (1988). Task specific devices and the perceptual bottleneck. *Human Movement Science, 7,* 225–264. Also in P. N. Kugler (Ed.) (1989), *Self-organization in human action.* Amsterdam: North-Holland.

Bingham, G. P. (1993). Scaling judgments of lifted weight: Lifter size and the role of the standard. *Ecological Psychology, 5,* 31–65.

Bingham, G. P. (1995). Dynamics and the problem of visual event recognition. In R. Port & T. van Gelder (Eds.), *Mind as motion: Dynamics, behavior and cognition* (pp. 403–448). Cambridge, MA: MIT Press.

Bingham, G. P. (2004a). A perceptually driven dynamical model of bimanual rhythmic movement (and phase perception). *Ecological Psychology, 16*(1), 45–53.

Bingham, G. P. (2004b). Another timing variable composed of state variables: Phase perception and phase driven oscillators. In H. Hecht & G. J. P. Savelsbergh (Eds.), *Theories of time-to-contact.* Boston: MIT Press.

Bingham, G. P., Rosenblum, L. D., & Schmidt, R. C. (1995). Dynamics and the orientation of kinematic forms in visual event recognition. *Journal of Experimental Psychology: Human Perception and Performance, 21*(6), 1473–1493.

Bingham, G. P., & Runeson, S. (1983, October). *On describing what is perceived: Seeing 'velocity' versus seeing 'push' in moving objects.* Paper presented at a meeting of the International Society for Ecological Psychology.

Bingham, G. P., Schmidt, R. C., & Zaal, F. (1999). Visual perception of the relative phasing of human limb movements. *Perception & Psychophysics, 61*(2), 246–258.

Bingham, G. P., Zaal, F. T., Shull, J. A., & Collins, D. R. (2001). The effect of frequency on the visual perception of relative phase and phase variability of two oscillating objects. *Experimental Brain Research, 136,* 543–552.

Blake, R. (1993). Cats perceive biological motion. *Psychological Science, 4,* 54–57.

Booth, A. E., Pinto, J., & Bertenthal, B. I. (2002). Perception of the symmetrical patterning of human gait by infants. *Developmental Psychology, 38*(4), 554–563.

Brady, M., Hollerbach, J. M., Johnson, T. L., Lozano-Perez, T., & Mason, M. T. (Eds.) (1982), *Robot motion: Planning and control.* Cambridge, MA: MIT Press.

Braunstein, M. L. (1994). Structure from motion. In A.T. Smith & R. J. Snowden (Eds.), *Visual detection of motion* (pp. 367–393). San Diego: Academic Press.

Cole, J. (1995). *Pride and the daily marathon.* Cambridge, MA: MIT Press.

Darwin, C. (1872). *The expression of emotions in man and animals.* London: John Murray.

Dittrich, W. H., Troscianko, T., Lea, S. E. G., & Morgan, D. (1996). Perception of emotion from dynamic point-light displays represented in dance. *Perception, 25,* 727–738.

Fowler, C. (1986). An event approach to the study of speech perception from a direct-realist perspective. *Journal of Phonetics, 14,* 3–28.

Fowler, C. (1989). Real objects of speech perception: A commentary on Diehl and Kluender. *Ecological Psychology, 1,* 145–160.

Gibson, J. J. (1966). *The senses considered as perceptual systems.* Boston, MA: Houghton-Mifflin.

Gibson, J. J. (1979). *The ecological approach to visual perception.* Boston: Houghton-Mifflin.

Giese, M. A., & Poggio, T. (2005). Neural mechanisms for the recognition of biological movements. *Nature Neuroscience Reviews, 4,* 179–192.

Goldfield, E. C. (1995). *Emergent forms.* New York: Oxford University Press.

Haken, H., Kelso, J. A. S., & Bunz, H. (1985). A theoretical model of phase transitions in human hand movements. *Biological Cybernetics, 51,* 347–356.

Harris, M. G. (1994). Optic and retinal flow. In A. T. Smith & R. J. Snowden (Eds.) (1994), *Visual detection of motion* (pp. 307–332). San Diego, CA: Academic Press.

Hollerbach, J. M. (1982). Computers, brains, and the control of movement. *Trends in Neurosciences, 5,* 189–192.

Jacobs, A., Pinto, J., & Shiffrar, M. (2004). Experience, context, and the visual perception of human movement. *Journal of Experimental Psychology: Human Perception and Performance, 30*(5), 822–835.

Jacobs, A., & Shiffrar, M. (2005). Walking perception by walking observers. *Journal of Experimental Psychology: Human Perception and Performance, 31*(1), 157–169.

Johansson, G. (1950). *Configurations in event perception.* Uppsala, Sweden: Almquist & Wiksell.

Johansson, G. (1973). Visual perception of biological motion and a model for its analysis. *Perception & Psychophysics, 14*, 201–211.

Johansson, G. (1976). Spatio-temporal differentiation and integration in visual motion perception. *Psychological Research, 38*, 379–393.

Jokisch, D., Daum, I., & Troje, N. F. (in press). Self recognition versus recognition of others by biological motion: Viewpoint-dependent effects. *Perception.*

Jokisch, D., & Troje, N. F. (2003) Biological motion as a cue for the perception of size. *Journal of Vision, 3*, 252–264.

Kelso, J. A. S. (1995). *Dynamic patterns: The self-organization of brain and behavior.* Cambridge, MA: MIT Press.

Knoblich, G., & Prinz, W. (2001). Recognition of self-generated actions from kinematic displays of drawing. *Journal of Experimental Psychology: Human Perception and Performance, 27*, 456–465.

Koenderink, J. J., & van Doorn, A. (1977). How an ambulant observer can construct a model of the environment from the geometrical structure of the visual flow. In G. Hauske & F. Butenandt (Eds.), *Kybernetik* (pp. 224–247). Munich: Oldenberg.

Lacquaniti, F., Terzuolo, C., & Viviani, P. (1983). The law relating the kinematic and figural aspects of drawing movements. *Acta Psychologica, 54*, 115–130.

Large, E. W., & Jones, M. R. (1999). The dynamics of attending: How people track time-varying events. *Psychological Review, 106*, 119–159.

Latash, M. (1993). *Control of human movement.* Champaign, IL: Human Kinetics Press.

Leduc, J.-P., Mujica, F., Murenzi, R., & Smith, M. (1997). Spatio-temporal wavelet transforms for motion tracking. *ICASSP-97, 4*, 3013–3016.

Liberman, A. M. (1996). *Speech: A special code.* Cambridge, MA: MIT Press.

Lind, M. (1996). Perceiving motion and rigid structure from optic flow: A combined weak perspective and polar-perspective approach. *Perception & Psychophysics, 58*, 1085–1102.

Loula, F., Prasad, S., Harber, K., & Shiffrar, M. (2005). Recognizing people from their movement. *Journal of Experimental Psychology: Human Perception and Performance, 31*(1), 210–220.

Magid, R. (1998, June). Making size matter. *American Cinematographer: The International Journal of Film and Digital Production Techniques, 79*(6), 1–3.

Magid, R. (2000, June). Making waves. *American Cinematographer: The International Journal of Film and Digital Production Techniques, 81*(6), 1–3.

McAuley, J. D. (1995). *Perception of time as phase: Toward an adaptive oscillatory model of rhythmic pattern processing.* Unpublished doctoral dissertation. Bloomington, IN: Indiana University.

McAuley, J. D., & Kidd, G. R. (1998). Effect of deviations from temporal expectations on temp on discrimination of isochronous tone sequences. *Journal of Experimental Psychology: Human Perception and Performance, 24*, 1786–1800.

McConnell, D. S., Muchisky, M. M., & Bingham, G. P. (1998). The use of time and trajectory forms as visual information about spatial scale in events. *Perception & Psychophysics, 60*(7), 1175–1187.

McGeer, T. (1990). Passive dynamics walking. *International Journal of Robotics Research, 9*, 62–82.

McMahon, T. A. (1984). *Muscles, reflexes and locomotion.* Princeton, NJ: Princeton University Press.

Mochon, S., & McMahon, T. A. (1979). Ballistic walking: An improved model. *Mathematical Biosciences, 52*, 241–260.

Muchisky, M. M., & Bingham, G. P. (2002). Trajectory forms as a source of information about events. *Perception & Psychophysics, 64*(1), 15–31.

Pavolova, M., & Sokolov, M. (2000). Orientation specificity in biological motion perception. *Perception & Psychophysics, 62*, 889–899.

Pittenger, J. B. (1985). Estimation of pendulum length from information in motion. *Perception, 14*, 247–256.

Pittenger, J. B. (1990). Detection of violations of the law of pendulum motion: Observers' sensitivity to the relation between period and length. *Ecological Psychology, 2*, 55–81.

Pratt, J. E., & Pratt, G. A. (1998). Exploiting natural dynamics in the control of a planar bipedal walking robot. *Proceedings of the Thirty-Sixth Annual Allerton Conference on Communication, Control and Computing.* Monticello, IL.

Pylyshyn, Z. (Ed.) (1987). *The robot's dilemma: The frame problem in artificial intelligence.* Norwood, NJ: Ablex.

Raibert, M. (1986). *Legged robots that balance.* Cambridge, MA: MIT Press.

Runeson, S. (1974). Constant velocity—not perceived as such. *Psychological Research, 37*, 3–23.

Runeson, S. (1977/1983). *On the visual perception of dynamic events.* (Acta Universitatis Upsaliensis: Studia Psychologica Upsaliensia 9). Stockholm: Almqvist & Wiksell.

Runeson, S., & Frykholm, G. (1981). Visual perception of lifted weight. *Journal of Experimental Psychology: Human Perception and Performance, 7*, 733–740.

Runeson, S., & Frykholm, G. (1983). Kinematic specification of dynamics as an informational basis for person and action perception: Expectations, gender recognition, and deceptive intention. *Journal of Experimental Psychology: General, 112*, 585–615.

Shipley, T. F. (2003). The effect of object and event orientation on perception of biological motion. *Psychological Science, 14*, 377–380.

Simpson, W. A. (1993). Optic flow and depth perception. *Spatial Vision, 1*, 35–44.

Stappers, P. J., & Waller, P. E. (1993). Using the free fall of objects under gravity for visual depth estimation. *Bulletin of the Psychonomic Society, 31*, 125–127.

Sumi, S. (1984). Upside-down presentation of the Johansson moving light-spot pattern. *Perception, 13*, 283–286.

Todd, J. T. (1983). Perception of gait. *Journal of Experimental Psychology: Human Perception and Performance, 9*, 31–42.

Todd, J. T. (1995). The visual perception of three-dimensional structure from motion. In W. Epstein & S. Rogers (Eds.), *Perception of space and motion* (pp. 201–226). San Diego, CA: Academic Press.

Troje, N. F., Westhoff, C., & Lavrov, M. (2005). Person identification from biological motion: Effects of structural and kinematic cues. *Perception & Psychophysics, 67*, 667–675.

Turvey, M. T. (1990). Coordination. *American Psychologist, 45*, 938–953.

Twardy, C., & Bingham, G. P. (2002). Causation, causal perception and conservation laws. *Perception & Psychophysics, 64*(6), 956–968.

Viviani, P., & McCollum, G. (1983). The relation between linear extent and velocity in drawing movements. *Neuroscience, 10*, 211–218.

Viviani, P., & Stucchi, N. (1992). Biological movements look uniform: Evidence of motor-perceptual interactions. *Journal of Experimental Psychology: Human Perception and Performance, 18*, 603–623.

Warren, W. H., Kim, E. E., & Husney, R. (1987). The way the ball bounces: Visual and auditory perception of elasticity and control of the bounce pass. *Perception, 16*, 309–336.

Warren, W. H., & Shaw, R. E. (Eds.) (1985). *Persistence and change: Proceedings of the First International Conference on Event Perception*. Hillsdale, NJ: Erlbaum.

Warren, W. H., Young, D. S., & Lee, D. N. (1986). Visual control of step length during running over irregular terrain. *Journal of Experimental Psychology: Human Perception and Performance, 12*, 259–266.

Watson, J. S., Banks, M. S., von Hafsten, C., & Royden, C. S. (1992). Gravity as a monocular cue for perception of absolute distance and/or absolute size. *Perception, 21*, 69–76.

Watson, T. L., Johnston, A., Hill, H. C. H., & Troje, N. F. (2005). Motion as a cue for view-point invariance. *Visual Cognition, 12*, 1291–1308.

Westhoff, C., & Troje, N. F. (in press). Kinematic cues for person identification from biological motion. *Perception & Psychophysics*.

Wickelgren, E., & Bingham, G. P. (2001). Infant sensitivity to trajectory forms. *Journal of Experimental Psychology: Human Perception and Performance, 27*(4), 942–952.

Wickelgren, E. A., & Bingham, G. P. (2004). Perspective distortion of trajectory forms and perceptual constancy in visual event identification. *Perception & Psychophysics, 66*, 629–641.

Wickelgren, E. A., & Bingham, G. P. (in press). Trajectory forms as information for visual event recognition: 3D perspectives on path shape and speed profile. *Perception & Psychophysics*.

Wilson, A., & Bingham, G. P. (2005a). Perceptual coupling in rhythmic movement coordination—stable perception leads to stable action. *Experimental Brain Research, 164*, 517–528.

Wilson, A., & Bingham, G. P. (2005b). Human movement coordination implicates relative direction as the information for relative phase. *Experimental Brain Research, 165*, 351–361.

Wilson, A., Craig, J. C., & Bingham, G. P. (2003). Haptic perception of phase variability. *Journal of Experimental Psychology: Human Perception and Performance, 29*, 1179–1190.

Winters, J. M., & Woo, S. L. (1990). *Multiple muscle systems: Biomechanics and movement organization.* New York: Springer-Verlag.

Zaal, F., Bingham, G. P., & Schmidt, R. C. (2000). Visual perception of relative phase and phase variability. *Journal of Experimental Psychology: Human Perception and Performance, 26*(3), 1209–1220.

Zhang, Z., & Troje, N. F. (2005). View-independent person identification from human gait. *Neurocomputing, 69,* 250–256.

11

Movement Style, Movement Features, and the Recognition of Affect from Human Movement

FRANK E. POLLICK & HELENA PATERSON

The goal of this chapter is to explain the recognition of affect from human movement within the broader context of the recognition of different styles of movement. To achieve this end we first define what we mean by movement style and move on to discuss possible theoretical constraints and what essential properties of a movement might support recognition. This leads to the notion of decomposing movements into features and a review of studies investigating the decomposition of movements into features. With this background we finally narrow our focus to explore the recognition of affect from human movement.

Movement Style

Two papers motivated our choice of the term "style" to describe differences among human actions. The first of these, by Tenenbaum and Freeman (2000), discusses the separation of style and content using bilinear models and provides examples of how these models could be used to extrapolate from a set of letters with known fonts to letters that had not been seen before. The other paper, by Brand and Hertzmann (2000), in the area of 3-D computer animation, presented "style machines" where hidden Markov models of action recognition could be inverted to inject "style" into a given movement. These two works deal with the issue that, for both objects and actions, there is substantial variability in physical stimuli capable of giving rise to the same basic evaluation. Moreover, this variability of the stimuli is not merely noise but creates an intrinsic part of the visual experience that carries its own aesthetic or semantic significance.

Although such notions of movement style are not commonly mentioned in the biological motion literature, the early results that showed competence in recognizing gender from point-light walkers (Kozlowski & Cutting, 1977) are an example of the recognition of movement style. Clearly, both male and female point-light walks are evaluated as examples of human locomotion, but the differences between how males and females achieve locomotion can lead to the appreciation of the gender of the walker.

Besides gender recognition, there are various other examples of what we call style recognition. These include the recognition of affect from dance (Brownlow, Dixon, Egbert, & Radcliffe, 1997; Dittrich, Troscianko, Lea, & Morgan, 1996; Walk & Homan, 1984), affect from arm movements (Paterson, Pollick, & Sanford, 2001; Pollick, Paterson, Bruderlin, & Sanford, 2001), identity (Cutting & Kozlowski, 1977; Hill & Pollick, 2000), and vulnerability (Gunns, Johnston, & Hudson, 2002). In addition to these more general kinds of style recognition, there are a variety of other classifications inherent in specific activities. For example, in tennis there are several different styles of serve (e.g. flat, slice, topspin) (Pollick, Fidopiastis, & Braden, 2001) that result in different physical outcomes, and a similar situation exists in cricket bowling (Abernethy & Russell, 1984). In dance such as ballet there are different schools that impose different regularities on the production of the same basic movements.

At first blush there would seem to be little issue with our examples of movement style. However, there are some questions that need to be addressed. These include (a) whether all these different examples of style are consistent with the same definition, (b) why different styles exist and under what conditions would they naturally arise, and (c) how, or whether, what we call style recognition relates to the concept of categorization. We address these questions in turn.

We gave the examples of gender, affect, identity, vulnerability, and tennis serve all as examples of movement styles and raised the question of whether these are all examples of the same phenomenon. At a simple level they all are, since they provide an example of a categorization judgment that individuals can be asked to make and—assuming the information is available—they would be able to make. However, each of these judgments depends on different properties of movement. For example, gender and identity are traits of an individual that are largely stable across time. Emotion and affect, on the other hand, describe the current state of the individual and could be expected to vary widely over time. What emotion, affect, identity, and gender have in common is that they will be overlaid with every action performed. This is in distinction to movement styles like tennis serves and ballet movements, where the action style arises from strategic or aesthetic considerations. This leads to general consideration of how the goals of the action relate to style difference and the finer distinction of whether or not a goal-directed action is transitive in the sense that the object the action is being directed toward is readily apparent. It would seem possible to construct a detailed system for describing movement styles, and perhaps even to argue the case for ecological validity for different types of organization. In this chapter, however, we leave this issue of how best to conceptually organize the different varieties of movement styles as beyond our current scope.

In the previous paragraph we already touched on some of the answer of why style differences should arise. In the case of goal-directed actions, the style might change to modify the specific strategic or aesthetic nature of the goal. For the cases of identity and gender, style differences might be determined by the biomechanics of body structure, and for affect there are potential benefits in social interaction to express one's internal state. However, we stated that affect might be overlaid upon a movement, and we need to provide some intuition as to why this could be so. The key point here arises from a primary aspect of human motor control. In other words, specifying the goal to be achieved does little to specify how that goal will be achieved—the problem is ill posed—and there are an infinite number of possible joint trajectories, joint torques, and muscle forces that can be used to achieve the goal (for a review see Wolpert, 1997). That is to say that the motor control system seems ideally suited to overlaying additional constraints on the production of movement, and these constraints could express multiple properties of the actor.

Given that we have a motor control system that appears inclined to generate different styles of movement and the variety of styles that might exist, we need an operational definition of "movement style" to proceed with discussions of style recognition. For this we will view movement style recognition in the framework of subordinate category recognition. A standard definition (Rosch, Mervis, Gray, Johnson, & Boyes-Braem, 1976) considers a basic-level category as the most common term for an object, and typically the first one learned by children. In addition, a subordinate-level category captures the fine distinctions among the members of the basic-level category. An example of this is the basic-level category of birds, with subordinate-level categories of robins, sparrows, etc. Regarding our problem of recognizing movement style, we could take any action (walking, drinking, lifting, tennis serve, dancing, etc.) as the basic-level category, and the subordinate-level categorization of any of these actions could be gender, affect, identity, emotion, or particular school of dance or type of tennis serve. The advantage of taking this operational definition is that it allows us to proceed with the task of trying to identify action properties that are used to recognize different movement styles. The disadvantage is that we might end up with nothing more than a bag of tricks—various feature sets that work for various tasks (Levin and Saylor discuss this point in Chapter 19 of this volume in terms of the issue of "conceptual heterogeneity"). As such it is useful to be mindful of other theoretically inspired approaches to categorizing actions (Lamberts, 2004).

Movement Features

To give substance to the notion of style recognition as movement categorization requires being able to describe how the various physical characteristics of a movement lead to its categorization. These different physical characteristics can be thought of as movement features, and the process of categorization as the process of mapping features to categories. We begin by discussing the concept of a movement feature and visit potential processing and theoretical constraints that might suggest particular movement features. Next, we touch upon techniques of automatic pattern recognition and how they can be used to quantify efficiency in recognition of human movement. Finally, we discuss research investigating how features can be manipulated within a defined movement space to reveal their importance.

Movement Features and Processing Constraints

Of course, to recognize a style of movement requires that there is some physical information in the movement that supports the process of recognition, and we can consider any such movement information to be a feature. This movement information can be a particular posture obtained during a movement, the instantaneous speed or location of one particular limb segment, or the relative timing of the different movement phrases. Given the complexity of human form and human motion and the kinematic redundancy within the human body, it is useful to start with the assumption that there is no single unique source of information to movement style. Instead we can consider many sources of information to be simultaneously available and assume that different information might be diagnostic for different recognition tasks. This assumption is consistent with models of object recognition as well as experimental results from the recognition of actions by elite athletes (Abernethy, Gill, Parks, & Packer, 2001). Finally, despite claims that humans have a visual system that is exquisitely tuned to understanding actions, there have to be limits. Depending upon the categorization task required, the particular viewing conditions, and the inherent variability of the movement, it might well be impossible to reliably recognize certain styles of movement (except for possibly all but the extreme exaggerated cases). Thus, what we currently face is a vast feature space, and what is needed is both theoretical understanding of the limits and intrinsic features of this space, as well as empirical results that can argue for the utility of particular features. This issue of the size of the feature space is particularly relevant to issues in learning and development, which are discussed in this volume in Chapters 4, 6, and 7.

One theoretical point that has attracted particular attention recently is that recognizing human action has a peculiar significance in psychology, since it stands in the middle of a variety of perception-action loops. An important distinction to make here is that people might want to observe an action to better understand their environment, or they might want to perform the same action themselves. This distinction leads to the two hypotheses of *visual matching* and *direct matching* in action understanding. In visual matching, it is held that we match visual events to sophisticated visual representations that might not, in principle, be different from the same mechanisms used to represent the event of a ball rolling down a slope. In direct matching, it is held that we match vision of an action to visuomotor representations with direct involvement in the production of one's own actions (Rizzolatti, Fadiga, Gallese, & Fogassi, 1996; Wilson & Knoblich, 2005). While neurophysiological evidence supports the existence of so-called mirror neurons that could subserve direct matching mechanisms by representing both the production and perception of an action, this evidence does not specify the precise computational principles by which direct matching can take place. Theoretical efforts are underway to understand how visual information about viewed movements could be mapped onto motor primitives to produce imitative movements (Demiris & Johnson, 2004; Schaal, Ijspeert, & Billard, 2003) and how this can be achieved in the context of paired forward-inverse models (Wolpert, Doya, & Kawato, 2003). However, a difficulty with this approach is that there is little consensus about what exactly specifies a "good" motor primitive. Moreover, the fact that we can manage to scratch our head, reach out to open a door, and keep our balance at the same time points out that these primitives must be able to be combined in complex ways. One theoretical approach to this complexity in the production of continuous action is to decompose the action into a posture component and a task component (Khatib, Sentis, Park, & Warren, 2004).

In summary, when considering the recognition of human movement style, the primary issue is that there is a vast potential feature space. While theoretical models of action recognition such as those provided by mirror neurons and direct matching can provide some guidance, they do not at present firmly constrain the study of style recognition or uniquely specify the exact motor primitives. Moreover, since direct matching relies upon one's own existing motor repertoire, it would seem that visual matching mechanisms are needed, at least for the process of learning new movements.

Automatic Classification and Estimating Efficiency

The question of how to decompose the vision of human movement into its essential features is problematic given the size of the potential feature space. One useful way to approach this problem is to apply well-defined methods for the recognition and decomposition of time-varying signals. For this approach automatic pattern recognition techniques are appropriate, and there are various examples of their application in the literature, including dynamic time warping (Wanderley, Bradley, Middleton, Mckay, & Hatch, 2005), Fourier decomposition (Unuma, Anjyo, & Takeuchi, 1995), and principal component analysis (Troje, 2002; see also Chapter 12 in this volume). However, a potential drawback of these techniques is that they do not necessarily allow a convenient interpretation of the results since, although movement is effectively represented for recognition, it is done via abstract features that do not necessarily have a direct physical or psychological interpretation. For example, techniques of Fourier decomposition and principal-components analysis produce features that are holistic in nature and thus do not facilitate identification of any feature that might be local. Thus, while they can inform the existence of systematic differences between, say, male and female gait (Troje, 2002), they do not necessarily indicate which limb segment(s) or time instant(s) within the movement are informative. Such difficulties can be ameliorated by using clever input representations or biologically inspired instantiations of the computational technique, but we leave discussion of this topic as beyond the scope of the present chapter. Instead we focus on one clear advantage of the techniques of automatic pattern classification: its ability to quantify the existence of abstract features and to quantify a level of performance using these features.

The ability to assess human performance in the recognition of biological motion is one area that has not received much attention. It has been often recognized that the ability to spontaneously organize a point-light walker appears extraordinary in terms of motion perception. Moreover, human thresholds in biological motion discrimination exceed those for translation (Neri, Morrone, & Burr, 1998). However, to appreciate this difference between discrimination of biological motion and translation it is necessary to have theoretical predictions of what performance would be obtained if all the possible available information could be used to make the discrimination (Lu, Yuille, & Lui, 2005). Similarly, to appreciate the ability of humans to recognize the style of human movement requires the ability to compare it to a standard measure. Automatic pattern classifiers provide such a tool. In the next paragraphs we explain the results of experiments that have used techniques of pattern classification to provide estimates of human efficiency at recognizing movement style.

One straightforward way to assess human performance at style recognition is to give observers a style recognition task and measure their accuracy at this task. However, there is an important issue with the use of accuracy as a measure of performance: low accuracy might be due to either exceptionally good performance at extracting information from an information-poor display or exceptionally bad performance at extracting information from an information-rich display. One way to deal with this issue is to obtain estimates of human efficiency, where human performance is compared to that of an algorithm that can be shown to use all the possible information (Barlow, 1978; Tanner & Birdsall, 1958). The efficiency measure generally used is the squared ratio of sensitivity (d') of the human observer to that of the algorithm that can utilize all the available information. This measure of efficiency can be used to compare performance across different tasks, and it is generally taken that efficiencies of over 10% can be taken to indicate exceptionally good performance (Liu, Knill, & Kersten, 1995). In the following paragraphs we review two studies that have examined the efficiency of human recognition.

A study by Pollick, Lestou, Ryu, and Cho (2002) examined the recognition of gender and affect from point-light displays of arm movements performing knocking, lifting, and waving actions. A database of approximately 1,500 movements was collected from 26 actors (13 male, 13 female) performing the actions in both a neutral and angry style. These movements were used both for psychological experiments on gender and affect recognition and to train a neural network to recognize either gender or affect. The neural network was used to estimate performance obtainable if all possible available information was used optimally, and as such it was noted that it did not strictly satisfy the criterion of an "ideal observer." Because of this the results of the efficiency calculations need to be interpreted as an upper-bound estimate of efficiency; if in fact a classifier can use more information, then efficiency would go down. However, even with this drawback the approach has the advantage of being able to compare recognition of gender and recognition of affect against the same standard. Overall, the network obtained d' values of approximately 3 regardless of whether recognizing gender or affect. However, human observers showed a large difference in performance—displaying d' values of around 1.5 for affect recognition and around 0 (chance level) for gender recognition. Computations of efficiency yielded upper-bound estimates of 32.5% for affect and 0.3% for gender recognition. From this we can reason that although the raw information was available for recognizing both gender and affect, the perceptual system was not able to utilize the information that signaled gender.

In the previous example we used features automatically defined by the neural networks and we did not have a physical interpretation of their meaning. One way to circumvent this issue is to measure efficiency relative to a known feature that has been defined manually. Although using this approach still fails to provide a proof that our manually defined feature encompasses all the available information, we do obtain a quantitative measure of human performance relative to our chosen feature. To illustrate the utility of this approach we will examine the efficiency of gender recognition from gait (Pollick, Kay, Heim, & Stringer, 2005). One cue that has been proposed for the recognition of gender from gait is center of moment, which assumes that the structural information in the size of the hips and shoulders informs gender recognition. To examine this using efficiency we need both an estimate of human performance and an estimate of optimal performance using center of moment. To estimate human performance we conducted a meta-analysis of 21 experiments examining gender from side views of gait that revealed an average level of performance of 66% correct (d' = 0.82). To estimate optimal performance we examined anthropometric databases to construct the distributions of male and female center of moment and used signal detection theory to derive optimal performance as 79% correct (d' = 1.63). This revealed an upper-bound estimate of efficiency of 26%. This result leads to an important conclusion regarding the potential utility of center of moment information—namely, if center of moment was not a particularly useful cue and there was a much more dominant cue, for example residual information in the side view to specify lateral sway (Mather & Murdoch, 1994), then we would predict that efficiency would be above 100% (i.e., individuals use more information than available in center of moment). However, such a finding was not obtained, and thus center of moment was not disconfirmed as a potentially useful cue in gender recognition.

In summary, the calculation of efficiency provides a valuable tool for examining the recognition of human movement. It provides a means to use methods of automatic pattern recognition and can also be extended to the case where a specific manually selected feature is examined. The results of the two studies above suggest that when humans can recognize a style of action they do so with high efficiency; however, with only limited data on the efficiency of style recognition and the theoretical limitations of these previous works, it is premature to make far-reaching conclusions. Of particular importance is the fact that, given the complexity of human motion, it is difficult to prove that any "ideal observer" is truly using all the information available. As such, a conservative view would be to take all these measures of efficiency as upper bounds that will necessarily decrease as better "ideal observers" can be found.

Feature Manipulation in Movement Spaces

As we saw above, the automatic approach to defining features has the benefit of analytical precision and the problem of physical interpretation, while the complementary approach of taking handcrafted features provides us with a means to explore the effectiveness of specific factors on style recognition, but by design is lacking an analysis of the complete feature set. In this section we discuss the creation of movement spaces that allow parametric manipulation of specific features. This approach relies upon first collecting 3-D data from actual movements that can be thought to span a relevant part of the movement's space. This notion of spanning the space involves collecting enough different actions and different styles of movements from enough actors to ensure that the inherent variability of movements is represented. Once we have this space we can choose particular movement properties and, with the use of analytical techniques, parametrically vary these properties to create new displays. By studying the influence of these manipulations upon observers' interpretations of the movements, we can infer the influence of these particular properties on style recognition.

Given that one has collected 3-D data for a large group of movements, the next issue is what aspect of these data to manipulate. As seen above in the case for gender recognition, it is possible to extract specific features, such as the distribution of the center of moment for males and females. One can even collect a specialized set of movements and study specific hypotheses on this set, as has been done in studies of self-recognition (Beardsworth & Buckner, 1981; Cutting & Kozlowski, 1977; Loula, Prasa, Harber, & Shiffrar, 2005). However, another approach is to attempt to explore more general properties of movements to use as features. An obvious choice here is to try to dissociate spatial from temporal properties. It has been proposed that the primary visual region involved in the processing of biological motion is the posterior region of the superior temporal sulcus, located at the confluence of the processing streams of form and motion (Giese & Poggio, 2003; Oram & Perrett, 1994; see also Chapters 13 and 14). Such a functional location is consistent with the idea that recognizing biological motion involves the combination of separate analyses of form and motion information. While for motion stimuli it is inherently impossible to entirely dissociate form (spatial) from motion (temporal), it could be the case that recognition of some movement style might rely more heavily on one feature than another. For example, a defining characteristic might be the spatial property of a precise posture or the temporal property of a precise rhythm among the subcomponents of the movement.

To explore the influence of spatial and temporal features on the recognition of movement style, we have borrowed a technique made popular in the study of face recognition, which took libraries of facial images and manipulated the underlying properties of the images to define new facial images (Benson & Perrett, 1994; Perrett et al., 1998; Young, Rowland, Calder, Etcoff, Seth, & Perrett, 1997). The essential difference between this technique and ours is that since movements unfold in time, it is necessary to consider not only spatial properties of particular static images but also temporal properties of how this unfolding takes place. In our examples below we will discuss how spatial and temporal properties are teased apart. However, before that we would like to present a basic overview of how the collection of 3-D movement data forms the basis for these manipulations.

As we stated earlier, the 3-D movements were collected so as to span a region of interest in movement space. If we consider every collected movement to be a point in space, then it is reasonable to question what new points within this collection of movements look like as well as what points outside the region of the collection of movements look like. Synthesizing of these new points within the collection can be accomplished via interpolation, and outside the collection via extrapolation. If we would take a point in the collection representing one style of movement and move away from it, then we would expect that, in general, recognition of style would diminish, since we are farther away from a good example of the movement. However, it turns out that this is not always the case, and if one is careful about selecting locations to generate these new points then it is possible to synthesize new movements that are more easily recognized. Below we discuss experiments that explored spatial exaggerations of the style of tennis serve (Pollick, Fidopiastis, et al., 2001), temporal exaggerations of identity from drinking movements (Hill & Pollick, 2002), and spatial and temporal exaggerations of facial emotion (Pollick, Hill, Calder, & Paterson, 2003).

To explore spatial exaggerations of tennis-serve style, we first obtained 3-D records of flat, slice, and topspin serves and animated these movements using tools of 3-D computer animation. Each tennis-serve movement was specified by a vector with about 4,000 dimensions corresponding to the 24 measurements on the body, each with 3 spatial coordinates and sampled at 60 Hz for around 1 second. Extrapolation in the direction from the grand average of all styles to the individual style averages was used to create exaggerated flat, slice, and topspin serves. Results of this study showed an effect of the exaggeration technique, most clearly for the flat serves. Individual difference indicated an effect of the exaggeration for slice serves only with the more "expert" tennis players. The criterion used to define expertise was obtained through an independent dissimilarity-rating task, which showed that "experts" equally weighted all three serves, while "novices" had small weightings for at least one serve. While these results are encouraging, there is still the concern that, because the exaggerated displays were created from individual frames, each of which had been exaggerated, it was possible that enhanced recognition could have been due to a single frame rather than to the movement itself.

Temporal exaggerations of movement can be created that remove the previous concern about the effect of particular static frames. This temporal exaggeration technique requires that the movement being studied can be broken down into distinct phrases so that the relative timing of the different phrases can be manipulated. For the drinking movements we studied, the motion was decomposed into five segments based on minima of velocity of the wrist; these segments were (1) moving the hand from the side of the body to contact the glass, (2) lifting the glass to the mouth, (3) tilting the glass back, (4) returning the glass to the table, and (5) returning the hand to the side of the body. A database of seven different drinkers was used to exaggerate the differences among the relative phrasing of the movements among the actors, and the results revealed enhanced recognition for the exaggerated displays. For these displays the spatial pattern of every individual was identical for all exaggeration conditions; all that ever changed in the displays shown to observers was the timing of the segments. Thus, with spatial patterns held constant across different levels of exaggeration, the exaggeration effect had to occur due to some temporal aspect of the motion.

The results of these two studies indicate that both spatial and temporal properties could be exaggerated to obtain enhanced recognition. Although the second experiment argues for temporal properties, another possible interpretation is that a spatiotemporal interaction such as velocity mediated the exaggeration effects obtained. Both of our exaggeration techniques changed the velocity profile of the movement as they acted to exaggerate the spatial or temporal information. We studied this effect further by performing both spatial and temporal exaggerations of facial emotion for point-light faces (Pollick et al., 2003). In separate experiments there was a clear effect of spatial exaggeration but no equivalent effect of temporal exaggeration. From this result with faces it is tempting to speculate that for different activities the essence of the movement style is present to different degrees in the spatial and temporal encoding of the movement.

Recognition of Affect from Human Movement

In this final section we turn our attention to the recognition of affect from human movement. Affect has been defined as an emotion or subjectively experienced feeling, and as such the terms "affect" and "emotion" can at times be used interchangeably. We prefer to use the term "affect" since some aspects we might want to recognize in a movement are clearly related to the disposition of an individual but are not emotions. Although the term "affect" is broader than "emotion," it is not clear that even it is broad enough to cover the range we hope to cover. For example, we will use "affect" to encompass "tired," "vulnerable," "weak," and even more abstract conditions such as "fragile" and "light." We begin our discussion of the recognition of affect by examining the issue of what type of actions might carry an affective message and offer a more detailed look at emotions. From this we move on to experiments that have used multidimensional scaling to examine the recognition of affect from the everyday movements of lifting and drinking as well as the less common movements of butoh dance. The results of both studies point to the differential use of spatial and temporal information in the representation of affect.

What Kinds of Actions Describe Affect?

While the style of an actor's movements is often determined by relatively stable elements such as his or her physiological composition, gender, and age, there are also transient elements that can contribute to style, such as emotions and more sustained characteristics such as mood or present physical state. Of course, movement is only one of several cues to affect; in particular, emotions may be evident in many kinds of dynamic signal, from vocal prosody to facial expression. Consequently, in a natural setting there are potentially many different dynamic cues to emotion in any given social event. Actions that convey affect can be divided into two types: those that can convey emotional states from almost any activity and those that convey short bursts of emotion which are in themselves reactions to environmental cues.

Emotions form an important subset of affects, and longstanding research on emotion has resulted in a very small subset of affects being considered suitable for study. The subset of emotional expressions that are usually examined are known as the six basic expressions (Ekman, Friesen, & Ellsworth, 1972): afraid, angry, disgusted, happy, sad, and surprised. It would seem that these six basic expressions are highly appropriate for investigating perception of emotion from static facial images; however, it is far from certain that they are appropriate for investigating emotion from human movement in its entirety. For instance, while a basic facial expression might be easily identified from almost any face, there are some emotions that might only be conveyed by specific actions or postures. It might yet be the case that there is a range of expression whose optimal basis of communication lies within movements and is complementary to that obtained via the basic facial expressions.

It is instructive to review the six basic emotions and how successfully they might be conveyed by movement, as well as how this success might interact with the different time scales on which affect will be displayed. First, it is useful to point out that any distinctions of time scale are not exclusive: some emotions can exist either as a prolonged state or a passing reaction to a particular situation. For instance, our reactions to a joke or a spike of annoyed anger are reactions to the situation around us, while we can also sustain a happy or angry mood for a relatively long period of time. In comparison, disgust and surprise are almost exclusively reactive emotions and very often have quite specific postures and actions associated with them. Just imagine trying to knock on a door in a surprised or disgusted way. The best way to convey the emotion might be to knock and then show some kind of reaction to the door. Finally, the emotion "sad" is possibly best conveyed as a sustained mood (apart from perhaps some very specific cases of intense grief) with slowed movements in all actions. Of the basic expressions, fear is probably the most difficult emotion to portray as an action. This is because while it is easy to imagine your reaction to some fearful event, it is less clear-cut how your actions would embody the emotions that you feel when going to a job interview. While it could be argued that this particular situation would bring on a nervous mood rather than fear, it raises the issue that the same basic emotion might change the character of its influence on movement as situations change.

The characteristics of emotions hence have implications for the kinds of actions that might be associated with them. Reactive emotions might be best described with goal-directed or even object-directed movements, so that, for instance, the actor can display a fearful, surprised, or disgusted reaction to an object that he or she has interacted with. In comparison, either goal-directed or intransitive (non-goal-directed) actions may be used to convey states or moods. As an example, imagine pacing backwards and forwards in an angry way. This is relatively easy to do, but in comparison try to imagine pacing in a surprised way—this will seem much harder. In the past, a range of actions have been used in psychological and neuroscience research to investigate the perception of emotion from human motion, including mimed emotions (Atkinson, Dittrich, Gemmell, & Young, 2004; Walk & Homan, 1984), dance (Dittrich et al., 1996), arm movements (Paterson & Pollick, 2001; Pollick, Paterson, et al., 2001), and walking (Ma, Paterson, & Pollick, 2006). These actions can be divided into two broad groupings, with the mime and dance showing actions that are choreographed independently for each emotion. This has the benefit of maximizing the possibility of detecting the emotion as well as being able to capture a wide variety of emotions. In comparison, the other groups of actions are choreographed so that the action remains the same for each emotion and hence only the specific emotional content changes. This has the benefit of enabling a researcher to compare almost exclusively the motion features associated with different emotions while minimizing noise due to differing actions. On the other hand, the range of emotions that may be compared becomes restricted, as the range of actions is restricted.

One drawback of using choreographed movements at all is that they are not necessarily representative of human behavior in "the wild." One example of research that used naturally occurring emotions is that of Troscianko and colleagues (2004). This research used CCTV clips captured in British towns and cities to test observers' abilities to predict the outbreak of violent events. While this approach profits greatly from the use of naturalistic stimulus material, without an immense corpus of well-cataloged events it is hard to systematically manipulate the properties of the actions being viewed to uncover the essential visual properties.

A Feature Space for the Structure of Affect

In an earlier section of the chapter we described means of quantifying efficiency in human movement recognition that used predefined or automatically defined features. In this section we describe the analogous psychometric technique of multidimensional scaling (Kruskal & Wish, 1978) for obtaining a feature space that underlies the perception of affective movements. Multidimensional scaling (MDS) commonly works by first constructing a distance table between all elements of a set of stimuli. Next, by properly considering the type of measurement scale used to obtain the "distances" (typically an ordinal scale), one can construct a low-dimensional map of appropriate locations for all the elements. While this guarantees a psychological representation, it is not necessarily accessible to any physical interpretation, and obtaining a physical interpretation can be difficult. In the following section we pursue a representation of affect by first recording a set of affective movements and then using judgments about them to construct a distance table that can be analyzed using MDS. From this we try to relate the structure of the psychological space to the physical characteristics of the movement.

To examine the recognition of affect from everyday movements, we obtained 3-D recordings of affective knocking and drinking movements in which only point-light displays of the arm were made available (Pollick, Paterson, et al., 2001). The movements were recorded with the actors depicting 10 affective styles (afraid, angry, excited, happy, neutral, relaxed, sad, strong, tired, and weak). Participants viewed these displays and tried to correctly identify which of the 10 affects had been presented to them. Results were converted to a matrix of dissimilarities and input to an MDS algorithm. In a first experiment using the natural 3-D recordings, results showed that the structure of this MDS solution was similar to the 2-D circumplex structure of affect obtained by Russell (1980), with one dimension varying along an activation axis (lethargic to energetic) and the other varying along a valence axis (unpleasant to pleasant). In a second experiment we inserted a random phase delay into each point and inverted the display to show it to observers who made the same judgments as to the exhibited affect in the display. The results of this experiment showed that the ordering of affects along the activation axis was preserved, but reorganization along the valence axis was found. In both experiments we were able to show a strong correlation between the actual movement kinematics and the location of a movement along the activation axis, with more activation correlated positively to greater velocity. However, no strong correlation between kinematics and the valence dimension was obtained for either experiment.

The results generally indicated that activation was more robustly recovered than valence. One possible reason for this is that, by its nature, movement is a more natural indicator of physiological arousal and its associated neural mechanisms. In addition, the continuous structure of the circumplex model parallels the smoothly varying range of speeds with which a movement can be performed. Thus, it would appear that the mapping between stimulus properties and representation of affect is a fairly direct one for the activation axis. However, such a direct connection between stimulus and representation has proven elusive for the second dimension of valence. Other research has suggested that subtle phase relations between the joints might possibly carry information about affect (Amaya, Bruderlin, & Calvert, 1996). Comparison of the results between our two experiments supports this view; however, the present data do not indicate which aspect of the phase relations is the crucial one.

To explore further whether this circumplex structure could be obtained for other types of affective movements, we examined the recognition of affect from movements from butoh dance (Macfarlane, Pollick, & Kulka, 2004). Butoh dance is a modern form of Japanese dance that provides a unique and dynamic movement style (Kurihara, 2000). To obtain stimuli, video sequences of butoh dance depicting the 10 affects of anger, calm, fear, fragility, happiness, lightness, rigidity, sadness, strength, and warmth were edited into low-resolution 15-second digital video clips. The conversion to low resolution was used to obscure the features of the face while preserving the integrity of the limb movements. Participants viewed these movements in pairs and gave ratings of dissimilarity between all possible pairings of the two clips. These dissimilarity ratings were next analyzed using MDS to obtain a 2-D solution of the psychological space. Although this experiment used dance movements instead of everyday movements, a different means of presenting the motion data, and a different means of obtaining responses, the results were remarkably similar: one axis appeared to span activation, with anger at one side and calm at the other, while the other axis appeared to span valence, with fear at one end and warm at the other. Although visual inspection of the movements was consistent with the placement of movements upon the activation axis, no quantitative measurement of the video data was attempted. However, appropriate techniques such as those developed by Camurri and colleagues do exist for quantifying movement in video data (Camurri, Volpe, & Lagerlöf, 2003), and in future work we hope to use such measurements to relate movement quantities to perception.

In summary, we have discussed general characteristics of human movement important for recognizing affect and presented results from experiments that argue for a psychological representation of affective movement that separately represents activation and valence. Important factors in the composition of affective movement are that the movements can be reactive or sustained and they can be either overlaid upon existing movements or generated as movements specific for the affect. These factors alone provide quite a diversity of affective movements. The proposed representation of affect appears capable of handling this diversity within the scope of the activation axis, where movement kinematics can be mapped to activation. However, at present the valence axis is problematic, as there does not yet exist a close mapping between a general physical property of movement and perceived valence.

Conclusion

We have tried to explain the recognition of affect from human movement. This explanation has proceeded in the directions of two somewhat independent strands of questioning. One strand has been directed toward the question of what human movement properties might appropriately be considered features for recognition. The other question has been how to systematize the recognition process and identify the appropriate taxonomy for categorizing different movement styles. In trying to tie together these two strands regarding the recognition of affect, we have presented evidence that it is possible to recognize affect even for everyday movements. Moreover, movement speed is a critical feature that can be mapped directly into the activation axis found in a circumplex representation of affect. Numerous loose ends and unanswered questions remain. However, we hope that with the direction and inspiration from the other chapters in this volume, progress in the study of affect recognition can illuminate the larger picture of understanding events.

References

Abernethy, B., Gill, D. P., Parks, S. L., & Packer, S. T. (2001). Expertise and the perception of kinematic and situational probability information. *Perception, 30*(2), 233.

Abernethy, B., & Russell, D. G. (1984). Advanced cue utilisation by skilled cricket batsmen. *Australian Journal of Science and Medicine in Sport, 16*(2), 2–10.

Amaya, K., Bruderlin, A., & Calvert, T. (1996). *Emotion from motion.* Paper presented at the Proceedings Graphics Interface '95, Toronto, Ontario.

Atkinson, A. P., Dittrich, W. H., Gemmell, A. J., & Young, A. W. (2004). Emotion perception from dynamic and static body expressions in point-light and full-light displays. *Perception, 33*(6), 717.

Barlow, H. B. (1978). The efficiency of detecting changes of density in random dot patterns. *Vision Research, 18*(6), 637.

Beardsworth, T., & Buckner, T. (1981). The ability to recognize oneself from a video recording of one's movements without seeing one's body. *Bulletin of the Psychonomic Society, 18*(1), 19–22.

Benson, P. J., & Perrett, D. I. (1994). Visual processing of facial distinctiveness. *Perception, 23*(1), 75–93.

Brand, M., & Hertzmann, A. (2000). Style machines. *Computer Graphics Proceedings. Annual Conference Series, 547*, 183–192.

Brownlow, S., Dixon, A. R., Egbert, C. A., & Radcliffe, R. D. (1997). Perception of movement and dancer characteristics from point-light displays of dance. *Psychological Record, 47*(3), 411–421.

Camurri, A., Volpe, G., & Lagerlöf, I. (2003). Recognizing emotion from dance movement: Comparison of spectator recognition and automated techniques. *International Journal of Human Computer Studies, 59*(1–2), 213.

Cutting, J. E., & Kozlowski, L. T. (1977). Recognizing friends by their walk: Gait perception without familiarity cues. *Bulletin of the Psychonomic Society, 9*(5), 353–356.

Demiris, Y., & Johnson, M. (2004). Simulation theory for understanding others: A robotics perspective. In K. Dautenhahn & C. Nehaniv (Eds.), *Imitation and social learning in robots, humans and animals: Behavioural social and communicative dimensions*. Cambridge: Cambridge University Press.

Dittrich, W. H., Troscianko, T., Lea, S., & Morgan, D. (1996). Perception of emotion from dynamic point-light displays represented in dance. *Perception, 25*(6), 727–738.

Ekman, P., Friesen, W. V., & Ellsworth, P. (1972). *Emotion in the human face: Guidelines for research and an integration of findings*. London: Pergamon Press.

Giese, M., & Poggio, T. (2003). Neural mechanisms for the recognition of biological movements. *Nature Reviews Neuroscience, 4*(3), 179–192.

Gunns, R. E., Johnston, L., & Hudson, S. M. (2002). Victim selection and kinematics: A point-light investigation of vulnerability to attack. *Journal of Nonverbal Behavior, 26*(3), 129–158.

Hill, H., & Pollick, F. E. (2000). Exaggerating temporal differences enhances recognition of individuals from point light displays. *Psychological Science, 11*(3), 223–228.

Khatib, O., Sentis, L., Park, J., & Warren, J. (2004). Whole-body dynamic behavior and control of human-like robots. *International Journal of Humanoid Robotics, 1*(1), 29–43.

Kozlowski, L. T., & Cutting, J. E. (1977). Recognizing the sex of a walker from a dynamic point-light display. *Perception and Psychophysics, 21*(6), 575–580.

Kruskal, J. B., & Wish, M. (1978). *Multidimensional scaling*. Beverly Hills and London: Sage Publications.

Kurihara, N. (2000). Hijikata tatsumi: The words of butoh. *Drama Review, 44*, 12–28.

Lamberts, K. (2004). An exemplar model for perceptual categorization of events. In B. Ross (Ed.), *Psychology of learning and motivation: Advances in research and theory*, Vol. 44 (pp. 227–260). San Diego: Academic Press.

Liu, Z., Knill, D. C., & Kersten, D. (1995). Object classification for human and ideal observers. *Vision Research, 35*(4), 549–568.

Loula, F., Prasad, S., Harber, K., & Shiffrar, M. (2005). Recognizing people from their movement. *Journal of Experimental Psychology: Human Perception and Performance, 31*(1), 210–220.

Lu, H., Yuille, A., & Lui, Z. (2005). *Configural processing in biological motion detection: Human versus ideal observers.* Paper presented at the Vision Sciences Society, Sarasota, FL.

Ma, Y. L., Paterson, H. M., & Pollick, F. E. (2006). A motion-capture library for the study of identity, gender and emotion perception from biological motion. *Behavior Research Methods, 38*(1), 134–141.

Macfarlane, L., Pollick, F. E., & Kulka, I. (2004). The representation of affect revealed by butoh dance. *Psychologia, 47*(2), 96.

Mather, G., & Murdoch, L. (1994). Gender discrimination in biological motion displays based on dynamic cues. *Proceedings of the Royal Society of London Series B, Biological Sciences, 258*(1353), 273–279.

Neri, P., Morrone, M. C., & Burr, D. C. (1998). Seeing biological motion. *Nature, 395*(6705), 894–896.

Oram, M. W., & Perrett, D. I. (1994). Responses of anterior superior temporal polysensory (stpa) neurons to "biological motion" stimuli. *Journal of Cognitive Neuroscience, 6*(2), 99–116.

Paterson, H. M., & Pollick, F. E. (2001). *Form and animacy in the perception of affect from biological motion.* Paper presented at the Vision Sciences Society First Annual Meeting, Sarasota, FL.

Paterson, H. M., Pollick, F. E., & Sanford, A. J. (2001). *The role of velocity in affect discrimination.* Paper presented at the Twenty-Third Annual Conference of the Cognitive Science Society, Edinburgh.

Perrett, D. I., Lee, K. J., Penton-Voak, I., Rowland, D., Yoshikawa, S., Burt, D. M., et al. (1998). Effects of sexual dimorphism on facial attractiveness. *Nature, 394*(6696), 884–887.

Pollick, F. E., Fidopiastis, C., & Braden, V. (2001). Recognising the style of spatially exaggerated tennis serves. *Perception, 30*(3), 323–338.

Pollick, F. E., Hill, H., Calder, A., & Paterson, H. (2003). Recognising facial expression from spatially and temporally modified movements. *Perception, 32*(7), 813–826.

Pollick, F. E., Kay, J. W., Heim, K., & Stringer, R. (2005). Gender recognition from point-light walkers. *Journal of Experimental Psychology: Human Perception and Performance, 31*(6), 1247–1265.

Pollick, F. E., Lestou, V., Ryu, J., & Cho, S.-B. (2002). Estimating the efficiency of recognizing gender and affect from biological motion. *Vision Research, 42*(20), 2345–2355.

Pollick, F. E., Paterson, H. M., Bruderlin, A., & Sanford, A. J. (2001). Perceiving affect from arm movement. *Cognition, 82*(2), B51–B61.

Rizzolatti, G., Fadiga, L., Gallese, V., & Fogassi, L. (1996). Premotor cortex and the recognition of motor actions. *Cognitive Brain Research, 3*(2), 131–141.

Rosch, E., Mervis, C. B., Gray, W. D., Johnson, D. M., & Boyesbraem, P. (1976). Basic objects in natural categories. *Cognitive Psychology, 8*(3), 382–439.

Russell, J. A. (1980). A circumplex model of affect. *Journal of Personality and Social Psychology, 39*(1 Suppl 6), 1161–1178.

Schaal, S., Ijspeert, A., & Billard, A. (2003). Computational approaches to motor learning by imitation. *Philosophical Transaction of the Royal Society of London: Series B, Biological, 358*(1431), 537–547.

Tanner, W. P. J., & Birdsall, T. G. (1958). Definition of d' and η as psychophysical measures. *Journal of Acoustic Society of America, 30*(10), 922–928.

Tenenbaum, J. B., & Freeman, W. T. (2000). Separating style and content with bilinear models. *Neural Computation, 12*(6), 1247.

Troje, N. F. (2002). Decomposing biological motion: A framework for analysis and synthesis of human gait patterns. *Journal of Vision, 2*(5), 371–387.

Troscianko, T., Holmes, A., Stillman, J., Mirmehdi, M., Wright, D., & Wilson, A. (2004). What happens next? The predictability of natural behaviour viewed through CCTV cameras. *Perception, 33*(1), 87–101.

Unuma, M., Anjyo, K., & Takeuchi, R. (1995). *Fourier principals for emotion-based human figure animation.* Paper presented at the International Conference on Computer Graphics and Interactive Techniques.

Walk, R. D., & Homan, C. P. (1984). Emotion and dance in dynamic light displays. *Bulletin of the Psychonomic Society, 22*(5), 437–440.

Wanderley, M. M., Bradley, W. V., Middleton, N., Mckay, C., & Hatch, W. (2005). The musical significance of clarinetists' ancillary gestures: An exploration of the field. *Journal of New Music Research, 34*(1), 97–113.

Wilson, M., & Knoblich, G. (2005). The case for motor involvement in perceiving conspecifics. *Psychological Bulletin, 131*(3), 460.

Wolpert, D. M. (1997). Computational approaches to motor control. *Trends in Cognitive Sciences, 1*(6), 209–216.

Wolpert, D. M., Doya, K., & Kawato, M. (2003). A unifying computational framework for motor control and social interaction. *Philosophical Transactions of the Royal Society of London Series B, Biological Sciences, 358*(1431), 593–602.

Young, A. W., Rowland, D., Calder, A. J., Etcoff, N. L., Seth, A., & Perrett, D. I. (1997). Facial expression megamix: Tests of dimensional and category accounts of emotion recognition. *Cognition, 63*(3), 271–313.

12

Retrieving Information from Human Movement Patterns

NIKOLAUS F. TROJE

Biological motion—that is, the movement patterns of animals and humans—provides a rich source of information that helps us to quickly and reliably detect the presence of another living being; to identify it as a predator, prey, or conspecific; and to infer its actions and intentions in order to respond with adequate behavior. Once we know that we are being confronted with another person, we are able to use motion as a source of information about identity, gender, age, emotional state, and personality traits and as a complex means for signaling and communications.

More than 30 years ago, the Swedish psychologist Gunnar Johansson (1973) introduced a stimulus into experimental psychology that allows us to disentangle to a large degree the information contained in the kinematics of a moving body from other sources of information about action and identity. His work showed that a few light dots placed strategically on a moving human or animal body are instantaneously organized into the coherent percept of a living creature (also see Chapter 11 in this volume). The observation goes back to the earlier work of the pioneers of cinematography (Muybridge, 1887/1979) and biomechanics (Marey, 1895/1972), but it was Johansson (1973) who first appreciated the significance of the tremendous saliency of biological motion point-light displays, and the effortless perceptual organization with which the visual system responds to them. Fewer than 10 isolated dots and display times of 200 ms are sufficient for a vivid percept of the articulated structure of a human body (Johansson, 1976).

Subsequent research concentrated on several aspects of this general phenomenon. It was shown that biological motion perception is very robust in the presence of many types of distracting masks (Cutting, Moore, & Morrison, 1988) and that it reveals more than just the presence of a person: point-light displays convey information about sex (Barclay, Cutting, & Kozlowski, 1978; Cutting, Proffitt, & Kozlowski, 1978; Kozlowski & Cutting, 1978) and identity of an agent (Cutting & Kozlowski, 1977), as well as emotional attributes (Dittrich, Troscianko, Lea, & Morgan, 1996; Pollick, Paterson, Bruderlin, & Sanford, 2001). Infants can perceive biological motion (Bertenthal, Proffitt, & Kramer, 1987; Fox & McDaniel, 1982), and it has been shown that at least pigeons and cats respond specifically to point-light displays (Blake, 1993; Dittrich, Lea, Barrett, & Gurr, 1998).

While the early work mainly concentrated on demonstrating the abilities of the visual system in processing biological motion, more recent studies have helped us understand how this is being achieved and which parts of the brain are involved. Recording from single cells in macaque cortex, Oram and Perrett (1994) first identified structures in the upper bank of the superior temporal sulcus (STS) as selectively responsive to human form and motion. A number of more recent brain imaging studies corroborate this finding and show that the posterior part of STS (STSp) is particularly active when looking at point-light displays of an upright human walker (Bonda, Petrides, Ostry, & Evans, 1996; Grossman, Blake, & Kim, 2004; Grossman et al., 2000; Peuskens, Vanrie, Verfaillie, & Orban, 2005). While STS is clearly responsive to biological motion, it is not clear how specific this area is. Stimuli such as speech (Beauchamp, 2005) or the sound of footsteps (Bidet-Caulet, Voisin, Bertrand, & Fonlupt, 2005), as well as motion confined to specific limbs, the eyes, or the mouth (Grezes, Costes, & Decety, 1998; Puce, Allison, Bentin, Gore, & McCarthy, 1998), also result in STSp activation. Besides STSp, other areas have been identified that are responsive to biological motion. They include the ventral surface of the temporal lobe (Vaina, Solomon, Chowdhury, Sinha, & Belliveau, 2001), the fusiform gyrus (Beauchamp, Lee, Haxby, & Martin, 2002), and the fusiform face area (Grossman & Blake, 2002; Peelen & Downing, 2005). For all these areas, it is rather unclear if they respond specifically to human motion or if they are triggered generally by biological motion. Very few imaging studies have contrasted responses to representations of humans versus nonhumans, and none of these used standard biological motion point-light displays (Buccino et al., 2004; Downing, Jiang, Shuman, & Kanwisher, 2001).

For a long time, biological motion has been treated as a single phenomenon. Only during the past few years has it become obvious that there are a number of different mechanisms involved that need to be distinguished both conceptually as well as experimentally. Here I am suggesting at least four different stages of information processing involved with biological motion perception.

1. **Detection of animate motion.** A fast and reliable system is required to detect the presence of an animal in the visual environment. Ideally, this mechanism should be independent of the particular nature of the animal, and in particular independent of its shape. It should respond to biological motion in the whole visual field, including the visual periphery. The evolutionary significance of such an early "life detector" is obvious. It is required either to trigger fast behavioral responses (flight, attack) or to guide attention to potentially threatening or otherwise interesting events. Troje and Westhoff (2006) identified the ballistic movements of the limbs of a terrestrial animal to provide such an invariant. The cue seems to work well not only for foveal vision but also in the visual periphery, and probably directs attention to an event of potentially vital significance. The underlying visual filter mechanism shows a pronounced inversion effect: if presented upside-down, our visual system is no longer able to retrieve information from the local motion of the limbs. The visual filter is expected to be evolutionarily old, innate rather than learned, and shared by other animals. Behavioral experiments on visually naïve, newly hatched chicks suggest that they in fact use the same cue to identify the object of filial imprinting (Vallortigara & Regolin, 2006; Vallortigara, Regolin, & Marconato, 2005).

2. **Structure from motion.** Once a living creature is detected, its movements can be used to perceptually organize it into a coherent, articulated body structure, resulting in "basic-level" (Rosch, 1988) agent recognition (e.g., Is this a human, a cat, a bird?). This mechanism does not work very well in the visual periphery (Ikeda, Blake, & Watanabe, 2005) and probably requires attention (Cavanagh, Labianca, & Thornton, 2001; Thornton, Rensink, & Shiffrar, 2002). In contrast to the early "life detection" stage, it requires learning and individual experience (Jastorff, Kourtzi, & Giese, 2006). It is also subject to an inversion effect, which, however, is independent of the one operating on the "life detection" mechanism and is instead similar to the orientation dependency of configural processing observed in face recognition (Farah, Tanaka, & Drain, 1995).

3. **Action perception.** On this level, structural and kinematic information is integrated into a system that classifies and categorizes actions and events. Ideally, efficient classification on this level should be invariant to actor, viewpoint, and the particular style of the action. Many of the chapters in this section of the book specifically address this processing level (see especially Chapters 10 and 11).

4. **Style recognition.** Once both agent and action are identified, pattern recognition at a "subordinate" (Rosch, 1988) level helps to retrieve further information about the details of both. For instance, once we know we are confronted with a human walker (rather than, say, a hunting tiger), we are able to use motion as a source of information about individual identity, gender, age, emotional state, and personality traits, and as a complex means for signaling and communications. Depending on the particular property, the results of initial data processing required to characterize and isolate diagnostic features might eventually feed into different neuronal circuits, and in that respect "style recognition" might not be due to a single mechanism but to several. Yet, at least from a computational point of view, it is likely that all of them share certain processing principles.

For the remainder of this chapter, I will concentrate on style recognition. The ability of the human visual system to sensitively detect and adequately interpret subtle nuances in the way people move is both a prerequisite and a consequence of the fact that the complex social structures characterizing our species require us to identify one another individually and to attribute emotion, personality, and intentions to our peers.

A number of different approaches to understanding style in human movement come both from the computer-vision community and from experimental psychology, and a large part of this work is well summarized in Chapter 11. In the present chapter, I want to present and discuss a particular computational framework that we used to retrieve stylistic information from visual human locomotion patterns over the past years. It was first developed to identify and analyze sex-specific differences between walkers (Troje, 2002a). We then changed and further improved the algorithm and applied it to a number of different problems and questions in the context of pattern recognition from biological motion. In the next section, I will first outline the general framework and then provide the details of the algorithm. In the third section, I will summarize some of the studies in which we applied the algorithm. In the final section, I will discuss the role of the proposed framework in understanding the very complex class of stimuli that our visual system copes with so easily, its value as a model for human perception, and potential ways to generalize and improve it.

A Framework for the Analysis and Synthesis of Human Walking Patterns

Our approach to understanding the mechanisms underlying biological motion perception focuses on the information provided by the stimulus itself. Understanding how information is encoded in biological motion patterns is a prerequisite for designing artificial vision systems, but is also helpful for understanding biological vision systems by means of "reverse engineering." How can we possibly retrieve structure from the complex spatiotemporal patterns of animate motion? Approaching biological motion perception as a pattern-recognition problem can teach us about principles and constraints that any system, regardless of whether it is artificial or biological, has to cope with when analyzing biological motion patterns.

The general idea of our approach is as follows. Starting with data obtained by means of a motion capture system (i.e., with the 3-D trajectories of discrete points on a person's body), the first step of the subsequent data processing is to transform the data into a representation that would allow us to apply standard methods from linear statistics and pattern recognition. Such representations have been termed "morphable models" (Giese & Poggio, 2000; Jones & Poggio, 1999; Shelton, 2000) in the computer-vision community, expressing the fact that the linear transition from one item to a second item of the data set represents a well-defined, smooth metamorphosis such that all intermediate stages maintain the structural characteristics defining the object class and are therefore qualitatively indistinguishable from the start and end points. Other terms that have been used in object recognition for similar kinds of models are "linear object classes" (Vetter & Poggio, 1997) and, in the context of human face recognition, "correspondence-based representations" (Troje & Vetter, 1998; Vetter & Troje, 1997). This latter term focuses on the fact that morphable models rely on establishing correspondence between features across the data set, resulting in a separation of the overall information into range-specific information on the one hand and domain-specific information on the other (Ramsay & Silverman, 1997). We also use the term "linearization" for the nonlinear transformation that is required to establish a representation that then enables us to treat the data as objects in linear space.

Linearization of the walker data mainly involves matching them in terms of frequency and phase. We do this by first computing the Fourier transform and then matching the data directly in the frequency domain. Note that this is slightly different from the way we have described data processing in earlier work (Troje, 2002a), where we used principal components analysis (PCA) to reduce dimensionality of the set of poses of a single walker. We found that the weights of the resulting Eigenposes (that is, the characteristic poses spanning the space of poses of an individual walker) vary sinusoidally with time. The decomposition resulting from PCA is therefore very similar to the one resulting from Fourier analysis. The main difference is that the roles of the terms that represent the basis functions and the terms that constitute the coefficients on these basis functions are interchanged (Troje, 2002b).

Once the data are linearized we apply PCA—however, this time we apply it not to the pose space but to the whole Fourier-based representations of a set of walkers. This reduces dimensionality of the linear walker space to the degree that the number of dimensions is much smaller than the number of data points that we use to establish this space. This step is important to avoid overfitting in the subsequent classification and to eventually construct a classifier that has predictive value.

The classifier itself is a very simple one. Based on the low-dimensional, linear space resulting from the previous two steps, we compute a linear discriminant function (LDF) by means of linear regression of the class indicator (e.g., indicating whether a particular walker in a training set is male or female) on the projections of the walkers into the resulting space.

One interesting feature of our approach is the fact that the transformations that map the time series of original motion capture data onto the morphable, low-dimensional walker space are more or less lossless and are therefore invertible. Consequently, any point in the morphable space—even points that do not correspond to original walkers—can be transformed back into a time series of marker positions and visualized as a point-light display. We will use this to exaggerate and caricature the set of diagnostic features that the classifier extracts, and to generate walking patterns with the respective properties and attributes.

The procedures described in the present study contain elements of earlier work on parameterizations of animate motion patterns (Bruderlin & Williams, 1995; Giese & Poggio, 2000; Guo & Roberge, 1996; Rose, Bodenheimer, & Cohen, 1998; Unuma, Anjyo, & Takeuchi, 1995; Urtasun, Glardon, Ronan, Thalmann, & Fua, 2004; Witkin & Popovic, 1995). Perhaps the most important one in the context of this paper is Unuma et al.'s (1995) study, which showed that blending between different human movements works much better in the frequency domain. At least for periodic motions, such as most locomotion patterns, Fourier decomposition can be used to achieve efficient, low-dimensional, linear decompositions. The fact that PCA applied to a time series of poses of a single walking person basically results in a discrete Fourier decomposition demonstrates that Fourier decomposition of walking data is nearly optimal in terms of explaining a maximum of variance with a minimum number of components (Troje, 2002b).

Data Collection

Most of our current work is based on data obtained by means of optical motion capture (Vicon 512, Oxford Metrics) from human subjects walking either on a treadmill or over ground. An array of 9 to 12 high-speed (120 Hz) cameras tracks the 3-D position of small (14 mm in diameter), passively reflecting markers with a spatial acuity in the order of 1 mm. Typically, participants wear swimsuits, and most of the markers are taped directly to their skin. Others, like the markers for the head, the ankles, and the wrists, are fixed to elastic bands, and the ones on the feet are taped onto the subjects' shoes. Currently, we are using a set of 41 markers (often referred to as the Helen-Hayes marker set; Davis, Ounpuu, Tyburski, & Gage, 1991). This set is designed such that, together with a few anthropometric measurements (such as the width of the knee, elbow, ankle, etc.), it provides the input to a biomechanical model that outputs accurate estimates for the location of the major joints of the human body. For most of our work, we use a set of 15 derived, "virtual" markers. They are located at shoulder joints, elbows, wrists, hip joints, knees, and ankles, and at the centers of the pelvis, clavicles, and head. The motion data that provide the input for the subsequent processing are therefore time series of poses (sampled at 120 Hz), each consisting of the 3-D Cartesian coordinates of 15 virtual markers. We call the 45-dimensional vector specifying their current location in space a "pose."

Whether data were collected from subjects walking on a treadmill or freely on the ground, we always asked our participants to walk for at least 5 minutes before we started data collection. On the treadmill, we allowed them to try different belt speeds to make sure that they felt as comfortable as possible. We did not tell the participants when actual data collection started. On the treadmill, we recorded a sequence of at least 10 full gait cycles. The volume available for free over-ground walking covered about four full gait cycles, and we typically recorded four passes throughout this volume for every participant.

Data Processing

The walk of an individual subject can be regarded as a time series of poses. Each pose can be described in terms of the position of the

15 markers in 3-D space. A single pose is therefore represented by a 45-dimensional vector:

$$p = (m1_x, m1_y, m1_z, m2_x, ...m15_z)^T \tag{1}$$

The time series of poses of a particular walker i can be decomposed into a discrete second-order Fourier series,

$$p_i(t) = p_{i,0} + p_{i,1} \sin(\omega_i t) + q_{i,1} \cos(\omega_i t) + p_{i,2} \sin(2\omega_i t) \\ + q_{i,2} \cos(2\omega_i t) + \mathrm{err}_i \tag{2}$$

where ω is the angular frequency derived from the gait frequency f as $\omega = 2\Pi f$. The first term $p_{i,0}$ describes the time-invariant average pose of walker i. It contains anthropometric structural information, for instance about the length of the limbs, the width of the shoulders, etc. The next two terms specify amplitudes and phases of the fundamental frequency, and the final two terms contain information about the second harmonic. Pairs of $p_{i,j}$ and $q_{i,j}$ can be translated directly into amplitudes $a_{i,j}$ and phases $\varphi_{i,j}$.

$$a_{i,j} = \sqrt{p_{i,j}^2 + q_{i,j}^2}, \quad \varphi_{i,j} = \arctan\left(\frac{q_{i,j}}{p_{i,j}}\right), \tag{3}$$

Here, Fourier analysis serves two purposes. First, it very effectively reduces redundancy and therefore provides compression of the data. For walking, the power carried by the residual term err in Equation 2 is less than 1% of the overall variance of the input data, and we usually discard it in all further computations.

Second, we use the Fourier representation to register the data in order to define correspondence between individual walking sequences. This is done by simply adjusting the phase and the frequency of the individual walking sequences. While the frequency of the walk is expressed in terms of the fundamental frequency ω_i, the absolute phase of the sequence and the relative phases between the 15 markers are contained in the relative contributions to the sine and the cosine terms (see Eq. 3). The absolute phase of a walking sequence depends only on the time at which we started data collection and contains no further information. We therefore adjusted the absolute phase of all sequences such that the average phase angle of the two ankle markers is 0 degrees.

A walk of a particular subject i is now approximated by specifying the average pose $p_{i,0}$, the four characteristic poses $p_{i,1}$, $q_{i,1}$, $p_{i,2}$, and $q_{i,2}$, and the fundamental frequency ω_i. The average pose and characteristic poses are all 45-dimensional vectors, while the fundamental frequency is a scalar. Thus, the dimensionality of the model at this stage is $5 \times 45 + 1 = 226$.

Although this number already reflects a considerable reduction in dimensionality as compared to the raw motion capture data, we expect the number of effective degrees of freedom within the database to be much smaller. For classification purposes it is necessary to reduce the dimensionality of the representation such that the number of dimensions becomes much smaller than the number of items represented in the resulting space.

The advantage of the above "linearized" representation (Eq. 2) is that it makes it possible to successfully apply linear operations to the set of motion data. At this stage, our representation has become a morphable model. Linear combinations of existing walking patterns result in new walking patterns that meaningfully represent the transitions between the constituting patterns (Troje, 2002a; Unuma et al., 1995). We can treat the 226-dimensional vector describing the walk wi of walker i as an object in linear space.

Classification

This representation also makes it possible to use PCA in order to further reduce dimensionality. Applying PCA to the set of walkers W results in a decomposition of each walker into an average walker v_0 and a weighted sum of Eigenwalkers v_j,

$$w_i = \sum_{j=1}^{m} k_{i,j} v_j \qquad (4)$$

or, in matrix notation,

$$W = V_0 = VK \qquad (5)$$

V_0 denotes a matrix with the average walker v_0 in each column. The matrix V contains the m Eigenwalkers as column vectors v_j. Matrix K contains the weights (or the coefficients) ki,j and is obtained by solving the linear equation system

$$VK = W - V_0 \qquad (6)$$

Given a set of n walkers, this procedure yields a total of $n-1$ Eigenwalkers. However, the variance covered by the first m Eigenwalkers is generally much larger than the fraction m/n of the overall variance. For instance, with the set of 100 walkers that we currently use, only four components are required to cover 50% of the overall variance, and 22 are required to cover 90%. The final choice of the number of Eigenwalkers m depends on the particular application. For classification purposes, it is recommended to use a relatively low number, resulting in better generalization. With a set of 100 walkers, we typically use 10 principal components for classification. For visualization purposes a larger number might be more suitable, since reconstruction is more accurate.[1]

Within the space spanned by the first m Eigenwalkers, a linear discriminant function can now be computed by simply regressing the class indicator (or any other variable quantifying an attribute of interest) on the projections of the walkers in the Eigenwalker space. This is achieved by finding the best (according to a least-square criterion) solution d of the overdetermined linear system

$$K^T d = r \qquad (7)$$

K^T is the transpose of matrix K, which contains the coefficients of each walker in the Eigenwalker space (Eq. 5). r is the column vector containing the n values r_i indicating the class to which walker i belongs (e.g., r_i

---

1. In our implementations, rather than submitting the matrix $W - V_0$ to the PCA, we first normalized each row of this matrix to get unit variance for each of them. The reasons for doing this, and the consequences it has for the subsequent computations and the way the resulting principal components are used, are beyond the scope of this chapter, and I chose to omit this detail here.

equals 1 if walker i is male and –1 if the walker is female) or another attribute that encodes the property of interest (e.g., a Likert scale rating given by an observer). The resulting column vector d then contains the coefficients of the linear discriminant function in the Eigenwalker space best accounting for the gender of the walkers.

The amount of variance explained by the regression (R^2) depends on the number of Eigenwalkers that have been used to span the walker space (m in Eq. 4). If all Eigenwalkers are used ($m = n - 1$), the value of R^2 will equal 1. However, in this particular case the predictive value of the classifier will be very low. The R^2 value, therefore, is not a good statistic to assess the quality of the classifier. A more useful way to do this is based on a leave-one-out cross-validation. A single walker is taken out, the discriminant function is computed on the set of the other $n - 1$ data samples, and the remaining walker is then used to test the classifier. This procedure is repeated for every single data sample. The classifier can then be evaluated in terms of the percentage of mis-classifications.

Feature Extraction

The vector d in Equation 7 describes the discriminant function in the low-dimensional space spanned by the first m Eigenwalkers. Given the matrix V containing the Eigenwalkers themselves, the corresponding discriminant function in the 226-dimensional representation is revealed as

$$v_d = Vd \qquad (8)$$

The discriminant walker v_d has the same format as any of the input walkers ωi (see Eq. 4). It can therefore be decomposed into its components according to Equation 2. Note that all of the components describe increments—that is, positive or negative additive terms that modify the average walker v_0. As described above, $p_{d,0}$ encodes structural, anthropomorphic features, whereas $p_{d,j}$ and $q_{d,j}$ represent kinematic information. Particularly, if the individual Fourier terms are transformed into amplitudes and phases (Eq. 3), the contribution of single body parts can also be quantified. Markers that are associated with large numbers in the discriminant walker vd are strongly affected by the attribute of interest, whereas those associated with small numbers do not change as the attribute changes.

Visualization

The decomposition of the time series of pose data into its Fourier components (Eq. 2) is invertible. A walking pattern that has been manipulated in the frequency domain can be transformed back into a time series of poses, which in turn can be animated in terms of a point-light display. This is a very useful property that helps to create well-defined stimuli for psychophysical experiments and provides tools to explore the nature of the discriminant function and linear classifiers described above. For instance, walkers w_α corresponding to a point that is α standard deviations away from the mean walker are represented as

$$w_\alpha = v_0 + \alpha v_d \tag{9}$$

As above, v_d denotes the discriminant walker and v_0 is the average walker. As α changes from negative to positive values, an animation of the walker v_α appears to change with regard to the attribute on which the classification was based. Large positive or negative α values can be used to generate exaggerated caricatures that help visualize these attributes.

An interesting additional feature of the methodology described here is the option to apply it to walking data that are reduced in information by normalizing it with respect to certain properties while retaining diagnostic information only in others. Below, I will describe a study in which we did that to explore the role of static versus kinematic information for sex classification. Similar manipulations have been used to investigate which parts of the overall information are being used for person identification (Troje, Westhoff, & Lavrov, 2005).

Examples

Sex Classification

Men and women show different walking patterns, and the human visual system is well able to distinguish between them (Barclay et al., 1978;

Cutting et al., 1978; Kozlowski & Cutting, 1977; Mather & Murdoch, 1994). A number of different features have been suggested that are possible candidates for conveying sex-specific diagnostic information. One of them was the "center of moment" (CoM) of the upper body. In an attempt to identify the point of maximal torsion, Cutting (1978) approximated the CoM as the point at which the diagonal lines connecting the shoulder with the contralateral hip intersect. This point is higher in women than in men. Even though the term "center of moment" suggests that this is a dynamic feature, its definition is basically structural. Cutting (1978) demonstrated that the CoM indeed affects sex classification, but later it was shown that this is the case only if no other information is available. A second cue that was investigated by Mather and Murdoch (1994) is the lateral sway of the upper body, which is more pronounced in male walkers than in female walkers. In experiments in which both cues were set into conflict, lateral body sway entirely dominated the CoM.

We applied the framework outlined above to the sex-classification problem (Troje, 2002a). The analysis was based on 20 male and 20 female walkers recorded while walking on a treadmill. The best classifier was based on the first four Eigenwalkers and produced only three misclassifications (out of 40 items), corresponding to an error rate of 7.5%. We then conducted the same analysis using only parts of the overall information. Rather than presenting all the available information to the classifier, we first normalized the data with respect to the size of the walkers and then ran classifications based either only on the remaining structural information ($p_{i,0}$ in Eq. 2) or only on the kinematic information ($p_{i,1}$, $q_{i,1}$, $p_{i,2}$, $q_{i,2}$). It turned out that size alone was a very good predictor for the sex of the walker. When normalized for size, the classification error increased to 17%. Depriving the data of other structural information did not have any effect; however, when kinematic information was removed, misclassifications further increased to 27% (Fig. 12.1). The finding that kinematic information is much more informative than structural information confirms Mather and Murdoch's (1994) results and suggests that the CoM plays only a minor role in sex classification from point-light displays.

To what extent does this result predict how the human visual system processes gender information from walking? We tested this by creating walker stimuli that were normalized with respect to either their structure (kinematics-only) or their kinematics (structure-only) (Troje, 2002a). For

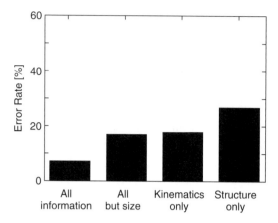

FIGURE 12.1. Percentage errors produced by the linear sex classifier when provided with all available information, size-normalized data, kinematic information only, or structural information only. Note that the information available to the classifier is three-dimensional.

the kinematics-only stimuli, for each individual walker i we replaced the component $p_{i,0}$ (Eq. 2) with the average of these components computed over all 40 walkers. Similarly, for the structure-only stimuli, we replaced the walker-specific components $p_{i,1}$, $q_{i,1}$, $p_{i,2}$, $q_{i,2}$ with their population averages. We then displayed these walkers as point-light displays from three different viewpoints and asked observers to guess the sex of the walkers. The results confirmed that kinematic information is more important than static, structural information for this task (Fig. 12.2). The effect of these manipulations is relatively small when the walkers are shown in frontal view but becomes very substantial for the half-profile and profile views. The results also confirm earlier findings (Mather & Murdoch, 1994) that sex-classification performance is better when walkers are shown in frontal view as compared to the half-profile and profile views.

The differences between male and female walkers can be visualized by animating point-light displays according to Equation 9. Animations of a sex-discriminant function based on the 40 walkers discussed here can be viewed at http://biomotionlab.ca/Demos/BMLgender.html. Visual inspection reveals a number of features that change between men and women. Several differences in the fronto-parallel plane are due to pose and anthropometric structure. Men have wider shoulders and slimmer hips, and their elbows are held farther away from their bodies. In terms of the kinematics, we observe that the upper body of the male shows

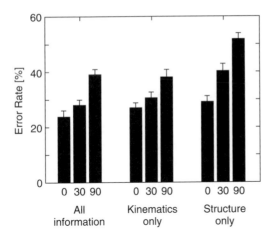

FIGURE 12.2. Percentage error rates (means and standard errors) of human observers who tried to determine the sex of point-light walkers. Point-light displays were shown from three different viewpoints (0 degrees: frontal view; 30 degrees: half-profile view; 90 degrees: profile view). Different groups of observers saw walkers that contained all available information (except size, which was normalized in all displays), kinematic information only, or structural information only. Data are based on 24 observers.

more pronounced lateral sway and that the movement of the hips, though not much larger in amplitude, is different in terms of the phase of its rotation with respect to the other parts of the body. Particularly in the exaggerated animations, it can be seen that the vertical movement of the hip is in counterphase with the vertical motion of knee and foot of the ipsilateral leg in women, while the hip moves almost in phase with the ipsilateral leg in men.

In contrast to previous work, our approach is not primarily hypothesis driven. Rather than focusing on a particular cue (e.g., CoM or lateral body sway), the discriminant function picks up on any feature that distinguishes between male and female walkers, and particularly on the correlations between them. Yet particular hypotheses can be tested and quantified by inspecting the numbers contained in the average walker v_0 and the discriminant function v_d (Eq. 9). For instance, in the average walker, the distance between the two shoulder markers is 350 mm and the distance between the two hip markers is 190 mm. The corresponding differences in the discriminant function are 19 mm for the shoulder and –5 mm for the hip, which means that a walker at a distance of 1 standard deviation (std) into the male part of the space has shoulders that are 19 mm wider and hips that are 5 mm narrower than in the average walker. Compared to a walker representing a point at a distance of 1 std into the female part of the space, the male walker's shoulders are 38 mm wider and his hips are 10 mm narrower. Transforming the sine and cosine terms of Equation 2 into amplitudes and phases (Eq. 3), we can determine the difference in amplitude of the lateral movement of the shoulders. While the shoulders sway with an amplitude of 20 mm on average (that is, a 40 mm difference between the leftmost and rightmost position) across all 40 walkers, a 1 std male walker sways with an amplitude that is 2.5 mm larger, and a 1 std female walker sways with an amplitude that is 2.5 mm smaller.

Retrieving Information about Other Attributes

In our previous example, the entry r_i of vector r in Equation 7 indicated the sex of walker i. As sex is a binary property, we used the number +1 (for male) and –1 (for female). Since our classifier is based on linear regression, we are not restricted to binary codes. In principle, the vector r can contain any score encoding any attribute. Scores can be derived from other information directly associated with the walkers—for instance, their weight or their age. However, the scores can also be based on questionnaires completed by the subjects themselves, or by their physicians or therapists. This allows for a number of applications in biomechanics, clinical psychology, and neurology. For instance, it is well known that patients suffering from depression show walking patterns that differ from those of healthy controls (Lemke, Wendorff, Mieth, Buhl, & Linnemann, 2000). In an ongoing study we are currently quantifying these differences with our method, and we are developing tools to objectively assess the success of different therapies for depressive disorders (Michalak, Troje, Fischer, Heidenreich, & Schulte, in preparation).

In vision research, we are particularly interested in the perception of biological motion with respect to emotional attributes, personality traits, and other characteristics that we seem to be able to derive visually from the way a person moves. In an animation available at http://biomotionlab.ca/Demos/BMLwalker.html, we show examples of axes driven by the results of perceptual rating experiments. In addition to a "gender axis" and one that is based on the body mass index of the walker, we show two axes that were obtained by means of an experiment in which observers were shown a total of 80 different walkers displayed as point-light displays on a computer monitor. Each display consisted of 15 white dots on a black background and was rendered from one of three different viewpoints (0 degrees = frontal view, 30 degrees, 90 degrees). A single rating session consisted of 80 trials, with each walker shown once for 7 s in a randomized order. All walkers within one session were shown from the same viewpoint. In order to indicate their rating, observers had to click one of six buttons displayed on the screen. Six observers participated in the experiments. For three of them the leftmost and rightmost buttons were labeled "nervous" and "relaxed," respectively. The other three observers were presented with the labels "happy" and "sad." Each observer carried out three sessions, one for each viewpoint, with short breaks between the sessions. The order of the three sessions was counterbalanced across observers.

The average of the ratings (across the three observers in each group and across the three different viewpoints) was used to form a vector r which in turn was used to compute the respective discriminant function v_d according to Equations 7 and 8. Animations along both the happy–sad axis and the nervous–relaxed axis give a clear percept of a change in the respective emotions of the walker. Visual inspection of the exaggerated walkers as well as quantitative examination of the discriminant function reveals the features that carry information about these attributes. Many of the differences between the nervous and the relaxed walker are due to the average pose and structure: walkers are perceived to be nervous when they have a skinny appearance with narrow pelvis and shoulders and when their shoulders and arms are pulled up tightly, whereas they are rated to be relaxed if they have wider frames and lower shoulders. With respect to their kinematics there is a shift of power for the horizontal movement of the markers, which is almost exclusively carried by the fundamental frequency in the relaxed walkers, to an increasing contribution of the second harmonic in the nervous walkers. Comparison of walkers along the happy–sad axis and inspection of the corresponding discriminant function shows that the main difference between walkers perceived to be sad or happy is the contribution of the second harmonic to the vertical movements. Here, the power of the second harmonic is relatively low for the sad walkers, while it is responsible for the appearance of bounciness in the happy walkers.

The data reported here are based on the relatively low number of only three observers per attribute. In fact, the power of the proposed method is so strong that it produces reasonable results from very short experiments run with single, individual observers. We therefore designed a Web-based system in which users can generate their own axis based on ratings of a set of walkers (http://biomotionlab.ca/Demos/BMLrating). Upon entering the system, users are presented with an input mask that requests a few personal data (age, sex, country of origin) and then asks them to input an attribute of their choice along with two labels indicating the two ends of a Likert rating scale. For instance, users might input the attribute "sex" and then the labels "male" and "female" for the two ends of the scale. However, they are free to choose any attribute and any labels. Once this is done, the user will be presented with individual point-light walkers on half of the screen and a Likert scale with six buttons on the other half of the screen. The whole display will be titled with the attribute the user chose (e.g., "sex") and the first and last buttons contain the chosen labels (Fig. 12.3; also see color insert). After rating at least 20 walkers (but being encouraged to complete many more ratings), the user clicks a "finish" button; the system will then compute and display a discriminant function based on the obtained ratings. A point-light walker is displayed along with a slider that allows the viewer to interactively change the position of the walker on the axis (α in Eq. 9).

The success in revealing an axis that really reflects the intended attribute depends on how it gets mapped into our motion space. Not all attributes are expected to be represented linearly. For instance, consider a case in which the user chooses the attribute "symmetry," labeling the two ends of the Likert scale with "very asymmetric" and "very symmetric." He or she would probably attribute a high value ("very symmetric") to walkers that are very close to the average walker v_0 (Eq. 4). A walker with a strong asymmetry—for instance, the right arm swinging with a much larger amplitude than the left arm—would probably be at some distance from the average walker and would be assigned a low symmetry rating. However, a walker that is as asymmetric but with the left arm swinging more than the right arm would be located as far away from the average walker as the first asymmetric walker, but in the opposite direction, and would be assigned with the same rating. Fluctuating asymmetry is not distributed linearly in our space but rather concentrically, and any attempt to capture it with linear regression will fail.

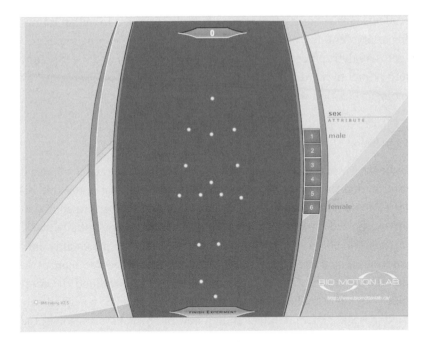

FIGURE 12.3. Layout of a Web-based demonstration. Observers can choose any attribute (e.g., "sex") along with two labels for the beginning and the end of a scale (e.g., "male" and "female") and then have to apply ratings to a series of individual point-light walkers. At the end they are presented with an animation that reflects their ratings in terms of a linear discriminant function.

Given this last consideration, it is surprising how many attributes are being successfully represented. While most users of our Web-based demonstration try attributes such as "sex," "attractiveness," "confidence," "mood," "weight," "age," "strength," "sportiness," etc., some came up with very creative ideas. For instance, we saw observers rate walkers according to their voting behavior (with labels "conservative" versus "liberal"), with very consistent outcomes, the discussion of which is beyond the scope of this chapter. One of my favorite axes was created by a user from Munich who rated walkers according to whether he would expect to see them in the rich and trendy neighborhood around Munich's Isartor or rather in a particularly shabby and rundown neighborhood characterized by cheap bars and plenty of nightlife.

We use this system to demonstrate the richness of information conveyed by human motion to the public visiting our Web site, as well as to students in lab courses. In addition, however, we use it to obtain ratings for a large number of trait terms, which eventually can be applied to factor-analytic procedures. This will help us to understand the topology and extract the cardinal dimensions of the perceptual space spanned by biological motion walking patterns.

Conclusion

Biological motion perception involves a complex hierarchy of visual information processing. A particularly interesting level is the one referred to as style recognition. Once an actor and the performed action are recognized on a basic level, style recognition can potentially reveal information about the specifics of an actor's identity, personality, and emotions. The framework we outlined in this chapter serves mainly two different functions. On the one hand, it helps us understand the complexity of the stimulus itself—a stimulus that is handled so effortlessly by our visual system. Understanding how our visual system solves the sophisticated problems involved in style recognition requires a comprehensive understanding of the constraints contained in the statistics of movement data and the encoding schemes for information in biological motion. Here, we approached the question of information encoding and retrieval from a pattern-recognition perspective. While we learned plenty about the way information is encoded in biological motion, the particular way it is retrieved by the human visual system may be very different from the way we did it here.

On the other hand, however, if considered as a model for information processing in the human visual system, our approach creates a number of hypotheses about its functioning that can well be tested. For instance, an artificial walker located 6 std away from the average walker on the sex axis is perceived completely unambiguously as male or female, even though such a walker probably has never been seen before in reality. Apparently, linear extrapolations in the proposed space result in walkers that are perceived as caricatures representing certain attributes even better than the real walkers—a strong argument for the idea that our visual system operates with similar representations. An item analysis with a close comparison between the artificial classification of individual walkers and the psychophysically obtained ratings also reveals striking similarities. The same walkers that are misclassified by the linear system tend to be misclassified by human observers, and this also argues for similar representational spaces and metrics within these spaces.

While we are working here with human walking patterns, the framework described here can be extended to other movements as well. Each class of movements, however, requires its own description. A model for running could be obtained similarly to the way we obtained the walking model. However, at least within the framework outlined here, it would not make sense to try to describe both walking and running patterns within the same model. Our model is based on morphability. Each item in the space must match any other item in a canonical, unambiguous way. The correspondence between two items defines the "morph" between them (i.e., a smooth transition from one item to the other). Of course, it is possible to blend a walking pattern into a running pattern, but the blending is not unique, since the correspondence between the two patterns can be defined in several different ways. Dynamic models of gait production (Alexander, 1989; Golubitsky, Stewart, Buono, & Collins, 1998, 1999) show that the transition between walking and running is characterized by a singularity, and therefore these gaits represent two principally different motion patterns.

Similarly to other implementations of morphable models, our framework relies on establishing correspondence between features across the data set, resulting in a separation of the overall information into range-specific information on the one hand and domain-specific information on the other hand (Ramsay & Silverman, 1997). Applied to the current model, the range-specific information is the positional information contained both in the average pose and in the Eigenposes. The domain-specific information is the information about when things are happening. This information is contained in the fundamental frequency and in the phase of the walk. The domain-specific (i.e., temporal) part of the walking information therefore has a comparatively simple description.

For nonperiodic motions, a more complex formulation has to be employed. A very explicit way to do this is to define the temporal behavior of a motion in terms of the deviations with respect to a prototype. The prototype can be any typical example of the respective motion pattern. The temporal behavior of any other item can then be formulated explicitly in terms of the time warp required to minimize the distance between the prototype and the time-warped version of the item. Implementations of such models have been described by Giese and Poggio (2000) and Ramsay and Silverman (1997). They could be incorporated in the framework described here in order to isolate information carrying biologically or psychologically relevant traits from actions that require more complex temporal descriptions, and to use it in turn to attribute personality and emotion to digital characters.

A number of modifications to the proposed model might further improve its value in classifying stylistic attributes and in identifying the features they are based on. Our approach is based on the attempt to linearize the data—that is, to transform it into a representation that describes it in terms of a low-dimensional convex linear manifold. Once this is achieved, we classify them by means of simple linear regression. Both the representation that we use as well as the classifier operating on it might not be optimal. For instance, there exist nonlinear methods for dimensionality reduction (e.g., Roweis & Saul, 2000) that might lead to latent variable representations that eventually result in a closer approximation to linearity than the combination of Fourier decomposition in the pose space and PCA in the walker space. There is also plenty of potential for improving the classifier. Linear regression is very sensitive to outliers. Even if we were assuming that the optimal classifier is eventually linear, methods like linear support vector machines (Cristianini & Shawe-Taylor, 2000) or robust PCA (De la Torre & Black, 2001) might improve classification. Nonlinear methods offer even more options.

By using these nonlinear methods, however, we might also have to sacrifice the ability to use the very same framework for the analysis of motion data on the one hand and synthesis and visualization on the other, which turn out to be of great help in combining pattern recognition approaches to biological motion perception with psychophysical methods. This combination, however, provides the basis for a mapping between a well-controlled, parameterized stimulus space and the perceptual spaces that biological motion research aims to explore.

References

Alexander, R. M. (1989). Optimization and gaits in the locomotion of vertebrates. *Physiological Reviews, 69*(4), 1199–1227.

Barclay, C. D., Cutting, J. E., & Kozlowski, L. T. (1978). Temporal and spatial factors in gait perception that influence gender recognition. *Perception & Psychophysics, 23*, 145–152.

Beauchamp, M. S. (2005). See me, hear me, touch me: Multisensory integration in lateral occipital-temporal cortex. *Current Opinion in Neurobiology, 15*(2), 145–153.

Beauchamp, M. S., Lee, K. E., Haxby, J. V., & Martin, A. (2002). Parallel visual motion processing streams for manipulable objects and human movements. *Neuron, 34*(1), 149–159.

Bertenthal, B., Proffitt, D. R., & Kramer, S. J. (1987). Perception of biological motion by infants: Implementation of various processing constraints. *Journal of Experimental Psychology: Human Perception and Performance, 13*, 577–585.

Bidet-Caulet, A., Voisin, J., Bertrand, O., & Fonlupt, P. (2005). Listening to a walking human activates the temporal biological motion area. *Neuroimage, 28*(1), 132–139.

Blake, R. (1993). Cats perceive biological motion. *Psychological Science, 4*(1), 54–57.

Bonda, E., Petrides, M., Ostry, D., & Evans, A. (1996). Specific involvement of human parietal systems and the amygdala in the perception of biological motion. *Journal of Neuroscience, 16*(11), 3737–3744.

Bruderlin, A., & Williams, L. (1995). Motion signal processing. Paper presented at the Proceedings of SIGGRAPH 95, Los Angeles.

Buccino, G., Lui, F., Canessa, N., Patteri, I., Lagravinese, G., Benuzzi, F., et al. (2004). Neural circuits involved in the recognition of actions performed by nonconspecifics: An FMRI study. *Journal of Cognitive Neuroscience, 16*(1), 114–126.

Cavanagh, P., Labianca, A. T., & Thornton, I. M. (2001). Attention-based visual routines: Sprites. *Cognition, 80*(1–2), 47–60.

Cristianini, N., & Shawe-Taylor, J. (2000). An introduction to support vector machines and other kernel-based learning methods. Cambridge: Cambridge University Press.

Cutting, J. E. (1978). Generation of synthetic male and female walkers through manipulation of a biomechanical invariant. *Perception, 7*(4), 393–405.

Cutting, J. E., & Kozlowski, L. T. (1977). Recognizing friends by their walk: Gait perception without familiarity cues. *Bulletin of the Psychonomic Society, 9*(5), 353–356.

Cutting, J. E., Moore, C., & Morrison, R. (1988). Masking the motions of human gait. *Perception & Psychophysics, 44*(4), 339–347.

Cutting, J. E., Proffitt, D. R., & Kozlowski, L. T. (1978). A biomechanical invariant of gait perception. Journal of Experimental Psychology: *Human Perception & Performance, 4*, 357–372.

Davis, R. B., Ounpuu, S., Tyburski, D., & Gage, J. R. (1991). A gait analysis data collection and reduction technique. *Human Movement Science, 10*, 575–587.

De la Torre, F., & Black, M. J. (2001). Robust principal component analysis for computer vision. Paper presented at the ICCV-2001, Vancouver.

Dittrich, W. H., Lea, S. E. G., Barrett, J., & Gurr, P. R. (1998). Categorization of natural movements by pigeons: Visual concept discrimination and biological motion. *Journal of the Experimental Analysis of Behaviour, 70*, 281–299.

Dittrich, W. H., Troscianko, T., Lea, S. E. G., & Morgan, D. (1996). Perception of emotion from dynamic point-light displays represented in dance. *Perception, 25*(6), 727–738.

Downing, P. E., Jiang, Y., Shuman, M., & Kanwisher, N. (2001). A cortical area selective for visual processing of the human body. *Science, 293*(5539), 2470–2473.

Farah, M. J., Tanaka, J. W., & Drain, H. M. (1995). What causes the face inversion effect? Journal of Experimental Psychology: *Human Perception and Performance, 21*(3), 628–634.

Fox, R., & McDaniel, C. (1982). The perception of biological motion by human infants. *Science, 218*(4571), 486–487.

Giese, M. A., & Poggio, T. (2000). Morphable models for the analysis and synthesis of complex motion patterns. *International Journal of Computer Vision, 38*, 59–73.

Golubitsky, M., Stewart, I., Buono, P. L., & Collins, J. J. (1999). Symmetry in locomotor central pattern generators and animal gaits. *Nature, 401*(6754), 693–695.

Golubitsky, M., Stewart, I., Buono, P.-L., & Collins, J. J. (1998). A modular network for legged locomotion. *Physica D, 115*, 56–72.

Grezes, J., Costes, N., & Decety, J. (1998). Top-down effect of strategy on the perception of human biological motion: A PET investigation. *Cognitive Neuropsychology, 15*(6–8), 553–582.

Grossman, E. D., & Blake, R. (2002). Brain areas active during visual perception of biological motion. *Neuron, 35*(6), 1167–1175.

Grossman, E. D., Blake, R., & Kim, C. Y. (2004). Learning to see biological motion: Brain activity parallels behavior. *Journal of Cognitive Neuroscience, 16*(9), 1669–1679.

Grossman, E. D., Donnelly, M., Price, R., Pickens, D., Morgan, V., Neighbor, G., et al. (2000). Brain areas involved in perception of biological motion. *Journal of Cognitive Neuroscience, 12*(5), 711–720.

Guo, S., & Roberge, J. (1996). A high-level control mechanism for human locomotion based on parametric frame space interpolation. In R. Boulic & G. Hegron (Eds.), *Computer animation and simulation '96* (pp. 95–107). New York: Springer.

Ikeda, H., Blake, R., & Watanabe, K. (2005). Eccentric perception of biological motion is unscalably poor. *Vision Research, 45*(15), 1935–1943.

Jastorff, J., Kourtzi, Z., & Giese, M. A. (2006). Learning to discriminate complex movements: Biological versus artificial trajectories. *Journal of Vision, 6*, 791–804.

Johansson, G. (1973). Visual perception of biological motion and a model for its analysis. *Perception & Psychophysics, 14*(2), 201–211.

Johansson, G. (1976). Spatio-temporal differentiation and integration in visual motion perception. *Psychological Research, 38*, 379–393.

Jones, M. J., & Poggio, T. (1999). Multidimensional morphable models: A framework for representing and matching object classes. *International Journal of Computer Vision, 29*, 107–131.

Kozlowski, L. T., & Cutting, J. E. (1977). Recognizing the sex of a walker from a dynamic point-light display. *Perception & Psychophysics, 21*(6), 575–580.

Kozlowski, L. T., & Cutting, J. E. (1978). Recognizing the sex of a walker from a dynamic point-light display: Some second thoughts. *Perception & Psychophysics, 23*(5), 459.

Lemke, M. R., Wendorff, T., Mieth, B., Buhl, K., & Linnemann, M. (2000). Spatiotemporal gait patterns during over ground locomotion in major depression compared with healthy controls. *Journal of Psychiatric Research, 34*(4–5), 277–283.

Marey, E.-J. (1895/1972). *Movement*. New York: Arno Press.

Mather, G., & Murdoch, L. (1994). Gender discrimination in biological motion displays based on dynamic cues. *Proceedings of the Royal Society of London Series B, 258*, 273–279.

Michalak, J., Troje, N. F., Fischer, J., Heidenreich, T., & Schulte, D. (in preparation). *The embodiment of depression: Gait patterns of currently and formerly depressed patients.*

Muybridge, E. (1887/1979). *Muybridge's complete human and animal locomotion*. New York: Dover.

Oram, M. W., & Perrett, D. I. (1994). Responses of anterior superior temporal polysensory (STPa) neurons to "biological motion" stimuli. *Journal of Cognitive Neuroscience, 6*(2), 99–116.

Peelen, M. V., & Downing, P. E. (2005). Selectivity for the human body in the fusiform gyrus. *Journal of Neurophysiology, 93*(1), 603–608.

Peuskens, H., Vanrie, J., Verfaillie, K., & Orban, G. A. (2005). Specificity of regions processing biological motion. *European Journal of Neuroscience, 21*(10), 2864–2875.

Pollick, F. E., Paterson, H. M., Bruderlin, A., & Sanford, A. J. (2001). Perceiving affect from arm movement. *Cognition, 82*(2), B51–B61.

Puce, A., Allison, T., Bentin, S., Gore, J. C., & McCarthy, G. (1998). Temporal cortex activation in humans viewing eye and mouth movements. *Journal of Neuroscience, 18*(6), 2188–2199.

Ramsay, J. O., & Silverman, B. W. (1997). *Functional data analysis*. New York: Springer.

Rosch, E. (1988). Principles of categorization. In A. Collins & E. E. Smith (Eds.), *Readings in cognitive science: A perspective from psychology and artificial intelligence* (pp. 312–322). San Mateo, CA: Morgan Kaufmann.

Rose, C., Bodenheimer, B., & Cohen, M. F. (1998). Verbs and adverbs: Multidimensional motion interpolation using radial basis functions. *Computer Graphics and Applications, 18*(5), 32–40.

Roweis, S. T., & Saul, L. K. (2000). Nonlinear dimensionality reduction by locally linear embedding. *Science, 290*(5500), 2323–2326.

Shelton, C. R. (2000). Morphable surface models. *International Journal of Computer Vision, 38*, 75–91.

Thornton, I. M., Rensink, R. A., & Shiffrar, M. (2002). Active versus passive processing of biological motion. *Perception, 31*(7), 837–853.

Troje, N. F. (2002a). Decomposing biological motion: A framework for analysis and synthesis of human gait patterns. *Journal of Vision, 2*(5), 371–387.

Troje, N. F. (2002b). The little difference: Fourier-based synthesis of gender-specific biological motion. In R. Würtz & M. Lappe (Eds.), *Dynamic perception* (pp. 115–120). Berlin: Aka Press.

Troje, N. F., & Vetter, T. (1998). Representations of human faces. In C. Taddei-Ferretti & C. Musio (Eds.), *Downward processing in the perception representation mechanism* (pp. 189–205). Singapore: World Scientific.

Troje, N. F., & Westhoff, C. (2006). The inversion effect in biological motion perception: Evidence for a "life detector"? *Current Biology, 16*(8), 821–824.

Troje, N. F., Westhoff, C., & Lavrov, M. (2005). Person identification from biological motion: Effects of structural and kinematic cues. *Perceptual Psychophysics, 67*(4), 667–675.

Unuma, M., Anjyo, K., & Takeuchi, R. (1995). *Fourier principles for emotion-based human figure animation.* Paper presented at the Proceedings of SIGGRAPH 95.

Urtasun, R., Glardon, P., Ronan, B., Thalmann, D., & Fua, P. (2004). Style-based motion synthesis. *Computer Graphics, 23*, 799–812.

Vaina, L. M., Solomon, J., Chowdhury, S., Sinha, P., & Belliveau, J. W. (2001). Functional neuroanatomy of biological motion perception in humans. *Proceedings of the National Academy of Sciences U S A, 98*(20), 11656–11661.

Vallortigara, G., & Regolin, L. (2006). Gravity bias in the interpretation of biological motion by inexperienced chicks. *Current Biology, 16*(8), R279–R280.

Vallortigara, G., Regolin, L., & Marconato, F. (2005). Visually inexperienced chicks exhibit spontaneous preference for biological motion patterns. *PLoS Biology, 3*(7), e208.

Vetter, T., & Poggio, T. (1997). Linear object classes and image synthesis from a single example image. *IEEE Transactions on Pattern Analysis and Machine Intelligence, 19*, 733–742.

Vetter, T., & Troje, N. F. (1997). Separation of texture and shape in images of faces for image coding and synthesis. *Journal of the Optical Society of America A, 14*, 2152–2161.

Witkin, A., & Popovic, Z. (1995). Motion warping. *Computer Graphics Proceedings of SIGGRAPH 95*, 105–108.

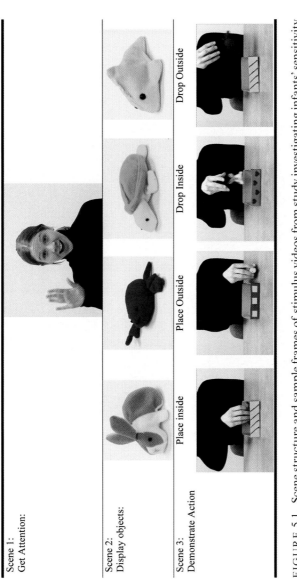

Scene 1:
Get Attention:

Scene 2:
Display objects:

Scene 3:
Demonstrate Action

Place inside   Place Outside   Drop Inside   Drop Outside

FIGURE 5.1. Scene structure and sample frames of stimulus videos from study investigating infants' sensitivity to manner and outcome in action processing.

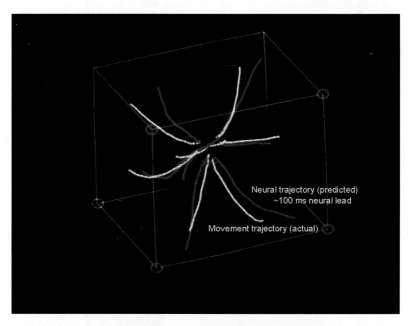

FIGURE 9.4. Neural population vector trajectories (predicted) and actual movement trajectories for eight reaching movements in 3-D space. (Adapted from Georgopoulos et al., 1988.)

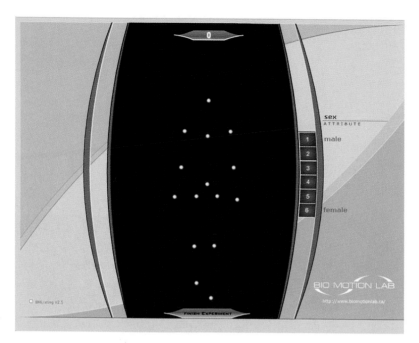

FIGURE 12.3. Layout of a Web-based demonstration. Observers can choose any attribute (e.g., "sex") along with two labels for the beginning and the end of a scale (e.g., "male" and "female") and then have to apply ratings to a series of individual point-light walkers. At the end they are presented with an animation that reflects their ratings in terms of a linear discriminant function.

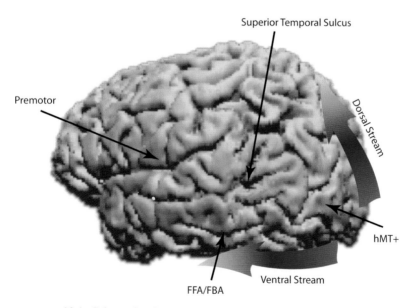

FIGURE 13.1. Schematic of the brain areas involved in action perception, as well as the dorsal and ventral pathways in visual cortex. FFA: fusiform face area; FBA: fusiform body area; hMT+: human middle temporal complex.

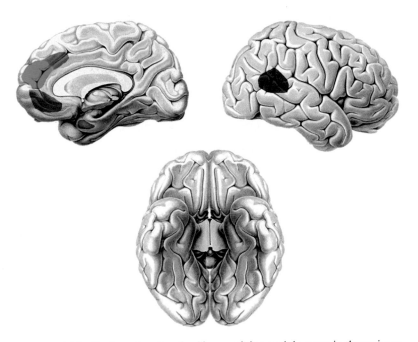

FIGURE 14.1. Brain regions involved in perceiving social events, in three views: medial (upper left), dorsal (upper right), and ventral (bottom). Two regions of medial prefrontal cortex, a more ventral one (in red) and a more dorsal one (in green); the amygdala (blue), buried deep in anterior medial temporal cortex; cortices around the temporo-parietal junction (purple); and the fusiform gyrus (orange). Note that in most cases these structures are implicated bilaterally, but here they are indicated only in the right hemisphere.

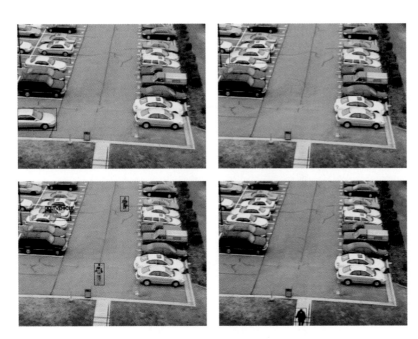

FIGURE 18.9. Example of a parking event.

FIGURE 18.10. Representative frames from sequences 1–4 for testing recognition of casing vehicles.

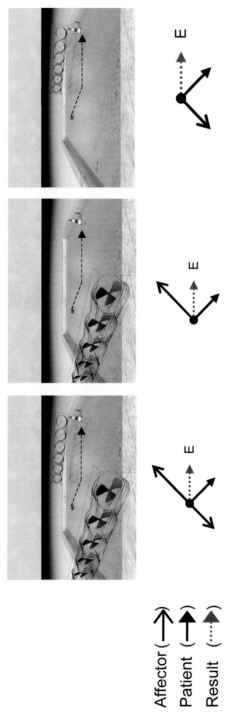

FIGURE 20.5. In each animation, the boat motors to the middle, the fans turn on, the boat changes course, and the boat hits the cone. Each animation is based on the same configuration of forces as shown in the first panel. However, in the second and third panels, only one of the two fans appears in the animation, as implied by the incomplete arrow diagrams.

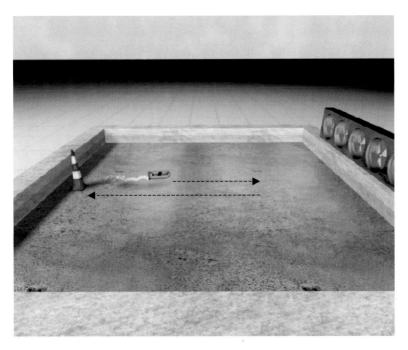

FIGURE 20.4. Frame from an animation used to instantiate a cause interaction.

FIGURE 20.6. The scene depicts a cause situation: the woman does not want to go to the cone (as indicated by the direction of her pointing), but the fans push her there nevertheless.

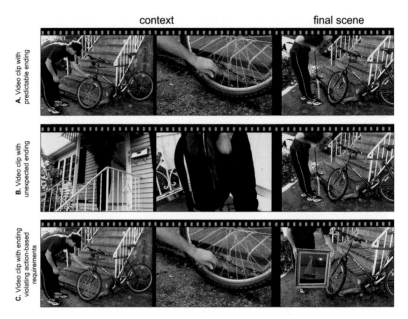

FIGURE 23.7. Frames taken from video clips (produced using a Canon GL1 digital video camcorder and Adobe digital editing software) used in our contextual congruency paradigm. For each video scenario, shown are two frames illustrating real-world events depicted as a context, followed by a single frame illustrating the predictable final scene (*A*), the unexpected final scene (*B*), and the final scene that both was unexpected and violated action-based requirements (*C*). The actual video clips may be viewed at http://www.nmr.mgh.harvard.edu/~tatiana/NCMHC.

13

Neurophysiology of Action Recognition

EMILY D. GROSSMAN

Most of us spend many hours each day listening and exchanging information with other individuals. Perhaps as a result of so much practice, we are quite skilled at recognizing the subtleties in body gestures, facial expressions, and eye movements that often accompany social interaction. The recognition of these changing features of the body, sometimes called "biological motion," plays an important role in anticipating and understanding the intentions of others. Understanding how such events are encoded by the brain is the first step toward learning how we are so successful at the task of social perception.

Human movement is perhaps the most salient form of visual motion experienced by an observer. Actions can be easily recognized when stripped from their carrier—the human form—a trick now commonly used in Hollywood to create computer-generated characters with natural body movements (e.g., the motion-captured "Gollum" in the *Lord of the Rings* trilogy). In visual science, action perception from kinematics is investigated using point-light animations in which a handful of lights are strategically placed on the joints of an actor. These animations were originally developed in the early 1970s by Gunnar Johansson, who recorded an actor in a dark room with small lamps attached to his joints.

Johansson erased any trace of the human form by adjusting the brightness and contrast of the television screen, leaving only the lamps on the joints visible. When these point-light displays are viewed as animations, observers easily recognize human actions in them, but single stationary frames are seen as meaningless clouds of dots (Johansson, 1973). Point-light displays are a critical tool in the study of action recognition because they allow action kinematics to be dissociated from static information about the human form. (For more information as to the richness of these displays, see Chapter 12 in this volume.)

Because humans are able to quickly and accurately interpret the movement of others, it would not be a unreasonable to suggest that our brains have evolved specialized machinery for interpreting this unique kind of motion. Indeed, large cortical networks appear to be involved in perceiving action events, including body recognition, action recognition, and action understanding. These networks include cortical areas more generally recruited during perception of dynamic events and object perception, as well as specialized circuits for human action recognition. In this chapter I will discuss the neural correlates of human action perception, specifically the perception of bodies and body movements. I will also provide a brief discussion on the likely connection of this network to additional cortical areas associated with more abstract properties of action perception, such as perceived intentionality (also see Chapter 14). But first, I offer an introduction to the primary perceptual pathways in visual cortex for generalized motion and form perception, as well as some preliminary evidence for specialized circuits dedicated to biological motion perception.

Parallel Processing Streams in Visual Perception

There is evidence for at least two anatomically distinct neural pathways originating in the retina and progressing into early visual cortex (Livingstone & Hubel, 1988; Schiller, Logothetis, & Charles, 1990). The parvocellular and magnocellular pathways, so called because of the distinct layers the two occupy in the lateral geniculate nucleus (LGN), receive different projection patterns from the retina and continue on to different sublayers of primary visual cortex (V1). It has been suggested that this segregation provides the basis for parallel processing in visual cortex in two channels, the dorsal and ventral streams (Milner & Goodale, 1998; Ungerleider & Haxby, 1994; Ungerleider & Mishkin, 1982).

The dorsal and ventral visual processing streams, which are defined anatomically and functionally, both originate in V1 but project into very different regions of cortex and are thought to subserve functionally different perceptual tasks. The ventral stream occupies the ventral surface of the temporal lobe, and physiological evidence strongly links this brain area with object recognition. Cells in inferior ventral cortex of monkeys are selective for complex stimuli such as geometric shapes and faces (e.g., Rolls, 2000; Sary, Vogels, & Orban, 1993; Tanaka, 1996). A vast number of neuroimaging studies in humans have identified regions in the inferior temporal cortex, including the ventral surface, in recognition and discrimination of objects and faces (e.g., Haxby et al., 1991; Kourtzi & Kanwisher, 2000b; Malach et al., 1995). Damage to ventral temporal cortex results in a number of visual deficits, generally characterized as difficulty with visual discrimination that requires awareness of object features such as shape and color (for a review, see Ettlinger, 1990; Farah, 2004; Logothetis, 1998). Combined, these studies provide evidence that the ventral temporal cortex, or the ventral stream, is integral for shape and color perception.

The dorsal stream occupies the occipital and parietal regions along the dorsal ridge of the two hemispheres in humans, and physiology links the dorsal stream to encoding of spatial location and visual cues for action planning (e.g., Andersen & Siegel, 1999; Colby & Goldberg, 1999). Cells in posterior parietal cortex encode memory for spatial location (Andersen, 1995, 1997), planning and executing eye movements (Andersen, Brotchie, & Mazzoni, 1992), and reaching and grasping (Jeannerod, 1994; Rizzolatti, Fadiga, Gallese, & Fogassi, 1996). Similar response properties have been identified in posterior parietal areas using neuroimaging techniques (Buccino et al., 2001; Culham & Kanwisher, 2001). Damage to dorsal stream brain areas results in visual ataxia, a deficit in the ability to execute visually guided reaching and grasping actions. Thus the dorsal pathway is important for the planning and execution of visually guided actions.

Situated between the dorsal and ventral steams in human cortex are the lateral parietal and temporal lobes, which are largely encompassed by the superior temporal and inferior temporal sulci and gyri (Fig. 13.1; also see color insert). It is this region of cortex, between the brain areas involved in object recognition and action execution, that much of the evidence has revealed neural substrates of action recognition.

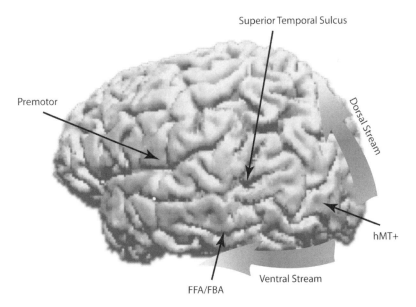

FIGURE 13.1. Schematic of the brain areas involved in action perception, as well as the dorsal and ventral pathways in visual cortex. FFA: fusiform face area; FBA: fusiform body area; hMT+: human middle temporal cortex.

Specialized Circuits for Action Perception: Some Case Reports

For centuries, neuropsychological studies of patients with localized brain injury or developmental disorders have been used to identify cortical specialization for behavior. Consider the following examples of individuals who have suffered acute brain damage to regions of the parietal, occipital, or temporal lobes and as a result have experienced difficulty in biological motion perception.

Patient A. L. suffered two strokes that damaged a large region of temporal lobe extending into posterior parietal cortex (Cowey & Vaina, 2000). Immediately following the stroke, A. L. was unable to recognize her friends and family by their face or gait, though she could identify them by their voices. A short time later she regained her ability to recognize familiar faces, but only if the individual remained still. She continued to report that she could not recognize people when they were moving. During psychophysical testing, A. L. continued to have difficulty recognizing objects that were defined by motion, such as by differential motion direction or flicker, but could easily recognize the objects if they were stationary. For example, A. L. was unable to discriminate a rotating cylinder consisting of a cloud of moving dots from an unstructured display of the same dots. A. L. was also unable to identify any human movements depicted in point-light animations, even after having been told the display showed human action. Thus the damage to temporal-parietal cortex resulted in a number of perceptual deficits specifically targeting motion-defined objects and including action recognition.

Schenk and Zihl (1997a,b) measured motion and form perception in two patients with bilateral lesions of the parietal lobe and extensive damage to the underlying white matter. The patients had no difficulty detecting directional motion signals in dot displays or segregating objects sketched as superimposed. These patients could also recognize human activities depicted in point-light animations when the figures were presented alone; however, they had great difficulty recognizing the actions when the figures were embedded in a field of static or random dots. These are conditions that would not effectively mask biological motion for normal observers (Bertenthal & Pinto, 1994). In this example, measures of simple motion perception or shape perception alone revealed no deficits, but there were significant perceptual failures when the motion and form cues had to be integrated for action recognition.

An additional recent study examined action recognition in two individuals with damage to right parietal cortex as a result of stroke (Battelli, Cavanagh, & Thornton, 2003). These individuals viewed point-light animations of actors walking and were asked to make simple judgments about the display, such as which of four actors was walking to the left versus the right, or which was "jumbled" so as to appear disjointed and limping. The right parietal patients were able to recognize the point-light animations as actors walking but had great difficulty with the simple judgments. The patients required many seconds of observation time as compared to approximately 1 second of viewing by normal observers, and the patients made many mistakes. Previous studies of patients with parietal lesions have demonstrated that these individuals suffer in a wide range of high-level motion tasks, specifically those tasks that require attentional mechanisms (Battelli et al., 2001; Cavanagh, Labianca, & Thornton, 2001). Although it is unlikely that the deficits these patients suffer from are limited to action recognition, this study provides strong evidence that an intact parietal system is required for normal perception of biological motion.

In contrast to the above examples, some individuals who easily recognize human actions have difficulty with simple motion and form perception, two processes thought to feed into action perception. For example, A. F. is an individual with bilateral lesions of the temporal-parietal-occipital junction extending into the posterior parietal cortex of the left hemisphere. A. F. can discriminate images based on shape and color but is unable to see shapes defined by depth or motion, and he has difficulty detecting directional motion signals in dot displays (Vaina, Lemay, Bienfang, Choi, & Nakayama, 1990). Despite these difficulties, A. F. can easily identify biological motion in point-light animations. He readily describes animations of a man climbing the stairs or riding a bicycle and details such as the direction of the walker. Clearly A. F.'s ability to see human movement is intact despite obvious difficulties in tasks designed to measure basic motion perception abilities.

These examples provide evidence that damage to brain regions near the parietal-occipital region can significantly impair action recognition, in both fully illuminated and the more degraded point-light animations. These deficits may exist without any indication of difficulty with motion or shape perception, or action recognition may be intact in individuals with damaged motion or shape recognition. These studies were the first to evidence a dissociation between the neural mechanisms supporting simple motion and form perception and those supporting the more complex biological motion perception. Based on the location of the lesions, the evidence suggests brain areas near the parietal-occipital junction, possibly extending into the parietal lobe, are important for human action recognition.

It is interesting to note that a number of developmental disorders have been linked to difficulty with action recognition. For example, individuals with schizophrenia and children with autism have difficulty discriminating point-light biological motion from motion-matched control stimuli (Blake, Turner, Smoskki, Pozdol, & Stone, 2003; Kim, Doop, Blake, & Park, 2005). Despite these deficits, neither group has difficulty detecting a stationary global form made of smaller parts. In contrast, children with Williams syndrome, a disorder characterized by moderate mental retardation and highly social behavior, perform *better* than mental-age-matched children in discriminating point-light biological motion (Jordan, Reiss, Hoffman, & Landau, 2002). This is perhaps even more surprising because these children have difficulty making global motion discriminations based on nonbiological patterns (Atkinson et al., 2001). Although these specialized populations may evidence perceptual difficulties, schizophrenia, autism, and Williams are better characterized by social and cognitive deficits. So in addition to further dissociating biological motion perception from simple motion and form perception, these studies provide evidence that human action recognition is linked to additional cortical circuits serving critical aspects of social perception.

Action Recognition on the Human Superior Temporal Sulcus

In recent years, the widespread use of neuroimaging techniques such as positron emission tomography (PET) and functional magnetic resonance imaging (fMRI) has led to an explosion of studies identifying brain areas involved in cognitive performance. Both techniques have been used extensively to study the neural correlates of action perception. Overall, the findings suggest that no single brain area is responsible for action recognition, but that many brain areas subserve body perception. One particular brain area, the human superior temporal sulcus (STS), has been identified in virtually all studies of action recognition using human movement and the movement of body parts.

The STS in humans is a large sulcus that extends from the most anterior aspects of the temporal lobe to the most posterior extent of parietal-occipital cortex. Many functional modalities, including speech, hearing, and visual perception, have been shown to activate discrete cortical areas on this large expanse of cortex. Perception of bodies, faces, and hands have all been found to activate regions on the posterior extent of the STS, near where the inferior temporal sulcus (ITS) and STS converge (Allison, Puce, & McCarthy, 2000).

Specialization on the STS for human action perception has been demonstrated in a number of ways. First, numerous studies have compared the neural responses on the STS during action perception to those generated when viewing other kinds of motion. For example, neural activity on the STS during point-light biological motion perception has been compared to that generated when viewing a variety of other dot-defined stimuli. Results show the STS to be more strongly activated during perception of point-light biological motion than during perception of motion-matched scrambled controls, simple coherent motion, animations that depict illusory boundaries, or motion-defined shapes (Grossman & Blake, 2002; Grossman et al., 2000; Howard et al., 1996; Peuskens, Vanrie, Verfaillie, &

Orban, 2005). Researchers have also compared STS activity to different kinds of familiar, moving events. For example, Beauchamp, Lee, Haxby, and Martin (2002) demonstrated the STS to be more activated by perception of biological motion than recognition of common tool motions such as a swinging hammer or twisting screwdriver. Even complex articulation (of nonhuman objects) is insufficient to drive STS activity. The STS is more strongly activated during action perception than during perception of everyday articulating objects (such as a grandfather clock), articulating but meaningless object motion, or novel articulating artificial biological motion (Pelphrey et al., 2003; Peuskens et al., 2005; Pyles, Garcia, Hoffman, & Grossman, in press).

Second, studies have demonstrated that neural activity on the STS is driven by body kinematics, not the surface features of the human form itself (such as the face, skin, clothing, etc.). The neural response on the STS does not differentiate between human actions as depicted in point-light animations, fully illuminated movies, or 3-D-rendered animations of human actions (Beauchamp, Lee, Haxby, & Martin, 2003; Grossman & Blake, 2002). The STS also responds robustly to animations of a robot walking when the movements of the robot are identical to those captured during natural human locomotion (Pelphrey et al., 2003).

Third, neuroimaging studies have demonstrated that in order to effectively drive cortical activity on the STS, the human body must be articulating as seen during natural action perception. For example, simply rotating a stationary image of the human body is insufficient to optimally drive the STS (Beauchamp et al., 2002; Peuskens et al., 2005). Breaking the body apart so that the limbs articulate in spatially fragmented pieces significantly reduces the neural signal on the STS (Thompson, Clarke, Stewart, & Puce, 2005).

Lastly, researchers have linked cortical activity on the STS to behavioral measures of human action sensitivity. For example, body perception and biological motion perception are orientation dependent. Discrimination of body postures and detection, discrimination, and time required for recognition of point-light biological motion are all impaired when the target figures are presented upside-down (Pavlova & Sokolov, 2000; Pavlova, Staudt, Sokolov, Birbaumer, & Krageloh-Mann, 2003; Reed, Stone, Bozova, & Tanaka, 2003; Sumi, 1984). The inversion effect for biological motion is similar to that found for faces (Yin, 1969) and is thought to reflect configural processing—perception of the whole mediated by relative position of the parts. Grossman and Blake (2001) found that inverting the animations results in approximately half the neural activity on STSp but still more neural response than nonbiological animations, corresponding nicely to the psychophysically measured inversion effect.

While neuroimaging studies identify cortical activity associated with a perceptual event, a recent study has argued that the STS is critical for biological motion perception. This study applied transcranial magnetic stimulation (TMS) pulses to the STS, temporarily disrupting the local patterns of neuronal firing within that local region. TMS has been used in a number of cognitive studies critically linking brain activity in localized regions to specific cognitive tasks, with the application of TMS typically impairing behavioral measures on a variety of perceptual and cognitive tasks (for a review, see Pascual-Leone, Walsh, & Rothwell, 2000). In the case of biological motion perception, TMS over the STS results in a significant decrease in sensitivity to point-light displays (Grossman, Battelli, & Pascual-Leone, 2005). Stimulation affects biological motion perception only if the animations are viewed in the upright, canonical orientation—sensitivity to inverted animations is unchanged. There is no change in sensitivity to biological motion (either the upright or inverted) following stimulation over the motion-sensitive human middle temporal complex (hMT+), associated more generally with motion perception. These results demonstrate the importance of the STS in biological motion perception, the lack of specialized computations in hMT+ for biological motion, and the dependence of biological motion and simple motion detection on dissociated neural mechanisms.

Finally, it should be noted that a number of studies have associated the STS with action perception using body parts instead of the entire body. For example, Wheaton, Thompson, Syngeniotis, Abbott, and Puce (2003) found STS activation when observers viewed hand, face, or leg motion, with strongest activation for the faces and hands and the weakest during hand-action perception. Bonda, Petrides, Ostry, and Evans (1996) showed the STS to be more strongly activated when observers viewed point-light animations of goal-oriented hand actions (e.g., reaching for a glass) compared to viewing whole body movement (e.g., a walker traveling in different directions). And animations depicting shifting eye gaze and changing mouth movements strongly activate the STS, but when the eyes and mouth are replaced with small moving checkerboards, brain activity on STS is reduced (Puce, Allison, Bentin, Gore, & McCarthy, 1998).

Given the diverse nature of the stimuli that have revealed activation on the STS, one might wonder whether these activation sites are the same across studies or represent different foci along the STS. Only one study has demonstrated consistent topography on the STS linked to perception of different body parts (Pelphrey, Morris, Michelich, Allison, & McCarthy, 2005). In that study, the researchers found viewing hand and eye movements to activate more posterior regions as compared to mouth movements. The researchers also noted considerable overlap between the cortical responses to these three types of biological motion. Although not a direct comparison, it should be noted that a meta-analysis by Allison et al. (2000) found a slightly different organization for these biological-motion-specific responses. Compiling foci of activation generated in a number of studies, these researchers found activations for hand perception to be more anterior than for eye and mouth activations, and a tendency for whole-body activation to be found on the most posterior regions of the STS. Thus, future studies are required to determine whether there actually is stable, somatotopic organization of the STS.

Action Recognition in the Monkey: Evidence for a Homologue to STS

Based on its anatomical location and preference for moving bodies over stationary bodies, the STS does not fit particularly well into the putative ventral or dorsal steams. Instead, this region appears to be situated in an intermediate region at the temporal-parietal-occipital intersection. What do we know about communication between the STS and ventral (object recognition) and dorsal (action planning and execution) brain areas? On the basis of anatomical connections to the possible monkey homologue of STS, it has been proposed that this region serves as an integration site for the two parallel processing streams (Boussaoud, Ungerleider, & Desimone, 1990; Cusick, 1996). Given this proposal, it is worth considering the physiology data measuring single-unit neuronal response during action recognition. These studies have identified a number of cells in the monkey anterior superior temporal polysensory area (STPa), thought to be the homologue to human STS, that respond robustly and selectively during action recognition.

A subset of the neurons in STPa appear to be very sensitive to viewing body movement or to the movements of discrete body parts (Oram & Perrett, 1994). These neurons fire when the monkey views a fully illuminated body walking across the field of view, rotating in space, and moving in and out of occlusion (Perrett, Smith, Potter, et al., 1985). In some cases, optimal firing of these cells is determined by the proper combination of form and movement. Many cells in STPa demonstrate a clear preference for particular actions, such as walking to the right or toward the viewer, and also for actions viewed from particular viewpoint perspectives (Wachsmuth, Oram, & Perrett, 1994). Thus a cell that fires when viewing someone walking to the left may not fire when the actor is facing the right and walking backward (Perrett, Smith, Mistlin, et al., 1985).

A small population of STPa cells also respond to body movement as depicted in point-light animations (Oram & Perrett, 1994), demonstrating selectivity for body kinematics over the surface features of the target. Like the findings using whole-body images, many of these cells are selective for direction of gait, viewpoint, or both. The cells do not respond well to non-biological-motion-matched controls. In addition, the researchers identify cells that respond when the figure shows articulation but do not fire when the figure rotates rigidly. This parallels neuroimaging findings on the human STS.

Finally, the researchers noted that cells with similar response selectivity (such as a preference for head rotations toward the animal) tended to be found in proximity to each other, such that the neurons were clustered according to motion and viewpoint preference. This preliminary evidence for clustering of common response selectivity in the monkey STS may be reflected in the early evidence for response-selectivity clustering found in the literature on humans.

STS and Action-Based Constructs

Before going further, it should be noted that some researchers have argued that neuroimaging studies identifying the human STS during action perception are actually mistaking the true nature of the neural representations driving this brain area. These researchers argue that STS neural activity reflects the attribution of cognitive states to dynamic social events, not the recognition of actions themselves. For example, studies have linked STS activity to the attribution of animacy in dynamic events (see Chapter 14 in this volume; Castelli, Happe, Frith, & Frith, 2000; Martin & Weisberg, 2003). In these studies, observers view animations of people, objects, or even simple geometric shapes that are moved so as to imply a social interaction, such as chasing or a parent–child relationship. Note that many of these events do not depict body articulation but instead convey social information that is often construed from action events.

Along a similar vein, Saxe, Xiao, Kovacs, Perrett, & Kanwisher (2004) argue that perceived goal-directed behavior, or intentionality of an agent, is actually driving neural activity on the STS. In their study, simple events (such as walking behind a bookcase) are constructed such that observers rate them as having more goal-directed behaviors (lingering behind the bookcase) as compared to control sequences (simply walking behind without pause). The authors find stronger neural signals on the STS during the goal-directed sequences compared to the controls. In the context of their findings, Saxe et al. argue that studies evidencing STS activation during action perception are actually measuring perceived intentionality of the kinematic event, uncontrolled by the experimenter.

The proposal that STS encodes perceived intentionality has some support from the literature on research in monkeys. Jellema, Baker, Wicker, and Perrett (2000) describe two populations of neurons within the STPa. The first population is selective for body movements and body parts; the second set is modulated by implied attentional state of the actor. The authors argue that the combination of these two populations would create a neural system that registers intentional states of an actor as depicted by articulated actions. The implication for human neuroimaging findings is that likely both body articulation and perceived intentionality will drive common cortical networks. Recent developments in neuroimaging techniques that push the boundaries on the spatial resolution limits of the BOLD response may be able to address this issue in the future.

Beyond STS: Additional Cortical Areas Recruited During Action Recognition

Evidence in the previous section argues that the STS is a critical node in the network of brain areas supporting action recognition. In the following section, three additional brain areas that are often identified in neuroimaging studies of action recognition will be described: the primary human motion area (the middle temporal area and its satellites, hMT+), the ventral temporal cortex (including the fusiform face and body areas), and the premotor cortex (F5)—areas known to play important and well-defined roles in motion perception, object recognition, and action execution, respectively. The following section briefly describes the defining characteristics of the neuronal responses in these areas and identifies their roles in the recognition of actions.

Human MT+, the Primary Motion Area

Striate and extrastriate cortex in humans has been mapped in great detail, and no fewer than 10 functional regions have been identified within Brodmann's areas 17, 18, and 19 (Press, Brewer, Dougherty, Wade, & Wandell, 2001). Among these is the human homologue to the monkey middle temporal area (MT, or sometimes called V5), which is referenced as hMT+ in humans (i.e., the human MT). The spatial resolution of standard neuroimaging techniques generally precludes delineating MT proper from its satellites (including MST, FST, FSTv, etc.); thus, human neuroimaging studies have adopted the nomenclature "hMT+" to describe the entire MT complex, including MT satellites (however, see Huk, Dougherty, & Heeger, 2002; Smith, Wall, Williams, & Singh, 2006). These issues notwithstanding, the hMT+ region is recognized as a general motion processing unit similar to that found in monkeys that is most strongly activated whenever an observer reports seeing motion (Huk et al., 2002; Orban et al., 1995; Tootell et al., 1995; Watson et al., 1993).

The evidence linking specialized computations within hMT+ to human action recognition is somewhat mixed, with some studies finding neural signals that differentiate action perception from other kinds of motion and other studies finding no such distinction. For example, Howard et al. (1996) found differential patterns of activation from the hMT+ region as measured by PET during point-light biological motion perception. The authors reported overlapping subcompartments within the hMT+ complex for a directional field of translating dots, optic flow patterns, and biological motion. Additionally, Peuskens et al. (2005) found stronger neural signals in hMT+ during biological motion perception than simple translational motion, which the authors suggest may reflect neural computation in one of the MT satellite regions. In contrast, Grossman et al. (2000) reported hMT+ to have nondifferential signals using the same kinds of stimuli. In other words, the neural responses in hMT+ were the same for point-light biological motion, motion-matched controls, and directional fields of translating dots. The above studies differ in the stimuli and comparisons used to generate their data, and most notably in their use of group versus individual subject analyses, which may be one of the factors contributing to the different findings. At this point, however, it is fair to say that the jury is still out on the specialization of the neural responses in this region for biological motion.

It should also be noted that in some studies, hMT+ has been found to activate when observers are not even seeing movement. This is particularly relevant for action perception, because actions can be implied by the postural cues of the human body in stationary images. For example, Peigneux et al. (2000) found activation in the lateral occipital region overlapping with MT when subjects viewed silhouette images of people in the midst of arm or torso gestures. Similarly, Kourtzi and Kanwisher (2000a) found MT+ to be more activated when subjects viewed stationary images of body postures that imply motion (e.g., a person with an arm poised to throw a ball) but not when viewing similar images that depict stationary postures (e.g., sitting). The authors conclude that implied kinetic postures are sufficient to activate hMT+, likely as a result of active imagery of the implicit dynamics of the events.

Recent psychophysical evidence has downplayed the importance of motion cues in recognition of actions, and studies of this nature may play a critical role in understanding the exact role of hMT+ activation in biological motion perception. For example, when point-light displays are generated that minimize local motion cues (such as by placing the dots between the joints instead of on the joints, or by limiting the amount of movement by any given dot), observers have little difficulty recognizing biological motion (Beintema & Lappe, 2002). This suggests that local motion is not necessary for extracting the biological configuration, and thus action, from point-light animations. Indeed, a recent neuroimaging study found increased neural activity in ventral temporal regions, not hMT+, during action recognition in these special displays (Michels, Lappe, & Vaina, 2005).

In contrast, Garcia and Grossman (2005) constructed point-light displays such that the animations depicted actions with only color contrast but no brightness cues (isoluminance). Isoluminance renders simple motion discriminations difficult, and observers' ability to recognize point-light biological motion fails entirely. Further psychophysical studies in conjunction with formal models and neuroimaging evidence are needed to better understand the importance of hMT+ computations in action recognition. A discussion of the importance of motion cues in recognition of the more abstract properties of human actions can be found in Chapters 11 and 12.

Ventral Temporal Cortex

In addition to the superior temporal sulcus, studies have identified brain areas in the ventral "form" pathway with neural signals that discriminate biological from nonbiological motion. For example, Vaina, Cowey, Eskew, LeMay, and Kemper (2001) measured neural activity while subjects viewed point-light animations of whole-body movements. They found brain areas on the ventral surface of the temporal lobe to be activated by the biological motion. Beauchamp et al. (2002) found regions on the lateral fusiform gyrus that are more responsive to body movement than to tool movement. Grossman and Blake (2002) showed that the "fusiform face area," a region previously identified as selective for faces (Kanwisher, McDermott, & Chun, 1997; Puce, Allison, Gore, & McCarthy, 1995; see also Gauthier, Tarr, Anderson, Skudlarski, & Gore, 1999), also contains neural signals that differentiate between biological and nonbiological motion.

It is perhaps not surprising to find action recognition in ventral temporal cortex. Human movement is, after all, the motion of a particular structure—the human body. Behavioral studies of bodies and body movements reveal many of the same dependencies as face and object recognition. For example, faces, bodies, and point-light animations of bodies all suffer from an inversion effect (Reed et al., 2003; Sumi, 1984; Yovel & Kanwisher, 2005). In the case of point-light animations, the human figure may even be rendered invisible by inverting the form (Pavlova & Sokolov, 2000, 2003), which may be a function of unfamiliarity with the inverted body shape and dynamics (Shipley, 2003).

More recently, Downing, Jiang, Shuman, and Kanwisher (2001) and Peelen and Downing (2005) have identified two regions in occipital and temporal cortex that respond preferentially to viewing stationary images of bodies. The extrastriate body area (EBA) responds optimally to stationary images of bodies, particularly when these images omit faces. A second study identified the fusiform body area (FBA) as a region adjacent to and overlapping with the fusiform face area (FFA). Peelen, Wiggett, and Downing (2006) argue that standard fMRI analysis techniques can not dissociate the FBA and FFA because the two brain areas are so close. Instead, these brain areas can be dissociated only on the basis of combined functional attributes and the more sophisticated voxel-by-voxel analyses. The previous reports of biological-motion-selective signals on the floor of the fusiform gyrus, and in some cases within the FFA, probably reflect body-selective neurons in the FBA.

The possible role of the EBA and FBA in action perception appears to be related to analyzing the form content in biological motion (fully illuminated and point-light). Both brain areas are identified using stationary images, not animated action events. However, both are activated when viewing human actions. Thus, it is likely that cortical activity in these brain areas reflects a more general mechanism for body-shape analysis that is engaged during action recognition.

Premotor Cortex

Action perception has also been linked to activity in premotor cortex of the frontal lobe. Located on the inferior frontal gyrus, premotor cortex in humans is thought to be the human homologue to monkey area F5, the region in which "mirror" cells have been identified (Gallese, Fadiga, Fogassi, & Rizzolatti, 1996). Mirror neurons are a special class of cells that fire both during execution of particular actions (typically hand and arm movements) and during perception of those actions. Mirror neurons are thought to play a critical role in action recognition, action understanding, and motor learning (Gallese et al., 1996; Rizzolatti, Fadiga, Gallese, et al., 1996).

In an early PET study of action recognition, Rizzolatti and colleagues (Rizzolatti, Fadiga, Matelli, et al., 1996) measured neural activity associated with viewing a hand grasping an object as compared to passive observation of an object. Illustrating the network of brain areas discussed throughout this chapter, observing grasping movements resulted in increased activation of the hMT+ region, the STS and premotor cortex. The same brain areas were identified in a recent study investigating point-light whole-body biological motion perception (Saygin, Wilson, Hagler, Bates, & Sereno, 2004).

Studies identifying neural activity in premotor cortex during action perception often set their findings in the context of action-observation networks, since viewing actions shares a common representation with those brain areas involved in producing actions. For a critical discussion of common action-perception networks in movement perception, see Chapter 10. Briefly, however, the idea that viewing an action and performing that action may be subserved by a common neural representation has some support from psychophysical findings. As an example, consider the experiment of Shiffrar and Freyd (1990), who demonstrated that the perceived path of a body limb in an apparent motion sequence can follow body constraints imposed by limb structure. In this study, subjects are shown two stationary images of a body posture chosen such that a limb is positioned in front of or behind another body part. For example, an arm is shown in front of the torso in one image and behind the torso in the other image. If sufficient time is allowed between presentation of the two images, observers report seeing smooth, apparent motion of the arm around the torso, a path "possible" with the movement constraints of the body. However, this interpretation is reported less frequently when the images are presented in rapid succession, and instead observers report seeing the impossible motion of the arm through the torso. In a subsequent imaging study, experimenters found higher neural activity levels in the superior temporal gyrus and primary motor and premotor cortices in the trials with long interframe intervals, favoring the impression of possible body movement, than in those trials favoring impossible biological motion (Stevens, Fonlupt, Shiffrar, & Decety, 2000).

Task dependencies also affect the extent to which the action-perception network is engaged. For example, Grezes, Costes, and Decety (1998) showed observers fully illuminated videos of hand movements that depicted either meaningful or meaningless pantomimes. The researchers found the same cortical network of activity to be activated for the two types of hand motion (meaningful or meaningless), including the hMT+ region and STS. However, when observers were asked to take note of the gestures because they would be required to imitate the pantomimes, viewing the meaningful hand actions also activated premotor cortex.

Using a slightly different approach, researchers have shown that observation of action, in conjunction with motor stimulation, facilitates motor evoked potentials measured on the peripheral muscles (i.e., the hand and arm). Fadiga, Fogassi, Pavesi, and Rizzolatti (1995) applied pulses of magnetic stimulation (TMS) to motor cortex responsible for the hand representation and simultaneously recorded hand and arm motor evoked potentials (MEPs). They found an increase in MEP amplitude during TMS if the observers simultaneously viewed the experimenter grasping various objects and making complex arm movements such as tracing a shape in space. There was no change in MEP amplitude when observers viewed the same objects without the experimenter manipulating them, or when observers had to perform a simple visual detection task. Thus the study found recruitment of muscles that would be used during action execution during the observation of those actions.

An Action Recognition Network

The finding of multiple brain areas with neural signals selective for biological motion is indicative of a network of brain areas supporting action perception (Fig. 13.2). The STS responds (perhaps in an obligatory manner) during all action perception, either of the whole body or body parts, and neural responses in this region prefer natural body move-

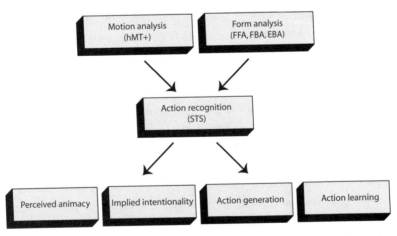

FIGURE 13.2. Suggested organization of perceptual processes and putative neural basis in action perception.

ments such as articulating, grasping, changes in eye gaze, and mouth movements. In addition to the STSp, hMT+ and ventral temporal and premotor brain areas have also been found to be involved in action perception. The hMT+ region is generally involved in motion perception, and thus it is not surprising to find activation, albeit most commonly nonselective activation, during action perception. The ventral temporal pathway is involved in the recognition of objects and bodies. Premotor cortex is important for motor planning and execution, and it is most commonly activated when observers view intentional arm movements (such as grasping) and are given the task of viewing the actions with the intent to later imitate that action. How do we link these findings together?

A recent computational model of biological motion perception argues that the STS is the integration site of stationary body recognition and dynamic motion information present in body actions (Giese & Poggio, 2003). In this model, ventral temporal regions encode "snapshots" of key body postures and compare those postures to static templates stored in memory. The motion-flow patterns characteristic of body kinematics are analyzed in the hMT+ region and, together with the body templates, feed-forward to STS. Activation of the FBA and adjacent regions during biological motion perception supports the hypothesis that cortical machinery dedicated to static body perception also supports dynamic biological motion perception. Further studies are required to determine the nature of the cortical representation in this region during action recognition. And while specialization for action perception in hMT+ is currently under debate, it is clear that the STS is most strongly driven by biological events depicting natural body articulation.

The role of additional cortical areas, including premotor cortex, is less clear. Some authors argue that a common action network is engaged during recognition and execution of human actions, and a number of brain imaging studies have identified premotor activation during action recognition. This finding remains one of the most unclear, with some studies failing to find evidence for premotor activity during biological motion perception. A reasonable interpretation of these studies is that action recognition interfaces with a number of additional cortical networks, one of which includes the mirror neuron system.

Conclusion

We live in a dynamic visual world, and one of its most biologically salient events is human movement. People are remarkably adept at recognizing the actions performed by others, even when the kinematic patterns of their movements are portrayed by nothing more than a handful of points of light attached to the head and major joints of the body. Over the past two decades, evidence has accumulated to suggest that the STS is a "hot spot" for early registration of sensory events related to socially relevant experiences (Allison et al., 2000). This hot spot of action recognition likely reflects the integration of body posture and kinematic information as depicted in action events and analyzed in "earlier" cortical regions such as ventral temporal cortex and hMT+.

In addition, it appears that the STS serves as the front-end to additional circuits registering more refined aspects of action events, many of which are discussed in other chapters of this volume. Briefly, examples include action imitation in learning (Jeannerod, 1997; Rizzolatti, Fogassi, & Gallese, 2001), recognition of intentional action in social situations (Blakemore & Decety, 2001; Meltzoff & Decety, 2003), and quick recognition of changeable aspects of personality such as emotion (e.g., Atkinson, Dittrich, Gemmell, & Young, 2004). For example, one likely consequence of spending so much time watching biological motion is that we learn how to create these behaviors ourselves. Infants as young as 2 to 3 weeks old (and possibly as young as 2 days old) can imitate facial movements such as mouth openings and tongue protrusions (Meltzoff & Moore, 1977, 1983). Meltzoff and Moore proposed that imitation is possible because we are able to directly compare production of our own movements with those body movements that we see, which implies a shared representation of the actions we see with those we generate. The physiological implementation of this comparison is presumably within the mirror system, known to be involved in some instances with action recognition.

An equally intriguing proposition for the importance of action recognition is in the ability to infer and attribute complex social behaviors, such as intentions and desires, to other individuals on the basis of their movements (Adolphs, 2001; Blakemore & Decety, 2001; Frith & Frith, 1999). Neuroimaging studies in humans find the STS to be activated when subjects attribute goal-directed intentions to clearly inanimate moving objects (Castelli et al., 2000; Martin & Weisberg, 2003). Winston, Strange, O'Doherty, and Dolan (2002) found STS activation to be elevated when subjects were required to make assessments of the trustworthiness of faces, as opposed to passively viewing them. Analysis of single-unit recordings from the likely monkey homologue of human STS suggests that neural responses are strongly modulated by implied intention. For example, neurons that fire robustly when the experimenter reaches toward the monkey will not fire when the experimenter performs the same action but appears to be paying attention to a different region of space (Jellema et al., 2000). Thus the STS may play an important role in our understanding of intent as conveyed in social interactions. It is interesting to note also that populations of individuals who have difficulty attributing mental states to other individuals (as occurs in autism and schizophrenia) also have difficulty recognizing biological motion in point-light animations.

The extent to which humans use body kinematics to extract subtle social cues is a relatively unexplored domain. We know, for example, that individuals can identify emotions and personalities from gait (Heberlein, Adolphs, Tranel, & Damasio, 2004), discriminate emotions portrayed by point-light dancers (Dittrich, Troscianko, Lea, & Morgan, 1996), infer affect from arm movements (Pollick, Paterson, Bruderlin, & Sanford, 2001), and estimate vulnerability from body movements (Gunns, Johnston, & Hudson, 2002). As more behavioral studies explore the ways in which we employ action recognition in our social interactions, the network of brain activation will also likely expand. Future work is needed to develop a framework that takes into account the perceptual computations required for action recognition, and the output of that system into more complex social activities that we experience with such ease in our everyday lives.

References

Adolphs, R. (2001). The neurobiology of social cognition. *Current Opinion in Neurobiology, 11*, 231–239.

Allison, T., Puce, A., & McCarthy, G. (2000). Social perception from visual cues: role of the STS region. *Trends in Cognitive Science, 4*(7), 267–278.

Andersen, K. C., & Siegel, R. M. (1999). Optic flow selectivity in the anterior superior temporal polysensory area, STPa, of the behaving monkey. *Journal of Neuroscience, 19*, 2681–2692.

Andersen, R. A. (1995). Encoding of intention and spatial location in the posterior parietal cortex. *Cerebral Cortex, 5*(5), 457–469.

Andersen, R. A. (1997). Multimodal integration for the representation of space in the posterior parietal cortex. *Philosophical Transactions of the Royal Society of London B: Biological Sciences, 352*(1360), 1421–1428.

Andersen, R. A., Brotchie, P. R., & Mazzoni, P. (1992). Evidence for the lateral intraparietal area as the parietal eye field. *Current Opinion in Neurobiology, 2*(6), 840–846.

Atkinson, A. P., Dittrich, W. H., Gemmell, A. J., & Young, A. W. (2004). Emotion perception from dynamic and static body expressions in point-light and full-light displays. *Perception, 33*, 717–746.

Atkinson, J., Anker, S., Braddick, O., Nokes, L., Mason, A., & Braddick, F. (2001). Visual and visuospatial development in young children with Williams syndrome. *Developmental Medicine of Children and Neurology, 43*(5), 330–337.

Battelli, L., Cavanagh, P., Intriligator, J., Tramo, M. J., Henaff, M. A., Michel, F., et al. (2001). Unilateral right parietal damage leads to bilateral deficit for high-level motion. *Neuron, 32*(6), 985–995.

Battelli, L., Cavanagh, P., & Thornton, I. M. (2003). Perception of biological motion in parietal patients. *Neuropsychologia, 41*, 1808–1816.

Beauchamp, M. S., Lee, K. E., Haxby, J. V., & Martin, A. (2002). Parallel visual motion processing streams for manipulable objects and human movements. *Neuron, 34*(1), 149–159.

Beauchamp, M. S., Lee, K. E., Haxby, J. V., & Martin, A. (2003). FMRI responses to video and point-light displays of moving humans and manipulable objects. *Journal of Cognitive Neuroscience, 15*(7), 991–1001.

Beintema, J. A., & Lappe, M. (2002). Perception of biological motion without local image motion. *Proceedings of the National Academy of Sciences of the United States of America, 99*(8), 5661–5663.

Bertenthal, B., & Pinto, J. (1994). Global processing of biological motion. *Psychological Science, 5*, 221–225.

Blake, R., Turner, L. M., Smoski, M. J., Pozdol, S. L., & Stone, W. L. (2003). Visual recognition of biological motion is impaired in children with autism. *Psychological Science, 14*(2), 151–157.

Blakemore, S.-J., & Decety, J. (2001). From the perception of action to the understanding of intention. *Nature Reviews Neuroscience, 2*, 561–566.

Bonda, E., Petrides, M., Ostry, D., & Evans, A. (1996). Specific involvement of human parietal systems and the amygdala in the perception of biological motion. *Journal of Neuroscience, 16*(11), 3737–3744.

Boussaoud, D., Ungerleider, L. G., & Desimone, R. (1990). Pathways for motion analysis: Cortical connections of the medial superior temporal and fundus of the superior temporal visual areas of the macaque. *Journal of Comparative Neurology, 296*, 462–495.

Buccino, G., Binkofski, F., Fink, G. R., Fadiga, L., Fogassi, L., Gallese, V., et al. (2001). Action observation activates premotor and parietal areas in a somatotopic manner: An fMRI study. *European Journal of Neuroscience, 13*(2), 400–404.

Castelli, F., Happe, F., Frith, U., & Frith, C. (2000). Movement and mind: A functional imaging study of perception and interpretation of complex intentional movement patterns. *NeuroImage, 12*(3), 314–325.

Cavanagh, P., Labianca, A. T., & Thornton, I. M. (2001). Attention-based visual routines: Sprites. *Cognition, 80*(1–2), 47–60.

Colby, C. L., & Goldberg, M. E. (1999). Space and attention in parietal cortex. *Annual Review of Neuroscience, 22*, 319–349.

Cowey, A., & Vaina, L. M. (2000). Blindness to form from motion despite intact static form perception and motion detection. *Neuropsychologia, 38*(5), 566–578.

Culham, J. C., & Kanwisher, N. G. (2001). Neuroimaging of cognitive functions in human parietal cortex. *Current Opinion in Neurobiology, 11*(2), 157–163.

Cusick, C. G. (1996). The superior temporal polysensory region in monkeys. In K. S. Rockland, J. H. Kaas, & A. Peters (Eds.), *Extrastriate cortex in primates,* 14 (pp. 435–468). New York: Plenum Press.

Dittrich, W. H., Troscianko, T., Lea, S. E., & Morgan, D. (1996). Perception of emotion from dynamic point-light displays represented in dance. *Perception, 25*, 727–738.

Downing, P. E., Jiang, Y., Shuman, M., & Kanwisher, N. (2001). A cortical area selective for visual processing of the human body. *Science, 293*(5539), 2470–2473.

Ettlinger, G. (1990). Object "vision" and "spatial vision": The neuropsychological evidence for the distinction. *Cortex, 26*(3), 319–341.

Fadiga, L., Fogassi, L., Pavesi, G., & Rizzolatti, G. (1995). Motor facilitation during action observation: A magnetic stimulation study. *Journal of Neurophysiology, 73*(6), 2608–2611.

Farah, M. J. (2004). *Visual agnosia.* Cambridge, MA: MIT Press.

Frith, C. D., & Frith, U. (1999). Interacting minds—a biological basis. *Science, 286,* 1692–1695.

Gallese, V., Fadiga, L., Fogassi, L., & Rizzolatti, G. (1996). Action recognition in the premotor cortex. *Brain, 119,* 593–609.

Garcia, J. O., & Grossman, E. D. (2005). *Perception of point-light biological motion at isoluminance.* Annual Meeting of the Vision Sciences Society, Sarasota, Florida.

Gauthier, I., Tarr, M. J., Anderson, A. W., Skudlarski, P., & Gore, J. C. (1999). Activation of the middle fusiform 'face area' increases with expertise in recognizing novel objects. *Nature Neuroscience, 2*(6), 568–573.

Giese, M. A., & Poggio, T. (2003). Neural mechanisms for the recognition of biological movements. *Nature Reviews Neuroscience, 4*(3), 179–192.

Grezes, J., Costes, N., & Decety, J. (1998). Top-down effect of strategy on the perception of human biological motion: A PET investigation. *Cognitive Neuropsychology, 15*(7/8), 553–582.

Grossman, E., Battelli, L., & Pascual-Leone, A. (2005). TMS over STSp disrupts perception of biological motion. *Vision Research, 45*(22), 2847–2853.

Grossman, E., & Blake, R. (2002). Brain areas active during visual perception of biological motion. *Neuron, 35*(6), 1157–1165.

Grossman, E., Donnelly, M., Price, R., Pickens, D., Morgan, V., Neighbor, G., et al. (2000). Brain areas involved in perception of biological motion. *Journal of Cognitive Neuroscience, 12*(5), 711–720.

Grossman, E. D., & Blake, R. (2001). Brain activity evoked by inverted and imagined biological motion. *Vision Research, 41*, 1475–1482.

Gunns, R. E., Johnston, L., & Hudson, S. M. (2002). Victim selection and kinematics: A point-light investigation of vulnerability to attack. *Journal of Nonverbal Behavior, 26*(3), 129–158.

Haxby, J. V., Grady, C. L., Horwitz, B., Ungerleider, L. G., Mishkin, M., Carson, R. E., et al. (1991). Dissociation of object and spatial visual processing pathways in human extrastriate cortex. *Proceedings of the National Academy of Sciences of the United States of America, 88*(5), 1621–1625.

Heberlein, A. S., Adolphs, R., Tranel, D., & Damasio, H. (2004). Cortical regions for judgments of emotions and personality traits from point-light walkers. *Journal of Cognitive Neuroscience, 16*, 1143–1158.

Howard, R. J., Brammer, M., Wright, I., Woodruff, P. W., Bullmore, E. T., & Zeki, S. (1996). A direct demonstration of functional specialization within motion-related visual and auditory cortex of the human brain. *Current Biology, 6*, 1015–1019.

Huk, A. C., Dougherty, R. F., & Heeger, D. J. (2002). Retinotopy and functional subdivision of human areas MT and MST. *Journal of Neuroscience, 22*(16), 7195–7205.

Jeannerod, M. (1994). The representing brain: Neural correlates of motor intention and imagery. *Behavioral and Brain Sciences, 17*, 187–245.

Jeannerod, M. (1997). *The cognitive neuroscience of action.* Oxford: Blackwell Publishing.

Jellema, T., Baker, C. I., Wicker, B., & Perrett, D. I. (2000). Neural representation for the perception of the intentionality of actions. *Brain and Cognition, 44*, 280–302.

Johansson, G. (1973). Visual perception of biological motion and a model for its analysis. *Perception and Psychophysics, 14*, 195–204.

Jordan, H., Reiss, J. E., Hoffman, J. E., & Landau, B. (2002). Intact perception of biological motion in the face of profound spatial deficits: Williams syndrome. *Psychological Science, 13*(2), 162–167.

Kanwisher, N., McDermott, J., & Chun, M. M. (1997). The fusiform face area: A module in human extrastriate cortex specialized for face perception. *Journal of Neuroscience, 17*(11), 4302–4311.

Kim, J., Doop, M. L., Blake, R., & Park, S. (2005). Impaired recognition of biological motion in schizophrenia. *Schizophrenia Research, 77*(2–3), 299–307.

Kourtzi, Z., & Kanwisher, N. (2000a). Activation in human MT/MST by static images with implied motion. *Journal of Cognitive Neuroscience, 12*(1), 48–55.

Kourtzi, Z., & Kanwisher, N. (2000b). Cortical regions involved in perceiving object shape. *Journal of Neuroscience, 20*(9), 3310–3318.

Livingstone, M., & Hubel, D. (1988). Segregation of form, color, movement, and depth: Anatomy, physiology, and perception. *Science, 240*(4853), 740–749.

Logothetis, N. K. (1998). Object vision and visual awareness. *Current Opinion in Neurobiology, 8*(4), 536–544.

Malach, R., Reppas, J. B., Benson, R. R., Kwong, K. K., Jiang, H., Kennedy, W. A., et al. (1995). Object-related activity revealed by functional magnetic resonance imaging in human occipital cortex. *Proceedings of the National Academy of Sciences of the United States of America*, *92*(18), 8135–8139.

Martin, A., & Weisberg, J. (2003). Neural foundations for understanding social and mechanical concepts. *Cognitive Neuropsychology*, *20*(3–6), 575–587.

Meltzoff, A. N., & Decety, J. (2003). What imitation tells us about social cognition: A rapprochement between developmental psychology and cognitive neuroscience. *Philosophical Transactions: Biological Sciences*, *358*(1421), 491–500.

Meltzoff, A. N., & Moore, M. K. (1977). Imitation of facial and manual gestures by human neonates. *Science*, *198*, 75–78.

Meltzoff, A. N., & Moore, M. K. (1983). Newborn infants imitate adult facial gestures. *Child Development*, *54*, 702–709.

Michels, L., Lappe, M., & Vaina, L. M. (2005). Visual areas involved in the perception of human movement from dynamic form analysis. *Neuroreport*, *16*(10), 1037–1041.

Milner, A. D., & Goodale, M. A. (1998). *The visual brain in action*. Oxford Psychology Series, 27. Oxford: Oxford University Press.

Oram, M. W., & Perrett, D. I. (1994). Responses of anterior superior temporal polysensory (STPa) neurons to "biological motion" stimuli. *Journal of Cognitive Neuroscience*, *6*, 99–116.

Orban, G. A., Dupont, P., De Bruyn, B., Vogels, R., Vandenberghe, R., & Mortelmans, L. (1995). A motion area in human visual cortex. *Proceedings of the National Academy of Sciences of the United States of America*, *92*(4), 993–997.

Pascual-Leone, A., Walsh, V., & Rothwell, J. C. (2000). Transcranial magnetic stimulation in cognitive neuroscience—virtual lesion, chronometry, and functional connectivity. *Current Opinion in Neurobiology*, *10*, 232–237.

Pavlova, M., & Sokolov, A. (2000). Orientation specificity in biological motion perception. *Perception and Psychophysics*, *62*, 889–898.

Pavlova, M., & Sokolov, A. (2003). Prior knowledge about display inversion in biological motion perception. *Perception*, *32*(8), 937–946.

Pavlova, M., Staudt, M., Sokolov, A., Birbaumer, N., & Krageloh-Mann, I. (2003). Perception and production of biological movements in patients with early periventricular brain lesions. *Brain*, *126*(Pt. 3), 692–701.

Peelen, M. V., & Downing, P. E. (2005). Selectivity for the human body in the fusiform gyrus. *Journal of Neurophysiology*, *93*(1), 603–608.

Peelen, M. V., Wiggett, A. J., & Downing, P. E. (2006). Patterns of fMRI activity dissociate overlapping functional brain areas that respond to biological motion. *Neuron*, *49*(6), 815–822.

Peigneux, P., Salmon, E., van der Linden, M., Garraux, G., Aerts, J., Delfiore, G., et al. (2000). The role of lateral occipitotemporal junction and area MT/V5 in the visual analysis of upper-limb postures. *Neuroimage*, *11*(6 Pt 1), 644–655.

Pelphrey, K. A., Mitchell, T. V., McKeown, M. J., Goldstein, J., Allison, T., & McCarthy, G. (2003). Brain activity evoked by the perception of human walking: Controlling for meaningful coherent motion. *Journal of Neuroscience*, *23*(17), 6819–6825.

Pelphrey, K. A., Morris, J. P., Michelich, C. R., Allison, T., & McCarthy, G. (2005). Functional anatomy of biological motion perception in posterior temporal cortex: An FMRI study of eye, mouth and hand movements. *Cerebral Cortex*, *15*(12), 1866–1876.

Perrett, D. I., Smith, P. A., Mistlin, A. J., Chitty, A. J., Head, A. S., Potter, D. D., et al. (1985). Visual analysis of body movements by neurones in the temporal cortex of the macaque monkey: A preliminary report. *Behavioral Brain Research*, *16*(2–3), 153–170.

Perrett, D. I., Smith, P. A., Potter, D. D., Mistlin, A. J., Head, A. S., Milner, A. D., et al. (1985). Visual cells in the temporal cortex sensitive to face view and gaze direction. *Proceedings of the Royal Society of London, B: Biological Sciences*, *223*(1232), 293–317.

Peuskens, H., Vanrie, J., Verfaillie, K., & Orban, G. A. (2005). Specificity of regions processing biological motion. *European Journal of Neuroscience*, *21*(10), 2864–2875.

Pollick, F. E., Paterson, H. M., Bruderlin, A., & Sanford, A. J. (2001). Perceiving affect from arm movement. *Cognition*, *82*(2), B51–B61.

Press, W. A., Brewer, A. A., Dougherty, R. F., Wade, A. R., & Wandell, B. A. (2001). Visual areas and spatial summation in human visual cortex. *Vision Research*, *41*(10–11), 1321–1332.

Puce, A., Allison, T., Bentin, S., Gore, J. C., & McCarthy, G. (1998). Temporal cortex activation in humans viewing eye and mouth movements. *Journal of Neuroscience*, *18*, 2188–2199.

Puce, A., Allison, T., Gore, J. C., & McCarthy, G. (1995). Face-sensitive regions in human extrastriate cortex studied by functional MRI. *Journal of Neurophysiology*, *74*(3), 1192–1199.

Pyles, J. P., Garcia, J. O., Hoffman, D. D., & Grossman, E. D. (in press). Visual perception and neural correlates of novel "biological motion." *Vision Research*.

Reed, C. L., Stone, V. E., Bozova, S., & Tanaka, J. (2003). The body inversion effect. *Psychological Science*, *14*(4), 302–308.

Rizzolatti, G., Fadiga, L., Gallese, V., & Fogassi, L. (1996). Premotor cortex and the recognition of motor actions. *Brain Research Cognitive Brain Research*, *3*(2), 131–141.

Rizzolatti, G., Fadiga, L., Matelli, M., Bettinardi, V., Paulesu, E., Perani, D., et al. (1996). Localization of grasp representations in humans by PET: 1. Observation versus execution. *Experimental Brain Research*, *111*(2), 246–252.

Rizzolatti, G., Fogassi, L., & Gallese, V. (2001). Opinion: Neurophysiological mechanisms underlying the understanding of imitation and action. *Nature Reviews Neuroscience*, *2*, 661–670.

Rolls, E. (2000). Functions of the primate temporal lobe cortical visual areas in invariant visual object and face recognition. *Neuron*, *27*(2), 205–218.

Sary, G., Vogels, R., & Orban, G. (1993). Cue-invariant shape selectivity of macaque inferior temporal neurons. *Science*, *260*(5110), 995–997.

Saxe, R., Xiao, D. K., Kovacs, G., Perrett, D. I., & Kanwisher, N. (2004). A region of right posterior superior temporal sulcus responds to observed intentional actions. *Neuropsychologia*, *42*(11), 1435–1446.

Saygin, A. P., Wilson, S. M., Hagler, D. J., Bates, E., & Sereno, M. I. (2004). Point-light biological motion perception activates human premotor cortex. *Journal of Neuroscience, 24*(27), 6181–6188.

Schenk, T., & Zihl, J. (1997a). Visual motion perception after brain damage I: Deficits in global motion perception. *Neuropsychologia, 35*, 1289–1297.

Schenk, T., & Zihl, J. (1997b). Visual motion perception after brain damage II: Deficits in form-from-motion perception. *Neuropsychologia, 35*, 1299–1310.

Schiller, P. H., Logothetis, N. K., & Charles, E. R. (1990). Functions of the colour-opponent and broad-band channels of the visual system. *Nature, 343*(6253), 16–17.

Shiffrar, M., & Freyd, J. J. (1990). Apparent motion of the human body. *Psychological Science, 1*, 257–264.

Shipley, T. F. (2003). The effect of object and event orientation on perception of biological motion. *Psychological Science, 14*(4), 377–380.

Smith, A. T., Wall, M. B., Williams, A. L., & Singh, K. D. (2006). Sensitivity to optic flow in human cortical areas MT and MST. *European Journal of Neuroscience, 23*(2), 561–569.

Stevens, J. A., Fonlupt, P., Shiffrar, M., & Decety, J. (2000). New aspects of motion perception: Selective neural encoding of apparent human movements. *Neuroreport, 11*(1), 109–115.

Sumi, S. (1984). Upside-down presentation of the Johansson moving light-spot pattern. *Perception, 13*(3), 283–286.

Tanaka, K. (1996). Inferotemporal cortex and object vision. *Annual Review of Neuroscience, 19*, 109–139.

Thompson, J. C., Clarke, M., Stewart, T., & Puce, A. (2005). Configural processing of biological motion in human superior temporal sulcus. *Journal of Neuroscience, 25*(39), 9059–9066.

Tootell, R. B., Reppas, J. B., Kwong, K. K., Malach, R., Born, R. T., Brady, T. J., et al. (1995). Functional analysis of human MT and related visual cortical areas using magnetic resonance imaging. *Journal of Neuroscience, 15*(4), 3215–3230.

Ungerleider, L. G., & Haxby, J. V. (1994). 'What' and 'where' in the human brain. *Current Opinion in Neurobiology, 4*(2), 157–165.

Ungerleider, L. G., & Mishkin, M. (1982). Two cortical visual systems. In D. J. Ingle, M. A. Goodale, & R. J. W. Mansfield (Eds.), *Analysis of visual behavior*. Cambridge, MA: MIT Press.

Vaina, L. M., Cowey, A., Eskew, R. T., Jr., LeMay, M., & Kemper, T. (2001). Regional cerebral correlates of global motion perception: Evidence from unilateral cerebral brain damage. *Brain, 124*(Pt 2), 310–321.

Vaina, L. M., Lemay, M., Bienfang, D. C., Choi, A. Y., & Nakayama, K. (1990). Intact "biological motion" and "structure from motion" perception in a patient with impaired motion mechanisms: A case study. *Visual Neuroscience, 5*(4), 353–369.

Wachsmuth, E., Oram, M. W., & Perrett, D. I. (1994). Recognition of objects and their component parts: Responses of single units in the temporal cortex of the macaque. *Cerebral Cortex, 5*, 509–522.

Watson, J. D., Myers, R., Frackowiak, R. S., Hajnal, J. V., Woods, R. P., Mazziotta, J. C., et al. (1993). Area V5 of the human brain: Evidence from a combined study using positron emission tomography and magnetic resonance imaging. *Cerebral Cortex*, *3*(2), 79–94.

Wheaton, K. J., Thompson, J. C., Syngeniotis, A., Abbott, D. F., & Puce, A. (2003). Viewing the motion of human body parts activates different regions of premotor, temporal, and parietal cortex. *NeuroImage*, *22*, 277–288.

Winston, J. S., Strange, B. A., O'Doherty, J., & Dolan, R. J. (2002). Automatic and intentional brain responses during evaluation of trustworthiness of faces. *Nature Neuroscience*, *5*(3), 277–283.

Yin, R. K. (1969). Looking at upside-down faces. *Journal of Experimental Psychology*, *81*, 141–145.

Yovel, G., & Kanwisher, N. (2005). The neural basis of the behavioral face-inversion effect. *Current Biology*, *15*(24), 2256–2262.

14

Animacy and Intention in the Brain: Neuroscience of Social Event Perception

ANDREA S. HEBERLEIN

While many movements look animate because they are derived from actual biological motion (as discussed in Chapters 11, 12, and 13), some movements are perceived as animate even when the moving objects are geometric objects or blobs. Further, these moving objects may not look merely alive; in many instances, they look like intentional agents, with goals, emotions, and personality traits. Viewers make such anthropomorphic attributions despite being fully aware that the shapes to which they are ascribing these anthropomorphic qualities are animated geometric objects: the impression that the shapes are alive and social is so compelling that it is not amenable to top-down information, as in classic perceptual illusions. When people make these social attributions, a suite of brain regions is recruited, including structures known to be important for processing cues related to people and to emotional information: the amygdala, the fusiform face area (FFA), the temporo-parietal junction (TPJ), and both ventral and dorsal medial prefrontal cortices (VMPFC and DMPFC; Fig. 14.1; also see color insert). Though some of these structures have roles that extend considerably beyond processing social information, this circuit has been dubbed the "social brain" (Adolphs,

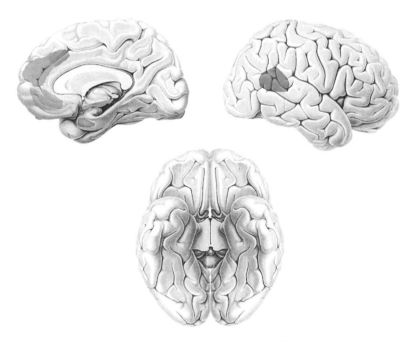

FIGURE 14.1. Brain regions involved in perceiving social events, in three views: medial (upper left), dorsal (upper right), and ventral (bottom). Two regions of medial prefrontal cortex, one more ventral and one more dorsal; the amygdala (shaded region in lower-middle portion of the upper-left figure), buried deep in anterior medial temporal cortex; cortices around the temporo-parietal junction (shaded region in upper-right figure); and the fusiform gyrus (lower left region of bottom figure). Note that in most cases these structures are implicated bilaterally, but here they are indicated only in the right hemisphere.

2003; Brothers, 1990; Skuse, Morris, & Lawrence, 2003) because its components are implicated across a wide variety of social processes.

In this chapter I will explore a set of related concepts, including judgments of animacy, judgments of agency or intentionality, and anthropomorphizing, focusing on the functional neuroanatomy of each process. Anthropomorphizing can be thought of as an illusion: stimuli possessing certain features appear to automatically elicit attributions of mental states and other qualities associated with people, in the face of declarative knowledge that the stimuli are not only not human but, in many cases, inanimate. Studies of illusions are particularly useful in revealing the organization of perceptual processes. Thus, I will focus on studies of anthropomorphizing—that is, the attribution of personhood and person-related features such as emotions, intentions, personality traits, and beliefs to inanimate objects. I will focus especially on the neural circuitry underlying social attributions based on the kind of minimal stimuli described above, relating these findings to other social processes in which the same neural regions have been implicated. Finally, I will propose a framework relating judgments of animacy, agency or goal, and emotion.

Social Judgments from Ambiguous Motion Stimuli: Animacy and Anthropomorphizing

Working separately in the early 1940s, Michotte (1946/1963) and Heider and Simmel (1944) examined the movement features that lead to attributions of psychological traits to simple geometric objects. Michotte, extending his work on physical causation, showed that different patterns of movement are interpreted as physically caused versus psychologically caused. For example, if one moving object contacts a second object which then immediately begins moving in the same direction as the initial moving object, the event is interpreted as a transfer of momentum—as physical causation. In contrast, if the second moving object begins moving after a pause, the event is interpreted as being caused by something internal in the second object (i.e., as psychological causation)—the second object moved of its own accord, having *decided* to move, perhaps because it was *convinced* to do so by the first object, or because it was *trying* to escape the other object.

In contrast to these very simple movements, Heider and Simmel's (1944) 2.5-minute-long[1] movie depicts the movements of three geometric objects: a large triangle, a smaller triangle, and a circle. These three objects move around and in and out of the outline of a rectangle, circling and bumping into each other in nonrandom patterns. With very few exceptions, viewers of this movie interpret it as the interactions of three people moving in and out of a house, and include intentions, emotions, personality traits, gender, and relationships in their spontaneous descriptions of the movie. For example, the big triangle is frequently

---

1. Oddly, successive studies using, allegedly, the original movie have described it as anywhere from 90 seconds to 2.5 minutes long (e.g., Berry et al., 1992; Heberlein & Adolphs, 2004). It is possible that when the original movie was converted to VHS, it was somehow shortened.

described as a *bully* who *intimidates* both of the other characters; the other two are *friends* (or a *couple*) who finally manage to *escape*.

Many studies have followed up both the initial Michotte studies and the Heider and Simmel paper (reviewed in Scholl & Tremoulet, 2000). Studies in the Michotte tradition have primarily attempted to determine which stimulus features lead to perceptions of animacy and agency. In contrast, studies in the Heider and Simmel tradition have focused more on studying the attribution of personality traits and of representational mental states, such as theory of mind. Though the two processes are related, the distinction is a significant one and parallels distinctions that have been made in both developmental and neuroimaging studies of mental state attribution (e.g., Saxe, Carey, & Kanwisher, 2004). In this section, I will first review psychological studies of animacy and agency perception and then discuss studies of anthropomorphizing, or attributing representational mental states based on similar kinds of motion stimuli.

Studies of single objects moving (e.g., Stewart, 1982, summarized in Gelman, Durgin, & Kaufman, 1995; Tremoulet & Feldman, 2000) have illuminated some features that influence animacy judgments. The necessity for a hidden energy source appears to play some role, though only some animations that would require this inference are seen as animate (Stewart, 1982); environmental and/or contextual cues also play some role, so that animacy percepts might be seen as arising from interactions between certain movement patterns and specific environmental cues (Gelman et al., 1995), and very simple featural cues, such as the local orientation of the moving objects, or combinations of velocity and direction changes, influence judgments of animacy (Tremoulet & Feldman, 2000).

Stimuli that contain two or more moving objects often appear more compellingly animate than those depicting only one object, perhaps because each object provides a more rich and variable "context" for the other. Several variations of this have been explored by Bassili (1976), Dittrich and Lea (1994), Opfer (2002), Blythe, Todd, and Miller (1999), and Zacks (2004). Proposing a role for observable goal-directedness before many of the above studies of single moving objects were performed, Bassili showed that temporal contingencies between the movements of two objects influenced whether the objects were perceived as animate (and interacting) or not. Further, the relative directions of the contingently moving objects influenced the kinds of interactions that were perceived, especially whether the interactions were seen as intentional (chasing, following) or not. When movement paths converged with temporal contingency between movements, both objects, and especially the following object, were seen as intentional, but when movement paths diverged or were random, temporal contingency had less of an effect in creating impressions of agency (Bassili, 1976). Looking specifically at the effect of "following" or pursuit movements, Dittrich and Lea showed subjects movies of multiple moving objects, in which all but one object moved randomly. The nonrandomly moving object followed one of the randomly moving objects, and, as in Bassili's study, the degree to which its movement was seen as animate was affected by variables relating the movement of the "chaser" to the randomly moving objects, especially how closely it tracked its target (Dittrich & Lea, 1994). Opfer (2002) developed two sets of stimuli that were identical in their depiction of a moving "blob" but differed in that one set had moving goal objects that the blob appeared to pursue. Adults and children as young as 5 years old consistently rated the goal-directed objects as more animate than the autonomously moving but not goal-directed blobs. Interestingly, adults and older children did not assign more psychological capacities to the blobs, implying that goal-directed movement is a better cue for animacy than for intentionality (Opfer, 2002).

In contrast to these three studies focusing on animacy from agency or goal-directedness cues, Blythe and colleagues (1999) attempted to parameterize the movement-specific cues that enable judgments of not just animacy but specific interaction intentions from the movements of pairs of objects. Their movement stimuli were created by having two subjects each control a cursor on a computer screen and interact according to assigned roles, including not only chaser/chased but also two individuals playing, fighting, or courting. Many of these displays were identifiable by a separate group of subjects in forced-choice settings, and furthermore they could be categorized correctly by an algorithm based on just a few motion parameters (Blythe et al., 1999). In contrast to Opfer's conclusions, then, Blythe et al.'s findings appear to show that sufficiently complex movement interactions—dependent perhaps on having two self-propelled moving objects, both of which are moving in goal-directed ways—convey not just biological but also psychological content. However, the primary response measure in this study was forced choice, leaving open the possibility that subjects would not have spontaneously inferred such high levels of intentionality. Zacks (2004) used a different method to explore the effects of movement features on viewers' interpretations of animated objects: viewers were asked to segment activity at "meaningful event boundaries," or the beginnings and ends of parts of a dynamic stimulus, in this case a short movie of two moving geometric objects. The timing of viewers' marked boundaries correlated highly with movement features when the stimuli were created randomly, but less well when the stimuli were created by people following scripts like those used by Blythe and colleagues, such as "chasing" or "fighting." This is particularly interesting because participants showed this pattern of response even when they were given no cues as to the intentions behind these nonrandom stimuli, and, further, even when they were not told that some of the stimuli were goal-directed. Zacks (2004) concluded that while movement features play a major role in how people perceive events, inferences about the goals of the moving objects (or of the agents moving the objects) interact with the information contained in movement features.

Affective information can also be derived from similar animations. Rimé, Boulanger, Laubin, Richir, and Stroobants (1985) used simple Michotte-esque stimuli consisting of two moving dots and asked subjects to rate the level of each of several affective states or traits associated with one of the two dots for each stimulus. Though their conclusion that the stimuli *evoke* emotional perceptions may not be warranted given the constrained nature of the responses, ratings demonstrated a high degree of consensus, including between European and U.S. raters, consistent with the interpretation that the stimuli lend themselves easily to emotional interpretation. Interestingly, when identical stimuli with simple human-like silhouettes were presented instead of dots as the moving objects, consensus between raters was markedly lower than for the dot stimuli (Rimé et al., 1985). People's ability to identify emotions based on fairly minimal movement stimuli is also shown in studies using point-light stimuli, including of both whole bodies (Dittrich, Troscianko, Lea, & Morgan, 1996) and, strikingly, of just single limbs (see Chapter 11 in this volume).

In summary, though autonomous motion itself is not a particularly strong cue for animacy, autonomous movements that appear goal-directed with respect to background contexts, especially when those contexts are themselves moving objects, are robustly perceived as animate by both adults and children.[2] This suggests that goal-directedness, or agency, is a kind of perceptual primitive and may itself underlie attributions of animacy (Dittrich & Lea, 1994; Scholl & Tremoulet, 2000; Tremoulet & Feldman, 2000). Some of the studies reviewed here, especially Blythe et al.'s (1999) study of different types of interaction, presage the next section on more complex movement stimuli, in which the movements of simple geometric objects elicit attributions not just of animacy but of intentionality and representational mental content as well.

As noted above, Heider and Simmel's original (1944) movie was much longer than Michotte's stimuli, and given the contributions of contextual elements to animacy judgments it should not be surprising that the objects in this movie are robustly seen as animate. The shapes are not merely animate, or goal-directed, however: in contrast to descriptions of the simple Michotte-esque stimuli explored by Opfer (2002), descriptions of Heider-esque stimuli appear to include both psychological and biological attributions (Hashimoto, 1966; Heberlein & Adolphs, 2004; Heberlein, Adolphs, Tranel, & Damasio, 2003; Heider & Simmel, 1944). These attributions appear to be due to movement features or changes in location over time, and not the difference in the objects' shapes: versions of the movie in which the movement information is disrupted via a strobe-like effect were not described in anthropomorphic terms, whereas versions in which the shape information is disrupted by blurring were described much like the original movie was (Berry, Misovich, Kean, & Baron, 1992). Similar stimuli are anthropomorphized in other cultures (Barrett, Todd, Miller, & Blythe, 2005; Hashimoto, 1966; Morris & Peng, 1994), though the specific content of attributions may differ markedly

---

2. Note that developing concepts of animacy and the cues that elicit animacy and agency categorizations in infants, toddlers, and preschoolers are a rich field of study. Infants under 1 year of age categorize moving objects in terms of their goal-directedness, use other animacy cues such as the presence of eyes and the contingency of behavioral responses to categorize objects as agents, and also appear to reason with regard to teleological intention. Furthermore, supporting the distinction inherent in the present chapter, there are distinct time courses for the development of reasoning about goals as compared to reasoning about representational content such as in theory of mind. I will not review this literature here; instead I point readers toward just a few of the many excellent recent reviews: Csibra, 2003; Johnson, 2003; Mandler, 1992; Rakison & Poulin-Dubois, 2001; and Saxe, Carey, & Kanwisher, 2004.

(Morris & Peng, 1994), and watching them one is struck by the seemingly automatic and obligatory nature of the anthropomorphic impression. Despite knowing that one is watching two-dimensional depictions of simple shapes, the feeling that the shapes have complex intentions, emotions, and personality traits is unsettlingly strong. It has been challenging, however, to devise satisfactory methods for measuring the content and nature of such impressions. Hashimoto (1966) told one group of subjects that the movements they were viewing were of inanimate entities and instructed them to describe them that way. His subjects nevertheless described the movie in anthropomorphic terms, and this has been interpreted as evidence for the automaticity and obligatoriness of this percept. However, this paper not only lacked a systematic coding scheme to assign ratings of levels of animacy but also apparently lacked any effort to blind the experimenter as to the condition in which participants' descriptions were elicited.

More recent studies examining subjects' descriptions of the original Heider and Simmel movie or similar stimuli have utilized a range of dependent measures to operationalize anthropomorphizing, from counting the instances of several categories of anthropomorphisms, such as actions, traits, and social roles (Berry et al., 1992), through very detailed analysis of specific types of anthropomorphic content, such as the percentage of propositions in the total description that contain affective content (Klin, 2000). In a recent study, my colleagues and I (Heberlein, Scheer, McGivern, & Farah, 2006) extended Hashimoto's finding using a more objective measure of anthropomorphizing: a computerized text analysis program known as Linguistic Inquiry and Word Count (Pennebaker, Francis, & Booth, 2001). This program counts words in 74 categories and thus provides an objective measure of the extent to which subjects are including references to or descriptions of anthropomorphic or animate content. Though it is not sensitive to context in the way that human-rater indices are, it has the twin advantages of very high speed and perfect replicability. Replicating Hashimoto (1966), we found that people who had been told before viewing that the movie depicted inanimate objects still included some anthropomorphic content in their descriptions; few described the movies in asocial, inanimate terms. However, relative to subjects given a neutral instruction, they used significantly fewer words in three categories that index such content: Affective and Emotional Processes (e.g., happy, evil), Social Processes (e.g., he, hers, talk, friend), and Insight (e.g., want, try). In contrast, they did not differ in their use of words in a control category, Motion (e.g., move, go). We tested a more stringent instruction focusing on the description (as compared with the perception) of the stimulus, explicitly forbidding subjects from anthropomorphizing or using language "implying that the shapes have emotions, intentions, or mental states." In this condition, we hypothesized that the percept of intentionality would be strong enough to leak through in verbal responses, despite subjects' efforts to describe it in inanimate terms. Indeed, we found that while subjects were successful to some extent in regulating their word use—they anthropomorphized significantly less than subjects given a completely neutral instruction—they regularly failed, implying that their percepts of animacy and anthropomorphism were too strong to fully override. Furthermore, the rate of speech in subjects given the instruction not to anthropomorphize is significantly slower than that of subjects given a neutral instruction (Heberlein et al., 2006). In summary, movement cues can create percepts of intentionality that are so strong that it is difficult to override them with instructions given before viewing or before describing the movements, supporting the idea that such processes are both stimulus-driven and modular.

I will turn now to an examination of the neural substrates subserving animacy perception and anthropomorphizing from movement cues, but will return to a discussion of the bottom-up and top-down contributions to these processes at the end of the chapter.

Functional Neuroanatomy of Animacy Perception and Anthropomorphizing

Functional neuroimaging studies have examined the neural circuitry subserving both animacy perception and the attribution of intentionality to simple moving objects. Notably, many of the structures involved in perceiving and interpreting these stimuli are also implicated in a variety of other social cognitive tasks. These structures principally include cortices along the posterior superior temporal sulcus (pSTS) and the temporoparietal junction more broadly, as well as bilateral amygdala, temporal poles, ventral occipital regions including the fusiform gyrus, and ventral and medial prefrontal cortices (see Fig. 14.1; also see color insert). This list overlaps to a striking degree with those regions proposed by Brothers

(1990) to make up the primate social cognitive brain, which she defined as a network of brain regions more or less specialized for perceiving and processing behavioral cues that are relevant for inferring mental states and predicting behavior based on them. Based primarily on neurophysiological studies in nonhuman primates, Brothers' social brain included orbitofrontal cortices, the temporal poles, amygdala, and STS cortices. An area in humans that appears to be homologous to macaque anterior STS, the posterior section of human STS (Logothetis, Guggenberger, Peled, & Pauls, 1999), has revealed regions responsive to the visual perception of human bodies (Downing, Jiang, Shuman, & Kanwisher, 2001); to representations of both whole-body movement and the movement of specific body parts such as mouths, eyes, and hands (reviewed in Allison, Puce, & McCarthy, 2000; also see Chapter 13 in this volume); and to the perception of animacy, goal-directedness, and intentionality.

In functional imaging studies of human subjects, participants have been scanned while viewing or making judgments about animate movements as depicted by simple geometric objects such as triangles or small dots. Because, as noted in the previous section, goal-directedness is a robust cue for animacy, the stimuli in many of these studies appear goal-directed. Brain regions implicated in animacy perception were isolated in contrasts of goal-directed movements as contrasted with physically random (J. Schultz, Imamizu, Kawato, & Frith, 2004), physically but not psychologically causal (Blakemore et al., 2003; Castelli, Happé, Frith, & Frith, 2000), or geometrically patterned movements (Castelli et al., 2000). Activations elicited by viewing such animations partly overlap with those elicited by viewing obviously human goal-directed movements, as contrasted with non-goal-directed movements (Decety et al., 1997; Pelphrey, Morris, & McCarthy, 2004) or with emotional movements (Bonda, Petrides, Ostry, & Evans, 1996). Notably, static animacy cues such as faces or human forms are also processed in a different set of overlapping brain regions; I will return to this point below. Some functional imaging studies did not distinguish between animate, goal-directed movement and intentional[3] movement, the interpretation

---

3. I use "intentional" in the sense of higher-order levels of intentionality; in the case of movement stimuli, one or more of the moving objects appears to take the intentional stance or, in other words, to attribute mental states to others, not just to have goal-directedness itself.

of which requires the attribution of mental states (i.e., mentalizing); still others focused specifically on mentalizing based on moving object stimuli. Perhaps not surprisingly, the brain regions implicated in this type of anthropomorphizing largely overlap those implicated in attributing mental states to unambiguously human targets.

Animacy and Agency Percepts: Superior Temporal Sulcus

In a clever isolation of animacy perception from movement, Schultz, Friston, O'Doherty, Wolpert, and Frith (2005) created animations of two autonomously moving discs, in which one appears to chase the other while the "chasee" appears to evade capture. By continuously varying the cross-correlation of the discs' motions, the authors could capture the interactive nature of the movements in a single continuous variable and relate it to both viewers' percepts and their brain activity. Interactive movement stimuli were seen as significantly more animate than control stimuli created by decoupling the movements of the two objects (thus replicating Bassili, 1976, and others discussed earlier), and ratings of animacy increased with the degree of cross-correlation. Bilateral regions of posterior STS/STG were more active when subjects viewed the cross-correlated movements relative to the uncorrelated movements, and activity in these regions increased parametrically with the increase in the relationship of the objects' movements. Notably, this was the case even when subjects were performing a task for which the relationship between the objects' movements was irrelevant (judging how fast both objects were moving), implying that this region is sensitive to animacy cues even in the absence of full attention to this feature (Schultz et al., 2005). However, though it may respond to animacy even with limited attentional resources, this posterior STS/STG region responds *more* to animate or goal-directed stimuli when attention *is* focused on this aspect of movement: instructing subjects to attend to the contingent nature of animate contingent animations (as opposed to physically contingent collision events and noncontingent animate and physical events) increased activity in posterior STS/STG (Blakemore et al., 2003), and instructing subjects to attend to the strategy employed by a chasing object (predict versus follow the target), as compared to attending to the outcome (success versus failure in catching it), had a similar effect (Schultz et al., 2004). These findings support the idea of a role for posterior STS/STG in processing animacy cues from goal-directed motion. Also consistent with such a role is the finding that the same pSTS region that is activated in response to biological motion cues demonstrates activity correlated with the moments in a simple animated stimulus that participants code as event boundaries (Zacks, Swallow, Vettel, & McAvoy, 2006). Because these authors used a biological motion localizer, they were able to demonstrate that certain features in the motion of circles and squares elicit activity from the same region that responds to nonrigid, articulated, whole-body movements. Notably, the same region is involved in processing specifically goal-directed human movements (Pelphrey et al., 2004), including in the context of imitation (Decety, Chaminade, Grezes, & Meltzoff, 2002; Grezes, Armony, Rowe, & Passingham, 2003), which appears to be facilitated by attention to goals.

Intentional and Anthropomorphic Attributions: pSTS, FFA, Amygdala, and mPFC

Posterior STS/STG, along with several other structures, is also implicated in processing more complex social movements, such as those that are seen as not merely goal-directed but also intentional or representational. Castelli et al. (2000) compared brain activity in participants viewing three types of Heider-and-Simmel-like animations: random or physically constrained movements (e.g., bouncing, star pattern, billiard balls); goal-directed movements (e.g., chasing, fighting); and movements implying higher-level mental content, which they termed "Theory of Mind movements" (e.g., coaxing, mocking, seducing). Four regions—temporoparietal cortex corresponding to pSTS, medial prefrontal cortex, the fusiform gyrus on the ventral occipitotemporal surface, and extrastriate regions of lateral occipital cortex—were more active during viewing of the goal-directed stimuli versus the random stimuli, and all of these were also significantly more active during the theory of mind movies than during the goal-directed ones. In addition, activity in these areas correlated with subjects' ratings of intentionality in the movies, regardless of the designated movie type (Castelli et al., 2000).

Two other studies employing similar stimulus contrasts have found largely complementary patterns of activation: viewing animated actions that look intentional and social (dancing, swimming, fishing, scaring) compared with objects that are not involved in any such actions (a cannon, a paper shredder, billiard balls), movies depicting random motion, and static stimuli yielded greater activity in lateral fusiform, right amygdala, bilateral pSTS, bilateral anterior STS, and ventromedial prefrontal cortex (Martin & Weisberg, 2003). These differences are especially noteworthy given the authors' report that subjects had to be actively prevented from attributing meaning to the random movement stimuli, as pilot testing showed that they would otherwise do so. This implies that some part of the activation difference observed is due to top-down effects, such as a dampening of response in the random movement case or in a ramping-up of response in the social case, or both; I will return to this issue shortly. In a similar study, subjects viewing animations of three interacting geometric objects while judging whether all the objects were "friends" showed greater activity in the fusiform gyrus, amygdala, temporal pole, medial PFC, and STS as compared to viewing somewhat different "bumper car" animations while judging whether all the objects weighed the same amount (Schultz et al., 2003). These experimenters focused particularly on a region of the fusiform cortex that has widely been reported to be critical for processing face information, the "fusiform face area" or FFA (Farah, Wilson, Drain, & Tanaka, 1995; Kanwisher, McDermott, & Chun, 1997; Puce, Allison, Asgari, Gore, & McCarthy, 1996). This region responds significantly more to visually presented faces than to any other visual stimulus, though it also responds to other visual stimuli with which the viewer has expertise, especially if processing of the said stimuli occurs holistically (Tarr & Gauthier, 2000). R. Schultz and colleagues localized the FFA on each subject's brain and confirmed that the fusiform activation—which was also observed by both Castelli and colleagues (2000) and Martin and Weisberg (2003)—was in fact in the face-responsive part of the fusiform gyrus.

There are at least two ways in which one might interpret FFA activity in a social judgment task not containing any faces: FFA might participate in social judgments even when those judgments are made based on nonface stimuli, or the FFA might be potentiated by input from a structure such as the amygdala, which might participate in the detection of socially relevant stimuli and the focus of attention by relevant visual cortices—including FFA and pSTS—onto such stimuli (Schultz et al., 2000). This latter view is consistent both with the finding of greater amygdala activity in two of the above studies (and both of the two fMRI studies) and with a recent lesion study: a subject with complete bilateral amygdala damage describes the original Heider and Simmel (1944) movie in strikingly inanimate (and therefore also nonanthropomorphic) terms (Heberlein & Adolphs, 2004). As noted above, it is difficult for neurologically intact subjects to describe the movie without references to animacy or mental content, and yet, on two separate testing occasions, patient S. M. gave remarkably consistent inanimate descriptions. For example, her first spontaneous (oral) description of the movie is as follows:

> OK, so, a rectangle, two triangles, and a small circle. Let's see, the triangle and the circle went inside the rectangle, and then the other triangle went in, and then the triangle and the circle went out and took off, left one triangle there. And then the two parts of the rectangle made like a [*sic*] upside-down V, and that was it. (Heberlein & Adolphs, 2004)

Amygdala, TPJ, and mPFC: Roles in Other Social Cognitive Processes

The amygdala is known to be important for a range of emotional and social processes, including fear conditioning (LeDoux, 1993; Phelps & Anderson, 1997); recognizing certain basic emotional facial expressions, most commonly fear (Adolphs & Tranel, 2000; Adolphs et al., 1999); processing facial cues relevant to trustworthiness ratings (Adolphs, Tranel, & Damasio, 1998; Winston, Strange, O'Doherty, & Dolan, 2002); and processing other-race faces (Cunningham et al., 2004; Hart et al., 2000; Phelps et al., 2000; but see Phelps, Cannistraci, & Cunningham, 2003). It receives visual information through both cortical and noncortical pathways, the latter via the superior colliculus and pulvinar nucleus of the thalamus (Jones & Burton, 1976), and projects widely, including extensive projections to visual and other sensory cortices, as well as to frontal and temporal regions (Amaral & Price, 1984). These projections are thought to reflect the amygdala's role in directing attention to salient environmental stimuli, including certain features of socially relevant stimuli such as emotional faces (Adolphs, 2002; Adolphs et al., 2005; Whalen, 1998; Whalen et al., 2004). Thus the amygdala's role in processing anthropomorphic movements may be related to the detection of specific movement features that communicate information about emotional or goal-directed content and the direction of attention to facilitate further processing of the relevant stimuli by, for example, FFA, pSTS, and prefrontal regions. Amygdala damage has also been linked to impairments in difficult theory of mind tasks (i.e., those requiring more complicated levels of processing than simple false belief tasks; Fine, Lumsden, & Blair, 2001; Shaw et al., 2004; Stone, Baron-Cohen, Calder, Keane, & Young, 2003), though it appears to have an effect primarily when damage was acquired early in life, suggesting that its role in such processes lies in acquiring relevant social knowledge and not in representing mental content in an online fashion (Shaw et al., 2004).

As noted above, pSTS cortices (and cortices around the temporo-parietal junction more generally) have been implicated in a wide range of social cognitive tasks (Allison et al., 2000). Several authors have hypothesized that the implication of posterior STS regions in animacy perception, biological motion perception, body-form perception, and mental state attribution is due to a common process underlying these different behaviors (e.g., J. Schultz et al., 2004). However, studies directly comparing two or more such processes in individual subjects imply that they are in fact dissociable. For example, by comparing areas of maximal activation in individual subjects, Saxe and colleagues have dissociated regions of TPJ that are activated during the representation of other people's mental states (but not physical representations of people; Saxe & Kanwisher, 2003) and for viewing goal-directed action (but not merely articulated body motion; Saxe, Xiao, Kovacs, Perrett, & Kanwisher, 2004). Note that both of these two regions are distinct from two other nearby regions: the extrastriate body area, which responds to representations of human body forms (Downing et al., 2001), and the pSTS region responsive to articulated biological motion (Grezes et al., 2001; Grossman et al., 2000; Servos, Osu, Santi, & Kawato, 2002). This distinction between attribution of goal states and theory of mind processes parallels a distinction seen in development, leading Saxe, Carye, and Kanwisher (2004) to conclude that these are not the same system at two levels of elaboration, but rather two distinct, and separately instantiated, cognitive systems. However, because these regions are very close together, they may not be distinct in group analyses, and thus it is difficult to compare the coordinates of regions activated across studies. Further careful comparisons across tasks focusing on animacy perception, goal attribution, and mental state attribution—to humans in narratives, to physical representations of moving humans, and to minimal stimuli such as geometric objects—will help to elucidate the relationships among the underlying processes.

The role of medial prefrontal cortices in mental-state attribution is similarly controversial. Substantial evidence exists supporting a role for mPFC in person-related cognition. However, interpretations differ as to its specialization, with data from some studies supporting a role in representing mental states (Amodio & Frith, 2006; Fletcher et al., 1995; Gallagher et al., 2000; Mitchell, Banaji, & Macrae, 2005a) and making trait judgments (Mitchell, Neil Macrae, & Banaji, 2005), as well as in making trait, emotion, and intention judgments relevant to one's self (den Ouden, Frith, Frith, & Blakemore, 2005; Gusnard, Akbudak, Shulman, & Raichle, 2001; Mitchell, Banaji, & Macrae, 2005b; Ochsner et al., 2004); in certain kinds of moral judgments (Greene & Haidt, 2002); and in semantic knowledge about people (Mitchell, Heatherton, & Macrae, 2002). However, bilateral lesions affecting medial prefrontal regions do not necessarily affect theory of mind abilities (Bird, Castelli, Malik, Frith, & Husain, 2004), implying that these cortices are not critical for mental state attribution. Consonant with this interpretation, Saxe and colleagues failed to find mPFC activation in a contrast between stories requiring theory of mind and stories containing physical descriptions of people, though a region in TPJ was robustly more active in this contrast (Saxe & Kanwisher, 2003); they interpret these findings to mean that mPFC is involved in representing people but not specifically mental states. The debate is far from settled, however: a recent paper by Mitchell, Banaji, and Macrae (2005a) found equivalent dorsal mPFC activity during a task requiring judgments of the applicability of psychological-trait words such as "friendly" (as compared to abstract concept adjectives such as "celestial") to people or to dogs. Judgments as to whether body parts were in fact present on people or on dogs (as compared to whether objects such as "bolt" were) did not yield a similar activation difference for either person or dog judgments. For the time being, one can summarize by saying that medial prefrontal regions appear to be important for many person-related judgments, especially but not consistently those requiring thinking about mental content such as beliefs or traits. Such a role is entirely consistent with the repeated finding of mPFC activity in interpreting the movements of geometric shapes in anthropomorphic terms, given that subjects imbue the shapes with intentions, personality traits, and beliefs as they watch the stimuli. However, it does not address how or why certain stimuli appear to elicit such interpretations.

Automaticity and Top-Down Versus Bottom-Up Contributions to Animacy and Intentionality

As noted above, certain stimuli, such as the original Heider and Simmel (1944) movie, seem to automatically elicit judgments of animacy and intentionality, despite the difficulty of measuring this automaticity. Interestingly, reports of neuroimaging studies using such stimuli have referred to the difficulty of keeping participants from interpreting similarly complex stimuli in anthropomorphic terms. For example, R. Schultz et al. (2003) noted that they did not use the original set of social stimuli while asking nonsocial questions because pilot testing revealed that participants "were not able to consciously stop seeing the films as social stories" (p. 417). Castelli et al. (2000) noted that a substantial minority of participants anthropomorphized in their descriptions of even the "random" stimuli; furthermore, they found no difference in activation between a condition in which participants viewed each movie after having been told what each type was ("a random movement," "a simple interaction," or "an interaction with feelings and thoughts") as compared to one in which they did not receive such cuing. This implies that the stimuli were sufficiently different in the dimension described by the cues that participants did not differ in how they saw the stimuli, whether they were biased by the cues or not; the activation differences and associated differences in the level of intentionality in participants' descriptions were driven completely by stimulus features. Consistent with a limited role for instruction, as compared to movement features, in how participants perceive intentions from animated shapes, Zacks and colleagues (2006; Zacks, 2004) have reported similar segmenting behavior and neural activity when the same set of stimuli are described as either goal-directed or random in nature.

A recent study by Wheatley, Milleville, and Martin (in press) specifically addresses the question of stimulus-driven versus top-down contributions in anthropomorphizing animated geometric objects. Participants viewed the same animated geometric objects superimposed onto two different backgrounds, one that biased an animate interpretation and one that biased an inanimate one. (For example, a spinning cone with a knob on top could look like an ice skater when spinning on a frozen pond but like a top when on a floor strewn with toys). The brain regions recruited more when visual contexts biased animate interpretations largely overlapped the social brain structures implicated in the interpretation of stimuli that look animate due to movement alone: lateral fusiform gyrus, STS, amygdala, insula, mPFC, and posterior cingulate cortex. Thus, top-down information affects the activity of these regions, and not just perceptual information. Wheatley and colleagues observed a similar pattern for merely *imagining* movements in the animate-biasing as compared to the inanimate-biasing background. They theorize that the social brain network may prime further social processing, such as attributions of emotions, personality traits, and mental states.

Conclusion

The network of social brain structures implicated across all of these studies of anthropomorphic animations appears to be recruited by certain movement features, but also by conceptual knowledge about animacy and agents in the absence of any movement differences.

What are the stimulus features that lead to anthropomorphic or intentional attributions (and, presumably, the recruitment of the social brain components)? Agency or goal-directedness cues alone do not appear to be sufficient: as J. Schultz (Schultz et al., 2004, 2005) and Blakemore (Blakemore et al., 2003) both note, animations that are animate by virtue of being goal-directed (Blakemore's stimuli also appeared to imply perceptual tracking) do not elicit intentional or mentalistic processing or recruit mPFC and other brain regions frequently associated with such processing. Contextual cuing alone is also insufficient to explain the existing data, as robust animate and intentional percepts or interpretations can be elicited from objects moving on backgrounds including only a single rectangle, as in the original Heider and Simmel (1944) movie or Castelli's more recent ones (2000). One clue might come from the finding, discussed above, of reduced anthropomorphizing subsequent to amygdala damage (Heberlein & Adolphs, 2004). The original Heider and Simmel movie contains several prominent emotionally laden interactions: the big triangle and the small triangle "fight"; the big triangle "corners" the circle inside the house, "threatening" it; the two smaller shapes "escape" and run away; the big triangle becomes angry and destroys the house. Note that most of these emotional events are negative ones: the sole positive interaction event is when the smaller triangle helps the circle escape from the house, and the two smaller shapes spin around one another, touching tenderly. Though most participants describe it as "kissing," "high-fiving," or "celebrating" when asked about this event, few participants include the interaction in their spontaneous oral descriptions; in contrast, the negative events, especially the fight and the destruction of the house, are almost always included (Heberlein et al., 2006). Negative events thus seem more salient, and in fact may prompt or bootstrap a social interpretation of the movie. Consistent with this interpretation, damage to the amygdala, a structure important for processing emotionally salient stimuli and especially threat-related cues, may lead to reduced anthropomorphizing in response to the Heider and Simmel (1944) movie because of abnormally low sensitivity to the emotional significance of certain movement features. It remains to be seen whether a similar deficit would be observed in responses to anthropomorphic movement stimuli in which the salient emotional events were positive; such studies are underway.

A general lack of sensitivity to emotional cues also affects spontaneous interpretations of the Heider and Simmel movie: patients with damage to right somatosensory cortices—a region known to be important for emotion recognition from tasks such as labeling or rating faces, vocal prosody, and body movements—not only use fewer emotional words in their descriptions of the Heider and Simmel (1944) movie but also use fewer words in other categories indicative of anthropomorphizing, such as gendered pronouns and social role words (Heberlein et al., 2003). However, the descriptions given by these patients are not as inanimate as that given by patient S. M., perhaps because their brain damage was incurred in adulthood, allowing normal development of social knowledge, or because their intact amygdalas allowed some awareness of the negative events of the movie to proceed and to bring online other social cognitive processing.

The existence of a negativity bias in agency attribution has recently been documented in studies of neurologically intact participants: Morewedge (2006) recently showed that negative outcomes are more likely to bias judgments of intentionality. For example, participants were more likely to believe that a person and not a computer was behind an unusually selfish offer in an ultimatum game, while unusually generous offers were thought to be generated by a computer. Similarly, unexpected negative outcomes were more likely to lead to anthropomorphisms of computers and cars than unexpected positive outcomes (Morewedge, 2006; we curse our computers for crashing, after all, but do not thank them for remembering to auto-save). Such a negativity bias makes sense given an influential theory for humans' evolved predisposition to anthropomorphize: humans and proto-humans who were biased to interpret rustles in the forest as predators and react accordingly, and to respond to approaching conspecifics as though they had (potentially aggressive) intentions, would be, in the long run, more successful, despite the potential costs associated with overinterpretation (such as positing forest elves and sacrificing to weather gods; Guthrie, 1995). Given this account, it may be unsurprising that negative events draw more social-attributional attention than positive ones; the costs associated with failing to detect potential benefactors are presumably less than those associated with failing to detect agents with the intent to end one's existence. This theory accounts for the observations of experimenters, noted above, that it is difficult to dissuade subjects from interpreting even random movements as inanimate; unless an obvious mechanical interpretation can be found, we seem curiously predisposed to attribute animacy and intention to ambiguous objects.

In conclusion, emotional cues, and possibly primarily negative emotional cues, may be featural primitives. Like agency or goal-directedness cues, we may automatically detect the presence of certain emotion-relevant features from static as well as dynamic cues, a process in which the amygdala would be hypothesized to play a critical role. Taking this into account, an account of how we perceive and interpret social events from motion might run something like this[4]: In parallel, the cortical

---

4. Note that it is never simple to ascribe a cognitive process to a given brain region, and in this case the levels at which I am specifying cognitive processes are likely to be far too complex. Given the non-social-cognitive tasks that engage these same, or largely overlapping, neural regions and the level of resolution at which we are discussing both neuroanatomy and cognitive process, any framework that attempts to lay out how a complex stimulus such as a social event is interpreted will doubtless be subject to considerable revision. With this major caveat, I'll still make an attempt at such a framework here.

and subcortical visual processing streams process movement and form information. More specialized extrastriate cortical regions respond to stimulus features normally associated with animate entities, which include pSTS regions for movement that appears biological by virtue of its path or its articulation and FFA for face-like configurations. Amygdalar responses to both static and dynamic cues could serve to direct attention, via projections to these and other cortical regions, to objects possessing emotion-relevant features like large sclera (Adolphs et al., 2005; Whalen et al., 2004) or, perhaps, certain movement features. By feed-forward mechanisms, conceptual information about mental-state contents and person-related features could be accessed and related to perceived behaviors via some combination of medial prefrontal cortices, TPJ, and other cortical regions. In cases of contextual cuing, activation of such information could prime pSTS, FFA, and amygdala by feedback mechanisms. In summary, the combined detection of emotional content and goal-directed agents may engage social attention for the perception and attribution of intentions, relationships, and social narratives—the complex and richly interwoven fabric that supports our daily social interactions.

Acknowledgments

I am grateful to Josh Greene, Carey Morewedge, Jeff Zacks, and an anonymous reviewer for helpful comments, and to Dan Wegner and Mahzarin Banaji for both mentorship and support.

References

Adolphs, R. (2002). Recognizing emotion from facial expressions: Psychological and neurological mechanisms. *Behavioral and Cognitive Neuroscience Reviews, 1*(1), 21–61.

Adolphs, R. (2003). Cognitive neuroscience of human social behaviour. *National Review of Neuroscience, 4*(3), 165–178.

Adolphs, R., Gosselin, F., Buchanan, T. W., Tranel, D., Schyns, P., & Damasio, A. R. (2005). A mechanism for impaired fear recognition after amygdala damage. *Nature, 433*(7021), 68–72.

Adolphs, R., & Tranel, D. (2000). Emotion recognition and the human amygdala. In J. P. Aggleton (Ed.), *The amygdala. A functional analysis* (pp. 587–630). New York: Oxford University Press.

Adolphs, R., Tranel, D., & Damasio, A. R. (1998). The human amygdala in social judgment. *Nature, 393*, 470–474.

Adolphs, R., Tranel, D., Hamann, S., Young, A. W., Calder, A. J., Phelps, E. A., et al. (1999). Recognition of facial emotion in nine individuals with bilateral amygdala damage. *Neuropsychologia, 37,* 1111–1117.

Allison, T., Puce, A., & McCarthy, G. (2000). Social perception from visual cues: Role of the STS region. *Trends in Cognitive Science, 4*(7), 267–278.

Amaral, D. G., & Price, J. L. (1984). Amygdalo-cortical projections in the monkey (*Macaca fascicularis*). *Journal of Comparative Neurology, 230*(4), 465–496.

Amodio, D. M., & Frith, C. D. (2006). Meeting of minds: The medial frontal cortex and social cognition. *National Review of Neuroscience, 7*(4), 268–277.

Barrett, H. C., Todd, P. M., Miller, G. F., & Blythe, P. W. (2005). Accurate judgments of intention from motion cues alone: A cross-cultural study. *Evolution and Human Behavior, 26*(4), 313–331.

Bassili, J. N. (1976). Temporal and spatial contingencies in the perception of social events. *Journal of Personality and Social Psychology, 33*(6), 680–685.

Berry, D. S., Misovich, S. J., Kean, K. J., & Baron, R. M. (1992). Effects of disruption of structure and motion on perceptions of social causality. *Personality and Social Psychology Bulletin, 18*(2), 237–244.

Bird, C. M., Castelli, F., Malik, O., Frith, U., & Husain, M. (2004). The impact of extensive medial frontal lobe damage on "Theory of Mind" and cognition. *Brain, 127*(Pt 4), 914–928.

Blakemore, S. J., Boyer, P., Pachot-Clouard, M., Meltzoff, A., Segebarth, C., & Decety, J. (2003). The detection of contingency and animacy from simple animations in the human brain. *Cerebral Cortex, 13*(8), 837–844.

Blythe, P. W., Todd, P. M., & Miller, G. F. (1999). How motion reveals intention: Categorizing social interactions. In G. Gigerenzer, P. M. Todd, & ABC Research Group (Eds.), *Simple heuristics that make us smart.* New York: Oxford University Press.

Bonda, E., Petrides, M., Ostry, D., & Evans, A. (1996). Specific involvement of human parietal systems and the amygdala in the perception of biological motion. *Journal of Neuroscience, 16*(11), 3737–3744.

Brothers, L. (1990). The social brain: A project for integrating primate behavior and neurophysiology in a new domain. *Concepts in Neuroscience, 1*(1), 27–51.

Castelli, F., Happé, F., Frith, U., & Frith, C. (2000). Movement and mind: A functional imaging study of perception and interpretation of complex intentional movement patterns. *NeuroImage, 12,* 314–325.

Csibra, G. (2003). Teleological and referential understanding of action in infancy. *Philosophical Transactions of the Royal Society of London B: Biological Science, 358*(1431), 447–458.

Cunningham, W. A., Johnson, M. K., Raye, C. L., Chris Gatenby, J., Gore, J. C., & Banaji, M. R. (2004). Separable neural components in the processing of black and white faces. *Psychological Science, 15*(12), 806–813.

Decety, J., Chaminade, T., Grezes, J., & Meltzoff, A. N. (2002). A PET exploration of the neural mechanisms involved in reciprocal imitation. *Neuroimage, 15*(1), 265–272.

Decety, J., Grezes, J., Costes, N., Perani, D., Jeannerod, M., Procyk, E., et al. (1997). Brain activity during observation of actions: Influence of action content and subject's strategy. *Brain, 120,* 1763–1777.

den Ouden, H. E., Frith, U., Frith, C., & Blakemore, S. J. (2005). Thinking about intentions. *Neuroimage, 28*(4), 787–796.

Dittrich, W. H., & Lea, S. E. G. (1994). Visual perception of intentional motion. *Perception, 23,* 253–268.

Dittrich, W. H., Troscianko, T., Lea, S. E., & Morgan, D. (1996). Perception of emotion from dynamic point-light displays represented in dance. *Perception, 25*(6), 727–738.

Downing, P. E., Jiang, Y., Shuman, M., & Kanwisher, N. (2001). A cortical area selective for visual processing of the human body. *Science, 293*(5539), 2470–2473.

Farah, M. J., Wilson, K. D., Drain, H. M., & Tanaka, J. R. (1995). The inverted face inversion effect in prosopagnosia: Evidence for mandatory, face-specific perceptual mechanisms. *Vision Research, 35*(14), 2089–2093.

Fine, C., Lumsden, J., & Blair, R. J. R. (2001). Dissociation between "theory of mind" and executive functions in a patient with early left amygdala damage. *Brain, 124,* 287–298.

Fletcher, P., Happé, F., Frith, U., Baker, S., Dolan, R., Frackowiak, R., et al. (1995). Other minds in the brain: A functional imaging study of "theory of mind" in story comprehension. *Cognition, 57*(2), 109–128.

Gallagher, H. L., Happé, F., Brunswick, N., Fletcher, P. C., Frith, U., & Frith, C. D. (2000). Reading the mind in cartoons and stories: An fMRI study of "theory of mind" in verbal and nonverbal tasks. *Neuropsychologia, 38*(1), 11–21.

Gelman, R., Durgin, F., & Kaufman, L. (1995). Distinguishing between animates and inanimates: Not by motion alone. In D. Sperber, D. Premack, & A. J. Premack (Eds.), *Causal cognition: A multidisciplinary debate* (pp. 150–184). Oxford: Clarendon Press.

Greene, J. D., & Haidt, J. (2002). How (and where) does moral judgment work? *Trends in Cognitive Science, 16*(12), 517–523.

Grezes, J., Armony, J. L., Rowe, J., & Passingham, R. E. (2003). Activations related to "mirror" and "canonical" neurones in the human brain: An fMRI study. *Neuroimage, 18*(4), 928–937.

Grezes, J., Fonlupt, P., Bertenthal, B., Delon-Martin, C., Segebarth, C., & Decety, J. (2001). Does perception of biological motion rely on specific brain regions? *NeuroImage, 13,* 775–785.

Grossman, E., Donnelly, M., Price, R., Pickens, D., Morgan, V., Neighbor, G., et al. (2000). Brain areas involved in perception of biological motion. *Journal of Cognitive Neuroscience, 12*(5), 711–720.

Gusnard, D. A., Akbudak, E., Shulman, G. L., & Raichle, M. E. (2001). Medial prefrontal cortex and self-referential mental activity: relation to a default mode of brain function. *Proceedings of the National Academy of Sciences of the United States of America, 98*(7), 4259–4264.

Guthrie, S. E. (1995). *Faces in the clouds: A new theory of religion.* Oxford: Oxford University Press.

Hart, A. J., Whalen, P. J., Shin, L. M., McInerney, S. C., Fischer, H., & Rauch, S. L. (2000). Differential response in the human amygdala to racial outgroup vs. ingroup face stimuli. *NeuroReport, 11*(11), 2351–2355.

Hashimoto, H. (1966). A phenomenal analysis of social perception. *Journal of Child Development, 2,* 3–26.

Heberlein, A. S., & Adolphs, R. (2004). Impaired spontaneous anthropomorphizing despite intact perception and social knowledge. *Proceedings of the National Academy of Sciences of the United States of America, 101*(19), 7487–7491.

Heberlein, A. S., Adolphs, R., Tranel, D., & Damasio, H. (2003). Social attribution depends on right-hemisphere brain structures involved in recognizing and simulating emotions. *Political Psychology, 24*(4), 705–726.

Heberlein, A. S., Scheer, K., McGivern, M., & Farah, M. J. (2006). Unpublished data.

Heider, F., & Simmel, M. (1944). An experimental study of apparent behavior. *American Journal of Psychology, 57,* 243–259.

Johnson, S. C. (2003). Detecting agents. *Philosophical Transactions of the Royal Society of London B: Biological Science, 358*(1431), 549–559.

Jones, E. G., & Burton, H. (1976). A projection from the medial pulvinar to the amygdala in primates. *Brain Research, 104*(1), 142–147.

Kanwisher, N., McDermott, J., & Chun, M. M. (1997). The fusiform face area: A module in human extrastriate cortex specialized for face perception. *Journal of Neuroscience, 17*(11), 4302–4311.

Klin, A. (2000). Attributing social meaning to ambiguous visual stimuli in higher-functioning autism and Asperger syndrome: The social attribution task. *Journal of Child Psychology and Psychiatry, 41*(7), 831–846.

LeDoux, J. E. (1993). Emotional memory systems in the brain. *Behavioral Brain Research, 58*(1–2), 69–79.

Logothetis, N. K., Guggenberger, H., Peled, S., & Pauls, J. (1999). Functional imaging of the monkey brain. *Nature Neuroscience, 2*(6), 555–562.

Mandler, J. M. (1992). How to build a baby: II. Conceptual primitives. *Psychological Review, 99*(4), 587–604.

Martin, A., & Weisberg, J. (2003). Neural foundations for understanding social and mechanical concepts. *Cognitive Neuropsychology, 20*(3–6), 575–587.

Michotte, A. (1946/1963). *La perception de la causalité* (T. M. a. E. Miles, Trans.). Louvain: Institut Supérior de Philosophie.

Mitchell, J. P., Banaji, M. R., & Macrae, C. N. (2005a). General and specific contributions of the medial prefrontal cortex to knowledge about mental states. *Neuroimage, 28*(4), 757–762.

Mitchell, J. P., Banaji, M. R., & Macrae, C. N. (2005b). The link between social cognition and self-referential thought in the medial prefrontal cortex. *Journal of Cognitive Neuroscience, 17*(8), 1306–1315.

Mitchell, J. P., Heatherton, T. F., & Macrae, C. N. (2002). Distinct neural systems subserve person and object knowledge. *Proceedings of the National Academy of Sciences of the United States of America, 99*(23), 15238–15243.

Mitchell, J. P., Neil Macrae, C., & Banaji, M. R. (2005). Forming impressions of people versus inanimate objects: Social-cognitive processing in the medial prefrontal cortex. *Neuroimage, 26*(1), 251–257.

Morewedge, C. K. (2006). *A mind of its own: Negativity bias in the perception of intentional agency.* Unpublished Ph.D. thesis. Cambridge, MA: Harvard University.

Morris, M. W., & Peng, K. (1994). Culture and cause: American and Chinese attributions for social and physical events. *Journal of Personality and Social Psychology, 67*(6), 949–971.

Ochsner, K. N., Knierim, K., Ludlow, D. H., Hanelin, J., Ramachandran, T., Glover, G., et al. (2004). Reflecting upon feelings: An fMRI study of neural systems supporting the attribution of emotion to self and other. *Journal of Cognitive Neuroscience, 16*(10), 1746–1772.

Opfer, J. E. (2002). Identifying living and sentient kinds from dynamic information: The case of goal-directed versus aimless autonomous movement in conceptual change. *Cognition, 86*(2), 97–122.

Pelphrey, K. A., Morris, J. P., & McCarthy, G. (2004). Grasping the intentions of others: The perceived intentionality of an action influences activity in the superior temporal sulcus during social perception. *Journal of Cognitive Neuroscience, 16*(10), 1706–1716.

Pennebaker, J. W., Francis, M. E., & Booth, R. J. (2001). *Linguistic inquiry and word count*. Mahwah, NJ: Erlbaum Publishers.

Phelps, E. A., & Anderson, A. K. (1997). Emotional memory: What does the amygdala do? *Current Biology, 7*(5), R311–314.

Phelps, E. A., Cannistraci, C. J., & Cunningham, W. A. (2003). Intact performance on an indirect measure of race bias following amygdala damage. *Neuropsychologia, 41*(2), 203–208.

Phelps, E. A., O'Connor, K. J., Cunningham, W. A., Funayama, E. S., Gatenby, J. C., Gore, J. C., et al. (2000). Performance on indirect measures of race evaluation predicts amygdala activation. *Journal of Cognitive Neuroscience, 12*(5), 729–738.

Puce, A., Allison, T., Asgari, M., Gore, J. C., & McCarthy, G. (1996). Differential sensitivity of human visual cortex to faces, letterstrings, and textures: A functional magnetic resonance imaging study. *Journal of Neuroscience, 16*(16), 5205–5215.

Rakison, D. H., & Poulin-Dubois, D. (2001). Developmental origin of the animate-inanimate distinction. *Psychological Bulletin, 127*(2), 209–228.

Rimé, B., Boulanger, B., Laubin, P., Richir, M., & Stroobants, K. (1985). The perception of interpersonal emotions originated by patterns of movement. *Motivation and Emotion, 9*(3), 241–260.

Saxe, R., Carey, S., & Kanwisher, N. (2004). Understanding other minds: Linking developmental psychology and functional neuroimaging. *Annual Review of Psychology, 55*, 87–124.

Saxe, R., & Kanwisher, N. (2003). People thinking about thinking people. The role of the temporo-parietal junction in "theory of mind." *Neuroimage, 19*(4), 1835–1842.

Saxe, R., Xiao, D. K., Kovacs, G., Perrett, D. I., & Kanwisher, N. (2004). A region of right posterior superior temporal sulcus responds to observed intentional actions. *Neuropsychologia, 42*(11), 1435–1446.

Scholl, B. J., & Tremoulet, P. D. (2000). Perceptual causality and animacy. *Trends in Cognitive Science, 4*(8), 299–309.

Schultz, J., Friston, K. J., O'Doherty, J., Wolpert, D. M., & Frith, C. D. (2005). Activation in posterior superior temporal sulcus parallels parameter inducing the percept of animacy. *Neuron, 45*(4), 625–635.

Schultz, J., Imamizu, H., Kawato, M., & Frith, C. D. (2004). Activation of the human superior temporal gyrus during observation of goal attribution by intentional objects. *Journal of Cognitive Neuroscience, 16*(10), 1695–1705.

Schultz, R. T., Gauthier, I., Klin, A., Fulbright, R. K., Anderson, A. W., Volkmar, F., et al. (2000). Abnormal ventral temporal cortical activity during face discrimination among individuals with autism and Asperger syndrome. *Archives of General Psychiatry, 57*(4), 331–340.

Schultz, R. T., Grelotti, D. J., Klin, A., Kleinman, J., Van der Gaag, C., Marois, R., et al. (2003). The role of the fusiform face area in social cognition: Implications for the pathobiology of autism. *Philosophical Transactions of the Royal Society of London B: Biological Science, 358*(1430), 415–427.

Servos, P., Osu, R., Santi, A., & Kawato, M. (2002). The neural substrates of biological motion perception: An fMRI study. *Cerebral Cortex, 12*(7), 772–782.

Shaw, P., Lawrence, E. J., Radbourne, C., Bramham, J., Polkey, C. E., & David, A. S. (2004). The impact of early and late damage to the human amygdala on "theory of mind" reasoning. *Brain, 127*(Pt 7), 1535–1548.

Skuse, D., Morris, J., & Lawrence, K. (2003). The amygdala and development of the social brain. *Annals of the New York Academy of Sciences, 1008*, 91–101.

Stewart, J. A. (1982). *Perception of animacy.* Philadelphia, PA: University of Pennsylvania.

Stone, V. E., Baron-Cohen, S., Calder, A., Keane, J., & Young, A. (2003). Acquired theory of mind impairments in individuals with bilateral amygdala lesions. *Neuropsychologia, 41*(2), 209–220.

Tarr, M. J., & Gauthier, I. (2000). FFA: A flexible fusiform area for subordinate-level visual processing automatized by expertise. *Nature Neuroscience, 3*(8), 764–769.

Tremoulet, P. D., & Feldman, J. (2000). Perception of animacy from the motion of a single object. *Perception, 29*, 943–951.

Whalen, P. J. (1998). Fear, vigilance, and ambiguity: Initial neuroimaging studies of the human amygdala. *Current Directions in Psychological Science, 7*(6), 177–188.

Whalen, P. J., Kagan, J., Cook, R. G., Davis, F. C., Kim, H., Polis, S., et al. (2004). Human amygdala responsivity to masked fearful eye whites. *Science, 306*(5704), 2061.

Wheatley, T., Milleville, S. C., & Martin, A. (in press). Understanding animate agents: Distinct roles for the "social network" and "mirror system." *Psychological Science.*

Winston, J. S., Strange, B. A., O'Doherty, J., & Dolan, R. J. (2002). Automatic and intentional brain responses during evaluation of trustworthiness of faces. *Nature Neuroscience, 5*(3), 277–283.

Zacks, J. M. (2004). Using movement and intentions to understand simple events. *Cognitive Science, 28*, 979–1008.

Zacks, J. M., Swallow, K. M., Vettel, J. M., & McAvoy, M. P. (2006). Visual motion and the neural correlates of event perception. *Brain Research, 1076*(1), 150–162.

Section 2
Segmenting Events

15

The Role of Segmentation in Perception and Understanding of Events

STEPHAN SCHWAN & BÄRBEL GARSOFFKY

In everyday perception we have the impression of witnessing a continuous stream of external events, beginning when we open our eyes in the morning and ending when we close them in the evening. On the other hand, when recounting our experiences, we generally report sequences of discrete events in a stepwise manner. In other words, somewhere along the line of cognitive processes going from perception to recounting, a transition must take place by which this continuous stream of events is segmented into a sequence of discrete units.

A number of research findings, which will be discussed in more detail in the current chapter, show that this process of segmentation (or "unitization") is located relatively early in the chain of cognitive processes. Therefore, according to some authors (Tversky, Zacks, & Lee, 2004), event segments, with specific "shapes" in terms of event boundaries, can be conceived of as building blocks with which our cognitive system operates in the temporal realm, just as objects are cognitive building blocks in the spatial realm.

The question of event segmentation is strongly coupled with a specific experimental paradigm, which was introduced by Darren Newtson

(1973) and will be described in the next section. Along with this paradigm, Newtson also developed a general model of the underlying perceptual and cognitive processes, which has been further refined in the last few years and which will be described further on in this chapter. According to this model, observers are not confined to one invariant type of segmenting over a given course of events. Instead, the definition of event segments results from a complex interplay of both characteristics of the observed event and of personal factors, the latter ranging from stable cognitive traits to observational goals, prior knowledge, and mood states.

As a consequence, variations in segmentations have been shown to have a substantial impact on higher cognitive processes such as memorization, causal attribution, decision making, or experience of time. Finally, some events, particularly in the media, already come in segmented form to their observers. The effects of these external segments on cognitive processes will be discussed in the final section of this chapter.

Segmenting Events: The Basic Paradigm

In order to study event segmentation, Darren Newtson (1973) devised a simple and straightforward procedure. He presented observers with film recordings of simple and familiar human activities, such as sorting a number of paper sheets or assembling a mechanical device. While watching the film, observers were given a hand-held button and were instructed to press the button whenever a meaningful (in their opinion) change occurred— that is, when one meaningful action ended and a different one began. By means of this procedure, each subject produced a number of "tags" by which the entire observed event was segmented in a number of discrete steps. In other words, these tags indicated the position of subjectively defined event boundaries (or "breakpoints" in Newtson's terminology).

From this procedure, two basic measures can be derived: the number of segmentations and their respective positions in the event stream. According to Newtson, the number of segmentations indicates the amount of information that an observer extracts from an event stream. Correspondingly, it has been used as both a dependent (for example, indicating that it is being affected by variations in prior knowledge of the observer or predictability of the observed events) and an independent (showing that it has an impact on the richness of the subsequent mental representation of the observed event) variable.

The position of event boundaries is typically measured by partitioning the event sequence into second-long intervals and determining the intervals in which a boundary occurred. Event boundaries can be described on either an individual or group level. In the latter case, the mean number of boundaries across observers is calculated for each interval, and those intervals whose frequency of boundaries lies above or below a certain threshold are identified. For example, in a study by Schwan, Garsoffky, and Hesse (2000), such intervals, whose tag frequency lay in the upper 5% of the frequency distribution (i.e., more than 1.65 standard deviations above the mean tag frequency of the intervals), counted as group-level event boundaries. Correspondingly, those intervals whose frequency lay in the lower 5% of the frequency distribution counted as nonboundaries. Therefore, group-level event boundaries represent boundaries that are positioned with a high interindividual agreement. In other words, they constitute boundaries that can be assumed to be commonly perceived by the majority of observers. In contrast, nonboundaries signify parts of the event where the segmentation rate is substantially reduced, thereby indicating that the majority of observers agree that this part does *not* constitute the boundary of an event segment. Keep in mind that the group-level boundary structure of an event sequence should not be conceived as "fixed" and "objective." Instead, it may vary in accordance with a number of factors (e.g., instruction) and is defined in relation to a given group of observers.

Event boundaries can also be determined on an individual level by means of a continuous analysis that does not rely on dividing the event stream into discrete time intervals. This method, which was introduced by Zacks, Tversky, & Iyer (2001), is mainly used for determining the partonomic relationship between segmentations of different grain. Basically, the average temporal distance of coarse-event boundaries to the nearest fine-event boundary is calculated for each participant and is tested against a null model that assumes that the coarse breakpoints are distributed randomly and uniformly across the event stream. Zacks, Tversky, et al. (2001) report that both discrete and continuous analysis lead to similar results and conclusions regarding the partonomic segmentation of events.

As an alternative to measuring event segmentation by means of button presses, some studies had observers describe events verbally and subsequently analyzed the descriptions in terms of the event units that were mentioned (Lichtenstein & Brewer, 1980; Reed, Montgomery, Schwartz, Palmer, & Pittenger, 1992; see Berry & Misovich, 1994, for an overview of methodological approaches to social event perception), with primarily similar results in terms of a general partonomic structure of event sequences. Recently, both methods have been combined by letting the observers concurrently describe the event verbally while segmenting the event stream. This combined approach allows researchers to study the criteria upon which the segmentation is based (e.g., reference to objects for coarse segmentations, reference to activities for fine segmentations), but it should be kept in mind that the concurrent verbalization also changes the segmentation process itself, leading observers to apply a more coherently partonomic type of segmentation (Zacks, Tversky, et al., 2001).

Perceptual and Cognitive Mechanisms of Event Segmentation

Newtson's Model: Segmentation as a Perceptual Cycle

Based on findings from this experimental paradigm, Newtson published a number of papers during the 1970s in which he successively developed a comprehensive model of the perceptual and cognitive mechanisms of event segmentation (Massad, Hubbard, & Newtson, 1979; Newtson, 1973, 1980; Newtson & Engquist, 1976; Newtson, Engquist, & Bois, 1977; Newtson & Rindner, 1979; Newtson, Rindner, Miller, & LaCross, 1978). By the end of the 1970s, the model was considered sufficiently elaborated upon so that research in the area slowed down. Recently, Zacks and Tversky (Zacks, 2004; Zacks & Tversky, 2001; Zacks, Tversky, et al., 2001) provided a new theoretical approach and thereby initiated a renewed interest in processes of behavior segmentation.

As its most basic premise, Newtson's model assumes that the continuous flow of events or activities is not perceived and mentally represented as such but instead is segmented into a sequence of discrete units. According to Newtson (1973), these segments constitute the basic perceptual units of ongoing events or human activities and therefore are the prior elements of event cognition, upon which subsequent mental operations are based. In other words, by means of segmentation, a structure is defined by which the stream of visible information is partitioned into bounded events. The relevance of this process is further emphasized by Tversky et al. (2004), who assume that such bounded events have the same cognitive status in the temporal realm that objects have in the spatial realm.

Although the segment structure of events can be shown to bear a strong relationship to particular characteristics of the visible stream of information, its definition should not be conceived as strictly determined by objective features, which have simply to be registered by observers in a passive manner. Instead, observers are playing an active part by cognitively projecting a structure into the observed stream of events, as evidenced by the fact that different observers at different times segment a given stream of activities in different ways.

Accordingly, Newtson, Engquist, and Bois (1977) have proposed that the process of segmentation can best be modeled as an interplay between perceptual, bottom-up processes, and inferential, top-down processes, in a manner similar to the concept of the perceptual cycle described by Neisser (1976). Observers start with an anticipatory schema as an initial framework of interpretation, which they use as a guide for comprehension. As part of the anticipatory schema, the viewer selects a set of observable features that are characteristic for anticipated events or activities. He or she then monitors the behavior stream for the occurrence of feature-relevant cues, which indicate a change of event or activity. When consistent information has been picked up and matched with the schema, an event boundary is defined. The boundary in turn forms the basis for a redefinition of the search, in that the boundary becomes a basis for the discrimination of the next action unit (Newtson et al., 1977). In other words, besides defining event boundaries and projecting a certain structure into an event stream, segmentation can also be interpreted as an indication of the quality and amount of information that an observer picks up from an event.

It should be kept in mind that this cycle of generation, testing, and confirmation or disconfirmation of hypotheses is influenced both by the intentions and the prior schematic knowledge of the observers, and also (e.g., in the case of unexpected activities) by characteristics of the behavior stream itself, as discussed in the following two sections.

Extracting Information by Monitoring Event Features

The model proposed by Newtson implies that segmentation results from an interplay between objective characteristics of the event stream and perceptual and cognitive attributes of the observing subject. Starting with the characteristics of the stream of events, it can be shown that bottom-up aspects of event segmentation operate in close relation to the process of feature detection, which Newtson has postulated as a main underlying perceptual mechanism of segmentation. Observers are assumed to select certain features from the behavior stream, which they continuously monitor for changes. Whenever a substantial transformation in one or more of these features occurs, that point within the flow of visible information is interpreted as the onset of a new activity in the chain of events—and, in the context of Newtson's experimental paradigm, a button is pressed and a corresponding event boundary is defined. In line with models of attention and working memory, the number of features that are monitored simultaneously is limited. For example, Newtson et al. (1977) analyzed sequences of activities with a notational coding scheme borrowed from dance choreography. By applying factor analysis, they found the positional changes, which occurred at event boundaries and which qualified as potential monitoring cues, could be described with a set of four to six dimensions.

At least in principle, every stimulus feature that can be cognitively encoded and monitored for change qualifies as a potential segmentation cue. Depending on the type of event, different factors may play different roles. Examples of features are changes in bodily position (or posture); states of objects; relations between persons or objects; and motion characteristics such as velocity, acceleration, or deceleration. Three types of events deserve special consideration. First, many instances of human behavior can be described as instrumental: an actor uses some objects or tools in order to pursue his or her intentions and to achieve certain goals. The vast majority of empirical studies on event segmentation fall into this category. Here, changes in objects or instruments in the course of the activity have been shown to constitute a feature set of particular importance; such changes are typically indicative of a switch in intentions or goals of the actor (Zacks & Tversky, 2001; Zacks, Tversky, et al., 2001). Second, another type of human behavior, which may be of equal importance, can be described as social-interactional. In this case, at least two human actors engage in activities that are dependent on each other. With regard to social-interactional behavior, it has been shown that observers tend to pay attention to the dyad instead of the individual actors (Ginsburg & Smith, 1993; Jensen & Schroeder, 1982).

Third, for temporally extended sequences of events (ranging from hours to days instead of minutes), higher-order features play an important role for segmentation. In particular, actor or location changes elicit segmentations, as Magliano, Miller, and Zwaan (2001) and Schwan, Hesse, and Garsoffky (1998) have shown for the unitization of narrative films.

Perceptual salience has been identified as another important criterion for feature selection—that is, the more easily a feature is perceived, the higher the probability that it will serve as a segmentation cue. Newtson et al. (1977) showed participants a video in which a person was assembling a number of questionnaires in a repetitive manner. The first page of each questionnaire was either white, and therefore similar to the other pages in the questionnaire, or black, and therefore distinguishable from the subsequent pages. In the latter case, the observers obviously monitored the occurrence of the salient pages as a perceptual feature, segmenting the activity accordingly and more homogeneously into corresponding coarse-grained units. In a similar line of research, it has been shown that enhancing the salience of relevant features by presentational cues like co-occurring film cuts also led to an increase in the corresponding segmentation rate (Schwan, Garsoffky, & Hesse, 2000).

Do event boundaries that result from feature monitoring characterize an easily perceivable, distinct state within the stream of activities, or do they instead gain their distinctiveness by means of contrast with their predecessors, thus reflecting a distinct change instead of a distinct state? In order to address this issue, Newtson et al. (1977) coded a series of behavior sequences according to a choreographic dance notation, which allows for specifying the position of the limbs and the body at different points of time. Based on this coding scheme, an index of position difference between pairs of points in time as a measure of position change was developed. By comparing different pairs of points in time, Newtson et al. (1977) found empirical evidence in favor of the distinct change hypothesis. Pairs of successive event boundaries showed a substantially higher difference in their position index than matched pairs of nonboundaries, indicating that a substantial change from one boundary to the next is an important determinant for segmentation. Also, for successive nonboundary/boundary pairs, a difference score was defined; this score was larger than for nonboundary pairs but less pronounced than for boundary pairs Finally, random pairs of an event boundary and a nonboundary did not differ significantly from random pairs of two nonboundaries. In sum, the pattern of results suggests that it is not the event boundary per se but rather some difference between that point and the previously defined boundary that forms the basis for the feature detection and the subsequent segmentation (Massad et al., 1979).

According to Newtson (1973), event boundaries not only partition a continuous stream of events into discrete units but also are assumed to mark points of time that are especially informative for the observed events, and therefore the observer engages in a process of information extraction.

Evidence for the notion that information sampling from continuous event streams proceeds in a discontinuous manner comes from developmental studies in which children were seated in a room with toys and a TV monitor showing a narrative movie for kids (Lorch, Anderson, & Levin, 1979). It was found that the children did not focus their attention in a continuous manner on the film but instead switched between playing with the toys and paying attention to the film. They were nevertheless as accurate in answering questions about the film as a group of children who watched the film continuously. This suggests that the children identified "strategic points" in the film that were sufficient to specify its contents. These findings suggest that information sampling operates in a discontinuous manner, reflecting moment-by-moment variations in information content.

Event boundaries constitute plausible candidates for strategic points. By possessing distinctive properties, they provide a kind of summary of the preceding segment, thus characterizing it as a whole. In other words, event boundaries appear to be selected in such a way that the information contained at successive boundaries is sufficient to reconstruct and interpret the event that occurred during the interval between them (Newtson et al., 1978). In support of this notion of higher information content at event boundaries, some empirical evidence has been presented by Newtson and Engquist (1976). Their research showed that the deletion of pictures from a sequence was more easily detectable at event boundaries than at nonboundaries. Also, pictures taken from event boundaries were more easily recognized, and sets of picture stills stemming from event boundaries lead to more appropriate verbal descriptions of the activity than matched sets of still pictures stemming from nonboundaries. Similarly, Schwan and Garsoffky (2004) have shown that film summaries of event sequences that consisted of event boundaries led to recall that more closely resembled a complete event presentation than film sum-maries of events that consisted of nonboundaries.

It is the position, as well as the number or density, of event bound-aries that seems to be indicative of information extraction. From the notion that each breakpoint marks the extraction of information, it fol-lows that the more an event sequence is broken down into its compo-nent parts, the more information about this sequence is extracted. That happens because each action may be used to rule out some interpreta-tions of the intentions and dispositions of the actor (Newtson, 1973), and the more segmentations an observer makes, the more actions he or she defines. A more fine-grained segmentation, as indicated by a higher density of event boundaries, indicates a higher amount of extracted in-formation.

Again, some empirical evidence has been presented in favor of this assumption. First, if one considers behavior perception as an act of formation and validation of a specific hypothesis, then, in the course of observing an activity, more and more alternative explanations of the activity in terms of goals and intentions should be ruled out. In other words, if, during the course of events, an interpretation is successively settled, the observer should become increasingly confident in his or her interpretation, and, accordingly, the necessity of extracting further in-formation from the behavior stream should decrease. Correspondingly, a decrease in segmentation rate over the course of an event presentation can be predicted, and this segmentation pattern has repeatedly been re-ported in several studies (Newtson, 1973; Newtson & Rindner, 1979).

In another line of research, the impact of predictability on segmen-tation has been investigated. According to the model of information extraction, the occurrence of unexpected events should invalidate the current hypothesis the observer is pursuing, thereby inducing the gen-eration of new, alternative hypotheses, which in turn should lead to an increased need for information. Again, several studies have found empirical evidence for this assumption (Newtson, 1973; Wilder, 1978a, 1978b). In one experiment, Wilder (1978a) varied the predictability of behavior on either the level of goals (molar level) or the level of specific activities (molecular level) and found that in both cases unpredictability led to a significantly finer segmentation of the stream of behavior. In a second experiment, Wilder (1978b) systematically varied the predict-ability of activities over the time course of an event stream. He found patterns of finer segmentation if the actor started with unpredictable behavior, and also in the case of an abrupt change from unpredictability to predictability or vice versa.

The perspective of a partonomical structure of events and activities offers an alternative explanation for the decrease in segmentation density over the course of an event. This pattern may reflect the tendency to adapt the segmentation density to the temporal scope of the activity, with temporally extended higher-level goals becoming successively more salient (Anderson, Alwitt, Lorch, & Levin, 1979). In other words, during the progression of an extended activity, as more and more low-level activity steps get completed, the observer comes across event boundaries that mark the transition between goals of an upper level of the partonomic hierarchy. To the observer, such transition points, therefore, offer the opportunity to switch to a higher-level conceptualization of the event, resulting in a more coarse-grained segmentation.

Structuring Event Streams by Means of Anticipatory Schemata

In one major finding of the research program initiated by Newtson, it turned out that the process of segmentation is not simply determined by "objective" characteristics of the event stream but may be influenced by a number of observer-related characteristics. For example, depending on the type of event sequence, Newtson (1980) reported segment lengths ranging from 0.5 to 18 seconds. In its simplest empirical demonstration, the number and position of event boundaries can partly be controlled by instructing the observer to segment the event stream into "fine units" or "coarse units," or to forego a special instruction, thereby inducing "natural units." Apparently, observers do not have any problems following these different instructions. This finding has been taken as a first indication that the segmentation process is open to deliberate control by the observer. In terms of the processing model as described above, observers possess some degrees of freedom in choosing an anticipatory schema, which in turn serves as a guide for monitoring relevant event features, picking up information accordingly, and, finally, deciding where event boundaries are located.

In addition to overt manipulation of the grain size of segmentation by means of direct instruction, a number of other observer-related factors have also been found to have a substantial impact on segmentation—in particular, the observer's goals, his or her prior knowledge and familiarity with the observed event, subjective relevance (Russell, 1979), personal traits such as the need for cognition (Lassiter, Briggs, & Bowman, 1991) or aggressiveness (Courtney & Cohen, 1996), and/or mood states such as dysphoria (Lassiter, Koenig, & Apple, 1996).

According to Cohen and Ebbesen (1979), the observer's goals define the purpose for which an individual intends to use the information that he or she has gathered by observing the behavior of an actor. Therefore, the formation of such a goal should have two consequences on the segmentation process. First, in comparison to having no such goal, the observer should be more focused on the event features that are relevant to the goal at hand, which in turn will alter segmentation behavior, making it more selective because less primarily goal-relevant information is picked up. In line with this argument, Lassiter, Geers, Apple, and Beers (2000) found that the provision of a specific goal led observers to place substantially fewer event boundaries, compared to having no such explicit goal. Second, different observer goals should lead to different event characteristics being attended to, thereby inducing patterns of event boundaries that are qualitatively, but not necessarily quantitatively, different. Again, this assumption has been empirically confirmed. Both Cohen and Ebbesen (1979) and Lassiter et al. (2000) had subjects segment event streams with the goal to either form an impression of the actor or learn the activity. In both studies, different goals led to significantly different patterns of segmentation in terms of differing spatiotemporal locations of segments.

Besides observational goals, prior knowledge may also trigger the selection and application of anticipatory schemas. In a study by Massad et al. (1979), observers were given different information about the events that they were to segment. The events used in the study consisted of cartoons of moving figures (triangles and circles). In one condition the events were described as a treasure hunt (a triangle guards a treasure and a circle wants to steal it), and in the other condition as an episode of bullying. Similar to the findings on observational goals, different prior information presumably leads to the selection of different schemas, which in turn leads to different, only partially overlapping segmentation patterns. Additionally, in line with findings from schema-based text processing (e.g., Graesser, Millis, & Zwaan, 1997), observers seemed to extract less information from an event stream if it was consistent with prior information (Graziano, Moore, & Collins, 1988).

Another factor that has been shown to have a strong impact on segmentation is the degree of familiarity with an event or activity. High familiarity implies that one has already developed a well-elaborated, appropriate schema for it. The possession of such a well-developed schema has implications for the pattern of segmentation. In particular, by means of such a schema one should be able to identify schema-relevant characteristics more accurately. This hypothesis was confirmed in a study reported by Newtson (1980). Skilled and unskilled archers were presented a video showing a person shooting arrows at targets and were instructed to segment the video into meaningful units. These data were used to identify event boundaries for the skilled and unskilled archers. Photographs taken at the times identified by the two sets of boundaries were prepared and presented to viewers with the instruction to memorize and describe the activity. The picture set representing the event boundaries of the skilled archers led to more accurate descriptions of the activity than the picture set derived from the event boundaries of unskilled archers. Another converging piece of evidence comes from a study by Markus, Smith, and Moreland (1985), who found that observers who were not familiar with a given activity had difficulties segmenting it on a fine level. Whereas observers who were familiar with the events adapted their segmentation behavior according to the instructions (i.e., segmenting finer when instructed to do so), this was not the case for observers who were unfamiliar with the events shown. Thus, the latter group apparently lacked sufficient knowledge to identify subtle details in the behavior stream associated with event boundaries.

According to the model of Newtson, anticipatory schemata are an important component of the segmentation process, and differences in schema activation and schema structure are the main sources of both intra- and interindividual variance in segmentation. Recently, Zacks and Tversky (2001) have proposed an alternative explanation for variations in segmentation; however, the models should not be considered to be mutually exclusive but rather complementary. In particular, Zacks and Tversky (2001) emphasize that a stream of activities should not be seen as simply a sequence of different steps of action; instead it may be thought of as being hierarchically–sequentially organized—that is, events and activities can be described as hierarchies of nested goals or intentions as well as of nested activities or movements from the perspective of the actor (e.g., Miller, Galanter, & Pribram, 1960; Vallacher & Wegner, 1987) and/or of the observer (Mandler, 1984; Shank & Abelson, 1977; Zacks, Tversky, et al., 2001). In other words, a single higher-level goal or activity can be decomposed into sequences of subgoals and activity steps, and each of the subgoals or activity steps can be further decomposed into lower-level goals and activities, and so on, leading to a partonomic structure of the overall event.

Therefore, from the perspective of the partonomic character of events, the issue of fine-grained versus coarse-grained segmentation patterns should not only be interpreted as a matter of amounts of information extracted but can also be considered as a matter of differing levels of conceptualizing an event—either as a sequence of few, temporally extended higher-level goals and activities or as a sequence of a larger number of low-level goals and shorter action steps. In other words, whereas differences in schema activation lead to different, only partially overlapping patterns of segmentation, conceptualizing a given event on different levels of the partonomy leads to variations in segmentation density, with patterns of finely segmented units coupled with patterns of coarse segmentation in a hierarchically nested way.

The partonomic character of events manifests itself in several ways. First, observers can switch between different levels of the partonomic hierarchy of a given stream of events and are therefore able to segment a given stream of events at different levels of grain size with apparent ease. Thus, a number of studies have successfully induced different levels of segmentation simply by instructing the observers to unitize on a more fine or more coarse level (e.g., Hanson & Hirst, 1989; Lassiter, Stone, & Rogers, 1988; Newtson, 1973; Zacks, Tversky, et al., 2001).

Moreover, coarse-level segment boundaries will tend to coincide with fine-level segment boundaries (Zacks, Tversky, et al., 2001). This alignment effect suggests that the event structures at both fine and coarse levels are not independent types of segmentation reflecting differences in schema activation or amount of information extraction but instead are strongly coupled in such a way that the coarse-level segments are constituted by chunks of fine-level units. The alignment effect can be strengthened by having observers describe the event units verbally during segmentation. In this case, corresponding knowledge structures about goals, intentions, or causal relationships are activated that help the observer to focus on the partonomic structure of the event, and this in turn causes a greater degree of alignment between fine-grained and coarse-grained segmentation patterns.

Finally, different levels of unitization are associated with different types of attended features. According to the action/object model, which was validated by linguistic analyses of event descriptions during segmentation (Zacks, Tversky, et al., 2001), fine-level segmentation appears to be associated with different types of activities with an object and with characteristics of movement, whereas coarse-level segmentation appears to be associated with different objects and with features that are primarily indicative of higher-level goals and intentions.

Intra- or interindividual variations in segmentation may be attributed to at least two different cognitive mechanisms. On the one hand, activating different anticipatory schemas may lead to qualitatively different, only partially overlapping segmentation patterns, and, on the other hand, different decisions about the partonomic level on which a given event is conceptualized lead to segmentation patterns that have different grain size but are nevertheless closely aligned.

To sum up, while event boundaries reflect a mechanism for partitioning a continuous stream of events into cognitively manageable units, which are partly based on the attributes of the observer and partly on the "objective" characteristics of the events themselves, they also reflect the quality and amount of information picked up during observation. Therefore, it can be hypothesized that patterns of segmentation have a substantial impact on subsequent cognitive processes like memorizing or causal attribution.

Effects of Event Segmentation on Memory and Cognition

We not only perceive discrete events and cognitively process them while they are happening, we also transform these percepts into more enduring mental representations which are stored in memory and can be assessed and retrieved at later points in time. Both cognitive research (Liechtenstein & Brewer, 1980; Reed et al., 1992) and linguistic analysis (Zacks, Tversky, et al., 2001a) indicate that discrete event steps, typically nested into partonomic hierarchies, play an important role in thinking and talking about events. Therefore, the process of segmentation that occurs during event perception defines the perceptual units that will in turn influence the encoding and mental representation of events.

Within this context, several questions arise: What role does event segmentation play for processes of event encoding? What is the relationship between segmentation and event memory? Aside from questions of representation, does segmentation also tap processes of social cognition?

With regard to the first question about the role of segmentation in the representation of events, event boundaries have been conceptually linked to syntactic markers in text understanding. In other words, they may mark points at which the previous unit is recoded in a format for transfer into long-term memory. Some evidence for this notion of "boundary encoding" has been found in the studies of Gernsbacher (1985) for picture stories and in the studies of Carroll and Bever (1976) involving film material. In particular, Carroll and Bever (1976) found evidence that at event boundaries, the amount of mental load increased, indicating the occurrence of additional cognitive processes. Also, Gernsbacher (1985) shows that after crossing an event boundary in picture stories, a substantial amount of surface information (e.g., left–right orientation) is lost, and that this phenomenon can be attributed to a shift from building one substructure to initiating another.

If specific kinds of recoding processes are initiated at event boundaries, it seems plausible that the segmental structure of event perception is, to a certain extent, also reflected in the structural organization of the mental representation of the event as it is stored in memory. Again, empirical evidence has accumulated in favor of this hypothesis.

First, the level of segmentation is strongly coupled with the amount and quality of subsequent event recall. Observers who have segmented a given stream of events into fine units also tend to recall significantly more event steps than observers who have segmented that stream only in a coarse manner (Hanson & Hirst, 1989; Lassiter, 1988; Lassiter & Shaw, 1991; Lassiter, Stone, & Rogers, 1988). This is in line with the previously mentioned hypothesis that coarse-grained unitization also indicates scarce information extraction. Coarse segments signal the formation of coarse cognitive units as summaries of extended parts of the stream of events, from which event details can not be easily reconstructed. But, as Hanson and Hirst (1989) have shown, the level of segmentation does not necessarily preclude the ability to remember details of the event sequence, as evidenced by measures of recognition. In other words, the segmentation process seems to define a kind of structural organization in combination with a preferred "entry level" for the representation of an event sequence, but it does not imply that the event is represented solely on this level. In particular, event details, which are relevant for causally related activities (Lassiter et al., 1988), as well as activity steps located near segment boundaries (Newtson & Engquist, 1976), tend to be easily recognized irrespective of the level of segmentation.

Second, the action/object relation, which has been found for concurrent descriptions during perceptual segmentation and which seems to reflect the features upon which observers base their unitization, also holds for subsequent verbal recountings of that event (Zacks, Tversky, et al., 2001). In other words, observers who have segmented an event stream during its presentation into fine units tend to focus their recall on different types of activities with a given object and on characteristics of movement, whereas observers who initially segmented the event presentation into coarse units tend to focus on multiple objects and on features primarily indicative of higher-level goals and intentions. Additionally, a high degree of structural overlap between verbal descriptions and visual presentations in terms of partonomic relationships has been established (Lichtenstein & Brewer, 1980; Reed et al., 1992; Zacks, Tversky, et al., 2001). Thus, perceptual segmentations and verbal event descriptions seem to be strongly intertwined. On the one hand, concurrent verbalizations do shape segmentation in terms of a top-down process; on the other hand, perceptual segmentation, in turn, has some influence on subsequent verbal recounting, reflecting a kind of reverse, bottom-up influence.

Finally, perceptual segmentation has been shown to exert a substantial impact on the subsequent memory representation of an event and on its interpretation. According to Newtson's model, segmenting a given activity into fine units indicates a high information state; that is, the observer is frequently sampling information about the behavior of an actor—a process resulting in dense information. Accordingly, observers who segmented an activity into fine units tend to report more differentiated impressions about the actor, as measured with trait rating. They are also significantly more confident in their impressions than coarse-unit segmenters (Newtson, 1973). Additionally, fine segmentation leads observers to make more dispositional attributions (Newtson, 1973; Wilder, 1978a, 1978b) and report more favorable impressions of the observed actor (Jensen & Rottmeyer, 1986; Lassiter, 1988; Lassiter & Stone, 1984). Finally, since the segmentation rate typically decreases over the course of an activity, a sampling bias has been observed with regard to attribution. In other words, earlier parts of an activity, which tend to be segmented on a more fine-grained level and from which, therefore, more information is extracted, tend to exert a greater impact on personal impressions and attributions. In contrast, information stemming from later parts of an event tends to be discarded because the viewer has already reached a point of subjectively sufficient information, as indicated by a coarse pattern of segmentation (Newtson, 1973; Newtson & Rindner, 1979).

To sum up, the notion of perceived event segments as building blocks of event cognition has received some empirical support. Event segments obviously are not confined to an early perceptual level; they influence mental representation, memory, and social cognition as well.

Experiencing Segmented Events

The current chapter started with the premise that during our waking hours, we experience a continuous stream of unfolding and changing events upon which our cognitive system projects a certain structure by segmenting it into discrete units. While in some sense the notion of a seamless continuity of events is obviously true, there are also major exceptions in the sense that some types of events come to us in a segment-like fashion.

In particular, although everyday experiences can be phenomenally continuous from the perspective of the observer, they may be considered discrete and incomplete because the events may not be observed in a continuous manner. Often there are situations (a party, for example) in which a number of events will unfold in parallel. As attention is limited, we can focus on only one of these events at a given point in time. In order to follow multiple events, we have to switch our attention back and forth between the different events. Additionally, neither observers nor events should be considered stationary, as they may change their location over time, whereby the trajectory of event and observer do not necessarily correlate. As a consequence, due to switches in attention and changes in position, observers often perceive unfolding events in a piecemeal fashion consisting of more or less extended segments.

Both introspection and empirical evidence suggest that the human cognitive system is well adapted to this situation, being able to make sense even of small and unsystematic segment samples of extended event chains. More specifically, unseen parts of events can often be accurately inferred on the basis of schematic knowledge structures like scripts, thereby leading to an integrated and coherent representation of the event chain as a whole (Jenkins, Wald, & Pittenger, 1986). Also, the sampling of event segments can be further improved by systematically distributing attention across simultaneous events in a strategic manner (Lorch et al., 1979). Additionally, even short activity segments that last less than 5 minutes (so-called "thin slices of behavior") seem to provide sufficient information to allow for accurate judgment of characteristics such as personality traits or intelligence (Ambady & Rosenthal, 1992; Borkenau, Mauer, Riemann, Spinath, & Angleitner, 2004). Similarly, the features of events can be specified by means of short segments in an economical way. For example, Valenti and Costall (1997) showed that observers could accurately discriminate between different weights of a lifted box if just a short segment of the activity of lifting was presented in a video. Some video segments were more effective than others, depending on which phase of the lifting event they represented. Also, the discrimination of the lifted weights was more reliable for short video segments than for static pictures.

This flexibility of event processing helps us understand the ways event sequences are depicted in media such as films or picture stories (Bordwell, 1986). For example, many films rely on the abilities of their viewers' cognitive systems to make sense of piecemeal events, both when switching abruptly between different lines of action and when characterizing extended events by means of a sequence of short (but well-chosen) event samples. In particular, different activities taking place simultaneously at distant places can be shown by crosscutting—that is, showing a short segment from event A, then showing a short segment from event B, then again showing a short segment from event A, and so on. The classic example of this strategy is the last-minute rescue in action films, where segments showing the victim in danger are mixed with segments showing the hero approaching the scene and rescuing the victim. Also, extended events (consider the hero of an action film taking a transatlantic flight) can be summarized appropriately by showing just a few characteristic segments of the whole event (e.g., check-in at the airport, taking a seat in the plane, the plane landing). The principles underlying such filmic summaries were investigated in a study by Schwan and Garsoffky (2004). They compared complete film versions of events with summaries in which either event boundaries or nonboundaries were deleted and found that the recall of the summaries in which the event boundaries were deleted were much more incomplete and differed much more extensively from the complete version than summaries in which the event boundaries were retained. In other words, to be understandable for the viewer, the selection of segments has to conform to the principles of event segmentation as specified in the models of Newtson (1973) and Zacks and Tversky (2001)—namely, keeping highly informative event boundaries while skipping the less informative nonboundaries.

Even when an activity or event is presented in a continuous and complete manner, media offer a rich repertoire of design possibilities by which the process of segmentation can be influenced. For example, variations in presentation speed can be utilized to induce a certain type of segmentation. Thus, slow motion leads viewers to finer segmentation, and time lapse, in turn, induces a more coarse segmentation (Newtson & Rindner, 1979). Additionally, formal features like cuts can be used to accentuate existing event boundaries, thereby facilitating the segmentation process. Several studies have shown that there is a positive relationship between the occurrence of such filmic features and segmentation (Magliano et al., 2001; Schwan et al., 1998, 2000). Closer analysis shows that such filmic features have an influence on segmentation only if they coincide with structural changes in the event sequence itself (i.e., with event boundaries; Kraft, 1986; Schwan et al., 2000). Accentuating event boundaries has an impact on segmentation and on a number of subsequent cognitive processes. Most importantly, the accuracy of event recall can be substantially improved when film cuts are placed at event boundaries (Schwan et al., 2000).

Taking this topic one step further, Boltz (1992, 1995) has investigated the impact of advertising breaks on the event structure of fictional films as an example of a massive disruption of the flow of events. She found that the placement of advertising breaks at event boundaries led to an improvement of recall of the content of the fictional film, whereas placing advertising breaks at nonboundaries severely reduced accuracy of recall (Boltz, 1992). The placement of breaks was also found to influence the experience of time—that is, if event boundaries of fictional feature films were accentuated by short advertising breaks, variability of duration estimation across observers decreased and accuracy of judgements increased. In contrast, if short advertising breaks were placed at nonboundaries, variability of duration estimation increased and accuracy of judgements decreased (Boltz, 1995).

Finally, strategically breaking events into discrete steps allows the viewer to partially control even complex social judgments. For example, Lassiter, Geers, Munhall, Ploutz-Snyder, and Breitenbecher (2002) presented viewers with three versions of a videotaped confession, each differing with regard to the viewpoint of the camera, with the focus primarily on the interrogator, primarily on the suspect, or on both persons in an equal manner. The three versions led to different segmentation patterns: the activity of the person who was the main focus of the camera was segmented more finely. This segmentation pattern, in turn, had a substantial impact on judgments of causality, as revealed by path analysis. In particular, the participants viewing the confession on a tape that focused more on the suspect judged the confession to be more voluntary than those filmed under the other conditions, where it was judged more coerced. In another line of research, Ariely and Zauberman (2000, 2003) showed that the partitioning of extended experiences by means of breaks had a strong influence on their subjective hedonic quality. In particular, increased partitioning of an experience reduced the effect of the overall trend and resulted in more equal weighting of its parts, indicating that components of sequences are evaluated similarly to the way whole sequences are evaluated. Overall, studies like Lassiter et al. (2002) and Ariely and Zauberman (2003) make clear that perceptual segmentation and its strategic facilitation by means of environmental structures like breaks or cuts is not only of academic interest but has important practical implications as well.

Conclusion

Starting with the seminal studies of Newtson in the early 1970s, the past three decades have brought much progress in our understanding of how humans deal with the continuous flow of events unfolding before their eyes. Segmenting the event stream into manageable units plays an important role in subsequent cognitive processing. Segmentation appears to be a central mechanism underlying event cognition because, independent of mode of observation or medium of presentation, event understanding obviously proceeds in a stepwise, partonomically structured manner.

From a more general standpoint, this focus on segmentation marks a double shift in perspective, both from questions of space and object to the problem of time and event, and from verbal descriptions of events to their direct visual perception, which goes hand in hand with a change in focus of interest from indirect to more direct modes of social knowing (McArthur & Baron, 1983).

The scientific investigation of event segmentation is, however, far from complete. In the past several years, the problem of event unitization has appeared in new areas of research, including clinical psychology (Zalla, Verlut, Franck, Puzenat, & Sirigu, 2004), developmental psychology (Sharon & Wynn, 1998), applied psychology (Lassiter et al., 2002; Zacks & Tversky, 2003), and, most importantly, cognitive neuropsychology (Speer, Swallow, & Zacks, 2003; Zacks, Braver, et al., 2001). Therefore, in the near future, both the practical applicability of principles of segmentation and the biological foundations of perceptual segmentation will surely bring new insights into the process of how humans make sense of events.

References

Ambady, N., & Rosenthal, R. (1992). Thin slices of expressive behaviour as predictors of interpersonal consequences: A meta-analysis. *Psychological Bulletin, 111*, 256–274.

Anderson, D. R., Alwitt, L. F., Lorch, E. P., & Levin, S. R. (1979). Watching children watch television. In G. A. Hale & M. Lewis (Eds.), *Attention and cognitive development* (pp. 331–361). New York: Plenum.

Ariely, D., & Zauberman, G. (2000). On the making of an experience: The effects of breaking and combining experiences on their overall evaluation. *Journal of Behavioral Decision Making, 13*, 219–232.

Ariely, D., & Zauberman, G. (2003). Differential partitioning of extended experiences. *Organizational Behavior and Human Decision Processes, 91*, 128–139.

Berry, D. S., & Misovich, S. J. (1994). Methodological approaches to the study of social event perception. *Personality & Social Psychology Bulletin, 20*, 139–152.

Boltz, M. G. (1992). Temporal accent structure and the remembering of filmed narratives. *Journal of Experimental Psychology: Human Perception and Performance, 18*, 90–105.

Boltz, M. G. (1995). Effects of event structure on retrospective duration judgements. *Perception & Psychophysics*, *57*, 1080–1096.

Bordwell, D. (1986). *Narration in the fiction film*. London: Routledge.

Borkenau, P., Mauer, N., Riemann, R., Spinath, F. M., & Angleitner, A. (2004). Thin slices of behavior as cues of personality and intelligence. *Journal of Personality & Social Psychology*, *86*, 599–614.

Carroll, J. M., & Bever, T. G. (1976). Segmentation in cinema perception. *Science*, *191*, 1053–1055.

Cohen, C. E., & Ebbesen, E. B. (1979). Observational goals and schema activation: A theoretical framework for behavior perception. *Journal of Experimental Social Psychology*, *15*, 305–329.

Courtney, M. L., & Cohen, R. (1996). Behavior segmentation by boys as a function of aggressiveness and prior information. *Child Development*, *67*, 1034–1047.

Gernsbacher, M. A. (1985). Surface information loss in comprehension. *Cognitive Psychology*, *17*, 324–363.

Ginsburg, G. P., & Smith, D. L. (1993). Exploration of the detectable structure of social episodes: The parsing of interaction specimens. *Ecological Psychology*, *5*, 195–233.

Graesser, A. C., Millis, K. K., & Zwaan, R. A. (1997). Discourse comprehension. *Annual Review of Psychology*, *48*, 163–189.

Graziano, W. G., Moore, J. S., & Collins, J. E. (1988). Social cognition as segmentation of the stream of behaviour. *Developmental Psychology*, *24*, 568–573.

Hanson, C., & Hirst, W. (1989). On the representation of events: A study of orientation, recall, and recognition. *Journal of Experimental Psychology: General*, *118*, 136–147.

Jenkins, J. J., Wald, J., & Pittenger, J. B. (1986). Apprehending pictorial events. In V. McCabe & B. Balzano (Eds.), *Event cognition: An ecological perspective* (pp. 117–133). Hillsdale, NJ: Lawrence Erlbaum.

Jensen, T.D., & Rottmeyer, L.W. (1986). Visual information-processing of television commercials: Cognitive effects. *Advances in Consumer Research*, *13*, 158–163.

Jensen, T. D., & Schroeder, D. A. (1982). Behavior segmentation in a dyadic situation. *Personality & Social Psychology Bulletin*, *8*, 264–272.

Kraft, R. N. (1986). The role of cutting in the evaluation and retention of film. *Journal of Experimental Psychology: Learning, Memory, and Cognition*, *12*, 155–163.

Lassiter, G. D. (1988). Behavior perception, affect, and memory. *Social Cognition*, *6*, 150–176.

Lassiter, G. D., Briggs, M. A., & Bowman, R. E. (1991). Need for cognition and the perception of ongoing behaviour. *Personality and Social Psychology Bulletin*, *17*, 156–160.

Lassiter, G. D., Geers, A. L., Apple, K. J., & Beers, M. J. (2000). Observational goals and behaviour unitization: A re-examination. *Journal of Experimental Social Psychology*, *36*, 649–659.

Lassiter, G. D., Geers, A. L., Munhall, P. J., Ploutz-Snyder, R. J., & Breitenbecher, D. L. (2002). Illusory causation: Why it occurs. *Psychological Science*, *13*, 299–305.

Lassiter, G. D., Koenig, L. J., & Apple, K. J. (1996). Mood and behavior perception: Dysphoria can increase and decrease effortful processing of information. *Personality & Social Psychology Bulletin, 22*, 794–810.

Lassiter, G. D., & Shaw, R. D. (1991). The unitization and memory of events. *Journal of Experimental Psychology: General, 120*, 80–82.

Lassiter, G. D., & Stone, J. I. (1984). Affective consequences of variation in behaviour perception: When liking is in the level of analysis. *Personality & Social Psychology Bulletin, 10*, 253–259.

Lassiter, G. D., Stone, J. I., & Rogers, S. L. (1988). Memorial consequences of variation in behaviour perception. *Journal of Experimental Social Psychology, 24*, 222–239.

Lichtenstein, E. H., & Brewer, W. F. (1980). Memory for goal-directed events. *Cognitive Psychology, 12*, 412–445.

Lorch, E. P., Anderson, D. R., & Levin, S. R. (1979). The relationship of visual attention to children's comprehension of television. *Child Development, 50*, 722–727.

Magliano, J., Miller, J., & Zwaan, R. A. (2001). Indexing space and time in film understanding. *Applied Cognitive Psychology, 15*, 533–545.

Mandler, J. M. (1984). *Stories, scripts, and scenes: Aspects of schema theory.* Hillsdale, NJ: Lawrence Erlbaum.

Markus, H., Smith, J., & Moreland, R. L. (1985). Role of the self-concept in the perception of others. *Journal of Personality and Social Psychology, 49*, 1494–1512.

Massad, C. M., Hubbard, M., & Newtson, D. (1979). Selective perception of events. *Journal of Experimental Social Psychology, 15*, 513–532.

McArthur, L. Z., & Baron, R. M. (1983). Toward an ecological theory of social perception. *Psychological Review, 90*, 215–238.

Miller, G. A., Galanter, E., & Pribram, K. H. (1960). *Plans and the structure of behavior.* New York: Holt.

Neisser, U. (1976). *Cognition and reality.* San Francisco: Freeman.

Newtson, D. (1973). Attribution and the unit of perception of ongoing behavior. *Journal of Personality and Social Psychology, 28*, 28–38.

Newtson, D. (1980). An interactionist perspective on social knowing. *Personality & Social Psychology Bulletin, 6*, 520–531.

Newtson, D., & Engquist, G. (1976). The perceptual organization of ongoing behaviour. *Journal of Experimental Social Psychology, 12*, 436–450.

Newtson, D., Engquist, G., & Bois, J. (1977). The objective basis of behaviour units. *Journal of Personality and Social Psychology, 35*, 847–862.

Newtson, D., & Rindner, R. J. (1979). Variation in behavior perception and ability attribution. *Journal of Personality and Social Psychology, 37*, 1847–1858.

Newtson, D., Rindner, R., Miller, R., & LaCross, K. (1978). Effects of availability of feature changes on behavior segmentation. *Journal of Experimental Social Psychology, 14*, 379–388.

Reed, E. S., Montgomery, M., Schwartz, M., Palmer, C., & Pittenger, J. B. (1992). Visually based descriptions of an everyday action. *Ecological Psychology, 4*, 129–152.

Russell, J. C. (1979). Perceived action units as a function of subjective importance. *Personality & Social Psychology Bulletin, 5*, 206–209.

Schwan, S., & Garsoffky, B. (2004). The cognitive representation of filmic event summaries. *Applied Cognitive Psychology, 18*(1), 37–55.

Schwan, S., Garsoffky, B., & Hesse, F. W. (2000). Do film cuts facilitate the perceptual and cognitive organization of activity sequences? *Memory & Cognition, 28*(2), 214–223.

Schwan, S., Hesse, F. W., & Garsoffky, B. (1998). The relationship between formal filmic means and the segmentation behavior of film viewers. *Journal of Broadcasting and Electronic Media, 42*(2), 237–249.

Shank, R., & Abelson, R. P. (1977). *Scripts, plans, goals, and understanding.* Hillsdale, NJ: Lawrence Erlbaum.

Sharon, T., & Wynn, K. (1998). Individuation of actions from continuous motion. *Psychological Science, 9*, 357–362.

Speer, N. E., Swallow, K. M., & Zacks, J. M. (2003). Activation of human motion processing areas during event perception. *Cognitive, Affective, & Behavioral Neuroscience, 3*, 335–345.

Tversky, B., Zacks, J. M., & Lee, P. (2004). Events by hand and feet. *Spatial Cognition & Computation, 4*, 5–14.

Valenti, S., & Costall, A. (1997). Visual perception of lifted weight from kinematic and static (photographic) displays. *Journal of Experimental Psychology: Human Perception and Performance, 23*, 181–198.

Vallacher, R. R., & Wegner, D. M. (1987). What do people think they're doing? Action identification and human behavior. *Psychological Review, 94*, 3–15.

Wilder, D. A. (1978a). Effect of predictability on units of perception and attribution. *Personality and Social Psychology Bulletin, 4*, 281–284.

Wilder, D. A. (1978b). Predictability of behaviours, goals, and unit of perception. *Personality and Social Psychology Bulletin, 4*, 604–607.

Zacks, J. M. (2004). Using movement and intentions to understand simple events. *Cognitive Science, 28*, 979–1008.

Zacks, J. M., & Tversky, B. (2001). Event structure in perception and conception. *Psychological Bulletin, 127*, 3–21.

Zacks, J. M., & Tversky, B. (2003). Structuring information interfaces for procedural learning. *Journal of Experimental Psychology: Applied, 9*, 88–100.

Zacks, J. M., Tversky, B., & Iyer, G. (2001). Perceiving, remembering, and communicating structure in events. *Journal of Experimental Psychology: General, 130*, 29–58.

Zacks, J. M., Braver, T. S., Sheridan, M. A., Donaldson, D. I., Snyder, A. Z., Ollinger, J. M., et al. (2001). Human brain activity time-locked to perceptual event boundaries. *Nature Neuroscience, 4*, 651–655.

Zalla, T., Verlut, I., Franck, N., Puzenat, D., & Sirigu, A. (2004). Perception of dynamic action in patients with schizophrenia. *Psychiatry Research, 128*, 39–51.

16

Geometric Information for Event Segmentation

THOMAS F. SHIPLEY & MANDY J. MAGUIRE

To interact with other humans, one must recognize and categorize actions in such a way as to understand intentions and predict future events. However, this is not possible from any temporally local cue. For example, the positions of a body have different meaning and can lead to very different events in different, broader spatiotemporal contexts: a raised open hand can precede a high-five or a slap in the face. Humans effortlessly recognize events, allowing them to differentiate a friendly gesture for a job well done from the beginnings of a fight. Without this ability we would be unable to interact with agents or objects in our environment.

How do humans make sense of a world with overlapping "blooming, buzzing" events? The chapters in this book grapple with this problem, offer a sense of the scope of the puzzle, and, we hope, position some of the important pieces. Our goal for this chapter is to sketch the outline of a critical piece: how perceptual processes help segment events, begin the complex process of giving meaning to the flux of change around each of us, and ultimately give us the social graces to differentiate friend from foe. Here we briefly consider the scope of this problem and then address in detail an analysis that focuses on how object paths play a vital role in event segmentation.

Scope

Why do we break up the continuous ebb and flow of events into discrete event packets? The discretization of events may serve, or reflect, an important function for humans: prediction of future events. Segmentation creates (or reflects) units of prediction. For each event unit, future changes within the unit may be predicted from what has occurred at earlier points in time within the unit. An event boundary is, then, the point where predictability breaks down (Zacks, Speer, Swallow, Braver, & Reynolds, in press).

In this chapter, to illustrate how humans make these predictions, we draw on work in another domain where segmentation is better understood: objects. As with events, objects can be discretized into units, the perception of which reveals statistical regularities of a world where bounded objects relate to local units of predictability. Because objects tend to be smooth and homogeneous in substance, it is possible to predict the location of unseen boundaries and surface properties within the object's boundaries (Brunswik & Kamiya, 1953). For smooth boundaries it is possible to predict where the boundary will continue, thus allowing visual extrapolation and interpolation (Kellman & Shipley, 1991; Shipley & Kellman, 2003). Similarly, the visual system can predict, or fill in, surface properties of regions that are not directly visible (Yin, Kellman, & Shipley, 2000). For object units, an object's boundaries represent the region of space where predictability breaks down.

The central idea here is that certain properties of the world change predictably within bounded regions of space and time. Whenever there is an abrupt change in some property, segmentation is likely to occur. For events, abrupt changes in the transformation of objects should be associated with event boundaries. For physical events abrupt changes may occur in objects' motion, orientation, collision, shape, surface properties, number, or existence (see the discussion of Gibson's categories of events in Chapter 1). Chapters 11 and 12 in this volume consider how the visual system processes shape changes to identify gender or emotion. In this chapter, we focus on object motion.

An important point to bear in mind is that this notion of predictability is a statistical issue. Predictability is not all or none but graded, so segment boundaries may be experienced when predictability drops below some threshold—for example, when an object moves outside of an envelope around a predicted path. Furthermore, predictability may be a function of temporal scale. Consider an animal traveling an irregular route from one point to another; at a fine scale its motion is hard to predict, but at a coarser scale it is moving consistently in one direction. This is analogous to natural objects, for example a tree, where at a fine scale the contours of the trunk are not smooth but at a coarser scale the trunk on the whole is smooth.

A Case Study

We begin the rather daunting task of specifying the potential perceptual features of event boundaries by focusing on the motion of individual objects through space. Here we use the term *path* to refer to the space-time trajectory of an object. There are three reasons to start here: (1) paths of objects provide important information about animate objects, and researchers have argued that paths are fundamental to event classification in language learning; (2) the formal mathematical tools are available for characterizing the information available in the world for segmentation of paths; and (3) preliminary findings indicate that path features are used by observers to segment events. We will consider each in turn.

Paths Are Fundamental to Cognition

One of the difficulties in studying events is that they contain many features. Even when studying an event that involves only one agent, there are many aspects of the event to which one might attend. Event features range from the direction of the agent's motion, the way in which the agent moves, and the intentions of the agent to the presumably less important aspects such as the agent's eye color. In theory any of these features could be used to segment events. It may be that when watching an ongoing event we would predict a "change" only when locations change (e.g., when the agent leaves a room), or only when the agent's manner changes (e.g., the agent shifts from running to jogging). However, although these features may play some role in segmentation for specific events or event types, research and theories in three areas—(1) how events are represented linguistically, (2) how event representations develop, and (3) computational models of event segmentation—converge on a single conclusion: that event paths are the most important feature for event representation and segmentation. Here we briefly review each in turn.

Linguists have noted the importance of event path across and within languages. Every event has many features and any of them *could* be labeled, but instead there are striking similarities across languages with respect to which features *are* encoded in relational terms (Braine, 1990; Braine, Reiser, & Rumain, 1984; Clark, 2001; Frawley, 1992; Langacker, 1987; Slobin, 2001, 2003; Talmy, 1985, 2000). Path is an event feature labeled by most languages. Indeed, it is integral to language, so much so that Talmy (1985) classified the world's languages based on how they encode paths—for example, whether path is conveyed outside of the verb, as in English prepositions (over, up, behind), or within the verb, as in Romance languages (descendere, partir). Although languages often omit the manner of the action, regularly omitting path information is rare. The universal emphasis on representing path information when discussing an event is a strong indicator of the importance of path in human event representation.

Further, developmental research suggests that path is crucial to understanding, categorizing, and labeling events (Mandler, 2006). Paths are one of the earliest motion features that infants recognize (Mandler, 2006). This is most likely because they provide critical information about the actors in an event. For example, an animate object is likely to stop before it hits a second object, whereas an inanimate object is likely to stop as the result of hitting another object. By 4 months of age, infants discriminate between objects that hit each other and those that do not, even if the gap is very small (Leslie, 1984). Path also provides information about the goal, or intent, of an actor. Actors are likely to change direction when they head toward a new goal, either because the last goal has been reached or because the new one is more important (Mandler, 2006). Thus, if attempting to deduce the goals of an actor, changes in direction of a path would be useful cues. Baldwin, Baird, Saylor, and Clark (2001) found that 10- and 11-month-old infants could exploit a change in the direction of an action as a cue to intentionality. They argued that statistical learning of a correlation between goal reaching and breaks in temporal regularities of the path motion may lead to an understanding of intentional acts.

Lastly, path appears to be vital in computational models of event segmentation. Early computational models of motion representation were based on object shape and the paths between static shapes (Marr & Vaina, 1982). Subsequently, path as an indicator of event boundaries has become a focus of artificial intelligence research (Engel & Rubin, 1986; Rubin & Richards, 1985; see also Chapter 18 in this volume). Path shape may be used to isolate, identify, and label an event (Mann & Jepson, 2002; Mann, Jepson, & Siskind, 1997; Siskind, 2001). The general approach is to try to identify and categorize the forces, the dynamics, present in an event. For example, Mann and Jepson (2002) discuss identifying the forces acting on a ball from the ball's movement (falling, bouncing, etc.). Research in this area of computer vision has both the pragmatic goal of achieving a useful level of segmentation for automated event recognition and the psychological goal of understanding how humans might segment events. Yet to date no research has directly tested these computer models.

Taken together, research in linguistics, developmental psychology, and artificial intelligence all points to the importance of paths in event representations. Paths are universally employed in linguistic representations of events, paths appear to be the first feature of events meaningfully encoded by infants, and path information has proved to be a useful feature for computational models of event segmentation.

A Formal Analysis

To conceive of a path as a space-time curve allows us to draw on a significant body of mathematical work on the segmentation of objects (spatial curves). The analogy between event and object segmentation is mathematically rich, meaning the geometry of edge segmentation and space-time path segmentation is similar. The approach of using object knowledge to inform event knowledge is far from novel. Miller and Johnson-Laird (1976), Quine (1985/1996), and Zacks and Tversky (2001) all note similarities between the two domains. As Zacks and Tversky point out, "Event perception can be regarded as the temporally extended analog of object perception: Events are objects in the manifold of the three dimensions of space plus the one dimension of time" (p. 5). Below, we outline the similarities and then consider a few of the differences.

The projection of a path defined over time by a point moving through space is identical to the projection of a curve (object boundary), as long as the observer does not move. Thus, any analysis of the geometric properties of curves will also apply to spatial paths of points. Obviously, we inhabit a world of extended objects, not points, so the projection over time of an object will define a space-time volume. Here we restrict the analysis to a space-time line, positing that the visual system might use the movement of a point to characterize the movement of an object. There are a number of perceptually realistic features of objects that are natural candidates for such a point. One example is an object's center of mass. The motion of this point would define a space-time line that describes the linear velocity and acceleration of the object.

We begin our consideration of the geometry of paths with a brief review of a geometric approach to object segmentation (Hoffman & Richards, 1984). Objects may be segmented based on geometric properties of their projected images. Whenever the images of two objects intersect (e.g., one object partially occludes another), a discontinuity in contour orientation change will be present. This is true because the contours on two objects are unlikely to have the same orientation, so at the point where their images intersect there will be an abrupt change in orientation (and thus a discontinuity in the first derivative of the edge orientation; Kellman & Shipley, 1991). Similarly, for objects composed of two or more objects, whenever one object interpenetrates another the surfaces will intersect to form discontinuities in the surface curvature (Hoffman & Richards, 1984). This will always be true because the probability that two surfaces will intersect in such a way that their surfaces are parallel to each other, thus forming a smooth junction, is mathematically zero. (Of course it could happen by design, but it has zero probability of occurring at random; for a formal proof see Appendix A in Kellman & Shipley, 1991.)

A surface curvature discontinuity is associated with the intersection of two objects, the point where surface properties are likely to change, and is thus a natural place to decompose objects into parts. Such discontinuities have an important optical property: they are projectively invariant, meaning that for all viewpoints there will be a discontinuity in the contour curvature of the projected image of the 3-D surface curvatures. Singh and Hoffman (2001) have extended this analysis from segmentation based on curvature discontinuities to segmentation based on curvature extrema. They argue that curvature minima in particular will be regions of objects that are topologically related to object parts and predict the perceptual segmentation of objects. A coffee mug provides a simple example: the joint between the handle and the cup is a curvature minima, and two parts are seen—the part you grip and the part that holds the coffee. The same analysis may be applied to more complex objects such as the human body. Humans perceptually segment the body into parts such as head, arms, and legs. The boundaries of each part are marked by curvature extrema (neck, armpit, etc).

In an object, curvature extrema correspond to regions of an object that are likely to have arisen from the joining of two objects. In events, regions of extreme curvature on a path correspond to the local application of forces. Consider the two broad categories of moving objects, animate and inanimate objects. Generally, an inanimate object will change direction only when an external force has been applied (e.g., something hits it). An animate object will change direction in response to both external forces and internal forces. Internal forces will be applied whenever the animate object changes its goal (either because an old goal has been achieved or a new goal has become more important; for instance, the sudden appearance of a predator causing an animal to run away). Abrupt application of a strong force will cause a discontinuity in path curvature. A local region of extreme curvature on a path corresponds to a more gradual application of forces (e.g., a runner altering his or her path to avoid a distant obstacle).

While the geometric analyses of part and object segmentation are closely related, humans reason differently about events and their parts and about objects and their parts. In object perception, objects are at a natural level of analysis that is qualitatively different from that of parts (for example, when naming objects the default is that new words refer to the entire object; special actions are required to map a new word to a part; Markman, 1991). Whether or not there is a natural grain of analysis in events is more controversial; see Chapter 17 in this volume for further discussion of this issue. While it is not self-evident that the geometric analogies between the two domains will hold up, the analysis developed here suggests a way to conceive of events and sub-events. The natural level of an event analysis may be points where predictability completely breaks down. Thus, curvature discontinuities may be treated as boundaries between different events, whereas curvature extrema in paths may be treated as boundaries of sub-events (just as discontinuities in contours generally, although not always, indicate overlapping images of distinct objects, and curvature extrema are associated with parts within an object). Thus, we propose using the term *events* to refer to spatiotemporal collections of actions and transformations that are statistically associated and independent of other transformation, and the term *sub-event* to refer to the components that are statistically related to one another and parts of a larger event unit. The two cases are associated with different levels of force (e.g., abrupt onset versus slow onset) and thus different levels of predictability of an object's path. Whether or not this distinction makes sense in practice is an open question, but it implies that there may be a certain level of statistical coherence of basic perception-action level goals, and that superordinate goals (e.g., getting to school—see Chapter 21 in this volume) may require responses to environmental conditions (e.g., avoiding a street due to traffic conditions) that make prediction from one sub-goal to the next very difficult; thus the actions within each event are independent.

Although spatial contour curvature minima are associated with differing objects and spatiotemporal contour curvature extrema are associated with forces, they both are associated with local minima in predictability. Thus, it may be possible to bootstrap a theory of event path segmentation using theoretical work in the more mature area of object perception. In the next section we present some specific hypotheses for geometric properties that will be associated with event boundaries.

Predictions

A geometric approach to object motion indicates that segmentation will occur whenever the path of an object becomes difficult to predict based on the geometric properties of the object's previous motion. Here we distinguish between two types of geometric properties: local and global. Local properties are geometric features that can be identified on the basis of a spatially or temporally local analysis. In contrast, global features require comparisons of multiple local geometric properties—comparing properties at one location to spatially or temporally distal properties. Noting an event boundary when an actor turns and leaves the stage would be an example of a local feature, whereas seeing one event by linking the disappearance of a train at one end of a tunnel and the reappearance at the other end of a tunnel would be an example of the use of global features. The relationship between the applications of forces and paths is relatively straightforward for local features and more complex for global features.

LOCAL GEOMETRIC PROPERTIES

When forces are applied to a moving object, its path changes shape, so the future motion of that object is hard to predict using the path seen up to the introduction of the new force. This means, as noted above, that segmentation may occur when a path contains a curvature discontinuity (the point on a path where the direction of motion changes abruptly). More generally, changes in curvature that are not abrupt should also be associated with event boundaries. A change in curvature will occur when there is a gradual application of a new force—for example, when the wind begins to blow an inanimate object off of its original course, or when an animal gradually changes direction to approach or avoid a new goal.

As path curvature becomes greater (i.e., the radius of curvature decreases), a smooth curve approaches the shape of a discontinuous curve (Fig. 16.1[A]). We hypothesize that there will be an inverse relationship between radius of curvature and probability of segmentation, with segmentation particularly likely for abrupt changes in direction and curves with very high curvature (very small radii of curvature) and lower probability of segmentation for more gradual curves. Such a relationship would be consistent with predictability in the various paths; the greater the force applied to a moving object, the higher the curvature of its path, and the greater the uncertainty in prediction of future path from the shape of the path before the force was applied.

Independent of curvature, curves may also be characterized by their turning angle (i.e., how far the contour continues along a curve of a given radius). Greater turning angles will be associated with longer applications of a force (see Fig. 16.1[B]). As was the case for curvature, longer applications of force would make prediction of future paths less reliable, so we predict that the probability of segmentation will increase with increases in turning angle. Both radius of curvature and turning angle in spatial curves have been argued to be related to segmentation on analogous grounds (Singh & Hoffman, 2001).

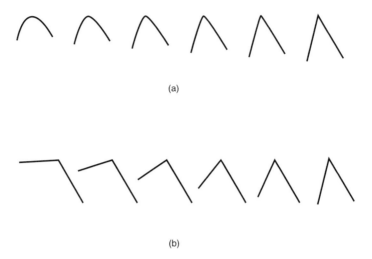

(a)

(b)

FIGURE 16.1. (*A*) Decreases in radius of curvature and (*B*) increases in turning angle of paths are associated with greater forces and are predicted to be
associated with greater likelihood of segmentation.

The magnitude of local geometric features, as well as their relationship
to the magnitude of change in an event, allows us to make predictions
about the relative priority of features for segmentation. However, local
features may only be useful for fine-grained segmentation; more complex
qualities of events require an analysis that captures relationships between
features. For example, identifying a goal requires noting a relationship
between the behavior of an organism and a spatially, and on occasion
temporally distant, object or event. The geometric approach may be
extended to describe invariant geometric features in the relations
between sub-events that are separated in space or time.

GLOBAL GEOMETRIC PROPERTIES

In simple events, the motion of an object is determined by the application of local forces. For more complex events, particularly social events,
where there exists some coordination between the forces acting on one
object and the forces acting on another (e.g., two people walking together and mutually adjusting their gaits to accommodate each other),
a similar geometric analysis in terms of object relative properties is also
possible; it requires an analysis at broad spatial and temporal scales.
The spatiotemporal relations between two or more local extrema may
define some of these geometric properties that allow us to characterize

coordination of forces. Again, there are some direct analogies to object segmentation, where relationships between parts have proven useful in understanding part segmentation. Here we consider five global properties and their analogs in object segmentation (Fig. 16.2).

Curvature Minima and Maxima

For bounded objects and closed paths (paths that begin and end in the same place), the direction of curvature can be defined relative to the entire contour. In objects, part boundaries are associated with curvature minima (because overall the curve will tend to curve back on itself to complete the closed form; Singh & Hoffman, 2001). Analogously, if the visual system takes advantage of this regularity for motion paths—the certainty that in the future an object will move in such a way as to return to the origin of motion—then we would expect more path segmentation

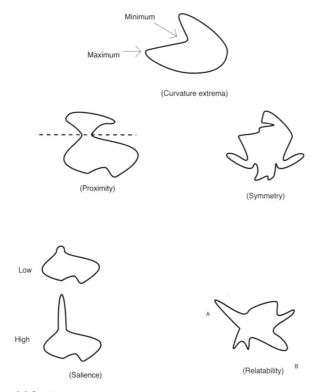

FIGURE 16.2. Illustrations of paths showing each of the five global properties that allow path predictability and thus might be related to segmentation.

to occur at curvature minima where the path deviates from the tendency to curve back on itself. There are two reasons to suspect that this geometric property will not be as useful in paths as it appears to be for objects. First, as noted by Zacks and Tversky (2001), no two events are literally identical, and paths can not be truly closed, as they can not return to the time they began, only the location in space. Although we frequently return to the same location (our home, office chair, etc.), this may be the exception in events. Most paths are likely motivated by a spatially distant goal which, once reached, ceases to be a goal. Second, the boundaries of an object define the inside of the object. In contrast, the inside region of a path has a much looser relationship to the path itself. There may be cases (e.g., skirting an obstacle) where what is inside a closed path is related to the path, but there is no necessary relationship. So, curvature minima may be important signals for segmentation of paths, but no more important than curvature maxima.

Proximity

In objects, proximal points of extreme curvature (e.g., the curved transitions from neck to shoulder) are likely to be related to each other and define a local part. The rationale for spatial proximity lies in part in the topology of intersecting objects (Singh, Seyranian, & Hoffman, 1999). If two objects of unequal size intersect, the shortest cut between curvature extrema will mark the part boundary of the smaller of the two objects.

For paths, spatiotemporally proximal curvature extrema are likely to reflect related forces (an area of high wind, or a location near a dangerous animal where other animals change course to avoid the danger). Thus any segment of a path bound by two proximal extrema may offer a meaningful path part within a larger event. However, we anticipate that this global property may be only weakly related to segmentation, as the beginnings and ends of a significant class of events—goal-related events—will not necessarily be proximate to each other. The beginning will be associated with wherever the organism detected or decided to pursue a new goal, and the end will be at the goal location.

Relatability

The edges of objects are relatively smooth, so when an edge is partially occluded, the visible pieces will tend to be aligned. The analogy between smooth paths and smooth edges is discussed in Chapter 1; here we restrict discussion to the formal geometric properties of aligned path parts. Two visible path fragments are more likely to be connected and seen as parts of a larger, continuous path if they form a straight line; more generally, they are likely to be connected if they show little evidence of an intervening force. Note that the concept of relatability is in some ways the flip side of discontinuity. Paths are likely to be connected if it is unlikely that the connection forms a curvature extrema. So, the lower the alignment between the visible paths (and presumably the greater the difference in velocity or acceleration), the less likely the two parts will be seen as going together to form a larger unit. This has been found in multiple object tracking studies by Scholl and Pylyshyn (1999).

Symmetry

All other things being equal, boundaries of an object that define a symmetrical form will be seen as a separate part of the object, segmented from other regions that are not part of the pattern. Analogously, perhaps we segment events that display some spatiotemporal symmetry. A casual consideration of events would suggest that both repetition and mirror symmetrical patterns could be the basis for some segmentation. Consider two cases, "retracing one's steps" and "imitation." A path to a destination and the same path away from that destination define a pattern that is symmetrical in time and should be segmented. For example, if there is a unique route to a goal (e.g., a mountain summit), then the approach and return along that route should be grouped and seen as an event, because the entire act is predictable from the initial steps. Similarly, whenever one actor imitates another, the resulting pattern will show repetition symmetry—the path of motion of the body and limbs of the first actor will be repeated at a different location and with some temporal delay by the imitator. Because the spatial repetition allows prediction of one actor's path from another's path, this event should also be segmented at the beginning and end of imitation.

Relative Salience

The theoretical world of object segmentation involving smooth, "nice" objects can be quite different from the real world, with objects that have complex boundaries (e.g., trees with rough bark). Despite the large number of contour extrema in such objects, there is agreement on the part structure. The branches of a tree are seen as the natural parts of a tree. The contour curvature extrema at the base of the branches define the part boundaries because they are the most salient of the curvature extrema (Singh & Hoffman, 2001). To say only that the more salient extrema are most important for part segmentation does not offer much predictive power if the only way to identify salience is to determine whether or not the extrema demarcate a part. However, one might a priori hypothesize that discontinuities, as well as curvature extrema, are processed at multiple levels of scale, and that larger-scale extrema will be more salient than smaller-scale ones. Thus the larger-scale curvature extrema will have priority in determining part boundary locations.

A similar approach to event analysis with multiple levels of spatiotemporal scale would prioritize segmentation at certain spatial and temporal scales. A focus on larger/longer levels of scale in a path analysis would allow observers to segment paths in such a way that they were able to capture the overall direction of motion of an object, and thus allow prediction of future motion without the confusion of smaller-scale deviations, those associated with going around obstacles or forces irrelevant to the goal. This scale problem must be taken into account in any attempt to construct a theory of event segmentation based on object motion. It is possible that constraints imposed by the properties of episodic memory may serve to limit the role of long spatiotemporal scales changes. Furthermore, paths may be of limited value in understanding events at longer scales (see the cogent discussion in Chapter 17 of this volume about differences between objects and events). So, there may be a relatively short temporal scale at which humans attend to path shape.

EVIDENCE

Support for a geometric approach to event segmentation, and specifically segmentation based on path geometry, comes from a series of studies on segmentation of single object paths (Shipley, Maguire, & Brumberg, 2004). The basic questions underlying these studies were, are object and event segmentation related? Moreover, will similar objects and events be segmented in similar ways? To answer these questions we developed a set of 10 unfamiliar objects and events that were matched for spatial properties. Seven of these forms were 2-D closed forms selected from Singh and Hoffman (2001) in order to highlight specific predictions that those researchers made about how geometric variables should influence object segmentation. The other three forms were 2-D open forms. In the object condition these appeared as squiggly lines with various turns; in the event condition these were paths in which the agent did not return to the start location (examples are shown in Fig. 16.3).

To mathematically match object and path stimuli, we used line-drawn forms as our objects and a single point of light moving along a path that was spatially identical to each spatial form as our event. The events were 6 seconds long for closed forms and 3 seconds long for open forms. Because we used a constant velocity for the moving point, the only variations occurred along spatial dimensions; thus, the information content of the spatial and spatiotemporal displays were equated.

Half of the subjects were assigned to the object condition. After being given an example in which they were asked to segment a line drawing of a watch into smaller parts, we asked subjects to segment the spatial forms by indicating the location of any part boundaries in each of the 10 forms. The subjects in the event condition were introduced to the

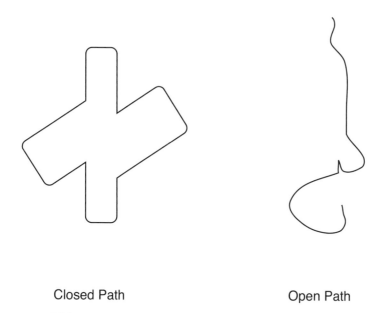

Closed Path   Open Path

FIGURE 16.3. Examples of closed and open paths used to test object and event segmentation. The closed form is similar to Figure 29(A) in Singh and Hoffman (2001).

idea of segmentation by a discussion of how the event of going to lunch could be divided into smaller events. They were then shown a video of a person performing a few tasks while walking around a room and asked to segment that video. Next, they were shown the 10 test videos. After subjects had watched each event, they indicated its boundaries by stepping through that event and indicating each event boundary.

The findings were clear. First, there was a high correlation between the spatial locations of object boundaries and event boundaries. Whatever the mechanisms underlying the segmentation in the two domains, it would appear that they share at least some formal properties; whatever stimulus features are associated with object parts, those features are also associated with event segmentation.

Curvature extrema were clearly associated with segmentation of both objects and events. In both the object and event conditions more than 50% of responses were near curvature extrema (i.e., they were within the distance moved by the dot each frame of the event video). The two conditions differed considerably in the association of segmentation and curvature minima. When only the closed forms were considered, segmentation appeared to be influenced by direction of curvature in objects, but not events. For objects, the tendency to continue in one direction, or to curve back to form a complete contour, appeared to play a role in dividing the object into parts: segmentation was associated with curvature minima, as predicted by Singh and Hoffman (2001). Overall, 72% of the segmentation responses for objects occurred at minima, and only 3% at maxima. In contrast, 36% of event segmentation responses occurred at minima and 20% at maxima.

Three specific hypotheses were tested. The first is that boundaries are more likely to occur at curvature discontinuities than points at continuous curves. To test this prediction, we compared object and event segmentation for shapes that differed only in the presence or absence of a curvature discontinuity. We found that for both objects and events, discontinuous points were more likely to be identified as event boundaries than continuous points. The second hypothesis was that increases in turning angle would be associated with increases in the probability of segmentation at that curve. Turning angle was a strong predictor of object segmentation, but only for closed forms. For events, turning angle was not predictive of boundary placement for either type of path. The third hypothesis was that part salience would be associated with segmentation, with the more salient parts more likely to be segmented from the larger whole. Part salience was predictive of segmentation for objects but not for events.

Thus, some geometric properties predicted boundary placement for events, while others did not. In particular, objects and events seem to be segmented in similar ways based on curvature extrema. However, turning angle and part salience seemed to be predictive of boundaries for closed objects and not for events. Looking at these specific predictions in simple visual displays (line drawings and a moving dot) helped us to identify some of the similarities and differences between object and event parsing. However, any useful theory of event segmentation should provide predictions of segmentation boundaries in more natural displays. To show that this approach can be extended beyond dots moving on a screen, we employed two different measures to investigate event segmentation of a person walking along a path in a field similar to the shapes used in the first experiment (although at a much slower screen speed; the average clip duration was 24.75 seconds). We found that when stepping through the movie frame by frame, 59% of all responses fell within 500 ms of the predicted locations (near curvature extrema) and 75% fell within 1 s.

Stepping frame by frame though a movie does not provide a subject with a natural flow of events, and it does not allow for online reports of event segmentation. So, we ran a second group of subjects with the widely used online reporting procedure pioneered by Newtson (1973). Subjects pressed a key whenever they felt an event boundary had been reached. Here we found that 71% of the segmentation boundaries were within 500 ms of a curvature extrema in the path of the walker. Furthermore, segmentation was relatively normally distributed around a point 190 ms after the curvature extrema. Although the curvature extrema account for much of the segmentation, variability was greater than that due simply to variation in time to press a key (standard deviation of 466). Several factors may have contributed to the spread, but the most important was probably the fact that for this analysis we included all curvature extrema, even those with a large radius of curvature.

Finally, there was greater variability in segmentation of events than objects. This is notable in light of developmental differences in cognitive processing of events and objects. While children readily attach a novel label to an object (e.g., learning the label "blick" for a kitchen item like a juicer), they struggle up through the age of 4 years to correctly label a novel verb with a novel label (i.e., learning the label "blicking" for a simple action like spinning the arms in circles). This difficulty may reflect in part the relatively low variability in object segmentation and the greater variability in event segmentation. Chapters 7 and 8 in this volume provide further discussion of this issue.

Limitations of a Geometric Approach

The primary criticism to be faced by any geometric approach is that it is a one-size-fits-all analysis, so it provides no accommodation for an observer's past experience. If segmentation is used to carve out units of predictable events, then individual experiences with any statistical regularity should also be used to segment events. So, the geometric approach may need to be supplemented with statistical learning to accurately predict segmentation.

A critical limitation of the path-based approach presented here is that it focuses on local geometric features, which can not capture interactions between two objects. Yet human understanding of events is relational in nature. Understanding an event requires a consideration of more than the actions of a single actor; it requires seeing how the actor is acting with respect to something. We know that goals and intentions are likely to predict segmentation; how might such cognitive constructs be accommodated in a geometric analysis? In human languages, verbs and propositions are relational (Gentner & Boroditsky, 2001). For example, the paths labeled by verbs represent how an object is transforming relative to another (e.g., stepping over a puddle). Even deictic verbs (e.g., ascend), which describe the path of a single object, describe a relationship—the changing relationship between the object of interest and an observer. One may conceive of the research presented in this chapter as demonstrating that subjects are sensitive to the geometry of deictic paths. This makes sense, as this geometry provides relevant, functional information about the motion of objects relative to an observer. The geometry of nondeictic paths, those determined relative to some ground object, will also provide functional information. The trick is identifying the relevant ground object for any given observer.

Thus, the future of a geometric approach to event segmentation will be devising an approach that allows for frames of reference (how an object is changing relative to another object), for geometric properties that involve multiple objects, and perhaps critically for a geometry that includes contact, which is critical for processing events that include hands.

Conclusion

The segmentation of events allows us to predict the future from the past and to represent past occurrences for future use. We may understand, in part, how segmentation is achieved by considering the motions of objects and the function of segmentation. Certain geometric properties of paths, such curvature extrema, are related to the presence of forces in an event and appear to be important for segmentation of physical events and biological events. Humans use the geometric properties of objects' paths to identify units of predictable object motion. A mature theory of events will surely be constructed from many pieces; we believe that a geometric approach to event parts offers a significant set of building blocks.

References

Baldwin, D. A., Baird, J. A., Saylor, M. M., & Clark, M. A. (2001). Infants parse dynamic action. *Child Development, 72*, 708–717.

Braine, M. D. S. (1990). The "natural logic" approach to reasoning. In W. F. Overton (Ed.), *Reasoning, necessity, and logic: Developmental perspectives* (pp. 133–157). Hillsdale, NJ: Lawrence Erlbaum.

Braine, M. D. S., Reiser, B. J., & Rumain, B. (1984). Some empirical justification for a theory of natural propositional logic. In G. H. Bower (Ed.), *The psychology of learning and motivation: Vol. 18. Advances in research and theory* (pp. 313–371). New York: Academic Press.

Brunswik, E., & Kamiya, J. (1953). Ecological cue-validity of "proximity" and of other Gestalt factors. *American Journal of Psychology, 66*, 20–32.

Clark, E. V. (2001). Emergent categories in first language acquisition. In M. Bowerman & S. C. Levinson (Eds.), *Language acquisition and conceptual development* (pp. 379–405). Cambridge: Cambridge University Press.

Engel, S. A., & Rubin, J. M. (1986). Detecting visual motion boundaries. *Proceedings of the IEEE Workshop on Motion: Representation and Analysis* (pp. 107–111). Washington, DC: IEEE Computer Society.

Frawley, W. (1992). *Linguistic semantics*. Hillsdale, NJ: Erlbaum Associates.

Gentner, D., & Boroditsky, L. (2001). Individuation, relativity, and early word learning. In M. Bowerman & S. C. Levinson (Eds.), *Language acquisition and conceptual development*. New York: Cambridge University Press.

Hoffman, D. D., & Richards, W. A. (1984). Parts of recognition. *Cognition, 18,* 65–96.

Kellman, P. J., & Shipley, T. F. (1991). A theory of visual interpolation in object perception. *Cognitive Psychology, 23,* 141–221.

Langacker, R. W. (1987). *Foundations of cognitive grammar. Vol. 1: Theoretical perspectives.* Stanford, CA: Stanford University Press.

Leslie, A. M. (1984). Spatiotemporal continuity and perception of causality in infants. *Perception, 13,* 287–305.

Mandler, J. M. (2006). Actions organize the infant's world. In K. Hirsh-Pasek & R. M. Golinkoff (Eds.), *Action meets word: How children learn verbs* (pp. 111–133). New York: Oxford University Press.

Mann, R., & Jepson, A. (2002). *Detection and classification of motion boundaries.* Eighteenth National Conference on Artificial Intelligence, American Association for Artificial Intelligence (pp. 764–769).

Mann, R., Jepson, A., & Siskind, J. M. (1997). The computational perception of scene dyntamics. *Computer Vision and Image Understanding, 65*(2), 113–128.

Markman, E. M. (1991). The whole-object, taxonomic, and mutual exclusivity assumptions as initial constraints on word meanings. In S. A. Gelman & J. P. Byrnes (Eds.), *Perspectives on language and thought: Interrelations in development* (pp. 72–106). Cambridge, England: Cambridge University Press.

Marr, D., & Vaina, L. (1982). Representation and recognition of the movements of shapes. *Proceedings of the Royal Society of London B, 214,* 501–524.

Miller, G. A. & Johnson-Laird, P. N. (1976). *Language and perception.* Cambridge, MA: The Belknap Press of Harvard University Press.

Newtson, D. (1973). Attribution and the unit of perception of ongoing behavior. *Journal of Personality and Social Psychology, 28,* 28–38.

Quine, W. V. (1996). Events and reification. In R. Castati & A. C. Varzi (Eds.), *Events* (pp. 107–116). Aldershot, England: Dartmouth. Reprinted from E. LePore & B. P. McLaughlin (Eds.) (1985), *Actions and events: Perspectives on the philosophy of Donald Davidson* (pp. 162–171). Oxford, England: Blackwell.

Rubin, J. M., & Richards, W. A. (1985). Boundaries of visual motion. *Artificial Intelligence Memo,* 835.

Scholl, B. J., & Pylyshyn, Z. W. (1999). Tracking multiple items through occlusion: Clues to visual objecthood. *Cognitive Psychology, 38,* 259–290.

Shipley, T. F., & Kellman, P. J. (2003). Boundary completion in illusory contours: Interpolation or extrapolation? *Perception, 32*(8), 985–1000.

Shipley, T. F., Maguire, M. J., & Brumberg, J. (2004). Segmentation of event paths. *Journal of Vision, 4*(8), 562.

Singh, M., & Hoffman, D. D. (2001) Parts-based representations of visual shape and implications for visual cognition. In T. F. Shipley & P. J. Kellman (Eds.), *From fragments to objects: Segmentation and grouping in vision* (pp. 401–459). Amsterdam: North-Holland.

Singh, M., Seyranian, G., & Hoffman, D. (1999). Parsing silhouettes: The shortcut rule. *Perception and Psychophysics, 61,* 636–660.

Siskind, J. M. (2001). Grounding the lexical semantics of verbs in visual perception using force dynamics and event logic. *Journal of Artificial Intelligence Research, 15,* 31–90.

Slobin, D. I. (2001). Form-function relations: How do children find out what they are? In M. Bowerman & S. C. Levinson (Eds.), *Language acquisition and conceptual development* (pp. 406–449). Cambridge: Cambridge University Press.

Slobin, D. I. (2003). Language and thought online: Cognitive consequences of linguistic relativity. In D. Gentner & S. Goldin-Meadow (Eds.), *Language in mind* (pp. 157–192). Cambridge, MA: MIT Press.

Talmy, L. (1985). Lexicalization patterns: Semantic structure in lexical forms. In T. Shopen (Ed.), *Language typology and syntactic description: Grammatical categories and the lexicon.* Cambridge: Cambridge University Press.

Talmy, L. (2000) *Towards a cognitive semantics, Vol. 1: Concept structuring systems.* Cambridge, MA: MIT Press.

Yin, C., Kellman, P. J., & Shipley, T. F. (2000). Surface integration influences depth discrimination. *Vision Research, 40,* 1969–1978.

Zacks, J. M. (2004). Using movement and intentions to understand simple events. *Cognitive Science, 28*(6), 979–1008.

Zacks, J. M., Speer, N. K., Swallow, K. M., Braver, T. S., & Reynolds, J. R. (2007). Event perception: A mind/brain perspective. *Psychological Bulletin, 133,* 273–293.

Zacks, J. M., & Tversky, B. (2001). Event structure in perception and conception. *Psychological Bulletin, 127,* 3–21.

17

The Structure of Experience

BARBARA TVERSKY, JEFFREY M. ZACKS,
& BRIDGETTE MARTIN HARD

Continuous Sensation/Discrete Mind

One way to regard the body is as a moving set of sensors, continuously
capturing light, sound, smell, touch, heat, and more from the surrounding world. Yet more sensors are inside the body, capturing information from the body's own movements and processes. Comprehending
everyday action and experience requires integrating that information
and making sense of it. Despite the fluctuating flow of information to
our senses, the impression is of a stable world. From the ever-changing
multimodal stream of information, the mind carves fixed entities, organizing and integrating sensations of light, sound, smell, and touch into
entities that are distinct from other lights, sounds, smells, and touches.
The perception is not just of separate entities but of specific objects
and organisms, each with its own shape, size, and parts. Although the
sensations are continuous and changing, the impression is discrete and
enduring. Activity, too, is discretized. Although the perception of activity is one of change over time, the change is thought of as changes—not
as constant change but as sequences of key moments.

Why the mind discretizes is a question that has answers on many levels. On the neurological level, neurons fire or don't. On the cognitive level, the continuous input is so rich and complex that much of it must be, and is, ignored; the input must be categorized to be effectively processed and understood. The categories the mind forms are not random; rather, the mind organizes information into packets that are easily recognized on the one hand and informative on the other. Such packets are useful not just for understanding what is happening but also for predicting what will happen. This case has been made forcefully for objects (Rosch, 1978; Tversky & Hemenway, 1984). As shall be seen, basic objects such as tables and dogs and violins are easy to detect by their shapes. These perceptual packets are not only readily discriminated but also readily associated with significant information about the objects—their behavior and functions. This correspondence between the appearance of things and their behaviors or functions provides a way for people to learn the information essential to organizing and planning their own behavior. It enables a working hypothesis that things that look alike behave alike and things that look different behave differently. Of course, this is a working hypothesis, a starting point, and the world presents both examples and counterexamples. Ultimately, the link between perceived features and functions or behavior renders the world more comprehensible and predictable. The link from appearance to function or behavior has been established for objects. One question raised here is whether the link holds for other important entities, notably events.

Ongoing experience is discretized in multiple ways. The perceptual world is parsed into distinct scenes, objects, and people. Interactions among people and objects are segmented into events. Discourse is decomposed into sentences, phrases, words, and sounds. As is evident from these examples, people do more than extract whole entities from ongoing experience; they go on to divide these wholes into parts. People perceive discrete objects and decompose them into discrete components (e.g., Hochberg, 1978). Similarly, people perceive discrete events and decompose them into discrete stages (e.g., Newtson, 1973; Newtson & Engquist, 1976; Zacks & Tversky, 2001; Zacks, Tversky, & Iyer, 2001). The process of partitioning is significant for many reasons: knowing the parts of a whole, how the parts are determined, how they are related, and what they do is a crucial part of understanding the whole. This analysis leads to a series of questions to be considered here:

- *Wholes:* How are wholes determined—that is, how are they distinguished from backgrounds?
- *Parts:* How are wholes partitioned into parts, and on the basis of what kind of information? Parts may be further partitioned into subparts; do the same bases for partition hold for the subparts?
- *Configuration:* How are the parts of a whole arranged?
- *Composition:* Each whole entity has a set of parts, which may be parts of other wholes as well. How does the entire set of parts get distributed to wholes?
- *Perception-to-function:* Are there relations between perception and appearance on the one hand and behavior and function on the other?

Although our central concern is the structure of events, considering the structure of other categories—specifically language, objects, and scenes—provides insights by comparison. Moreover, these categories interact in actual experience. Objects, scenes, and events are the primary categories forming the stage for human activities. They also compose central topics of language as it is used: people are usually someplace in some activity with something. Objects have served as the paradigm example of entity since antiquity (e.g., Casati & Varzi, 1996, 1999; Jacob & Jeannerod, 2003; Quine, 1985) as their many uses, including the concept "reify," attest. Objects are typically inseparable parts of events, and events invariably occur in scenes. But before we begin, a short detour into alternative ways of organizing knowledge, by parts and by kinds.

Partonomies and Taxonomies

As indicated, the focus here is event partonomies. Partonomies are hierarchies formed by "part of" relations. The human body is a prototypical example. Some of the body's parts are arms, legs, head, feet, hands, chest, and back. Hands, in turn, have parts: thumb, fingers, palm, and back. Partonomies contrast with another hierarchical organization of the world: taxonomies (see Miller & Johnson-Laird, 1976; Tversky, 1990; Tversky & Hemenway, 1984). Taxonomies are hierarchies formed by "kind of" relations. A familiar example is the animal kingdom: vertebrates and invertebrates are kinds of animals; fish, amphibians, reptiles, birds, and mammals are kinds of vertebrates. In a taxonomy the same individual is simultaneously in all the classes superordinate to it, so a robin is a bird, and also a vertebrate, an animal, and a living thing. Given that an individual belongs to so many nested categories, a question that has fascinated psychologists is how to choose the level for reference (Brown, 1958; Rosch, 1978). It turns out that one level is preferred across many contexts and tasks, perceptual, behavioral, and linguistic: the *basic level*, the level of bird and chair (Rosch, 1978). The basic level bridges perception or appearance with function or behavior, allowing inferences from one to the other; moreover, parts distinguish the basic level, linking partonomic and taxonomic organizations (Tversky & Hemenway, 1984).

Language

Wholes and Parts

We begin with language, whose structure and organization have been studied for generations. Indeed, the structure of language has served as an instructive analogy for that of bodies, scenes, and events, and vice versa. Here, we overview the features of language that have served the analogies. Language has distinctive characteristics—at the levels of frequency, phonology, and more—that allow it to be distinguished from the background of other sound. Language decomposes into parts on many levels: discourse has as parts sentences or utterances, utterances have as parts words or morphemes, morphemes have as parts sounds or phonemes. Each higher level serves as the whole for a more elementary level. The bases for segmenting into components as well as the rules of combination of components change at each level, and in fact vary with the individual language. The level of phonemes (units of sound) and the level of morphemes (units of meaning) are most relevant here.

Phonemes: Configuration, Composition, and Perceptual-Function Links

For every language, there is a small set (20 to 40) of phonemes that combine to make words (see Chapters 4 and 10 in this volume). There are strong perceptual correlates for phonemes, so much so that continuous changes in sounds are perceived to have categorical boundaries corresponding to phonemes. Phonemes are at the same time a unit of speech perception, as well as a unit of speech production. This, along with other findings, has led some to claim that the same perceptual-motor mechanisms that underlie production of speech also underlie perception of speech—that is, that we understand speech through the motor mechanisms that produce it (Liberman, Cooper, Shankweiler, & Studdert-Kennedy, 1967; Liberman & Mattingly, 1985). Every language has rules for arranging phonemes. These rules of combination do not allow certain sequences of phonemes, such as *tv* (in English), at the beginning of words, but they are free enough to allow far more combinations than any language is likely to need, even with a small alphabet. Phonemes are indeed combined in a multitude of ways, challenging poets and delighting readers. Within languages, the sequencing constraints are strong enough that there are statistical dependencies for sequences of phonemes that even infants and other new language learners rapidly pick up, providing a basis for distinguishing words (e.g., Brent, 1999; Saffran, Aslin, & Newport, 1996; Saffran, Newport, Aslin, & Tunnick, 1997).

Morphemes: Configuration, Composition, and Perceptual-Functional Links

Despite their complexity, distinguishing and configuring phonemes seems easy in contrast to distinguishing and configuring morphemes or words. The perceptual basis for distinguishing words from utterances is multifaceted and language-dependent, as anyone acquiring a new language can confirm. Discerning individual words or morphemes in spoken language relies not only on the phonemes of the particular word but also on the phonemes of the surrounding morphemes, the syntactic structure, and the semantic context. Languages have a large vocabulary of morphemes or, loosely, words, numbering in the tens of thousands. The rules of combining morphemes—the syntax—are intricate and constrained, expressed sometimes in arrangements of words and sometimes in inflective changes within words. There are statistical dependencies in arrangements of morphemes just as there are in the arrangements of phonemes (e.g., Landauer, 1998; Landauer & Dumais, 1996; Miller, 1963). We *peel* apples but not books, just as we *read* books but not apples. The statistical dependencies or redundancies at both levels, phonemes and morphemes, may facilitate comprehension as well as production. In contrast to phonemes, it is not straightforward to tie mechanisms used to distinguish morphemes with those used to produce them.

The cases of phonemes and morphemes have been revealing. Within language, the principles of segmentation, composition, and configuration vary depending on the level at which language is analyzed. Each creates large numbers of wholes, but differently. Phonemes combine to create many morphemes by using a small number of elements and loose constraints on combination. Morphemes combine to create many utterances by using a large number of elements and tight constraints on combination. Phonemes have a strong perceptual basis, tightly linked to production; not so for morphemes.

As we have seen, language is structured on many levels—on the level of sound, on the level of meaning, and on the level of discourse. These levels cooperate and interact but are not completely reducible (e.g., Clark, 1996). Language serves many human activities. One important service of language is providing a means for describing and remembering the things, places, and activities that occur in the world. We turn now to those.

Objects

Wholes: Distinguishing Objects from Backgrounds

Thinking about partonomies brings us to the first question about objects, an old one that continues to challenge researchers: how are objects partitioned from a scene—that is, how are figures distinguished from ground? More simply, what makes a good object? To answer that question, the Gestalt psychologists proposed principles for organizing perception, providing insights that continue to fascinate artists and scientists alike. Good objects are more likely to have closed, continuous, convex contours; they are also more likely to have parts with a common fate—that is, parts that move together (e.g., Hochberg, 1978; Peterson, 1994; Spelke, Gutheil, & Van der Valle, 1995). Contours, if presupposed, are nevertheless key to object integrity: contours that are continuous and closed, especially under movement, suggest that what is contained by the contour has an existence independent of the background. This is not to say that there are necessary and sufficient conditions for objecthood; there are borderline cases and cases that are ambiguous in context, and these are provocative, puzzling, and illuminating. Despite such ambiguities, many common objects can be recognized from their contours, especially at canonical orientations (e.g., Palmer, Rosch, & Chase, 1981; Rosch, 1978)

Parts: Partitioning Objects

Partitioning objects from backgrounds leads to the next question: how are objects themselves partitioned? There is more than one way to partition an object: an object can be partitioned into the stuff it's made from; it can be partitioned into its sides, front, back, top, and bottom; it can be partitioned into the pieces it breaks into when it falls. Here, we are interested in a different sense of part from any of those; we are interested in what might be called *compositional* parts or *integral* parts, the kinds of parts that people name when asked to give the parts of an object, say a body or a car. Because external, visible parts are those available to direct perception, we are not interested here in internal parts such as hearts and lungs.

The clues the Gestalt psychologists provided for distinguishing objects seem to apply to distinguishing parts of objects; what makes a good part is also what makes a good object—continuity, closure, convexity, and common fate. This suggests that the same principles that underlie discriminating objects appear to underlie discriminating parts of objects—that is, the same perceptual features that serve as clues to wholes should serve as clues to parts. Although the features that make an object good seem also to be the features that make a part of an object good, the analyses of object segmentation have come from perspectives other than Gestalt. Some analyses of object segmentation have been inspired by Attneave's (1954) observation that natural boundaries are likely to be points of large changes in information. For objects, one important change in information is relative discontinuity in contour, particularly local minima in the curvature of contours (e.g., Hoffman & Richards, 1984; Hoffman & Singh, 1997). These local minima occur at the junctures of parts—for example, where the fingers attach to the hand or where the arms and legs attach to the body. The parts picked out by these local minima in curvature are relatively closed, continuous, and convex. Good parts have a perceived independence—detachability from their wholes analogous to the detachability of objects from scenes, if not in actuality then in perception.

Compelling as this view is, it has limitations. For one thing, objects have an infinite number of contours, depending on the point of view. Some points of view are far easier to recognize than others, notably those that show the critical features of the objects (Palmer, Rosch, & Chase, 1981). Because objects are typically three-dimensional, they may have parts that do not affect the contour from certain views—for example, noses from frontal views of faces. Even so, a frontal view of a face will provide some information about the shape of the nose; that is, even a single view of an object has clues that reveal the three-dimensional structure of the object. Thus, the visual system has more to work from when parsing objects than inflection points in contours.

Another approach to object partition relies on local convergences of edges irrespective of viewing angle. As Biederman and his collaborators noted in the "recognition by components" theory of object recognition, the visual system is sensitive to a host of local properties of object contours, such as lines at various orientations, pairs of lines, vertices, convex curves, and more (Biederman, 1987; Hummel & Biederman, 1992). These and other attributes are called nonaccidental properties, as they are likely to arise from enduring features of objects rather than accidents of perspective. Groupings of such attributes activate *geons*, generalized cones that form shapes such as cylinders, blocks, wedges, and cones. Geons can take many meanings, depending on their size and their configuration in objects. A cylinder might be the leg of a person or chair or an ear of corn. A block might be a brick or a layer of a stupa. A curved cylinder might be the handle of a coffee cup or a piece of macaroni. An ovoid might be a Brancusi head or an egg.

Composition: Components of Objects

Biederman (1987) has drawn analogies between phonemes and geons. Just as phonemes are the building blocks of words, geons are the building blocks of objects. Just as there is a small set of phonemes that can be combined to form the words of a language, there also is a small set of geons that can be combined to form all objects. Just as phonemes vary depending on the neighboring phonemes, geons vary depending on the neighboring geons. For example, whether a *p* is aspirated or not depends on the neighboring phonemes. However, the particular characteristics of geons—size and shape—seem to depend more on global than local features of objects. The size and the shape of a curved cylinder seem to derive from qualities of an entire object, even its function, whether it's the spout of a teapot or the handle of a suitcase. As is the case for phonemes, there appear to be statistical dependencies among parts of objects (e.g., Rosch, 1978; Malt & Smith, 1982). Animate things that have legs also have heads with eyes and mouths; things that have feathers also have wings and beaks. Certainly the integrity, and hence recognizability, of parts (or geons) is important in object recognition. When portions of line drawings of contours of objects are deleted so that part boundaries—the nonaccidental properties—are intact, objects are more readily recognized than when the same amount of contour is deleted at part boundaries (Biederman, 1987).

From Perceptual Parts to Functional Parts

Geons are perceptually defined object parts, but geons may or may not correspond to the parts people name when asked to list parts of objects. The horizontal and vertical components of the tail of an airplane are probably two geons, but they form a single part. When asked to rate object parts for "goodness," people give high ratings to those parts that have contour distinctiveness and functional significance, such as legs of pants or tables, either for the object or for the user of the object (Tversky & Hemenway, 1984). Parts that are perceptually distinct also have different functions; people hold the handle of a knife and slice with the blade; they blow into the mouthpiece of a clarinet and open and close its holes with their fingers. The legs of a chair or a person or a pair of pants have different functions from the seat of a chair or the arms of a person or the waist of pants. In some cases, the appearances of parts give clues to their functions. For example, long, thin parts are likely to be good for reaching, and flat, horizontal ones of a certain size and height are likely to be good for putting or for sitting. The very names of parts suggest links from perception to function: *seat*, *leg*, and *handle* refer sometimes to appearance, sometimes to function, sometimes to both; on many occasions it is not clear, or doesn't even matter, whether part names refer to appearance or to function.

Connecting geons, the perceptual parts of objects, to the functional parts of objects is not straightforward and may not be feasible. Functional parts such as *handles*, *legs*, *bodies*, and *frames* have a broad range of specific forms, differing in geons. The seat of a bicycle bears little resemblance to the seat of an armchair. The leg of a chair may be close to a cylinder, but the leg of a horse and the leg of a crab are not. This points to a difference between geons and phonemes. Phonemes are at once parts of perceiving language and parts of producing language. Geons are perceptual parts but not functional ones. Moreover, the building blocks of objects may be closer to functional parts than to perceptual parts. Rabbit legs and camel legs look different, but they serve rabbits and camels in similar ways, respectively, just as bicycle seats and armchair seats look different but serve humans similarly.

Configurations of Parts

Whatever their view on the status of object parts, most approaches recognize that an object is more than just a collection of parts; the parts must be properly arranged. A pile of arms, legs, torsos, and heads is a pile of parts, not a set of bodies. Names of parts reflect the significance of configuration; many part names derive from their position in a configuration (*top, bottom, middle, side*). As for phonemes and morphemes, or morphemes and phrases, the organization of the parts of objects is critical to meaning. A highly constrained configuration of parts does not appear in all domains, as shall be discussed in the analysis of scenes.

Objects of all kinds are all around us, but they are not distributed helter-skelter. If there's a refrigerator, there's probably a sink and a stove nearby. Objects that serve related ends typically appear together in contexts, specifically in scenes.

Scenes

Wholes and Parts

The first thing to notice about scenes in contrast to objects is that they don't have shapes or clear boundaries. Scenes are the contexts for objects, the grounds from which objects are distinguished. They are also the contexts for events. Scenes typically surround us, include us. Perhaps for this reason, the problem of distinguishing a scene from its background has not occupied psychologists. The background would have to be an even larger context encompassing more than one scene. The related problem of recognizing scenes, distinguishing one scene from another, has occupied psychologists, and scene recognition is surprisingly quick, requiring less than a second of exposure, even for schematic line drawings of scenes (Biederman, 1981).

Scenes don't seem to have shapes, in contrast to objects. This being the case, how are they distinguished and recognized? What features of scenes underlie their rapid recognition? There are clues from research on scene taxonomies and partonomies (Tversky & Hemenway, 1983). In that research, one group of participants was asked to list categories of scenes and subcategories of scenes. For those scenes that were frequently mentioned, other informants listed parts of scenes and activities performed in scenes. The top-level categories were *indoors* and *outdoors*; outdoor scenes included beaches, forests, and cities; indoor scenes were schools, restaurants, and stores, each of these with subcategories. Could it be that scenes are recognized by their parts? The parts of scenes informants listed were the objects that are common in them: sand and water for beaches, desks and tables and blackboards for schools. Informants also listed activities appropriate for different scenes. Activities were the things people do in scenes: hike in forests and eat in restaurants. The features of scenes—that is, their appearance— and the activities performed in scenes—that is, their functions—are linked. For example, swimming and boating go with water and sand, writing and reading go with desks and blackboards, and eating goes with tables and dishes.

Scenes, then, are both different from and similar to objects. Gestalt features like closure or continuity, or features analogous to them, do not partition the world into scenes. Unlike objects, scenes don't have shapes; they seem to be recognized by the kinds of things they contain—the objects large and small—and not shapes.

Configuration, Composition, and Perceptual-Functional Links

For objects, the spatial arrangement of the parts is highly constrained: the legs of a chair must be under the seat, at far corners from each other; the back of the chair must be above the seat and at its edge. Similarly, the legs of a giraffe must be below its body and at far corners. The spatial arrangement of the parts of a scene is more loosely constrained, partly by gravity and the physics of the world, partly by function. For schools, desks should be on the ground, blackboards on the wall, lights on the ceiling. Desks should have chairs nearby and chalk should be near the blackboard, but the exact configuration of objects in scenes is not as constrained as, say, the configuration of the parts of a desk (e.g., Mandler & Parker, 1976). A kitchen needs a stove, refrigerator, sink, cabinets, and countertops, but the relative positions of the major appliances and the overall shape of the kitchen do not matter within a large range. Scenes have a potentially large number of parts, but they appear in a correlated fashion. Schools have desks and chairs and books and chalkboards, and supermarkets have produce and canned goods and aisles and cash registers. Thus sharp changes in information may distinguish one scene from another, but the information changes are in the objects and activities, not in anything analogous to a contour. The features that allow scenes to be recognized so quickly are not perceptual features like contour minima or geons but rather larger features, objects, which have been interpreted and assigned meanings. Like object parts, scene parts, mostly objects, have different appearances and serve different functions.

Scenes are characterized not just by the objects appearing in them but also by the activities occurring in them. In fact, the characteristic objects determine the activities. Stoves, refrigerators, countertops, and tables support cooking and eating. Desks, chairs, books, and chalkboards support teaching and learning. Just as object parts afford actions, linking perception and function, so scene parts (objects) afford actions and link perception and function.

Scenes, like objects and words, are rapidly recognized, a strong indication of their perceptual distinctiveness and significance. Scenes have characteristic parts, typically objects, but the configuration of those parts is loosely constrained. Moreover, recognition of parts does not seem to occur prior to recognition of scenes (e.g., Biederman, 1981). Although the features underlying the rapid discrimination and recognition of scenes are not yet well understood (e.g., Epstein & Kanwisher, 1998; Henderson & Hollingworth, 1999), there does appear to be a part of the cortex selective for recognizing scenes (Epstein & Kanwisher, 1998). Scenes link objects and activities; they provide the settings for objects and for human activities, with different objects and different activities associated with different scenes. We now turn to human activities, from categories existing in space to categories existing in time.

Events

Our lives are a string of events, from the mundane—for example, going to a movie—to the extraordinary (e.g., getting married). One way of looking at events is as segments of time, analogous to objects as segments of space—but this view is misleading. It is misleading first because events have a spatial status in addition to a temporal one, and objects have a temporal status—buildings are constructed, remodeled, destroyed, reconstructed—as well as a spatial status. But the view is misleading for yet another reason: objects aren't merely segments of space, they exist in space and also in time; what's more, their positions in space can change. Similarly, events aren't segments of time; they exist in time and also in space; events as types rather than specific episodes can also change their spatial–temporal positions. A wedding, a meeting, or a parade can be held in many places or times. Events contrast with activities; running is an activity, but running a race is an event. Events have been characterized as achievements or accomplishments; as such, events are associated with outcomes as well as processes. Thus, as Casati and Varzi (Chapter 2 in this volume) argue, it is appropriate to regard both objects and events as entities with internal spatiotemporal structure, not as homogenous regions. Within the structure, some parts are more central to function than others—the seat of a chair is more central than the armrests, and blowing out candles is more central to a birthday party than pouring juice.

Wholes and Parts: Distinguishing and Partitioning Events

Just as a scene can contain many objects, it can also contain many events, like a three-ring circus. Think of a busy parent preparing dinner after work, monitoring a toddler, answering the phone, setting the table, and chatting with a spouse about the events of the day. Intuition suggests that each of these events can be comprehended, and the actions associated with each distinguished, so that reaching for the phone is not usually confused with chopping the vegetables, either in enactment or in perception. Of course, these events are familiar to us; how those unfamiliar with such events would separate them awaits investigation. As will be seen, what probably allows partitioning a scene into separate, coherent events is that events are typically characterized as sets of related actions on the same object or associated objects.

Event Contours

Do events have shapes, as objects do? Or are events like scenes, without clear shapes? For objects, contour serves as a one-dimensional description, one that is powerful, if incomplete; it is the boundary between an object and the surrounding world, but for observers this boundary exists only from a particular perspective. A candidate for an analogous one-dimensional description of an event is an activity contour, the moment-to-moment change in amount of physical activity over time. By analogy, an activity contour can be regarded as the "boundary" between the activity of the event of interest and the background activity. Abrupt changes, either increases or decreases, in moment-to-moment levels of activity may signal changes in event parts, just as contour discontinuities are a clue to object parts. Why might this happen? Event segments correspond to completions of goals and subgoals (Zacks, Braver, et al., 2001). After a goal or subgoal is accomplished, such as putting on a sheet or scrambling an egg or buying a movie ticket, there might be an increase in activity in preparation for the next subgoal or goal. Or, after a large task is finished—for example, vacuuming the living room—there might be a pause, a slowing down, before another task is begun—for example, washing the clothes. Either way, there would be a dramatic change in level of activity. Seen this abstractly, events, like objects, can be partitioned at many levels and still be made of the same stuff: activity. This one-dimensional summary ignores the numerous qualitative differences that characterize events and their segments. However, the question raised here is whether there is any psychological validity to an event contour.

One common way to study parts of events is to ask observers to segment films of events, such as a person making a bed or assembling a saxophone, into parts as they watch them (e.g., Newtson, 1973; Newtson & Engquist, 1976; Hard, 2006; Hard, Tversky, & Lang, in press; Zacks, 2004; Zacks, Tversky, et al., 2001; see Chapter 15 in this volume for an overview). In many experiments, observers have been asked to segment events at two levels on separate viewings: coarse and fine. In *coarse* segmentation, they are asked to identify the largest segments that make sense, and in *fine* segmentation, the smallest. There is remarkable agreement across and within observers on locations of segment boundaries, called *breakpoints*. Knowledge about events is hierarchically organized; that is, boundaries of fine units coincide with boundaries of coarse units more often than could occur by chance (e.g., Hard, Lozano, & Tversky, 2006; Zacks, Braver, et al., 2001). Hard et al. developed a variant measure of hierarchical organization indexing the frequency with which the corresponding fine unit occurs at or before the related coarse unit; this *enclosure* measure better reflects the containment of fine units in coarse units.

Observational studies of naturally occurring behavior suggest that sharp perceptual discontinuities form the basis for identifying parts of events. In a large in vivo study aimed at capturing what ordinary people do on ordinary days, observers recorded people's behavior throughout the day in "behavior episodes." These behavior episodes corresponded to events at varying levels of granularity: eating a meal, reading a book, crossing a street. The changes from one behavioral episode to another were characterized as changes in the "sphere" of behavior—verbal to social to intellectual, for example— changes in the active part of the body, changes in the object interacted with, changes in the spatial direction, changes in the tempo, or changes in the behavioral setting or scene (Barker & Wright, 1954). These are physical changes that signal changes in the nature, especially the purpose, of the activity.

This project was observational, and the observations were insightful, but the approach was atheoretical. It did not consider the possibility that these kinds of changes may be correlated—for example, that different parts of the body may be active in different spheres and with different objects. For objects and scenes, key features are correlated. Nor did this approach distinguish different breadths or levels of events. The event of getting through a day can include making a bed, going to work, and eating in a restaurant, and eating in a restaurant includes the events of ordering, eating, and paying. The discontinuities at different levels may well differ in quantity as well as quality of activity, and evidence from several studies of a variety of events suggests that they do.

In one project directed at investigating the link between perceptual change and event boundaries, participants segmented everyday events filmed from a single camera angle several times, each time at a different level of granularity (Hard, 2006). Still frames were selected from the filmed events at 1 s intervals and filtered for contours, eliminating irrelevant factors such as ambient lighting and yielding sharpened images of people and objects on backgrounds. The pixel-to-pixel change from frame to frame was computed. Comparisons of the segment boundaries to the pixel-change measure revealed that segment boundaries corresponded to large physical changes—in fact, to local maxima. Averaging the relative pixel change over all the coarse breakpoints for all the events yielded a regular event contour: a sharp rise in pixel-to-pixel activity at each coarse breakpoint, followed by a slow decline. The pattern was the same for the finer breakpoints, but far less dramatic. Thus, the coarse event segment boundaries were physically distinctive from the other captured moments of the events. In a companion experiment, participants watched the still frames from the video in sequence, free to examine each slide as long as they liked. Looking time was longer at breakpoints, even controlling for pixel change. This finding shows that breakpoints elicit heightened attention, suggesting that they are especially informative. The finding also makes it apparent that high relative change, while characteristic of perceived event boundaries, is not the only factor contributing to their meaning.

The dramatic correlation between event boundaries and relative degree of pixel change suggests that discontinuities in activity might allow people to segment events that are novel or difficult to understand. A physical basis for segmentation would allow observers to bootstrap the perceptual information to segment novel events into parts to start making sense of them. Another project has addressed that process. That project required segmenting films of abstract events in which geometric figures moved in ways that were difficult to comprehend on first viewing but became meaningful after repeated viewings (Hard, Tversky, & Lang, in press). One video was based on the well-known film of Heider and Simmel (1944) in which a large geometric figure is perceived to bully and chase two smaller ones who taunt the larger one; another was based on hide-and-seek. Observers segmented the videos at both coarse and fine levels. Observers' verbal descriptions of what happened in each segment indicated that these interpretations were not evident on first viewing. However, after viewing the animations five times and writing a narrative describing them, most observers were able to interpret the actions as a related sequence of intentional actions.

In spite of the differences in interpretation, observers both familiar and unfamiliar with the animations segmented the events the same way, suggesting that movement change rather than comprehension was the basis for segmentation. To ascertain whether event boundaries corresponded to changes in physical activity, the videos were coded by type of movement rather than measuring pixel-to-pixel change. The movements coded were when the geometric figures stopped, started, turned, and so on. As before, though with a different measure, the quantity of movement changes distinguished breakpoints. Analogous to line junctures and line angles in objects, the nervous system seems tuned to such changes in motion: stops, starts, changes in direction, changes in velocity, etc. Coarse segment boundaries were associated with more changes in movement, as for the previously discussed work on human events. This makes sense; completing a relatively large goal should be associated with greater change in activity than completing a subgoal.

A third project, using yet different stimuli and different measures, also showed correspondences between degree of physical change and event segment boundaries. This project compared moment-to-moment movement of objects and event segmentation quantitatively (Zacks, 2004). Participants viewed movies of simple abstract animations in which the movements of two geometric objects were determined either by two people playing a video game or by a stochastic algorithm. As they watched, participants segmented the movies into fine or coarse segments. The two-dimensional trajectories were analyzed to provide a detailed quantitative characterization of the object's movement, including the velocity and acceleration of each object, the distance between the objects, and their relative velocity and acceleration. Features of the objects' movements were associated with observers' segmentation in all conditions. The most predictive features were discontinuities: local minima in the distance between the objects and points of high acceleration. Thus, three projects using different stimuli and different measures provide support for the claim that activity contours are correlated with event boundaries, and that segment boundaries tend to occur when there are sharp changes in amount of activity. Event contours bear some analogies to object contours.

Conceptual Influences on Event Segmentation

As we have seen, there is compelling evidence for a bottom-up, perceptual basis for event segmentation, though it is by no means a complete account. The fact that events can be segmented fairly well on the basis of the perceptual input alone simplifies the task of understanding complex human activities. The correspondences between changes in physical activity and event boundaries, impressive as they are, are nevertheless insufficient for identifying events or for understanding them. Top-down knowledge of goals and causes also influences event segmentation. These influences are apparent even in unfamiliar, abstract events that are difficult to interpret, such as those studied by Hard, Tversky, and Lang (in press) and by Zacks (2004). Those movies can be interpreted as actions of agents relative to each other and to the environment, but such interpretations must be achieved without the rich set of cues available in real-life behavior. In them, the geometric figures are without faces, bodies, or limbs, and the context is minimal. These studies also suggest that social interactions and intentional states are important for partitioning events. In the project just described, showing relations between motion change and event segmentation, participants commonly reported looking for the achievement of goals in order to decide when to segment activity (Zacks, 2004). One experiment provided a focused look at how the segmentation of random movements is influenced by observers' beliefs about the intentionality of the activity (Zacks, 2004, Experiment 3). One group of observers was told that the activity was generated randomly, but the other group was told that the activity was generated by humans trying to achieve goals. For the group who thought the activity was randomly generated, the movements of individual objects were the best predictors of event segmentation, particularly moments of high acceleration. For the group who thought the activity was intentional, the distance between objects was the single best predictor of segmentation. This suggests that when people believe activity is intentional, they are sensitive to features of the activity that are relevant to the intentions of the actors—in this case, configural movement features that capture the objects' interactions. Similarly, in Hard et al.'s (in press) study, participants segmented abstract events by relying on the same discontinuities that predict changes in goals and intentions for people, such as initiations of movement, reorientations, and contact with objects. In this case, when the events had been viewed five times as opposed to one, intentional descriptions of the actions increased from 45% to 75%.

A final piece of evidence (Schwan & Garsoffky, 2004) that event breakpoints correspond to discontinuities in physical or conceptual information comes from a manipulation analogous to eliminating contour information at part (geon) junctures or between part junctures

(Biederman, 1987). In Biederman's studies, recognition of objects declined when part junctures were eliminated. Schwan and Garsoffky (2004) tested memory for filmed events that had deletions at event boundaries or deletions between event boundaries. Later memory of the events was poorer when frames were deleted at event boundaries than between event boundaries—more evidence that event boundaries are especially informative.

Together, these projects highlight an important fact about the relationship between physical change and conceptual interpretations: they often are correlated, and so have discontinuities in the same places (Zacks & Tversky, 2001). In other words, when one goal is completed and another initiated, there is a change of activity.

Events by Feet and Events by Hands

The schematic films discussed so far were of motion paths of geometric figures, interpreted as agents moving around in environments. Thus they can be viewed as "events by feet," in contrast to events that can be viewed as "events by hands," such as making a bed or doing the dishes (Tversky, Zacks, & Lee, 2004). The actions that make up events by feet are relatively simple; they consist of whole-body movements and can be summarized by a moving dot or a stationary line. A paradigmatic example is the route taken from home to work. Thinking of events by feet as cumulative paths inspires comparisons of event paths to object contours (Shipley, Maguire, & Brumberg, 2004). Here the analogy from object contours is to the actual path inscribed by the event, not to the more abstract degree of activity. Inflection points in both would presumably underlie segmentation. However, a naked path is not the same kind of summary of an event by feet as a contour is of an object. The line inscribing the outline of an object is closed, summarizing a three-dimensional form, in the best case, of a canonical view (e.g., Palmer, Rosch, & Chase, 1981). The line inscribing the path of an agent is an abstraction of a path of motion, not an entity in and of itself. On a finer level, the meaning of changes in line direction, or inflection points, is different for object contours than for event paths. For objects, the changes in contour reflect the internal structure of the object, its inherent parts. For events, the changes in path are a consequence of the intentions of the agent in an environment, for example, to approach or avoid or accompany other agents or features of the environment. Without clues as to the external terrain, a path can not be interpreted (Gelman, Durgin, & Kaufman, 1995). Thus, an object contour can be understood on its own, but an event path can not. The differences between object contours and abstractions of motion paths are revealed in studies by Shipley and colleagues (2004) in which segmentation of the two types of stimuli differed.

Event Contours and Object Contours

This difference between lines that inscribe event paths and object contours illustrates a fundamental difference between objects and events. Actions that are parts of events typically occur with respect to something else, usually an object; that is, of necessity they involve not just an action but also an object that is acted on or with respect to. For paths, actions occur with respect to objects in the external environment—for example, turning at landmarks or chasing another agent. Studies of events by hands will draw out this point further. The actions that compose events performed prototypically by hands are far more complex than those performed by feet, entailing intricate interactions with objects and object parts rather than simple turns.

As we have seen, event contours, whether conceived concretely as paths of motion or more abstractly as activity contours, bear analogies to object contours. Sharp changes of contour signal new parts for both. However, there is a yet another critical disanalogy between object and event contours: objects can normally be recognized by their contours—that is, when the view is canonical and recognition occurs at the basic level, for example, the identification of or differentiation between chairs, giraffes, and trees (Palmer et al., 1981; Rosch, Mervis, Gray, Johnson, & Boyes-Braem, 1976). Events such as going to the store or making a bed, by contrast, can not be identified or recognized by either their path contours or their activity contours. Research suggests that recognition of everyday events depends on articulated actions on objects in scenes.

Action–Object Couplets as Event Parts

Earlier, we described research showing that event segments selected by observers correlate with points of relatively large changes in overall activity. However, event parts marked by activity changes are not in themselves meaningful event segments. Descriptions of event segments while segmenting reveal that there is more to segmenting events than quantitative changes in action. For these studies, common basic-level events were chosen (e.g., Hemeren, 1996; Morris & Murphy, 1990; Rifkin, 1985). In one project, observers segmented basic-level events such as making a bed or assembling a saxophone at both coarse and fine levels (Zacks, Braver, et al., 2001). Some observers described what happened in each segment as they segmented. As before, there was considerable agreement across observers in event boundaries, event levels, and event descriptions. The descriptions were illuminating. More than 95% of the descriptions were actions on objects: "he spread the sheet," "she attached the mouthpiece." In effect, the descriptions were of achievements of subgoals. The descriptions also distinguished coarse and fine levels. The changes from one coarse segment to another were primarily changes in objects: the bottom sheet, the top sheet, the pillowcases. In contrast, the changes from one fine segment to another were primarily changes in actions on the same object: "he spread the bottom sheet," "he tucked in one corner," "he tucked in another corner," "he smoothed the sheet." These play-by-play descriptions of ongoing action also correspond to event descriptions produced from memory of the films (Zacks, Braver, et al., 2001) as well as to descriptions of generic events such as going to a restaurant or visiting a doctor (Bower, Black, & Turner, 1979).

This evidence reveals that events are understood as action–object couplets. The entire set of action verbs used in the descriptions of four very different events was not large; that is, the same verbs were used in many different contexts (Zacks, Braver, et al., 2001). Common verbs include *putting, taking, lifting, inserting, pushing, pulling,* and *spreading*. These action verbs do not describe components of events the way nouns alone can describe components of objects and entire objects. Verbs are relational terms (e.g., Gentner, 1981; see also Chapters 7 and 8 in this volume); a list of action verbs alone is difficult to understand. Consider, for example, the following list: *take, spread, fold, put*. Without knowledge of the objects being acted on, we can not know if this is about baking a cake or putting away the laundry (in Chapter 8 of this volume, Maguire and Dove argue that this is why verbs are harder to learn than nouns, as Gentner argued earlier). Folding flour into a batter and folding a sheet, or spreading icing on a cake and spreading a sheet on a bed, are achieved with very different movements of the body, as well as different auxiliary objects. Indeed, the very movements depend on the object. Events are not simply partitioned into movements, they are partitioned into action–object couplets (this observation provides support for the contention of Casati and Varzi in Chapter 2 of this volume that objects play a special role in determining the structure of events, whereas events may determine objects only in a weaker sense). Neither movements nor objects alone suffice as parts of events. This fact means that event parts differ in a fundamental way from object parts. Event parts include two ontologically different categories: movements on the one hand and objects on the other.

Perception-to-Function Hypothesis

Just as for objects, for events perception is connected to function through parts. Parts of events are typically actions on objects—that is, they include perceptually identifiable behaviors as well as perceptually identifiable objects. At nearly every stage there is an accomplishment, a goal, a function. That is how events and event parts are understood—as a sequence of accomplishments. For unfamiliar events, this may be effortful. The work on unfamiliar events suggests that with repeated exposure, the actions that are first perceived as movements come to be perceived and comprehended in terms of goals—in other words, functions (Hard et al., in press).

How might event segmentation support understanding? Segmenting reduces the amount of information into manageable chunks. Segmenting appears to occur naturally, even under passive viewing of everyday events (Zacks, Braver, et al., 2001). The perception-to-function hypothesis proposes that a large change in activity signals that something important has happened. Increased inspection of what happened in the segment reveals clues as to the nature of what has happened. The illuminating clues are actions on objects. With increasing familiarity, actions on objects come to be understood as completions of goals or subgoals. The bootstrapping from large perceptual changes to functional understanding in events parallels processes linking part structure to part function in objects (Tversky, 1989). This reasoning can be extended to scenes as well, where the parts are objects, and the objects present give clues to the likely behaviors and functions.

Composition of Event Parts

Are action–object couplets like the phonemes of the sound system of language or like the morphemes of the meaning system of language? In other words, is there a small number of them that are used in many combinations to form different events, as phonemes combine to yield an abundance of words? Or is there a large number that are used in correlated fashion as words combine to utterances? The idea that events consist of parts that have internal coherence and can be excised and reassembled in different temporal configurations is appealing. It has been proposed and has received some support through cartoons (Avrahami & Kareev, 1994; see Chapter 4 in this volume) and primate behaviors (Byrne, 2002). Classical ballet is to some extent composed that way: a sequence of steps that have names and are used and reused to create many different dances. But for typical events that fill human lives, it appears that there is a large vocabulary of action–object couplets and that there are strong correlations between the parts that co-occur. Making a bed involves a different set of actions, objects, and object–action couplets than going to a restaurant or seeing a doctor. Mixing and matching the parts won't create sensible events. Actions and objects constrain each other; not every action can be applied to every object. Actions constrain the objects they can be applied to; eating a meal entails a different set of objects than making a bed or assembling a saxophone. Conversely, different objects afford different actions; balls and Frisbees can be tossed, bananas and bread can be sliced, milk and wine can be poured. Object–action couplets co-occur in events. On this analysis, events appear to be more like scenes than like objects or language. Both have a large set of components that aren't mixed and matched but, rather, appear in a correlated fashion (see also Chapter 4 in this volume). Scenes like schools have a different set of parts—objects and activities—than beaches, and beaches than movie theaters.

At a higher level, events can be arranged and rearranged to some extent. The bed can be made before or after fixing breakfast (or not at all). These events, along with many others, constitute the larger event of living a day. This is not meant to imply that making a bed and eating breakfast are necessary parts of living a day, just that they are typical ones. Even so, the events of making a bed and eating breakfast tend to occur at the beginning of a day, so their position is somewhat constrained, much as the positions of chairs and desks are constrained in a classroom. At the basic level of making the bed or eating breakfast, there appear to be a multitude of event parts, and these tend to occur in a correlated fashion; tucking in sheets and fluffing pillows go with the bed, and making toast and brewing coffee go with the breakfast.

Just as object parts have a spatial structure—the parts of the body have a specific spatial arrangement—so event parts have a temporal structure. They also have a spatial structure. In making a bed, the bottom sheet goes on before the top one. The temporal and spatial configurations of many events, however, are flexible. At a birthday party, the games can come before or after the cake and ice cream. Grocery shopping can be done in any order, though some are more efficient than others.

Seen this way—the way observers see it—the set of event parts seems more like the set of morphemes than the set of phonemes. There is a large and open class of events and event parts. Parts are correlated within events; ice cream and cake go with the birthday party, and sheets and pillowcases with making the bed; they co-occur just as the morphemes used to describe those events co-occur.

Returning to the Questions

Returning to the opening questions, what can be said about the structure of events? Events have two structural bases: one at the raw level of changes in amount of activity, the other at the level of understanding; one bottom-up, one top-down. Observers' segmentation of events corresponds to sharp changes in level of activity, suggesting that either people are using changes in activity for segmentation or that the features they are using correlate with changes in activity. For unfamiliar events, descriptions of what occurs in event segments are in terms of movement, but as events become familiar they are described in terms of accomplishments of goals and subgoals. Events are distinguished from activities by achievements or accomplishments. Events can be conceived of at many levels: a lifetime can be a single event, but so can eating a meal or folding a shirt. What distinguish events from backgrounds are their accomplishments or achievements. Similarly, accomplishments or achievements partition entire events into segments and subsegments. The parts of events have both temporal and spatial configurations, but in many cases those configurations are flexible and can be rearranged. The number of event parts is enormous in contrast to the number of phonemes, yet, rather than being combined and recombined like phonemes, event parts tend to co-occur. Finally, the parts of events (when viewed as action–object couplets), like the parts of objects, connect perception and appearance on the one hand and behavior and function on the other.

Pulling It Together

The world provides a multitude of sensations from which the mind delineates a multitude of experiences. Life is experienced as a series of events, events that ordinarily involve objects in places and which are facilitated by language. To reduce the overwhelming inundation of information, to make sense of it, and to predict and prepare for what will happen next, the mind segments, groups, and categorizes. The mind structures each of these domains critical to existence—language, objects, events, and scenes. They are experienced as meaningful, organized, and related wholes and parts, distinct from backgrounds. The comparisons of the structures across domains have been instructive.

The focus here has been events—not monumental events such as the French Revolution but events that involve one person and one place, events short enough to be studied in real time in the laboratory. These typify the events that fill the day, the events that people readily enact and comprehend even though they weren't born with those skills or that knowledge. Events are about action—not simple action but action that ends in accomplishment or achievement. The sheer amount of activity ebbs and flows as the events progress; the ebbs and flows correlate with the parsing of events into segments. The segment boundaries also coincide with achievements and accomplishments of goals. Objects, chunks in space, are the closest analogue to events, which are chunks in time and space. For objects, contours are distinctive and informative, so much so that many can be recognized as silhouettes (e.g., Rosch et al., 1976). Discontinuities in object contours correlate and seem to serve as a signal to parse object parts. The ebbs and flows of activity in events form one-dimensional contours that bear analogies and disanalogies to object contours. As for objects, the partition boundaries fall at points of change. The analogy extends in that the separate parts of objects and events are both salient in perception and serve as clues to behavior or function. These links from the perceptually salient to the functionally significant promote understanding of new events. But the contour analogy fails at an essential point: objects can be recognized by spatial contour, but events can not be recognized by activity contour. For events, higher-level qualitative information, namely actions on objects, is needed for recognition.

Partitioning the "blooming, buzzing confusion" the world presents is the first step to comprehending it. Some partitioning is so instantaneous and automatic that perception of the world is not of multimedia mixtures of continuously changing sensations but rather of coherent objects, events, and scenes. The mind goes on to parse those elements and to look for structure among the parts. Typically there is a perceptual basis for part structure. Truly understanding each of these elements of our lives requires assigning meaning to their parts. Simply chopping up the flow of experience into chunks does not, by itself, allow comprehension of the world or action in it. However, in the world, the parts of objects, of scenes, of language, and of events covary with the functions of those things. According to the perception-to-function hypothesis, the perceptual identification of parts allows bootstrapping to meaning. What is remarkable about the segmentation of activity into events, then, is that the discovery of parts in perception provides links to their significance in conception.

Acknowledgments

The authors are indebted to Tim Shipley for his insightful comments and discussion and for catching some, but undoubtedly not all, misstatements. B. T. wishes to express her appreciation to the Russell Sage Foundation for a congenial and scholarly atmosphere for thought and work. We are grateful to Irv Biederman, Jerry Fodor, and Norma Graham for illuminating conversations, and to the thinking of Roberto Casati and Achille Varzi, and we offer apologies for any misconceptions, omissions, and other distortions. Portions of this work were supported by grants NIH R01-MH70674 and NSF BCS-0236651 to J. Z. and NSF REC-0440103 to B. T.

References

Attneave, F. (1954). Some informational aspects of visual perception. *Psychological Review, 61*, 183–193.
Avrahami, J., & Kareev, Y. (1994). The emergence of events. *Cognition, 53*, 239–261.

Barker, R. G., & Wright, H. F. (1954). *Midwest and its children: The psychological ecology of an American town*. Evanston, IL: Row, Peterson and Company.

Biederman, I. (1981). On the semantics of a glance at a scene. In M. Kubovy & J. R. Pomerantz (Eds.), *Perceptual organization* (pp. 213–252). Hillsdale, NJ: Erlbaum.

Biederman, I. (1987). Recognition-by-components: A theory of human image understanding. *Psychological Review, 94*, 115–117.

Bower, G. H., Black, J. B., & Turner, T. J. (1979). Scripts in memory for text. *Cognitive Psychology, 11*, 177–220.

Brent, M. R. (1999). An efficient, probabilistically sound algorithm for segmentation and word discovery. *Machine Learning, 34*, 71–105.

Brown, R. (1958). How shall a thing be called? *Psychological Review, 65*, 14–21.

Byrne, R. (2002). Seeing actions as hierarchically organized structures: Great ape manual skills. In A. Meltzoff & W. Prinz (Eds.), *The imitative mind: Development, evolution and brain bases* (pp. 122–130). Cambridge: Cambridge University Press.

Casati, R., & Varzi, A. C. (1996). *Events*. Aldershot, England; Brookfield, VT: Dartmouth.

Casati, R., & Varzi, A. C. (1999). *Parts and places: The structures of spatial representation*. Cambridge, MA: MIT Press.

Clark, H. H. (1996). *Using language*. Cambridge: Cambridge University Press.

Epstein, R., & Kanwisher, N. (1998) A cortical representation of the local visual environment. *Nature, 392*, 599–601.

Gelman, R., Durgin, F., & Kaufman, L. (1995). Distinguishing between animates and inanimates: Not by motion alone. In D. Sperber, D. Premack, & A. J. Premack (Eds.), *Causal cognition: A multidisciplinary debate* (pp. 150–184). Oxford: Clarendon Press.

Gentner, D. (1981). Some interesting differences between verbs and nouns. *Cognition and Brain Theory, 4*, 161–178.

Hard, B. M. (2006). Reading the language of action: Hierarchical encoding of observed behavior. Ph.D. Dissertation. Palo Alto, CA: Stanford University.

Hard, B. M., Lozano, S. C., & Tversky, B. (2006). Hierarchical encoding: Translating perception into action. *Journal of Experimental Psychology: General, 135*, 588–608.

Hard, B. M., Tversky, B., & Lang, D. (in press). Making sense of abstract events: Building event schemas. *Memory and Cognition*.

Heider, F., & Simmel, M. (1944). An experimental study of apparent behavior. *American Journal of Psychology, 57*, 243–259.

Hemeren, P. E. (1996). Frequency, ordinal position and semantic distance as measures of cross-cultural stability and hierarchies for action verbs. *Acta Psychologica, 91*, 39–66.

Henderson, J. M., & Hollingworth, A. (1999). High-level scene perception. *Annual Review of Psychology, 50*, 243–271.

Hochberg, J. (1978). *Perception*. Englewood Cliffs, NJ: Prentice-Hall.

Hoffman, D. D., & Richards, W. A. (1984). Parts of recognition. *Cognition, 18*, 65–96.

Hoffman, D. D., & Singh, M. (1997) Salience of visual parts. *Cognition, 63,* 29–78.

Hummel, J. E., & Biederman, I. (1992). Binding in a neural network for shape recogniton. *Psychological Review, 99,* 480–517.

Jacob, P., & Jeannerod, M. (2003). *Ways of seeing: The scope and limits of visual cognition.* Oxford: Oxford University Press.

Landauer, T. K. (1998). Learning and representing verbal meaning: The latent semantic analysis theory. *Current Directions in Psychological Science, 7,* 161–164.

Landauer, T. K., & Dumais, S. T. (1997). A solution to Plato's problem: The latent semantic analysis theory of acquisition, induction, and representation of knowledge. *Psychological Review, 104,* 211–240.

Liberman, A. M., Cooper, F. S., Shankweiler, D. P., & Studdert-Kennedy, M. (1967). Perception of the speech code. *Psychological Review, 74,* 431–461.

Liberman, A. M., & Mattingly, I. G. (1985). The motor theory of speech perception revised. *Cognition, 21,* 1–36.

Malt, B. C., & Smith, E. E. (1982). The role of familiarity in determining typicality. *Memory & Cognition, 10,* 69–75.

Mandler, J. M., & Parker, R. E. (1976) Memory for descriptive and spatial information in complex pictures. *Journal of Experimental Psychology: Human Learning and Memory, 2,* 38–48.

Miller, G. A. (1963). *Language and communication.* New York: McGraw-Hill.

Miller, G. A., & Johnson-Laird, P. N. (1976). *Language and perception.* Cambridge, MA: Harvard University Press.

Morris, M. W., & Murphy, G. L. (1990). Converging operations on a basic level in event taxonomies. *Memory & Cognition, 18,* 407–418.

Newtson, D. (1973). Attribution and the unit of perception of ongoing behavior. *Journal of Personality and Social Psychology, 28,* 28–38.

Newtson, D., & Engquist, G. (1976). The perceptual organization of ongoing behavior. *Journal of Experimental Social Psychology, 12,* 436–450.

Palmer, S., Rosch, E. & Chase, P. (1981). Canonical perspective and the perception of objects. In J. B. Long & A. D. Baddeley (Eds.), *Attention and performance, IX.* Hillsdale, NJ: Erlbaum.

Peterson, M. A. (1994). Shape recognition can and does occur before figure-ground organization. *Current Directions in Psychological Science, 3,* 105–111.

Quine, W. V. (1985/1996). Events and reification. In R. Casati & A. C. Varzi (Eds.), *Events* (pp. 107–116). Aldershot, England: Dartmouth. Reprinted from E. LePore & B. P. McLaughlin (Eds.), *Actions and events: Perspectives on the philosophy of Donald Davidson* (pp. 162–171). Oxford: Blackwell.

Rifkin, A. (1985). Evidence for a basic level in event taxonomies. *Memory & Cognition, 13,* 538–556.

Rosch, E. (1978). Principles of categorization. In E. Rosch & B. Lloyd (Eds.), *Cognition and categorization* (pp. 27–48). Hillsdale, NJ: Lawrence Erlbaum Associates.

Rosch, E., Mervis, C. B., Gray, W., Johnson, D., & Boyes-Braem, P. (1976). Basic objects in natural categories. *Cognitive Psychology, 8,* 382–439.

Saffran, J. R., Aslin, R. N., & Newport, E. L. (1996). Statistical learning by 8-month-old infants. *Science, 274*, 1926–1928.

Saffran, J. R., Newport, E. L., Aslin, R. N., Tunick, R. A., & Barrueco, S. (1997). Incidental language learning: Listening (and learning) out of the corner of your ear. *Psychological Science, 8*, 101–105.

Schwan, S., & Garsoffky, B. (2004). The cognitive representation of filmic event summaries. Applied Cognitive Psychology, 18, 37–55.

Shipley, T. F., Maguire, M. J., & Brumberg, J. (2004). Segmentation of event paths. *Journal of Vision, 4*, 562.

Spelke, E. S., Gutheil, G., & Van der Valle, G. (1995). The development of object perception. In D. Osherson (Ed.), *An invitation to cognitive science,* Vol. 2 (pp. 297–330). Cambridge, MA: MIT Press.

Tversky, B. (1989). Parts, partonomies, and taxonomies. *Developmental Psychology, 25*, 983–995.

Tversky, B. (1990). Where partonomies and taxonomies meet. In S. L. Tsohatzidis (Ed.), *Meanings and prototypes: Studies in linguistic categorization* (pp. 334–344). London: Routledge.

Tversky, B., & Hemenway, K. (1983). Categories of scenes. *Cognitive Psychology, 15*, 121–149.

Tversky, B., & Hemenway, K. (1984). Objects, parts, and categories. *Journal of Experimental Psychology: General, 113*, 169–193.

Tversky, B., Zacks, J. M., & Lee, P. (2004). Events by hand and feet. *Spatial Cognition and Computation, 4*, 5–14.

Zacks, J. M. (2004). Using movement and intentions to understand simple events. *Cognitive Science, 28*, 979–1008.

Zacks, J. M., Braver, T. S., Sheridan, M. A., Donaldson, D. I., Snyder, A. Z., Ollinger, J. M., et al. (2001). Human brain activity time-locked to perceptual event boundaries. *Nature Neuroscience, 4*, 651–655.

Zacks, J. M., & Tversky, B. (2001). Event structure in perception and conception. *Psychological Bulletin, 127*, 3–21.

Zacks, J., Tversky, B., & Iyer, G. (2001). Perceiving, remembering, and communicating structure in events. *Journal of Experimental Psychology: General, 130*, 29–58.

Part IV
Representing and Remembering
Events

Part IV

Representing and Remembering Events: Overview

In the previous section we read much evidence that perception encodes experience to some extent in discrete quanta—events—and that these function as basic units of conscious experience. However, the quanta picked out as perceptual events also are good candidates for basic units of cognition about activity that is not directly available to perception, as noted by Schwan and Garsoffky in Chapter 15. But how are these units stored in the mind/brain? What is their representational format? The chapters in this section address this question from the point of view of perception, attention, judgment, and memory. The first two chapters extend the previous section's concerns with perception, addressing representational issues in the context of perception. Chellappa, Cuntoor, Joo, Subrahmanian, and Turaga in Chapter 18 review artificial intelligence approaches to several aspects of event perception, including recognition of events and segmentation. To build a working model that solves one of these perceptual problems requires being explicit about representational format in a way that much psychological theorizing does not. One important conclusion of their review is that event representations likely capture a lot of raw statistical information about the co-occurrence of components of events, which allows for the abstraction of relevant patterns. However, for many problems this statistical information by itself is insufficient to support abstractions that work.

Thus, one needs to bring to bear knowledge about the specific structure of the domain of activity, including how entities interact causally. In Chapter 19, Levin and Saylor argue from perceptual studies that event representations are necessarily selective. Attention samples the sensory world more heavily at some times than others; these times are boundaries between events, and are overrepresented in event representations. Attention also samples different sorts of information at different times. Attentional sampling does not just passively reflect the structure of the world. Instead, it has its own intrinsic dynamics that may in part determine the lower bound on the duration of the units we can experience as perceptual events.

So, event representations are abstracted and selective. What sorts of information are retained by the operations of abstraction and selection? Information about causes and effects, for one. Representing causal structure allows an organism to reason and make judgments about events, to predict outcomes and adapt behavior accordingly. Chapter 20, by Wolff, focuses on the representation of causal structure in events. The chapter presents a theory of the representation of causal structure. According to the theory, concepts of cause are grounded in the physical configuration of forces in an event. As the chapter reviews, this representational claim is supported by analyses of the structure of language and by observers' judgments about causes in perceptual events.

Representational issues are crucial not only for reasoning about events but also for remembering the events of our lives. Chapter 21, by Williams, Conway, and Baddeley, asks about the representational format of the events that make up one's autobiographical memory. Consistent with the attentional theory proposed by Levin and Saylor, autobiographical memories do not distribute different sorts of information evenly across the representation of an event. Instead, representations of the beginnings and endings of events capture different sorts of qualities: beginnings tend to represent actions, and endings tend to represent facts. This asymmetry is tied to the asymmetry of the passage of time and has implications for how people retrieve information about their lives and use it to reason.

Autobiographical memory is concerned with particular events that occurred in one's life. People also have knowledge about events in general and how they typically transpire. This semantic knowledge contributes to the formation and recall of episodic autobiographical memories, and also is very important for reasoning and prediction. The final two chapters in this section address the structure of semantic knowledge about events and its neural basis. In Chapter 22, Krueger and Grafman argue that the prefrontal cortex is specialized for storing semantic knowledge about events. This knowledge is represented in the form of structured event complexes, which capture information about the sequential and hierarchical organization of activity in time. Structured event complexes vary on several dimensions, including the frequency of the event type, its emotional tone, and time scale. Prefrontal cortex and other brain areas may spatially distribute semantic event knowledge based on these qualities. In the final chapter, Sitnikova, Holcomb, and Kuperberg focus on two particular aspects of event semantic knowledge, which echo one of the distinctions proposed by Chellappa et al. One aspect is associative knowledge, which is basically statistical in nature. The other aspect is principles-based, which reflects the role of causes and constraints on possible event sequences. The use of these two types of information in event perception gives rise to different patterns of brain activity, as indexed by electroencephalography.

So, the results of perception are representations of events that are abstracted and selective, transmuting sensory data into conceptual information. The dimensions that are abstracted inform our knowledge about events in general, and this constrains our memories of particular events in our lives.

Section 1
Representing Events

18

Computational Vision Approaches for Event Modeling

RAMA CHELLAPPA, NARESH P. CUNTOOR,
SEONG-WOOK JOO, V. S. SUBRAHMANIAN,
& PAVAN TURAGA

Given raw video, our objective is to discern events from motion patterns so that activities can be represented as a sequence of events. The emphasis is on developing computationally efficient ways of detecting events that conform to common human experience.

Event modeling systems provide a semantic interpretation of sequences of pixels that are captured by a video camera. The design of a practical system has to take into account the following three main factors: low-level preprocessing limitations, computational and storage complexity of the event model, and user interaction. In the past decade, low-level preprocessing algorithms for detecting foreground and moving objects, extracting motion trajectories, computing optical flow, and so forth have made significant strides. They continue to be challenged, however, by problems arising from insufficient or changing illumination, low contrast between foreground and background objects, and imperfect tracking. It is therefore necessary to develop robust event models that can incorporate these uncertainties. As the low-level algorithms continue to improve, the uncertainties can be reduced, though not completely eliminated.

Arguably, computational efficiency of the event model is the weakest link in the proverbial chain. The model has to be a realistic reflection of the data. At the same time, algorithms should be able to compute parameters of the model quickly and efficiently. It is no surprise that the hidden Markov model (HMM) and its variants have been widely used to model both speech and video signals. Computational efficiency of the Baum-Welch and the Viterbi algorithms has been a leading reason for the popularity of the HMM.

Since the objective is to detect events in video sequences that are meaningful to humans, one might want to provide space in the design loop for a user who can specify events of interest. We explore this line of thought using semantic approaches that not only use features extracted from raw video streams but also incorporate metadata and ontologies of activities. Creating a set of events defined by a user and specifying ontologies allows us to incorporate domain knowledge more readily.

We present three approaches for applications such as event recognition: anomaly detection, temporal segmentation, and ontology evaluation. The three approaches discussed are statistical methods based on HMMs, formal grammars, and ontologies. We illustrate the effectiveness of these approaches using video sequences captured both indoors and outdoors: the indoor UCF human action dataset (Rao, Yilmaz, & Shah, 2003), the TSA airport tarmac surveillance dataset (Vaswani, Roy-Chowdhury, & Chellappa, 2003), and the bank monitoring dataset (Vu, Bremond, & Thonnat, 2002).

Over the past 10 years several approaches have been proposed for modeling events. We provide a brief review of related work in event modeling and recognition involving humans and vehicles.

Literature Review

Artificial Intelligence Approaches

One of the earliest works on action recognition comes from the field of artificial intelligence (AI), where Tsuji, Morizono, and Kuroda (1977) used simple cartoon films for representation. Neumann and Novak (1983) proposed a hierarchical representation of event models. At each level, a template of a verb of locomotion is matched to the observed data. Sandewall and Ronnquist (1986) described an action structure that is partially ordered in time, where actions are defined by preconditions, postconditions, and prevailing conditions. Vu et al. (2002) defined a description of activity consisting of actors, logical predicates, and temporal relations between sub-events. Guestrin, Koller, Gearhart, and Kanodia (2003) proposed a Markov decision-process framework for planning in new environments. A regression tree is learned using a set of training features and used to generate actions and events in a new world. Even as learning-based approaches continue to proliferate, there have been several approaches that use predefined semantic concepts to model events.

Ontology consists of a vocabulary for describing a domain of interest and a set of explicit assumptions about the domain. Recently there have been attempts to create a standard set of ontologies for several domains of interest. These came about partly as a result of the Video Event Challenge workshops (2003). At these workshops, ontologies were defined for six domains of video surveillance: perimeter and internal security, railroad crossing surveillance, visual bank monitoring, visual metro monitoring, store security, and airport-tarmac security. Chen, Yang, and Wactlar (2004) used ontologies for analyzing social interaction in nursing homes. Hakeem and Shah (2004) categorized meeting videos using ontologies. Georis, Maziere, Bremond, and Thonnat (2004) described the ontologies of common activities in a bank monitoring scenario. Cupillard, Avanzi, Bremond, and Thonnat (2004) used finite state machines and "and/or" trees to model sequential and temporal constraints in sequences. Ghanem, Dementhon, Doermann, and Davis (2004) formulated a querying language based on Petri nets for surveillance scenarios in a parking lot. Shet, Harwood, and Davis (2005) described the architecture of a visual surveillance system that combines real-time computer vision algorithms with logic programming to represent and recognize events in activities involving interactions among humans, packages, and the environment. The low-level computer vision algorithms log primitive events of interest, while the higher-level Prolog-based reasoning engine uses these events in conjunction with predefined rules to recognize events. Francois, Nevatia, Hobbs, and Bolles (2005) described a framework for video event representation and annotation. The Video Event Representation Language (VERL) and the Video Event Markup Language (VEML) were introduced to describe the

ontologies and manually annotate events. Albanese, Moscato, Picariello, Subrahmanian, and Udrea (2006) developed a Probabilistic Activity Detection System (PADS) in which actions are represented in a logic
that is more expressive than Prolog and where probabilistic information
on the content of video is available. They developed fast algorithms to
find all video segments that contain the given event with a probability
exceeding a given threshold, as well as algorithms for online activity
detection.

Grammar-Based Approaches

Ivanov and Bobick (2000) described an event-modeling approach that
uses predefined semantics to enhance the capability of a purely statistical approach. Activity recognition is separated into two processes: event
detection using trained sub-HMMs, and parsing the output of HMMs
using stochastic context-free grammars. In particular, ambiguities in the
input symbols were resolved by substitution error correction, whereas
misdetections and interference were handled by insertion error correction. The error correction method was based on the probabilities of explicit alternative parses. The parser can handle concurrent tracks from
separate objects. Moore and Essa (2002) used domain-specific heuristics
for detecting primitive events based on the location and appearance of
objects obtained from low-level machine vision system.

State Space Approaches

State space models have been applied in many problems ranging from
gesture (Starner & Pentland, 1995; Wilson & Bobick, 1999) and gait
(Izo & Grimson, 2004; Kale et al., 2004) to complex activities (Brand,
Oliver, & Pentland, 1997; Vaswani et al., 2003). In particular, HMMs and
their variants have been a popular choice in many applications. Brand
et al. (1997) model human actions involving multiple parts such as the
hands and the head using coupled HMMs, where conditional probabilities connect the hidden state sequences of two HMMs. Oliver, Horwitz,
and Garg (2002) described an approach based on coupled HMMs for
learning and recognizing human interactions. Dynamic Bayesian networks (DBNs) have been used to capture causal structure between observations and hidden states. DBNs, which represent probabilities using

an acyclic graph structure, can be viewed as a generalization of HMMs. Koller and Lerner (2000) described a sampling approach for learning parameters of a DBN. Hamid, Huang, and Essa (2003) presented a DBN framework for tracking and recognizing complex, multi-agent activities. Hongeng, Nevatia, and Bremond (2004) developed a system that includes techniques for object detection, tracking, and recognition of multi-agent events. Simple or primitive events were represented by a Bayesian network, while single-thread events were represented using finite-state automata. Multi-thread events were represented by an event graph depicting the temporal relations between the sub-events.

Shape Space Theory

Many human activities involve the motion of multiple moving objects. The location of objects in each frame, referred to as landmarks, may be connected by an arc to form a landmark configuration. When the effects of location, scale, and rotation are filtered out, the remaining geometric information in the landmark configuration is said to be the shape. This was described statistically by Kendall, Barden, Carne, and Le (1999) and is commonly referred to as Kendall's shape space. It can be shown that shape space is $(2k-4)$ dimensional, where k is the constant number of landmarks. Vaswani, Roy-Chowdhury, & Chellappa (2003) developed shape space models for a group of moving or landmarks or point objects. Since the number of objects in the scene need not be constant, the curve connecting the ordered objects is resampled to obtain a constant cardinality k. The shape configuration deforms due to dynamics of the objects in the scene. Assuming that the changes are small in shape space, continuous state HMMs are used to capture the deformations in the tangent space. The hypothesis is that dynamics of normal activities are confined to tangent spaces, whereas those due to anomalous trajectories may deviate from the trained HMMs. Two types of errors were defined to detect anomalies: the tracking error and the expected log likelihood (ELL). Experiments have demonstrated that tracking error may be used to detect drastic changes, whereas ELL is sensitive to slow changes. Roy-Chowdhury and Chellappa (2003) reformulated the shape space representation of motion trajectories using the factorization framework originally proposed by Tomasi and Kanade (1992) and extended to nonrigid shapes by Torresani and Bregler (2002). Each activity can be represented as a linear combination of 3-D basis shapes. The location of tracked features is recorded in a measurement matrix W of order $2F \times P$, where F is the number of frames and P is the number of feature points or landmarks. The matrix W is rank-deficient and can be factorized using singular value decomposition (SVD) as $W=QB$, where Q is of order $2F \times 3K$ and B is of order $3K \times P$. K is the number of basis shapes. Given a test video sequence, activities are identified by projecting onto each basis shape obtained during training. If the projection does not cluster as expected, an anomaly is declared.

Action Recognition

Aggarwal and Cai (1999) presented a survey of human motion analysis. An unsupervised system for classification of activities was developed by Stauffer and Grimson (2000). Motion trajectories collected over a long period of time were quantized into a set of prototypes representing the location, velocity, and size of objects. Assuming that the sequence of prototypes in each trajectory consists of a single activity, a co-occurrence matrix representing the probability that a pair of prototypes both occur in the same sequence was estimated and used for classification. Syeda-Mahmood, Vasilescu, and Sethi (2001) used generalized cylinders to represent actions. Assuming that the start and end points were known, they formulated the task as a joint action recognition and fundamental matrix recovery problem. Zelnik-Manor and Irani (2001) considered events as long-term temporal objects at multiple temporal scales. The χ^2 distance between empirical distributions is used to compare such event sequences. Parameswaran and Chellappa (2003) computed view-invariant representations for human actions in both 2-D and 3-D. In 3-D, actions are represented as curves in an invariance space, and the cross-ratio is computed to find the invariants. Efros, Berg, Mori, and Malik (2003) introduced a motion descriptor based on optical flow measurements in a spatiotemporal volume of regions in the images for recognizing human actions at a distance. The region of interest is localized, and the image of a person is stabilized within the bounding box. The motion descriptors are computed using the horizontal and vertical components of the optical flow field and compared using normalized correlation. A nearest-neighbor rule is used to recognize actions. Rao et al.

(2003) treated activities as a sequence of dynamic instants or points of high curvature of motion trajectories, which are quasi–view invariant. Stauffer (2004) presented a factored representation for activities in far-field surveillance videos. Short-time trajectories of moving objects are used to segment the activity into K characteristics using factored latent analysis.

Statistical Approaches for Event-Based Activity Representation

A fundamental task in human activity modeling is finding a suitable representation of events in video sequences. The motivation for modeling activities comes from diverse domains such as surveillance and monitoring, storing and indexing home videos, and detecting abnormal human motion in biomedical applications. There is a need for developing automatic methods that represent activities and infer events and behaviors using features extracted from video streams. This necessity is magnified by the large amount of video data generated by the escalating ubiquity of video cameras. In this section, we focus on developing statistical models that represent activities as a sequence of semantically significant events.

It may be illuminating to illustrate the decomposition of activities into a sequence of events using examples. Consider the trajectory traced out by a hand as it performs the activity of opening a door. The shape of the trajectory depends on the person opening the door, the initial position of the hand, the camera's viewing direction, and so forth. Modeling these variations is neither easy nor relevant to opening the door. The relevant event of the door being opened occurs within a few frames once the hand makes contact with the door. The sequence of events—extending the hand, grabbing the handle, and opening the door—is a sufficient representation. As another illustration, consider the activity "going home after work." We may use the events *leave office, enter car, exit campus, pick a route*, and *reach home* to convey the information in the activity. These phrases capture the essence of the activity. They may not specify the complete activity for reconstructing motion trajectories, but they provide an adequate representation of the activity. It is reasonable, therefore, to model activities as a sequence of some important events. These events mark the boundaries between primitive segments of activities.

Events are thought of as instantaneous occurrences. In light of the discussions in several other chapters in this book (Chapters 2, 8, 15, 16, & 20), this may seem to be a restrictive notion of events. There are two main mitigating factors in the proposed model of events. It is a practical choice, as demonstrated in the experiments section below. Also, it provides a representation that is largely view invariant (Cuntoor, Yegnanarayana, & Chellappa, 2005). (Besides, we claim the title of Chapter 3, " Events Are What We Make of Them," in our defense!) The characterization of events that divide activities into coherent units is consistent with the arguments in Chapters 15 and 16. We elaborate the importance of segmentation for modeling activities below.

There are several choices of models that can encode events. A user could describe the relevant events using domain knowledge. Statistical approaches (including our methods presented in this section) tend to place a lesser emphasis on user-defined events because of scalability, computational efficiency, and low-level preprocessing limitations. In other words, it may not be possible to easily extend a set of rules or events defined by a user to model new events. Events specified by the user may rely on low-level preprocessing assumptions that are difficult to realize in practice. Alternatively, we may hypothesize that persistent and dominant frames constitute events (Zhong, Shi, & Visontai, 2004). It may not be suitable, however, for detecting subtle changes. Instead, we may look for events that mark changes in the data. These changes could represent transitions between primitives of an activity, as illustrated in the examples above. Further, events based on changes are more directly suited for anomaly detection.

Event detection methods can be broadly categorized into data-driven and model-based methods. Data-driven methods (Cuntoor & Chellappa, 2006; Rao et al., 2003) detect events using the extracted data or features, whereas model-based methods (Ivanov & Bobick, 2000) estimate a best-fitting generative model and detect events based on these models. Rao et al. (2003), motivated by the need for view-invariant representations, treated points of maximum curvature as events. Cuntoor and Chellappa (2006) proposed a general characterization of events based on changes using anti-eigenvalues, which are sensitive to changes, whereas eigenvalues, which capture the dominant characteristics, represent the direction of maximum spread of the data. The position and speed of the moving point objects were assumed to be modeled by a linear transformation.

The average anti-eigenvalue of these operators is treated as a measure of change in the data. Model-based methods, unlike data-driven ones, allow for events to be defined at higher levels of abstraction.

Event Probability Sequences

Statistical models for time-series signals such as video and speech have evolved from template matching and vector quantization to state space models. If limited data are available, it may be prudent to use data sequences as templates for matching. As the amount of available data increases, the samples can be clustered using vector quantization, where each data point is assigned to its nearest cluster center. State space models can be thought of as a soft clustering technique that incorporates time evolution at the state level. Instead of assigning a data sample to its nearest state (roughly, the cluster center), the probability of the data sample being generated by every state is computed. The sequence of states that maximizes this probability is said to be the optimal state sequence. Among state space approaches, the HMM and its variants and the dynamic Bayesian network have become popular mainly because of their elegance and efficient implementation.

Many existing approaches use the HMM as a " black box" for activity modeling. Given a set of training video sequences of an activity, the parameters of an HMM are efficiently estimated using the Baum-Welch algorithm (Baum, Petries, Soules, & Weiss, 1970). The learned model serves as a compact signature of the activity. Given a new video sequence, the probability of its generation by the learned model is computed using the Viterbi algorithm (Viterbi, 1967). A few approaches provide a physical interpretation of the states of the HMM (Brand et al., 1996). In Cuntoor et al. (2005) we introduced an event representation called the event probability sequence that uses the HMM in an attempt to interpret certain stable state sequences to find physically meaningful events.

Before describing the event probability sequences, we briefly summarize the HMM (Rabiner, 1989). It models an observed data sequence $O=\{o1,o2,...,oT\}$ of length T in a generative manner using a state sequence $Q=\{q1,q2,...,qT\}$. The state qt emits ot according to a probability distribution that is learned from training data. At every time t, qt can take any value from the discrete set $\{1,2,...,N\}$, where N is the known model order. Usually the model order is chosen based on experience.

Alternatively, it may be estimated using one of several information theoretic criteria. Each of the N states is associated with an output probability distribution (e.g., Gaussian or mixture of Gaussian).

The time evolution of the state sequence is assumed to be Markovian; in other words, given the present and all past states, the conditional probability distribution of all future states depends only on the present state and not on any of the past states. The state sequence is not observed but has to be estimated from the observed data (hence the term "hidden"). In an N-state HMM, since the state variable can take N possible values at every time instant, a state sequence of length T has N^T possible state sequences. Each of these N^T state sequences can generate the observed data with some probability. The optimal state sequence, which is one among these N^T sequences, maximizes this probability and has been used extensively in many modeling approaches. The optimal state sequence, however, need not be useful for detecting events in activities. So we examine other state sequences based on the hypothesis that events are reflected as significant state-level changes in motion properties.

The state $q_t = i$ at time t can change to state $q_{t+1} = j$ at time $t+1$ for some i,j in $\{1,2,...,N\}$. The probability of this transition for all possible pairs of states i,j, conditioned on the observed sequence, can be measured efficiently using the forward and backward variables in the Baum-Welch algorithm along with the model parameters. Using this as a building block, a stable change is said to be one that remains in state i for p frames, changes to state j, and remains in state j for p frames. The probability of a stable change is computed for all distinct pairs of states (i,j) using the observed data sequence. Suppose the probability is maximized by a pair of states (k,l). This stable change associated with the transition from state k to state l over the $2p$ frame window (state k for p frames, changing to state l, and remaining in state l for p frames) is interpreted as an event. Algebraically, this can be expressed as:

$$\text{Stable Change: } \eta_t^p = P(q_{t-p} = i, q_{t-p+1} = i,...,q_t = i, q_{t+1}$$

$$= j,...,q_{t+p+1} = j \mid O, \lambda) \qquad (18.1)$$

$$\text{Event: } e_t^p(k.l) = \max_{i,j} \eta_t^p(i,j) \qquad (18.2)$$

where λ represents the HMM, $i,j,k,l \ \varepsilon \ \{1,2,...,N\}$, N is the model order, and p is a parameter, $p = 2,3,...,P$.

Approach

Figure 18.1 shows a block diagram of event modeling (training) and recognition (testing) using event probability sequences. The training process may be divided into three phases: preprocessing, modeling, and event detection. In the preprocessing phase, moving objects of interest are automatically detected and tracked. The extracted motion trajectory forms the observed sequence O. The modeling phase consists of estimating parameters of an HMM for each activity from multiple trajectories using the Baum-Welch algorithm (Baum et al., 1970). If the appearance of motion trajectories of an activity varies drastically, multiple HMMs are trained.

The event probability sequences are computed in the third phase. An event probability sequence is computed for every motion trajectory in the training set using the activity's HMM learned in the previous phase. This is done during the training phase alone, where the activity to

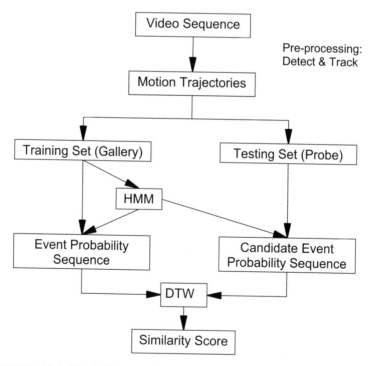

FIGURE 18.1. Block diagram showing an overview of event modeling using event probability sequences.

which each motion trajectory belongs is known. The event probability sequence, along with the HMM used in its computation, forms a signature of the activity.

Given a new (test) video sequence, its motion trajectory is extracted as before. Candidate event probability sequences are computed using each HMM learned during the training stage. The candidate event probability sequences are compared with the event probability sequences in the database (computed in the three-phase process). A straightforward matching would compare event probability in frame *1* of the candidate sequence with that in frame *1* of the trained sequence, frame *2* with frame *2*, and so on. This is unrealistic since an activity need not be repeated at the same pace. To allow for changes in the rate of execution of activities, we use the dynamic time warping (DTW) algorithm when comparing event probability sequences. It is a dynamic programming technique that provides nonlinear time normalization in matching.

Experiments

We illustrate the usefulness of event probability sequences for activity recognition and anomaly detection using the UCF human action dataset (Rao et al., 2003) and the TSA airport tarmac surveillance dataset (Vaswani et al., 2003).

The UCF dataset consists of 60 trajectories of common activities. Figure 18.2 shows sample images from the dataset. We divide these into seven classes: *open door, pick up, put down, close door, erase board, pour water into cup,* and *pick up object and put down elsewhere.* The starting position of the hand is initialized using a skin detector, and the trajectory is extracted by mean-shift tracking. The trajectories are smoothed using anisotropic diffusion (Perona & Malik, 1990). A detailed description of the dataset and tracking and smoothing operations is available in Rao et al. (2003). We illustrate the application of event probability sequences for activity recognition using the UCF dataset. HMMs for the different activities are learned from multiple trajectories using the Baum-Welch algorithm. For each trajectory, its event probability sequence is computed at P scales using the trained model for the activity as given in Equations 18.1 and 18.2. Figure 18.3 shows events at multiple

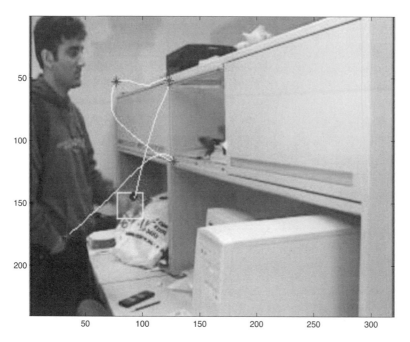

FIGURE 18.2. Sample images from the UCF dataset with hand trajectories.

scales for picking up an object. As expected, we observe fewer events as the value of P is increased. Given a test trajectory for recognition, candidate event probability sequences are computed using the models learned during training. Similarity scores between these candidates and the event probability sequences in the database are obtained using dynamic time warping. The overall similarity score can be calculated in three ways: integrating scores across P scales, at the conditionally optimal parameter values, or at the jointly optimal parameter values. The recognition rates are summarized in Figure 18.4. The results are compared with those reported in Rao et al. (2003).

The TSA airport tarmac surveillance dataset consists of airport surveillance videos captured by a stationary camera that operates at approximately 30 frames per second. The image size is 320 × 240. It contains approximately 230,000 frames or 120 minutes of data. Activities include movement of ground crew personnel, vehicles, planes, and passengers embarking and disembarking. In our experiments, we extracted the trajectories corresponding to vehicles, passengers, and

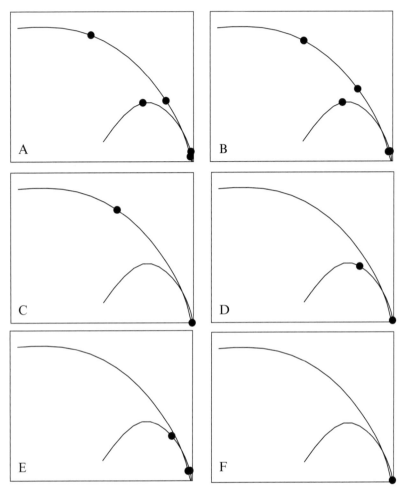

FIGURE 18.3. Events detected at different scales for trajectory of picking up an object. The scale parameter p varies from (*A*) p = 3 to (*F*) p = 8

luggage carts. We used simple background subtraction with periodic reinitialization of the background to detect the objects, and the KLT tracker (Lucas & Kanade, 1981) to extract the motion trajectories. Figure 18.5 shows the extracted motion trajectories. We trained HMMs for three activities that occur around the plane: passengers embarking, passengers disembarking, and the luggage cart going to and from the plane. During the training phase, we estimated the model parameters and the event probability sequences using the learned models. Given a test trajectory, we computed the event probability sequence using each

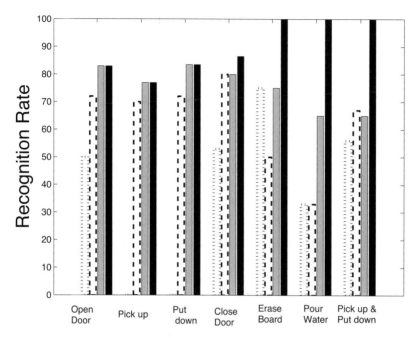

FIGURE 18.4. Recognition rate for UCF database.

FIGURE 18.5. Motion trajectories in TSA airport surveillance dataset.

of the models in the database to generate as many candidate event probability sequences as the number of models in the database. We compared these candidates with the trained event sequences using dynamic time warping. In the experiments, we used 10 trajectories of passengers embarking, 10 of disembarking, and 5 of luggage carts. All the activities were correctly recognized.

We consider normal trajectories of people disembarking from the plane and walking toward the gate to demonstrate the application of event probability sequences for anomaly detection. Anomalies may be caused by deviations from normal activities that are too subtle to be statistically significant. For this reason in part, it is impractical to view anomalies as deviations from an overall statistical model. On the other hand, if an activity is represented as a sequence of certain important events, we may say that deviations from these events constitute an anomaly. This uses an activity representation that is localized in time and space. Also, it measures deviations that are localized not only physically but also in parameter space.

Figure 18.6 shows sample images from the TSA airport surveillance dataset along with the extracted motion trajectories of people and vehicles in the scene. The event probability sequences for three normal trajectories of passengers walking to the gate after disembarking are shown in Figures 18.6(A)–(C). The events partition the path into regions. If we use a left-to-right model, these regions roughly correspond to the states of the HMM at a sufficiently fine scale. In other words, at the appropriate scale $p1$, we may expect $N-1$ events, where N is the number of states at regularly spaced intervals. Since we do not have any instances of anomalous trajectories, we simulate one by considering deviation from the path as an anomaly. We introduce various extents of deviation by setting the deviation $\sigma^2 = 2, 4, 16$. Using the set of normal trajectories, a five-state HMM is trained, assuming a left-to-right model (see Figs. 18.6[A]–[C]). Given a new (anomalous) trajectory, we use the model in the database to compute the event probabilities. If the anomaly is present in some part of the trajectory and normal activity is resumed after some time, then this is reflected in the events detected. The method does not accumulate errors at all time instants, only those based on the times when events occur or when an event was expected to occur as seen in the training data. To declare the presence of an anomaly, we use both

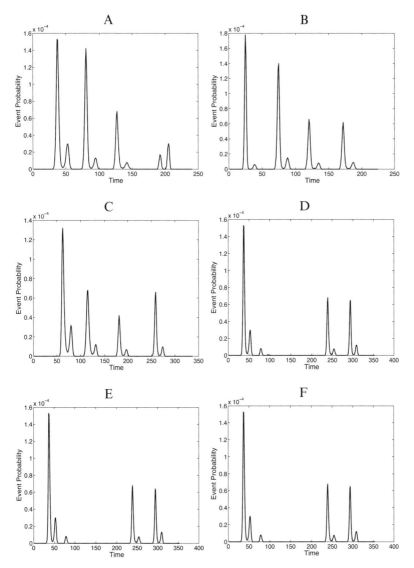

FIGURE 18.6. (*A*) through (*C*) show the event probability sequences for three normal trajectories of people deplaning and walking toward the terminal. There are four dominant events in the normal trajectories, irrespective of the exact paths that people follow. (*D*) through (*F*) show probability sequences for deviating trajectories with increasing extents of deviation.

the number of events detected (spurious and missing events are both anomalies) and the location of the detected events. Figures 18.6(*D*)–(*F*) show the event probability sequences for a person who deviates from the normal path and later rejoins the virtual path. We observe that the latter two dominant peaks in the anomalous trajectories resemble the latter half of the normal event sequences, whereas a missing event in the first half indicates an anomaly.

Behavior-Driven Mixed-State Models for Nonstationary, Multi-object Activities

In the previous section, activities were decomposed into a sequence of instantaneous events based on significant changes in motion properties of objects. Events partition the video sequence into dynamic segments by coherent behavior. Instead of modeling events, we can identify these dynamic segments and detect events that mark the boundary between two such segments. Whereas motion trajectories are continuous-valued, behavior such as start/stop, split/merge, and moving along a straight line are discrete-valued. This necessitates a mixed-state model that can handle both continuous- and discrete-valued variables.

In general, the activity structure and the number and sequence of behavioral segments may not be known a priori. It requires an activity model that can not only adapt to changing behavior but also learn incrementally and "on the fly." Many existing approaches assume that the structure of activities is known. A fixed number of free parameters are allocated based on experience or by estimating the model order. The structure then remains fixed. This may be a reasonable assumption for activities such as walking and running but becomes a serious limitation when modeling complex activities in surveillance and other scenarios. We are interested in these classes of activities. Instead of assuming a fixed global model order, the problem is translated into one whose local behavioral complexity is limited using a basis of behaviors. The basis of behaviors is chosen to reflect generic motion properties that occur in the domain of interest. For example, in surveillance settings, the basis elements represent motion with constant velocity along a straight line, curved motion, and so forth.

Chapter 15 discussed the validity of segmenting activities into a sequence of coherent "units." Though the observed world consists of continuous signals (e.g., motion), we as humans are able to aggregate the gathered information into a series of discrete units. This is explained using event regularities in Chapter 16; in this section we address this idea computationally.

As an illustration of the types of activities of interest, consider an airport surveillance scenario. We may observe segments of activities such as movement of ground crew personnel, arrival and departure of planes, movement of luggage carts to and from the plane, and embarkation and disembarkation of passengers. The video sequences are usually long and contain several motion trajectories. We may be interested in segmenting the video sequences for convenient storage. Classifying segments of video sequences based on constituent activities greatly aids the human expert in sifting through data. It also provides a way to compare two streams of activities to check for anomalous behavior. Using the identified segments, it is possible to reason at a higher level of abstraction. The reasoning engine need not be tied to a particular form of modeling; Bayesian statistics, ontology, or a combination of the two techniques could be used.

Mixed-State Model for Human Activities in Video

Activity modeling can be regarded as a mapping from raw video sequences to events that are meaningful to humans. It is convenient to introduce an intermediate stage that converts the sequences of moving pixels to building blocks of activities. These building blocks in turn can be used to represent the higher-level activity. Accordingly, the tasks can be split into three levels—low-, mid-, and high-level vision—similar to those of the human visual system, where low-level vision occurs at the retina (e.g., light adaptation) and high-level vision involves cognitive processes encompassing knowledge of objects, materials, and scenes. Mid-level vision consists of a range of processes connecting the low and high levels. Typical steps involved in these levels (of computational vision) are outlined below.

Low-level vision is concerned with extracting features such as motion trajectories from raw video data. Given a video sequence, moving objects are detected and tracked. Generally, segmentation of the foreground (moving object) from the background becomes increasingly challenging as the video sequence grows longer. This is mainly because of changes in illumination and background motion, which can drastically alter background statistics. A robust solution to this problem incorporates an adaptive background model (Haritaoglu, Cutler, Harwood, & Davis, 1999).

High-level vision algorithms describe the other end of the process. The level of detail with which the higher-level reasoning is captured depends on the scenario. For instance, in a far-field surveillance scenario one may be interested in movement of humans and their interaction within the scene, unlike near-field scenarios, where motion of individual parts of the body may be of interest. Representation at the mid-level is designed to aid in the interpretation of the low-level outputs for high-level tasks. It is guided by the high-level requirements while being cognizant of limitations of low-level algorithms.

In our approach, mid-level vision is modeled by mixed-state systems consisting of a continuous dynamic model and a discrete model that is indexed by behavior at the higher level. Dynamic systems are a natural choice for modeling behavior due to motion, since they capture changes in position and velocity of an object within video segments. It is well known that linear systems can represent a range of trajectories such as those along straight-line, curved, and circular trajectories. They are distinguished by the location of eigenvalues of the system matrix (Vidyasagar, 1993). This choice of representation provides a connection between middle and high levels that is both physically significant and mathematically appealing.

Any computational model of activities has to take practical limitations at the low level into account (e.g., performance of object detection techniques, quality of background subtracted data, reliability and generality of tracking algorithms). By generality we mean avoiding fine-tuning of parameters in the tracking algorithm in different video sequences. Each building block at the middle level is limited in complexity in time and space so that it can model trajectories that follow linear dynamics.

There is another aspect of mixed-state models that may be worth noting, since dynamics is discussed in Chapter 20 as well. Chapter 20 uses forces and dynamics to model causal relationships. Inspired by the operations of forces in physics, force-like quantities are described. In the present discussion, however, the use of dynamic systems is not intended to invoke physical forces (as in Chapters 11 and 12). For instance, though we use linear dynamic systems to model humans walking in a scene, we are not attempting to recover forces exerted on the ground. Rather, we use mixed-state systems as a tool to model motion to facilitate activity recognition and other applications.

Before describing the mixed-state model we take a short detour to explore events at the different levels of vision mentioned above. At the low level the camera sees a sequence of pixels, some of which belong to the moving foreground and others to the background. We may say that an event occurs at the boundary that separates these two classes in every frame. By consolidating low-level detections, event categories of objects and shapes may be constructed. Similarly, events may be constructed along the time domain in which an event separates behaviors of differing kinds. At present, we focus on events defined along the time domain. Ultimately, high-level vision determines the existence and characterization of events. In mid-level vision, event concepts are not immediately obvious. At any rate, it is advantageous to decompose activities into their constituent building blocks, which are relatively simple to analyze and compute. Chapter 16 extends this line of reasoning to complex social events such as wars and elections.

Modeling Behavior Using Trajectories

The mid-level component is described in this section. Let the sequence of discrete states be $\{q(1),q(2),...,q(T)\}$, where $q(i) \in \{1,2,...,N\}$ indexes the discrete valued behavior. In general, we do not know the number of allowed behavior segments or the switching times between them. We present offline and online behavior-driven mixed-state models to model behavior within such segments. In the offline model, the parameters of behavior in segments are learned from training data, whereas in the online model the parameters are not known.

The state dynamics can be written as:

$$dz/dt = A_{q(t)}z(t) + u(t), z(0) = z0 \qquad (18.3)$$

$$q(t+1) = g(q(1),...,q(t-1),z(1),...,z(t-1),n(t)) \qquad (18.4)$$

where $u(t)$ and $n(t)$ represent system and measurement noise respectively, and $A_{q(t)}$ is a square matrix with real-valued entries.

The continuous state dynamics $A_{q(t)}$ depends on the discrete state $q(t)$. It captures the notion that a higher-level behavior evolves in time and generates correlated, continuous-valued states $z(t)$. The discrete state $q(t)$ evolves according to $g(.)$ and depends not only on the previous discrete state but also on the past values of the observed data. This makes the evolution of discrete state non-Markovian when the state equations are translated into probabilities.

Approach

This section consists of an outline of estimation of mixed-state systems that form building blocks of activities in the proposed model. (The mathematical details are beyond the scope of this chapter.) The estimation task in both offline and online models consists of two main steps: computing the parameters of the behavioral segments and identifying switching times between segments. Given the switching times, parameters of segment-wise dynamics can be computed so that the squared error is minimized. Estimating the switching times, however, is computationally challenging. It may be tempting to use the Expectation-Maximization (EM) algorithm in this case (Baum et al., 1970). The EM algorithm involves iteration over the E-step to choose an optimal distribution over a fixed number of hidden states and the M-step to find the parameters of the distribution that maximize the data likelihood. Unlike the classical HMM, however, the E-step is not tractable in switched state space models (Ghahramani & Hinton, 1998). To work around this, Ghahramani and Hinton (1998) presented a variational approach for estimating the parameters of switched state space models. On the other hand, Isard and Blake (1998) presented a sampling approach. Either of these approaches is suitable for the offline mixed-state model, but neither is suitable for the online case. We propose an algorithm that has two main components: a basis of behavior for approximating behavior within segments and the Viterbi-based algorithm (Viterbi, 1967).

The Viterbi algorithm was introduced in Viterbi (1967) as an error-correcting technique for communication over noisy channels. It has since been applied in several fields, including speech recognition, computational linguistics, bioinformatics, and computer vision. The algorithm is a dynamic programming technique that finds a sequence of hidden states so that the probability of the observed sequence is maximized. Usually it is applied in the following setting: the number of hidden states is known and the time evolution of the hidden state is Markovian—that is, the hidden state at time t depends only on the hidden state at time $t-1$. Algorithmic efficiency is obtained using the principle of optimality in dynamic programming that breaks up the global estimation into a series of local optimizations. The overall optimal solution (the hidden state sequence that maximizes the probability of generating the observed data sequence) is found by stringing together the local solutions during backtracing the path from the final time.

This algorithm can be extended to estimate the switching times in the offline mixed-state model in a relatively straightforward manner. The main difference from the above-mentioned classical case is that the hidden state is not Markovian but depends on the most recent past values of the observed data sequence as well. Accordingly, the hidden state is augmented so that the effective state consisting of the original hidden state and a time window of recently observed data sequence becomes Markovian. A similar trick is performed in Hinton and Ghahramani (1998). The augmentation, however, makes it difficult to compute the transition probabilities between hidden states; specifically, the normalization term in the effective state evolution can not be evaluated. Isard and Blake (1998) address this issue using sampling. Given the inequitable distribution in different components of activities (very few samples of some cases and large samples of others), it is not easy to devise an effective sampling strategy.

In place of probabilities we introduce switching and approximation costs. The switching cost is defined at the boundary between behaviors as the cost incurred in making a transition from the current behavior to a different behavior in the segment at the next time step. The approximation or running cost is defined as the cost incurred in persisting in a behavior when the parameters are optimized to fit the observed data sequence.

The costs are evaluated using the chosen basis of behaviors as the reference model. Using costs associated with the basis of behaviors is a way of incorporating semantics in the design of building blocks of activities within a statistical framework. The trellis structure in the implementation of the Viterbi algorithm is maintained, thus preserving its computational advantage.

Applications

We will now demonstrate the usefulness of the online mixed-state model for temporal segmentation and the offline mixed-state model for anomaly detection using the TSA airport tarmac surveillance dataset (Vaswani et al., 2003) and the bank surveillance dataset (Vu et al., 2002).

TEMPORAL SEGMENTATION: TSA AIRPORT TARMAC SURVEILLANCE DATASET

We divide the TSA dataset discussed above into 23 blocks of about 10,000 frames each. We refer to sets of 10,000 frames as blocks. Figure 18.4 shows two such blocks along with detected motion trajectories. We demonstrate temporal segmentation using the online mixed-state model. We choose a basis of behavior whose elements can produce the following types of motion: constant velocity along a straight line, constant acceleration along a straight line, curved trajectories with constant velocity, and start and stop. The segmentation results for the two blocks shown in Figure 18.4 are summarized in Tables 18.1 and 18.2.

TEMPORAL SEGMENTATION: BANK SURVEILLANCE DATASET

The bank dataset consists of staged videos collected at a bank (Vu et al., 2002). There are four sequences, each approximately 15 to 20 seconds ($\approx$400 frames) long. The actors demonstrate two types of scenarios:

- an *attack* scenario, in which a person coming into the bank forces his way into the restricted area (this is considered an anomaly), and
- a *no attack* scenario in which people enter and exit the bank and conduct normal transactions. This depicts a normal scenario. The normal process of transactions is known a priori, and we train an offline mixed state model using these trajectories.

We retain the same basis of behavior that was used for the TSA dataset above. Though the TSA data are captured outdoors and the bank data indoors, both captures are surveillance videos. They retain similarity at the primitive or behavior level. For the *no attack* scenario, segmentation using the online mixed-state model yields two parts. In the first segment, we see two people entering the bank successively. The

TABLE 18.1. TSA Dataset: Temporal Segmentation of Two Blocks Using Online Mixed-State Model

#	Block in Figure 18.4(*A*)	Comment
1	2 GCP split, walk away	Det.
2	GCP across tarmac	Det.
3	Truck arrives, GCP	Det.
4	GCP across tarmac	Det.
5	Truck	Det.
6	GCP movement	Det.
7	Plane I arrives	Det.
8	Luggage cart to plane	Det.
9	Truck crossing scene, Plane II arrives	TF
10	GCP & luggage cart approach plane I	Det.
11	–	Extra segment
12	PAX disembark	Det.

GCP: ground crew personnel; PAX: passengers; Det.: segment detected; TF: tracking failed.

TABLE 18.2. TSA Dataset: Temporal Segmentation of Two Blocks Using Online Mixed-State Model

#	Block in Figure 18.4(*B*)	Comment
1	2 GCP movement	Det.
2	Luggage cart	TF
3	GCP movement	TF
4	Plane II arrives	Det.
5	GCP movement	TF
6	Luggage cart to plane II	Det.
7	Plane III arrives	Det.
8	PAX embark	Det.
9	Truck movement	Det.
10	GCP near plane II	TF
11	Luggage cart from plane II	Det.
12	PAX embark	Det.

GCP: ground crew personnel; PAX: passengers; Det.: segment detected; TF: tracking failed.

first person goes to the area where paper slips are kept, and the second person goes to the counter. In the second segment, the two people leave the bank. We store the parameters of these behavioral segments as representations of normal activities.

For an *attack* scenario, the online mixed-state model yields three segments. In the first segment, a person enters the bank and proceeds to the area where the deposit/withdrawal slips are kept. This is similar to the first segment in the *no attack* case. During the second segment, he follows another person into the restricted area behind the counter. The third segment consists of the person leaving the bank.

ANOMALY DETECTION: BANK SURVEILLANCE DATASET

The parameters of an offline mixed-state model are estimated using the *no attack* scenario. To detect the presence of an anomaly, we compute the error accumulated along the optimal state sequence using the test trajectory. It is difficult to assess the performance of this naïve scheme since we have very few samples. Alternatively, we use the online mixed-state model to detect anomalies. If we assume that the *attack* scenarios were normal activities while the *no attack* scenario was an anomaly, we may expect the comparison scores of the different *attack* scenarios to be clustered together. For each of the four scenarios in the dataset, parameters of their online mixed-state models are computed. We form a similarity matrix of size 4×4 in order to check whether the *attack* scenarios cluster separately. The L_1 distance between histograms of parameters of learned behavior is used as the similarity score. Table 18.3 shows the distance between the different *attack* examples with the *no attack* case. We observe that *attack* scenarios are more similar to each other compared to the *no attack* scenario.

Semantic Approaches for Activity Representation

Complex activities may exhibit significant variations in appearance that challenge statistical approaches. Instead of a pure data-driven approach, domain knowledge can be used to represent the activity consisting of agents, environment, and relationships between them. Formal grammars can express the structural relationships in activities by delineating a set of finite-length strings over an alphabet. We discuss different kinds

TABLE 18.3. Comparing No Attack and Attack Scenarios in Bank Surveillance Data

#	No Attack	Attack 1	Attack 2	Attack 3
No Attack	0	310	424	362
Attack 1	310	0	218	278
Attack 2	424	218	0	180
Attack 3	362	278	180	0

L1 distance between histograms of parameters of online mixed-state model is used as similarity score.

of grammars: attribute grammars, stochastic grammar, and multi-threaded events for activity modeling. Formal grammars are concerned with structural relationships between objects, whereas ontology deals with the nature of the objects and their relationships. We analyze and evaluate ontologies of surveillance activities.

Grammars for Activities

In this section we explore event recognition approaches using grammar-based syntactic pattern recognition. String grammars are suitable for representing events and the corresponding temporal ordering of sub-events. Hopcraft and Ullman (1979) define string *grammar G* as four-tuple $G = (V_N, V_T, P, S)$ where V_N is a finite set of *nonterminal symbols* (or *variables*) and V_T is a finite set of *terminal symbols*. Sets V_N and V_T are disjointed. P is a finite set of *production rules* in the form of $x \to y$, meaning x can be replaced by y where x and y are strings over $V_N \cup V_T$, and S is a special nonterminal symbol called the *start symbol*. Henceforth, symbols x, y, and z denote strings of arbitrary length over $V_N \cup VT$.

Multiple rules with a common left-hand side, such as $x \to y$, $x \to z$ mean either y or z may replace x. For notational convenience, the rules may be written as $x \to y \mid z$. The set of all strings generated by grammar G defines the *language L(G)*. The process of finding a sequence of production rules that generates a string is referred to as *parsing*. The simplest sub-patterns of activities are called primitive events and are associated with terminal symbols.

Types of Grammars

Depending on the complexity of the event structure, different types of grammar may be used for representation, the simplest being *regular* or *finite-state* grammar. In regular grammar, all the production rules are of the form[1] $A \rightarrow xB$ or $A \rightarrow x$, where A and B are variables and x denotes any substring consisting of terminal symbols. Intuitively, the strings generated by regular grammars have the property that a symbol in any location depends only on a finite number of symbols on the left. For example, walking may be expressed as:

$S \rightarrow L \mid R$

$L \rightarrow$ *left-leg-front* $R \mid$ *left-leg-front*

$R \rightarrow$ *right-leg-front* $L \mid$ *right-leg-front*,

where the phrases represent primitive events. Regular languages can be represented by equivalent *finite-state automata*, which are graphic representations consisting of a finite number of nodes and arcs, corresponding to states and terminal symbols, respectively. Figure 18.7 shows a simple finite-state automaton for a person leaving an object behind. The primitive events used are *start*, *stop*, and *object-appear*. Since humans usually stop when putting down a large object, we assume that *start* and *stop* events do not occur consecutively. Parsing is done by traversing the graph as the input symbols are sequentially matched with the arcs. The time complexity of this algorithm is $O(n)$, where n is the length of the input string.

As another example, consider traffic passing though a one-way, multi-lane tunnel seen at the two ends. It can be described as a string consisting of matching pairs of entering and exiting cars. Since the *enter* and

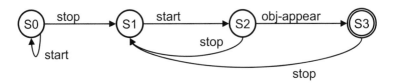

FIGURE 18.7. Finite-state automaton for a person leaving an object behind.

---

1. This form of production generates a string sequentially from left to right and hence is called right-linear. Regular grammars can also be in the left-linear form, $A \rightarrow Bx$ or $A \rightarrow x$.

exit events can be arbitrarily far apart, regular grammars do not have sufficient expressive power to describe this event. This requires *context-free grammars*, which allow production rules of the form $A \rightarrow x$, where A represents a single variable, and which can be described as: $S \rightarrow enter$ $S\ exit \mid SS \mid enterexit.$

Parsing of a context-free language results in a tree structure where internal nodes correspond to variables and leaf nodes represent terminal symbols. Each internal node branches into its children using a suitable production rule. The parsing algorithm involves storing arbitrarily large contextual information resulting from multiple applications of production rules. The order in which the information is stored and retrieved can be restricted to the last-in/first-out order. Earley (1970) proposed an online algorithm for parsing general context-free languages whose typical time complexity is $O(n)$ and worst-case time complexity is $O(n^3)$. Some events are better expressed by context-free grammars rather than regular grammars.

The production rules of *context-sensitive grammars* are of the form $xAy \rightarrow xzy$, where the length of z is greater than zero. Thus x and y are seen as the context in which A can be replaced with w. An event that includes a matching number of occurrences of three or more sub-events requires this kind of grammar. For instance, in a shopping event, the number of items put into the shopping cart should match the number of items taken out of the cart for checkout and the number put into the shopping bag.

ATTRIBUTE GRAMMARS FOR EVENT REPRESENTATION

It is desirable to use additional attributes or features associated with primitive events to describe an event. *Attribute grammars* for context-free grammars, introduced by Knuth (1968), have been used in syntactic pattern recognition (Fu, 1982), natural language processing (Allen, 1995), and programming languages (Alblas, 1991). Attribute grammars consist of the grammar, a set of attributes, *attribute evaluation rules*, and *semantic conditions* associated with production rules of the grammar. The attributes are initially given with the terminal symbols, which are passed up the tree and evaluated during parsing.[2] Attributes can provide

---

2. These kinds of attributes are called *synthesized attributes*. It is also possible to define *inherited attributes* where the values are evaluated top-down from the root of the tree.

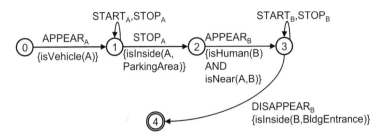

FIGURE 18.8. Attributed finite-state automaton for a parking event.

semantic information such as the time interval of the event or location of a sub-event, which can not be expressed by the syntax of the event string. In addition, the syntax of the grammar may be restricted by the condition on the attributes. Figure 18.8 shows an attributed finite-state automaton representing a parking event in a parking lot. Through the use of conditions on the attributes, the sequence *appear, stop, appear, disappear* is restricted to a sequence of more meaningful events representing a car entering the scene, the car parking, a person exiting the car, and that person entering the building. A sample video corresponding to sub-events for the automaton is shown in Figure 18.9 (also see color insert). The conditions on the attributes allow a context-free attribute grammar to describe a context-sensitive language. For the context-sensitive *check out after shopping* event, synthesized numerical attributes named *num-cart*, *num-checkout*, and *num-bag* can be defined, each representing the number of items put into the shopping cart, the number of items taken out of the cart for checkout, and the number put into the shopping bag. Each of these attributes can be incremented by one whenever the associated production rules are used. The grammar allows for arbitrary repetitions of each sub-event. At the top level, a condition to match the values of the three attributes is imposed. The following is an attributed grammar for the (self-checkout) shopping event.

SELFCHECKOUT → appear SHOP CHECKOUT disappear
(isInside(X1.location, shop-entrance) ∧ isInside(X4.location, shop-exit)
$X2.num\text{-}in\text{-}cart := X3.num\text{-}scanned$
SELFCHECKOUT → appear disappear

SHOP → in-cart SHOP
X0.*num-in-cart* := X2.*num-in-cart* + 1 (isInside(X1.location,
shopping-area))
SHOP → in-cart
X0.*num-in-cart* := 1 (isInside(X1.location, shopping-area))
CHECKOUT → enter-checkout[0] SCAN pay
X0.*num-scanned* := X2.*num-scanned* (X2.*num-scanned* :=
X2.*num-in-cart*)
SCAN → scan-item SCAN X0.num-scanned := X2.*num-scanned* + 1
SCAN → in-cart SCAN X0.num-in-cart := X2.*num-in-cart* + 1
SCAN → scan-item   X0.*num-scanned* := 1
SCAN → in-cart   X0.*num-in-cart* := 1

The symbols with which the attributes are associated are referenced
by the notation X*i*, where *i* is the index of the symbol in the production
rule (X0 denotes the variable on the left-hand side). The conditions are
enclosed in parentheses.

FIGURE 18.9. Example of a parking event.

Attribute grammars can also be used to achieve compactness of a context-free grammar. In the earlier example of casing cars, two separate rules for *C* and *F* can be combined as $S \rightarrow E\ Cl\ L$ with attributes *by-car* and *on-foot* associated with *E* and *L*. Attributes are also useful where the number of primitive events is unbounded, such as in an event involving arbitrary number of objects, each having distinct primitive events associated with it. In this case, a unique object identification number can be used as the attribute of the primitive event. Context-free parsers can be extended to parsing with an attribute grammar. In particular, a simple modification of Earley's parser can be used if the evaluation of each attribute of a symbol depends only on the ones on the left of the symbol.

STOCHASTIC GRAMMAR

An event may have different variations in its subpatterns, some of which occur more frequently than others. In addition, primitive events detected by low-level computer vision techniques are imperfect due to occlusions, noise, and so forth. Stochastic grammars address these issues by assigning probabilities to the production rules. Stochastic regular grammars are equivalent to probabilistic finite automata (Vidal, Thollard, de la Higuera, Casacuberta, & Carrasco, 2005), which are similar to HMMs. Unlike the states in an HMM, the states in a probabilistic finite automaton corresponding to a grammar have a well-defined meaning. Training algorithms, however, may not be able to learn useful grammars from examples (Manning & Schütze, 1999). Stolcke (1995) described a probabilistic extension to Earley's parser. In the case of attribute grammars, the uncertainty in an attribute may be expressed by a probability distribution over the possible values. In this case, the semantic conditions can be evaluated as a probability instead of logical values.

Multi-Thread Events

Events may involve interaction between multiple agents, which move independently except when they interact. The representation should be capable of modeling multiple parallel streams of events. The structure of such a *multi-thread* event (François et al., 2005) is described by a *partial ordering* of the sub-events instead of a *total ordering*. String grammars are not best suited since they require a single stream of symbols as input. A common formalism for modeling concurrent processes is the *Petri-Net* (Murata, 1989). Web grammars (Pfaltz & Rosenfeld, 1969) also naturally represent the partial ordering between symbols. Since the languages generated by web grammars are graphs, the parser should determine the thread to which each primitive event belongs.

Experiments

We demonstrate the usefulness of grammars for casing cars in a parking lot, which is a typical surveillance scenario. "Casing" can be described as a person walking into a parking lot, walking close to multiple cars, and then walking out of the lot. The person may also drive in and out of the lot before and after the casing takes place. An attribute grammar for casing cars is shown in Table 18.4.

A probability value is assigned to each of the production rules such that it reflects the frequency of the rule being used. For instance, a higher probability is given to the behavior of entering and leaving on foot, compared to entering and leaving by car. Also, for the actual casing behavior we use a soft thresholding function for the fuzzy condition on the distance to a vehicle. We have used four different image sequences for recognizing the vehicle casing event; Figure 18.10 shows representative frames from each sequence (also see color insert). In Sequence 1, a person enters the lot on foot, cases vehicles, and exits on foot. Sequence 2 consists of a person driving into the parking lot, casing vehicles on foot, and driving out of the lot. Sequence 3 contains a person parking a car and leaving the lot on foot; the person stops twice without casing vehicles. Finally, Sequence 4 shows a person

TABLE 18.4. Attribute Grammar for Casing Vehicles

Sequence	Recognized	Likelihood of parse
1	yes	0.480
2	yes	0.247
3	yes	0.059
4	no	–

FIGURE 18.10. Representative frames from sequences 1–4 for testing recognition of casing vehicles.

walking through parked vehicles without casing any vehicles (also see color insert).

Table 18.5 summarizes the recognition results. Sequences 1 and 2 were correctly recognized as the casing event with higher likelihood for Sequence 1 because the person moved closer to the vehicles than in Sequence 2, and a higher probability is given to the production rule for the case of walking in and out of the lot ($p = 0.5$) compared to driving in and out ($p = 0.3$). Sequence 3 was syntactically parsed as a casing event but with a (semantically) very low likelihood compared to Sequences 1 and 2. Thus the use of probabilistic conditions contributes to the robustness of the recognition. Sequence 4 is correctly parsed as a noncasing event.

Ontology for Activities

Recently there has been significant interest in modeling common activities in surveillance scenarios. Activities can be decomposed into a sequence of simpler events that satisfy certain spatiotemporal constraints.

TABLE 18.5. Recognition Results for Casing Vehicles

Production Rules	p	Attribute Rules and Semantic Conditions
S → CASEVEHICLES	1.0	
CASEVEHICLES → appear CASING disappear	0.5	(isPerson(appear.class) ∧ ~isInside(appear.loc, ParkingLot) ∧ ~isInside(disappear.loc, ParkingLot))
CASEVEHICLES → DRIVEIN CASING DRIVEOUT	0.3	
CASEVEHICLES → appear CASING DRIVEOUT	0.1	(isPerson(appear.class) ∧ ~isInside(appear.loc, ParkingLot))
CASEVEHICLES → DRIVEIN CASING disappear	0.1	(~isInside(disappear.loc, ParkingLot))
DRIVEIN → appear^1 DSTOP appear^1	1.0	(isVehicle(appear.class) ∧ isNear(appear.loc, DSTOP.loc) ∧ isPerson(appear.class))
DSTOP^1 → start stop DSTOP^2	0.9	DSTOP^1.loc := DSTOP^2.loc
DSTOP → start stop	1.0	DSTOP.loc := stop.loc
DRIVEOUT → stop disappear start DEXIT	1.0	(isNear(disappear.loc, start.loc))
DEXIT → stop start DEXIT	0.9	
DEXIT → disappear	1.0	
CASING → start stop start CASING^2	1.0	CASING.mindist:= min(stop.dist,CASING2. mindist)(p_isSmall(CASING. mindist))
CASING2 → stop start CAS-ING2	1.0	CASING2.mindist := min(stop. dist, CASING2.mindist)
CASING2 → stop start	1.0	CASING2.mindist := stop.dist

These constraints may depend on the user analyzing the activity. It is necessary to standardize events and constraints to allow portability, motivating the need for ontology. Gruber (1995) defines ontology as an explicit specification of a conceptualization. It is a systematic representation of our knowledge about the domain of interest. Ontologies can be used to represent temporal coupling such as concurrency and sequentiality among events.

There is considerable variation in the literature about what exactly constitutes an ontology. These vary from using full first-order logic to less expressive description logics (Calvanese, Lenzerini, & Nardi. 1998) to Web standards such as RDF (Lassila & Swick, 1998) that are less expressive but more efficient to compute with. Specialized ontologies have been developed for a wide variety of domains (e.g., ontobroker.com; daml.org) ranging from travel to university hierarchies to wine. In this section, we will discuss how a few of these variants of ontologies have been used for activity modeling and detection.

The principle of decomposing events into primitive sub-events is also a feature of taxonomy, which is a categorization of concepts into primitives or components. Each component is placed on a hierarchical tree so that parent–child relationships may be used in representation. However, taxonomy is not suitable for modeling activities because we are interested not only in the primitives but also in the sequence of primitives. For example, consider the activity of a car cruising in a parking lot. We might say that it is composed of the following primitives: *car enter, car move in circuit*, and *car exit*. Car-parking activity can also be seen as being composed of the same primitives as car-cruising. The difference lies in the temporal span of the *car move in circuit* primitive. It can be described by the following primitives and constraints:

```
PROCESS(cruise-parking-lot(vehicle v, parking-lot lot),
Sequence(enter(v, lot),
set-to-zero(i),
Repeat-Until(
AND(move-in-circuit(v), inside(v, lot), increment(i)),
equal(i, n)),
exit(v, lot)))
```

This ontology keeps track of the number of times a car loops around within a parking lot. When the number of loops matches a predefined threshold *n*, a car-cruising-parking-lot event is declared.

Ontology is more powerful than taxonomy and provides a detailed characterization among components of activities. Also, several activities can share the same set of primitives but differ in their sequencing.

Gruber (1995) defines five important criteria for ontology design: clarity, coherence, extendibility, minimal encoding bias, and minimal ontological commitment.

1. Clarity requires conceptualizations to be conveyed unambiguously. Ontological definitions need to be independent of social or computational contexts.
2. Coherence allows for meaningful inferences to be drawn that are consistent with definitions and axioms.
3. If an ontology is extensible, new concepts can be defined based on the existing vocabulary without a need for revising definitions.
4. An ontology with minimal encoding bias has conceptualizations that are symbol-independent. An encoding bias may result when a representation choice is made purely for convenience of notation or implementation.
5. If an ontology makes as few assumptions as possible about the world being modeled, it is said to be minimally committed.

In the section below titled "Ontology Evaluation," we illustrate how domain-specific ontologies can be evaluated based on these criteria.

Design of Ontologies for Activities

An ontology describes entities, environment, the interaction between them, and the resulting sequence of events, which is semantically identified with an activity. It specifies how an activity can be constructed using lower-level primitive events by identifying the role played by each entity in the sequence of events. As described in Chapter 16, it is perhaps instructive to start with known domains where a detailed description of entities and interactions is available. Building ontologies for a domain may be broadly classified into the following steps:

1. Identification of entities: Animate and inanimate entities relevant to an activity are identified. The list includes humans, vehicles, and environment such as the scene location, buildings, and so forth. The properties of each entity, such as physical attributes and appearance, are also specified.

2. Description of activities: The activities describe the relationship between entities and specify the level of granularity at which the relationships are described.

3. Identification of events: Primitive events involving each entity individually and in relation to two or more objects are described. Primitiveness of an event is intrinsically linked to the granularity at which the activity is described.

4. Description of changes: The physical properties of entities and relationships between two or more entities may change with time. All the possible changes are described in order to specify a complete ontology.

5. Choice of representation: A suitable computational framework that can represent the entities, their properties, and the relationships between them is chosen.

If properties of entities and primitive events can be reliably extracted from video streams, deterministic methods such as deterministic finite-state automata (DFA), Petri nets (Ghanem et al., 2004), and logic-based systems (Shet et al., 2005; Vu et al., 2002; Vu, Bremond, & Thonnat, 2003) can be used for recognizing events defined by ontologies. DFAs are best suited for single-threaded activities, whereas Petri nets are better equipped to handle multi-threaded and concurrent activities. Logic-based systems are basically rule-based methods, which can express arbitrarily complex relationships. In order to handle uncertainties in the low-level event extraction processes from video streams, probabilities can be incorporated to build a robust system. Stochastic context-free grammar (Ivanov & Bobick, 2000) can be used to represent events in a hierarchical structure. Probabilistic parsing techniques provide effective ways of handling errors and uncertainties in detection of primitive events. In our experiments we have used DFAs to model ontologies in a bank monitoring scenario (see the section below titled "Logical Ontologies and Probabilistic Detection").

It may be worth noting that the five-step classification described above is artificial in the sense that these steps can not be considered completely independent of each other. For example, the description of activities has to make realistic assumptions about the capabilities of the imaging modules and the choice of representation. As an illustration, in a surveillance scenario in a parking lot, it may not be possible to extract high-resolution images of people such that the arms and legs are clearly visible. This makes it challenging to recognize fine-grained activities such as making hand gestures.

Ontology Evaluation

In this section we illustrate the use of ontologies and analyze their properties according to Gruber's criteria (discussed above) using examples from the Video Event Challenge workshop (2003).

Low-level properties such as location and speed of objects are extracted from video sequences using background subtraction and tracking algorithms (Joo & Zheng, 2005). These are used to extract primitive events such as *start/stop*, *pick up*, and so on based on heuristics. A sequence of these primitives forms an activity, which is described using regular expressions. We use DFA to parse the activity. The DFA can produce false alarms and misdetections if the ontology is not minimal.

CLARITY

In perimeter and internal security ontology, tailgating is defined as follows:

Ontology 1 (Video Event Challenge Workshop, 2003):
SINGLE-THREAD(tailgate(entity x, entity y, facility f)
AND(portal-of(entrance, f)),
Sequence(AND(approach(x, y)behind(x,y)),
tail-behind(x, y),
get-access(y, entrance),
enter(y,facility),
NOT(get-access(x, entrance)),
enter(x, facility)))

where the *tailgate* event is described by the following sequence of sub-events: person x and person y approach the portal of facility f with x behind y; person y gets access to the entrance and enters the facility; x enters the facility without explicitly getting access to the entrance (by means of swiping a card, for example). In Ontology 1, there is no concept of time other than sequentiality. The *tail-behind* sub-event should occur before the *enter* sub-event for *x*, and the *enter* sub-event for x should occur between the time *y* gains access to the entrance and the time the entrance to the facility closes. For this, we need the definitions for *before* and *between* in temporal relations. This indicates a lack of clarity in this ontology.

MINIMAL COMMITMENT

We illustrate the principle of minimal commitment using tarmac and perimeter security ontologies (Video Event Challenge Workshop, 2003).

Ontology 2 (Tarmac Security):
$((v1$: fuel carrier vehicle),$(z1$: airplane),$(eq1$:fuel tank opening of plane), $(eq2$:fuel pump of carrier))
components:
$((c1$:approach$(v1,z1))$
$(c2$:open$(eq1))$
$(c3$:inside of$(eq2,eq1))$
$(c4$:together$(v1,z1))$
$(c5$:close$(eq1))$
$(c6$:leave$(v1,z1)))$
constraints:
(sequence$(c1,c4,c6)$
$(c2,c3,c5$ during $c4)$
sequence$(c2,c3,c5))$

We observe here that event $c4$, which corresponds to the fuel vehicle being near the plane, can not be put in any order with activities $c2$, $c3$, and $c5$ as it is concurrent with these processes. This is a minimally committed ontology. Attempts at further simplification could lead to misdetections or ambiguities.

Ontology 3 (Perimeter Security):
SINGLE-THREAD(suspicious-load(vehicle *v*, person *p*, entity *obj*, facility *fac*),
AND(zone(loading-area),
near(loading-area, *fac*),
portable(*obj*),
Sequence(approach(*v, fac*), AND(stop(*v*), near (*v, fac*),

NOT(inside(v, loading-area))),
AND(approach(p, v), carry(p, *obj*)),
AND(stop(p), near (p, v)),
cause(p, open(portal-of(v))),
enter (*obj*, v),
cause(p, close(portal-of(v))),
leave(v, *fac*))))

In Ontology 3, the vehicle's portal has to be open to load a suspicious object. This does not encompass other possible scenarios. For example, the suspicious load can be placed onto the trailer of a truck that is open from the top, without using the portal. Or it can be an explosive placed under the vehicle. Also, it is not necessary for the vehicle to stop; a person inside the vehicle could grab a bag from a pedestrian through the window. Hence, minimized ontology should only include the object being on the vehicle's exterior and then being transferred to the vehicle's interior while it is in a restricted zone.

Logical Ontologies and Probabilistic Detection

Another interesting use of ontologies is the PADS system (Albanese et al., submitted). In PADS, the authors propose that full first-order logic be used to model activities; this is in contrast to the work of Shet et al. (2005), who propose using Prolog to model activities. According to the PADS system, in order to model an activity of a passenger throwing a package out of the car, a specification is written as follows:

(exists f) (in(v,f) AND
in(p,v,f) AND
holding(p,pkg,f) AND
(exists f') f' >= f AND
In(p,v,f') AND
~holding(p,pkg,f') AND
Outside-car(pkg,f').

The above is a partial specification saying that for this condition to be true, there must exist a frame f in the video that shows a vehicle v and a passenger p in the vehicle who is holding a package pkg, and a later frame f' in which the passenger is no longer holding the package and the package is out of the car. Note that this is a simple representation of how a passenger can get rid of a package; this can be made more realistic (and complicated).

Two points are noteworthy. First, frames are explicitly referenced in these activity specifications through variables such as f and f' above. Second, partial ordering of events is also explicitly specifiable—in the above example, the constraint $f' \geq f$ ensures that f' is a frame that occurs after f in the video. The PADS framework allows predicates such as "holding" and "outside-car" in the above specification to invoke image processing algorithms to perform the requisite checks.

PADS also assumes the existence of a *probabilistic frame labeling*. A labeling specifies, for each frame, a set of properties that are true in the frame (with some probability). This can be done by applying a standard suite of image-processing algorithms to recognize objects or motions in the video. Such a labeling may, for example, state that a given frame f contains a car and a passenger inside the car. But it may say that the passenger is holding a package with only 60% probability.

PADS then provides fast matching algorithms. These algorithms take an activity specification as input, together with a frame labeling, and find minimal segments of the video that contain the activity with a probability exceeding a given threshold.

Experiments

The bank monitoring dataset discussed above consists of video sequences showing normal activities at a bank and different scenarios of attacking the bank safe. We illustrate the design of ontology (Video Event Challenge Workshop, 2003) for this domain and evaluate it based on Gruber's criteria. The agents involved in this domain are the bank employees, the customers, and the robbers. The inanimate entities of interest are different parts of the bank such as the entrance, the counter, and the area where the deposit/withdrawal slips are kept. The entities may be involved in a normal activity where customers enter the bank, conduct transactions, and exit. Or, in an anomalous case, a robber enters the bank, gains unauthorized access to the bank safe situated behind the counter, and exits the bank.

In Ontology 4, several safe-attack (i.e., attacking the bank safe) scenarios, with minor differences corresponding to deviations in the path of
the attackers, have been defined. There are several multi-thread versions
involving two robbers and minor deviations for each robber and the gate.
This suggests a need to exhaustively define all possible scenarios, which is
impractical. It violates the minimal ontological commitment criterion.

Ontology 4 (Video Event Challenge Workshop, 2003):
composite_event Safe_attack_1person_baçk_counter
physical_objects:
((p : Person), *($z1$*: Back_Counter), ($z2$: Safe))
components:
($c1$: primitive_event Changes_zone ($p, z1, z2$))
constraints:
($c2$ before $c1$)
composite_event   Safe_attack_1person_back_counter_and_door_
opened
physical_objects:
((p : Person), ($z1$: Back_Counter), ($z2$: Safe), (g: Gate))
components:
($c1$: composite_event Safe_attack_1person_back_counter($p, z1, z2$))
constraints:
(g is opened)

We can simplify the safe-attack scenarios by observing that there is an
unauthorized access to the safe in all such scenarios. Figure 18.11 shows
detection of safe-attack using the following simplified ontology:

Ontology 5 (Video Event Challenge Workshop, 2003):
safe attack: usage: safe attack($mo1, z1$) physical objects:
(($mo1$:mobile object),($z1$:zone))
components:
(($c1$:approach($mo1, z1$))
($c2$:inside zone($mo1, z1$)))
($c3$:leave($mo1, z1$)))
($c4$:NOT(employee(($mo1$))))
temporal constraints:
(sequence($c1, c2, c3$))

FIGURE 18.11. Bank surveillance dataset: intruder attacking the bank safe.

Conclusion

The need for building useful representations of video sequences may be driven by varied tasks such as event modeling (or its inverse problem of path planning for robotic navigation) and temporal segmentation and event detection for indexing or anomaly detection. All these applications offer compelling challenges to computational vision systems at many levels, ranging from low-level vision tasks for detection and segmentation of objects to high-level models that capture the essential characteristics at increasing levels of abstraction.

Ontologies provide a rich description of entities and events in activities but rely on an expert's ability to completely specify the given scenario. Their main advantage is the complete description, irrespective of whether some scenarios are observed or not. At the same time, ontologies are limited by this factor because describing all possible sequences of events can be tedious. Also, the use of ontologies emphasizes the expert's ability to predict all possible scenarios in an activity. Given such ontologies, a suitable grammar can be used to parse the sequence of events. Statistical approaches, on the other hand, yield compact models of observed data. By design, they are best suited to mathematical manipulations. They may be useful for extracting repeated patterns from the data but generally are not adept at finding higher-level structure in the data. A multidisciplinary approach that incorporates statistical methods, semantic descriptions, and human–computer interactions can aid in building effective models for activities.

Acknowledgments

This work was partially supported by the ARDA/VACE program under contract 2004H80200000 and the ARL CTA program under agreement DAAD19-01-2-008.

References

Aggarwal, J., & Cai, Q. (1999). Human motion analysis: A review. *Computer Vision & Image Understanding*, *73*(3), 428–440.

Albanese, M., Moscato, V., Picariello, A., Subrahmanian, V. S., & Udrea, O. (submitted). *PADS: A Probabilistic Activity Detection System*.

Alblas, H. (1991). Introduction to attribute grammars. In H. Alblas & B. Melichar (Eds.), *Lecture Notes in Computer Science: Proceedings on Attribute Grammars, Applications and Systems* (pp. 1–15). London: Springer-Verlag.

Allen, J. (1995). *Natural language understanding* (2nd ed.). Redwood City, CA: Benjamin/Cummings.

Baum, L., Petrie, T., Soules, G., & Weiss, N. (1970). A maximization technique occurring in the statistical analysis of probabilistic functions of Markov chains. *Annals of Mathematical Statistics*, *41*(1), 164–171.

Brand, M., Oliver, N., & Pentland, A. (1997). Coupled hidden Markov models for complex action recognition. *Proceedings of the IEEE Computer Society Conference on Computer Vision & Pattern Recognition*, 994–999.

Calvanese, D., Lenzerini, M., & Nardi, D. (1998). Description logics for conceptual data modeling. In J. Chomicki & G. Saake, *Logics for databases & information systems* (pp. 229–263). Norwell, MA: Kluwer Academic Publishers.

Chen, D., Yang, J., & Wactlar, H. (2004). Towards automatic analysis of social interaction patterns in a nursing home environment from video. *Proceedings of the SIGMM International Workshop on Multimedia Information Retrieval*, 283–290.

Cuntoor, N. P., & Chellappa, R. (2006). Key frame-based activity representation using antieigenvalues. *Proceedings of the Asian Conference on Computer Vision, 2*, 499–508.

Cuntoor, N. P., Yegnanarayana, B., & Chellappa, R. (2005). Interpretation of state sequences in HMM for activity representation. *Proceedings of the IEEE International Conference on Acoustics, Speech, and Signal Processing, 2*, 709–712.

Cupillard, F., Avanzi, A., Bremond, F., & Thonnat, M. (2004). Video understanding for metro surveillance. *Proceedings of the IEEE International Conference on Networking, Sensing and Control, 1*, 186–191l.

Earley, J. (1970). An efficient context-free parsing algorithm. *Communications of the ACM, 13*(2), 94–102.

Efros, A. A., Berg, A. C., Mori, G., & Malik, J. (2003). Recognizing action at a distance. *Proceedings of the IEEE International Conference on Computer Vision, 1*, 726–733.

François, A. R. J., Nevatia, R., Hobbs, J., & Bolles, R. C. (2005). VERL: An ontology framework for representing & annotating video events. *IEEE MultiMedia, 12*(4), 76–86.

Fu, K. S. (1982). *Syntactic pattern recognition & applications.* Englewood Cliffs, NJ: Prentice Hall.

Georis, B., Maziere, M., Bremond, F., & Thonnat, M. (2004). A video interpretation platform applied to bank agency monitoring. In *Proceedings of the 2nd IEEE Workshop on Intelligent Distributed Surveillance Systems* (pp. 46–60). London: IEEE.

Ghahramani, Z., & Hinton, G. E. (1998). Variational learning for switched state space models. *Neural Computation, 12*, 969–996.

Ghanem, N., Dementhon, D., Doermann, D., & Davis, L. (2004). Representation and recognition of events in surveillance video using Petri nets. In *Proceedings of the IEEE Workshop on Event Mining*, Vol. 7 (pp. 112–117). Washington, DC: IEEE.

Gruber, T. R. (1995). Toward principles for the design of ontologies used for knowledge sharing. *International Journal of Human Computer Studies, 43*, 907–928.

Guestrin, C., Koller, D., Gearhart, C., & Kanodia, N. (2003). Generalizing plans to new environments in relational MDPs. *Proceedings of the International Joint Conference on Artificial Intelligence, 1*, 1003–1010.

Hakeem, A., & Shah, M. (2004). Ontology and taxonomy collaborated framework for meeting classification. *Proceedings of the IEEE International Conference on Pattern Recognition, 4*, 219–222.

Hamid, R., Huang, Y., & Essa, I. (2003). Argmode: Activity recognition using graphical models. *Proceedings of the IEEE Computer Society Conference on Computer Vision and Pattern Recognition, 4*, 38–43.

Haritaoglu, I., Cutler, R., Harwood, D., & Davis, L. (1999). Backpack detection of people carrying objects using silhouettes. *Proceedings of the IEEE Computer Society Conference on Computer Vision & Pattern Recognition, 1*, 102–107.

Hongeng, S., Nevatia, R., & Bremond, F. (2004). Video-based event recognition: Activity representation and probabilistic recognition methods. *Computer Vision and Image Understanding, 96*(2), 129–162.

Hopcroft, J. E., & Ullman, J. D. (1979). *Introduction to automata theory, languages and computation.* Reading, MA: Addison-Wesley.

Isard, M., & Blake, A. (1998). A mixed state condensation tracker with automatic model switching. *Proceedings of the IEEE Computer Society Conference on Computer Vision & Pattern Recognition, 1,* 107–112.

Ivanov, Y. A., & Bobick, A. F. (2000). Recognition of visual activities and interactions by stochastic parsing. *IEEE Transactions Pattern Analysis Machine Intelligence, 23,* 852–872.

Izo, T., & Grimson, W. E. L. (2004). Simultaneous pose estimation and camera calibration from multiple views. *Proceedings of the IEEE Workshop on Motion of Non-Rigid and Articulated Objects, 1,* 14–21.

Joo, S., & Zheng, Q. (2005). A temporal variance-based moving target detector. *Proceedings of the IEEE Workshop on Performance Evaluation of Tracking & Surveillance* [electronic version]. Beijing, China: IEEE.

Kale, A., Rajagopalan, A. N., Sundaresan, A., Cuntoor, N., Roy-Chowdhury, A. K., Kruger, V., et al. (2004). Identification of humans using gait. *IEEE Transactions Image Processing, 13,* 1163–1173.

Kendall, D., Barden, D., Carne, T., & Le, H. (1999). *Shape & shape theory.* West Sussex, UK: John Wiley & Sons.

Knuth, D. E. (1968). Semantics of context-free languages. *Mathematical Systems Theory, 2*(2), 127–145.

Koller, D., & Lerner, U. (2000). Sampling in factored dynamic systems. In A. Doucet, N. de Freitas, & N. Gordon (Eds.), *Sequential Monte Carlo methods in practice* (pp. 470–490). New York: Springer.

Lassila, O., & Swick, R. R. *Resource Description Framework (RDF) model and syntax specification: W3C Working Draft 1998.* Retrieved August 8, 2007, from http://www.w3.org/TR/WD-rdf-syntax/.

Lucas, B. D., & Kanade, T. (1981). An iterative image registration technique with an application to stereo vision. *Proceedings of the International Joint Conferences on Artificial Intelligence, 1,* 674–679.

Manning, C. D., & Schütze, H. (1999). *Foundations of statistical natural language processing.* Cambridge, MA: MIT Press.

Moore, D., & Essa, I. (2002). Recognizing multitasked activities from video using stochastic context-free grammar. *Proceedings of the National Conference on Artificial Intelligence, 1,* 770–776.

Murata, T. (1989). Petri nets: Properties, analysis & applications. *Proceedings of the IEEE, 77*(4), 541–580.

Neumann, B., & Novak, H. J. (1983). Event models for recognition & natural language descriptions of events in real-world image sequences. *Proceedings of the International Joint Conferences on Artificial Intelligence, 1,* 724–726.

Oliver, N., Horvitz, E., & Garg, A. (2002). Layered representations for human activity recognition. In *Proceedings of the IEEE International Conference on Multimodal Interfaces* (pp. 3–7). Pittsburgh, PA: IEEE.

Parameswaran, V., & Chellappa, R. (2003). View invariants for human action recognition. In *Proceedings of the IEEE Computer Society Conference on Computer Vision & Pattern Recognition, 2*, 613–619.

Perona, P., & Malik, J. (1990). Scale-space and edge detection using anisotropic diffusion. *IEEE Transactions Pattern Analysis & Machine Intelligence, 12*(7), 1213–1243.

Pfaltz, J. L., & Rosenfeld, A. (1969). Web grammars. *Proceedings of the International Joint Conferences on Artificial Intelligence*, 609–620.

Rabiner, L. R. (1989). A tutorial on hidden Markov models and selected applications in speech processing, *Proceedings of the IEEE, 63*, 257–285.

Rao, C., Yilmaz, A., & Shah, M. (2003). View-invariant representation and recognition of actions. *International Journal of Computer Vision, 63*, 257–285.

Roy-Chowdhury, A. K., & Chellappa, R. (2003). A factorization approach for activity recognition. In *Proceedings of the IEEE Workshop on Event Mining*, Vol. 4 (pp. 41–46). Madison, WI: IEEE.

Sandewall, E., & Ronnquist, R. (1986). A representation of action structures. *Proceedings of theNational Conference on Artificial Intelligence*, 89–97.

Shet, V. D., Harwood, D., & Davis, L. S. (2005). VidMAP: Video Monitoring of Activity with Prolog. In *IEEE International Conference on Advanced Video & Signal-Based Surveillance (AVSS)* (pp. 224–229). Como, Italy: IEEE

Starner, T., & Pentland, A. (1995). Real-time American Sign Language recognition from video using hidden Markov models. In *Proceedings of the IEEE International Symposium on Computer Vision* (pp. 265–270). Coral Gables, FL: IEEE.

Stauffer, C. (2004). Learning a factorized segmental representation of far-field tracking data. In *Proceedings of the IEEE Workshop on Event Mining*, Vol. 7 (pp. 115–121). Washington, DC: IEEE.

Stauffer, C., & Grimson, E. (2000). Learning patterns of activity using real-time tracking. *IEEE Transactions Pattern Analysis & Machine Intelligence, 22*(8), 747–757.

Stolcke, A. (1995). An efficient probabilistic context-free parsing algorithm that computes prefix probabilities, *Computational Linguistics, 21*(2), 65–201.

Syeda-Mahmood, T., Vasilescu, A., & Sethi, S. (2001). Recognizing action events from multiple viewpoints. In *Proceedings of the IEEE Workshop on Detection & Recognition of Events in Video* (pp. 64–72). Vancouver, BC, Canada: IEEE.

Tomasi, C., & Kanade, T. (1992). Shape and motion from image streams under orthography: A factorization method. *Internal Journal of Computer Vision, 9*(2), 137–154.

Torresani, L., & Bregler, C. (2002). Space-time tracking. *Proceedings of the European Conference on Computer Vision, 1*, 801–812.

Tsuji, S., Morizono, A., & Kuroda, S. (1977). Understanding a simple cartoon film by a computer vision system. *Proceedings of the International Joint Conferences on Artificial Intelligence*, 609–610.

Vaswani, N., Roy-Chowdhury, A. K., & Chellappa, R. (2003). Activity recognition using the dynamics of the configuration of interacting objects. *Proceed-

ings of the IEEE Computer Society Conference on Computer Vision & Pattern Recognition, 2, 633–639.

Vidal, E., Thollard, F., de la Higuera, C., Casacuberta, F., & Carrasco, R. C. (2005). Probabilistic finite-state machines. *IEEE Transactions on Pattern Analysis & Machine Intelligence, 27*(7), 1013–1039.

Video Event Challenge Workshop (2003). Retrieved August 8, 2007, from http://www.ai.sri.com/~burns/EventOntology/ [restricted-access page].

Vidyasagar, M. (1993). *Nonlinear systems analysis.* Englewood Cliffs, NJ: Prentice Hall.

Viterbi, A. J., (1967). Error bounds for convolutional codes and an asymptotically optimal decoding algorithm. *IEEE Transactions on Information Processing, 13*(2), 260–269.

Vu, V. T., Bremond, F., & Thonnat, M. (2002). Temporal constraints for video interpretation. *Proceedings of the 15th European Conference on Artificial Intelligence* [electronic version].

Vu, V. T., Bremond, F., & Thonnat, M. (2003). Automatic video interpretation: A novel algorithm for temporal scenario recognition. *Proceedings of the International Joint Conferences on Artificial Intelligence* [electronic version].

Wilson, A. D., & Bobick, A. F. (1999). Parametric hidden Markov models for gesture recognition. *IEEE Transactions Pattern Analysis & Machine Intelligence, 21*, 884–900.

Zelnik-Manor, L., & Irani, M. (2001). Event-based analysis of video. *Proceedings of the IEEE Computer Society Conference on Computer Vision and Pattern Recognition, 2*, 123–130.

Zhong, H., Shi, J., & Visontai, M. (2004). Detecting unusual activity in video. *Proceedings of IEEE Computer Vision & Pattern Recognition, 2*, 819–826.

19

Shining Spotlights, Zooming Lenses, Grabbing Hands, and Pecking Chickens: The Ebb and Flow of Attention During Events

DANIEL T. LEVIN & MEGAN M. SAYLOR

Researchers have long used a series of rich metaphors to describe visual attention, and some have argued that these metaphors have played a crucial role in shaping scientific theories of attention (Fernandez-Duque & Johnson, 1999). For example, visual attention has been likened to a spotlight, a zoom lens, and a hand. All of these metaphors are apt, particularly as descriptions of attention as it has been studied in typical lab tasks. However, recent research has revealed a series of striking limits to the results of attending that do not seem to fit with these metaphors. The contrast between the earlier work and more recent work represents, in part, a shift from studying visual capacity in situations where people are forced to process as much visual information as fast as they can to situations where we study typical visual behavior as people navigate real-world situations. These situations often involve the kinds of highly structured events that are the topic of this book. Perceiving structured events may involve more thought and less continuous contact with the visual world than previous understandings of visual attention have assumed. Therefore, we propose a new metaphor to guide research on visual attention, at least in some situations. Instead of a spotlight, hand, or zoom lens, we propose that attention is sometimes better likened to a pecking chicken. This metaphor may capture visual attention in situations where it only sometimes samples the visual world and does not track all objects over space and time.

In the pages that follow, we first review a set of metaphors for visual attention and discuss some of the ways in which these metaphors arise from the tasks used to study visual attention. Then we describe research documenting a range of failures of visual awareness that has questioned this understanding. Based on these findings and recent work exploring the analysis of dynamic action sequences, we discuss some implications for a model of attention that is less continuous than previous models but which produces a close link between knowledge and perceptual information during the specific moments when perceivers need to understand a visual scene.

Spotlights, Zoom Lenses, Grabbing Hands

One of the major points of this chapter, and this book more generally, is that visual attention and visual awareness have been studied in a relatively narrow range of situations, and for that reason we have developed a somewhat distorted picture of how they work. One of the key ways in which lab tasks mischaracterize visual attention is that they often give the impression that visual processing is continuous. This assumption often entails a deep and prolonged awareness of concrete visual features that may not be characteristic of everyday visual processing. This aspect of lab tasks is often reflected in the metaphors used to describe attention. In this section, we will review the most common of these metaphors and suggest that, as a group, they mischaracterize attention in some situations. Then, we will propose a new metaphor based on recent research that captures the dynamics of visual attention as it ebbs and flows over time. We should point out that this review focuses primarily on attentional metaphors that attempt to specify visual selective mechanisms, as opposed to more general resource models. We also focus on relatively active and top-down models of endogenous attention, leaving exogenous attention and stimulus-driven competition models in the background for the moment. For an excellent review of attention metaphors that encompasses these models, see Fernandez-Duque and Johnson (1999, 2002).

The Spotlight Metaphor

The spotlight metaphor originated in the 1960s as a way of describing spatial attention. Early research validating it used a spatial cueing paradigm in which an initial stimulus predicted the occurrence of a later stimulus. For example, Posner, Snyder, and Davidson (1980) asked subjects to respond to the appearance of a stimulus at one of four locations arrayed horizontally on a computer screen. These imperative stimuli were preceded by a cue that predicted the location of the imperative stimulus in 80% of trials. Subjects were faster to respond when the spatial location of the cue was the same as that of the target, and they obtained a smaller but still significant advantage when the cue was not in the same location but was nearby. Also important, cueing had no effect when a second-most-likely target was spatially separated from the most likely target by an intervening stimulus. In contrast, the second-most-likely stimulus did receive a benefit when it was adjacent to the target.

Together, these results establish several important features of the spotlight metaphor. First, just as a spotlight can be directed to illuminate only one region of a scene, leaving other parts of the scene dark, attention facilitates detection of targets in the spatial region where it is directed while leaving unattended regions "dark," possibly outside of awareness, and certainly not responded to. Second, a number of authors have suggested that this spotlight has a penumbra—a peripheral region within which illumination falls off but does not fail completely. For example, LaBerge and Brown (1989) suggest that either the spotlight has a penumbra or attention should instead be considered a more stationary gradient. Another key feature of the spotlight is that it is designed to be moved from one location to another and can not be subdivided. This latter feature has been the subject of a number of recent experiments suggesting that people can in some cases attend to two discontinuous locations, especially if they are occupied by objects that move as a group (see, for example, Driver & Baylis, 1989).

Many entailments of these metaphors have been the focus of subsequent research, which has generally provided support for the notion that contiguous regions within the spotlight are facilitated (with an occasional caveat about the precise shape of the region) and that the spotlight can not be subdivided. The metaphor of a moving bounded region of attention has proven particularly useful in the visual search literature, in which it often serves as the alternative to a parallel pre-attentive search. So, if a target can not be detected in parallel across the entire visual field, one must push the spotlight around the display, examining each location until the target is isolated. The spotlight metaphor is a particularly good fit for findings suggesting that serial search proceeds group by group, because the spotlight can illuminate several nearby items simultaneously (Pashler, 1987; Treisman & Gormican, 1988).

One interesting aspect of the spotlight metaphor is that it captures a very compelling "extramissionist" view of attention—that is, the source of attention is the perceiver, and it sometimes feels as if it consists of some sort of radiance that arises from the perceiver's eyes to illuminate different regions in the world. Thus, people think they can "feel" unseen stares, and a popular fantasy is the power to affect others from a distance with fiercely directed attention, even to the point of strangling them, as occurs with some regularity in the *Star Wars* movies. The suitability of an extramissionist system such as a spotlight for vision is particularly salient when one considers fictional depictions of potent supernatural energies. So, when a superhero acts on another thing at a distance, the requisite energy usually comes from his or her eyes or hands. It is particularly interesting to note that no fiction that we know of has involved auditory extramissions: have you ever seen a character kill an enemy by orienting his ear toward the villain and shooting lightning bolts (or sound waves) from it? A Google search of "superhero vision" produces 239 hits, while "superhero hearing" produces 67 hits, and "superhero smell" produces only 31 hits (the same pattern holds when substituting "eyes," "ears," and "nose" for "vision," "hearing," and "smell"). Indeed, adults will often endorse descriptions of vision that involve something emanating from the eyes, a misconception that is robust over a wide range of circumstances and quite resistant to all but the most direct educational interventions (see Winer & Cottrell, 2004, for a review). This metacognitive error may result from overgeneralizing the cognitive push inherent to endogenous visual attention to the inherently passive mechanics that allow the eyes to receive light.

It is particularly interesting to note that a rarely incorporated part of the spotlight metaphor is the notion that real spotlights can be turned on and off, usually to create fairly salient or even dramatic moments. When the spotlight comes on, its target is often a performer, who is then also "on." Conversely, when the spotlight is shut off the performance is over, and in some examples of fiction meaningful life itself ends at that moment. These entailments nicely highlight the more social aspects of attention, but the key to both of them is that the light stays on in the interim. It is this part of the spotlight that may constitute a problematic entailment of the metaphor. Many metaphorical treatments of the spotlight treat it as a harsh glare, and it is often treated as something that must always have something to shine on. So, when the spotlight is on you it is inescapable, and when it is gone it moves on to someone else.

In considering the specific pattern of connections between the spotlight as the metaphor's source domain and attention as a target domain, it becomes clear both that the source domain may constrain the questions we ask about the target domain and that the tasks used to understand the target domain have limited the connections made with the source domain. In particular, the tasks most closely associated with the spotlight, visual search and spatial priming, place a strong emphasis on the moments when attention is shifting from one thing to another, at the expense of exploring the possibility that attention turns on and off.

The Zoom Lens Metaphor

The zoom lens metaphor captures several important aspects of attention. It was first suggested by Charles Eriksen (Eriksen & Rohrbaugh, 1970; Eriksen & Yeh, 1985) as an alternative to strict dichotomies between diffuse and focal attention (e.g., Jonides, 1983). Similar to the spotlight metaphor, the zoom lens metaphor describes attention by assuming that it is applied to a limited region of space and can not be divided into disjoint subregions. Its key distinguishing feature is the idea that attention can be focused on a very small region or a large region, and that a key aspect of many tasks is the need to continuously adjust the size of the attended region. Also important in Eriksen's formulation is that the telephoto end of the zoom range increases the resolving power of the visual system. When we need to perceive additional visual features of some object, we "zoom in," confining the attentional window to the object of interest and allowing increased extraction of information from that object.

The zoom lens metaphor was originally developed to explain the re-sults of cueing experiments in which subjects searched for an alphanu-meric target in an array of letters. In Eriksen and Yeh (1985), subjects searched for an S or a Y in an array of eight letters presented in a fixed set of locations arranged in a circle. On some trials a partially predic-tive visual cue was presented. The key to this experiment was that the target was not only more likely to appear in the cued location but, on some trials, was also more likely to appear in a secondary location, de-fined as the diametrically opposite location in the circle. When all loca-tions in the array were filled with targets and distracters, subjects were fastest to detect cued targets and slowest to detect targets in uncued locations; intermediate results were demonstrated with the secondary locations. In contrast, when there were no distracters, subjects were fast-est in the cued location and showed slower and equivalent performance in the secondary and noncued locations. This implies that subjects had to search locations serially when there were distracters, so they checked the cued location, followed by the secondary location, followed by the noncued location. In contrast, when there were no distracters, subjects could start by checking the target location and then complete the task by "zooming out" to look at all of the other locations, giving them an equal chance of finding the target at secondary and noncued locations.

More recent findings are also consistent with the idea that the breadth of attention varies over time, both as a consequence of relatively au-tomatic processes underlying search and detection tasks and as part of more strategic refocusing between analytic and holistic processing. Recent analyses of visual search have demonstrated that at the begin-ning of a trial, visual attention is first broadly spread to encompass an entire array and then "zooms in" to encompass progressively smaller regions until it centers on the targets. A particularly vivid empirical sign of this process can be seen in Zelinsky, Rao, Hayhoe, and Ballard (1997), who asked subjects to search for a specific real-world object while they tracked subjects' eye movements. The stimuli were arranged in a semicircular array. Although subjects did not search the scene in parallel (slopes were 28 ms/item), they also apparently did not engage in a location-by-location search involving a shifting spotlight. Instead, the fixation analysis demonstrated that they first processed the scene as a whole, fixating on the center of the screen. Then, they shifted their eyes toward the hemifield containing the target, fixating in the left- or right-center of the screen, in a region that contained no objects. Finally, from this fixation, subjects usually moved their eyes again, typically to the target itself. This pattern of fixation implies that subjects initially processed the scene globally and detected a probable target. Then, they progressively narrowed their focus until they fixated on the target and responded. A key aspect of this finding is that attention, as reflected by fixation points (an assumption that is generally reliable, although not perfect), encompasses regions of space that increase or decrease in size systematically over the course of a task.

The zoom lens is also a suitable metaphor for tasks in which subjects need to force themselves to focus on the whole or parts of an object or scene. The best-known example of this phenomenon is a task in which subjects view a compound stimulus that instantiates one target category when viewed as a whole and another when its parts are the focus (Navon, 1977). For example, a large E can be made of small S's, and subjects can be asked to respond to either. One nice feature of this kind of task is that it can cause carryover effects in which the breadth of attention induced by processing the compound stimulus can carry over to a subsequently processed stimulus, causing it to be processed in the same way (see, for example, Austen & Enns, 2000). Thus, the last setting of the zoom lens, whether it is wide-angle or telephoto, remains unless a new task demands otherwise.

Generally, the zoom lens and spotlight metaphors are similar in that they emphasize the orienting of attention in space, and they differ in that the zoom lens is designed to vary the area that is illuminated. Although a spotlight can also do this, focusing a spotlight does not give as vivid an impression of increased resolving power when focused tightly. However, it is clearly not necessary for spatially constricted focus to be associated with increased information extraction per unit area—the other, and equally important, purpose of a narrow focus is to exclude distracting or conflicting information. A dynamically resizable spotlight (or even some sort of annulus) might be a more suitable description of attention in situations where the primary purpose of selective attention is to exclude information.

However, it is interesting to note that the spotlight metaphor seems more extramissionist than the zoom lens metaphor. The spotlight shoots light at something to illuminate it, whereas a zoom lens receives reflected light. Both are more generally "active" and selective because a zoom lens lends itself nicely to intentional control—we are all familiar with the idea of pointing a video camera to different locations and zooming in to points of interest. Given the extramission research, it would be particularly interesting to assess experimentally the degree to which lay intuition is consistent with these two metaphors, and to determine whether individual differences in acceptance of extramissionist views of vision are associated with increased preference for the spotlight model of attention.

Another difference between the spotlight and zoom lens metaphors is that the notion of turning on and off is less central to the functioning of a zoom lens than a spotlight. The duration of input is controlled by the camera, not the lens. Therefore, if the spotlight tends to imply a system that is always on, the zoom lens does so even more strongly. The lens of a camera is a chronically open system accepting information that some other system (e.g., the camera) may or may not process. Accordingly, this metaphor may be more consistent with a late-selection view of attention that implies a relatively large amount of processing prior to selection, whereas the spotlight is consistent with an early-selection view that would be characterized by less processing prior to filtering.

Attention as Fingers and Hands

The major feature that binds the spotlight and zoom lens metaphors is that they are spatial—that is, attention focuses on a given region of space, and the objects or features that happen to be inside of the region get processed more deeply. However, a competing tradition of research suggests that attention is often defined more by objects and less by the region of space they occupy. Thus, it is possible to observe situations in which subjects attend to a given object or part that suddenly moves to a new region of space and demonstrate facilitated responding to the object in its new location (Tipper, Driver, & Weaver, 1991), or to demonstrate that subjects find it easier to respond to two features of one object than to respond to the same features if they are parts of different objects (Duncan, 1984). Theories of object-based attention may be more suited to situations illustrating extreme limits on visual awareness, particularly because they emphasize the selection of some specific thing, not a region of space within which all objects are processed. So it is not surprising that the well-known object-based metaphors have been used to understand situations in which failures of visual awareness are common. In this section, we briefly review findings documenting a series of failures in visual awareness that might be problematic for the spotlight/ zoom lens metaphors, and we then discuss relatively recent finger and hand metaphors that may better account for these tasks.

Over the past 10 years psychologists have repeatedly demonstrated that people are poor at detecting between-view visual changes, so long as the transient that would normally signal a change is masked (for reviews see Rensink, 2002; Simons & Levin, 1997). For example, Levin and Simons (1997) showed subjects a short video depicting a conversation between two people. The film included a series of transitions (cuts) between different shots, and on each cut some visual property was changed. For example, in one shot the actors were sitting at a table with red plates on it, and in the next the same table was visible from a different point of view but the plates had suddenly become white. Despite the seeming salience of the changes, when subjects viewed the films they noticed none of them. This phenomenon, known as "change blindness," can be observed using a wide range of methodologies. For example, similar visual changes can go unnoticed when different versions of a photo are alternated, as in Rensink's "flicker paradigm" (Rensink, O'Regan, & Clark, 1997). Another means of eliminating the change-signaling transient is to ensure that it occurs as eye movements are occurring (Grimes, 1996; Henderson & Hollingsworth, 2003), and yet another is to ensure that other transients are included in the scene to eliminate the uniqueness of the change-transient (O'Regan, Rensink, & Clark, 1999).

These findings reveal striking limits to visual awareness and implicate a surprising amount of selectivity inherent to visual attention. However, in all of the above-mentioned change blindness findings, subjects missed changes in parts of scenes that they were not necessarily attending to while the change occurred. Accordingly, this would be consistent with a spotlight metaphor. If something changes while it is in the spotlight, the change will be noticed, and if it changes outside of the spotlight it will not be noticed. However, other findings extend the change blindness phenomenon into the realm of attended objects. For example, Levin and Simons (1997) and Simons and Levin (1998) found that subjects missed changes even in nominally attended objects. They showed subjects films in which the sole actor changed into another person across a cut, and they created a situation in which a subject's real-world conversation partner changed into another person across a brief occlusion. In both cases, about 50% of subjects missed the change. Change blindness in attended objects has been replicated both in other real-world situations (Levin, Simons, Angelone, & Chabris, 2002) and in the lab (Angelone, Levin, & Simons, 2003; O'Regan, Deubel, Clark, & Rensink, 2000). These findings are problematic for the spotlight and zoom lens metaphors because participants appear to be missing salient changes that occur within the boundaries of visual attention.

A key conclusion from this line of research is that we are aware of the world only in thin slices. These slices represent selections that are restricted not only in space but also in aspect and point of view—that is, sometimes attention focuses processing on some region of space, sometimes it focuses on some specific object, and sometimes it focuses on some specific feature of some specific object (O'Regan et al., 2000; Simons & Levin, 1998). The spotlight and lens metaphors might be reasonable in the first case and passable in the second, but both seem to have difficulty encompassing a phenomenon such as change blindness in attended objects.

If spotlights and lenses have difficulty with change blindness in attended objects, then more recent finger and hand metaphors might be more suitable. The finger metaphor comes from work by Pylyshyn using the Multiple Object Tracking (MOT) task (Pylyshyn & Storm, 1988). In this task, subjects are first shown a screen containing a set of identical objects, some of which are designated targets, as signaled by flickering for a moment. After subjects know their targets, all of the objects start moving in random directions, and the subject's job is to track the targets while ignoring the other distracting objects. Subjects are able to do this efficiently with up to four targets at a time, in the face of randomly moving and bouncing targets that are interspersed with distracters at irregular spacings. Even brief occlusions do not interfere appreciably with performance in this task (Scholl & Pylyshyn, 1999). Clearly, this constitutes another situation that is not well described by an attentional spotlight, and recent data show that salient nontracked objects sometimes go entirely unnoticed (Most, Scholl, Clifford, & Simons, 2005), despite the fact that they repeatedly travel inside of whatever spotlight would be defined by the targets. Pylyshyn hypothesized that the objects are tracked by a mechanism that instantiates object tokens and tracks them over time, but does not store perceptual information. Given that the mechanism can track a maximum of four or five objects at a time, Pylyshyn and Storm likened it to a set of fingers that maintain contact with objects as they move, and they coined the acronym "FINSTs" (fingers of instantiation).

Although FINSTs are not really a description of attention (rather, they provide an initial selection of objects for attention to operate upon), a similar metaphor was proposed by Rensink (2000), who used it as part of a theory of attention that could account for change blindness. Rensink's coherence theory is much like feature integration theory (Treisman & Gelade, 1980) in that it proposes an early, preattentive parallel stage of processing that develops representations of objects that include descriptions of basic features. However, these features are not bound into object representations and are spatially and temporally unstable until they are further processed by attention. The arrival of attention on an object or location makes these representations stable in space and time. This stability is what allows subjects to detect changes to a given object—without it, subjects may process some of the changing features but will be unable to assign them to a correctly individuated object, and therefore will not detect the change. A key part of this theory is that once attention leaves a location, the coherent object representations immediately revert back to their incoherent state. Thus, to see an object change, a subject needs to attend to it both before and after it changes.

In coherence theory, attention is likened to a hand that rummages through the visual world, grabbing a succession of objects and holding them in a coherent state for the rest of the cognitive system to inspect. In the original formulation, there is only one hand, implying a one-object visual capacity. Other research demonstrating a visual capacity of four or five items can be reconciled with this by assuming that the hand can create coherence by touching things with its four or five fingers, as in FINST theory, or by assuming that the items are collectively processed as a single object.

In any case, the hand metaphor is particularly compelling, and it is well suited for understanding change blindness because it is so active. The impression of vision that one gets based on the change blindness literature is that a significant representational effort is necessary to detect changes to objects and features. To see a change, you really have to reach out and grab an object, holding it while it changes. Anything short of this will result in change blindness, and perhaps a failure to be aware of the object at all (Mack & Rock, 1998). Although much research suggests that we may create long-lasting representations without this kind of effortful retention and comparison, these representations are not sufficient to detect changes and may be insufficient for other purposes, such as explicit recognition (e.g., Levin, Simons, Angelone, & Chabris, 2002).

But why does attention necessarily need to be so "grabby" (or maybe "holdy" is more appropriate)? Clearly we sometimes need to track things over space and time, but not always, and maybe not even usually. After all, the best-known anatomical and functional distinction in the visual system assigns only half of it to the task of tracking objects over time (Goodale et al., 1994). The other half is devoted to identifying objects, which does not necessitate tracking. The hand metaphor was developed to explain the entailments of detecting a visual change—attention has to be focused on something long enough to process pre- and post-change features; only then will a change be seen. The point, however, is that changes often are not seen, and according to the hand notion this occurs because the hand was grabbing something else when the change occurred, grabbed on to the thing after it changed, or let go before it changed.

In the next section, we review three lines of research that suggest the need for a new metaphor to describe attention that is, indeed, less holdy. The key to all of these is that visual attention is often focused on the task of identification and, further, that the real world not only does not require attentive tracking but may sometimes even discourage it.

New Views of Attentional Selection

The metaphors we have reviewed above are all good descriptions of attention, especially for the sorts of tasks that have been studied in the lab. However, these tasks may not be fully representative of the kinds of things we need attention for in the real world. In particular, we often must attend to meaningful events that unfold over time. Watching someone as he or she makes bread is far different from searching for a target or using arbitrarily paired cues and imperative stimuli. As attested to by the chapters in this book, recent research has begun to focus on how people perceive and make sense of events that unfold over time. In this section we describe several lines of research that suggest the need for a new understanding of attention. The first includes research closely related to the change blindness research described above. It shows that people represent only the information they need, and only when they need it for the task at hand. This research sets the stage for a description of research on event perception that converges to suggest a similarly constricted need for awareness of visual information. The event perception research, combined with research exploring momentary failures of visual awareness and more recent findings documenting similar but broader failures, converge to suggest the need for a new approach to visual attention.

Selection During a Real-World Task

A number of authors in vision research have begun to explore attention in real-world dynamic settings, and one key insight from this research is that we should account carefully not only for visual attention in space and relative to objects but also for the ebb and flow of attention over the different time courses inherent to unfolding events (Hayhoe, 2000). In Ballard, Hayhoe, and Peltz (1995), subjects were asked to complete a block assembly task in which they used LEGO blocks to copy a sample configuration of blocks. The task therefore involved a series of eye and hand movements in which subjects looked at the sample, at the resource area containing the blocks they were to use to assemble the pattern, and at the target area where they were assembling the blocks. A key observation from this task is that subjects looked from the sample to the resource area, grabbed a block, and then looked back to the sample before placing the block. Ballard et al. hypothesized that subjects first represented the color of the next block they were going to use, then looked to the resource area to retrieve it, and finally looked back to the target to represent the location of the block before finally placing it. Therefore, even though subjects had the capacity to simultaneously represent both the color and location of the block, they did not do so. Instead they represented only one of these at a time, preferring the alternative of making additional eye movements. On this view, we may attend to and represent only the specific features we need at the particular moment in which we need them.

This research was instrumental to the development of our understanding of the representational limits implied by change blindness. Recent research on change blindness has, in turn, produced evidence not only that visual representations are closely tied to the task at hand but that what we do with the representation is task-dependent. In particular, in some situations people appear to represent a very small number of features, but they may track those features over time. In other situations they may represent a larger number of features but fail to track many of those features. For example, Levin, Simons, Angelone, and Chabris (2002) tested the degree to which change blindness in a real-world person-change was associated with success on a recognition test for the pre-change experimenter. Consistent with Simons and Levin (1998), they found that a substantial number of subjects missed the change. In addition, they found that subjects who missed the change were unable to recognize the pre-change experimenter in the lineup, whereas subjects who saw the changes were reasonably accurate on this lineup. This implies that subjects miss changes when they fail to represent the changing details, but when they see changes it is because they did represent the pre-change experimenter and then compared this representation with the post-change experimenter. In contrast, a lab experiment using a similar paradigm demonstrated that change detection is sometimes unassociated with later recognition. Angelone, Levin, and Simons (2003) showed subjects videos of person substitutions and of other feature changes, and again gave subjects lineups in which they attempted to choose the changing object from among distracters. In this case, subjects who saw changes and those who missed them exhibited equivalent and above-chance performance. In addition, large between-condition and between-experiment differences on overall change detection were unassociated with overall lineup accuracy, which was consistently above chance. These findings break the close relationship between change detection and recognition, implying that in this case subjects represented features that they were later able to access for the recognition lineups, but they failed to track them over time to use for change detection. One interesting question is, what caused the contrasting pattern of recognition-change detection relationships between these two sets of experiments? Clearly, two major factors distinguish them—the Levin et al. study used subjects who did not know they were in an experiment, whereas in the Angelone et al. study subjects viewed videos and knew they were in an experiment. Although we have not systematically tested each of these possible differences, our bet is that subjects' knowledge of the experimental setting led them to purposely encode many features, which they failed to compare. Regardless of the specific source of this contrast, these findings are similar to Ballard, Hayhoe, and Peltz (1995) in demonstrating that people can sometimes represent and remember features, but they compare them across views only when they recognize the need to.

Lapses in Attention During Rapid Sequences of Stimuli

Among the more traditional lab paradigms, research demonstrating *repetition blindness* and *attentional blink* both have clear implications for attention during dynamic events. In the attentional blink paradigm, subjects are shown a rapid series of pictures, letters, or words and are asked to determine the number of target-category items that appear in the series (a rapid serial visual presentation, or "RSVP," paradigm). For example, they might be asked to determine how many letters appear in a mixed string of numbers and letters. The rate of presentation is adjusted so that subjects are reasonably good at detecting one of them, and the question is, what happens when they must detect two? When the second target is presented shortly after the first, subjects often fail to report it. In contrast, subjects are more successful in reporting the second target if several nontargets intervene between it and the first target (Raymond, Shapiro, & Arnell, 1992). The idea is that while subjects are processing the first target, limited-capacity attentional resources are engaged, and it is impossible to bring a second target into awareness while this is happening (Chun & Potter, 1995). Thus there is a cost to attending to a target deeply enough so that it can be reported later, and this may prevent awareness of a second task-relevant stimulus for a moment.

Repetition blindness is similar in that it involves a failure of awareness during an RSVP sequence. In this case, a stimulus identical to the target is repeated. So, subjects might be asked to determine whether a word is repeated in an RSVP sequence. In the face of good performance on individual words, subjects often have difficulty detecting the repeated word. This occurs even in situations where the repeated words are necessary to make a grammatical sentence—thus subjects might see a serial presentation of the grammatical sentence, "When she spilled the *ink* there was *ink* all over" but report the nongrammatical version, "When she spilled the ink there was all over" (Kanwisher, 1987). In this case, subjects not only have failed to detect the target, they have also failed to fill in a contextually likely gap in the sequence.

To explain these results, Kanwisher (1987) argued that the effect was caused by a failure in token individuation. This hypothesis relies on a type/token distinction that differentiates processes of identification from those necessary for tagging specific spatiotemporal objects with individual identities. Thus, the visual system not only needs to use specific features to identify "dog" out there; it also needs to associate those features with some specific thing. Otherwise, the only way of distinguishing between one dog and many dogs would be to assess the amount of "dog"-feature in the world—hardly a reliable means of distinguishing between a single stray and a pack of dozens. In the case of a repeated stimulus in an RSVP display, the two targets are tracked using the same token, even though they are separated by one or more intervening stimuli. Both of these lines of evidence reinforce the degree to which visual attention can be tightly constrained in time and, further, that there are clear costs to attending to a stimulus sufficiently to become aware of it (namely lack of awareness of a subsequent stimulus). It is important to note that in both of these situations there are different kinds of attention. First, prior to the target, subjects are attending to the sequence, and once the target appears they attend to the target more deeply, consolidating it so that it can be reported. On one view, this deeper kind of processing might be considered post-attentive cognitive elaboration. However, this kind of deeper processing is necessary for many basic kinds of information acquisition, and therefore arguably fits within the category of attention. In the case of RSVP, it is the kind of processing that allows us to tokenize and report an event, and in the case of change detection it allows sufficient spatiotemporal stability to compare features across views. If we were to use a spotlight or zoom lens metaphor, this would be analogous to distinguishing between an initial diffuse attention that affords some processing of an entire scene or perceptual channel and the more narrowly focused, "telephoto" attention necessary to report on and/or track a specific object over time (for similar distinctions see Chun & Wolfe, 2000; Zelinsky et al., 1997). However, these metaphors become strained when considering the fact that repetition blindness and inattentional blindness demonstrate a clear cost to focal attention. When we narrow the beam of focus to report on a single object, we can not, for a time, report on other objects or events, and so one would have to posit that the beam somehow shuts off after focusing.

A key implication of repetition blindness and attentional blink is that our perceptual and cognitive systems would be most useful if they sampled visual information only when it would prove informative. Thus, there is a clear demand for efficient allocation of attention over time as well as space. Just as attention in space might use the structure of natural scenes to guide efficient selection (for a review see Oliva, 2005), attentional allocation over time might take advantage of natural event structures to guide efficient sampling. In the next section, we briefly describe research on event perception, with an eye toward the hypothesis that events shape attention.

Attention During Dynamic Events

One's view of others moving about the world has the potential to devolve into a muddle. Real-world events—such as peanut-butter-sandwich construction and box moving—are continuous, dynamic, and evanescent. Bodies move rapidly in contact with diverse sets of objects, and there are no clear pauses to delineate the end of one action and the beginning of another. However, previous research demonstrates that observers of such action (adults and infants alike) do not perceive a chaotic jumble of motion but rather extract a sensible, discrete series of actions from the complex flow (e.g., Baird, Baldwin, & Malle, 1999; Baldwin, Baird, Saylor, & Clark, 2001; Saylor, Baldwin, Baird & Labounty, 2007; Zacks, Tversky, & Iyer, 2001). There is even method to the madness: the units extracted are commensurate with actors' goals and intentions and exist in hierarchical relation to one another, with larger units subsuming smaller units (for a fuller treatment of these issues, see Baird et al., 1999; Zacks et al., 2001; and Chapters 15 and 17 in this volume).

ACTION ANALYSIS AND EVENT PARSING

Classic and contemporary research on action analysis has elucidated the structure of dynamic events. In particular, observers typically identify distinct acts in others' everyday behavior, though the motions themselves flow continuously from one action to the next (Asch, 1952; Heider, 1958; Newtson, 1973). For example, in a series of classic studies, Newtson and colleagues (e.g., Newtson, 1973; Newtson, En-quist, & Bois, 1977) presented adults with videotapes of human action (e.g., model assembly, lighting a cigarette). Participants were asked to indicate meaningful juncture points within the action stream. Across several studies, participants were highly consistent in their detection of "breakpoints" within continuous action sequences. One recent study has demonstrated that such breakpoints are aligned with an analy-sis of actors' goals and intentions. In Baird et al. (1999), participants were shown videos of dynamic human action (e.g., kitchen cleaning). In a first study, one group of participants segmented the continuous sequences into consistent units coinciding with the actors' goals and in-tentions. In a second study, the intention boundaries were found to be psychologically salient during action processing: participants showed better memory for tones placed at intention boundaries than for tones placed in the midst of actions. Together, these findings clearly imply that boundaries between intentional actions have some special status in adults' processing of human action. A basic message arising from this research is that people seem to perceive events that unfold in time as having a clear structure, with individual acts being bounded by tran-sitions signaling the completion of one action and the beginning of another. It is interesting to note that this action structure appears early: research with infants has revealed similar findings (e.g., Baldwin et al., 2001; Saylor et al., in press).

One might reasonably hypothesize not only that this structure is re-flected by the ongoing dynamics of visual attention in a given situation but, more generally, that our attentional system might in a more basic way embody the spatial and temporal constraints of events (see Say-lor & Baldwin, 2004, for a similar argument). One of the key implica-tions of this structure is that there are some moments when we are more likely to allocate attention to events than others. During the transitions between events, for example, it is necessary not only to code visual in-formation but also to be fully aware of it. From a functional stand-point, this is because a new event must be perceived, related to current knowledge, and potentially acted upon. So, when you are having dinner with someone and he or she is holding a hot dog while looking around at the table, you need to identify relevant objects (the person, the hot dog), process the details (the look of the table, the lack of ketchup on the hot dog), and make meaningful links among these stimuli to infer that your dining partner desires ketchup. You might then determine that the bottle is closer to him or her than it is to you, so there is no need to stop eating. However, once an event has started there is little need to be aware of additional visual information. While your dining partner is reaching for the ketchup, little new information is being provided as the event occurs in a manner consistent with your initial assessment. Movements continue in expected directions, there are no new shifts of gaze, and already established visual properties are very unlikely to change in an important way.

There are at least two potentially compatible accounts of why attention may be allocated more strongly to transitions between intentions during dynamic events. On the one hand, attention may be allocated to such points as a direct result of an intentional analysis of action. On the other hand, transitions may grab attention because of salient basic perceptual features (e.g., the hand movement that is characteristic of moving from one object to the next). Results of one of Newtson's classic studies (Newtson & Enquist, 1976) are compatible with the first interpretation. In this study, participants were shown two types of still shots of action sequences: those from breakpoints/transitions and those from non-breakpoints. Participants were more successful at predicting the overall action when shown the breakpoint than non-breakpoint still shots. This finding suggests that at some level adults' analysis of transitions between actions is guided by an intentional analysis. However, it fails to answer the question of why attention might be drawn to such points during action analysis. (Because the study used still photographs, it does not give information about the time course of attention allocation during action analysis.) Recent research by Baldwin and colleagues and research underway in our labs will clarify these issues.

FAILURES TO DETECT LARGE-SCALE DISRUPTIONS

If there is a cost to attending to visual features, as the attentional blink and repetition blindness literatures suggest, then not only is there no need to be aware of visual information mid-event, but we really should avoid attending to mid-event visual information. This leads to the hypothesis that people should experience something like attentional blink or repetition blindness during real-world events. In a sense, the transitions between individual acts are analogous to the initial target in these paradigms, and succeeding information is probably processed to some degree, but not very deeply. So, it should be possible to ask subjects to view real-world events and have them miss significant disruptions occurring in the midst of the events.

Recently, Levin and Varakin (2004) created just such a situation. They asked subjects to view films of simple events and told them to pay close attention to the films because they were going to be "asked questions about them." In one of the films, an actor is seen entering a room, sitting at a table, putting a newspaper on it, turning the pages, and copying some information onto a small notepad. In a second film, two actors are seen walking toward each other in a series of alternating shots. One is carrying a stack of boxes, which falls to the ground when the two meet and collide. Each film lasted for less than 1 minute, and in each there was a large disruption to the ongoing event toward the end. In the newspaper film, while the actor was turning a page the entire picture was replaced with a low-spatial-frequency motion field (created by doing a fast pan with the lens thrown out of focus) for a variable number of frames. These disruptions were placed within the collision film just after the two actors hit each other. After they had viewed films (in small groups ranging in size from one to four participants) with these disruptions, we assessed the degree to which subjects had detected the disruptions by asking them a series of questions, starting with a general question about the degree to which they noticed anything unusual during the film and ending with a question asking specifically about the disruptions.

When we ran an initial version of this experiment, we found that most subjects failed to detect 200 ms disruptions. We then ran another experiment using 200, 400, and 600 ms disruptions to test the limits of the phenomenon. We were, however, shocked to find no effect of lengthening the disruptions—nearly 80% of subjects missed the 600 ms disruption. Like many change detection experiments, the experience of sitting behind a group of subjects who are oblivious to such a large and relatively lengthy disruption tends to change one's understanding of visual experience. Given that the disruptions were motion fields that were consistent with the motion of onscreen events, we tested whether the globally consistent motion was necessary to carry subjects through the disruption by simply changing the disruptions to blank screens (that were approximately equiluminant with the average of the pre- and post-disruption frames). Again, this had no effect. Subjects were no more likely to report the complete elimination of the stimulus sequence than they were to report the motion fields. (In addition, they were no more likely to report motion fields that were opposite to the direction of on-screen events.)

There are, of course, several issues to consider when evaluating this kind of failure in visual awareness. First, were the subjects who missed the event simply "spacing out" and completely inattentive to either the entire sequence or some part of it? This is particularly important for this kind of incidental perception experiment because subjects have no real task aside from "paying attention," and therefore we do not verify subjects' focus online. We tested this hypothesis by asking subjects a series of questions about the visual contents of the scene that were only answerable using information that was visible during the few seconds before and after the disruptions. For example, for the collision video, we asked subjects about the relative heights of the two colliding actors, and for the newspaper video we asked which direction the actor turned the pages in. We compared the responses of subjects who did and did not report the disruption with a group of control subjects who saw the videos with the critical seconds containing the disruptions and the surrounding events edited out. Thus, the control group could only guess about the answers to the questions, unless the broader context of the films somehow implied the answers. Subjects who missed the disruption were very nearly as accurate (74.4%) in answering these questions as the subjects who saw the disruption (81.8%), and they were far more accurate than subjects who saw the videos with the critical moments edited out (48.4%).

Another important question is whether subjects were aware of the disruption but failed to report it, either because they forgot about it or because our questions were not sensitive enough to tap their memory for it. The first possibility is difficult to rule out, but we would point out that the event itself posed no real memory load—subjects did not have to remember any specific identifiers to be able to tell us what they saw. In addition, although the disruption may have reached some sort of momentary awareness, it was far less accessible than subjects' memory for the actual events in the movie. Thus, whatever representation existed for the disruption, it was weaker than other representations of the event. This result makes clear the value of a functional approach to attention and awareness. We attend to things and are aware of them for a range of important purposes. High on this list would be the need to incorporate visual information into our plans and to be able to relate our experience to others. In this experiment, the disruption did not create a representation sufficient to do this, so in an important way it was missed. More generally, though, we sought to eliminate the possibility that subjects simply failed to understand what we were asking about by adding a recognition test to our experiments in which we replayed the disruption and the events surrounding it, carefully pointing the disruption out to subjects. They all saw it for the test, and were no more likely to report having seen it in the previous video than they were for the purely verbal recall questions.

Based on these data, we hypothesize that subjects miss the disruptions because they are generally unaware of specific visual information at the moment the disruptions occur. So, the key question to answer is, when are people aware of visual information? One good answer to that question would be to refer to the ongoing structure of events. People need to be aware of visual information when it is necessary to determine the nature of an event. This awareness allows one to bring a full complement of cognitive and perceptual resources to bear when deciding what is coming next. However, while an event is unfolding in an expected manner it may not be necessary to be aware of visual information. In fact, the lesson from the attentional blink and repetition blindness literatures is that this kind of awareness has costs, so not only is it unnecessary to be aware of visual information mid-event but the efficient allocation of attention may demand far less contact with the visual world than has previously been appreciated. We have collected some preliminary data in support of this hypothesis by placing disruptions either in the middle of events or during periods prior to the onset of an event. So, for the collision event, the disruption occurred several seconds before the collision while the actor carrying the boxes was turning a corner, and for the newspaper-reading event the disruption occurred while the actor was reading the paper and not moving. When disruptions occurred with no event context, they were noticed by approximately 50% of subjects, as compared with 10% to 15% detection of mid-event disruptions (see Saylor & Baldwin, 2004, for a description of similar findings).

So, what do these data have to say about visual attention? It appears that we may sometimes be aware of no specific visual information in a scene. The key questions, then, are: what are subjects in these experiments aware of, and how does visual attention contribute to this awareness? In this experiment, subjects are clearly attending to the video at some level, and they also must be processing the visual information in it. A late-selection view of attention would seem to be suitable here, with a few minor modifications. First, it seems important to distinguish between no attention, broadly focused attention, and a sort of attention that is responsible for bringing specific visual information into awareness. There are clearly situations in which subjects entirely fail to attend to something and do not process it at all, even though it is visually available. However, in the situation we have tested, subjects were probably processing quite a bit of visual information on an ongoing basis, because they were attending to the video and were successful on the later recognition test. Using a zoom lens metaphor, subjects may be doing "wide-angle" processing that resolves little detail. The trouble is that the zoom lens metaphor isn't particularly apt here, because wide-angle, diffuse attention should still have been sufficient to allow detection of the complete disappearance of the attended channel, and the same is true for the spotlight. The notion of a hand works slightly better, if one assumes that the hand is constantly grabbing and dropping things, but this kind of application does not fall directly out of the hand metaphor, which puts more emphasis on the notion that features are encoded and held for some amount of time.

Conclusion

The research reviewed in this section explores the temporal dynamics of visual attention over the course of unfolding events. Several key findings arise from the confluence of these findings, and they converge across a wide variety of natural and artificial tasks and stimuli. First, the picture one gets of attention is quite different from that given by the tasks reviewed in the first section. Most important is the idea that we often attend to things for very tightly circumscribed purposes. This leads to specific feature codings that last for specific durations. Second, the repetition blindness and attentional blink findings suggest that the kind of attention necessary for awareness of specific objects is associated with brief costs that prevent the awareness of subsequent events. Finally, failures to detect unexpected disruptions during natural events show that people are often entirely unaware of visual stimuli for a time, and that these moments of unawareness may be predictable based on the ongoing structure provided by real-world events. These findings suggest that in many situations internal attentive processes should be closely synchronized to the dynamics of the external world, and that this will inevitably require a balance between awareness of critical stimuli and openness to subsequent stimuli.

Visual Attention as a Pecking Chicken

To help understand attention in situations where vision is tightly coupled with ongoing events, we propose that visual attention might sometimes be more akin to a pecking chicken than a spotlight, zoom lens, or hand. Just as a chicken continuously searches for grain but engages the ground only in momentary pecks to eat a bit of grain, visual attention leads to awareness of specific visual information in a series of more or less closely spaced momentary samplings. A key feature of this metaphor is that these moments of deep engagement are often brief and may not involve ongoing tracking of visual information over time. Instead, visual samples are sometimes most efficient when they produce an immediate elaboration that forestalls awareness of subsequent visual information. So, if the system samples information at the beginning of an event, it will generally be necessary to elaborate upon it. There may be a "safe period" following this, during which it is unlikely that additional visual features will need to be elaborated because real-world events take time, and it is unlikely that two events will begin at very short temporal intervals. This may justify a "recoil" to attention—just as the chicken pecks and then immediately disengages from the ground. This idea is, of course, much like that illustrated by the attentional blink, a phenomenon that has a nicely metaphorical name in itself.

The recoil inherent to a peck is the primary feature that distinguishes the pecking chicken from the hand metaphor. We would argue that this makes pecking particularly well suited to understanding attention during the perception of real-world events. In this case, meaning-driven temporal structure may strongly differentiate effective sampling strategies from poor ones. If we select visual information for elaboration only at the moments when the information is necessary in order to understand an event, then we can understand events, consider their meaning, and incorporate novel visual information into our processing without losing the opportunity to elaborate on unexpected events. Thus, the chicken metaphor captures an interesting hypothesis regarding the efficient use of limited-capacity resources. One particularly nice thing about this description of efficiency is that it goes beyond traditional notions of filtering or inhibition to suggest an interlocked temporal sequence in which one actively focuses on some things (elaborating on an initial stimulus) and not others (further elaboration on subsequent stimuli). In metaphorical terms, the chicken can only peck at some things, and therefore should hit as much grain and as few pebbles as possible (for a related discussion likening visual search to foraging, see Gilchrist, North, & Hood, 2001).

In a sense, this tradeoff is straightforward, but it is useful to consider a concrete example of the predictions that follow from the idea. For example, imagine an experiment in which subjects are induced to elaborate on some visual property at various moments during a real-world event. They might be asked to report the color of an object that is cued by a probe dot or surrounded by a box. In one condition, they might be induced to do such elaborations during segment boundaries, consistent with a typical pattern of pecking. In another, they might be probed during mid-events, forcing them to elaborate at nonoptimal moments. There are a number of interesting predictions here. First, we might expect that subjects would be less likely to correctly remember the incorrectly cued events. Another interesting prediction is that subjects might have more difficulty integrating visual information with knowledge about the event. For example, they may have difficulty matching properties with actors in the event, correctly remembering the color of a shirt but forgetting who wore it (an event-based version of illusory conjunctions; Treisman & Schmidt, 1982).

A key element of these predictions is that there may be particularly opportune moments to combine visual information with more abstract, semantic knowledge (for a closely related discussion of information pickup at different points in the continuous action stream, see Chapter 1 in this volume). So, the transitions between individual actions or events within a continuous sequence may be just the time to "peck" because visual information (e.g., objects coming into contact with one another, characteristic movement vectors) will be useful in specifying the event, and once this information is encoded it can be elaborated upon for a time, allowing a wide range of knowledge to be recruited in understanding the scene. One could imagine a system that is tuned to the temporal dynamics of real-world events such that moments of conscious visual elaboration occur when they are most useful and are brief enough to allow encoding of subsequent events. How long does the system have until the next bit of visual information needs to be elaborated? If one assumes that fine segment boundaries are the soonest possible moment when a new bit of information needs to be elaborated upon, then the system has about 1 second to ready itself, a period that fits well with the theories of Ballard et al. (1995). If we assume that the duration of the attentional blink reflects a maximum possible rate of serial elaboration, then the typical fine event represents about half of the maximum event-perception speed. So, we should observe that it is very difficult for subjects to process more than about two or three events per second. At this speed, events should be very difficult to perceive in order, to replicate, and perhaps even to identify. Although this seems to be outside the realm of real-world experience, it isn't. For example, a good typist can type about 300 characters per minute, or about 5 characters per second. We might, therefore expect that it would be very difficult to perceive the individual key presses coherently, to detect a target key press, and perhaps to perceive the difference between a correctly typed word and an incorrect one. The same goes for a wide range of skilled behaviors—consider a musician's finger movements when he or she plays the guitar or piano, or even the hand movements that go into tying a shoe. All of these actions might be individually imperceptible, or at least impossible to elaborate upon and remember, especially for novices in the relevant domain.

Pecks represent moments when visual information is integrated with knowledge to produce a sophisticated understanding of the visual world that goes beyond the present, and beyond the immediately apparent. So, these may be the moments when actions are related to intentions, novel stimuli are related to existing knowledge, and actions are integrated with one another. Accordingly, there are a range of situations in which a peck might occur. Clearly, when the system has detected the transitions between individual acts we could assume such a sample, but other situations might cause them as well. For example, when an individual forms an intention to act or begins an action, one would expect a peck. Also, when the elaboration completed on one peck leads to the need for an additional sample, perhaps timed relative to the ongoing event, a peck might be planned.

Of course, when one mentions that a process needs to be "planned," the question of what does the planning usually comes up. In part, we would follow tradition here and point to the usual array of executive processes, past associations, and knowledge. However, a key insight that might be derived when considering visual attention during real-world events is that these extravisual control processes need not always stem from some unexplainable, vast knowledge base or from an executive homunculus. Instead, a large proportion of pecks might be understood as responses to the reasoning that stems from a relatively limited set of assumptions that followed from previous pecks, combined with slightly more elaborate knowledge about typical interactions between actions and objects. For example, Tversky, Zacks, and Hard (Chapter 17 of this volume) argue that much of the knowledge necessary to comprehend and segment events might be organized into a library of "action–object couplets." Such a library might serve as a powerful guide to attention, both spatially and temporally, if it sufficiently fine-grained information about the time course of the relation between specific movements and specific aspects of the objects being acted upon.

Before concluding, one final issue is the degree to which pecking chickens are a good metaphor for both exogenous and endogenous attention. In introducing the metaphors described in this chapter, we put our focus on endogenous attention, but it is possible that more stimulus-driven attention is also suitably described by pecking. A key issue here is that many processes are probably a mix of exogenous and endogenous attention (Egeth & Yantis, 1997), and perceiving natural events is probably a prime example of this mix. Event perception represents an online combination of perception of simple kinematic cues, identification of more complex perceptual categories, and consideration of more abstract goals and intentions. This leads one to expect a rapid interchange between stimulus-driven orienting and top-down guidance of attention. Thus, although the pecking-chicken metaphor most directly models endogenously driven sampling, the application of this metaphor to event perception instantiates a much broader ecology of attention that includes the chicken along with a whole barnyard full of stimuli and goals.

To summarize, the pecking-chicken metaphor has two parts. The first is that in some situations people engage in occasional elaborative samplings of the visual world, just as a chicken occasionally pecks for grain.

When no peck is occurring, we are aware of no specific visual information and may therefore miss brief disappearances of the attended visual channel. This is not to say that no processing is going on—the chicken is still looking for grain, and our visual system is processing information in an attended channel. However, much of this information does not rise to the level of awareness. The second entailment of this metaphor is the notion of recoil. A peck is followed by a moment of elaboration, and during this time further visual information can not be elaborated upon. This represents an important temporal limit on visual perception, and research on event perception may be critical in understanding how these limits will play themselves out in the real world.

"Which Is Right?" Versus "When Is Which Right?" Versus "For What Is Which Right?"

Of course, if one proposes a new metaphor, it seems necessary to argue that it is more "correct" than others. However, we would like to avoid this. We agree with Fernandez-Duque and Johnson (1999), who suggested that visual attention is a complex and diverse phenomenon that will probably best be described using a diverse set of theories associated with a similarly rich set of metaphors (for a similar argument see Chun & Wolfe, 2000). We would also follow them in arguing that this collection of metaphors does not constitute a set of temporary explanatory patches pending the development of "real" theories of attention but rather reflects a series of principles that will help formulate specific hypotheses in each of the subdomains that make up research on attention.

Even so, we do not want to imply that this conceptual heterogeneity is an invitation to proliferate a series of narrow explanations of attention that fail to generalize. Instead, we would advocate the same middle ground that researchers in cognitive development and concepts have developed (for a review see Hirschfeld & Gelman, 1994). Both of these fields have recognized the difficulty of developing theories of cognition that are broadly applicable without reducing to relatively blank generalizations about learning or similarity that at best explain little in any given situation, and at worst are tautological restatements of a problem (Keil, Smith, Simons, & Levin, 1998). Recent critiques of research on attention have made this point (Zelinsky, 2003). It may therefore be profitable to work toward understandings of how attention operates for each of a relatively small number of broadly inclusive basic domains. This approach strikes a middle ground between the need to develop broad generalizations and the need to make useful predictions about behavior in specific situations.

So, what will these domains look like? We do not know for sure but can make an informed guess. We suspect that the well-known division between dorsal and ventral vision can provide a good starting point for this set of domains. However, it remains unclear whether this anatomical and functional distinction should constitute a superordinate category for our domains or specify a pair of dimensions on which different domains vary. For example, one good candidate for a domain is something one might refer to as "intentional vision"—in other words, the set of visual tasks involving perceiving other people, inferring their internal representational states, and modifying behavior in accordance with those. Key criteria for such domains should be that they represent broad functions, develop in early childhood, and perhaps be neurologically dissociable. Intentional vision satisfies these criteria—a large branch of developmental psychology is focused on studying children's emerging understanding of other minds and how this relates to vision (for a review see Flavell, 2004), and serious neurological disorders such as autism may have their basis in a failure in this kind of visual/intentional task (Baron-Cohen, 1995). Most important, intentional vision is a broad domain. It is probably the basis for a wide range of social tasks and the perception of a wide range of visual events.

It is also interesting to note that much of the practice of motion picture editing is structured around precisely the set of visual tasks inherent to intentional vision. Film editors routinely must direct attention in a coherent way by inducing audiences to ask questions about characters' intentional representations; the editors answer these questions by showing the targets of intentions (for example, by cutting to the object or person an actor is looking at) and then cutting again to other intention-relevant objects, creating a cycle of "looks" between representational states and the external world (Levin & Beck, 2004). One common situation where this is salient is the creation of "eyeline matches" in which close-ups of two conversing characters must give the impression that each actor is looking at, and responding to, the actions or words of the other. This is typically done by ensuring that each actor looks offscreen at the other in a consistent direction. Thus, actor A will consistently look offscreen to the left to see actor B, who always returns the gaze by looking offscreen to the right at A. In a well-edited scene, this interchange can be quite complex; we see a pair of actors looking, behaving, and interpreting with their partner to give a rich sense not only of a spoken dialogue but of a deeper, more subtle interchange of desires and intentions that are hidden or visible to varying degrees. (For a related discussion of both the relationship between motion picture perception and event segmentation and the idea that research on event perception would be facilitated by a typology of events, see Chapter 15 in this volume.)

In addition to intentional vision, one could imagine other domains, many of which are already the subjects of considerable research. For example, a visual domain involving nonsocial object-to-object interactions might be worth considering, and existing research on visually guided locomotion and navigation is another excellent candidate for a domain. The key is that these might be the focus of an effort to sort out a set of domains that collectively might constitute a reasonably complete set of arenas in which visual attention operates.

This kind of effort not only might help us understand vision but also has the potential to put vision researchers at ease. We can avoid having to decide which metaphor is right, while also avoiding the creeping sense that we are proliferating explanations that will become progressively more narrow, less organized, and less like the kind of science we would like to have.

Acknowledgments

Thanks to Tim Shipley and Stephen Killingsworth for reading and commenting on this chapter. This work was supported by the National Science Foundation under Grant No. 0433653 to D. T. L. and M. M. S.

References

Angelone, B., Levin, D. T., & Simons, D. J. (2003). The relationship between change detection and recognition of centrally attended objects in motion pictures. *Perception, 32*, 947–962.

Asch, S. E. (1952). *Social psychology*. Englewood Cliffs, NJ: Prentice-Hall.

Austen, E., & Enns, J.T. (2000). Change detection: Paying attention to detail. *Psyche, 6*(11).

Baird, J. A., Baldwin, D. A., & Malle, B. F. (1999). *Adults' parsing of continuous action: The role of intention-based units.* Unpublished manuscript. Eugene: University of Oregon.

Baldwin, D. A., Baird, J. A., Saylor, M. M., & Clark, M. A. (2001). Infants detect structure in human action: A first step toward understanding others' intentions? *Child Development, 72,* 708–718.

Ballard, D, Hayhoe, M., & Peltz, J. (1995). Memory representations in natural tasks. *Cognitive Neuroscience, 7,* 66–80.

Baron-Cohen, S. (1995). *Mindblindness: An essay on autism and theory of mind.* Cambridge, MA: MIT Press.

Chun, M. M., & Potter, M. C. (1995). A two-stage model for multiple target selection in rapid serial visual presentation. *Journal of Experimental Psychology: Human Perception and Performance, 21,* 109–127.

Chun, M. M., & Wolfe, J. M. (2000). Visual attention. In E. B. Goldstein (Ed.), *Blackwell handbook of perception* (pp. 272–310). Malden, MA: Blackwell.

Driver, J., & Baylis, G. C. (1989). Movement and visual attention: The spotlight metaphor breaks down. *Journal of Experimental Psychology: Human Perception and Performance, 15,* 448–456.

Duncan, J. (1984). Selective attention and the organization of visual information. *Journal of Experimental Psychology: General, 4,* 501–517.

Egeth, H. E., & Yantis, S. (1997). Visual attention: Control, representation, and time course. *Annual Review of Psychology, 48,* 269–297.

Eriksen, C. W., & Rohrbaugh, J. W. (1970). Some factors determining the efficiency of selective attention. *American Journal of Psychology, 83,* 330–342.

Eriksen, C. W., & Yeh, Y. (1985). Allocation of attention in the visual field. *Journal of Experimental Psychology: Human Perception and Performance, 11,* 583–597.

Fernandez-Duque, D., & Johnson, M. L. (1999). Attention metaphors: How metaphors guide the cognitive psychology of attention. *Cognitive Science, 23,* 83–116.

Fernandez-Duque, D., & Johnson, M. L. (2002). Cause and effect theories of attention: The role of conceptual metaphors. *Review of General Psychololgy, 6,* 153–165.

Flavell, J. H. (2004). Development of knowledge about vision. In Levin, D. T. (Ed.), *Thinking and seeing: Visual metacognition in adults and children* (pp. 13–36). Cambridge, MA: MIT Press.

Gilchrist, I. D., North, A., & Hood, B. (2001). Is visual search really like foraging? *Perception, 30,* 1459–1464.

Goodale, M. A., Meenan, J. P., Buelthoff, H. H., Nicole, D. A., Murphy, K. J., & Racicot, C. I. (1994). Separate neural pathways for the visual analysis of object shape in perception and prehension. *Current Biology, 4,* 604–610.

Grimes, J. (1996). On the failure to detect changes in scenes across saccades. In K. Akins (Ed.), *Perception (Vancouver studies in cognitive science),* Vol. 2 (pp. 89–110). New York: Oxford University Press.

Hayhoe, M. (2000). Vision using routines. *Visual Cognition, 1–3,* 43–64.

Heider, F. (1958). *The psychology of interpersonal relations.* New York: Wiley.

Henderson, J. M., & Hollingworth, A. (2003). Global transsaccadic change blindness during scene perception. *Psychological Science, 14*(5), 493–497.

Hirschfeld, L. A., & Gelman, S. A. (1994). Toward a topography of mind: An introduction to domain specificity. In L. A. Hirschfeld & S. A. Gelman (Eds.), *Mapping the mind: Domain specificity in cognition and culture* (pp. 3–35) New York: Cambridge University Press.

Jonides, J. (1983). Further toward a model of the mind's eye. *Bulletin of the Psychonomic Society*, *21*, 247–250.

Kanwisher, N. G. (1987). Repetition blindness: Type recognition without token individuation. *Cognition*, *27*, 117–143.

Keil, F. C., Smith, W. C., Simons, D. J., & Levin, D. T. (1998). Two dogmas of conceptual empiricism: Implications for hybrid models of the structure of knowledge. *Cognition*, *65*, 103–135.

LaBerge, D., & Brown, V. (1989). Theory of attentional operations in shape identification. *Psychological Review*, *96*, 101–124.

Levin, D. T., & Beck, M. R. (2004). Thinking about seeing: Spanning the difference between metacognitive failure and success. In D. T. Levin (Ed.), *Thinking and seeing: Visual metacognition in adults and children*. Cambridge, MA: MIT Press.

Levin, D. T., & Simons, D. J. (1997). Failure to detect changes to attended objects in motion pictures. *Psychonomic Bulletin and Review*, *4*, 501–506.

Levin, D. T., Simons, D. J., Angelone, B. L., & Chabris, C. F. (2002). Memory for centrally attended changing objects in an incidental real-world change detection paradigm. *British Journal of Psychology*, *93*(3), 289–302.

Levin, D. T., & Varakin, D. A. (2004). No pause for a brief disruption: Failures of visual awareness during ongoing events. *Consciousness and Cognition*, *13*, 363–372.

Mack, A., & Rock, I. (1998). *Inattentional blindness*. Cambridge, MA: MIT Press.

Most, S. B., Scholl, B. J., Clifford, E. R., & Simons, D. J. (2005). What you see is what you set: Sustained inattentional blindness and the capture of awareness. *Psychological Review*, *112*(1), 217–242.

Navon, D. (1977). Forest before trees: The precedence of global features in visual perception. *Cognitive Psychology*, *9*, 353–383.

Newtson, D. (1973). The dynamics of action and interaction. In L. B. Smith & E. Thelan (Eds.), *A dynamic systems approach to development: Applications* (pp. 241–264). Cambridge, MA: MIT Press.

Newtson, D., & Engquist, G. (1976). The perceptual organization of ongoing behavior. *Journal of Experimental Social Psychology*, *12*, 436–450.

Newtson, D., Engquist, G., & Bois, J. (1977). The objective basis of behavior units. *Journal of Personality and Social Psychology*, *35*, 847–862.

Oliva, A. (2005). Gist of a scene. In L. Itti, G. Rees, & J. Tsotsos (Eds.), *Neurobiology of attention* (pp. 251–256) Burlington, MA: Academic Press.

O'Regan, J. K., Deubel, H., Clark, J. J., & Rensink, R. A. (2000). Picture changes during blinks: Looking without seeing and seeing without looking. *Visual Cognition*, *7*, 191–211.

O'Regan, J. K., Rensink, R. A., & Clark, J. J. (1999). Change blindness as a result of "mudsplashes." *Nature*, *398*, 34.

Pashler, H. P. (1987). Detecting conjunctions of color and form: Reassessing the serial search hypothesis. *Perception and Psychophysics*, *41*, 191–201.

Posner, M. I., Snyder, C. R. R., & Davidson, B. J. (1980). Attention and the detection of signals. *Journal of Experimental Psychology: General, 109,* 160–174.

Pylyshyn, Z. W., & Storm, R. W. (1988). Tracking multiple independant targets: Evidence for a parallel tracking mechanism. *Spatial Vision, 3,* 179–197.

Raymond, J. E., Shapiro, K. L., & Arnell, K. M. (1992). Temporary suppression of visual processing in an RSVP task: An attentional blink? *Journal of Experimental Psychology: Human Perception and Performance, 18,* 849–860.

Rensink, R. A. (2000). The dynamic representation of scenes. *Visual Cognition, 7,* 17–42.

Rensink, R. A. (2002). Change detection. *Annual Review of Psychology, 53,* 245–277.

Rensink, R. A., O'Regan, J. K., & Clark, J. J. (1997). To see or not to see: The need for attention to perceive changes in scenes. *Psychological Science, 8,* 368–373.

Saylor, M. M., & Baldwin, D. A. (2004). Action analysis and change blindness: Possible links. In D. T. Levin (Ed.), *Thinking and seeing: Visual metacognition in adults and children* (pp. 37–56). Cambridge, MA: MIT Press.

Saylor, M. M., Baldwin, D., Baird, J. A., & Labounty, J. (2007). Infants' on-line segmentation of dynamic human action. *Journal of Cognition and Development, 8,* 113–128.

Scholl, B. J., & Pylyshyn, Z. W. (1999). Tracking multiple items through occlusion: Clues to visual objecthood. *Cognitive Psychology, 38,* 259–290.

Simons, D. J., & Levin, D. T. (1997). Change blindness. *Trends in Cognitive Sciences, 1,* 261–267.

Simons, D. J., & Levin, D. T. (1998). Failure to detect changes to people during a real-world interaction. *Psychonomic Bulletin and Review, 5,* 644–649.

Tipper, S. P., Driver, J., & Weaver, B. (1991). Object-centered inhibition or return of visual attention. *Quarterly Journal of Experimental Psychology, 43A,* 289–298.

Treisman, A., & Gelade, G. (1980). A feature integration theory of attention. *Cognitive Psychology, 12,* 97–136.

Treisman, A., & Gormican, S. (1988). Feature analysis in early vision: Evidence from search asymmetries. *Psychological Review, 95,* 15–48.

Treisman, A., & Schmidt, H. (1982). Illusory conjunctions in the perception of objects. *Cognitive Psychology, 14,* 107–141.

Winer, G. A., & Cottrell, J. E. (2004). The odd belief that rays exit the eye during vision. In D. T. Levin (Ed.), *Thinking and seeing: Visual metacognition in adults and children* (pp. 97–120). Cambridege, MA: MIT Press.

Zacks, J., Tversky, B., & Iyer, G. (2001). Perceiving, remembering and communicating structure in events. *Journal of Experimental Psychology: General, 130,* 29–58.

Zelinsky, G. J. (2003). Detecting changes between real-world objects using spatiochromatic filters. *Psychonomic Bulletin and Review, 10,* 533–555.

Zelinsky, G. J., Rao, R. P. N., Hayhoe, M. M., & Ballard, D. H. (1997). Eye movements reveal the spatiotemporal dynamics of visual search. *Psychological Science, 8,* 448–453.

20

Dynamics and the Perception
of Causal Events

PHILLIP WOLFF

To imagine possible events, we use our knowledge of causal relationships. We also use these relationships to look deep into the past and
infer events that were not witnessed or to infer what can not be directly
seen in the present—for instance, the existence of planets around distant stars, or the presence of subatomic particles. Knowledge of causal
relationships allows us to go beyond the here and now. In this chapter I
introduce a new theoretical framework for how this very basic concept
might be mentally represented.

In effect, I propose an epistemological theory of causation—that is, a
theory that specifies the nature of people's knowledge of causation, the
notion of causation used in everyday language and reasoning. In philosophy, epistemological theories are often contrasted with metaphysical
theories, or theories about the nature of reality. Since people's concepts
of causation are assumed to be in error, most metaphysical theories of
causation seek to reform rather than describe the concept of *cause* in
people's heads (see Dowe, 2000; Mackie, 1974). Theories of causation
in psychology have followed suit by linking people's representations of
causation to the outward manifestations of causation rather than to
the quantities in the world that produce those manifestations. In this

chapter, I explore another possibility, one that assumes that people can peer beyond the veil of the visible to represent the (invisible) elements of the world that are essential to causal events. In the theory of causation to be presented, I propose that while the essential elements of causation are invisible, they are also are highly inferable because they are lawfully connected to the visible properties of events. As a consequence, people's representations of causation partially reproduce causation in the world. In short, I propose an epistemological theory that could, in many respects, also serve as a metaphysical theory.

Theories of Causation of the Humean Tradition

The distinction between causation in the mind and in the world is notably discussed by Hume (1737/1975). He stated that when people first observe a causal relationship, they may be able to detect spatial-temporal contiguity, a succession of events and, in particular, covariation, but not what is most central to people's ordinary concept of causation—that is, force, necessary connection, causal power and/or energy. Since notions such as these can not be determined from observation, let alone from reasoning, Hume held that people's ordinary notion of causation had no clear basis in reality (Dowe, 2000; Mackie, 1974).

Hume's arguments have greatly influenced psychological theories of causation. The invisibility of causation has led many researchers to conclude that causal relationships can be induced only from event frequencies. Induction from event frequencies implies that causal relations are represented in terms of their observable outcomes, rather than in terms of the physical quantities that actually produce those outcomes. Such theories are exemplified by, for example, Cheng and Novick's (1991, 1992) *probabilistic contrast model.* In this theory, causal relations are based on the covariation people observe between a candidate cause and effect within a "focal set" of events. Specifically, facilitative causation (CAUSE) is inferred when the probability of the effect in the presence of a candidate cause, $P(E|C)$, is noticeably greater than the probability of the effect in the absence of the cause, $P(E|\neg C)$—that is, when the difference between these two probabilities, ΔP, is positive. Inhibitory causation (PREVENT) is inferred when ΔP is negative. While the probabilistic contrast model is primarily a model of causal induction, it also implies a theory of causal representation in which causal relationships are associated with statistical dependencies. Cheng's (1997) power PC theory of causation extends the probabilistic contrast model by proposing that people's causal judgments are based on a theoretical entity—causal power—that can be estimated from covariation, provided certain conditions are honored (see Luhmann & Ahn, 2005, for a critical analysis of these assumptions). The power PC model fleshes out Hume's (1748/1975) intuition that people's ordinary notions of causation involve the notion of causal power and that this notion is derived from covariational information. Importantly, however, causal power in the power PC model is still very much a statistical entity: it is determined purely on the basis of co-occurrence patterns across multiple events, not on the physical quantities in the world that bring about those patterns (just as Hume would have liked).

Another recent approach to representation of causal relationships is captured in Bayesian network models of causation. In Bayesian models, causal factors are linked together in a network of nodes and arrows indicating causal connections (Gopnik et al., 2004; Pearl, 2000; Sloman, 2005; Sloman & Lagnado, 2002; Sobel, Tenenbaum, & Gopnik, 2004; Tenenbaum & Griffiths, 2001). While Bayesian networks go beyond prior approaches to causation in being able to address phenomena associated with causal reasoning, they remain very much theories based only on the visible. Before a Bayesian network can reason, it must first be constructed, typically on the basis of statistical dependencies (Gopnik et al., 2004). As stated above, statistical dependencies are summary representations that are tabulated and stored in people's minds, not in the world. Such networks do not directly represent the processes and quantities that bring about causal relationships in the world. As pointed out by Bunge (1959), to treat statistical dependency approaches as theories of causation is to confuse causation for one of its tests.

In addition to probability approaches to causation, Hume's views have influenced accounts of causal perception, most notably Michotte's (1946/1963). Michotte examined in great detail the stimulus conditions that give rise to the impression of causation. He focused primarily on what he called launching events. In the canonical launching event, an object A approaches and hits a stationary object B, sending it into motion. One of the main findings from this research is that even small changes in the stimulus conditions could greatly affect the impression of causation (Scholl & Tremoulet, 2000). For example, a temporal gap between the two objects can sometimes disrupt the impression of causation (Michotte, 1946/1963; Thinès, Costall, & Butterworth, 1991). Importantly, when people are asked to describe launching events, their descriptions typically include more than a mere specification of the objects' motions (Choi & Scholl, 2004; Michotte, 1946/1963). In billiard-ball collisions (a type of launching event), for example, people not only see changes in motion in two objects but also view one of the balls as causing the other's motion. The pattern of motion instantiated by the launching event leads to the apprehension of an invisible causal agency. However, Michotte (1946/1963) emphasized that this causal agency was not a direct representation of forces or energies in the world. Rather, it was a perceptual phenomenon, or illusion, possibly triggered by an innate perceptual mechanism.

Challenges for Theories of the Humean Tradition

Many current models of causation are based on Hume's assumption that the physical quantities that give rise to causal events are unavailable to the human perceiver. But on this assumption, I will argue, Hume was mistaken. While people can not directly see forces and energies, this does not mean that such quantities can not be directly recovered from the sensory input. Newtonian physics indicates that, in principle, such recovery is possible because of the lawful mapping between kinematics and dynamics. Kinematics specifies the observable properties of an event—the shapes, sizes, spatial relations, velocities, and accelerations of the various entities in a motion event (Gilden, 1991; Joskowicz & Sacks, 1991; Schwartz, 1999). In contrast, a motion event's dynamics concern the invisible properties of an event (Schwartz, 1999), specifically the forces, potential energies, pressures, powers, elasticities, and masses that bring about an event. Some of the mapping between kinematics and dynamics is captured in Newton's laws of motion. For example, if an object suddenly turns to the right, Newton's First Law states that the change in velocity implies acceleration, which entails the presence of a force. Newton's Second Law, $F = m\mathbf{a}$, implies that the direction of the force, $\mathbf{F}$, is exactly the same as the direction of acceleration, $\mathbf{a}$. Thus, by observing an instance of change in velocity and the direction of that change, people can, in principle, detect the presence of a force and the direction of its influence. The process of computing forces from kinematics is known as *inverse dynamics*.

Within the field of physics understanding, there is general agreement that people are capable of performing inverse dynamics, at least to a limited extent (Gilden, 1991; Hecht, 1996; Kaiser & Proffitt, 1984; Kaiser, Proffitt, Whelan, & Hecht, 1992; Pittenger,1990; Proffitt & Gilden, 1989; Twardy & Bingham, 2002). According to Runeson and his colleagues, people's ability to infer the dynamic properties of an event is quite good, because people's perceptual systems allow them to "see" the dynamics of an event via its kinematics, a proposal known as the principle of kinematic specification of dynamics (KSD; see Runeson & Frykolm, 1983; Runeson, Juslin, & Olsson, 2000; Runeson & Vedeler, 1993). Others have been more conservative in their estimates of people's ability to infer the dynamics of an event, suggesting that people may be able to recover a portion of these properties via perceptual heuristics (see Gilden, 1991; Hecht, 1996; Proffitt & Gilden, 1989). Clearly, people's ability to infer dynamic properties is not perfect (e.g., McCloskey, 1983; McCloskey & Kohl, 1983; McCloskey, Washburn, & Felch, 1983). People sometimes fail to notice certain kinds of dynamic properties or impute properties that do not exist (Clement, 1983; McCloskey, 1983). Nevertheless, the process of inducing dynamic properties is not completely arbitrary. This is especially true when the dynamic properties of a situation do not depend on the geometry of the objects, in which case the moving entities in a scene can be treated as particles (Gilden, 1991; Hecht, 1996; Kaiser, Proffitt, Whelan, & Hecht, 1992; Proffitt & Gilden, 1989).

Beyond the empirical literature, our ability to infer the presence of dynamic properties is supported by everyday experience. Human bodies can detect energy. When we touch a hot pan, we feel not only the solidness of the pan but also the heat it gives off. Bigelow, Ellis, and Pargetter (1988) provide a similar example in the case of forces. If something bumps us and we stumble, we feel the force. We can argue that it is the force that is felt—rather than just the object—because the same object feels different when it bumps us gently or hard. Hume's assumption that people do not have access to the agencies that bring about causal events is inconsistent with work in physics understanding, as well as with common sense. Just because forces and energies can not be seen does not mean that their existence can not be sensed in other ways, or that their presence can not be inferred, relatively directly, from visual input. Therefore, one of the basic assumptions motivating models in the Humean tradition is false: people have at least partial access to the quantities that bring about causation in the world.

Physicalist Models of Causation

In contrast to Humean models, physicalist models hold that people's representations of causation may partially copy or reproduce what goes on in the real world. The basic idea in physicalist approaches to causation is that people's representations of causation specify physical quantities in the world, such as energy, momentum, linear and angular momentum, impact forces, chemical forces, and electrical forces, among others. For example, according to Aronson's (1971) Transference Theory, causation implies contact between two objects in which a quantity possessed by the cause (e.g., velocity, momentum, kinetic energy, heat) is transferred to the effect. Another transference theory is proposed by Fair (1979), who holds that causes are the source of physical quantities, energy, and momentum that flow from the cause to the effect. According to Salmon's (1994, 1998) Invariant Quantity theory, causation involves an intersection of world lines that results in transmission of an invariant quantity. The proposals of Aronson, Fair, and Salmon come from the philosophy literature. Similar proposals from the psychology literature have been termed generative theories of causation. According to Bullock, Gelman, and Baillargeon (1982), adults believe that causes bring about their effects by a transfer of causal impetus. Shultz (1982) suggests that causation is understood as a transmission between materials or events that results in an effect. According to Leslie (1994), physical causation is processed by a "Theory of Bodies" (ToBy) that schematizes objects as bearers, transmitters, and recipients of a primitive notion of force.

A recent proposal from the philosophy literature breaks from earlier physicalist models by not requiring a one-way transmission of energy or momentum. According to Dowe's Conserved Quantity theory (2000), there are two main types of causation: persistence (e.g., inertia causing a spacecraft to move through space) and interactions (e.g., the collision of billiard balls causing each ball to change direction). Causal interactions occur when the trajectories of two objects intersect and there is an *exchange* of conserved quantities (e.g., an exchange of momentum when two billiard balls collide). Unlike transfers, exchanges are not limited to a single direction (e.g., from cause to effect).

Assumptions of Physicalist Theories

Physicalist approaches to causation share several assumptions. First, they assume that an interaction can be identified as causal on the basis of properties that belong solely to that interaction. Second, defining causal relationships in terms of physical quantities imposes a relatively "local" level of granularity on the analysis of causal relationships. Transfer of energy, for example, can occur only through local interactions between objects. Third, at the "local" level of granularity, causal relationships are deterministic (Goldvarg & Johnson-Laird, 2001; Luhmann & Ahn, 2005): the physical quantities that instantiate direct causal relationships are either present or absent, not present to a probabilistic degree. Fourth, the "local" nature of causal connections implies that when there is a causal connection between two non-contiguous events, there must be a causal chain of intermediate links, each contiguous to the next (Russell, 1948). Hence, physicalist theories imply the need for causal mechanisms, as has been supported by work in psychology (Ahn & Bailenson, 1996; Ahn & Kalish, 2000; Ahn, Kalish, Medin, & Gelman, 1995; see also Bullock et al., 1982; Shultz, 1982). The fifth commonality is that most physicalist theories reduce causal relationships to quantities that can not be directly observed. In the language of physics, physicalist models hold that people represent causal relationships in terms of their dynamics rather than kinematics. The sixth assumption is that physical causation is cognitively more basic than nonphysical causation (e.g., social or psychological causation). In support of this assumption, the ability to perceive physical causation begins to develop earlier in infants (around 3 to 4 months) than the ability to perceive social causation (around 6 to 8 months; Cohen, Amsel, Redford, & Casasola, 1998; Leslie, 1994; Oakes, 1994). A final assumption is that nonphysical causation is in some way modeled after physical causation (Leslie, 1994; Talmy, 1988). This modeling may occur via a process of analogy in which notions such as "effort" and "intention" are construed as energies and forces.

Evaluation of Physicalist Accounts of Causations

Physicalist models hold that people's representations of causation refer to physical quantities in the world. As a consequence, such theories can provide a precise characterization of the physical agencies that bring about causal events. They can also provide an account of how causal relationships might be inferred on the basis of a single observation. This is possible because the information needed to infer causal relationships is available in the occurrence of individual events. While physicalist models have several strengths, they also have several limitations. Arguably the most important test of a theory of causation is whether it has extensional adequacy. A theory of causation should be able to pick out the range of situations that people judge to be causal while excluding situations that people judge to be noncausal. However, current physicalist models do not categorize causal situations in the same way as people. In particular, the physicalist models discussed so far conflate the concepts of *cause* and *enable*. These concepts are similar but not synonymous; in most contexts they are not interchangeable, as illustrated by the sentences below:

1. a. Hinges enabled the crutches to fold in half.
   b. A weak spot in the welding caused the crutches to fold in half.

2. a. Hinges caused the crutches to fold in half.
   b. A weak spot in the welding enabled the crutches to fold in half.

The sentences in 1(a) and 1(b) are perfectly acceptable. However, if the verbs in 1(a) and 1(b) are switched, the resulting sentences in 2 sound odd. Importantly, however, in all of the scenarios described in sentences 1 and 2 there is a transmission or exchange of energy. Another limitation of current physicalist theories is that they do not easily represent the concept of *prevent* (Dowe, 2000). If prevention is characterized by the lack of transfer or exchange of energy, it does not differ from the absence of any kind of interaction, and if it is characterized by a transfer or exchange of energy then it does not differ from causation. (See Dowe, 2000, for an in-depth discussion of the problem of prevention.) The problem with the physicalist models discussed so far is that transmission or exchange of energy is too coarse a criterion for distinguishing causation from other kinds of events that also involve a transmission or exchange of energy. To distinguish causation from other kinds of relationships, a finer level of representation is required.

The Dynamics Model

The *dynamics model* is a physicalist model of causation. As such, it holds that people represent causal relations in a manner that copies or reproduces the way in which causal relationships are instantiated in the real world. While it is primarily based in physical causation, it can be extended to nonphysical causation by analogy. However, unlike other physicalist models, the dynamics model does not equate causation with the transfer or exchange of a physical quantity. Rather, it associates causation with a pattern of forces and a position vector that indicates an endstate. Previous researchers have suggested that causation is closely linked to the notion of force (Ahn & Kalish, 2000, Bigelow et al., 1988; Leslie, 1994). In particular, Bigelow and Pargetter (1990) proposed that causation might be associated with a specific pattern of several forces, though they did not specify the exact pattern. Important parts of the dynamics model are also reflected in diSessa's (1993) phenomenological primitives, as well as in White's (2000) influence and resistance model, in which causal judgments are likened to the passage of energy in a physical system.

The importance of force in the representation of causation is illustrated by the causal (but static) situations described in 3.

3. a. Pressure will cause the water to remain liquid at slightly below 0°C.
   b. Dirt caused the valve to stay open.
   c. Tiny barbs on the stinger cause it to remain in the wound.
   d. Guide wires prevented the Christmas tree from falling.

In each of the situations described in 3, nothing happens. Because nothing happens, there is no regular sequence of events, or transfer or exchange of energy, at least at the macro level. What is present in each of these situations is a configuration of forces. According to the dynamics model, it is this configuration of forces that makes these situations causal (3[a–c]) or preventive (3[d]).

The dynamics model is based on Talmy's (1985, 1988) *force dynamics* account of causation (see also Jackendoff, 1990; Pinker, 1989; Siskind,

2003; Verhagen, 2002; Verhagen & Kemmer, 1997; Wolff, 2003, 2007; Wolff & Zettergren, 2002). By analyzing the concept of cause into patterns of forces, Talmy showed that the concept of cause could not only be grounded in properties of the world but also be used to define other related concepts, such as *enable*, *prevent*, and *despite*. He also showed how this approach to causation could be extended to many domains of experience, including the physical, intrapsychological, social, and institutional. I incorporate many of Talmy's key ideas into the dynamics model of causation. However, I also introduce several new distinctions and make significant changes to the theory's underlying semantics.[1]

The dynamics model holds that the concept of *cause* and related concepts involve interactions between two main entities: an affector and a patient (the entity acted on by the affector). The nature of this interaction can be described at two levels of analysis. The *category* level specifies summary properties of various cause-related concepts. Distinctions at this level are sufficient to distinguish different classes of causal verbs (see Wolff, Klettke, Ventura, & Song, 2005). The *computational* level re-describes the distinctions at the category level in terms of units of cognition that represent physical quantities in the world. It is at this level that causes and related concepts are explicitly linked to configurations of force.

The Category Level of Representation

The dynamics model holds that, at the category level, the concept of cause and related concepts can be understood in terms of three dimensions (Wolff & Song, 2003). Specifically, as summarized in Table 20.1, the concepts of *cause*, *enable*, *prevent*, and *despite* can be captured in terms of (1) the *tendency* of the patient for the endstate, (2) the presence or absence of *concordance* between the affector and the patient, and (3) *progress toward the endstate*.

The semantics of these three dimensions are illustrated by the sentences in 4. Consider the example of causation in 4(a). In this sentence, the patient (the boat) does not have a tendency for the endstate (heeling). The affector (wind) is not in concordance with the patient, and the result occurs. In enabling situations, as in 4(b), the tendency of the

---

1. See Wolff (2007) for summary of the key differences between the two accounts.

TABLE 20.1. Representations of Cause, Enable, and Prevent

	Patient Tendency for Endstate	Affector-Patient Concordance	Result: Endstate Approached
Cause	N*	N	Y
Enable	Y	Y	Y
Prevent	Y	N	N

* Y = Yes; N = No.

patient (the body) is for the result (to digest food). The affector (vitamin B) does not oppose the patient, and the result occurs. In preventing situations, as in 4(c), the patient (the tar) has a tendency for the result (bonding). The affector (the rain) opposes the tendency of the patient and the result does not occur.

4. a. Wind caused the boat to heel.
   b. Vitamin B enables the body to digest food.
   c. Rain prevented the tar from bonding.

The Computational Level of Analysis

The computational level of the dynamics model re-describes the three dimensions of tendency, concordance, and result in terms of patterns of forces, or vectors. In discussing such vectors I make a distinction between vectors in the world and vectors in people's minds. Vectors in the world are quantities that have a point of origin, a direction, and a magnitude. The vectors in people's representations of causation are more qualitative. Specifically, vectors in people's representations are predicted to be relatively accurate with respect to direction, but somewhat imprecise with respect to magnitude. People may be able to infer the relative magnitude of two vectors—that one is greater than another. Uncertainty about the magnitude of the vectors adds a certain amount of indeterminacy to people's representations of force dynamic concepts. It is hypothesized that our mental notion of force vectors can represent not only physical forces but also social and psychological forces. Like physical forces, social and psychological forces can be understood as quantities that influence behavior in a certain direction. In this chapter, all vectors are in boldface (e.g., **P**).

The dynamics model specifies that four types of force vectors are relevant to the mental representation of cause-related concepts. **A** represents the force exerted on the patient by the affector; **P** represents the force (i.e., thrust) produced by the patient itself or, in the absence of such a force, its weight (e.g., gravity) and/or resistance to motion due to frictional forces; and **O** represents the summation of the remaining other forces acting on the patient. The patient's path through space is determined by **R**, the resultant force acting on the patient based on the vector addition of **A**, **P**, and **O**. In addition to these four forces, people's mental representation of the patient's location with respect to an endstate is specified by the vector **E**, which begins at the patient and ends at the endstate, as shown in Figure 20.1.

With these definitions and assumptions in place, the relationship between the category and computational levels of the dynamics model can be specified, as summarized in Table 20.2.

TENDENCY

As shown in Table 20.2, the patient can be viewed as having a tendency for the endstate when the force associated with it, **P**, is in the direction of the endstate, **E**. For example, in the free-body diagrams illustrating

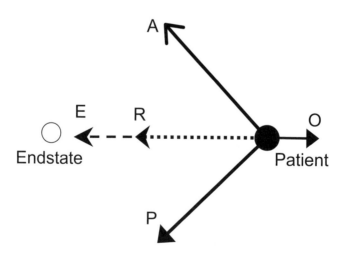

FIGURE 20.1. Forces associated with the affector **A**, patient **P**, and other forces O combine to produce a resultant force **R** that is directed toward the endstate, as specified by the position vector **E**.

TABLE 20.2. Dimensions in Dynamics Model

Tendency (of patient for endstate)	**P** & **E** in same direction
Concordance (of affector & patient)	**A** & **P** in same direction
Result: Endstate approached	**R** & **E** in same direction

enable, prevent, and *despite* in Figure 20.2, **P** lies in the same direction as **E**, indicating that the patient has a tendency for the endstate. In the *cause* configuration, **P** does not point in the same direction as **E**, indicating that the patient does not have a tendency for the endstate.

CONCORDANCE

The patient and the affector are in concordance when the patient's tendency, **P**, is in the same direction as the force associated with the affector, **A**. As shown in Figure 20.2, collinearity holds in the case of *enable* but not in the cases of *cause, prevent,* and *despite*.

RESULT

The patient will approach the endstate and eventually reach it, barring changes in the forces acting on the patient, when the sum of the forces acting on the patient, **R**, is in the direction of the endstate **E**.

Spanning Restriction and Heuristic

The dynamics model places constraints on what constitutes a valid configuration. Valid configurations are those in which the resultant could

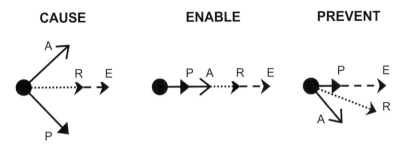

FIGURE 20.2. Configurations of forces associated with *cause, enable,* and *prevent.*

be produced from the vector addition of the component vectors. Thus, according to the dynamics model, understanding causal relationships involves evaluating whether **R** reflects the sum of the vectors **A**, **P**, and **O** in the real world. The model assumes that people are sensitive to the way in which forces interact in the real world. However, since vectors in the mind do not have exact magnitudes, their representations do not allow for exact vector addition to assess **R**. Instead of exact vector addition, I propose that people use a qualitative criterion for deciding whether a resultant could have been produced from the vector addition of two vectors. An implication of the parallelogram law of vector addition is that the resultant of two vectors will always lie on top of or within, or *span*,[2] the region bounded by the vectors being added, as depicted in Figure 20.3.

If the resultant lies outside the span of the two vectors being added, the configuration violates the *spanning restriction*. According to the dynamics model, people refer to the spanning restriction in a heuristic— the *spanning heuristic*—to make rough guesses about whether a resultant was produced from the vector addition of the component forces. When a resultant—as indicated by a patient's motion—lies within the span bounded by two vectors, the spanning heuristic warrants the inference that the resultant was produced from the vector addition of the two component vectors. When a resultant lies outside the span, the spanning heuristic holds that the result was not due to the addition of the two component vectors alone.

Testing the Dynamics Model

The dynamics model makes predictions about how people will interpret scenes that instantiate different configurations of forces. In particular, the dynamics model makes predictions about what kinds of events will count as causation, as opposed to enablement or prevention. Here I

---

2. The word "span" is used here in a more restricted sense than is used in mathematics. In its usual sense, "span" refers to, for example, the set of resultant vectors, $\mathbf{u}i$, that can be formed from the equation $\mathbf{u} = c_1\mathbf{v}_1 + c_2\mathbf{v}_2$, where $\mathbf{v}_1$ and $\mathbf{v}_2$ are vectors and c_1 and c_2 are scalars. When using "span" in the context of the dynamics model, I restrict c_1 and c_2 to values that are equal to or greater than zero, thus limiting the resultant vectors, $\mathbf{u}i$, to the region bounded by and including $\mathbf{v}_1$ and $\mathbf{v}_2$.

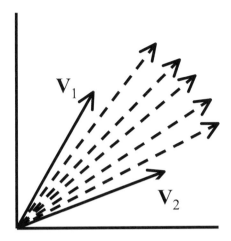

FIGURE 20.3. Despite uncertainty about the magnitudes of V1 and V2, we can infer that the resultant of the two vectors will reside within the area bounded by V1 and V2.

provide a summary of the experiments reported in Wolff and Zettergren (2002) and Wolff (2007). In these experiments, participants viewed 3-D animations that depicted a boat (the patient) moving in a pool of water toward a cone (the endstate); a bank of fans beside the pool (the affector) affected the speed and direction of the boat (Fig. 20.4; also see color insert). The boat's path through the water was completely determined by a physics simulator, which allowed the dynamics of the situation, in particular the forces acting on the boat, to be independently manipulated. After viewing an animation, participants chose from several linguistic descriptions or "none of the above" (Wolff, 2007). All of the descriptions were the same (*The fans* ____ *the boat to [from] hit[ting] the cone*) except for the main verb, which was either *caused*, *helped*, or *prevented*.

We predicted that *cause* descriptions would be chosen when the boat initially moved away from the cone (Tendency = N) but eventually hit it because of the fans' blowing in the direction of the cone (Concordance = N; Endstate approached = Y). We predicted that *enable* descriptions would be chosen when the boat moved toward the cone (Tendency = Y), the fans blew in the same direction (Concordance = Y), and the boat ultimately reached the cone (Endstate approached = Y). We predicted that *prevent* descriptions would be chosen when the boat moved toward the cone

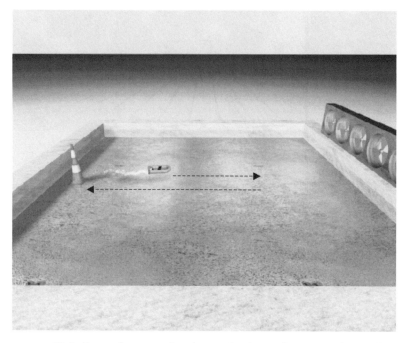

FIGURE 20.4. Frame from an animation used to instantiate a cause interaction.

(Tendency = Y) but the fans blew in another direction (Concordance = N) such that the boat missed the cone `(Endstate approached = N). Finally, we predicted participants would choose the option "none of the above" when none of the above configurations were instantiated.

The predictions of the dynamics model were fully borne out by the results. The lower portion of Table 20.3 shows the percentage of times people chose each of the four options for each of the vector configurations. Importantly, participants did not choose *prevent* for all scenes in which the boat missed the cone (6 through 8). Instead, *prevent* was restricted to just those situations in which the boat had an initial tendency for the endstate (4). Likewise, participants did not choose *cause* or *help* just because the boat hit the cone (5). Since two vectors must be evaluated to determine concordance, this last result strongly suggests that participants considered the relationships among the vectors when choosing the description, just as predicted by the theory.

The dynamics model easily extends beyond the one-dimensional interactions used in Experiment 1 to two-dimensional interactions. Wolff (2007; see also Wolff & Zettergren, 2002) demonstrated this using the

TABLE 20.3. Experiment 1 in Wolff (2007), Along with Associated Predictions and Results

Config. #	1	2	3	4	5	6	7	8
Affector (↑) Patient (↑) Result (⋯▶)	E	E	E	E	E	E	E	E
	CAUSE	ENABLE	ENABLE	PREVENT	Unspecified	Unspecified	Unspecified	Unspecified
Predicted								
"Cause"	94%	11%	6%	-	-	-	6%	-
"Help"	6%	89%	94%	-	11%	-	-	-
"Prevent"	-	-	-	100%	6%	-	-	6%
"No verb"	-	-	-	-	83%	100%	94%	94%

configurations shown in Table 20.4. Also as shown in Table 20.4, participants' choices matched the predictions of the theory.

The results from Wolff (2007) are consistent with the hypothesis that people's causal concepts are based on configurations of force. The results also support the dynamics model's account of how people determine causation on the basis of a single observation. According to the model, people identify causal relationships by constructing representations of the forces acting on the patient. However, the data so far are open to an alternative possibility; specifically, they could be explained in terms of kinematics rather than dynamics. In a kinematics account, only visible movements—specifically, the velocities—are considered in the classification of interactions. For example, causation might be defined as an interaction in which the patient was not moving toward the endstate at first, but then moved toward the endstate after the affector made contact with it. Enablement could be defined as an interaction in which the patient was moving toward the endstate to start andthen moved more quickly toward the endstate once the affector made contact with it. Finally, prevention might be defined as an interaction in which the patient was moving toward the endstate but then moved away from the endstate after the affector made contact with it.

One way to test between kinematics and dynamic approaches to causation would be to examine whether people are aware of the way in which forces are added. If people's causal judgments are based on kinematics, their causal judgments should be insensitive to such violations in the way the forces are added. On the other hand, if causal judgments are based on the dynamics of an event, people should notice when an object moves in a way that is not consistent with the way forces are added.

As discussed earlier, it is assumed that people use a qualitative criterion, the *spanning heuristic*, to determine whether a particular resultant could be derived from a particular set of forces. When a patient moves in a direction that lies within the area between the forces acting on the patient (see Fig. 20.4; color insert), the spanning heuristic should lead people to assume that the resultant is produced from the vector addition of those forces. Conversely, when the resultant does not reside within the span of the component vectors, it can be said that the configuration violates the *spanning restriction*.

The spanning heuristic provides a rough method of evaluating whether the net force acting on a patient is derivable from the overt

TABLE 20.4. Configurations Used in Experiment 2 of Wolff (2007), with Associated Predictions and Results

Config. #	1	2	3	4	5	6	7	8	9	10
Affector (→) Patient (→) Result. (⊶▸)										
Predicted	CAUSE	ENABLE	PREVENT	PREVENT	PREVENT	PREVENT	Unspec-ified	Unspec-ified	Unspec-ified	Unspec-ified
"Cause"	89%	11%	-	-	-	-	-	-	-	-
"Help"	0.1%	83%	-	-	-	-	-	-	-	-
"Prevent"	-	-	94%	94%	89%	89%	-	17%	-	11%
"No verb"	-	6%	6%	6%	11%	11%	100%	83%	100%	89%

forces acting on the patient. However, in certain circumstances, the heuristic may lead people to incorrectly infer that the net force acting on the patient is fully explained in terms of the perceived forces when, in fact, there are other forces in play. Such an illusion of sufficiency is most likely to occur when there is more than one external force acting on the patient—that is, when the magnitude of other forces, **O**, is greater than zero. For example, consider the three scenes and free-body diagrams in Figure 20.5 (also see color insert). The forces entered into the physics simulator for all the scenes are depicted in the first free-body diagram. In the first animation, a boat motors to the middle of a pool, two sets of fans turn on, and the boat moves toward the cone, ultimately hitting it. The second panel shows a frame from an animation that is exactly the same as the one on the left except that one of the fans is not shown (though its force is still present). In this animation, the boat moves into the area bounded by the overt forces; hence, according to the spanning heuristic, the fan may be construed as a cause of the boat's hitting the cone. The third panel shows an animation that is also exactly the same as the one in the first panel except that the opposite fan is not shown. In this scene, based on a single visible fan, the boat's direction lies outside the area bounded by the perceived forces. According to the spanning heuristic, then, the visible fan can not be construed as a cause of the boat's hitting the cone.

These predictions were tested in an experiment in which participants saw four pairs of animations (Wolff, 2007). Like the middle and

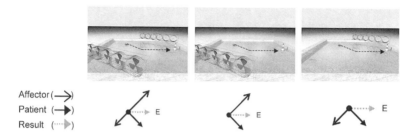

FIGURE 20.5. In each animation, the boat motors to the middle, the fans turn on, the boat changes course, and the boat hits the cone. Each animation is based on the same configuration of forces as shown in the first panel. However, in the second and third panels, only one of the two fans appears in the animation, as implied by the incomplete arrow diagrams.

rightmost animations in Figure 20.5, these animations depicted situations in which two external forces were in play but only one was shown. One member of each minimal pair depicted a situation in which the resultant was within the span of the observable forces and the other member depicted a situation in which the resultant was not within that span. As predicted, participants were quite willing to say that the fan "caused" the boat to hit the cone when the resulting direction of the boat was within the span of the two observable forces (percent "caused" = 84%). Also, as predicted, participants were quite unwilling to say that the fan "caused" the boat to hit the cone when the boat moved in a direction that was outside of the area spanned by the two observable forces (percent "caused" = 18%). When the boat moved outside of the area span of the observable forces, people decided that it was not physically possible for the result to be due to the observable forces alone.

In both kinds of scenarios, the boat changed direction immediately after the fans began to blow, so neither temporal nor spatial contiguity was a determining factor in participants' judgments. The two kinds of animations were equally "physically accurate" since they were based on exactly the same underlying forces. They were also equally "incomplete" in that only one of the two forces acting on the boat was shown. Finally, both kinds of animations were equally "natural" in the sense that we are likely to encounter scenes in which any of a number of external forces may be hidden.

Support for the spanning heuristic also makes it clear that that people's judgments of causation do not require knowledge of the exact magnitudes of the forces. In the spanning conditions, the animations did not provide enough information to determine whether the boat's course was due to the force associated with just the one fan or due to that force in combination with (an)other hidden force(s). Nevertheless, when the boat moved within the span of the overt forces, people agreed that the fan "caused" the boat to hit the cone. Thus, precise knowledge of magnitudes is not necessary for classifying the situation as causal. What appears to be necessary, instead, is awareness of the direction of the forces, which supports the hypothesis that people think about causation in terms of vectors. In sum, the results of this experiment support three main assumptions of the dynamics model: namely, that people think about causal situations in terms of vectors, that they perform vector addition via the spanning heuristic, and that their causal judgments are based on the dynamic properties of an event, which are derived from the kinematics.

In addition to these results, several other problems remain for a kinematics-only account of causation. As discussed above, the concept of *cause* extends to situations in which there are conflicting forces but no change occurs (e.g., *The rubber bottom caused the cup to stay in place*). A kinematics-based account can not distinguish these static causal situations from situations that are static but simply spatial (e.g., *The tree causes the roof to be under the branch*). Another limitation to a kinematics approach is that it does not easily explain our language for nonphysical causation. In describing social causation, we rarely talk about "social velocities" or "peer accelerations." Rather, we talk about "social forces" and "peer pressures." Our language for describing social interactions implies that we think about these interactions in terms of dynamic properties. We can talk about "psychological forces," as when we describe someone as strong-willed or internally conflicted. Ordering someone to do something is easily viewed as imparting an invisible, directional influence that may or may not produce an effect.

These patterns in language suggest that the dynamics model might be extended to account for people's causal judgments of scenes involving intentions and desires. Consider, for example, the scenario depicted in Figure 20.6, in which a woman is standing in a raft and pointing in a particular direction (also see color insert). She indicates the direction she wants to move in by pointing. If intentions are analogous to physical forces, as assumed in the dynamics model, people should prefer to say that the fans *caused* the woman to reach the cone when the woman is pointing away from the cone and that the fans *enabled* her to reach the cone when the woman is pointing toward the cone. In addition, they should report that the fans *prevented* her from reaching the cone when she points toward the cone but is pushed away from it.

These possibilities were tested in an experiment involving intentional forces (Wolff, 2007). Participants saw two kinds of animations. Half of the animations were based on physical forces only, just as in the previous experiments. In the remaining animations, the underlying configurations of forces were exactly the same as those used in the physical-only animations. The main difference was that the patient's tendency was indicated by a woman's intention (as represented by her pointing). Specifically, in physical-and-intentional animations, the motor boat was replaced with

CAUSE

 E

FIGURE 20.6. The scene depicts a cause situation: the woman does not want to go to the cone (as indicated by the direction of her pointing), but the fans push her there nevertheless.

a round rubber raft with a woman inside of it. Because the boat did not have an engine, the tendency of the patient (i.e., the woman in the round rubber raft) could not be specified by its self-motion. Rather, for these animations, the patient's tendency was specified by the woman pointing in a certain direction. Thus, for the *cause* animations, the tendency of the patient was indicated by the boat motoring away from the cone in the physical force-only condition and by the woman pointing away from the cone in the physical-and-intentional force condition. In the *enable* and *prevent* animations, the tendency of the patient was indicated by the boat motoring toward the cone and the woman pointing toward the cone.

As in the previous experiments, participants saw the animations and described them by choosing sentences containing either cause-verbs (*cause, get, make*), enable-verbs (*enable, help, let*), prevent-verbs (*block, keep, prevent*), or the option "none of the above." The results showed that people treated the woman's intention as if it were a physical force. In the animations in which both forces were physical, the results were the same as in previous experiments: people preferred cause-verbs for the *cause* animations (94%), enable-verbs for the *enable* animations (89%), and prevent-verbs for the *prevent* animations (100%). The pattern of responses was the same when the patient's tendency was determined by where the woman was pointing: people preferred cause-verbs for the *cause* animations (94%), enable-verbs for the *enable* animations (83%), and prevent-verbs for the *prevent* animations (100%). The results indicated that the dynamics model can be extended to situations involving nonphysical forces. In an earlier work (Wolff, 2007), I show that the dynamics model extends to situations in which all of the forces are either intentions or desires.

Summary

The dynamics model describes how people's representations of causation reproduce causation in the real world. It explains how people's representations of causation are specified in terms of forces, which are the very quantities that cause events in the real world. The assumptions embodied in the dynamics model contrast with those of Hume and models of the Humean tradition. Hume (1748/1975) maintained that people's conceptualization of causation went beyond kinematics to include such notions as force, necessary connection, causal power, and/or energy. Importantly, however, he also held that because such notions could not be directly seen, they were constructs of the mind rather than reflections of what went on in the world. Because these quantities could not be seen, Hume argued, they must emerge from the observation of a regular succession of events.

Michotte's (1946/1963) assumptions about causation in launching events were very similar to Hume's assumptions about causation in general. Like Hume, Michotte argued that people's notion of causation extended beyond the kinematics of an event: when an object A strikes an object B and sends it into motion, people infer the presence of a causal relationship, not just a sequence of motions. Also like Hume, Michotte felt that the impression of causation did not directly reflect the dynamics of the event. Instead, he felt that the impression was a visual illusion formed from a (possibly innate) perceptual mechanism. Michotte's view of causation differed from Hume's in that he held that the causal impression could be formed on the basis of a single observation rather than requiring multiple occurrences for its apprehension.

The dynamics model shares certain assumptions with Michotte's account of causation for launching events. Both accounts hold that people's representations of causation extend beyond kinematics and that the induction of causation can occur on the basis of a single observation. However, unlike Michotte's and Hume's accounts, the dynamics model holds that people's representations of causation copy, or replicate, certain aspects of the dynamics of an event, and as a consequence people's causal representations capture important aspects of the quantities that bring about causation in the world. This does not imply that people are able to recover all of the dynamic properties of an event; work in physics understanding shows that this clearly does not happen. However, people do appear to be able to construct partial representations of an event's dynamics. In particular, they appear to be relatively good at recovering the direction of forces.

Launching Events and Dynamics

Given the close similarities between the dynamics model and Michotte's account of causation, one might wonder why Michotte chose to argue against a dynamics account of the causal impression. As reviewed below, the evidence that Michotte used to argue against a dynamics account of causation is open to alternative explanations. In addition, when we look more closely at Michotte's own experiments, we find that many of his results provide evidence against his own hypotheses and support for dynamics.

MICHOTTE'S ARGUMENTS AGAINST DYNAMICS

One reason for Michotte's feeling that the causal impression was not due to dynamics is that people sometimes reported perceiving causation in events that he viewed as physically impossible. For example, people reported perceiving causation in situations in which objects A and B are moving, object A faster than object B, and object A stops and object B slows down when the two make contact (Michotte, 1946/1963, p. 71). On the basis of such results, Michotte concluded that the causal impression is not based on past experience with the world: had people referred to past experience, they would have expected object B to speed up, not slow down, after being hit. However, while such a sequence of events may be unusual, it is not necessarily at odds with Newtonian physics. Friction can change dramatically over the course of an object's movement, as when a ball rolls off an asphalt road and onto a gravel driveway. Michotte's "impossible" event is not, in fact, impossible in the world, and so his finding does not necessarily rule out the role of dynamics in the perception of causation.

Another of Michotte's arguments for the independence of the launching effect and real world causation is that sometimes the causal impression failed to obtain for trajectories that people experience in the real world. In support of this point, Michotte conducted several experiments (34 and 35) in which object A hits object B directly and B travels at an angle away from its expected straight-line path. The degree of deviation from B's expected straight path ranged from 25 to 90 degrees; as the size of the angle increased, the impression of causation grew weaker. Michotte points out that this result is at variance with our real-world experience in which two colliding objects can travel at angles (besides 180 degrees) and still be viewed as causal (e.g., billiards, marbles). However, Michotte's collision events were quite different from those involving billiard balls and marbles. In particular, since object A hit object B directly, Newtonian physics would predict that object B should move straight ahead, not at an angle. In addition, in Michotte's Experiment 35, from which it seems most of his conclusions were derived, the objects were rectangles instead of circles. If a rectangle were to hit another rectangle straight on, it would, indeed, be quite surprising and inconsistent with Newtonian physics if the second rectangle veered off at an angle, especially a right angle. Thus, in complete contrast to Michotte's stated conclusions, his work showing how changes in direction weaken the causal impression actually supports the conclusion that there is a tight relationship between the causal impression and dynamics in the world.

Yet another reason why Michotte believed the causal impression was only a perceptual phenomenon is that people experience the causal impression even when the objects involved are spots of light, shadows, or lines painted on a rotated disk. In other words, people perceive causation while also knowing that such causation does not occur in the real world (1946/1963, pp. 84–85). However, a dynamics approach to causation does not imply that people can not be subject to illusions of causation. A particular configuration of forces will produce only one kinematic pattern, but a single kinematic pattern is potentially consistent with more than one configuration of forces. This asymmetry explains why causal illusions can sometimes occur: people may infer the wrong configuration of forces from a particular kinematic pattern. This is especially likely when the actual forces driving the kinematics are obscured, as in the case of Michotte's launching events. Further, the process of inducing forces is likely to be at least partially automatic (Runeson & Frykolm, 1983), so causal illusions may occur even when the inferred configuration of forces is inconsistent with prior knowledge of the situation.

HOW MICHOTTE'S FINDINGS INDICATE THE ROLE OF DYNAMICS IN THE PERCEPTION OF CAUSATION

Michotte emphasized that the causal impression was not a mere copy or reproduction of what goes on in the real world. If anything, however, many of Michotte's findings indicate just the opposite. For example, Michotte observed that the causal impression disappeared fully when there was a gap of around 150 ms between the moment objects A and B made contact and the moment B began to move. This finding is readily explained by the dynamics model. When object A hits object B, the force imparted on B is instantaneous. If object B begins moving well after it is hit, its movement can not be due to the force imparted by object A. Another finding of Michotte's is that the perception of causation is strongest when object A makes physical contact with object B. This finding is also consistent with a dynamics approach, since contact forces can not exist unless objects make contact with one another.

Yet another finding of Michotte's concerns a phenomenon he referred to as the *radii of action*. The radii of action are the portions of the paths traveled by A and B that subjectively appear to be relevant to the impression of causation. In particular, when B travels beyond A's radius of action, it appears to be moving on its own, not as a consequence of the collision. Michotte found that object B's radius of action increased with the speed of object A. Michotte offered no explanation for the phenomenon of radii of action. However, the dynamics model offers a natural explanation for this effect: as object A's speed increases, the force it imparts on B increases, and, in turn, so will the distance B travels as a consequence of the impact of A (for a related proposal, see Hubbard & Ruppel, 2002).

Finally, according to Michotte, the causal impression should be strongest when the two parts of a launching event constitute a single continuous movement, whereby the motion of the first object extends into the second and there is an "ampliation of motion." According to this hypothesis, any differences in velocity between the first and second objects should decrease the causal impression, since any differences in velocity would make the sequence of events less continuous. However, in contrast to this prediction, Michotte found that the causal impression was stronger when the speed of object B was slower than that of object A. Specifically, in Experiments 15 and 39, people reported a much stronger causal impression when the ratio in speed of objects A and B was 4:1 than when the ratio was 1:1. This result is consistent with the dynamics model, which predicts that the second object should move less rapidly than the first because the second object resists moving in the direction of the force acting on it. That resistance, due to friction and inertia, means that the second object will move more slowly than the first (and ultimately will come to a stop). When object B's speed is the same as object A's, the dynamics model predicts that the causal impression should be weaker because of the absence of evidence for such resistance.

Conclusion

Humean theories of causation do not deny that people's everyday notions of causation are associated with invisible quantities such as energy or force, but they do imply that such notions are better viewed as part of the occult than the actual world. For these theories, *out of sight* is *out of mind*.

A physicalist approach does not deny the importance of kinematic features, but such features do not form the basis for people's causal representations; rather, they are the keys for unlocking the dynamics of an event. People's ability to infer these properties is by no means perfect, but nor is it arbitrary. In particular, people may be reasonably good at inferring the presence of forces and their direction but relatively insensitive to their magnitude. The dynamics of events are central to people's concept of causation because they are central to causation in the actual world. Because dynamic properties can be sensed, a physicalist approach to causation not only grounds causation in the world, it also explains how causation might be experienced in our own bodies, and why such notions of causal power, energy, and force are not just side effects of statistical dependencies.

References

Ahn, W., & Bailenson, J. (1996). Mechanism-based explanations of causal attribution: An explanation of conjunction and discounting effect. *Cognitive Psychology, 31,* 82–123.

Ahn, W., & Kalish, C. W. (2000). The role of mechanism beliefs in causal reasoning. In F. C. Keil & R. A. Wilson (Eds.), *Explanation and cognition* (pp. 199–225). Cambridge, MA: MIT Press.

Ahn, W., Kalish, C. W., Medin, D. L., & Gelman, S. A. (1995). The role of covariation versus mechanism information in causal attribution. *Cognition, 54,* 299–352.

Aronson, J. L. (1971). On the grammar of 'CAUSE.' *Synthese, 22,* 414–430.

Bigelow, J., Ellis, B., & Pargetter, R. (1988). Forces. *Philosophy of Science, 55,* 614–630.

Bigelow, J., & Pargetter, R. (1990). Metaphysics of causation. *Erkenntnis, 33,* 89–119.

Bullock, M., Gelman, R., & Baillargeon, R. (1982). The development of causal reasoning. In W. Friedman (Ed.), *The developmental psychology of time* (pp. 209–255). London: Academic Press.

Bunge, M. (1959). *Causality: the place of the causal principle in modern science.* Cambridge, MA: Harvard University Press.

Cheng, P. W. (1997). From covariation to causation: A causal power theory. *Psychological Review, 104,* 367–405.

Cheng, P. W., & Novick, L. R. (1991). Causes versus enabling conditions. *Cognition, 40,* 83–120.

Cheng, P. W., & Novick, L. R. (1992). Covariation in natural causal induction. *Psychological Review, 99,* 365–382.

Choi, H., & Scholl, B. J. (2004). Effects of grouping and attention on the perception of causality. *Perception & Psychophysics, 66,* 926–942.

Clement, J. (1983). A conceptual model discussed by Galileo and used intuitively by physics students. In D. Gentner & A. L. Stevens (Eds.), *Mental models* (pp. 299–324). Hillsdale, NJ: Lawrence Erlbaum.

Cohen, L. B., Amsel, G., Redford, M. A., & Casasola, M. (1998). The development of infant causal perception. In A. Slater (Ed.), *Perceptual development: Visual, auditory, and speech perception in infancy* (pp. 167–209). East Sussex, UK: Psychology Press.

diSessa, A. (1993). Towards an epistemology of physics. *Cognition and Instruction, 10,* 105–225.

Dowe, P. (2000). *Physical causation.* Cambridge: Cambridge University Press.

Fair, D. (1979). Causation and the flow of energy. *Erkenntnis, 14,* 219–250.

Gilden, D. L. (1991). On the origins of dynamical awareness. *Psychological Review, 98*, 554–568.

Goldvarg, E., & Johnson-Laird, P. (2001). Naive causality: A mental model theory of causal meaning and reasoning. *Cognitive Science, 25*, 565–610.

Gopnik, A., Glymour, C., Sobel, D., Shulz, L., Kushnir, T., & Danks, D. (2004). A theory of causal learning in children: Causal maps and Bayes nets. *Psychological Review, 111*, 1–31.

Hecht, H. (1996). Heuristics and invariants in dynamic event perception: Immunized concepts or nonstatements? *Psychonomic Bulletin & Review, 3*, 61–70.

Hubbard, T. L., & Ruppel, S. E. (2002). A possible role of naive impetus in Michotte's "Launching Effect:" Evidence from representational momentum. *Visual Cognition, 9*, 153–176.

Hume, D. (1737/1978). *A Treatise of human nature* (L. A. Selby-Bigge, Ed.). Second ed., revised by P. H. Nidditch. Oxford: Oxford University Press.

Hume, D. (1748/1975). *Enquiry concerning human understanding.* In L. A. Selby-Bigge (Ed.), *Enquiries concerning human understanding and concerning the principles of morals*, 3rd ed., revised by P. H. Nidditch. Oxford: Clarendon Press.

Jackendoff, R. (1990). *Semantic structures*. Cambridge, MA: MIT Press.

Joskowicz, L., & Sacks, E. (1991). Computational kinematics. *Artificial Intelligence, 51*, 381–416.

Kaiser, M. K., & Proffitt, D. R. (1984). The development of sensitivity to causally-relevant dynamic information. *Child Development, 55*, 1614–1624.

Kaiser, M. K., Proffitt, D. R., Whelan, S. M., & Hecht, H. (1992). The influence of animation on dynamical judgments. *Journal of Experimental Psychology: Human Perception and Performance, 18*, 669–690.

Leslie, A. M. (1994). ToMM, ToBy, and agency: Core architecture and domain specificity. In L. Hirschfield & S. Gelman (Eds.), *Mapping the mind: Domain specificity in cognition and culture* (pp. 119–148). Cambridge: Cambridge University Press.

Luhmann, C. C., & Ahn, W. (2005). The meaning and computation of causal power: Comment on Cheng (1997) and Novick and Cheng (2004). *Psychological Review, 112*, 685–692.

Mackie, J. L. (1974). *The cement of the universe*. Oxford: Oxford University Press.

McCloskey, M. (1983). Naïve theories of motion. In D. Gentner & A. L. Stevens (Eds.), *Mental models* (pp. 299–324). Hillsdale, NJ: Lawrence Erlbaum.

McCloskey, M., & Kohl, D. (1983). Naïve physics: The curvilinear impetus principle and its role in interactions with moving objects. *Journal of Experimental Psychology: Learning, Memory, and Cognition, 9*, 146–156.

McCloskey, M., Washburn, A., & Felch, L. (1983). Intuitive physics: The straight-down belief and its origin. *Journal of Experimental Psychology: Learning, Memory, and Cognition, 9*, 636–649.

Michotte, A. E. (1946/1963). *The perception of causality*. New York: Basic Books.

Oakes, L. M. (1994). The development of infants' use of continuity cues in their perception of causality. *Developmental Psychology, 30*, 869–879.

Pearl, J. (2000). *Causality: Models, reasoning, and inference*. Cambridge, UK: Cambridge University Press.

Pinker, S. (1989). *Learnability and cognition: The acquisition of argument structure*. Cambridge, MA: MIT Press.

Pittenger, J. B. (1990). Detection of violations of the law of pendulum motion: Observers' sensitivity to the relation between period and length. *Ecological Psychology, 2*, 55–81.

Proffitt, D. R., & Gilden, D. L. (1989). Understanding natural dynamics. *Journal of Experimental Psychology: Human Perception and Performance, 15*, 384–393.

Runeson, S., & Frykholm, G. (1983). Kinematic specification of dynamics as an informational basis for person and action perception: Expectation, gender recognition, and deceptive intention. *Journal of Experimental Psychology: General, 112*, 585–615.

Runeson, S., Juslin, P., & Olsson, H. (2000). Visual perception of dynamic properties: cue heuristic versus direct-perceptual competence. *Psychological Review, 107*, 525–555.

Runeson, S., & Vedeler, D. (1993). The indispensability of precollision kinematics in the visual perception of relative mass. *Perception & Psychophysics, 53*, 617–632.

Russell, B. (1948). *Human knowledge*. New York: Simon and Schuster.

Salmon, W. (1994). Causality without counterfactuals. *Philosophy of Science, 61*, 297–312.

Salmon, W. (1998). *Causality and explanation*. Oxford: Oxford University Press.

Scholl, B. J., & Tremoulet, P. D. (2000). Perceptual causality and animacy. *Trends in Cognitive Sciences, 4*, 299–309.

Schwartz, D. L. (1999). Physical imagery: Kinematic versus dynamic models. *Cognitive Psychology, 38*, 433–464.

Shultz, T. R. (1982). Rules of causal attribution. *Monographs of the Society for Research in Child Development, 47*, 1–51.

Siskind, J. M. (2003). Reconstructing force-dynamics models from video sequences. *Artificial Intelligence, 151*, 91–154.

Sloman, S. (2005). *Causal models: How people think about the world and its alternatives*. Oxford: Oxford University Press.

Sloman, S. A., & Lagnado, D. A. (2005). Do we "do"? *Cognitive Science, 29*, 5–39.

Sobel, D. M., Tenenbaum, J. B., & Gopnik, A. (2004). Children's causal inferences from indirect evidence: Backwards blocking and Bayesian reasoning in preschoolers. *Cognitive Science, 28*, 303–333.

Talmy, L. (1985). Force dynamics in language and thought. In W. Eilfort, P. Kroeber, & K. Peterson (Eds.), *Papers from the parasession on causatives and agentivity at the 21st regional meeting, Chicago Linguistics Society* (pp. 293–337). Chicago: Chicago Linguistics Society.

Talmy, L. (1988). Force dynamics in language and cognition. *Cognitive Science, 12*, 49–100.

Tenenbaum, J. B., & Griffiths, T. L. (2001). Structure learning in human causal induction. In T. Leen, T. Dietterich & V. Tresp (Eds.), *Advances in neural information processing systems 13* (pp. 59–65). Cambridge, MA: MIT Press.

Thinés, G., Costall, A., & Butterworth, G. (Eds.) (1991). *Michotte's experimental phenomenology of perception.* Hillsdale, NJ: Erlbaum.

Twardy, C. R., & Bingham, G. P. (2002). Causation, causal perception, and conservation laws. *Perception & Psychophysics, 64,* 956–968.

Verhagen, A. (2002). Interpreting usage: Construing the history of Dutch causal verbs. In M. Barlow & S. Kemmer (Eds.), *Usage-based models of language.* Stanford, CA: CSLI Publications.

Verhagen, A., & Kemmer, S. (1997). Interaction and causation: A cognitive approach to causative constructions in Modern Standard Dutch. *Journal of Pragmatics, 27,* 61–82.

White, P. A. (2000). Naive analysis of food web dynamics: A study of causal judgment about complex physical systems. *Cognitive Science, 24,* 605–650.

Wolff, P. (2003). Direct causation in the linguistic coding and individuation of causal events. *Cognition, 88,* 1–48.

Wolff, P. (2007). Representing causation. *Journal of Experiment Psychology: General, 136,* 82–111.

Wolff, P., Klettke, B., Ventura, T., & Song, G. (2005). Categories of causation across cultures. In W. Ahn, R. L. Goldstone, B. C. Love, A. B. Markman, & P. Wolff (Eds.), *Categorization inside and outside of the lab: Festschrift in honor of Douglas L. Medin* (pp. 29–48). Washington, DC: American Psychological Association.

Wolff, P., & Song, G. (2003). Models of causation and the semantics of causal verbs. *Cognitive Psychology, 47,* 276–332.

Wolff, P., & Zettergren, M. (2002). A vector model of causal meaning. In W. D. Gray & C. D. Schunn (Eds.), *Proceedings of the twenty-fourth annual conference of the Cognitive Science Society* (pp. 944–949). Mahwah, NJ: Lawrence Erlbaum.

Section 2
Remembering Events

21

The Boundaries of Episodic Memories

HELEN L. WILLIAMS, MARTIN A. CONWAY, & ALAN
D. BADDELEY

Episodic memories must have beginnings and endings, but what are
these? Are they systematic, always being of a certain type of autobiographical knowledge? Are they the same for all memories? Are they
discrete or fuzzy boundaries? How does the cognitive system "know"
when to form a memory? These are all fundamental questions about the
nature of human episodic memory, but curiously they are rarely asked
and even less frequently answered. Below we report two initial exploratory studies that attempted to identify the beginnings and endings of
various recent and remote episodic memories. Before describing these in
detail we first briefly consider the nature of episodic and autobiographical memory, as well as what is known about the perception of event
boundaries, which must surely play a role in the formation of memories
of experienced events.

Episodic Memories, Autobiographical Memory, and Goals

One current approach to autobiographical memory makes a sharp distinction between episodic memories and autobiographical knowledge

(Conway 2001, 2005; Conway & Pleydell-Pearce, 2000; Conway, Singer, & Tagini, 2004). Autobiographical knowledge consists of conceptual, generic, and schematic knowledge about one's life, which is not represented in memory as a single experience. Autobiographical knowledge, like all conceptual knowledge, is represented independently of the context in which it was acquired—it is experience-distant. Episodic memories, on the other hand, consist of sensory-perceptual-conceptual-affective information derived from single experiences. Episodic memories are samples of experience, although they are not usually literal or veridical copies of experience but rather represent psychological or cognitive summaries of experience. They are then "experience-near" and originate in working memory (Baddeley, 1986), where they derive from mental models of "online" experience configured in what Baddeley (2000) has termed the *episodic buffer*.

This approach to autobiographical memory (which consists of both autobiographical knowledge and episodic memories) proposes that one of the central functions of human memory is to monitor, constrain, and focus goal processing. Autobiographical knowledge is concerned with long-term goal processing (e.g., work, home, relationship goals) whereas episodic memory is concerned with the short-term goals that populate a day's experience (e.g., starting work on a paper, giving a lecture, attending meetings). Episodic memory serves the critical function of providing evidence, in the form of recent experience-near memories, on progress in recent and current goal processing. According to this view, many episodic memories are formed every day. Indeed, looking back over a day most people can recall that day's events in detail, with the important, mundane, and even the trivial being recalled well. These episodic memories are, in the main, rapidly forgotten. If an episodic memory becomes linked to or integrated with long-term autobiographical memory knowledge structures because of its goal relevance, then access to it may be retained; otherwise, access is lost. Within this framework an event is defined by its goal history, and an important issue here is the grain size of goals. Short-term goals have specific aims and specific associated action sequences—for example, getting to work in the morning. In contrast, long-term goals can be pursued in many different ways and satisfied by many different actions—for example, getting a job in the first place. Memory reflects the grain size of goals in the form of episodic memories for short-term goals and autobiographical knowledge for long-term goals.

Perceiving Events

When individuals are performing behaviors, they are provided with a continuous influx of information from a variety of sensory modalities as well as information obtained from the cognitive monitoring and control of their behavior. The process by which people are able to parse behavior, both their own and that of others, into distinct related actions has been explored using various approaches, and a number of models of event perception and construction have been developed. For example, in narratives and texts (e.g., Brewer & Lichtenstein, 1982; Zwaan & Radvansky, 1998), in the neuropsychology of action (e.g., Schwartz, Montgomery, FitzpatrickDeSalme, Ochipa, Coslett, Mayer, 1995), and in the perception of action sequences (e.g., Newtson, Engquist, & Bois, 1977). Here, however, we focus on the *event segmentation theory* (EST) of Zacks, Speer, Swallow, and Braver (2007), which encompasses many aspects of the earlier models but is grounded in theories of perception and the neurological representation of events. One central proposal of the EST model is that event segmentation is a spontaneous outcome of ongoing perception and arises at points where perceptual predictions begin to fail or change. This change in perceptual predictions is considered to occur at many different levels simultaneously and is a consequence of the failure of a currently active set of predictions, which are rapidly dysfacilitated and superceded by a more accurate set of predictions. The period or epoch between two such consecutive changes in current mental models is an *event* (see Zacks et al., 2007, for a review of the extensive body of data demonstrating high sensitivity to event boundaries). In experiencing events, segmentation of events into discrete actions or smaller events has been found to correspond well with perceived goals. Within this a hierarchical organization has been observed, with superordinate goals corresponding to coarse (or large) units and sub-goals corresponding to fine units of action, indicating that people are able to monitor the goal/sub-goal hierarchies of behavior (Hard, Lozano, & Tversky,

2006; Zacks, Tversky, & Iyer, 2001) and that events are conceptually organized in terms of goals.

An event, then, has two major components: a stable mental model and an updating mental model. The stable component is stable because the goals active in the epoch remain active. In the updating of mental models, goals, at some level of description or grain size, change; they are accomplished, deferred, or abandoned and superceded by new goals. Thus, there are two highly goal-relevant sets of information in an event; these derive from stable goal processing and from the periods of changes in goal processing. A discrete event will be influenced by two such periods of changes in goal processing (the period of change preceding the event and those changes related to the end of that event) and one period of stability (the middle of the event). By the present view, episodic memories preserve in summary form information about these highly goal-relevant components of events. Of special importance here are the points of goal change, which will feature important information about current goal processing that will be preserved in an episodic memory or set of memories of the event. It is the points of change in one's online perception of events and how they later feature during recall of episodic memories of these events in which we are particularly interested in the present studies.

As a starting point for our investigations into the beginnings and endings of episodic memories, we decided to initially focus on the set of memories recalled for a common everyday event for our subjects: the morning journey into school (the University of Leeds). This event provides an example of the core of the taxonomic category of "events" as specified by Zacks et al. (2007): it involves goal-directed human activity, is of modest duration, and has objectively identifiable temporal boundaries.

Experiment 1

In Experiment 1, we asked our participants to freely recall all they could about their journey into the university that morning; no constraints were placed on order or content of recall. Following the original work of Newtson (1976), we then asked our participants to divide what they had recalled into units they considered to be discrete memories. The analyses then focused on those (episodic) details that formed the *first* and *final* part of each of these discrete memories, the *boundaries* of each discrete memory chunk. We also repeated the recall 1 week later in the hope of detecting changes in the nature of episodic memory.

Method

PARTICIPANTS

Nineteen participants took part in this experiment, 16 women and 3 men. The mean age of participants was 22.9 years. The majority of participants were University of Leeds students who took part in the experiment for payment.

DESIGN

A within-subjects design was used in which participants completed two experimental sessions 1 week apart. At Time 1, participants were asked to recall everything they could from their journey to the university that morning. At Time 2, participants repeated this recall (of their journey from the week before). The dependent variables were the types of episodic detail used at the start and end boundaries of the memories, the recollective experience with which the memories were recalled, the number of memories recalled, the number of words written, and the values assigned to the different memories on various scales (e.g., vividness).

PROCEDURE

Participants were tested in groups of up to three but were not allowed to confer. At all stages of the experiment, participants had no prior knowledge of what they would be asked to recall. At Time 1 participants were asked to "write down, in as much detail as you are able to remember, every single thing you did between when you left the house this morning and arrived at the first building you entered when you arrived at the university." The events were to be recalled in the order in which they came to mind and written on a sheet provided. This phase of the experiment typically took about 10 minutes.

Participants were then asked to go back and divide what they had written into what they considered to be discrete memories. They typically did this by drawing a backslash or line to separate their memory descriptions. They were verbally instructed that there was no set way to do this but that they should use their own judgment to decide where one memory ended and another began. It was emphasized that we were interested in how each person divided up his or her recall into discrete memories, and so participants should mark it as they saw it. For an example narrative and outline of how the participant divided this narrative into discrete memories, see Figure 21.1. Having completed this task, participants then numbered the discrete memory chunks in the temporal order in which they had occurred. For each of the discrete memories identified by the participant, questions were asked regarding the participant's recollective experience or awareness associated with the memory and from which perspective he or she recalled the memory. These questions are shown in Table 21.1. Participants then rated each separate memory on 5-point scales measuring the vividness, rehearsal, emotional intensity, surprise, and ease of recalling the memory (1 = low, 5 = high). Participants were also asked to state the approximate time at which each discrete event had occurred.

In the retest at Time 2, participants were asked to recall everything that had occurred on their journey when they had come into the university 1 week earlier (as reported in the first part of the experiment). The only change between the test booklets used at Time 1 and Time 2 was the inclusion of a question at Time 2 asking whether each individual memory was recalled because the participant could remember writing about that event in the previous session, because he or she could actually remember the event occurring, or because the memory was a mixture of both these sources.

CODING OF MEMORIES

To analyze the episodic details of the memories, two independent raters (H. L. W. and M. A. C.) coded seven memory scripts from a pilot study, and through discussion of these scripts appropriate coding categories were determined. The remaining memory scripts were coded by H. L. W. Twelve mutually exclusive categories were used initially to code the content of the memories. However, due to a shortage of reporting of types of memory content such as visual perceptions and external facts, these 12 categories were then condensed into 4 overarching categories or memory details: actions, thoughts, sensations, and facts. Table 21.2 outlines all levels of the categorization process. Examples of discrete

Walked to the University along the edge of the park. // It was raining a bit but not enough to get wet. // Was busy talking // so walked past the Psychology building and only noticed when we were at the [Student's] Union. Turned back and went into Psychology building. // Remember thinking that there weren't many students about. All the roads seemed quite quiet. // Walked up the hill, the worst part of the walk. //

FIGURE 21.1. An example narrative of a participant's journey into the University. "//" denotes the points at which the participant chose to divide the overall recall narrative into discrete memories.

memory chunks and their detail categories are shown in Figures 21.2 and 21.3. Although each detail of each discrete memory was coded, because this study was primarily interested in the boundaries of episodic memories only the Start and End details of each discrete memory chunk are the focus of the subsequent analysis.

TABLE 21.1. Explanations of the Levels of Recollective Experience and Perspective as Given to Participants

Experience—this refers to how you recalled the memory:

R   You REMEMBERED the event occurring; this could have included seeing the event recurring in your mind's eye and/or having a sense of yourself in the past.

F   You had a feeling of FAMILIARITY that the event had occurred, but you could not remember details of it and did not have a sense of yourself in the past.

K   You simply KNEW that the event had occurred without having a full remembering experience, i.e., you did not have a sense of yourself in the past and/or you could not remember any details of the memory.

S   The event was like a SCRIPT, i.e., it is something you do every day and you think it occurred on the day in question, but you can't remember any details of the event and you do not have a sense of yourself in the past.

G   You simply GUESSED that the event occurred on the day in question but you can't be sure.

Perspective—this refers to how you saw your memory:

Y   You could see YOURSELF in the memory.

O   You could not see yourself but had something like your ORIGINAL view.

TABLE 21.2. Description of Coding Categories

Overarching category	Detailed category	Description and category example
ACTION	Action	An action performed by the participant: "*I cycled*"
	Other action	An action performed by someone else: "*George walked up to me*"
	Collective action	An action performed by the participant as a member of a group: "*We crossed the road*"
THOUGHT	Thought	A thought had by the participant during the event: "*and I thought to myself, why didn't I think of living on campus*"
	Evaluation	A statement referring to the quality, value or importance of an element of the event: "*the worst part of the walk*"
	Collective thought	A thought attributed as reflecting the opinion of a group of people: "*we all thought she looked a mess*"
SENSATION	Feeling	A feeling experienced by the participant: "*feeling a bit sleepy and tired*"
	Visual perception	Something seen by the participant during the event and/or a specific visual detail, e.g., color: "*I noticed a silver car stop suddenly*"
	Auditory perception	Something heard by the participant during the event: "*I overheard the girls walking in front of me talking about another girl*"
	Collective feeling	An affectual feeling attributed to more than one person: "*we both felt hung-over*"
FACT	Internal fact	A factual detail internal to the event memory: "*I was running late*"
	External fact	A factual detail external to the event itself, e.g., general knowledge, ongoing events: "*Samy is Frank's girlfriend*"

Walked to the University	Action
along the edge of the park	Fact
//	//
It was raining a bit	Fact
but not enough to get wet	Thought (Evaluation)
//	//
Was busy talking	Action
//	//
so walked past the Psychology building	Action
and only noticed	Sensation (Visual Perception)
when we were at the [Student's] Union.	Fact
Turned back	Action
and went into Psychology building	Action
//	//
Remember thinking that there weren't many students about.	Thought
All the roads seemed quite quiet	Thought (Evaluation)
//	//
Walked up the hill,	Action
the worst part of the walk	Thought (Evaluation)

FIGURE 21.2. Categorization of the details in the discrete memories that make up the narrative displayed in Figure 21.1.

Results and Discussion

ANALYSIS OF GENERAL MEMORY PROPERTIES

One of our initial areas of interest was how much participants were able to recall and how many discrete memories, or "chunks," participants split their narrative into. Figure 21.1 displays an example recall. From this we can see that this participant wrote 77 words in her recall and then determined that this was made up of six discrete memories; she so marked the boundaries of these memory chunks on her narrative. Of interest also were the subsequent average number of words per memory for each participant, the number of memories recalled out of temporal

I took a	Action
'short cut'	Thought (Evaluation)
to my lecture theatre,	Fact
by this time I was	Fact
feeling a bit sick	Sensation (Feeling)
as I stayed out	Fact
too late the night before	Thought (Evaluation)
and only got a few hours sleep	Fact
…..	…..
[I] walked	Action
down [the] hill,	Fact
saw big timber truck	Sensation (Visual Perception)
trying to reverse,	Fact
silver golf	Sensation (Visual Perception)
had to wait	Fact
…..	…..
[We] walked along [the] path	Action (Collective)
slower than I would have liked	Thought (Evaluation)
– felt a little stressed as	Sensation (Feeling)
I thought I was going to be late for lectures,	Thought
but felt relieved as they [my friends] were in the same situation	Sensation (Feeling)

FIGURE 21.3. An example of three self-defined discrete episodic memories (from different participants) and the categorization of their details.

order, and, finally, the perspective from which the participant viewed the memory. The means for each of these properties are displayed in Table 21.3. A series of paired-sample t-tests compared these values for each participant at Time 1 and Time 2; no reliable differences were observed. As can be seen in Table 21.3, at both Time 1 and Time 2 participants divided their narrative into approximately 9.5 discrete memory chunks, consisting of approximately 20 words per chunk.

TABLE 21.3. Means of General Memory Properties

Memory property	Mean (SD)	
	Time 1	Time 2
Number of memory "chunks"	9.84 (4.89)	9.32 (4.00)
Number of words written	198.21 (204.28)	139.89 (75.06)
Number of words per memory	21.15 (11.74)	17.01 (12.15)
Number of memories recalled out of temporal order	0.47 (1.02)	0.84 (1.39)
Percentage of memories seen from a third-person perspective	28.87 (38.88)	24.53 (33.13)

Participants were also asked to rate each of their discrete memories for vividness, ease of recall, surprise, rehearsal, and emotional intensity associated with the memory. Mean values for each of these properties can be seen in Table 21.4. To examine the relationship between ratings and time a series of t-tests were performed. Vividness and ease were found to be rated reliably higher at Time 1 than at Time 2, $t(18) = 7.26$, $p < 0.001$ and $t(18) = 4.69$, $p < 0.001$, respectively. No further reliable differences were observed; memories were rated as little-rehearsed, unsurprising, and of average emotional intensity.

TABLE 21.4. Mean Ratings Given to Memories at Time 1 and Time 2

Property	Mean rating (SD)	
	Time 1	Time 2
Vividness	3.17[++] (0.44)	2.50 (0.53)
Rehearsal	1.48 (0.33)	1.64 (0.54)
Ease	3.72[++] (0.60)	2.96 (0.61)
Surprise	1.72 (0.43)	1.70 (0.45)
Emotional Intensity	2.37 (0.65)	2.17 (0.54)

[++] Rating was reliably higher at Time 1 than Time 2 (p < 0.001).

ANALYSIS OF MEMORY AWARENESS

For each part of their recall that participants identified as a discrete memory, they also provided judgments of memory awareness. This measure was included for several reasons, the main reason being to determine the status of each "memory" as a memory rather than, for example, recall of routine or schematic information about their usual journey into the university (see Table 21.1). In particular, we expected that the number of memories judged to be recollectively experienced in the original recall would be high, showing good recall of actual memories, and that this would reliably diminish in the retest. Thus, we expected a fall in recollective experience over the two tests. Differences in memory awareness at Time 1 and Time 2 were analyzed in a 2 (time) × 3 (memory awareness) within-subjects ANOVA. The three levels of memory awareness were remember (R), knowing/feeling (KF), and script/guess (SG). The latter two levels both combine two levels of the original measure.

A reliable main effect of awareness was found, $F(2,36) = 34.45$, $MS_e = 0.103$, $p < 0.001$, as was a reliable interaction between time and awareness, $F(2,36) = 12.75$, $MS_e = 0.035$, $p < 0.001$.[1] As can be seen from Table 21.5, a memory had a much higher probability of being recalled with recollective experience than with any of the other levels of awareness at both Time 1 and Time 2. Planned comparisons revealed that this difference was reliable at Time 1: the probability of a memory being recalled with R was reliably higher than the probability of a memory being recalled with KF, $t(18) = 6.80$, $p < 0.001$. At Time 2 a reliable difference was not observed, $t(18) = 1.29$, $p = 0.21$ (NS). However, the probability of a memory being recalled with KF was found to be reliably higher than the probability of a memory being recalled as SG at both Time 1, $t(18) = 2.79$, $p = 0.012$, and Time 2, $t(18) = 3.54$, $p = 0.002$. Furthermore, planned comparisons found, as predicted, that a memory had a much higher probability of being recalled with R at Time 1 than at Time 2, $t(18) = 4.09$, $p = 0.001$, and conversely that a memory had a much lower probability of being recalled with KF, $t(18) = -3.10$, $p = 0.006$, and SG, $t(18) = -2.61$, $p = 0.018$, at Time 1 than at Time 2. These changes in memory awareness, a fall in recollection and a rise in

---

1. As the probabilities at each time for each participant sum to exactly 1, no effect of time could be computed.

TABLE 21.5. Mean Probabilities of Memories Being Recalled at Time 1 and Time 2 with Each Level of Awareness

	Level of Awareness (SD)		
	R	KF	SG
Time 1	0.78**+ (0.20)	0.19** (0.20)	0.03 (0.11)
Time 2	0.54 (0.29)	0.37***+ (0.30)	0.09+ (0.10)

* The probability of a memory being recalled with this level of awareness was reliably higher than the probability of a memory being recalled with the next-lower level of awareness ($p < 0.001$).
** The probability of a memory being recalled with this level of awareness was reliably higher than the probability of a memory being recalled with the next-lower level of awareness ($p < 0.05$).
+ The probability of a memory being recalled with this level of awareness at this time was reliably higher than the probability of a memory being recalled with this level of awareness at the opposing time ($p < 0.01$).

knowing, are precisely what would be expected if memories were being recalled. Thus, the pattern of findings supports our claim that memories were in fact recalled in this experiment, not just routine or schematic information.

This also ties in with a final question that participants were asked at Time 2: how each discrete memory was recalled—did they remember the event itself, did they just remember recalling the event at Time 1, or did their memory comprise both of these elements? Reponses demonstrated that 25% of memories were recalled fully from memory, 20% were recalled purely from the prior experimental recall, and 55% comprised both of these factors. The issue of the effects of repeated testing is returned to in Experiment 2.

ANALYSIS OF CLASSIFICATION OF MEMORY CONTENT

To examine our central area of interest, the type of content that lay at the boundaries of each of the discrete memories, the details that made up each memory chunk were coded by the experimenter as being Actions, Thoughts, Sensations, or Facts (see Table 21.2 for an explanation of the coding categories). The probability of each type of detail being used separately as a Start and End detail of a memory chunk was then calculated. As can be seen in Table 21.6, the probability of a memory chunk Starting with an Action and Ending with a Fact was much higher, at both Time 1 and Time 2, than the probability of a memory Starting or Ending with any other type of detail.

To explore the differences between Start and End details directly, a series of paired-sample t-tests were performed between the probability of each type of detail being used at the Start and End of memories. Actions were found to be reliably more likely to be used at the Start of a memory as opposed to at the End of a memory at both Time 1, $t(18) = 4.26$, $p < 0.001$, and Time 2, $t(18) = 4.52$, $p < 0.001$. At Time 2, when participants were instructed to repeat their recall of their journey

TABLE 21.6. Mean Probabilities of a Memory Chunk Starting and Ending with Each of the Detail Types: Action, Thought, Sensation, or Fact

Mean Probability (and SD) of Each Type of Detail Being Used as a START Detail

	Action	Thought	Sensation	Fact
Time 1	0.49*(0.23)	0.07(0.11)	0.11(0.12)	0.33(0.23)
Time 2	0.49*(0.20)	0.11(0.13)	0.11(0.15)	0.29**(0.19)

Mean Probability (SD) of Each Type of Detail Being Used as an END Detail[a]

	Action	Thought	Sensation	Fact
Time 1	0.21*(0.17)	0.13(0.19)	0.10(0.12)	0.44(0.17)
Time 2	0.19*(0.21)	0.09(0.11)	0.15(0.18)	0.46**(0.24)

* A reliable difference between the probability of this type of detail being used at this boundary of a memory and the probability of it being used at the opposing boundary ($p < 0.001$).
** A reliable difference between the probability of this type of detail being used at this boundary of a memory and the probability of it being used at the opposing boundary ($p < 0.05$).
[a] A further 11% of memories recalled were so short that they only consisted of one memory detail (e.g., *I got in the car*); this singular detail was classified as a Start detail and the memory was considered not to have an End detail.

to the university from a week earlier, facts were also found to be less likely to be used at the Start of a memory than at the End of a memory, $t(18) = -2.19$, $p = 0.042$. No other reliable differences were found; thoughts and sensations were not found to be reliably more likely to be used at either boundary of an episodic memory.

The present findings demonstrate that memories of an extended (cf., Barsalou, 1988) but trivial everyday event could be isolated on a variety of measures, including memory awareness, memory vividness, and ease of recall, and changed over time as memories would be expected to change over time. The accounts do, then, appear to be based on episodic memories of specific moments of experience. The Start and End details of these memories also differed in the content of the information they represented. Memories of the Start of discrete event units that together make up the superordinate event of the morning journey to campus predominantly, but not solely, contained information about actions. We suggest that this reflects the importance of goals in episodic memory and that the actions are intended to achieve a variety of goals relating to the overall goal of getting to the university. It should be noted that these actions were heterogeneous in nature and varied across participants. They did not consist only of "closing/locking the front door," although this was mentioned by some participants. See Figure 21.2 to see how one participant recalled four different kinds of actions in her narrative—walking, talking, turning, and entering.

Experiment 2

In Experiment 1, the retest would inevitably have been influenced by the original recall in several different ways. In order to remove the potential effects of retesting, the present experiment sampled recall of the journey to the campus only once and at a delay of 7 days. Seven days prior to this testing session, participants took part in an apparently separate experiment in which they recalled memories from a holiday. In their second experimental session, participants were asked to recall their journey to the university on the day 1 week earlier when they had taken part in the recall-of-a-holiday experiment. The inclusion of the holiday recall also allowed us to compare the Start and End details of recent and remote episodic memories. The two conditions, recall-a-holiday and recall your journey to campus 1 week ago, are referred to as the *remote* condition and *delayed-recent* condition, respectively.

Method

PARTICIPANTS

Eighteen participants took part in this study, 17 women and 1 man, with a mean age of 23.4 years. The majority of participants were University of Leeds students who took part in the experiment for payment.

DESIGN

A within-subjects design was used with two experimental sessions 1 week apart: the *remote* condition and the *delayed-recent* condition. In the remote condition, participants were asked to recall events from a holiday that had taken place between 1 and 5 years earlier. In the delayed-recent condition, participants were asked to recall events from their journey to the university the previous week, when they came in to take part in the first experimental session. The dependent variables were the details used at the Start and End boundaries of the memories, the recollective experience with which the memories were recalled, the number of memories recalled, the number of words written, and the values assigned to the different memories on various scales (e.g., vividness).

PROCEDURE

Participants were tested in groups of up to three and were instructed not to confer. At all stages of the experiment participants had no prior knowledge of what they would be asked to recall. In this experiment, in the remote condition participants were asked to recall events from a holiday that had taken place between 1 and 5 years earlier. Participants were asked to recall events that had lasted for minutes, hours, or 1 day, but no longer. They were instructed to write each memory in a separate paragraph and write down memories as they came to mind, without editing them. Participants were then asked the questions regarding the recollective experience associated with each memory and from which perspective they recalled the memory. They then completed rating scales on the imagery, rehearsal, emotional intensity, surprise, and ease of recalling each memory.

The delayed-recent condition took place 1 week after the remote condition. In the delayed-recent condition, a surprise-free recall procedure was used and participants were asked to recall their journey to the university the previous week, when they had come in to take part in the first experimental session. The procedure and test booklet for this condition were the same as those used at Time 1 in Experiment 1.

CODING OF MEMORIES

Coding of memory details was performed in the same manner as in Experiment 1. Again, although each detail of each memory was coded, because this study was primarily interested in the boundaries of episodic memories only the Start and End details of each discrete memory chunk are the focus of the subsequent analysis. Three remote memories of events from holidays and their category details are shown in Figure 21.4.

Results

Data preparation and analyses were the same as those used previously.

ANALYSIS OF GENERAL MEMORY PROPERTIES

As in Experiment 1, the first data to be examined were the number of separate episodic memories into which the participants split their narrative, the number of words each participant wrote, the subsequent average number of words per memory for each participant, the number of memories recalled out of temporal order, and finally the perspective from which the participant viewed the memory. The mean ratings for each of these properties in the remote condition and the delayed-recent condition are displayed in Table 21.7.

A series of paired-samples t-tests compared these values given by participants in the two conditions. A reliable difference between the mean number of words written in each condition was found, $t(17) = 3.94$, $p = 0.001$, and between the related figure of the mean number of words per memory chunk in each condition, $t(17) = 4.14$, $p = 0.001$. These results show that reliably more words were written, and were divided up into longer memory chunks, in the remote condition when participants were asked to write about events from a holiday than in the delayed-recent condition when participants wrote about their

[I remember] waiting	Action
in the departure lounge and	Fact
thinking that the plane looked	Thought
extremely small.	Thought (Evaluation)
We then began to worry as	Sensation (Collective feeling)
the cabin crew were Greek	Fact
and did not speak very good English.	Thought (Evaluation)
The plane was very small and	Fact
old fashioned and	Thought (Evaluation)
the journey was an hour longer than expected	Fact
due to the weather.	Fact
…..	…..
[I remember] making something	Action
for the local playground.	Fact
A big group of us managed to carve	Action (Collective)
a huge	Thought (Evaluation)
lion out of an old tree trunk	Fact
…..	…..
We went to watch the football final,	Action (Collective)
Portugal Vs Greece.	Fact
I wasn't that bothered about it	Thought (Evaluation)
so I went down to the beach	Action
with Noah.	Fact
I walked along	Action
on my own	Fact
and thought about things that had been troubling me.	Thought
Greece won the football.	Fact

FIGURE 21.4. An example of three memory chunks from remote memories and the categorization of their details.

TABLE 21.7. Means of General Memory Properties

Memory property	Mean (SD)	
	Remote	Delayed-Recent
Number of episodic memories	8.28 (4.31)	9.28 (4.96)
Number of words written	359.11[+] (228.57)	201.67 (119.33)
Number of words per memory	47.99[+] (27.64)	24.39 (12.51)
Number of memories recalled out of temporal order	NA	2.11 (3.55)
Percentage of memories seen from a third-person perspective	41.36 (31.32)	44.39 (34.02)

[+] Mean in the remote condition is reliably larger than in the delayed-recent condition ($p < 0.01$).

journey to campus the week before. No other reliable differences were observed. Comparisons of these data to the data from Experiment 1 are discussed later.

Participants were also asked to rate each memory chunk on the vividness, ease of recall, surprise, rehearsal, and emotional intensity associated with the memory. Mean values for each of these ratings can be seen in Table 21.8.

To examine the relationship between ratings and condition, a series of t-tests was performed. Vividness, rehearsal, surprise, and emotional intensity were all found to be rated reliably higher in the remote condition,

TABLE 21.8. Mean Ratings of Properties of Memories in the Remote Condition and the Delayed-Recent Condition

Property	Mean Rating (SD)	
	Remote	Delayed-Recent
Vividness	3.26[+] (0.47)	2.75 (0.77)
Rehearsal	2.51[++] (0.60)	1.40 (0.42)
Ease	3.33 (0.74)	3.06 (0.97)
Surprise	2.27[++] (0.63)	1.53 (0.50)
Emotional Intensity	2.74[++] (0.47)	1.90 (0.70)

[++] Rating was reliably higher in the remote condition than in the delayed-recent condition ($p < 0.001$).
[+] Rating was reliably higher in the remote condition than in the delayed-recent condition ($p < 0.01$).

where participants recalled self-selected events from a holiday, than in the delayed-recent condition, where participants were instructed to recall their journey to the university after a 1-week delay: vividness, $t(17) = 2.93$, $p = 0.009$; rehearsal, $t(17) = 7.73$, $p < 0.001$; surprise, $t(17) = 4.33$, $p < 0.001$; emotional intensity, $t(17) = 5.06$, $p < 0.001$. No reliable difference between ease of recall was observed, $t(17) = 1.45$, $p = 0.17$ (NS).

ANALYSIS OF MEMORY AWARENESS

In this experiment we were again interested in memory awareness, as this reflects the recall of specific memories rather than, say, the recall of a narrative or script. To examine the relationship between memory awareness and condition, a 2×3 within-subjects ANOVA was performed. There were two conditions (the remote condition versus the delayed-recent condition), and memory awareness had three levels—remember (R), knowing/feeling (KF), and script/guess (SG). As in Experiment 1, the latter two levels both combine two levels of the original measure.

Analysis of the means shown in Table 21.9 found a reliable main effect of awareness, $F(2,34) = 29.68$, $MS_e = 0.107$, $p < 0.001$. There was no reliable interaction between condition and awareness. As can be seen from Table 21.9, memories had a much higher probability of being recalled with recollective experience (being assigned to the R category) than being recalled with any of the other levels of awareness in both the

TABLE 21.9. Mean Probabilities of Memories Being Recalled in the Remote Condition or in the Delayed-Recent Condition with Each Level of Awareness

| | Level of Awareness | | |
	R	KF	SG
Remote	0.75* (0.27)	0.24* (0.25)	0.01 (0.04)
Delayed-recent	0.59* (0.33)	0.23 (0.20)	0.18+ (0.31)

R = remember; KF = knowing/feeling; SG = script/guess.
* The probability of a memory being recalled with this level of awareness was reliably higher than the probability of a memory being recalled with the next-lower level of awareness ($p < 0.01$).
+ The probability of a memory being recalled as a Script or Guess was reliably greater in the delayed-recent compared to the remote condition ($p < 0.05$).

remote condition and the delayed-recent condition. Planned comparisons confirmed that the probability of a memory being recalled with R was reliably higher than the probability of a memory being recalled with KF in both the remote condition, $t(17) = 4.10$, $p = 0.001$, and in the delayed recent condition, $t(17) = 3.41$, $p = 0.003$. However, only remote memories had a higher probability of being recalled with KF than with SG, $t(17) = 4.11$, $p = 0.001$. Memories were also more likely to be recalled as SG in the delayed-recent condition as opposed to in the remote condition, $t(17) = -2.31$, $p = 0.034$. Unsurprisingly, although the event had taken place more recently, memories of trivial everyday events sampled in the delayed-recent condition were recalled with less recollective experience than memories of self-selected events from the more remote, but more vivid and emotional, experiences recalled from a past holiday.

ANALYSIS OF CLASSIFICATION OF MEMORY CONTENT

As in Experiment 1, our central focus was on the type of content that lay at the boundaries of each of the discrete episodic memories recalled. To examine this, the probabilities of each type of detail (Actions, Thoughts, Sensations, and Facts) being used separately as Start and End details were again calculated. As can be seen in Table 21.10, the probability of a memory Starting with an Action and Ending with a Fact was much higher in both the remote condition and the delayed-recent condition than the probability of a memory Starting or Ending with any other type of detail.

To explore the differences between Start and End details directly, a series of paired-sample t-tests were performed between the probability of each type of detail being used at the Start and End of memories. Actions were found to be reliably more likely to be used at the Start of a memory as opposed to at the End of a memory in both the remote, $t(17) = 5.16$, $p < 0.001$, and in the delayed-recent, $t(17) = 5.85$, $p < 0.001$, conditions. In the delayed-recent condition, when participants were instructed to recall, for the first time, their journey to the university from a week earlier, Facts were found to be reliably more likely to be used at the End of a memory than at the Start of a memory, $t(17) = 2.70$, $p = 0.015$. In this experiment Thoughts were also found to be reliably more likely to be used at the End of a memory than at the Start of a memory in both the remote, $t(17) = 6.24$, $p < 0.001$, and the

TABLE 21.10. Mean Probabilities of a Memory Chunk Starting and Ending with Each of the Detail Types: Action, Thought, Sensation, or Fact

	Mean probability (SD) of Each Type of Detail Being Used as a Start Detail			
	Action	Thought	Sensation	Fact
Remote	0.49*	0.07*	0.11	0.34
	(0.28)	(0.12)	(0.18)	(0.21)
Delayed-recent	0.51*	0.04**	0.11	0.33**
	(0.30)	(0.72)	(0.12)	(0.24)

	Mean probability (SD) of Each Type of Detail Being Used as an End Detail[a]			
	Action	Thought	Sensation	Fact
Remote	0.14*	0.27*	0.13	0.46
	(0.13)	(0.15)	(0.13)	(0.20)
Delayed-recent	0.10*	0.16**	0.09	0.58**
	(0.15)	(0.14)	(0.14)	(0.28)

* A reliable difference between the probability of this type of detail being used at this boundary of a memory and the probability of it being used at the opposing boundary ($p < 0.001$).

** A reliable difference between the probability of this type of detail being used at this boundary of a memory and the probability of it being used at the opposing boundary ($p < 0.05$).

[a] In the remote condition a further 1% of memories recalled were so short that they only consisted of one memory detail (e.g., *I got in the car*); this singular detail was classified as a Start detail and the memory was considered not to have an End detail. In the delayed-recent condition this was true for 8% of memories.

delayed-recent, $t(17) = 2.93$, $p = 0.009$, conditions. No other reliable differences were found.

Comparison of Experiments

To examine whether the repeated recall influenced properties of the discrete memories recalled in Experiment 1, data from Time 2 were compared to data from the delayed-recent condition of Experiment 2. Memories of the journey into campus recalled at Time 2 in Experiment 1 had already been recalled at Time 1, 1 week before. Memories recalled in the delayed-recent condition of Experiment 2 had been encoded 1 week previously but had been subject to no other experimental recall. As was shown earlier, in Experiment 1 there were no reliable differences between the number of words written and the number of discrete memory chunks the narrative was divided into, and so forth, at Time 1 and Time 2. Comparing data from the delayed-recent condition of Experiment 2 with data from Experiment 1, Time 2, allows us to investigate whether data from Experiment 1, Time 2, were influenced by the prior recall. As different participants took part in the two experiments, a series of independent-groups t-tests were performed to compare the data sets.

Although the results did not reach conventional significance levels, a number of interesting trends emerged. Examining Table 21.11 we can see that in the delayed-recent condition (of Experiment 2), participants wrote longer narratives than at Time 2 in Experiment 1, $t(35) = 1.90$, $p = 0.066$; that participants wrote many more words per memory chunk, $t(35) = 1.82$, $p = 0.077$; and that a larger percentage of memories were recalled from the third-person perspective, $t(35) = 1.80$, $p = 0.081$. No other differences were observed. In conjunction with the finding that at Time 2 75% of memory chunks were identified as having been influenced by memories of having recalled that event at Time 1 and that a fall in recollection and a rise in knowing was found between Time 1 and Time 2, these data suggest that repeated testing had influenced recall at Time 2 appreciably. Due to prior recall at Time 1, memories may have

TABLE 21.11. Mean Ratings of Properties of Memories at Time 2 in Experiment 1 and in the Delayed-Recent Condition of Experiment 2

Memory property	Mean Rating (SD)	
	Experiment 1: Time 2	Experiment 2: Delayed-recent
Number of episodic memories	9.32 (4.00)	9.28 (4.96)
Number of words written	139.89 (75.06)	201.67 (119.33)
Number of words per memory	17.01 (12.15)	24.39 (12.51)
Percentage of memories seen from a third-person perspective	24.53 (33.13)	44.39 (34.02)

become more generic or semanticized by Time 2, whereas with no prior recall memories recalled in the delayed-recent condition consisted of vivid episodic memories.

General Discussion

Overall, the findings of the present two experiments show that the beginnings and endings of (self-defined) episodic memories are quite variable in type. Nevertheless, a distinctive pattern did emerge over the four conditions, and beginning or Start details were found to predominantly refer to *actions*, whereas End details were found to predominantly refer to *facts*. We term this the *Action-Fact* (AF) structure of episodic memories. In the discussion that follows, we focus on this predominant AF pattern. However, we emphasize here that other structures, although less frequent, are possible and were observed. Our general view is that the organization of details in an episodic memory will be determined in large measure by the goals that guided processing during the experience and by the subsequent integration of an episodic memory with other long-term knowledge structures. Nonetheless, the AF structure may be a basic form of organization in episodic memories, and one that can represent a wide and diverse range of events.

According to the present perspective, autobiographical memory is a cognitive system that has evolved to support effective short- and long-term goal attainment (Conway, 2005). By this view, event details, including Start and End details, are summary representations of perceptual and other predictions as these are conceived of in the EST model of Zacks and colleagues (2007). Perceptual predictions and their outcomes are embedded in a complex hierarchy of goal processing, and event details are suggested to reflect this. Thus, a series of details such as "Walked to the University along the edge of the park.// It was raining a bit but not enough to get wet.// Was busy talking . . ." (full narrative shown in Figures 21.1 and 21.2) summarizes a series of interconnected perceptual predictions and their outcomes, which are linked in the perceptual continuum by changes in perceptual predictions–event boundaries in the EST model. The details that constitute the Start of each discrete memory are thought to introduce a new goal context and often appear to do so by representing an activity that achieves an initial part of a plan, the aim of which is, of course, goal attainment.

An event, then, is an epoch of goal processing during which a particular goal structure dominates cognition. A goal structure might be thought of as a partonomic hierarchy (Barsalou, 1988) in which sub-goals are "part of" some larger goal. So the goal of "getting to campus" might consist of a set of sub-goals such as "leaving the house," "getting the bus," "meeting friends," "walking across the park," "entering the psychology building," which are all part of the larger, superordinate goal. Sub-goals are summaries of the histories of perceptual and other predictions that guided processing during the experience of the sub-goal event(s). In our experiments they generally formed the units self-defined by participants as episodic memories. We term these *simple episodic memories* and suggest that they are an output of the working memory system and in particular of the episodic buffer (Baddeley, 2000).

Simple episodic memories represent events on a small scale and are experience-near. The type of event in this study, which was goal-directed, of modest duration, and constrained by definite temporal boundaries, was chosen to reflect short-term goals, or goals with a small grain size. The superordinate goal, which participants were assumed to have held at the time of encoding, was the goal of "getting from home to the university." When then asked to split their recall into discrete episodic memories, the placement of episodic boundaries seems to have been informed by sub-goals of even smaller grain size and changes in perceptual predictions that were being updated at the time of the event and that were encoded as part of the episodic memories. Segmentation of events using differing grain-size instructions has been found to be hierarchically organized, with coarse grains and fine grains corresponding well to goals and sub-goals (Hard et al., 2006; Zacks et al., 2001). The current experiments did not set out to distinguish between different grain sizes, as we were interested in examining how a real-world event that had been *experienced* by the participant was recalled, rather than a participant's perception of an event he or she observed. Our primary interest was also where event boundaries would be placed if no explicit instructions were given regarding grain size, though manipulating grain-size instructions in memory retrieval studies of this nature would be of interest in future work. Asking participants to identify where their goals changed during their recall of their journey or a similar event would also be of interest, though with a starting point of such a small grain size ("getting to the university") participants may find it difficult to explicitly pinpoint goals of an even smaller grain size within this.

The AF structure is highly goal related in that an action has a specific goal and a factual end detail typically marks the close of the epoch of processing of the goal (see Figures 21.1 and 21.2). However, we also found that End details were more varied than Start details (see Tables 21.6 and 21.10). Thus, an action implementing part of a plan for goal attainment can reach a conclusion in many different ways (i.e., in thoughts, sensations, or even another action). Start details were predominantly actions or, to a lesser degree, facts (usually scene-setting), but only rarely were they thoughts or sensations. It may then be the case that Start details, because of their greater degree of uniformity, and hence greater predictability, feature more prominently in memory retrieval, perhaps being accessed before other details/memories. Start details may then be especially important in memories for experienced events, and we suggest that this is so because Start details provide important information about goals. Linking to the EST of Zacks et al. (2007), as goals and perceptual predictions are being updated, the details being encoded and then recalled at the Start of a simple episodic memory are proposed as being those that are first encoded after a period of change (when the stable mental model of the event is modified by the updating mental model), causing a change to be adopted in the stable mental model of the superordinate event. It seems that it is predominantly new actions, though not only actions and not always actions, that constitute a large enough change in recall of an event to bring about an episodic boundary being placed before them—in other words, the change in perceptual prediction or goal associated with experiencing the action during encoding leads to the action constituting the Start of a new simple episodic memory at recall.

Here we have shown that if asked to do so, people are able to segment their memories of a typical everyday event into simple episodic memories, and that although these divisions were based on the individual's own judgment and were therefore idiosyncratic, the Action-Fact pattern of the placing of these event boundaries was evident across all four conditions. Although participants were found to be able to place episodic boundaries somewhat consistently, another interesting question regarding knowledge of episodic boundaries is, are people consciously aware of any boundaries when recalling events from memory? In conducting these experiments we became aware, through informal discussions with the present participants and with participants taking part in other autobiographical memories in our laboratory, that there may be an additional factor involved in event segmentation and the creation of episodic memories that we had not formally assessed. This factor is to do with a *feeling* that is associated with the close of an event or with a change in goal processing. This feeling was variously mentioned and appeared to take different forms—for example, a sense of change, a sense of closure, a feeling of accomplishment, a strong need to attend to some other action, and so forth. The role of emotions and feelings in event segmentation and in the creation of episodic memories has not received any attention in research in this area thus far. This is perhaps a little unusual in that at least one set of major theories of emotion view emotions as arising in response to interruptions in goal processing, and even as internal signals about the current state of goal-processing (see Oatley, 1992). More generally, a view we are currently developing proposes that many different forms of processing are accompanied by or associated with what we have termed *cognitive feelings* (Moulin, Conway, Souchay, & O'Connor, in preparation). Cognitive feelings allow the individual to *experience* knowledge. By this view a person not only knows that he or she has just closed the door when leaving the house but also has a feeling, an experience, of a transition from one event to another. Our informal discussions with participants suggested that one potentially fruitful direction for further research might lie in the investigation of cognitive feelings arising at event boundaries and in the resulting formation of "action-fact" episodic memories.

Acknowledgments

Martin A. Conway is supported by a Professorial Fellowship, RES-051–27–0127, from the Economic and Social Research Council (ESRC) of Great Britain, and Helen L. Williams by a Research Assistantship also from the ESRC. The present research is part of a larger project on episodic memory being conducted by the authors in the Leeds Memory Group.

References

Baddeley, A. D. (1986). *Working memory*. Oxford: Clarendon Press.
Baddeley, A. D. (2000). The episodic buffer: A new component of working memory? *Trends in Cognitive Science, 4*, 417–423.

Barsalou, L. W. (1988). The content and organization of autobiographical memories. In U. Neisser & E. Winograd (Eds.), *Remembering reconsidered: Ecological and traditional approaches to the study of memory* (pp. 193–243). Cambridge: Cambridge University Press.

Brewer, W. F., & Lichtenstein, E. H. (1982). Stories are to entertain: A structural-affect theory of stories. *Journal of Pragmatics, 6,* 473–486.

Conway, M. A. (2001). Sensory perceptual episodic memory and its context: Autobiographical memory. *Philosophical Transactions of the Royal Society of London, 356,* 1297–1306.

Conway, M. A. (2005). Memory and the Self. *Journal of Memory and Language, 53*(4), 594–628.

Conway, M. A., & Pleydell-Pearce, C. W. (2000). The construction of autobiographical memories in the self memory system. *Psychological Review, 107,* 261–288.

Conway, M. A., Singer, J. A., & Tagini, A. (2004). The self and autobiographical memory: Correspondence and coherence. *Social Cognition, 22,* 495–537.

Hard, B. M., Lozano, S. C., & Tversky, B. (2006). Hierarchical encoding of behavior: Translating perception into action. *Journal of Experimental Psychology: General, 135,* 588–608.

Moulin, C. J. A., Conway, M. A., Souchay, C., & O'Connor, A. R. (in preparation). Cognitive feelings. To be submitted to *Consciousness and Cognition.*

Newtson, D. (1976). Foundations of attribution: The perception of ongoing behaviour. In J. H. Harvey, J. W. Ickes, & R. F. Kidd (Eds.), *New directions in attribution research,* Vol. 1 (pp. 41–67). Hillsdale, NJ: Lawrence Erlbaum Associates.

Newtson, D., Engquist, G., & Bois, J. (1977). The objective basis of behaviour units. *Journal of Personality and Social Psychology, 35,* 847–862.

Oatley, K. (1992). *Best laid schemes: The psychology of emotions.* Cambridge: Cambridge University Press.

Schwartz, M. F., Montgomery, M. W., Fitzpatrick-DeSalme, E. J., Ochipa, C., Coslett, H. B., & Mayer, N. H. (1995). Analysis of a disorder of everyday action. *Cognitive Neuropsychology, 12*(8), 863–892.

Zacks, J. M., Speer, N. K., Swallow, K. M., Braver, T. S., & Reynolds, J. R. (2007). Event perception: A mind/brain perspective. *Psychological Bulletin, 133*(2), 273–293

Zacks, J. M., Tversky, B., & Iyer, G. (2001). Perceiving, remembering, and communicating structure in events. *Journal of Experimental Psychology: General, 130,* 29–58.

Zwaan, R. A., & Radvansky, G. A. (1998). Situation models in language comprehension and memory. *Psychological Bulletin, 123*(2), 162–185.

22

The Human Prefrontal Cortex Stores Structured Event Complexes

FRANK KRUEGER & JORDAN GRAFMAN

Event sequence knowledge is necessary for learning, planning, and performing activities of daily living. Clinical observations suggest that the prefrontal cortex (PFC) is crucial for goal-directed behavior such as carrying out plans, controlling a course of actions, or organizing everyday life routines (Eslinger & Damasio, 1985; Fuster, 1997; Janowsky, Shimamura, & Squire, 1989; Milner, Petrides, & Smith, 1985; Shallice, 1982; Shallice & Burgess, 1991; Stuss & Benson, 1984). Researchers have proposed a number of theories of PFC function (e.g., Duncan, 2001; Fuster, 1991; Miller & Cohen, 2001; Shallice & Burgess, 1998), many of which center around the representations or processes that are mediated by the PFC (for further discussion and comparisons of different models of PFC function see Wood & Grafman, 2003).

Overall, the "processing" approach takes the view that cognition in the PFC can be described in terms of performance without specifying the representation that underlies these "processes." In this view, processes such as switching, maintenance, and inhibitory control are computational procedures or algorithms that are independent of the nature or modality of the stimulus being processed, and they operate upon knowledge stored in posterior parts of the brain. In our opinion, the

617

"processing" approach to PFC function is a fundamental shift away from how cognitive neuroscientists have previously tried to understand information storage in memory. It further implies that the PFC is minimally committed to long-term storage of knowledge, as compared to posterior cortical regions in the temporal, parietal, and occipital lobes.

We propose a "representational" approach to PFC function, which assumes that the PFC (a) stores long term memories of goal-oriented event sequence knowledge and (b) seeks to establish the format and categories according to which such information is stored (Wood & Grafman, 2003). According to this approach, storage and processing are integrally related and dependent on the same neuronal infrastructure. The PFC processes goal-oriented structured event complexes by encoding and retrieving the sequence of event components. In parallel, the PFC interacts with knowledge stored in posterior cortical regions. Specifically, event components interact and give rise to event sequence knowledge through three binding mechanisms: (1) sequential binding for linking event components within the PFC (Weingartner, Grafman, Boutelle, Kaye, & Martin, 1983); (2) temporal binding for linking event components with anatomically highly connected regions in the posterior cortex (Engel & Singer, 2001); and (3) third-party binding for linking event components with anatomically loosely connected regions through synchronized activity induced by the hippocampus (O'Reilly & Rudy, 2000; Weingartner et al., 1983). In our opinion, the representational approach is much more compatible with how neuroscience seeks to understand the functions of posterior cortical regions such as motor and visual representations.

In this chapter, we argue that the human PFC stores a unique type of knowledge in the form of structured event complexes (SECs). SECs are representations composed of higher-order goal-oriented sequences of events that are involved in the planning and monitoring of complex behavior (Grafman, 1995, 2002; Wood & Grafman, 2003). We will first summarize the key elements of the biology and structure of the PFC. Specifically, we will argue that the SEC framework is consistent with what is known about the structure, connectivity, development, neurophysiology, and evolution of the PFC. Then, we will describe the characteristics and principles of the SEC framework. We will review the different lines of evidence supporting the framework, focusing on both the effects of PFC lesions and functional neuroimaging experiments that reveal specific patterns of regional PFC activation in mediating event sequence knowledge.

Properties of the Human Prefrontal Cortex

We have argued in previous publications for the validity of a representational approach to understanding the cognitive function of the human PFC (Grafman & Krueger, 2006; Huey, Krueger, & Grafman, 2006; Moll et al., 2006; Wood & Grafman, 2003). We proposed that SECs are higher-order goal-oriented event sequences that are stored as knowledge in the PFC. Before we detail the principles of the framework and review different lines of evidence, we will summarize the key elements of the biology and structure of the PFC and argue for a rationale that emphasizes a representational approach to PFC function in mediating event sequence knowledge.

Structure

The human PFC occupies approximately one-third of the entire human cerebral cortex and has a columnar design like other cortical regions. Some regions of the PFC have a total of six layers; other regions are agranular (without a granular cell layer). The PFC can be subdivided into lateral, medial, and orbitofrontal regions (Fig. 22.1), in which Brodmann's areas (8, 9, 10, 11, 23, 24, 25, 32, 44, 45, 46, 47) provide the cytoarchitectonic subdivision within each of these gross regions (Barbas, 2000; Brodmann, 1912). Medial and lateral PFC belong to two distinct architectonic trends within the human PFC (Pandya & Yeterian, 1996). The medial trend is phylogenetically and ontogenetically older than the lateral trend, which is especially well developed in humans (Stuss & Benson, 1986). Comparing the human with the primate PFC, it has been claimed that the human PFC (and Brodmann's area 10 in particular) is proportionally larger compared to the rest of the cerebral cortex (Rilling & Insel, 1999; Semendeferi, Armstrong, Schleicher, Zilles, & van Hoesen, 2001; Semendeferi, Lu, Schenker, & Damasio, 2002). Moreover, it has also been suggested that in humans the PFC has a more sophisticated internal and differentially organized neural architecture (Chiavaras, LeGoualher, Evans, & Petrides, 2001; Elston, 2000; Elston & Rosa, 2000).

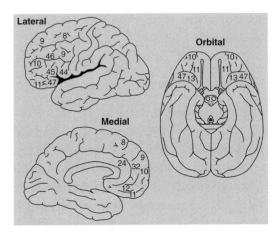

FIGURE 22.1. Anatomy of the human prefrontal cortex (PFC). The PFC can be subdivided into lateral, medial, and orbitofrontal regions. Prefrontal areas are numbered according to Brodmann's cytoarchitectural map. (*Source:* Fuster, J. M. (2001). The prefrontal cortex—an update: Time is of the essence. *Neuron*, 30, 320. Used with permission.)

Connectivity

All PFC regions are interconnected with other areas of the brain, and almost all of these pathways are reciprocal. There exist at least five distinct PFC regions, each of which is independently involved in separate cortico-striatal loops (Alexander, Crutcher, & DeLong, 1990; Masterman & Cummings, 1997). The PFC also has strong limbic system connections via its medial and orbital efferent connections terminating in the amygdala, thalamus, and parahippocompal regions (Groenewegen & Uylings, 2000; Price, 1999), and long pathway connections to association cortices in the temporal, parietal, and occipital lobes.

Development

The PFC undergoes relatively late development during ontogenesis compared to other cortical association areas (Conel, 1939; Flechsig, 1920; Huttenlocher, 1990; Huttenlocher & Dabholkar, 1997). Imaging studies indicate that the PFC does not fully mature until adolescence or early adulthood (Chugani, Phelps, & Mazziotta, 1987; Diamond, 1991; Durston et al., 2001; Giedd et al., 1999; Paus et al., 1999; Sowell, Thompson, Holmes, Jernigan, & Toga, 1999), and research on primates suggests that PFC lesions occurring early in development do not affect performance on tasks presumably subserved by PFC until the monkey's PFC matures (Diamond, 1991; Goldman-Rakic, 1987, 1992).

Neurophysiology

A key property of neurons in the PFC of monkeys and humans is their ability to fire during an interval between a stimulus and a delayed probe (Levy & Goldman-Rakic, 2000). Besides the property of sustained firing, a unique structural feature of neurons in the PFC has recently been found (Elston, 2000; Elston & Rosa, 2000). Pyramidal cells in the PFC of macaque monkeys (and presumably humans) are significantly more spinous compared to pyramidal cells in other cortical areas, making them capable of handling a larger amount of excitatory inputs. This could be one explanation for the PFC's ability to integrate input from many sources in order to implement more abstract behaviors.

EVOLUTION

There is an evolutionary cognitive advance from primates to humans in the ability of neurons to sustain their firing and code the temporal and sequential properties of ongoing events in the environment or mind over longer and longer periods of time (Rueckert & Grafman, 1996). Longer sustained firing and the ability to integrate input from many sources has enabled the human brain to code, store, and retrieve long and complex sequences of behavior (Nichelli, Clark, Hollnagel, & Grafman, 1995; Rueckert & Grafman, 1998).

In summary, the structure and connectivity of PFC regions, the physiological properties of its neurons, and evolutionary principles are strongly suggestive of its role in the integration of sensory and memory information and in the representation and control of actions and behavior. Along with extended firing of neurons, specialized neural systems were developed that enabled the encoding of these behaviors into sequentially linked but individually recognizable events. The event sequence itself must be parsed as each event begins and ends in order to explicitly recognize the nature, duration, and number of events that compose this sequence (Zacks, Braver, et al., 2001; Zacks & Tversky, 2001). These event sequences, in order to be goal-oriented and cohere, must obey a logical structure. This structure can be conceptualized as a representation (i.e., a "permanent" unit of memory) that, when activated, corresponds to a dynamic brain state signified by the strength and pattern of neural activity in a local brain sector. In this sense, over the course of evolution, the PFC became capable of representing knowledge of more complex behaviors or behaviors that occurred over a longer period of time. We have labeled these representational units in the PFC as SECs (Grafman, 1995).

Principles and Evidence for the SEC Framework

SECs are representations composed of higher-order goal-oriented sequences of events that are involved in the planning and monitoring of complex behavior. For example, an SEC with the goal "get ready for work" would consist of a sequence of events such as waking up, getting out of bed, using the bathroom, taking a shower, getting dressed, eating breakfast, and so forth. Event sequence knowledge has been described elsewhere as scripts or schemas (Rumelhart, 1980; Schank & Abelson, 1977). However, we use the term *SEC* to refer to the unique type of knowledge stored in the human PFC (Grafman, 1995). In our view, SECs are the underlying representations for cognitive structures such as plans, actions, rules, scripts, schemas, and mental models.

SECs are formed on the basis of repeated experience with events. Events within an SEC can be defined in terms of centrality, frequency of occurrence, relative position, duration, and temporal structure. Like objects that have boundaries in space, events have boundaries in time (Zacks, Tversky, & Iyer, 2001). For example, an object such as a ball takes up a certain amount of space of a certain shape. By analogy, an event such as "pitch a ball" takes place for a certain amount of time with a beginning and an end. SECs link a set of events to knowledge structures that store both the goals and boundaries of events. Specifically, each SEC has a beginning event that specifies a setting (e.g., "wake up"), a following set of events (e.g., "take a shower," "get dressed") that specify goals and activities to achieve these goals, and an event that signifies the setting that deactivates the SEC (e.g., "arrive at work"). Besides physical constraints, the sequential order of events obeys cultural and individual constraints. In the United States, for example, individuals generally shower on a daily basis in the morning before breakfast (cultural constraint), and some people brush their teeth twice in the morning—once before and once after eating breakfast (individual constraint).

During childhood, individual events are initially represented as independent memory units. For instance, SECs associated with "kitchen," "bar," and "restaurant" cluster around the event "ingestion of food," whereas "bus," "train," "airplane," and "bicycle" cluster around the physical event "moving oneself around." Later in development, these primitive SECs expand into large multi-event units, based on repeated exposure. In addition, the boundaries of event sequences become more firmly established. Therefore, in adulthood, SECs will range from specific episodes to context-free and abstract SECs. For example, the abstract SEC "eating" includes specific episodes representing evenings at a specific restaurant, SECs representing the actions and rules of how to behave at different types of restaurants (such as at a fast-food restaurant, at a coffeehouse, or on an airplane), and an abstract SEC representing actions related to "eating" that are context-independent.

The SEC framework lends itself to the generation of testable predictions regarding the properties and localization of SECs in the PFC. By combining two methods of research, we strengthen the inferences we can make in linking the processing of event sequence knowledge with specific brain areas. On the one hand, we apply lesion studies to examining deficits caused by specific brain damage in humans. On the other hand, we use functional neuroimaging such as positron emission tomography (PET) and functional magnetic resonance imaging (fMRI) to measure regional brain activity in healthy subjects while they perform behavioral tasks involving event sequence knowledge. Note that subjects are not actually involved in carrying out those behaviors during the experimental tasks. However, to solve the tasks subjects have to access the stored SECs about their sequential organization. Therefore, it appears reasonable to assume that performing our tasks engages the same sorts of representations that are activated during planning, monitoring, and executing those behaviors. We have started to investigate the differential contributions of PFC subregions to specific formats of representation and categories of knowledge.

Sequence Structure

Longer-sustained firing and the ability to integrate input from many sources have enabled the human PFC to code, store, and retrieve long and complex sequences of behavior. These event sequences, in order to be goal-oriented and cohere, must obey a logical structure. We argue that SECs are higher-order goal-oriented event sequences that are stored as unique knowledge in the PFC.

Our research group investigated script generation and evaluation in patients with lesions in prefrontal and posterior brain regions and in normal subjects (Sirigu et al., 1995, 1996). The script generation tested access to script information, while script evaluation tested how subjects could organize and manipulate this event sequence knowledge in the process of planning an activity. We found that prefrontal lesion patients did not differ from posterior lesion patients or normal subjects in the number of events evoked and mean evocation time. However, the prefrontal lesion group committed more errors in ordering the correct temporal sequence and remaining within the stated script boundaries, and these individuals failed to close scripts.

Further, we demonstrated a double dissociation in performances between event sequence and sentence ordering by comparing anterior PFC lesion patients with Broca's area lesion patients (Sirigu et al., 1998). Subjects were asked to produce either a grammatically correct sentence or a logically consistent short narrative based on the temporal sequence of segments of words or actions, respectively. Although both tasks involved ordering of verbal stimuli, patients with anterior PFC lesions had difficulty in performing the event sequencing task involving ordering events correctly to form a logical sequence of a script, but they made virtually no errors in the syntax task involving ordering words correctly in syntactically well-formed sentences. The opposite performance was observed in patients with Broca's area lesions. The results suggest that representation of ordering depends on the underlying knowledge structure being processed. There exist at least two different networks within the frontal lobes for verbal sequence processing—one network for SEC syntax and another for sentence syntax. The more posterior frontal Broca's region, which is closely tied to motor processing, may be better suited for handling the rapid analysis of word order in the context of online speech production, whereas the more anterior PFC region is more tied to knowledge-linked event sequence processing.

Moreover, using fMRI we investigated whether specific prefrontal regions are involved in script-event compared to sentence-word processing. For the script-event order task, subjects were requested to detect an error in the order of two familiar scripts (e.g., "get dressed/take a shower"). In contrast, for the sentence-word order task, subjects had to detect an error in the sequence of words depicting a sentence (e.g., "the message twice/announced was"). Both tasks were found to activate partially overlapping areas in the left frontal, parietal, and temporal cortices, which are known to be implicated in language processing (Crozier et al., 1999). In addition, the script-event order task activated a large area in the dorsolateral PFC (Brodmann areas [BA] 6 and 8) bilaterally, as well as the left supplementary motor area and angular gyrus (BA 39). The results suggest that these prefrontal areas may be more specifically involved in the process of analyzing sequential links in the action category.

In another fMRI study, we investigated the involvement of the PFC in temporal order and membership judgments of scripts (e.g., shopping) and category items (e.g., holidays) (Knutson, Wood, & Grafman, 2004). In the order task, subjects were asked to determine whether the stimuli were shown in the correct sequential order; in the judgment task they were asked if the stimuli belonged to the same category. Both tasks activated the middle frontal gyrus bilaterally (BA 6 and 8), but in addition the event order task activated the right inferior frontal gyrus (BA 44, 45, and 47) while the chronological order task activated the left inferior frontal gyrus (BA 44 and 46).

Altogether, these results corroborate our view that the PFC mediates higher-order goal-oriented event sequences that are stored as SECs. Overall, there exist different, though largely overlapping, neural substrates for event, sentence, and chronological knowledge during temporal ordering.

Category Specificity

The PFC can be divided into regions that have predominant connectivity with specific cortical and subcortical brain regions. This has led to the hypothesis that SECs are stored in different regions of the PFC on a category-specific basis.

In general, patients with ventral or medial PFC lesions are especially impaired in performing social and reward-related behavior (Dimitrov, Phipps, Zahn, & Grafman, 1999; Milne & Grafman, 2001), whereas patients with lesions to the dorsolateral PFC appear most impaired on mechanistic planning tasks (Burgess, Veitch, de Lacy Costello, & Shallice, 2000; Goel & Grafman, 2000). In a PET study, our research group showed category specificity in terms of localization of emotional versus nonemotional SECs within the PFC (Partiot, Grafman, Sadato, Wachs, & Hallett, 1995). For the nonemotional task, subjects were asked to "imagine silently the sequence of events and feelings concerned with preparation and dressing before [their] mother comes over for dinner." In contrast, for the emotional task subjects were asked to "imagine silently the sequence of events and feelings concerned with preparation and dressing to go to [their] mother's funeral." Different patterns of PFC activation were revealed while the subjects generated the emotional and nonemotional script. The nonemotional script activated the right superior frontal gyrus (BA 8) and the bilateral middle (BA 8 and 9) and medial frontal gyri (BA 6 and 10), whereas the emotional script activated the left anterior cingulate (BA 24 and 32), bilateral medial frontal gyrus (BA 8 and 9), and anterior medial temporal lobe (BA 21).

Using fMRI, we showed further that social and nonsocial SECs are localized independently in the PFC (Wood, Romero, Makale, & Grafman, 2003). We applied a modified go/no-go paradigm in which subjects had to classify either words (semantic: e.g., menu, order) or phrases (scripts: e.g., read the menu, order the food) according to category (social versus nonsocial). Frontal activation for social activities was restricted to the left superior frontal gyrus (BA 8 and 9), whereas frontal activation for nonsocial activities was restricted to the right superior frontal gyrus (BA 8), left medial frontal gyrus (BA 6), and bilateral anterior cingulate (BA 25). Orbitofrontal activation (BA 11) was not evident in that study. Visual inspection of the functional images showed a signal dropout in the orbitofrontal region, and therefore the present data can not address the question of whether this region is implicated in the storage of social SECs. However, lesion data strongly support this viewpoint (Fuster, 1997; Milne & Grafman, 2001). Therefore, the fMRI findings were elaborated on by a lesion study in which patients with lesions of the PFC and matched controls were given a classification task and a modified go/no-go paradigm (Wood, Tierney, Bidwell, & Grafman, 2005). Subjects were asked to classify events from social and nonsocial activities (e.g., read the menu, order the food) and related semantic items (e.g., menu, order) in terms of whether they belonged to a target activity. The results demonstrated that damage to the right orbitofrontal cortex results in impairment in the accessibility of script and semantic representations of social activities.

Finally, in another fMRI study we investigated the psychological structure of event sequence knowledge and then used multidimensional scaling to identify its neural correlates (Wood, Knutson, & Grafman, 2005). Multidimensional scaling is a qualitative analysis technique that has been applied to explain the underlying structure of appropriate representations (e.g., Halberstadt & Niedenthal, 1997; Kruskal & Wish, 1978; Taylor, Brugger, Weniger, & Regard, 1999). We applied multidimensional scaling to similarity ratings of pairs of events (e.g., "reading the menu" paired with "get the detergent" or "order the food") including events from social and nonsocial activities (Rosen, Caplan, Sheesley, Rodriguez, & Grafman, 2003). Three dimensions were identified by regressing the dimension coordinates against ratings on preselected variables of interest (age of acquisition, frequency of performance, socialness, commonality, emotional valence, level of involvement, and rule knowledge). The experience dimension was best explained by the variables "rule knowledge," "commonality," and "frequency"; the engagement dimension by the variables "level of involvement" and "social relatedness"; and the social valence dimension by the variables "emotional valence" and "social relatedness." During the fMRI experiment, subjects were asked to decide whether events of activities were social (e.g., going out for dinner) or not (e.g., doing the laundry). Parametric analyses of event-related fMRI data were applied to establish which brain regions exhibited activation that covaried for the events with the values for each of the three dimensions identified in the multidimensional scaling experiment. The experience dimension specifically activated the medial PFC (BA 10), the engagement dimension activated the left orbitofrontal cortex (BA 47), and the social valence dimension activated the amygdala and right orbitofrontal cortex (BA 11 and 47). The results demonstrated that the psychological structure of event sequence knowledge appears to be broadly organized along the dimensions of experience, engagement, and social valence, which are differentially stored across the human PFC.

In summary, overall these studies suggest that SECs are stored in different regions of the PFC on a category-specific basis. Specifically, nonsocial SECs are represented in the dorsolateral PFC and social

SECs in the ventromedial PFC. The results are consistent with the anatomical reciprocal connectivity of these regions, with the dorsolateral PFC being primarily connected to nonemotional sensory and motor areas and the ventromedial PFC being primarily connected to social and reward-related areas.

Frequency

Since SECs are long-term memory representations, the strength of representation of an event sequence should be partly dependent on how often a person enacts or observes an activity. For example, an activity such as "getting ready for work" includes a sequence of events that is executed more often than the events executed in an activity such as "having your picture taken." Therefore, we argue that low-frequency and high-frequency event sequence knowledge should be subserved by different neural substrates within the PFC.

There is neuropsychological evidence that supports the hypothesis that low-frequency and high-frequency event sequence knowledge are mediated by different neural substrates. Patients with anterior PFC damage show frequency effects in event knowledge tasks, with high-frequency event sequence knowledge being better preserved than low-frequency event sequence knowledge (Sirigu et al., 1995). In a recent fMRI study, our research group aimed to identify regions within the PFC specialized for different daily life activities that varied in frequency of experience (Krueger, Moll, Zahn, Heinecke, & Grafman, 2006). Daily life activities from a normative study, in which individuals recorded their daily activities for 7 consecutive days (Rosen et al., 2003), were used. The activities ranged along a frequency continuum from activities reported only once by a single individual during the week (e.g., going to an audition) to activities reported more than once by most or all of the individuals during the week (e.g., getting ready for work). After seeing the activity header (e.g., get ready for work) and a pair of events (e.g., wake up–get out of bed) subjects had to decide which one of the events occurred first in the chronological sequence of this activity. The results revealed a frequency gradient along the anterior-to-posterior axis of the medial PFC (MPFC), in which the anterior MPFC (BA 10) was engaged in low-frequency activities and the posterior MPFC (BA 10) in high-frequency activities. The frequency effect was independent of task difficulty as measured by response times and accuracy.

We believe that the anterior MPFC codes more complex cognitive information about an event sequence. As an event sequence becomes more frequently used, an economy of representation develops in which the posterior MPFC, activated in parallel with the anterior MPFC, codes sparser cognitive information about the same event sequence. This coding format leads to different profiles of MPFC activation depending upon the frequency of the event sequence the person executes. It would allow simpler representational codes to rapidly instruct lower-level systems (e.g., motor) in order to implement action sequences. In other words, the same activity can be performed quickly (e.g., by using a heuristic based on sparser coding) or slowly (e.g., by using deliberate reflection based on detailed coding) depending upon situational demands on the stored event sequence knowledge.

Interestingly, each of the frequency-dependent MPFC regions falls onto one of the three architectonic subdivisions of human BA 10 proposed by Ongur, Ferry, and Price (2003). These subregions have a similar cellular pattern but vary in the degree of granularity and the development of cortical layer III (and layer IV), with the most prominent and well-developed layer, III, located in the polar area, which is not observed in nonhuman primates (Creutzfeldt, 1995). This architectural complexity increase along the medial axis toward the frontopolar cortex may be an indication of the underlying frequency-dependent knowledge represented in each of the medial subregions.

In conclusion, the results suggest that low- and high-frequency event sequence knowledge are subserved by different neural substrates within the PFC. Representation of SECs is partly dependent on how often a person enacts or observes these event sequences.

In summary, we have started to investigate the differential contributions of PFC subregions to specific formats of representation and categories of event sequence knowledge. There is positive evidence that the PFC is implicated in storage of event sequence knowledge in the form of SECs. However, many predictions of the SEC framework have not been fully explored to date and await more precise testing. For example, the distinction between predictable and unpredictable SECs, as well as the roles of the left and right hemispheres in mediating SECs, needs explicit testing.

PREDICTABILITY

Medial and lateral PFC belong to two distinct architectonic trends within the human PFC (Pandya & Yeterian, 1996), in which the medial trend is phylogenetically and ontogenetically older than the lateral trend (Stuss & Benson, 1986). There is also strong evidence for a functional dissociation between medial and lateral PFC (Burgess, Scott, & Frith, 2003; Gilbert, Spengler, Simon, Frith, & Burgess, 2006a; Gilbert et al., 2006b; Koechlin, Corrado, Pietrini, & Grafman, 2000). In sequence learning, for example, lateral PFC regions are engaged in performing sequences contingent upon unpredictable events, whereas the medial PFC region is engaged in situations when predictable sequences of stimuli are encountered (Koechlin, Corrado, Pietrini, & Grafman, 2000). Given these distinctive properties, we argue that highly predictable SECs are represented in the medial PFC, whereas less predictable SECs are stored in the lateral PFC. Predictable SECs have a clear, definable goal, with all the cognitive and behavioral rules available for the sequence of events to occur. They can guide one's action and expectations during the sequence of behavior. For example, individuals with an SEC about "eating in a restaurant" are quite confident that once they have been seated at a table and have read the menu, someone will appear to take their order. In contrast, unpredictable SECs require the individual to adapt to arbitrary events using analogical reasoning or similarity judgments to determine the sequence of actions online (by integrating previously experienced events from memory with novel events) as well as developing a quickly fashioned goal. For example, if you are in a bank on a cold winter day at lunchtime and see someone enter the bank wearing a ski mask, with a bulge in his or her coat pocket and carrying a paper bag, you could make sense of these events by the time of the day you are in the bank and the current weather, or you might also activate a less frequently experienced SEC such as a bank robbery.

Hemispheric Lateralization

Lesion and fMRI data (Goel & Grafman, 2000; Huettel, Song, & McCarthy, 2005; Paulus et al., 2001) point to structural differences in the capacity of left and right PFC for encoding and manipulating certain types of representations (Beeman & Bowden, 2000; Goldberg, Podell, &

Lovell, 1994). In particular, the left PFC is more adept at constructing determinate, precise, and unambiguous representations of the world, whereas the right PFC is more adept at constructing and maintaining fluid, indeterminate, vague, and ambiguous representations of the world (Goel, 1995; Goel et al., 2006). Given this background, the SEC framework predicts different formats of representation within the left and right hemisphere. Specifically, we argue that the left PFC is specialized to activate the primary meaning of within-event information, sequential dependencies between single adjacent events, and coding for the boundaries between events. On the other hand, the right PFC is better suited to activating and integrating information across events in order to obtain the goal of the SEC. This dual coding should occur in parallel with individual shifting between the two depending on environmental and strategic demands.

Overall, the representational forms of the SECs and their proposed localizations within the PFC are summarized in Figure 22.2. Aspects of SECs are represented independently but are encoded and retrieved as an episode. All subcomponents can contribute to the formation of an SEC, with the different subcomponents being differentially weighted in importance depending on the nature of the SEC and moment-by-moment behavioral demands. For example, the left anterior ventromedial PFC would be expected to represent detailed information about event sequences representing social information integrating the meaning of within-event information, sequential dependencies between single adjacent events, and coding for the boundaries between events.

There has been little in the way of negative studies for this framework. Nevertheless, one study reported that frontal-lobe damage alone is not sufficient to cause impairment in everyday tasks (Humphreys & Forde, 1998). Specifically, a patient with frontal-lobe damage was good at recalling the component actions from stored action scripts and performing these everyday tasks, despite poor performance on "executive" tests. Another study reported no disruption of action representation in patients with frontal lobe lesions (Zanini, Rumiati, & Shallice, 2002). In action production and temporal sequencing tasks, these patients were as accurate as normal controls both in terms of the details reported and in maintaining the temporal sequence. Despite these rare negative studies, neuroimaging results are generally in agreement with patient data, providing strong evidence that the PFC is implicated in the storage of event

STRUCTURED EVENT COMPLEX
PREFONTAL CORTEX

HEMISPHERIC LATERALIZATION

LEFT PFC		RIGHT PFC

Single event integration
- Meaning and feature between
  single adjacent events to code for
  boundaries between events
		Across events integration
		- Meaning and features across
		  events to obtain goal of sequence

PREDICTIBILITY

LATERAL PFC		MEDIAL PFC

Unpredictable partial order SECs
- Frequently modified sequences
  that are used to adapt to special
  circumstances
		Predictable total order SECs
		- Overlearned sequences that have
		  clear definable goals and all
		  behavioral rules available

CATEGORY SPECIFICITY

DORSOLATERAL PFC		VENTROMEDIAL PFC

Non-social SECs
- Event sequences representing
  mechanistic plans and actions
		Social SECs
		- Event sequences representing
		  social rules and scripts

FREQUENCY

ANTERIOR PFC		POSTERIOR PFC

Complex SECs
- Detailed information about event
  sequences
		Non-complex SECs
		- Spare information about event
		  sequences

FIGURE 22.2. SEC framework. The representational forms of the structured event complexes (SECs) and their proposed localizations within the prefrontal cortex (PFC).

sequence knowledge. However, additional experimental studies will lead to a richer corpus of evidence that enables the verification or invalidation of the SEC framework.

Conclusion

In this chapter, we have emphasized the idea that the human PFC stores event sequence knowledge in the form of SECs. Specifically, SECs are representations composed of higher-order goal-oriented sequences of events that are involved in the planning and monitoring of complex behavior. They are the underlying representations for cognitive structures such as plans, actions, rules, scripts, schemas, and mental models. We argued for a "representational" approach of PFC function that seems to be most consistent with the structure, neurophysiology, and connectivity of the PFC as well as with a modern cognitive neuroscience view of how the brain stores aspects of certain kinds of stimuli (e.g., words or objects) in posterior cortex. The provided evidence for the SEC framework from neuropsychological studies of brain-injured patients and functional neuroimaging in healthy individuals confirms the importance and uniqueness of the human PFC for mediating event sequence knowledge. These knowledge structures are the key to understanding the human ability to build and execute daily life activities. We believe there is now a substantial set of research that suggests studying the nature of SECs is a fruitful way to characterize and identify the distribution of event sequence knowledge. The evidence collected so far has brought us one step closer to an understanding of the contribution of the PFC to uniquely human behavior.

Acknowledgment

This research was supported by the Intramural Research Program of the National Institutes of Health/National Institute of Neurological Disorders and Stroke/Cognitive Neuroscience Section.

References

Alexander, G. E., Crutcher, M. D., & DeLong, M. R. (1990). Basal ganglia-thalamocortical circuits: Parallel substrates for motor, oculomotor, "prefrontal" and "limbic" functions. *Progress in Brain Research, 85*, 119–146.

Barbas, H. (2000). Complementary roles of prefrontal cortical regions in cognition, memory, and emotion in primates. *Advances in Neurology, 84*, 87–110.

Beeman, M. J., & Bowden, E. M. (2000). The right hemisphere maintains solution-related activation for yet-to-be-solved problems. *Memory & Cognition, 28*, 1231–1241.

Brodmann, K. (1912). Neue Ergebnisse ueber die vergleichende histologische Lokalisation der Grosshirnrinde mit besonderer Beruecksichtigung des Stirnhirns. *Anatomischer Anzeiger, 41* (suppl), 157–216.

Burgess, P. W., Scott, S. K., & Frith, C. D. (2003). The role of the rostral frontal cortex (area 10) in prospective memory: A lateral versus medial dissociation. *Neuropsychologia, 41*, 906–918.

Burgess, P. W., Veitch, E., de Lacy Costello, A., & Shallice, T. (2000). The cognitive and neuroanatomical correlates of multitasking. *Neuropsychologia, 38,* 848–863.

Chiavaras, M. M., LeGoualher, G., Evans, A., & Petrides, M. (2001). Three-dimensional probabilistic atlas of the human orbitofrontal sulci in standardized stereotaxic space. *Neuroimage, 13,* 479–496.

Chugani, H. T., Phelps, M. E., & Mazziotta, J. C. (1990). Positron emission tomography study of human brain functional development. *Annals of Neurology, 22,* 487–497.

Conel, J. L. (1939). *The postnatal development of the human cerebral cortex,* Vols. 1–6. Cambridge, MA: Harvard University Press.

Creutzfeldt, O. (1995). *Cortex cerebri: Performance, structural and functional organization of the cortex.* Oxford: Oxford University Press.

Crozier, S., Sirigu, A., Lehericy, S., van de Moortele, P. F., Pillon, B., Grafman, J., et al. (1999). Distinct prefrontal activations in processing sequence at the sentence and script level: An fMRI study. *Neuropsychologia, 37,* 1469–1476.

Diamond, A. (1991). Guidelines for the study of brain-behavior relationships during development. In H. S. Levin, A. Eisenberg, & A. L. Benton (Eds.), *Frontal lobe function and dysfunction.* New York: Oxford University Press.

Dimitrov, M., Phipps, M., Zahn, T., & Grafman, J. (1999). A thoroughly modern Gage. *Neurocase, 5,* 345–354.

Duncan, J. (2001). An adaptive coding model of neural function in prefrontal cortex. *Nature Reviews Neuroscience, 2,* 820–829.

Durston, S., Hulshoff Pol, H. E., Casey, B. J., Giedd, J. N., Buitelaar, J. K., & van Engeland, H. (2001). Anatomical MRI of the developing human brain: What have we learned? *Journal of the American Academy of Child and Adolescent Psychiatry, 40,* 1012–1020.

Elston, G. N. (2000). Pyramidal cells of the frontal lobe: All the more spinous to think with. *Journal of Neuroscience, 20,* RC95.

Elston, G. N., & Rosa, M. G. (2000). Pyramidal cells, patches, and cortical columns: A comparative study of infragranular neurons in TEO, TE, and the superior temporal polysensory area of the macaque monkey. *Journal of Neuroscience, 20,* RC117.

Engel, A. K., & Singer, W. (2001). Temporal binding and the neural correlates of sensory awareness. *Trends in Cognitive Science, 5,* 16–25.

Eslinger, P. J., & Damasio, A. R. (1985). Severe disturbance of higher cognition after bilateral frontal lobe ablation: Patient EVR. *Neurology, 35,* 1731–1741.

Flechsig, P. (1920). *Anatomie des menschlichen Gehirns und Rueckenmarks auf myelogenetischer Grundlage.* Leipzig: Thieme.

Fuster, J. M. (1991). The prefrontal cortex and its relation to behavior. *Progress in Brain Research, 87,* 201–211.

Fuster, J. M. (1997). *The prefrontal cortex: Anatomy, physiology, and neuropsychology of the frontal lobe.* New York: Raven Press.

Giedd, J. N., Blumenthal, J., Jeffries, N. O., Castellanos, F. X., Liu, H., Zijdenbos, A., et al. (1999). Brain development during childhood and adolescence: A longitudinal MRI study. *Nature Neuroscience, 2,* 861–863.

Gilbert, S. J., Spengler, S., Simons, J. S., Frith, C. D., & Burgess, P. W. (2006). Differential functions of lateral and medial rostral prefrontal cortex (area 10) revealed by brain-behavior associations. *Cerebral Cortex, 16,* 1783–1789.

Gilbert, S. J., Spengler, S., Simons, J. S., Steele, J. D., Lawrie, S. M., Frith, C. D., et al. (2006). Functional specialization within rostral prefrontal cortex (Area 10): A meta-analysis. *Journal of Cognitive Neuroscience, 18,* 932–948.

Goel, V. (1995). *Sketches of thought.* Cambridge, MA: MIT Press.

Goel, V., & Grafman, J. (2000). The role of the right prefrontal cortex in ill-structured problem solving. *Cognitive Neuropsychology, 17,* 415–436.

Goel, V., Tierney, M., Sheesley, L., Bartolo, A., Vartanian, O., & Grafman, J. (2006). Hemispheric specialization in human prefrontal cortex for resolving certain and uncertain inferences. *Cerebral Cortex* [online journal]. Available at http://cercor.oxfordjournals.org/cgi/content/abstract/bhl132v1.

Goldberg, E., Podell, K., & Lovell, M. (1994). Lateralization of frontal lobe functions and cognitive novelty. *Journal of Neuropsychiatry & Clinical Neuroscience, 6,* 371–378.

Goldman-Rakic, P.S. (1987) Circuitry of primate prefrontal cortex and regulation of behavior by representational memory. In F. Plum & V. Mountcastle (Eds.), *Handbook of physiology* (pp. 373–517). Washington, DC: The American Physiological Society.

Goldman-Rakic, P. S. (1992). Working memory and the mind. *Scientific American, 267,* 110–117.

Grafman, J. (1995). Similarities and distinctions among current models of prefrontal cortical functions. In J. Grafman, K. J. Holyoak, & F. Boller (Eds.), *Structure and functions of the human prefrontal cortex* (pp. 337–368). New York: New York Academy of Sciences.

Grafman, J. (2002). The human prefrontal cortex has evolved to represent components of structured event complexes. In J. Grafman (Ed.), *Handbook of neuropsychology,* Vol. 7 (pp. 157–174). Amsterdam: Elsevier.

Grafman, J., & Krueger, F. (2006). Volition and the human prefrontal cortex. In N. Sebanz & W. Prinz (Eds.), *Disorders of volition* (pp. 347–372). Cambridge, MA: MIT Press.

Groenewegen, H. J., & Uylings, H. B. (2000). The prefrontal cortex and the integration of sensory, limbic and autonomic information. *Progress in Brain Research, 126,* 3–28.

Halberstadt, J. B., & Niedenthal, P. M. (1997). Emotional state and the use of stimulus dimensions in judgment. *Journal of Personality & Social Psychology, 72,* 1017–1033.

Huettel, S. A., Song, A. W., & McCarthy, G. (2005). Decisions under uncertainty: Probabilistic context influences activation of prefrontal and parietal cortices. *Journal of Neuroscience, 25,* 3304–3311.

Huey, E. D., Krueger, F., & Grafman, J. (2006). Representations in the human prefrontal cortex. *Current Directions in Psychological Science, 15,* 167–171.

Humphreys, G. W., & Forde, E. M. (1998). Disordered action schema and action disorganization syndrome. *Cognitive Neuropsychology, 15,* 771–811.

Huttenlocher, P. R. (1990). Morphometric study of human cerebral cortex development. *Neuropsychologia, 28,* 517–527.

Huttenlocher, P. R., & Dabholkar, A. S. (1997). Regional differences in synaptogenesis in human cerebral cortex. *Journal of Comparative Neurology, 387,* 167–178.

Janowsky, J. S., Shimamura, A. P., & Squire, L. R. (1989). Source memory impairment in patients with frontal lobe lesions. *Neuropsychologia, 27,* 1043–1056.

Knutson, K. M., Wood, J. N., & Grafman, J. (2004). Brain activation in processing temporal sequence: An fMRI study. *Neuroimage, 23,* 1299–2307.

Koechlin, E., Corrado, G., Pietrini, P., & Grafman, J. (2000). Dissociating the role of the medial and lateral anterior prefrontal cortex in human planning. *Proceedings of the National Academy of Science USA, 97,* 7651–7656.

Krueger, F., Moll, J., Zahn, R., Heinecke, A., & Grafman, J. (2006). Event frequency modulates the processing of daily life activities in human medial prefrontal cortex. *Cerebral Cortex* [online journal]. Available at http://cercor.oxfordjournals.org/cgi/content/abstract/bhl143v1.

Kruskal, J. B., & Wish, M. (1978). *Multidimensional scaling.* Beverly Hills and London: Sage Publications.

Levy, R., & Goldman-Rakic, P. S. (2000). Segregation of working memory functions within the dorsolateral prefrontal cortex. *Experimental Brain Research, 133,* 23–32.

Masterman, D. L., & Cummings, J. L. (1997). Frontal-subcortical circuits: The anatomic basis of executive, social and motivated behaviors. *Journal of Psychopharmacology, 11,* 107–114.

Miller, E. K., & Cohen, J. D. (2001). An integrative theory of prefrontal cortex function. *Annual Review of Neuroscience, 24,* 167–202.

Milne, E., & Grafman, J. (2001). Ventromedial prefrontal cortex lesions in humans eliminate implicit gender stereotyping. *Journal of Neuroscience, 21,* RC150 (1–6).

Milner, B., Petrides, M., & Smith, M. L. (1985). Frontal lobes and the temporal organization of memory. *Human Neurobiology, 4,* 137–142.

Moll, J., Krueger, F., Zahn, R., Pardini, M., de Oliveira-Souza, R., & Grafman, J. (2006). Human fronto-mesolimbic networks guide decisions about charitable donation. *Proceedings of the National Academy of Science USA, 103,* 15623–15628.

Nichelli, P., Clark, K., Hollnagel, C., & Grafman, J. (1995). Duration processing after frontal lobe lesions. *Annals of the New York Academy of Science, 769,* 183–190.

O'Reilly, R. C., & Rudy, J. W. (2000). Computational principles of learning in the neocortex and hippocampus. *Hippocampus, 10,* 389–397.

Ongur, D., Ferry, A. T., & Price, J. L. (2003). Architectonic subdivision of the human orbital and medial prefrontal cortex. *Journal of Comparative Neurology, 460,* 425–449.

Pandya, D. N., & Yeterian, E. H. (1996). In A. R. Damasio, H. Damasio, & Y. Christen (Eds.), *Neurobiology of decision making* (pp. 13–46). Berlin: Springer.

Partiot, A., Grafman, J., Sadato, N., Wachs, J., & Hallett, M. (1995). Brain activation during the generation of non-emotional and emotional plans. *Neuroreport, 6,* 1397–1400.

Paulus, M. P., Hozack, N., Zauscher, B., McDowell, J. E., Frank, L., Brown, G.G., et al. (2001). Prefrontal, parietal, and temporal cortex networks underlie decision-making in the presence of uncertainty. *Neuroimage, 13,* 91–100.

Paus, T., Zijdenbos, A., Worsley, K., Collins, D. L., Blumenthal, J., Giedd, J. N., et al. (1999). Structural maturation of neural pathways in children and adolescents: In vivo study. *Science, 283,* 1908–1911.

Price, J. L. (1999). Prefrontal cortical networks related to visceral function and mood. *Annals of the New York Academy of Science, 877,* 383–396.

Rilling, J. K., & Insel, T. R. (1999). The primate neocortex in comparative perspective using magnetic resonance imaging. *Journal of Human Evolution, 37,* 191–223.

Rosen, V. M., Caplan, L., Sheesley, L., Rodriguez, R., & Grafman, J. (2003). An examination of daily activities and their scripts across the adult lifespan. *Behavioral Research Methods Instruments & Computers, 35,* 32–48.

Rueckert, L., & Grafman, J. (1996). Sustained attention deficits in patients with right frontal lesions. *Neuropsychologia, 34,* 953–963.

Rueckert, L., & Grafman, J. (1998). Sustained attention deficits in patients with lesions of posterior cortex. *Neuropsychologia, 36,* 653–660.

Rumelhart, D. E. (1980). Schemata: The building blocks of cognition. In R. J. Spiro, B. C. Bruce, & W. F. Brewer (Eds.), *Theoretical issues in reading comprehension: Perspectives from cognitive psychology, linguistics, artificial intelligence, and education* (pp. 33–58). Hillsdale, NJ: Erlbaum.

Schank, R., & Abelson, P. (1977). *Scripts, plans, goals and understanding.* Hillsdale, NJ: Erlbaum.

Semendeferi, K., Armstrong, E., Schleicher, A., Zilles, K., & van Hoesen, G. W. (2001). Prefrontal cortex in humans and apes: A comparative study of area 10. *American Journal of Physical Anthropology, 114,* 224–241.

Semendeferi, K., Lu, A., Schenker, N., & Damasio, H. (2002). Humans and great apes share a large frontal cortex. *Nature Neuroscience, 5,* 272–276.

Shallice, T. (1982). Specific impairments of planning. *Philosophical Transactions of the Royal Society of London B: Biological Science, 298,* 199–209.

Shallice, T., & Burgess, P. (1998). The domain of supervisory processes and the temporal organization of behaviour. In A. C. Roberts, T. W. Robbins, & L. Weiskrantz (Eds.), *The prefrontal cortex: Executive and cognitive functions.* Oxford: Oxford University Press.

Shallice, T., & Burgess, P. W. (1991). Deficits in strategy application following frontal lobe damage in man. *Brain, 114*(Pt. 2), 727–741.

Sirigu, A., Cohen, L., Zalla, T., Pradat-Diehl, P., Van Eeckhout, P., Grafman, J., et al. (1998). Distinct frontal regions for processing sentence syntax and story grammar. *Cortex, 34,* 771–778.

Sirigu, A., Zalla, T., Pillon, B., Grafman, J., Agid, Y., & Dubois, B. (1995). Selective impairments in managerial knowledge following pre-frontal cortex damage. *Cortex, 31,* 301–316.

Sirigu, A., Zalla, T., Pillon, B., Grafman, J., Agid, Y., & Dubois, B. (1996). Encoding of sequence and boundaries of scripts following prefrontal lesions. *Cortex, 32,* 297–310.

Sowell, E. R., Thompson, P. M., Holmes, C. J., Jernigan, T. L., & Toga, A. W. (1999). In vivo evidence for post-adolescent brain maturation in frontal and striatal regions. *Nature Neuroscience, 2*, 859–861.

Stuss, D. T., & Benson, D. F. (1984). Neuropsychological studies of the frontal lobes. *Psychological Bulletin, 95*, 3–28.

Stuss, D. T., & Benson, D. F. (1986). *The frontal lobes.* New York: Raven Press.

Taylor, K. I., Brugger, P., Weniger, D., & Regard, M. (1999). Qualitative hemispheric differences in semantic category matching. *Brain Language, 70*, 119–131.

Weingartner, H., Grafman, J., Boutelle, W., Kaye, W., & Martin, P. R. (1983). Forms of memory failure. *Science, 221*, 380–382.

Wood, J. N., & Grafman, J. (2003). Human prefrontal cortex: Processing and representational perspectives. *Nature Reviews Neuroscience, 4*, 139–147.

Wood, J. N., Knutson, K. M, & Grafman, J. (2005). Psychological structure and neural correlates of event knowledge. *Cerebral Cortex, 15*, 1155–1161.

Wood, J. N., Romero, S. G., Makale, M., & Grafman, J. (2003). Category-specific representations of social and nonsocial knowledge in the human prefrontal cortex. *Journal of Cognitive Neuroscience, 15*, 236–248.

Wood, J. N., Tierney, M., Bidwell, L. A., & Grafman, J. (2005). Neural correlates of script event knowledge: A neuropsychological study following prefrontal injury. *Cortex, 41*, 796–804.

Zacks, J. M., Braver, T. S., Sheridan, M. A., Donaldson, D. I., Snyder, A. Z., Ollinger, J. M., et al. (2001). Human brain activity time-locked to perceptual event boundaries. *Nature Neuroscience, 4*, 651–655.

Zacks, J. M., & Tversky, B. (2001). Event structure in perception and conception. *Psychological Bulletin, 127*, 3–21.

Zacks, J. M., Tversky, B., & Iyer, G. (2001). Perceiving, remembering, and communicating structure in events. *Journal of Experimental Psychology General, 130*, 29–58.

Zanini, S., Rumiati, R. I., & Shallice, T. (2002). Action sequencing deficit following frontal lobe lesion. *Neurocase, 8*, 88–99.

23

Neurocognitive Mechanisms of Human Comprehension

TATIANA SITNIKOVA, PHILLIP J. HOLCOMB,
& GINA R. KUPERBERG

As humans make sense of the world, such as when processing language or watching events unfold around them, they must combine separate aspects of the incoming stimuli into a coherent gestalt of overall meaning. Comprehending an individual event depends on determining the nature of its central action and the roles (often termed "thematic roles") played by the people and objects in this action (Klix, 2001; Nowak, Plotkin, & Jansen, 2000). For example, at a birthday party, an observer of an event "woman cutting a cake with a knife" would understand that the action is "cutting," that the woman plays the role of an Agent (the person who is doing the cutting), that the cake is a Patient (the object that is being cut), and that the knife is an Instrument (the object that is used for cutting). Moreover, each event must be understood in the context of the preceding events (Klix, 2001; Knutson, Wood, & Grafman, 2004; Wood & Grafman, 2003). For example, if, before the cake is cut, one of the children at the party blows out the candles on the cake, the observer would understand the relationships between these two events: at a birthday party, blowing out the candles on a cake is a prerequisite for cutting it. This chapter reviews research suggesting that there are two separate neurocognitive mechanisms mediating such comprehension processes. The first mechanism relies on relationships of various strengths stored in comprehenders' semantic memory of the world (we term this knowledge "graded semantic representations"). The second mechanism relies on discrete, rule-like knowledge of what is necessary for the real-world actions (we term this knowledge "action-based requirements").

The notion of structured semantic memory representations has a long history in the theory of comprehension. Individual concepts in semantic memory are thought to have connections of various strengths, depending on factors such as their feature similarity or how often they have been experienced in the same context (Fischler & Bloom, 1985; Hutchison, 2003; Meyer & Schvaneveldt, 1971; Neely, 1991; Rosch, 1975; Rosch & Mervis, 1975; Stanovich & West, 1983). These graded semantic representations are continuously accessed and used as comprehension takes place in real time (online), being especially useful in familiar circumstances. Perceiving only a few details allows comprehenders to access representations of the related concepts and, as a result, to rapidly grasp the likely overall meaning of everyday situations and to prepare for what would be expected to come next. By mapping the perceptual input on these graded semantic representations, comprehenders can build expectations at various levels ranging from specific entities that are likely to play a given role in a real-world action (Ferretti, McRae, & Hatherell, 2001; McRae, Hare, Elman, & Ferretti, 2005) to the probable spatiotemporal relationships between individual events (Abelson, 1981; Bower, Black, & Turner, 1979; Schank & Abelson, 1977; van der Meer, Beyer, Heinze, & Badel, 2002). For example, the representational network of a conventional birthday party scenario would include strong associations between the Agent role of the cutting action and such features as <adult> and <able to perform volitional actions>, between the Patient role and such features as <has frosting> and <unsturdy>, and between the Instrument role and such features as <has handle> and <has a sturdy, sharp edge>. At a more global level, this information would be linked to the events that usually precede and follow cutting the cake at a birthday party. During comprehension, as one views, for instance, a boy blowing out candles on a birthday cake, accessing the related representations in semantic memory would allow this observer to anticipate that the boy's parent would soon be using a knife to cut the cake.

Such graded semantic representations, however, are relatively rigid in that what is stored is descriptive in nature, without regard as to whether any given component is *necessary* for a particular action. As a result, accessing these representations has limited utility for comprehending unfamiliar and unusual situations, and can not readily account for humans' remarkable ability to make sense of such situations quickly and intuitively. In the above example of cutting the birthday cake, only the Agent's property <able to perform volitional actions>, the Patient's property <unsturdy>, and the Instrument's property <has a sturdy sharp edge> are necessary for the cutting action. We suggest that it is these discrete, rule-like representations of what is essential for real-world actions that are crucial for flexible comprehension, as they can be applied to any novel combination between actions and entities (Sitnikova, 2003). A given action and its thematic roles (constituting an event) would be understood as long as the perceptual input meets the corresponding minimal requirements.

For instance, imagine that, at a birthday party, a woman starts wriggling a stretch of dental floss across the cake. The observers would probably have little trouble understanding that the woman is cutting the cake, albeit in an unusual way. Now imagine that the woman is wriggling a tissue paper across the cake. This time the observers will probably have no idea what is going on. Nonetheless, the dental floss and tissue paper are both unusual objects at a birthday party and both have semantic properties very different from those of a knife (the object that one expects to be used to cut a cake; e.g., both do not have properties such as <has handle>). We argue that to make such distinctions as between the floss and the tissue paper in the above scenarios, observers would access their knowledge of requirements of the cutting action. The dental floss but not the tissue paper has an edge that is sturdy and sharp enough to cut a relatively unsturdy cake.

It is also possible that comprehenders use action-based requirements to understand the relationships between events. The sequential order of events in most goal-directed activities is not random but is defined by which actions are possible given the current state of environment. For example, in a birthday party scenario, many of the events are possible only if the state of the cake and/or candles matches the requirements for the performed action (e.g., serving a piece of a cake is possible only after it has been cut). These enabling relationships between the events might be established based on the requirements for each individual action. A similar hypothesis is posed in Chapter 20 in this volume, with the suggestion that observers distinguish between causal, enabling, and preventing relationships between events by calculating how each event influences the current state of the environment in relation to the requirements of the central actions in other events.

In the paragraphs that follow, we first discuss evidence for distinctions between two semantic comprehension systems in the language domain: a system that maps the perceived information on graded semantic representations and a system that utilizes particular semantic requirements of verbs. We then review similar research using static and motion pictures. We suggest that the two mechanisms of language comprehension might be analogous to the systems that use graded semantic representations and action-based requirements to make sense of the visual world.

The experiments that are reviewed in this chapter examine questions of both how comprehenders understand relationships between the elements within individual events and how they understand the relationships between events. Furthermore, throughout the review, we highlight experiments that have used event-related potentials (ERPs). ERPs are electrophysiological brain responses that are recorded via electrode sensors placed on a participant's scalp and are time-locked to the onset of experimental trials of interest (e.g., presentation of target words, object pictures, or visual scenes). They measure brain activity online with a temporal resolution of milliseconds (Cohen, Palti, Cuffin, & Schmid, 1980; Williamson, Kaufman, & Brenner, 1978). This excellent time resolution is valuable in characterizing rapid comprehension processes.

In a typical ERP study, electrophysiological data are collected using 40 to 60 trials per experimental condition and are selectively averaged to obtain a single waveform for each condition. The changes in the neurophysiological activity that give rise to ERPs appear as positive-going or negative-going deflections in the recorded waveform, often referred to as ERP components. These components vary in their distribution across the scalp. Usually, differences in the polarity and/or topography of ERP components between experimental conditions are interpreted as reflecting distinctions in their underlying neuronal sources (Holcomb, Kounios, Anderson, & West, 1999; Kutas, 1993). In the studies described here, such polarity and topography information is used to distinguish between the neural mechanisms mediating different comprehension processes. In contrast, changes merely in the amplitude or timing of a component across experimental conditions are usually interpreted as indexing modulation of the same neurocognitive process(es) (Holcomb et al., 1999; Kutas, 1993). In the studies described below, the onset, peak latency, and duration of such amplitude changes are used to characterize the time course of the corresponding neurocognitive processes.

Language Comprehension

Graded Semantic Representations in Language Comprehension

BEHAVIORAL STUDIES

In the language domain, it has long been known that in familiar situations, comprehenders tend to fill in information missing from an utterance by using their knowledge of what would normally be expected (Abelson, 1981; Anderson, 1980; Bower et al., 1979; Rumelhart & Ortony, 1977; Schank & Abelson, 1977). For example, imagine a boy talking to his mother: "I've got an invitation to Johnny's birthday party, and I know he really wants a Starfighter Transformer toy. Mom, please!" Clearly, the mother of this boy would understand exactly what he is asking for. This has been argued to be possible because comprehenders store all the likely details of familiar situations in semantic memory within such knowledge structures as schemata (Anderson, 1980; Biederman, Rabinowitz, Glass, & Stacy, 1974; Rumelhart & Ortony, 1977; Zacks & Tversky, 2001; Zacks, Tversky, & Iyer, 2001) or scripts (Abelson, 1981; Bower et al., 1979; Schank & Abelson, 1977). As a result, it is unnecessary to mention all the particulars when people talk about familiar situations; instead it can be safely assumed that listeners will understand the message as long as certain critical components of the situation are mentioned. Experimental evidence for such comprehension by mapping the perceived information on the semantic memory structures comes from, for instance, the reconstructive memory of text (Bower et al., 1979). After reading text passages describing common activities such as eating in a restaurant or visiting a dentist, participants were poor at distinguishing between the statements that were presented in the text and lures that conveyed plausible elements of the described situations but that were not actually presented in the text. Comprehenders also appeared to tap into their knowledge of the typical temporal order of events in common activities. After reading text passages with sentences presented in a scrambled order, events tended to be recalled in a typical order.

More recent studies have employed a reaction time measure to demonstrate that semantic memory structures are accessed online as comprehenders build up a mental representation of meaning. For example, McRae and colleagues (Ferretti et al., 2001; McRae et al., 2005) demonstrated that online language processing is influenced by common thematic relationships between a given verb and its surrounding noun phrases (NPs). In sentences such as "She was arrested by a cop/crook," expected words such as "cop" were processed faster than unexpected words such as "crook." Note that both types of target words were semantically associated with the target action (e.g., "arresting"); therefore, the processing differences between these conditions suggest that event representations in semantic memory have thematic structure rather than simply tie together related concepts. Three other studies demonstrated that common spatial and temporal relationships between concepts and events are also used in online language comprehension. Richardson, Spivey, Barsalou, and McRae (2003) obtained evidence that verbs access typical spatial properties of their corresponding actions. In their paradigm, participants listened to verbs that commonly refer to vertical actions (e.g., "smash") or horizontal actions (e.g., "point"). Participants were found to be slower in detecting visually presented stimuli of the corresponding relative to different spatial orientation (e.g., processing "smash" interfered with discriminating targets on the top and bottom of the screen, but not on the left or right). Van der Meer and colleagues showed that verbal stimuli might access knowledge about the common temporal relationships both within and between events. In their studies, pairs of verbal stimuli (including combinations between individual words, word phrases, and sentences) were processed faster when they were presented in the common chronological order than when they were presented in the reversed order (e.g., "shrinking-small" was processed faster than "small-shrinking"—Nuthmann & van der Meer, 2005; "The boy bites off a juicy apple—chew" was processed faster than "The stomach digests the food—swallow"—van der Meer et al., 2002).

An extensive group of studies provides support for the hypothesis that concepts in semantic memory have graded connections, and that during online language comprehension the perceived information is mapped on these graded representations. Most of these studies used a semantic priming protocol to show that processing time of target words (e.g., "doctor") decreases from the items preceded by an unrelated prime word (e.g., "cat") to the items preceded by a moderately related prime (e.g., "accident"), to the items preceded by a strongly related prime (e.g., "nurse"; this is true for the relationships based on feature similarity and association strength—for a review see Hutchison, 2003). An analogous contextual congruency paradigm was also employed for target words embedded in whole sentences. For example, participants might be presented with a sentence stem, "She cleaned the dirt from her," followed by a target word either predictable (e.g., "shoes") or acceptable but less probable (e.g., "umbrella"). Comprehenders consistently took longer to respond to unexpected words than to words that were predictable in their preceding context (Fischler & Bloom, 1985; Stanovich & West, 1983). Additional evidence comes from studies examining eye fixations: the duration of readers' eye fixations tends to be shorter on critical words that are expected relative to those that are unexpected in the preceding context (Morris, 1994; Zola, 1984). Thus, it appears that words can be processed more easily if their corresponding representation is more closely related to the specific field in semantic memory activated by the context.

ERP STUDIES

More recently, ERP studies have provided further evidence that graded semantic representations are rapidly accessed during language comprehension (within 400 ms after target word onset). These studies recorded ERPs time-locked to the onset of target words in contextual congruency paradigms and identified an electrophysiological marker of the behavioral expectancy effects described above. At approximately 300 ms after word onset, content words evoke a negative-going ERP component that peaks at around 400 ms and accordingly is termed the N400. The magnitude of this N400 is inversely correlated with both the strength of the relationship between the prime and target words in semantic priming paradigms (e.g., Grose-Fifer & Deacon, 2004; Holcomb, 1988, 1993; Kutas & Hillyard, 1989) and the predictability of the target word in the preceding context in sentence paradigms (Kutas & Hillyard, 1980, 1984). For example, in sentences, the final word on trials such as "It was his first day at *work*" elicits a smaller N400 than the final word on trials such as "He took a drink from the *waterfall*," whereas the final word on trials such as "He took a drink from the *transmitter*" evokes the largest N400. This N400 electrophysiological response has also been reported to critical words that are incongruous with the preceding global context provided by groups of sentences in discourse (van Berkum, Hagoort, & Brown, 1999; van Berkum, Zwitserlood, Hagoort, & Brown, 2003; Van Berkum, Brown, Zwitserlood, Kooijman, & Hagoort, 2005). Moreover, the modulation of the N400 by congruency is seen both when language is presented visually (reading, e.g., Kutas & Hillyard, 1980) and when language is presented auditorily (speech comprehension, e.g., Holcomb & Neville, 1991a, 1991b). Taken together, these results suggest that the difficulty of mapping the target word on graded semantic representations is reflected by the N400: the closer the relationship between the representation of the eliciting item and the specific semantic memory field activated by the preceding context, the less demanding this mapping process, and the smaller the amplitude of the N400.

Verb-Based Semantic Requirements in Language Comprehension

Even though information stored in graded semantic memory networks can exert powerful effects on language comprehension, these descriptive representations may not be sufficient to achieve accurate comprehension. For example, how would readers arrive at a veridical interpretation of the statement "The humanoid space alien mailed a pencil"? This sentence describes an event that most humans would agree they had never experienced before, and therefore they would not have a prestored representation of this particular event.

Classic linguistic theory posits that, to communicate the relationships between concepts in verbal descriptions, speakers rely on their knowledge of syntactic and semantic requirements governing the correct use of verbs (Fillmore, 1968). Together, these requirements determine which NPs (the verb's arguments) are assigned which thematic roles in a statement that includes a given verb. For example, in a statement involving the verb "mail," two thematic roles have to be considered: the role of an Agent—the entity who is doing the mailing; the role of a Patient—the entity that is being mailed. Syntactically, these roles are expressed by a subject NP and an object NP, respectively. Semantically, the Agent of the verb "mail" must be able to mail (e.g., be able to perform a volitional action), and its Patient must be "mailable" (e.g., be transportable). Knowing these syntactic and semantic requirements would allow comprehenders to determine the relationships between the verb and its arguments in a sentence. Thus, readers of the statement "The humanoid space alien mailed a pencil" would evaluate each NP against the above requirements so that, for example, the Agent role of the verb "mail" would be assigned to the argument that is a subject NP and is able to mail—to the NP "the humanoid space alien."

Experimental research provided evidence that such assignment of thematic roles is a rapid online process that heavily depends on syntactic information but may also take into account verb-based semantic requirements (Altmann & Steedman, 1988; Caplan, Hildebrandt, & Waters, 1994; Clifton, 1993; Clifton, Traxler, & Mohamed, 2003; Ferreira & Clifton, 1986; Frazier & Clifton, 1997; Glenberg & Robertson, 2000; Kaschak & Glenberg, 2000; Kuperberg, Sitnikova, Caplan, & Holcomb, 2003; Marslen-Wilson, Brown, & Tyler, 1988; McElree & Griffith, 1995, 1998; Osterhout, Holcomb, & Swinney, 1994). Most importantly, this research suggests that when comprehenders use verb-based semantic requirements to help them in determining relationships between concepts in a sentence, the engaged neurocognitive processes might be different from those that mediate mapping of the input on graded semantic representations.

BEHAVIORAL STUDIES

Behavioral research has established that violations of semantic requirements of verbs are rapidly detected during online language comprehension (Caplan et al., 1994; McElree & Griffith, 1995, 1998). For example, McElree and Griffith (1995) showed that it took readers only a few hundred milliseconds to report such violations in sentences like "Some people *alarm books*" (i.e., books do not have semantic properties necessary for them to become alarmed). In another study, Marslen-Wilson et al. (1988) found that, when monitoring for target words in sentences containing different types of violations, participants were slower to detect words that violated semantic requirements of verbs than to detect nonviolated words. For example, subjects took longer to respond to a target word "guitar" in sentences such as "The crowd was waiting eagerly. John drank the guitar," than in the control sentences such as "The crowd was waiting eagerly. John grabbed the guitar." Interestingly, the time to detect the target words in sentences with verb-based semantic violations was also longer than to detect unexpected target words that did not violate verb-based requirements (e.g., in "The crowd was waiting eagerly. John buried the guitar."), which suggested that processing verb-based semantic requirements might have a different time course from the process of mapping the target word on graded semantic representations.

The processing distinctions between semantic requirements of verbs and graded semantic representations were more carefully examined in a series of studies by Glenberg and colleagues (Glenberg & Robertson, 2000; Kaschak & Glenberg, 2000). In these experiments, participants' judgments suggested that they relied on their knowledge of verb-based semantic requirements when asked to comprehend verbally described unusual events.[1] However, the patterns of their responses could not be accounted for by using event representations stored in graded semantic representations. To give an illustration of this line of research, in one of the experiments by Kaschak and Glenberg (2000) participants were asked to read short text passages (e.g., a story about a girl who wanted to prove that she could hit well in baseball; she borrowed a crutch from a person recovering from a twisted ankle and used the crutch to hit an apple). After reading each scenario, participants verified the truth value of a probe statement that was (a) highly relevant for the central action described in the passage (e.g., "the crutch is sturdy"—the crutch sturdiness was necessary for it to be used as a baseball bat), (b) relatively unimportant for the central action (e.g., "the crutch is long"), or (c) irrelevant for the central action but described a scenario that is frequently associated with the critical object (e.g., "the crutch can help with injuries"). Even though the first two probe types were similar in their degree of semantic relatedness to the contextual passages, participants were faster to verify the probes that were highly relevant for the described

---

1. In some of these experiments the actions were not described by a single verb; rather, their meaning became clear from the overall context—in fact, similar effects were found both with conventional verbs (e.g., "to hit") and novel verbs (e.g., "to crutch"). As a result, this data provides some evidence that not only semantic constraints stored in verbs' memory representations in the language system but also requirements of real-world actions are used in language comprehension.

central action (sturdy) than the less relevant probes (long). As a measure of semantic relationships between stimuli, most of the experiments by Glenberg and colleagues used Latent Semantic Analysis (Landauer & Dumais, 1997), a computer program that calculates an index of co-occurrence of sets of words in similar contexts. This analysis has been demonstrated to simulate semantic relatedness judgments given by human participants. Interestingly, the highly relevant probes (sturdy) were responded to even faster than the frequent associate probes (injuries), demonstrating that comprehenders did not simply access the most common role played by the target object in the real life but rather used the knowledge of verb-based semantic requirements to integrate these words with the passage context.

ERP STUDIES

ERP investigations have provided additional insights into how the language comprehension system analyzes verb-based semantic requirements. In our laboratory, we have used the contextual congruency paradigm to compare this mechanism to the processing based on graded semantic representations (Kuperberg, Sitnikova, et al., 2003). We asked participants to read three types of sentences such as the ones below while we recorded ERPs to the target verbs (italicized).

1. Although the young model is completely unaware her fans always *admired* . . .
2. Although the young model is completely unaware her fans always *grieved* . . .
3. Although the young model is completely unaware her hair always *admired* . . .

In sentences like (3), the target verbs are semantically associated with the preceding context[2] (e.g., "admiring" is related to the concept of being a young model who would be expected to have beautiful hair), but their preceding NP argument violates the semantic requirements of these

---

2. A separate rating study has shown that these target verbs were semantically associated with both the preceding subject NPs and the other content words in the preceding context (see Kuperberg, Caplan, et al., 2006; Kuperberg, Sitnikova, et al., 2003).

verbs. In these verb-argument violations, the syntax assigns a thematic role of an Agent around the target verb ("admired") to the preceding subject NP ("her hair"). However, this subject NP does not have semantic properties necessary to perform the described action (e.g., hair can not admire). In contrast, in sentences like (2), the target verb ("grieved") can assign the syntactically defined Agent role to the preceding subject NP ("her fans") because verb-based semantic requirements are not violated (e.g., fans can grieve). In this case, comprehension difficulties arose specifically at the level of relating these sentences to what commonly happens in the real world (e.g., celebrities usually have fans who admire rather than grieve). Our results are shown in Figure 23.1. Confirming prior research, unexpected verbs evoked an increased N400 effect relative to the predictable verbs (Fig. 23.1[*A*]). However, a different pattern of the brain electrophysiological response was evoked by the verb-argument violations. In this condition, the difficulties in integrating the semantically incompatible NPs with their syntactically defined thematic roles were reflected by a later, positive-going ERP wave that started at approximately 500 ms after target verb onset and peaked between 600 and 700 ms (Fig. 23.1[*B*]). Similar results have been also reported by other laboratories (e.g., Hoeks, Stowe, & Doedens, 2004; Kim & Osterhout, 2005; for a review see Kuperberg, 2007).

The late positivity observed in the verb-argument violations was remarkably similar to the P600 ERP component that previously had

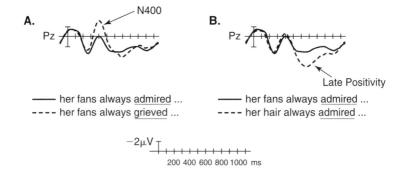

FIGURE 23.1. (*A*) Event-related potentials (ERPs) time-locked to unexpected target words compared to ERPs time-locked to predictable target words. (*B*) ERPs time-locked to violations of verb-based semantic requirements compared to ERPs time-locked to predictable target words. Negative voltages are plotted upward. ERPs shown are at a parietal electrode site.

been found for words that could not be easily integrated into the syntactic structure of the preceding sentence (e.g., to syntactic errors—Hagoort & Brown, 2000a; Osterhout & Holcomb, 1992—or when syntactic ambiguity was resolved toward an unpreferred syntactic structure—Osterhout et al., 1994). In fact, in our follow-up study, we directly compared the late positivity to verb-argument violations with the P600 evoked by syntactically anomalous verbs, such as the verb "admires" in (4) below (Kuperberg, Caplan, Sitnikova, Eddy, & Holcomb, 2006):

4. Although the young model is completely unaware her fans always *admires* . . .

The results are shown in Figure 23.2, which plots the difference waves obtained by subtracting the ERPs to predictable, syntactically correct target words (e.g., in [1] above) from the ERPs to verb-argument violations (e.g., in [3] above) and syntactic violations (e.g., in [4] above). The two types of violations evoked late positivity effects that were similar in their scalp distribution and timing. Both of these effects were largest at the parietal electrode sites (e.g., Pz) but were less prominent in the more anterior sites (e.g., Fz). Moreover, these effects were similar in their onset (at approximately 500 ms after target verb presentation), peak (at approximately 650 ms), and offset latencies (at approximately 1,000 ms). One interpretation of these similarities might be that the verb-argument violations evoked the late positivity because they were recognized by the processing system as being syntactic, rather than semantic, in nature. Indeed, as discussed above, some evidence suggests that the typical event structure retrieved from graded semantic representations may be used in the online assignment of thematic roles to NPs around the verb (e.g., Ferretti et al., 2001; McRae et al., 2005) and consequently may rapidly influence the syntactic processing of sentences. Perhaps the late positivity is evoked in sentences like (3) above because the subject NP (e.g., hair) is a likely candidate for the Patient role around the target verb (e.g., admired), and as a result these verbs are perceived as morphosyntactic violations (e.g., are perceived as a syntactic error in a sentence "her hair *was* always admired"—this phenomenon has been termed "semantic attraction" of the subject NP to the Patient role—see Kim & Osterhout, 2005).

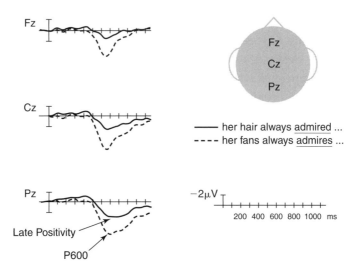

FIGURE 23.2. Difference waves obtained by subtracting the event-related potentials (ERPs) time-locked to predictable target words from the ERPs time-locked to violations of verb-based semantic requirements and from the ERPs time-locked to syntactic violations. Shown are waveforms at frontal, central, and parietal electrode sites, whose relative locations on the scalp are indicated on the head diagram (upper right).

An alternative interpretation of the late positivity to verb-argument violations might be that it reflects a semantic integration analysis that is functionally similar to the processing evoked by syntactic anomalies. On this account, it might reflect the process whereby the thematic roles are assigned to the NP arguments by evaluating the *semantic* properties of NPs against the minimal requirements of the target verb (Sitnikova, 2003). Thematic integration between the target verb and its NP arguments, based on at least some of the verb-based semantic requirements, has been suggested to be reflected by a posterior positivity evoked between approximately 200 and 600 ms after the verb presentation (e.g., Bornkessel, Schlesewsky, & Friederici, 2002; Bornkessel, Schlesewsky, & Friederici, 2003). The late positivity evoked by the verb-argument violations may reflect continuing efforts to integrate the target verb with the preceding subject NP by considering whether the properties of the NP match the semantic requirements for some other thematic role around the verb, not the one specified by the syntax. We examined these alternative explanations—based on semantic attraction and processing of verb-based semantic requirements—by recording ERPs to predictable target words and to two different types of verb-argument violations (Kuperberg, Caplan, et al., 2006). In one sentence type with the violations, such as (3) above, the semantic properties of the subject NP made it a likely candidate for the Patient role around the target verb. In contrast, in the second type of sentences with the violations, such as (5) below, the subject NP does not have the semantic properties required for the Patient role (e.g., it is not possible that "seats would be attended").

5. Although the lectures are excellent the seats hardly *attend* . . .

If semantic attraction between the subject NP and the Patient thematic role is the main trigger of the late positivity, this effect would be expected in sentences like (3) above but not in sentences like (5). Our results revealed robust late positivity effects to critical verbs in both sentence types (3) and (5) relative to the predictable target verbs, consistent with the hypothesis that this effect reflects attempts to repair the sentences by assigning thematic roles based on verb-based semantic requirements. The obtained ERPs are shown in Figure 23.3. Interestingly, verbs in sentences of type (5) with the Patient-incompatible subject NPs evoked larger late positivities than verbs in sentences of type (3), whose subject NP is compatible with the Patient role. As across these sentence types, semantic association between the target verbs and the preceding context[3] and syntactic complexity are matched, this increase in the positivity effect is likely to reflect an additional mental effort engaged by the attempts to re-assign thematic roles based on verb-based semantic requirements. The late positivity is larger when it

---

3. This experiment was carried out using *two types of video stimuli*: in one study, the video clips were continuous with no cuts between scenes (Sitnikova et al., 2003); in the other study, the final scene was shown after a cut (Sitnikova, 2003; Sitnikova et al., in press). This experiment was also carried out using *two different task instructions*: in one study, participants were asked to explicitly decide whether the presented sequence of events would commonly be witnessed in everyday life or not (Sitnikova et al., 2003). In contrast, in the other study participants were not instructed to classify the scenarios and instead answered occasional questions about their content (Sitnikova, 2003). These manipulations helped us to demonstrate that cuts in video clips or performing an additional classification task do not disrupt naturalistic comprehension. Shown are the ERPs evoked in video clips with cuts while participants performed the scenario classification task.

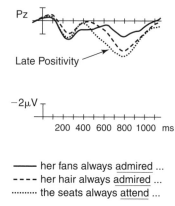

FIGURE 23.3. Event-related potentials (ERPs) time-locked to violations of verb-based semantic requirements that were preceded by subject noun phrases either compatible or incompatible with an alternative thematic role of a Patient, compared to ERPs time-locked to predictable target words. Shown are ERPs at a parietal electrode site.

is not possible to find an alternative thematic role for the subject NP around the target verb.

Our final follow-up study provided additional evidence that the late positivity to verb-argument violations is not related to the semantic association of the target verb to the context. In this experiment we again recorded ERPs to predictable target words and to two different types of verb-argument violations (Kuperberg, Kreher, Sitnikova, Caplan, & Holcomb, 2007). However, this time we compared semantically associated verb-argument violations (some of these sentences were like (3) and some were like (5) above) to verb-argument violations that were not semantically associated with their preceding context. For example, in (6) below, "grieved" is a verb-argument violation (hair can not grieve), and it is semantically unrelated to the "young model and hair" context:

6. Although the young model is completely unaware her hair always *grieved* . . .

As shown in Figure 23.4, the semantically unassociated verb-argument violations evoked a late positivity effect that was even larger than that to the semantically associated verb-argument violations, consistent with the interpretation of the late positivity as reflecting repair attempts based on verb-based semantic requirements.

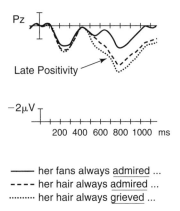

FIGURE 23.4. Event-related potentials (ERPs) time-locked to violations of verb-based semantic requirements that either were or were not semantically related to the context, compared to ERPs time-locked to predictable target words. Shown are ERPs at a parietal electrode site.

Taken together, the above ERP findings suggest that during the on-line sentence processing, comprehenders evaluate NPs against semantic requirements of verbs, and that this analysis is reflected by the late positivity—an ERP component distinct from the N400. This result demonstrates neuroanatomical and temporal distinctions between the processing based on graded semantic representations and verb-based semantic requirements. It is interesting that the late positivity evoked by verb-argument violations is similar to the P600 evoked by syntactic violations, suggesting that these types of anomalies evoke temporally similar processing that is mediated by overlapping neural regions.

Language Comprehension: Summary

One line of research on language comprehension has focused on how people rapidly retrieve their knowledge of the world stored within graded representations in semantic memory and use this information as a template for understanding ongoing verbal input in common situations. The other perspective, starting from classic linguistic theory, has been concerned with how comprehenders access their knowledge of semantic requirements stored around verbs and relate this information to NPs within sentences. ERP studies provide evidence that these two streams of cognitive processing may be neurophysiologically distinct.

Mapping the perceived information on graded semantic representations appears to be reflected by the N400 ERP component. Evaluating NPs against verb-based semantic requirements appears to be reflected by the late positivity.

Visual Real-World Comprehension

It is now well established that graded semantic representations are engaged during comprehension not only of language but also other real-world stimuli, including visual images. In contrast, the semantic requirements of verbs have traditionally been assumed to be stored with verbs' lexical entries in the linguistic knowledge system. Even though these requirements may be acquired through learning about the functional requirements of actions in the real world (Pinker, 1989), little is known about whether such requirements play a role in comprehension of real-world events.

Below, we first give an overview of the studies that examined use of graded semantic representations in processing of static pictures. We then examine evidence that, when presented both with the linguistic and visual-world input, comprehenders rapidly integrate properties of the visual environment with verb-based semantic requirements in sentences. Finally, we go on to describe a set of ERP experiments performed in our laboratory that used video clips to examine comprehension of real-world events. These data provide intriguing evidence that to make sense of their visual environment, comprehenders access both graded semantic representations and discrete, rule-like requirements of real-world actions.

Graded Semantic Representations in Visual-World Comprehension

BEHAVIORAL STUDIES

Just as in language, observers of the visual world have been documented to map the perceptual input on their semantic knowledge of common real-world situations. After viewing a scene and then being asked to recount what they saw, viewers frequently incorporate into their accounts expectations of what they think must have been present, even if it was not actually perceived. The phenomenon of boundary extension

(Intraub & Richardson, 1989; Intraub, Bender, & Mangels, 1992; Intraub & Bodamer, 1993; Intraub, Gottesman, Willey, & Zuk, 1996) is one example of such memory distortions. The boundary extension is evidenced by participants' drawings of the previously viewed visual scenes, which often incorporate added elements (e.g., a tree branch over the yard fence that was not present in the original picture). It is also evidenced by recognition tests, in which originally seen visual scenes are often reported as their close-up views and wide-angle foils are frequently reported as old pictures. Similar memory distortions have been reported after viewing video depictions of common sequences of real-life events (e.g., eating at a restaurant; Brewer & Dupree, 1983; Lichtenstein & Brewer, 1980). Viewers are relatively inaccurate in distinguishing the events they have perceived in video clips from plausible foils. The expected order of events in common activities is also known to influence later recall. Even when presented in a scrambled order in videos, the events tend to be later recalled in a usual order (Brewer & Dupree, 1983; Lichtenstein & Brewer, 1980). Importantly, this mapping on semantic memory representations occurs extremely rapidly. The boundary extension effect in memory for visual scenes has been observed even when pictures were presented for only 250 ms at a rate of three stimuli per second (Intraub et al., 1996).

Studies that used semantic priming paradigms with pictures, just as in language, have yielded results suggesting that comprehenders map the perceptual input online on graded representations in their semantic memory. In these studies, pictures that followed a semantically related word or picture were processed faster than pictures that followed semantically unrelated items (Bajo, 1988; Carr, McCauley, Sperber, & Parmelee, 1982; McCauley, Parmelee, Sperber, & Carr, 1980; Sperber, McCauley, Ragain, & Weil, 1979; Theios & Amrhein, 1989). Moreover, the strength of the prime-target connection also influenced the processing times of target pictures (e.g., McEvoy, 1988).

It remains a matter of debate whether pictures and language access the same semantic representations in the brain. According to a *single-code theory* of semantic memory, any stimulus activates common, amodal representations (e.g., Caramazza, Hillis, Rapp, & Romani, 1990; Kroll & Potter, 1984; Pylyshyn, 1980). In contrast, a *multiple-code theory* postulates several forms of semantic knowledge (e.g., visual, verbal, auditory), stored within distinct brain regions and being activated to a different degree by pictures and words (e.g., Paivio, 1971; 1986; 1991; Shallice, 1988; 1993). Behavioral findings do not clearly support either of these models. For instance, Potter, Kroll, Yachzel, Carpenter, and Sherman (1986) found that plausibility judgments were made just as quickly regarding sentences including just words as sentences in which the final word was replaced with a corresponding picture. For instance, after reading a sentence stem "Paul came to work soaking wet because he forgot his," participants responded just as fast to the word "umbrella" as to a picture of an umbrella. This was taken to support the single-code theory. In contrast, Paivio (1974) provided evidence that the verbal and image processing mechanisms may be independent, supporting the alternative, multiple-code theory. In this study, participants performed a free recall task after viewing a list of words and pictures. Whereas an immediate repetition of two identical items (either two words or two pictures) in a list produced less than additive effects on free recall, a presentation of an object's name immediately followed or preceded by the object's picture resulted in an additive enhancement of recall.

ERP STUDIES WITH STATIC PICTURES

ERP findings in a variety of contextual congruency paradigms suggest that comprehenders map visual images on graded semantic representations within approximately 400 ms after stimulus onset. Semantic priming studies have reported smaller N400s to pictures of objects preceded by related compared to unrelated picture primes (Barrett & Rugg, 1990; Holcomb & McPherson, 1994; McPherson & Holcomb, 1999). Again, the amplitude of this N400 effect was proportional to the relationship strength between the prime and target pictures (e.g., McPherson & Holcomb, 1999). Similarly, object pictures preceded by congruous written sentence contexts evoked a smaller N400 than pictures preceded by incongruous contexts (Federmeier & Kutas, 2001; Ganis, Kutas, & Sereno, 1996). Ganis and Kutas (2003) also showed an N400 effect to individual objects presented in appropriate relative to inappropriate visual scenes. For example, when shown in a "soccer match" background scene, objects such as a soccer ball evoked a smaller N400 than objects such as a toilet paper roll.

Finally, a study from our laboratory showed an N400 effect to final pictures in series of successively presented visual scenes conveying stories (West & Holcomb, 2002). Congruous final scenes (e.g., after being presented with a series of pictures showing a girl run a race and then fall down, participants viewed the final scene "the girl watching her competitors cross the finish line") elicited attenuated N400s relative to incongruous final scenes (e.g., "a girl carrying a pot" in the above context).

ERP studies have also addressed the single- versus multiple-code debate about semantic memory: do words and pictures access the same semantic memory representations in the brain? The results generally come out in favor of multiple-code theory: while both linguistic and picture stimuli evoke the N400 component, the distribution of this waveform across the surface of the scalp is different for pictures than for words, suggesting distinct underlying neuronal sources. Whereas the N400 evoked by verbal stimuli is characterized by a parietal-occipital scalp topography (Friederici, Pfeifer, & Hahne, 1993; Hagoort & Brown, 2000b; Holcomb et al., 1999; Kutas & Van Petten, 1994; van Berkum et al., 1999), the negativities elicited by pictures are typically distributed over more anterior electrode sites (Barrett & Rugg, 1990; Hamm, Johnson, & Kirk, 2002; Holcomb & McPherson, 1994; McPherson & Holcomb, 1999; West & Holcomb, 2002). This is illustrated in Figure 23.5, displaying the N400 effects during comprehension of sentences (Kuperberg, Holcomb, Sitnikova, Greve, Dale, & Caplan, 2003) and picture stories (West & Holcomb, 2002). Shown are the difference waves obtained by subtracting the ERPs to predictable target items from the ERPs to unexpected target items. Note that the N400 effect evoked to visual scenes is characterized by a more prolonged time course (beginning at approximately 300 ms after scene onset and lasting until the end of the recording epoch) relative to the N400 effect evoked to written words. One reason for this could be that mapping semantic information about several people and/or objects included within visual scenes on semantic memory representations could unfold over a few hundreds of milliseconds, thus sustaining the enhanced N400 to the incongruous scenario endings. Most importantly, throughout its entire time course, the N400 effect to visual scenes displays more anterior scalp topography than the N400 effect to words. While the verbal effect is maximal at the parietal sites (e.g., Pz), the visual scene effect is primarily evident at the fronto-central sites (e.g., Fz and Cz).

There are also ERP data suggesting that the above neurophysiological distinctions between word and picture stimuli stem from differences in the semantic code that they preferentially access. Within the verbal

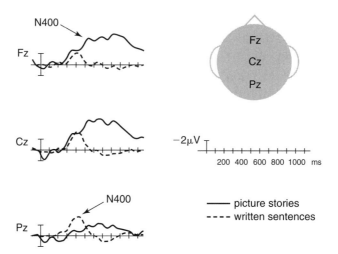

FIGURE 23.5. Difference waves obtained by subtracting the event-related potentials (ERPs) time-locked to predictable targets from the ERPs time-locked to unexpected targets in written sentences and picture stories. Shown are waveforms at frontal, central, and parietal electrode sites whose relative locations on the scalp are indicated on the head diagram (upper right).

domain, the N400 elicited by concrete, easily imageable words (e.g., "dog") is characterized by a more anterior scalp topography than that evoked by abstract words (e.g., "truth"; Holcomb et al., 1999; Kellenbach, Wijers, Hovius, Mulder, & Mulder, 2002; Kounios & Holcomb, 1994; West & Holcomb, 2000). In fact, we have shown that the N400 effect to concrete words (but not abstract words) had a similar anterior topography to the N400 evoked by pictures of individual objects (cf. Holcomb et al., 1999, versus McPherson & Holcomb, 1999). This is demonstrated in Figure 23.6, which includes difference waves (subtractions of ERPs to congruous targets from the ERPs to semantically unrelated targets) obtained for pictures, concrete words, and abstract words.

Taken together, these results have been taken to suggest that the N400 component comprises at least two separable negativities that may reflect processing within distinct semantic neural networks (see Holcomb & McPherson, 1994; Holcomb et al., 1999; Kellenbach et al., 2002; McPherson & Holcomb, 1999; Sitnikova, Kuperberg, & Holcomb, 2003; Sitnikova, West, Kuperberg, & Holcomb, 2006; West & Holcomb, 2002). The more anterior negativities elicited by visual images and concrete words might reflect access to graded semantic representations of the visual real world.

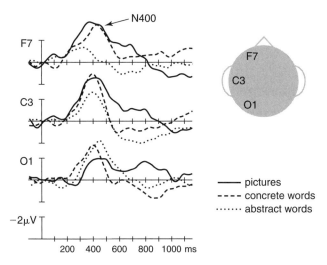

FIGURE 23.6. Difference waves obtained by subtracting the event-related potentials (ERPs) time-locked to congruous targets from the ERPs time-locked to semantically unrelated targets, obtained separately for pictures, concrete words, and abstract words. Shown are waveforms at frontal, central, and occipital electrode sites whose relative locations on the scalp are indicated on the head diagram (upper right).

In contrast, the posterior N400 might reflect activation of the brain regions selectively mediating verbally coded representations.

Action-Based Requirements in Visual-World Comprehension: Behavioral Evidence

As discussed in the introduction to this chapter, mapping the perceptual input on graded semantic representations might guide comprehension in familiar situations, such as a traditional birthday party. Such a mechanism, however, is not efficient in less familiar situations and can not explain how people are able to build veridical representations of events that include entities and actions that have not been previously experienced together. We suggest that accurate and flexible comprehension of events in the real world depends on a second semantic mechanism that utilizes discrete, rule-like knowledge of what is necessary for real-world actions.

Several seminal behavioral studies examining interactions between the processing of language and visual environment have established that object properties perceived in their visual inspection can be rapidly integrated into the online thematic processing of verb-based semantic requirements in sentences (Altmann & Kamide, 1999; Chambers, Tanenhaus, & Eberhard, 2002; Chambers, Tanenhaus, & Magnuson, 2004). For example, Chambers et al. (2004) tracked eye movements of participants who listened to spoken instructions about visual displays of real objects. Thus, participants might be presented with four items: an empty bowl, some flour on a cutting board, and two eggs. One of the eggs would be in a bowl and one in a different container. While viewing this display, participants would hear an instruction: "Pour the egg in the bowl over the flour." The critical manipulation involved semantic properties of the viewed eggs. In the first, control, condition, both of the eggs were liquid, and hence the display provided no information that would help to disambiguate the object NP "the egg." In contrast, in the second condition only the egg in the bowl was liquid and therefore could be poured, which disambiguated the NP "the egg." This study found that participants used such action affordances, perceived in the visual display, to interpret thematic relationships between constituents in the verbal instructions. In the second but not in the first condition, the propositional phrase "in the bowl" was misinterpreted as a location where the egg had to be poured, as was evident by participants' anticipatory eye movements toward the empty bowl in the visual display. Similar results were also obtained when the critical variable was the size of objects in visual displays (Chambers et al., 2002).

A similar experiment by Knoeferle, Crocker, Scheepers, and Pickering (2005) suggested that spatial properties of visual-world events also can be combined with the thematic cues in sentences. This study recorded eye movements while participants were presented with static pictures conveying unusual visual events and the corresponding spoken descriptions. Each picture depicted three animate characters involved in two actions; each action involved two characters who performed different roles in the action. For instance, a picture might show a fencer painting a princess who, in turn, was washing a pirate. The verbal descriptions referred to one of the observed actions and were conveyed either by German active sentences (e.g., "Die Prinzessin wird sogleich den Pirat waschen"/"The princess will soon wash the pirate") or passive sentences (e.g., "Die Prinzessin wird soeben von dem Fechter gemalt"/ "The princess is currently painted by the fencer"). The results revealed that as soon as the linguistic syntactic information that disambiguated the thematic role of the first NP was presented (e.g., "Die Prinzessin" was disambiguated as an Agent or Patient by the temporal adverbs "sogleich/soeben von," biasing toward the active or passive structure), participants tended to make anticipatory eye movements toward the image of the second character, who was about to be mentioned in the spoken description. Importantly, the only visual information that disambiguated the role of the central character (conveyed by the first NP) in each action was his or her spatial orientation, which made it impossible for the character to play an Agent role in one of the two conveyed actions. Therefore, the above finding indicates that participants were able to use such basic spatial information in assigning the thematic roles to the characters in the pictures.

Taken together, these results suggest, first, that comprehenders are able to rapidly evaluate whether properties of real-world objects meet the semantic requirements of a given verb. This, in turn, leads to a possibility that such processing relies on the knowledge representations analogous to verb-based semantic requirements in language—notably, requirements of real-world actions. Second, the semantic properties of objects appear to be combined with spatial information and possibly also temporal information as comprehenders determine the thematic structure of real-world events.

Based on these findings we put forward a hypothesis for a cognitive mechanism that is able to build veridical representations of real-world events (Sitnikova, 2003). In the visual-world domain, a set of requirements including the semantic properties of entities and the spatiotemporal relationships between them can uniquely constrain specific actions. For example, the cutting action requires that the entity in the Agent role be able to perform cutting (e.g., <have ability for volitional actions>), the entity in the Instrument role have physical properties necessary for cutting (e.g., <have a sturdy sharp edge>), and the entity in the Patient role be cuttable (e.g., <unsturdy>). There are also minimal spatiotemporal requirements for the cutting action (e.g., <the Instrument and the Patient must come in physical contact>). In comprehension of visual events, the correspondence between the perceptual input and the requirements of a given real-world action would allow viewers to identify the event's central action and assign the roles to the involved entities. Of note, employing these discrete, rule-like semantic representations is fundamentally different from any integration by accessing graded connections between concepts in semantic memory in that this analysis takes into account only a subset of the semantic properties of the visual event—those that are necessary to carry out a given real-world action. As a result, this analysis has great flexibility, as it can be applied to combinations of entities and actions that have not previously been encountered. For example, observers would interpret "wriggling the dental floss across the cake" as "cutting," even if they see such an event for the first time, because the semantic properties of dental floss are consistent with the required properties for cutting a cake. Thus, one interesting possibility is that during visual comprehension a semantic analysis based on the requirements of real-world actions may serve a combinatorial role similar to that played by syntactic processing in language.

ERP Studies in Video Clips: Relationships Between People, Objects, and Actions in Common and Unconventional Visual Real-World Events

Above, we suggested that the comprehension of visual real-world events might involve both mapping on graded semantic representations and the use of discrete, action-based requirements, analogous to the comprehension mechanisms used in language. We have also seen that, in the linguistic domain, ERP data suggest that these two mechanisms might be mediated by the anatomically and temporally distinct neural processes. Difficulties in mapping on graded semantic representations appear to be reflected by the modulation of the N400 waveform. In contrast, difficulties in the thematic analysis based on verb-based semantic requirements appear to be reflected by a somewhat slower late positivity waveform.

In our laboratory, we have recently employed ERPs to determine whether processing based on graded semantic representations and action-based requirements would be neurophysiologically dissociable during visual real-world comprehension (Sitnikova, 2003; Sitnikova et al., 2003; Sitnikova, Holcomb, & Kuperberg, in press). We reasoned that if these neurocognitive mechanisms are similar to their counterparts in language comprehension, their engagement should evoke similar ERP effects. Mapping of visual events on graded semantic representations would evoke the N400, while evaluating the events against action-based requirements would elicit the late positivity.

We explored this hypothesis using naturalistic depictions of real-world events in video clips. Although humans frequently do process static pictures (e.g., in magazines and books), a much more common form of visual comprehension involves the viewing of dynamic images juxtaposed in a continuous flow. Video clips preserve these dynamic properties of the visual environment and are known to evoke perceptual experiences that are remarkably similar to those elicited during comprehending events in the real world (e.g., Levin & Simons, 2000).

In our experiments, we used a contextual congruency paradigm analogous to the one that we previously employed to study semantic processing in the ERP studies of language (Kuperberg, Caplan, et al., 2006; Kuperberg, Kreher, et al., 2007; Kuperberg, Sitnikova, et al., 2003). We produced silent video clips that were about 10 s long. All of these videos were structured in a similar way: a common real-world activity was depicted in a lead-up context and was followed by a congruous or incongruous final scene. ERP recordings were time-locked to the onset of these target scenes.

We used two variations of this contextual congruency paradigm. In the first, we aimed to modulate the difficulty of mapping the final event on graded semantic representations, and in the second we aimed to examine the effects of taxing the analysis based on action-based requirements. In both versions of the paradigm, we used the same set of congruous video clips ending with a predictable final scene. A target object that was introduced in the scenario ending was not seen in the lead-up to these final scenes. For example, in one clip the lead-up context depicted a man squeezing the tire of his bicycle, which appeared soft, and then unscrewing the valve cap on the tire; in the final scene, he used a bike pump (the target object) to fill the tire (Fig. 23.7[A]; also see color insert). As described below, the anomalous versions of the scenarios differed depending on whether we aimed to examine the processing based on graded semantic representations or action-based requirements.

MAPPING VISUAL EVENTS ON GRADED SEMANTIC REPRESENTATIONS
    AND THE N400>

In our first experiment, we manipulated the predictability of the final scenes in their preceding context (Sitnikova, 2003; Sitnikova et al., in press), extending our earlier work using static pictures described above (West & Holcomb, 2002). The incongruous videos in this experiment were created by replacing the original context shot in each video with a context shot from another scenario. For example, as outlined above, in the congruous condition, participants would see a man squeeze a tire of his bike, unscrew the tire valve cap, and then use a bike pump to fill the tire (see Fig. 23.7[*A*]; color insert). In the incongruous condition, participants would see a man attempt to open the front door of his house, which turns out to be locked, and fumble in his bag; then the man would use a bike pump to fill a bike tire (see Fig. 23.7[*B*]; color insert). We expected that final scenes in congruous videos would evoke relatively small N400s, as these scenes were predictable and could be easily mapped on the fields in semantic memory activated by the preceding context. In contrast, the incongruous final scenes were expected to evoke increased N400s, as these scenes introduced information that was inconsistent with the semantic representation of the preceding contextual events.

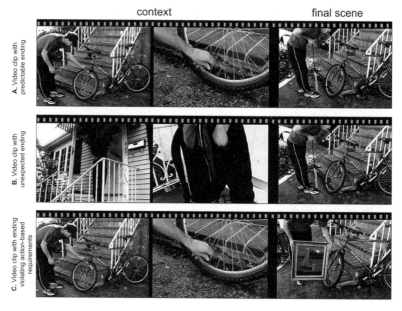

FIGURE 23.7. Frames taken from video clips (produced using Canon GL1 digital video camcorder and Adobe digital editing software) used in our contextual congruency paradigm. For each video scenario, shown are two frames illustrating real-world events depicted as a context, followed by a single frame illustrating the final scene. (*A*) shows a predictable final scene, (*B*) shows an unexpected final scene, and (*C*) shows a final scene that is unexpected and violates action-based requirements. The actual video clips may be viewed at http://www.nmr.mgh.harvard.edu/~tatiana/NCMHC.

Results of this experiment are shown in Figure 23.8. Starting at approximately 200 ms after their presentation, the final scenes in video depictions of real-world events evoked a robust negative-going ERP that was attenuated by the congruency of the preceding video context. Overall, the morphological, functional, and temporal properties of this effect suggest that it is similar to the N400 previously reported in verbal and static picture paradigms manipulating stimuli predictability (e.g., Ganis et al., 1996; Kutas & Hillyard, 1980; West & Holcomb, 2002). These findings confirm our hypothesis that during comprehension of visual events, the perceptual input is mapped on graded semantic representations. Moreover, they suggest that this mapping starts within a similar time frame as during language comprehension.

The time course of the N400 effect evoked by the video stimuli, however, was more prolonged than what is common for the studies with

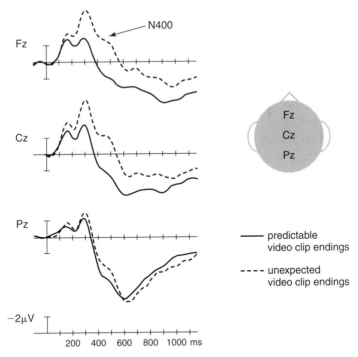

FIGURE 23.8. Event-related potentials (ERPs) time-locked to unexpected final scenes compared to ERPs time-locked to predictable final scenes in video scenarios. Shown are waveforms at frontal, central, and parietal electrode sites whose relative locations on the scalp are indicated on the head diagram (upper right).

visually presented words (cf. Fig. 23.1[A]). The N400 modulation to incongruous relative to congruous final scenes continued for more than 900 ms. This prolonged time course was in keeping with our previous findings with static visual scenes (West & Holcomb, 2002) and could be accounted for by the richness of semantic information conveyed in visual events. Another reason for the prolonged effect could be that presentation of incongruous information in video scenes unfolded continuously over several hundreds of milliseconds, which would lead to the prolongation of the semantic analysis. In line with the latter explanation, similar extended N400s are observed in association with spoken language that also involves processing of critical information over time as the eliciting word unfolds phoneme by phoneme (e.g., Holcomb & Neville, 1991a, 1991b).

Another difference between the N400 effects evoked by video scenes and words was in the scalp topography. Just as in our previous studies using static pictures (McPherson & Holcomb, 1999; West & Holcomb, 2002), the N400 to dynamic visual events presented in video clips was evident predominantly over more anterior electrode sites (e.g., Fz electrode site in Fig. 23.8). This finding is consistent with the multiple-code theory of semantic memory: comprehending the visual world and language might preferentially access graded semantic representations supported by distinct neurocognitive systems.

EVALUATING VISUAL EVENTS AGAINST ACTION-BASED REQUIREMENTS
AND THE LATE POSITIVITY

In our next study with video clips, we used the contextual congruency paradigm, which included violations of action-based requirements in addition to manipulations of the final scene's predictability (Sitnikova, 2003; Sitnikova et al., 2003; Sitnikova et al., in press). In this experiment, anomalous scenario endings introduced a single context-inappropriate object that the main character involved in the interaction with another entity in the video clip. For example, after checking the bike tire pressure and unscrewing the tire valve cap, a man twirled a framed painting against the opening of the bike tire valve (see Fig. 23.7[C]; color insert). Just as in our previous experiment, these final scenes were unexpected (e.g., twirling a framed painting is not usual when someone is fixing a bike). However, unlike in our previous experiment, these scenes were clearly a continuation of the activity conveyed earlier in the video clip, but did not meet the requirements of the final action constrained by the preceding context (e.g., twirling a framed painting does not meet the requirements of the action "pumping"). To make any sense of these scenes, participants would need to reevaluate whether the involved entities and their spatiotemporal relationships met the requirements for an alternative action that was also acceptable in the given video scenario (e.g., the framed painting has pointy and sturdy corners: perhaps it is being used to scrape off some relatively soft mud that is stuck to the opening in the tire valve). We anticipated that in addition to evoking an enhanced N400, these target scenes that both were unexpected and violated the requirements of the contextually constrained final action would evoke a large late positivity similar to the one evoked by violations of verb-based semantic requirements in language.

Our results are shown in Figure 23.9.[3] Relative to congruous video endings, the anomalous scenes evoked an increased anterior N400, confirming that it was more difficult to map these unexpected endings on graded semantic representations. In addition, over more posterior scalp regions, these scenes violating action-based requirements evoked an enhanced late positivity. Again, these ERP effects to video materials had a prolonged time course, possibly due to the richness and prolonged presentation of the semantic information. However, their onset latency and overall temporal pattern were similar to the language studies: the N400 started at approximately 250 ms, whereas the late positivity was delayed until approximately 500 ms after target scene presentation. Most importantly, the late positivity effect evoked in video clips resembled in its scalp topography the linguistic late positivity evoked to violations of verb-based semantic requirements—it was widely distributed over more posterior electrode sites, peaking over the parietal sites (a parietal electrode site Pz is shown in Figure 23.9—cf. the late positivity to words in Figures 23.1 and 23.2). These results are interesting as they provide evidence that the processing of action-based requirements during visual-world comprehension might engage neurocognitive mechanisms similar to those mediating the thematic analysis of verb-based semantic requirements in language.

Visual Real-World Comprehension: Summary

Experiments with static and motion pictures suggest that comprehension of the visual world might engage two separate mechanisms, one

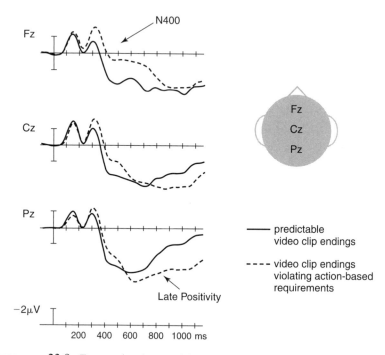

FIGURE 23.9. Event-related potentials (ERPs) time-locked to final scenes that were unexpected and violated action-based requirements, compared to ERPs time-locked to predictable final scenes. Shown are waveforms at frontal, central, and parietal electrode sites whose relative locations on the scalp are indicated on the head diagram (upper right).

relying on graded semantic representations and the other relying on the discrete knowledge of action-based requirements. Behavioral studies provide evidence for the mapping of visual-world stimuli on graded semantic representations, and also demonstrate that viewers can rapidly evaluate the visual environment against the semantic requirements of auditorily presented verbs. ERP investigations extend this line of research by revealing neurophysiological distinctions between the two semantic mechanisms during visual real-world comprehension. Several studies with static pictures have demonstrated that contextually unexpected stimuli that are relatively difficult to map on graded semantic representations evoke a large N400. More recently, a set of studies from our laboratory used video depictions of events to dissociate the N400 expectancy effect from the late positivity effect evoked by introducing an additional violation of action-based requirements. Intriguingly, both of these observed ERP effects to video scenes morphologically, functionally, and temporally resemble the N400 and late positivity evoked in response to semantic violations during language comprehension. The most parsimonious interpretation of this result is that there may be some similarities in the neurocognitive systems involved in language and visual-world comprehension.

Two Semantic Neurocognitive Mechanisms of Comprehension: A Hypothesis and Future Directions

In this chapter we propose a novel hypothesis that attempts to tie together research findings on language and visual-world comprehension. We have outlined prior behavioral and ERP evidence and have presented our own ERP findings suggesting that, in both verbal and visual-world domains, comprehension might be supported by two neuroanatomically and temporally distinct semantic mechanisms. The first mechanism, reflected by the N400 ERP component, appears to continuously access the world knowledge stored in graded semantic representations. The second mechanism, reflected by the late positivity ERP component, appears to access discrete requirements of real-world actions (depicted by verbs in language). There may be a tradeoff between these two types of semantic representation in their utility for integrating the people, objects, and actions during event comprehension, in which the first mechanism is better suited for familiar situations and the second mechanism is better suited for novel situations. In the remainder of this chapter, we consider some of the further questions in this line of research and review some clues to their answers stemming from the currently available data.

One important task for future research is to describe the neural networks mediating each comprehension mechanism. Interestingly, in the nonhuman primate brain, it is well established that there is a functional dichotomy of structures along the anterior–posterior dimension: the posterior cortex appears to specialize in representing sensory information, whereas the frontal lobe is devoted to representing and executing actions. A similar division of labor has been proposed in the human brain (e.g., Fuster, 1997). From this perspective we put forward a question: Is it possible that during event comprehension, graded semantic representations reflecting all prior perceptual experiences and requirements specific to real-world actions are selectively mediated within the posterior and prefrontal cortices, respectively? To examine this hypothesis, it will be important to use techniques such as functional magnetic resonance imaging and magnetoencephalography that can localize the neural activity in the brain with superior spatial resolution to ERPs.

The currently available neuroimaging data provide evidence for the involvement of primarily the temporal and prefrontal cortices in semantic processing of both language (for a review see Van Petten & Luka, 2006) and visual images (static scenes—e.g., Blondin & Lepage, 2005; video clips—Sitnikova, Coty, Robakis, Holcomb, Kuperberg, & West, 2004). In our laboratory, we have begun the work in the language domain to dissociate between processes based on graded semantic representations and verb-based semantic requirements (Kuperberg, Sitnikova, & Lakshmanan, 2007). Our findings show increased activity in the superior-rostral prefrontal cortex (BA 9) to verb-argument violations (relative to expected verbs) in sentences, suggesting that this brain region may be involved in processing verb-based semantic requirements. Importantly, this activation is not observed to the verbs that are merely unexpected in their preceding sentence context (relative to expected verbs). Other neuroimaging studies have implicated similar superior-rostral prefrontal regions in comprehending relationships between goal-directed and causally related events (Ferstl & von Cramon, 2001, 2002; Kuperberg, Lakshmanan, Caplan, & Holcomb, 2006; Ruby, Sirigu, & Decety, 2002; Tinaz, Schendan, Schon, & Stern, 2006; Xu, Kemeny, Park, Frattali, & Braun, 2005) that, as we argued in the introduction to this chapter, might depend on processing action-based requirements (also see Chapter 22 in this volume, which reviews the role of the prefrontal regions in processing temporal order relationships between real-world events).

The currently available neuropsychological findings also are consistent with the idea that graded semantic representations are mediated within the temporal cortex while action-based requirements are supported within the prefrontal cortex. Patients with temporal lobe damage show severe deficits in word comprehension and picture naming, and the profound temporal damage in semantic dementia tends to result in speech devoid of semantic content while the phonology and grammar are relatively preserved (for a review see Price, 2000). In contrast, patients with frontal lobe damage usually have little difficulty with execution of simple familiar routines but are unable to engage in behaviors that are weakly established and require understanding of a goal and the means to achieve it (Shallice & Burgess, 1991). Several studies have suggested that access to graded semantic representations in these patients is relatively spared: they have no difficulty determining which events tend to co-occur in common real-world activities (Sirigu, Zalla, Pillon, Grafman, Agid, & Dubois, 1995, 1996), and they are selectively impaired in sequentially ordering uncommon or unfamiliar rather than routine event sequences (Goel, Grafman, Tajik, Gana, & Danto, 1997; Sirigu et al., 1995). However, these patients with prefrontal damage have difficulties in comprehending relationships between goal-directed and causally related events (Ferstl, Guthke, & von Cramon, 2002; Zalla, Phipps, & Grafman, 2002) and ordering events in goal-directed sequences (Sirigu, Cohen, Zalla, Pradat-Diehl, Van Eeckhout, Grafman, & Agid, 1998).

The second important task for future studies is to delineate functional differences in neural processing between the two comprehension systems. Some insights with regard to the neural mechanisms able to support graded semantic representations and discrete, rule-like, action-based requirements come from research in computational neuroscience. In connectionist networks, acquisition and use of graded semantic knowledge have been simulated by means of variation in synaptic weights representing connection strengths (based on feature similarity or association strength) between the learned concepts (for a review see Hutchison, 2003). However, more recent studies have demonstrated that the neurobiological mechanisms specific to the prefrontal cortex (which support updating of active maintenance contingent on the presence of a reward) can lead to self-organization of discrete, rule-like representations coded by patterns of activity (e.g., distinct sets of units with high synaptic weights—e.g., Rougier, Noelle, Braver, Cohen, & O'Reilly, 2005). This computational model supports adaptive processing in novel situations by searching for the appropriate pattern of activity, which eliminates the need to learn a new set of connection strengths. Even though so far this model has only been shown to simulate human participants' performance on specific rule-driven behavioral tasks designed for experimental settings (e.g., the Stroop task), it is possible that the neural mechanisms within the prefrontal cortex can also support patterns of activity coding requirements of real-world actions. Specifically, through breadth of learning experience with actions that achieved or failed to achieve their goal (i.e., either resulted in a "reward" or not), these prefrontal mechanisms can identify the pattern of activity present across all instances of achieving a specific goal.[4] In comprehension, searching for such a pattern of activity, representing the parameters necessary for a given action, would allow flexibility in recognizing actions in novel circumstances.

Based on this model of coding action-based requirements as patterns of neuronal activity, we can make a specific prediction for future research. As a given pattern of neuronal activity only represents the properties necessary for a given action, this mechanism should be insensitive to event properties that are not necessary for the perceived action. For example, in the "cutting the cake" scenario, very different objects such as a plate, a tape measure, or dental floss, when they are used as Instruments of cutting, should access the same pattern of neuronal activity coding the requirement <the Instrument of the cutting action must have a sturdy sharp edge>. Interestingly, electrophysiological studies in nonhuman primates have already obtained some evidence that prefrontal neurons display such a discrete pattern of response to categories of visual stimuli (Freedman, Riesenhuber, Poggio, & Miller, 2001, 2002, 2003) and match-mismatch relationships (Wallis, Anderson, & Miller, 2001; Wallis & Miller, 2003) that are defined by their functional relevance (for a review see Miller, Freedman, & Wallis, 2002; Miller, Nieder, Freedman, & Wallis, 2003).

Yet another research task will be to determine how the two neurocognitive mechanisms of comprehension interact with each other in real time. Rapid reciprocal influences between these processing streams can be mediated by cortico-cortical axons interlinking cortical regions (e.g., Fuster, 1997). Recent ERP data in language comprehension give some evidence for these rapid interactions: outputs of one stream appear to immediately influence processing within the other (for review see Kuperberg, 2007). For example, detection of the violated verb-based semantic requirements (e.g., in "Although the young model is completely unaware her hair always *grieved* . . ."—Kuperberg, Kreher, et al., 2007) seems to reduce attempts to map the target word on graded semantic representations—words like "grieved" that are semantically

---

4. It is also possible that the same prefrontal mechanisms can code requirements of mental activities such as "admiring" that might be learned through feedback (from other individuals) about correct and incorrect attributing of such mental activities to oneself and surrounding entities.

unrelated to the context did not evoke a large N400. On the other hand, to motivate an extended processing based on verb-based semantic requirements, it might be necessary that the sentence activate a specific field in graded semantic representations. In sentences with less constraining context, the verb-argument violations (e.g., in "The library books had been *regretting* . . .") evoked an N400 effect rather than the late positivity (Kim & Osterhout, 2005). Given the functional similarities between the semantic integration processes between language and visual event comprehension that we discussed above, it is likely that similar dynamics might take also place during visual real-world comprehension.

Conclusion

In this chapter, we suggest that comprehenders in the real world engage two distinct neurocognitive mechanisms that may be analogous to those employed during language processing. One system might be adapted for efficiency in everyday predictable life. Another might be fine-tuned for flexible ability to rapidly make sense of even novel or unusual situations. Although most of the existing evidence for this perspective is in the language domain, we have presented recent electrophysiological data suggesting that this framework might generalize to real-world comprehension. Future experiments will need to test this theoretical perspective.

References

Abelson, R. P. (1981). Psychological status of the script concept. *American Psychologist, 36*, 715–729.

Altmann, G., & Steedman, M. (1988). Interaction with context during human sentence processing. *Cognition, 30*(3), 191–238.

Altmann, G. T., & Kamide, Y. (1999). Incremental interpretation at verbs: Restricting the domain of subsequent reference. *Cognition, 73*(3), 247–264.

Anderson, J. R. (1980). Concepts, propositions, and schemata: What are the cognitive units? *Nebraska Symposium on Motivation, 28*, 121–162.

Bajo, M. T. (1988). Semantic facilitation with pictures and words. *Journal of Experimental Psychology: Learning, Memory, & Cognition, 14*(4), 579–589.

Barrett, S. E., & Rugg, M. D. (1990). Event-related potentials and the semantic matching of pictures. *Brain Cognition, 14*(2), 201–212.

Biederman, I., Rabinowitz, J. C., Glass, A. L., & Stacy, E. W., Jr. (1974). On the information extracted from a glance at a scene. *Journal of Experimental Psychology, 103*(3), 597–600.

Blondin, F., & Lepage, M. (2005). Decrease and increase in brain activity during visual perceptual priming: An fMRI study on similar but perceptually different complex visual scenes. *Neuropsychologia, 43*(13), 1887–1900.

Bornkessel, I., Schlesewsky, M., & Friederici, A. D. (2002). Beyond syntax: language-related positivities reflect the revision of hierarchies. *Neuroreport, 13*(3), 361–364.

Bornkessel, I., Schlesewsky, M., & Friederici, A. D. (2003). Eliciting thematic reanalysis effects: The role of syntax-independent information during parsing. *Language & Cognitive Processes, 18*(3), 269–298.

Bower, G. H., Black, J. B., & Turner, T. J. (1979). Scripts in memory for text. *Cognitive Psychology, 11*(2), 177–220.

Brewer, W. F., & Dupree, D. A. (1983). Use of plan schemata in the recall and recognition of goal-directed actions. *Journal of Experimental Psychology: Learning, Memory, & Cognition, 9*(1), 117–129.

Caplan, D., Hildebrandt, N., & Waters, G. S. (1994). Interaction of verb selectional restrictions, noun animacy and syntactic form in sentence processing. *Language & Cognitive Processes, 9*(4), 549–585.

Caramazza, A., Hillis, A. E., Rapp, B. C., & Romani, C. (1990). The multiple semantics hypothesis: Multiple confusions? *Cognitive Neuropsychology, 7*(3), 161–189.

Carr, T. H., McCauley, C., Sperber, R. D., & Parmelee, C. M. (1982). Words, pictures, and priming: On semantic activation, conscious identification, and the automaticity of information processing. *Journal of Experimental Psychology: Human Perception & Performance, 8*(6), 757–777.

Chambers, C. G., Tanenhaus, M. K., & Eberhard, K. M. (2002). Circumscribing referential domains during real-time language comprehension. *Journal of Memory & Language, 47*(1), 30–49.

Chambers, C. G., Tanenhaus, M. K., & Magnuson, J. S. (2004). Actions and affordances in syntactic ambiguity resolution. *Journal of Experimental Psychology: Learning, Memory, & Cognition, 30*(3), 687–696.

Clifton, C., Jr. (1993). Thematic roles in sentence parsing. *Canadian Journal of Experimental Psychology, 47*(2), 222–246.

Clifton, C. J., Traxler, M. J., & Mohamed, M. T. (2003). The use of thematic role information in parsing: Syntactic processing autonomy revisited. *Journal of Memory & Language, 49*(3), 317–334.

Cohen, D., Palti, Y., Cuffin, B. N., & Schmid, S. J. (1980). Magnetic fields produced by steady currents in the body. *Proceedings of the National Academy of Sciences of the USA, 77*(3), 1447–1451.

Federmeier, K. D., & Kutas, M. (2001). Meaning and modality: Influences of context, semantic memory organization, and perceptual predictability on picture processing. *Journal of Experimental Psychology: Learning, Memory & Cognition, 27*(1), 202–224.

Ferreira, F., & Clifton, J., C. (1986). The independence of syntactic processing. *Journal of Memory & Language, 25,* 348–368.

Ferretti, T., McRae, K., & Hatherell, A. (2001). Integrating verbs, situation schemas, and thematic role concepts. *Journal of Memory & Language, 44,* 516–547.

Ferstl, E. C., Guthke, T., & von Cramon, D. Y. (2002). Text comprehension after brain injury: Left prefrontal lesions affect inference processes. *Neuropsychology, 16*(3), 292–308.

Ferstl, E. C., & von Cramon, D. Y. (2001). The role of coherence and cohesion in text comprehension: An event- related fMRI study. *Brain Research Cognitive Brain Research, 11*(3), 325–340.

Ferstl, E. C., & von Cramon, D. Y. (2002). What does the frontomedian cortex contribute to language processing: Coherence or theory of mind? *Neuroimage, 17*(3), 1599–1612.

Fillmore, C. (1968). The case for Case. In E. Bach & R. Harms (Eds.), *Universals in linguistic theory*. New York: Holt, Reinhart and Winston.

Fischler, I. S., & Bloom, P. A. (1985). Effects of constraint and validity of sentence contexts on lexical decisions. *Memory & Cognition, 13*(2), 128–139.

Frazier, L., & Clifton, C., Jr. (1997). Construal: Overview, motivation, and some new evidence. *Journal of Psycholinguistic Research, 26*(3), 277–295.

Freedman, D. J., Riesenhuber, M., Poggio, T., & Miller, E. K. (2001). Categorical representation of visual stimuli in the primate prefrontal cortex. *Science, 291*(5502), 312–316.

Freedman, D. J., Riesenhuber, M., Poggio, T., & Miller, E. K. (2002). Visual categorization and the primate prefrontal cortex: Neurophysiology and behavior. *Journal of Neurophysiology, 88*(2), 929–941.

Freedman, D. J., Riesenhuber, M., Poggio, T., & Miller, E. K. (2003). A comparison of primate prefrontal and inferior temporal cortices during visual categorization. *Journal of Neuroscience, 23*(12), 5235–5246.

Friederici, A. D., Pfeifer, E., & Hahne, A. (1993). Event-related brain potentials during natural speech processing: Effects of semantic, morphological and syntactic violations. *Brain Research Cognitive Brain Research, 1*(3), 183–192.

Fuster, J. M. (1997). Network memory. *Trends in Neuroscience, 20*(10), 451–459.

Ganis, G., & Kutas, M. (2003). An electrophysiological study of scene effects on object identification. *Brain Research Cognitive Brain Research, 16*(2), 123–144.

Ganis, G., Kutas, M., & Sereno, M. I. (1996). The search for "common sense": An electrophysiological study of the comprehension of words and pictures in reading. *Journal of Cognitive Neuroscience, 8*(2), 89–106.

Glenberg, A. M., & Robertson, D. A. (2000). Symbol grounding and meaning: A comparison of high-dimensional and embodied theories of meaning. *Journal of Memory & Language, 43*(3), 379–401.

Goel, V., Grafman, J., Tajik, J., Gana, S., & Danto, D. (1997). A study of the performance of patients with frontal lobe lesions in a financial planning task. *Brain, 120*(Pt 10), 1805–1822.

Grose-Fifer, J., & Deacon, D. (2004). Priming by natural category membership in the left and right cerebral hemispheres. *Neuropsychologia, 42*(14), 1948–1960.

Hagoort, P., & Brown, C. M. (2000a). ERP effects of listening to speech compared to reading: The P600/SPS to syntactic violations in spoken sentences and rapid serial visual presentation. *Neuropsychologia, 38*(11), 1531–1549.

Hagoort, P., & Brown, C. M. (2000b). ERP effects of listening to speech: Semantic ERP effects. *Neuropsychologia, 38*(11), 1518–1530.

Hamm, J. P., Johnson, B. W., & Kirk, I. J. (2002). Comparison of the N300 and N400 ERPs to picture stimuli in congruent and incongruent contexts. *Clinical Neurophysiology, 113*(8), 1339–1350.

Hoeks, J. C., Stowe, L. A., & Doedens, G. (2004). Seeing words in context: The interaction of lexical and sentence level information during reading. *Brain Research: Cognitive Brain Research, 19*(1), 59–73.

Holcomb, P. J. (1988). Automatic and attentional processing: An event-related brain potential analysis of semantic priming. *Brain Language, 35*(1), 66–85.

Holcomb, P. J. (1993). Semantic priming and stimulus degradation: Implications for the role of the N400 in language processing. *Psychophysiology, 30*(1), 47–61.

Holcomb, P. J., Kounios, J., Anderson, J. E., & West, W. C. (1999). Dual-coding, context-availability, and concreteness effects in sentence comprehension: An electrophysiological investigation. *Journal of Experimental Psychology: Learning, Memory & Cognition, 25*(3), 721–742.

Holcomb, P. J., & McPherson, W. B. (1994). Event-related brain potentials reflect semantic priming in an object decision task. *Brain Cognition, 24*(2), 259–276.

Holcomb, P. J., & Neville, H. J. (1991a). The electrophysiology of spoken sentence processing. *Psychobiology, 19*, 286–300.

Holcomb, P. J., & Neville, H. J. (1991b). Natural speech processing: An analysis using event-related brain potentials. *Psychobiology, 19*(4), 286–300.

Hutchison, K. A. (2003). Is semantic priming due to association strength or feature overlap? A microanalytic review. *Psychonomics Bulletin Review, 10*(4), 785–813.

Intraub, H., Bender, R. S., & Mangels, J. A. (1992). Looking at pictures but remembering scenes. *Journal of Experimental Psychology: Learning, Memory & Cognition, 18*(1), 180–191.

Intraub, H., & Bodamer, J. L. (1993). Boundary extension: Fundamental aspect of pictorial representation or encoding artifact? *Journal of Experimental Psychology: Learning, Memory & Cognition, 19*(6), 1387–1397.

Intraub, H., Gottesman, C. V., Willey, E. V., & Zuk, I. J. (1996). Boundary extension for briefly glimpsed photographs: Do common perceptual processes result in unexpected memory distortions? *Journal of Memory & Language, 35*(2), 118–134.

Intraub, H., & Richardson, M. (1989). Wide-angle memories of close-up scenes. *Journal of Experimental Psychology: Learning, Memory & Cognition, 15*(2), 179–187.

Kaschak, M. P., & Glenberg, A. M. (2000). Constructing meaning: The role of affordances and grammatical constructions in sentence comprehension. *Journal of Memory & Language, 43*(3), 508–529.

Kellenbach, M. L., Wijers, A. A., Hovius, M., Mulder, J., & Mulder, G. (2002). Neural differentiation of lexico-syntactic categories or semantic features? Event-related potential evidence for both. *Journal of Cognitive Neuroscience, 14*(4), 561–577.

Kim, A., & Osterhout, L. (2005). The independence of combinatory semantic processing: Evidence from event-related potentials. *Journal of Memory & Language, 52*(2), 205–225.

Klix, F. (2001). The evolution of cognition. *Journal of Structural Learning and Intelligence Systems, 14*, 415–431.

Knoeferle, P., Crocker, M. W., Scheepers, C., & Pickering, M. J. (2005). The influence of the immediate visual context on incremental thematic role-assignment: Evidence from eye-movements in depicted events. *Cognition, 95*(1), 95–127.

Knutson, K. M., Wood, J. N., & Grafman, J. (2004). Brain activation in processing temporal sequence: An fMRI study. *Neuroimage, 23*(4), 1299–1307.

Kounios, J., & Holcomb, P. J. (1994). Concreteness effects in semantic processing: ERP evidence supporting dual-coding theory. *Journal of Experimental Psychology: Learning, Memory & Cognition, 20*(4), 804–823.

Kroll, J. F., & Potter, M. C. (1984). Recognizing words, pictures, and concepts: A comparison of lexical, object, and reality decisions. *Journal of Verbal Learning and Verbal Behavior, 23*, 39–66.

Kuperberg, G. R. (2007). Neural mechanisms of language comprehension: Challenges to syntax. *Brain Research, 1146*, 23–49.

Kuperberg, G. R., Caplan, D., Sitnikova, T., Eddy, M., & Holcomb, P. J. (2006). Neural correlates of processing syntactic, thematic and semantic relationships in sentences. *Language and Cognitive Processes, 21*, 489–530.

Kuperberg, G. R., Holcomb, P. J., Sitnikova, T., Greve, D., Dale, A. M., & Caplan, D. (2003). Distinct patterns of neural modulation during the processing of conceptual and syntactic anomalies. *Journal of Cognitive Neuroscience, 15*(2), 272–293.

Kuperberg, G. R., Kreher, D. A., Sitnikova, T., Caplan, D. N., & Holcomb, P. J. (2007). The role of animacy and thematic relationships in processing active English sentences: Evidence from event-related potentials. *Brain and Language, 100*(3), 223–237.

Kuperberg, G. R., Lakshmanan, B. M., Caplan, D. M., & Holcomb, P. J. (2006). Making sense of discourse: An fMRI study of causal inferencing across sentences. *NeuroImage, 33*(1), 343–361.

Kuperberg, G. R., Sitnikova, T., Caplan, D., & Holcomb, P. J. (2003). Electrophysiological distinctions in processing conceptual relationships within simple sentences. *Brain Research Cognitive Brain Research, 17*(1), 117–129.

Kuperberg, G. R., Sitnikova, T., & Lakshmanan, B. (2007). Semantic violations of action and morphosyntactic agreement violations recruit an overlapping neural network: Evidence from functional magnetic resonance imaging (submitted).

Kutas, M. (1993). In the company of other words: Electrophysiological evidence for single-word and sentence context effects. *Language & Cognitive Processes, 8*(4), 533–572.

Kutas, M., & Hillyard, S. A. (1980). Reading senseless sentences: Brain potentials reflect semantic incongruity. *Science, 207*(4427), 203–205.

Kutas, M., & Hillyard, S. A. (1984). Brain potentials during reading reflect word expectancy and semantic association. *Nature, 307*(5947), 161–163.

Kutas, M., & Hillyard, S. A. (1989). An electrophysiological probe of incidental semantic association. *Journal of Cognitive Neuroscience, 1*, 38–49.

Kutas, M., & Van Petten, C. K. (1994). Psycholinguistics electrified: Event-related brain potential investigations. In M. A. Gernsbacher (Ed.), *Handbook of psycholinguistics* (pp. 83–143). San Diego, CA: Academic Press.

Landauer, T. K., & Dumais, S. T. (1997). A solution to Plato's Problem: The latent semnatic analysis theory of acquisition, induction, and representation of knowledge. *Psychological Review, 104,* 211–240.

Levin, D. T., & Simons, D. J. (2000). Perceiving stability in a changing world: Combining shots and integrating views in motion pictures and the real world. *Media Psychology, 2,* 357–380.

Lichtenstein, E. D., & Brewer, W. F. (1980). Memory for goal-directed events. *Cognitive Psychology, 12,* 412–445.

Marslen-Wilson, W., Brown, C. M., & Tyler, L. K. (1988). Lexical representations in spoken language comprehension. *Language & Cognitive Processes, 3*(1), 1–16.

McCauley, C., Parmelee, C. M., Sperber, R. D., & Carr, T. H. (1980). Early extraction of meaning from pictures and its relation to conscious identification. *Journal of Experimental Psychology: Human Perception Performance, 6*(2), 265–276.

McElree, B., & Griffith, T. (1995). Syntactic and thematic processing in sentence comprehension: Evidence for a temporal dissociation. *Journal of Experimental Psychology: Learning, Memory, & Cognition, 21*(1), 134–157.

McElree, B., & Griffith, T. (1998). Structural and lexical constraints on filling gaps during sentence comprehension: A time-course analysis. *Journal of Experimental Psychology: Learning, Memory, & Cognition, 24*(2), 432–460.

McEvoy, C. L. (1988). Automatic and strategic processes in picture naming. *Journal of Experimental Psychology: Learning, Memory & Cognition, 14*(4), 618–626.

McPherson, W. B., & Holcomb, P. J. (1999). An electrophysiological investigation of semantic priming with pictures of real objects. *Psychophysiology, 36*(1), 53–65.

McRae, K., Hare, M., Elman, J. L., & Ferretti, T. (2005). A basis for generating expectancies for verbs from nouns. *Memory & Cognition, 33*(7), 1174–1184.

Meyer, D. E., & Schvaneveldt, R. W. (1971). Facilitation in recognizing pairs of words: Evidence of a dependence between retrieval operations. *Journal of Experimental Psychology, 90,* 227–234.

Miller, E. K., Freedman, D. J., & Wallis, J. D. (2002). The prefrontal cortex: Categories, concepts and cognition. *Philosophical Transactions of the Royal Society of London B: Biological Sciences, 357*(1424), 1123–1136.

Miller, E. K., Nieder, A., Freedman, D. J., & Wallis, J. D. (2003). Neural correlates of categories and concepts. *Current Opinion Neurobiology, 13*(2), 198–203.

Morris, R. K. (1994). Lexical and message-level sentence context effects on fixation times in reading. *Journal of Experimental Psychology: Learning, Memory & Cognition, 20*(1), 92–103.

Neely, J. H. (1991). Semantic priming effects in visual word recognition: A selective review of current findings and theories. In D. Besner & G. W. Humphreys (Eds.), *Basic processes in reading.* Hillsdale, NJ: Laurence Erlbaum Associates.

Nowak, M. A., Plotkin, J. B., & Jansen, V. A. (2000). The evolution of syntactic communication. *Nature, 404*(6777), 495–498.

Nuthmann, A., & van der Meer, E. (2005). Time's arrow and pupillary response. *Psychophysiology, 42*(3), 306–317.

Osterhout, L., & Holcomb, P. J. (1992). Event-related potentials elicited by syntactic anomaly. *Journal of Memory & Language, 31*, 785–806.

Osterhout, L., Holcomb, P. J., & Swinney, D. A. (1994). Brain potentials elicited by garden-path sentences: Evidence of the application of verb information during parsing. *Journal of Experimental Psychology: Learning, Memory & Cognition, 20*(4), 786–803.

Paivio, A. (1971). *Imagery and verbal processes*. New York: Holt, Rinehart, and Winston.

Paivio, A. (1974). Spacing of repetitions in the incidental and intentional free recall of pictures and words. *Journal of Verbal Learning & Verbal Behavior, 13*, 497–511.

Paivio, A. (1986). *Mental representations: A dual coding approach*. New York: Oxford University Press.

Paivio, A. (1991). Dual coding theory: Retrospect and current status. *Canadian Journal of Psychology, 45*, 255–287.

Pinker, S. (1989). *Learnability and cognition: The acquisition of argument structure*. Cambridge, MA: MIT Press.

Potter, M. C., Kroll, J. F., Yachzel, B., Carpenter, E., & Sherman, J. (1986). Pictures in sentences: Understanding without words. *Journal of Experimental Psychology: General, 115*(3), 281–294.

Price, C. J. (2000). The anatomy of language: Contributions from functional neuroimaging. *Journal of Anatomy, 197*(Pt 3), 335–359.

Pylyshyn, Z. W. (1980). Computation and cognition: Issues in the foundations of cognitive science. *Behavioral and Brain Sciences, 3*, 111–132.

Richardson, D. C., Spivey, M. J., Barsalou, L. W., & McRae, K. (2003). Spatial representations activated during real-time comprehension of verbs. *Cognitive Science, 27*(5), 767–780.

Rosch, E. (1975). Cognitive representations of semantic categories. *Journal of Experimental Psychology: General, 104*, 192–233.

Rosch, E., & Mervis, C. B. (1975). Family resemblances: Studies in the internal structure of categories. *Cognitive Psychology, 7*, 573–605.

Rougier, N. P., Noelle, D. C., Braver, T. S., Cohen, J. D., & O'Reilly, R. C. (2005). Prefrontal cortex and flexible cognitive control: Rules without symbols. *Proceedings of the National Academy of Sciences of the USA, 102*(20), 7338–7343.

Ruby, P., Sirigu, A., & Decety, J. (2002). Distinct areas in parietal cortex involved in long-term and short-term action planning: A PET investigation. *Cortex, 38*(3), 321–339.

Rumelhart, D. E., & Ortony, A. (1977). The representation of knowledge in memory. In R. C. Anderson, R. J. Spiro, & W. E. Montague (Eds.), *Schooling and the acquisition of knowledge* (pp. 97–135). Hillsdale, NJ: Erlbaum.

Schank, R. C., & Abelson, R. P. (1977). *Scripts, plans, goals, and understanding: An inquiry into human knowledge structures*. Hillsdale, NJ: Erlbaum.

Shallice, T. (1988). Specialisation within the semantic system. *Cognitive Neuropsychology, 5*(1), 133–142.

Shallice, T. (1993). Multiple semantics: Whose confusions? *Cognitive Neuropsychology, 10*(3), 251–261.

Shallice, T., & Burgess, P. W. (1991). Deficits in strategy application following frontal lobe damage in man. *Brain, 114*(Pt 2), 727–741.

Sirigu, A., Cohen, L., Zalla, T., Pradat-Diehl, P., Van Eeckhout, P., Grafman, J., et al. (1998). Distinct frontal regions for processing sentence syntax and story grammar. *Cortex, 34*(5), 771–778.

Sirigu, A., Zalla, T., Pillon, B., Grafman, J., Agid, Y., & Dubois, B. (1995). Selective impairments in managerial knowledge following pre-frontal cortex damage. *Cortex, 31*(2), 301–316.

Sirigu, A., Zalla, T., Pillon, B., Grafman, J., Agid, Y., & Dubois, B. (1996). Encoding of sequence and boundaries of scripts following prefrontal lesions. *Cortex, 32*(2), 297–310.

Sitnikova, T. (2003). *Comprehension of videos of real-world events: Electrophysiological evidence.* Unpublished doctoral dissertation. Medford, MA: Tufts University.

Sitnikova, T., Coty, A., Robakis, D., Holcomb, P. J., Kuperberg, G. R., & West, W. C. (2004). FMRI correlates of comprehending real-world events. *Neuroscience 2004, the Society for Neuroscience's 34th Annual Meeting. Society for Neuroscience Abstracts.*

Sitnikova, T., Holcomb, P. J., & Kuperberg, G. (in press). Two neurocognitive mechanisms of semantic integration during the comprehension of visual real-world events. *Journal of Cognitive Neuroscience.*

Sitnikova, T., Kuperberg, G., & Holcomb, P. J. (2003). Semantic integration in videos of real-world events: An electrophysiological investigation. *Psychophysiology, 40*(1), 160–164.

Sitnikova, T., West, W. C., Kuperberg, G. R., & Holcomb, P. J. (2006). The neural organization of semantic memory: Electrophysiological activity suggests feature-based segregation. *Biological Psychology, 71*(3), 326–340.

Sperber, R. D., McCauley, C., Ragain, R. D., & Weil, C. M. (1979). Semantic priming effects on picture and word processing. *Memory and Cognition, 7*(5), 339–345.

Stanovich, K. E., & West, R. F. (1983). On priming by a sentence context. *Journal of Experimental Psychology: General, 112*(1), 1–36.

Theios, J., & Amrhein, P. C. (1989). Theoretical analysis of the cognitive processing of lexical and pictorial stimuli: Reading, naming, and visual and conceptual comparisons. *Psychological Review, 96*(1), 5–24.

Tinaz, S., Schendan, H. E., Schon, K., & Stern, C. E. (2006). Evidence for the importance of basal ganglia output nuclei in semantic event sequencing: An fMRI study. *Brain Research, 1067*(1), 239–249.

Van Berkum, J. J., Brown, C. M., Zwitserlood, P., Kooijman, V., & Hagoort, P. (2005). Anticipating upcoming words in discourse: Evidence from ERPs and reading times. *Journal of Experimental Psychology: Learning, Memory & Cognition, 31*(3), 443–467.

van Berkum, J. J., Hagoort, P., & Brown, C. M. (1999). Semantic integration in sentences and discourse: Evidence from the N400. *Journal of Cognitive Neuroscience, 11*(6), 657–671.

van Berkum, J. J., Zwitserlood, P., Hagoort, P., & Brown, C. M. (2003). When and how do listeners relate a sentence to the wider discourse? Evidence from the N400 effect. *Brain Research: Cognitive Brain Research, 17*(3), 701–718.

van der Meer, E., Beyer, R., Heinze, B., & Badel, I. (2002). Temporal order relations in language comprehension. *Journal of Experimental Psychology: Learning, Memory & Cognition, 28*(4), 770–779.

Van Petten, C., & Luka, B. J. (2006). Neural localization of semantic context effects in electromagnetic and hemodynamic studies. *Brain Language, 97*(3), 279–293.

Wallis, J. D., Anderson, K. C., & Miller, E. K. (2001). Single neurons in prefrontal cortex encode abstract rules. *Nature, 411*(6840), 953–956.

Wallis, J. D., & Miller, E. K. (2003). From rule to response: Neuronal processes in the premotor and prefrontal cortex. *Journal of Neurophysiology, 90*(3), 1790–1806.

West, W. C., & Holcomb, P. J. (2000). Imaginal, semantic, and surface-level processing of concrete and abstract words: An electrophysiological investigation. *Journal of Cognitive Neuroscience, 12*(6), 1024–1037.

West, W. C., & Holcomb, P. J. (2002). Event-related potentials during discourse-level semantic integration of complex pictures. *Brain Research: Cognitive Brain Research, 13*(3), 363–375.

Williamson, S. J., Kaufman, L., & Brenner, D. (1978). Latency of the neuromagnetic response of the human visual cortex. *Vision Research, 18*(1), 107–110.

Wood, J. N., & Grafman, J. (2003). Human prefrontal cortex: Processing and representational perspectives. *Nature Reviews Neuroscience, 4*(2), 139–147.

Xu, J., Kemeny, S., Park, G., Frattali, C., & Braun, A. (2005). Language in context: Emergent features of word, sentence, and narrative comprehension. *Neuroimage, 25*(3), 1002–1015.

Zacks, J. M., & Tversky, B. (2001). Event structure in perception and conception. *Psychological Bulletin, 127*(1), 3–21.

Zacks, J. M., Tversky, B., & Iyer, G. (2001). Perceiving, remembering, and communicating structure in events. *Journal of Experimental Psychology: General, 130*(1), 29–58.

Zalla, T., Phipps, M., & Grafman, J. (2002). Story processing in patients with damage to the prefrontal cortex. *Cortex, 38*(2), 215–231.

Zola, D. (1984). Redundancy and word perception during reading. *Perceptual Psychophysiology, 36*(3), 277–284.

Author Index

Subject Index